Adventuring with Books

A complete list of all contributors to this publication may be found on pages 599–604.

 Bibliography Series

Adventuring with Books

A Booklist for Pre-K–Grade 6

12th Edition

Kathryn Mitchell Pierce, Editor,

with Cathy Beck, Dick Koblitz, Shari Nelson-Faulkner,
Anne O'Connor, Susan Wolf, and the Committee to Revise
the Elementary School Booklist

With a Foreword by

Jane Yolen

National Council of Teachers of English
1111 W. Kenyon Road, Urbana, Illinois 61801-1096

Prepress Services: Precision Graphics

Production Editor: Kurt Austin

Interior Design: Doug Burnett

Cover Design: Tom Jaczak and Joellen Bryant

Series Cover Design: R. Maul

The cover illustration by Christopher Myers is from the cover of *Harlem* by Walter Dean Myers, illustrated by Christopher Myers. New York: Scholastic, 1997. Used with permission.

NCTE Stock Number: 00775-3050

ISSN 1051-4740

ISBN 0-8141-0077-5

Patricia Tefft Cousin
April 19, 1951–July 1, 1999

Dr. Patricia Tefft Cousin touched our lives and gave us new ways to think about ourselves and others. She listened to us, told us stories, focused on our strengths and potential, and showed us how we could learn by working together.

Pat taught us to make spaces for the voices of all children and to listen to their stories with care. She never stopped learning from her students or her friends. We celebrated learning and life with her in ways that changed us and gave us new appreciation for the power of teaching and caring. Her stories about children, and our stories about learning in her company, continue to create new possibilities for us and the children that are the center of our work.

In her honor we hope *Adventuring with Books* will encourage others to listen carefully to children, to honor their stories, and to share with them the best stories we have to offer. We hope her life will inspire all of us to see collaboration as a way of learning with and for one another.

About the NCTE Bibliography Series

The National Council of Teachers of English is proud to be part of a tradition that we want to share with you. In our bibliography series are four different booklists, each focused on a particular audience and each updated regularly. These are *Adventuring with Books* (pre-K through grade 6), *Kaleidoscope* (multicultural literature for grades K through 8), *Your Reading* (middle school/junior high), and *Books for You* (senior high). Together these volumes list thousands of recent children's and young-adult trade books. Although the works included cover a wide range of topics, they all have one thing in common: They're good books that students and teachers alike enjoy.

How are these volumes put together? The process begins when an educator who knows literature and its importance in the lives of students and teachers is chosen by the NCTE Executive Committee to serve as booklist editor. That editor then works with teachers and librarians who review, select, and annotate hundreds of new trade books sent to them by publishers. It's a complicated process, one that can last three or four years. But because of their dedication and strong belief in the need to let others know about the good literature that's available, these professionals volunteer their time in a way that is commendable and serves as an inspiration to all of us. The members of the committee that compiled this volume are listed in the front of the book, and a complete list of contributing reviewers is included on pages 599–604. We are truly grateful for their hard work.

As educators know, no single book is right for every reader or every purpose, so inclusion in this booklist is not necessarily an endorsement from NCTE. It does indicate that the professionals who make up the booklist committee feel that the work in question is worthy of teachers' and students' attention, whether for its informative or aesthetic qualities. Similarly exclusion from an NCTE booklist is not necessarily a judgment on the quality of a given book or publisher. Many factors—space, time, availability of certain books, publisher participation—may influence the final shape of the list.

We hope that you'll find this booklist a useful resource in discovering new titles and authors, and we hope that you will want to collect other booklists in the series. Our mission is to help improve the teaching and learning of English and the language arts, and we hope you'll agree that the quality of our booklists contributes substantially toward that goal.

Zarina M. Hock
Senior Editor

Contents

Acknowledgments

This edition of *Adventuring with Books* represents the work of a nationwide collaboration of teachers, librarians, university faculty, school and university students, and parents. We wish to acknowledge and offer thanks for the work completed by the many groups across the country who have contributed chapters to this book, as well as to the schools and universities that supported their involvement in this project.

We are equally indebted to the many publishers who so generously supported this project by providing review copies of the books considered for inclusion in this volume. Without their ongoing and generous support, such a project would not have been possible.

The entire staff at NCTE—particularly Michael Greer, Karen Smith, Marlo Welshons, Peter Feely, and Kurt Austin—has supported us throughout this project, and Kirsten Dennison of Precision Graphics has provided expert assistance throughout the production process. We thank them for all of their efforts.

Four other very important people have made significant contributions to this project. Susie Bargiel worked with our editorial leadership team during the proposal and early design phases of the project, and we acknowledge her input. Joan Von Dras and Jan Keenoy joined the editorial leadership team for the final year of this project, assuming primary responsibility for one of the chapters in this book and lending their insights and expertise. Last, but certainly not least, Shari Nelson-Faulkner, a parent at The Family Center in our district, stepped forward as a volunteer to help us with extensive final manuscript preparations and then agreed to assume responsibility for a chapter added near the end of the process.

Finally we are particularly grateful to the School District of Clayton, Missouri—to the school principals, who allowed us release time to work on this project and encouraged our participation; to Assistant Superintendent Linda Henke, who provided us with space for our books and funds for our summer work; to the Board of Education, which supported this and other professional development experiences in the District; and to Dale Sechel, who single-handedly moved every box of books that arrived in the District, as well as every box that was repacked for shipment to one of the satellite groups around the country.

Kathryn Mitchell Pierce

Foreword: Mage/Image/Imagination

I want you to think of the word *mage*.

What comes to mind? A pale old man with a long grey beard, wearing a midnight blue robe and a pointed hat spangled with stars? A magic maker. Is that what you see? You get five points for partial recognition, zero points for originality.

Try again.

Think of the word *mage*. The root is *magus*. Although that does mean magic maker, it does not specify the age. Why does that magic maker have to be old? Why not young? Like Ursula Le Guin's Ged in *The Wizard of Earthsea*. Like Diane Duane's Nita and Kit in *So You Want to Be a Wizard*. Like the young Merlin in my book *Passager*. They are all child mages.

Why does the magic maker have to be male? Why not female? Like Ozma of Oz. Like Patricia McKillip's Sybel in *The Forgotten Beasts of Eld*. Magic has no gender boundaries, certainly not in literature.

Why does the magic maker have to be white? Why not brown? Ged is brown. Why not Hispanic? Kit is Hispanic. Why not Chinese or Jewish or Native American or . . .

This is a magic maker we are talking about. In a book. There are no rules, hard and fast, about magic makers here.

Now think of the word *mage*. At this point, I hope you each have a new and different picture in mind. But add this to your portrait. The secondary meaning of the word *mage* is "a person of wisdom and learning."

How learned is a child? How wise? Where on the scale of wisdom is childhood? Is it at the beginning or at the end? Is naiveté wisdom? Is innocence? Is a sense of wonder—that neotenic sense that only a few of us are able to carry into old age—a component of wisdom? And aren't the greatest children's books about the journey to wisdom, whether the main character is a child or an adult?

I am asking you a lot of questions because in the getting of this particular wisdom, we must all seek the answers. Seeking—not getting—is a way of partaking in the magus inside.

Let's move from the word *mage* to a word that sounds as if it is a cognate, but is not: the word *image*. What comes to mind? A picture? An idol? An icon? Full points if those were your guesses. The word means an artificial imitation or representation of the external form of any object. So a mage, doing magic (a mage's work), will work with images.

When did you get it? I am not just talking about mages, I am describing a writer or an artist at work. Well, yes . . . I write books that are artificial representations of life. The better I am, the more lifelike and the less artificial my work seems.

But in that description I have left out the most important third step.

Now think of the word *imagination*. It comes from the word *image*. And without such a thing, the mage is helpless. But what is imagination? I believe it is wisdom fueled by wonder. It is wonder centered by wisdom. It is standing in the full sunlight and recalling the starry night. It is walking under the cauldron of stars and remembering the blue slate of morning sky.

It is story.

We are story. We are images. We are all magi.

And so are our children.

In fact, humans are not just a bundle of nerves and sinew and blood and bone. Such does not distinguish us from the rest of all the living creatures on earth. The human creature is made up of story. We can remember the past in story, reconstruct the present in story, foretell the future in story. Storying is our most distinctive ability. We can create images that laugh and cry and love and hate and lie and dissemble and plot and protest. We can invent purple trees and yellow skies and flying horses and talking wolves and heroic spiders and make them real. We can say a mouse is a child, a child falls down a rabbit hole, a rabbit goes against his mama's wishes into a garden, a garden rejuvenates an ailing boy, a boy grows up with a pack of wolves, or anything else we like. And those stories become part of children's lives and the lives of their own children to come.

I get letters every day from my readers, but some stick out.

> Dear Ms. Yolen:
> I love the meddlefurs in your book OWL MOON.
> Love, Stacey

When I wrote back to Stacey, I explained that in fact I didn't really know if there were any meddlefurs in OWL MOON. (Only I called them metaphors of course. I am nothing if not pedagogically sound!) I explained to Stacey that writers didn't count metaphors or similes or dependent clauses or gerundive phrases as we write. We simply work hard at the most felicitous telling, hoping the reader will indeed fall through the words into the story.

Words are, in fact, quirky, ungracious, and often slippery little things that get in the way of the tale we are trying to tell. But it's all we've got to work with. And so, as Humpty Dumpty reminded Alice about words, "The question is which is to be master—that's all."

P.S. I never heard back from Stacey. I do not know if she got lost in the struggle between pleasing her teacher and listening to a real live author. But I do know that Stacey had not come up with the concept of meddlefurs on her own. Yes it was Stacey's pen on the paper, but her teacher's hand was clearly atop Stacey's.

So how do we get to our children who may be struggling with stories in school and coming up only with dumbed-down mush or meddlefurs?

How do we teach them to love reading?

How do we give them that mantra: mage/image/imagination?

Start with the ear.

Caress it with story. Coax story past the outer ear and through the tympanum. Drum story into them. Read aloud until story has made its way along the labyrinth, until the youngsters can only follow that wonderful golden thread of story though the reading maze.

For maze it is: dangerous, forbidden, strange, aweful in the old sense, and wonder-filled.

As Lee Bennett Hopkins says in *Let Them Be Themselves*, "All children should be read to every day."

Story will always surprise the young readers that way, even if they already know a particular story well. Because your voice will remake story for them. And when they get to read the story themselves, it will be yet another revelation. Every time we meet an old story, we meet it anew, investing it with our own needs, worries, fears. It is an old coat on new shoulders; each reader wears it differently. Or—as the great editor Ursula Nordstrom reminded one writer who was just starting to venture into the world of children's literature—"The children are new though we are not."

All my life I have loved stories. Relied on stories. Respected them.

I love stories—not predicates. Not verbs. Not comma splices and dangling participles. (Although I could enjoy a good round now and then arguing with friends about copyediting. And my novel *The Wild Hunt* stars a boy named Gerund who is a running, tumbling, skittering, falling presence.)

How long have I loved story? Since forever.

As a child, I used to curl up on the window seat of our Manhattan apartment reading volumes like *The Phoenix and the Carpet* and *The Wind in the Willows* and *The Thirteen Clocks* and every one of Andrew Lang's color fairy books. Reading so absorbed me that I never even heard what went on in the street four stories below. Even earlier, when we lived in Hampton Roads, Virginia, with my grandparents while my father was away in Europe saving the world from the Nazis, I read *Babar* and *Madeline* and *Andy and the Lion* and *Ferdinand*—that last book I must have taken out of the library a hundred times over. These stories defined me to myself. They were more than mere entertainment. They were precursors to my adult life and concerns.

Education guru Frank Smith has said succinctly and wisely: "The brain is a narrative device that needs story."

That need is so great, it has given humans the ability to be both story makers and story listeners, the two things leaning upon one another.

That need is so great, we have all become magi, bringing to the world our greatest gift—stories.

Jane Yolen

For over three decades Jane Yolen has been delighting readers of all ages with a wide range of books from poetry and picture books to science fiction, high fantasy, and traditional tales. Whether it is unicorns and wizards or owls at night and the precious gift of water, Jane Yolen weaves words with magic to inspire, delight, and inform readers.

Introduction

As Jane Yolen explains in her foreword to this book, stories are our greatest gifts. Parents, teachers, librarians, and others important in the learning lives of children share the gift of story when they surround children with outstanding books to read. We do this because stories have the power to delight, inform, and inspire. Stories can lead us into new worlds and return us to ourselves as changed individuals. By inviting us to live through the eyes of characters, stories can make us more human (Huck, 1990). *Adventuring with Books* is an annotated bibliography of powerful stories that have the potential to impact children's lives and help redefine their futures. This potential to imagine, and to re-imagine, is the gift we offer when we share books with children.

Our Goal

Our goal in this project has been to build on the excellent work reflected in previous editions of *Adventuring with Books* by continuing to provide an annotated bibliography of books published for elementary children in the past three years (1996–1998). In addition, we specifically wanted to reach out to classroom teachers like ourselves by adding a further dimension to the reviews: We wanted to include children's comments and reactions, reflections on the ways we have used these books in our classrooms, and other ideas we had for sharing these books with children.

To achieve this goal, we had to make a very difficult decision about the number of books we included and the amount of information we provided about each book. We found a compromise position: We have included extensive information about our favorite books in what we refer to as *primary reviews,* and we have included brief annotations for other worthy books in what we refer to as *secondary reviews.* This enabled us to include approximately the same number of books as were included in previous editions of *Adventuring with Books,* while being able to further develop the reviews of our favorite books.

The Process

From the beginning, we felt strongly that this should be a collaborative project that included both school-based and university-based contributors. We invited NCTE colleagues from across the country with expertise in particular areas of children's literature to create collaborative groups to review the books. These review committee leaders worked with teachers, librarians, university faculty, school-age and university students, and parents to establish the criteria used to select and review books, to create a working bibliography of books to be included in their chapters, to write the reviews of individual books, and to contribute to decisions about the overall structure of the finished book. These review committees functioned as special study groups focused on selecting, using, and reviewing the best books published for children in the past three years. They deepened their own understandings of literature published for children, and offered a depth and breadth to the project that could not have been achieved by a single committee working in a single geographic area.

Each of these chapters, then, reflects the work of different committees. In the introduction to each chapter, the committees share their process, the criteria they developed, the issues they grappled with as they selected and reviewed their books, and the decisions they made about the most supportive way of organizing the books in their chapter. We hope you will find their introductions as instructive as the book reviews themselves.

Contents and Organization of the Book

We spent considerable energy wrestling with the best organizational structure for this book. Traditionally this booklist and others like it have organized books based on established categories of literature for children. We used these traditional categories as a starting place for our own work. We also took into consideration the ways we search for and use books ourselves as classroom teachers. Although we often think about and group books by category or genre, more often we organize books around topics, themes, and broad concepts (Short and Harste 1996). At times we select books to support readers in different phases of the learning-to-read process—books that could be considered supportive texts for readers (Watson 1998). Our final table of contents reflects a blending of these approaches for organizing books.

The table of contents evolved throughout the course of this project, too. When new books arrived, we tested our working table of contents by making decisions about which committee(s) should review each book. When we found books that didn't seem to fit anywhere in our table of contents—or everywhere—we made adjustments. Near the end of the three-year timeline for this project, we felt the need for an additional chapter. We had a large collection of high-quality picture story books that had not been claimed by any existing committee, and we didn't want these books to be overlooked. Shari Nelson-Faulkner, a parent from The Family Center in our district and a volunteer on this project, offered to work with other parents to review these books with their children and to create the "Picture Books" chapter.

Creating an entire chapter devoted strictly to picture books sparked further decisions. Rather than cross-reference all picture books included in *Adventuring with Books*, we have chosen to indicate *picture book* at the end of the bibliographic entry for each picture book.

Although the primary focus of this booklist is K–6, we have included many books that are appropriate for preK–8. The authors of the "Supporting Critical Conversations in Classrooms" chapter, through their example, led us to indicate *sophisticated chapter book* following the bibliographic entry for any books that may require additional consideration before being used with children. These were the books with mature themes or explicit content—books that the reviewers felt had significant merit, but that would be most accessible to children if mediated by a caring adult.

Many of the best books defy categorization. Where appropriate, we have cross-referenced books in more than one chapter. The review appears only once and in the chapter where we felt the book would most commonly be included. The bibliographic information is included in other chapters where the book also seems topical, and a cross-reference to the reviewed entry is included in boldface type at the end of the bibliographic information.

The subject index at the end of the book is designed to assist readers interested in selecting books on other topics not included in the table of contents.

Special Index Chapters

We asked several of our review committees to assume primary responsibility for identifying, critiquing, and reviewing books representing groups that often have been underrepresented in literature published for children. We felt strongly that such books should not be segregated from other books in this volume, yet we wanted readers to be able to find easily information about such books. We created special index chapters to achieve this purpose. Therefore, while we have included an index chapter that lists all books in this volume that address Native American experiences, the actual reviews of these books are included throughout *Adventuring with Books* in the appropriate chapters. So a book of Native American poetry would be listed in the bibliography for chapter 18, "Native American Voices and Experiences," while the review would be included in chapter 10, "Poetry." We are hopeful that this organizational structure will encourage greater use of these books in a broad range of contexts. The index chapters include chapter 15, "African and African American Voices and Experiences"; chapter 16, "Asian, Asian American, and Hawaii Pacific Voices and Experiences"; chapter 17, "Hispanic/Latino, Hispanic American, and Latino American Voices and Experiences"; chapter 18, "Native American Voices and Experiences"; and chapter 19, "Gender Issues: Spunky, Clever, Caring, and Endearing Girls and Boys in Children's Literature." The contributors for these chapters are listed on the appropriate chapter openers while the reviews they have written appear in other chapters throughout the book.

The final index chapter has been handled differently. The authors of chapter 20, "Supporting Critical Conversations in Classrooms," invite us to view literature as an opportunity to engage children in the "what if" discussions that have the potential to challenge the status quo. Because the reviews of books included in this chapter are so specific to critical issues, we have chosen to include those reviews in the index chapter and to list the bibliographic entry in other chapters where appropriate. Many of the books included in this chapter have been reviewed in other chapters as well. In many instances we have chosen to include in this volume both reviews—the reviews in chapter 20 that highlight the kinds of critical conversations a book might stimulate, and the reviews in other chapters that explore the content of the book itself more deeply. In such cases, a cross-reference to the other review are included at the end of the annotation in each chapter.

In the back of the book we have included more traditional indexes such as an "Author Index," an "Illustrator Index," and a "Subject Index." The book concludes with a complete list of contributors.

How You Might Use This Book

We hope the content and organizational structure of this book will be useful to parents, classroom teachers, librarians, and curriculum specialists, as well as university faculty and students in child development, children's literature, reading, language arts, and curriculum. Those interested in genre study will want to check the table of contents to locate a chapter that highlights the particular genre they are interested in, and then check the subject index for additional related books. Those interested in theme studies or explorations of broad concepts will find an extensive list of popular themes and concepts in both the table of contents and the "Subject Index." We invite you to develop your own index chapters by listing the topics, themes, and concepts you search for most often along with the review numbers of books you find that address these topics, themes, and concepts. The blank pages at the end of the book may be a handy place to keep these notes. The additional space at the end of each chapter may provide a convenient place to list new books you find that fit into the various chapters. In other words, we hope that this volume serves as a living document for you—an invitation to organize the books you currently use, to consider new books we have found useful or new ways to use familiar books, and to make notes about newer books as they are published.

Conclusions and an Invitation

As with many curriculum projects or other projects of this scope, those directly involved in the decision-making processes and the development of the project itself learn a great deal along the way. Much of what is learned cannot be shared easily with others outside the group. For most of us, the experience of participating in a study group centered around a particular group of books published for children has challenged us to deepen our understanding of the role this literature plays in the lives of our children and in our classrooms, to broaden our knowledge of recently published books and trends in the publishing industry, to familiarize ourselves with new authors and illustrators, and to learn in the company of others who share our commitment to children and their literature. We invite you to form your own literature study groups—to meet regularly with friends and colleagues committed to using the best of literature for children, and to engage in your own collaborative professional inquiries into literature and its role in the lives of children. We are certain, based on our own experiences, that you and the children with whom you work will benefit from the experience.

Works Cited

Huck, Charlotte. 1990. The Power of Literature. In *Talking about Books: Creating Literate Communities*, eds. Kathy Short and Kathryn Mitchell Pierce. Portsmouth, NH: Heinemann.

Short, Kathy, and Jerome C. Harste, with Carolyn Burke. 1996. *Creating Classrooms for Authors and Inquirers*. 2nd ed. Portsmouth, NH: Heinemann.

Watson, Dorothy. 1998. Beyond Decodable Text: Supportive and Workable Literature. *Language Arts* 74 no. 8: 635–643.

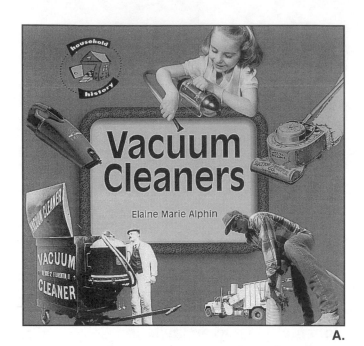

A.

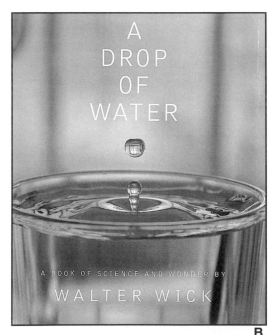

B.

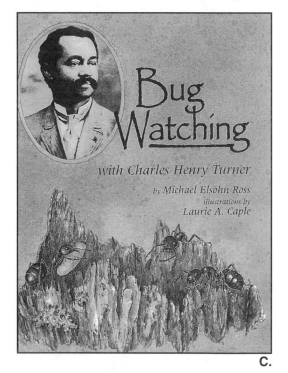

C.

A. *Vacuum Cleaners,* Elaine Marie Alphin (**1.32**). **B.** *A Drop of Water,* Walter Wick (**1.55**). **C.** *Bug Watching with Charles Henry Turner,* Michael Elsohn Ross/Laurie A. Caple (**1.51**).

1 Stories of the Universe: From Questions and Observations to Discoveries and Inventions

David J. Whitin

Phyllis E. Whitin

The authors wish to thank the following students enrolled in the M.A.T. Program at the University of South Carolina, 1998–1999, for their initial reading of and comments on many of the books included in this chapter: Ami Abramson, Carly Bennett, Doris Cochran, Stephen Corsini, Tonnette Dantzler, Jill Darr, Angela Davis, Shelley Ducworth, Carmen Ervin, Mandy Eskew, Kristi Giles, Rachael Ginn, Gina Howell, Marion Kelly, Dana Matyjasik, Brenda Morton, Cynthia Rainey, Rita Raley, Amber Ray, Andrea Ribelin, Amy Schofield, Pauley Smith, Robbie Spruill, Beth Steffens, Erin Till, Kimberley Trotter, Barbara Watkins, and Susan Wilbanks.

In this chapter, readers will find books that address such topics as mysteries, explorations, and disasters; health and medicine; inventions, discoveries, and statistics; and looking closely at the natural world. Books about mysteries, explorations, and disasters include stories about a Martian fossil on earth, the tragedy of the *Titanic*, and archaeological sites in Scotland and the American Southwest. Books that delve into issues of health include works that discuss the history of American medicine, present interviews with health professionals, and describe a teen's struggle with alcohol. Books that discuss interesting discoveries and inventions address such topics as the history of shoes, eyeglasses, and vacuums; important scientific discoveries such as light, magnetism, and radioactivity; the Internet; and different modes of transportation. Finally, books that focus on the natural world include those that provide a close examination of dirt and grime, a magical ride inside a honeybee hive, and a zoological guide to the body systems of insects, fish, birds, and invertebrates.

Books That Reflect an Inquiry Stance

Too often science texts portray science as a clearly defined set of fixed beliefs that are merely transmitted from one generation to the next. In reviewing the books for this chapter, we paid particular attention to those books that showed science not as a static body of knowledge but rather as the outcome of an inquiring mind. This inquiring stance is best reflected in books that show that scientific activity involves curiosity, doubt, collaboration, and close observation.

In *Martian Fossils on Earth?* (Bortz 1997), the author discusses this curiosity in the first sentence of the book: "Why are scientists so excited about a rock? Because scientists love the excitement of discovery, they sometimes love the search for answers even more than the answers themselves" (7). Questions about meteorite ALH 84001 form the framework of this fascinating scientific puzzle: How can we tell that it came from Mars? Where on Mars did it come from? How did it get to Earth? Did Martian microbes make these chemicals and crystals? What do these findings suggest about life in the universe? This same persistent inquisitiveness is also revealed in *Bug Watching with Charles Henry Turner* (Ross 1997). Turner was a premier African American entomologist whose interest in bugs began when he was a small boy growing up in post–Civil War America. He was always asking questions and conducting experiments about the observations he made: Are bees color-blind? Do spiders construct webs based on instinct, or can they adapt the shape of the web to their surroundings? Can a cockroach learn by trial and error? This incessant questioning demonstrates to readers the inquisitive basis of scientific explorations.

Of course, curiosity is a close cousin to careful observation. For this reason, we looked for books that portrayed the role of observation in scientific investigations. In *Clyde Tombaugh and the Search for Planet X* (Wetterer 1996), readers learn about a farm boy who discovers Pluto at the age of twenty-four. He accomplishes this feat by painstakingly examining hundreds of photographs, each containing 50,000 to 400,000 tiny dots of light. He finally detects a slight movement of one of these dots by comparing several photographs, thereby discovering the existence of our ninth planet. The power of close observation also is demonstrated by the spectacular photographs in *A Drop of Water* (Wick 1997). Wick uses his camera to stop the action of water and to show its various states in exquisite detail, such as the changing shape of a drop of water descending from the faucet. He uses time-lapse photographs to show condensation and evaporation. He magnifies intricately detailed snowflakes and glistening drops of water on a spider's web. Looking at the ordinary in extraordinary ways highlights the benefits of noticing the little details of our world.

According to Descartes, science is born of doubting. We looked for books that captured this spirit by portraying science as a tentative, provisional endeavor. One of the best examples is *Stone Age Farmers beside the Sea: Scotland's Prehistoric Village of Skara Brae* (Arnold 1997). Readers get a glimpse of the speculative work of archaeologists as these scientists try to piece together this puzzle from 3000 B.C.E. For instance, theories about the clothing worn have to be based on the tools that are found, and knowledge about plant foods is sketchy since these foods were not preserved. The reasons for the abandonment of the village remain unclear, although scientists offer several different hypotheses in this book. It is these missing pieces of data and this construction of multiple theories that gives readers an insight into the tentative nature of scientific conclusions.

Science is also a collaborative enterprise. If readers have ever entered the classroom of Ms. Frizzle, they will recognize this right away. In one of her recent explorations, entitled *The Magic School Bus: Inside a Beehive* (Cole 1996), the adventuresome Ms. Frizzle leads her students into the hive of a honeybee. As the children ask questions and write reports, the whole class benefits from their collaborative efforts. On this particular trip, the children wrote reports on where beeswax comes from, the dance of bees, why bees sting, and who's who in the hive. Collaboration also can be found in *Mission Earth* (English and Jones 1996), where space technology is used to try to solve ecological problems on Earth. This book describes the collaborative NASA mission (in conjunction with Italian and German scientists) in which special cameras and radar equipment were used to assess the ecological health of Earth. The radar probed beneath the sands of the Sahara to find clues about Earth's past climates and enable scientists to better predict future climatic conditions. Other equipment measured carbon monoxide pollution as it traveled through the atmosphere. Readers see that scientists grow through such collaborative ventures involving NASA engineers and astronauts and an international team of scientists.

Other Criteria for Judging Books

In addition to looking for these characteristics of scientific inquiry, we also used other criteria for judging the books in this section. First, how well do the photographs and illustrations complement and extend the written text? For instance in *Dinosaur Ghosts* (Gillette 1997), an archaeological mystery concerning the sudden disappearance of the dinosaur Coelophysis is depicted in an effective way. The author uses photographs of the original archaeological site as well as imaginative illustrations of the dinosaurs themselves to describe both the actual setting and the proposed scientific theories.

Second, how well do authors use metaphors or other comparisons to convey scientific principles or statistical information? In *Funny Bones and Other Body Parts* (Ganeri 1997), readers learn that skin is like a wetsuit and ligaments function like elastic bands. In *The World in One Day* (Ash 1997), the author states that the number of aluminum cans discarded in the United States every day would be enough to build sixteen DC-10 airliners. These are helpful comparisons for understanding.

Third, how well do authors tell engaging scientific stories for younger readers? Sometimes the content can be trivialized or oversimplified in books for younger children (e.g., explaining in a single sentence how volcanoes erupt). We looked for books that contained both language and content that preserved the integrity and complexity of the issue or concept. In this way the true nature of science is reserved not just for older students, but instead is made accessible to all students in an authentic, honest manner. A good example of this criterion is *Spacebusters: The Race to the Moon* (Wilkinson 1998), in which readers live the excitement and danger of the Apollo 11 space mission to the moon.

Fourth, how well do the inclusion of various details support the main points of the story? We looked for books in which details added focus and depth rather than distracted the reader. *The Magic School Bus: Inside a Beehive* (Cole 1996) is a prime example of a book in which details add depth to the discussion rather than detract from the story with unnecessary clutter.

Finally, how well does the author invite the reader into the scientific conversation? We have noted several successful strategies. One technique is to suggest experiments for students to try that are related to important concepts in the text. Books by Michael E. Ross offer excellent examples of this technique. Including primary sources is an effective tool for making historical stories come alive. In *Just What the Doctor Ordered* (Miller 1997), the author uses journal entries, woodcuts, and photographs to depict the history of modern medicine. A sense of humor also engages readers with the text. In *The Beginner's Guide to Animal Autopsy* (Parker 1997), readers discover that sharks never need a dentist because these creatures continually grow new teeth, and penguins move quickly in the water by practicing the flapstroke, not the backstroke! Finally, allowing children the opportunity to tell the story is another effective way to engage readers. In *Stones, Bones, and Petroglyphs: Digging into Southwest Archaeology* (Goodman 1998), students retell their experiences assisting archaeologists in trying to solve one of the great mysteries of Southwest archaeology.

---

*The titles listed below each subheading are organized into Primary Reviews and Secondary Reviews. The Primary Reviews describe outstanding books in each subheading. The Secondary Reviews provide brief information about other books worthy of consideration. Some titles listed below are **not** reviewed in this chapter; entries for these titles are not annotated and contain only bibliographic information. In such cases, a cross reference to the annotated entry contained elsewhere in this volume is provided in boldface type at the end of the bibliographic information.*

Mysteries, Explorations, and Disasters

Primary Reviews

1.1   Arnold, Caroline (1997). **Stone Age Farmers beside the Sea: Scotland's Prehistoric Village of Skara Brae.** Photographs by Arthur Arnold. New York: Clarion. 48 pp. ISBN: 0-395-77601-5. Chapter Book.

Before the Egyptians built their pyramids and before the Chinese built the Great Wall, people lived at Skara Brae. One of Europe's oldest known prehistoric settlements, Skara Brae is located on a windswept island on the tip of Scotland. This book tells the story of this archaeological treasure that was first discovered in 1850. People lived at Skara Brae for about six hundred years, from 3100 to 2500 B.C.E. It is unusual because it was a village of several families rather than a single family settlement. The book discusses the design of the village and how the buildings were built. Excellent photographs give readers a clear sense of how the village was organized. One of the strengths of this fascinating story is its honest portrayal of the tentative nature of archaeological conclusions. Speculation about the clothing worn is based on the tools that were found. Little is known about the plant foods that were eaten since these were not preserved. The reasons for burial with animal bones, and the mystery behind the rings of standing stones, are still unclear. Children may come away from this book with some of their own theories to explain the life and times of this intriguing village from the past.

1.2 Bortz, Alfred (1997). **Martian Fossils on Earth? The Story of Meteorite ALH 84001.** Brookfield, CT: Millbrook. 72 pp. ISBN: 0-7613-0270-0. Chapter Book.

"This book is about questions rather than answers," Fred Bortz states in the author's note. The book is framed by thirteen compelling questions that surround the yet unsolved mystery of Meteorite ALH 84001, which was discovered in Antarctica in 1984. Although the biggest question—Does the meteorite hold evidence for life on Mars?—is especially debatable, scientists may have answered some of the others. For instance, scientists were able to measure the presence of gases inside the meteorite, which matched samples of gases found on Viking expeditions. However, Bortz warns, "Scientists are a very cautious group . . . They will say that the parent body *is probably* Mars." His honest skepticism serves as an impressive demonstration for readers. Real scientific inquiry involves making conjectures, conducting multiple tests, and accepting the tentativeness of theories that may crumble in the wake of new evidence. Despite the uncertainty of its conclusions, the book describes amazing technological tools and brilliant work by scientists in understandable language. The text is supplemented with a glossary, index, and a recommended Web site to learn about new developments in this mystery.

1.3 Branley, Franklyn M. (1998). **Floating in Space.** Illustrated by True Kelley. New York: HarperCollins. 32 pp. ISBN: 0-06-025432-7. Picture Book.

One of the selections in the Let's-Read-and-Find-Out Science series, this book presents key ideas about gravity and weightlessness by inviting the reader to join a space voyage. The narrative text is simple and clear, and the large accompanying pictures and diagrams give additional information with touches of humor. The text explains that in space, people and objects can stay on a wall or ceiling if they remain undisturbed. Pictures show an astronaut standing upside down and another suspended sideways. Another diagram is labeled with a caption that reads, "Tray has magnets and velcro strips underneath so it can be attached to the table or even the wall." Although packed with information, the pages remain uncluttered. The book details the logistics of the astronaut's daily routines (such as eating, sleeping, exercising, and going to the bathroom), work, and play. Young children will enjoy discovering that astronauts legitimize playing with their food as they suspend liquid drops in the air or toss candy aloft before catching it in their mouths. They will also learn of the special challenges and dangers presented by the need to repair the Hubble telescope. Although the book lacks a glossary and index, it is a valuable resource for children.

1.4 Brewster, Hugh (1997). **Inside the *Titanic*.** Illustrated by Ken Marschall. Boston: Little Brown. 32 pp. ISBN: 0-316-55716-1. Picture Book.

The tragic story of the *Titanic* is told through the eyes of some of the passengers who survived. Frank Goldsmith, age nine, was going with his parents to America, where his father hoped to find work in Detroit. In contrast to the Goldsmiths' third-class accommodations, the Carter family enjoyed all the amenities of first-class travel. The Carters brought with them a new Renault automobile as well as a chauffeur. Although this contrast in socioeconomic status is made apparent, the preferential treatment given to first-class passengers during the filling of the lifeboats is not. Nevertheless, one of the strengths of the book is the large, cutaway illustrations that show boiler rooms, lounges, reception rooms, and engine rooms. Actual photographs of some of the crew and passengers, including some of the Goldsmiths and Carters, emphasize the human element of this story. Older students might enjoy reading a book that Frank Goldsmith wrote later in his life (listed in the recommended reading section) that describes his reflections about this tragic voyage.

1.5 Cole, Joanna (1997). **The Magic School Bus and the Electric Field Trip.** Illustrated by Bruce Degen. New York: Scholastic. 48 pp. ISBN: 0-590-44682-7. Picture Book.

In this latest edition of the Magic School Bus series, Ms. Frizzle and her class embark on one of their most exciting field trips yet— a journey to a power plant to learn about how electricity is made. As in their previous books, author Joanna Cole and illustrator Bruce Degen combine their talents to make the complex subject of electricity accessible to young readers. Through narrative, humorous conversation, and student research, they explain the composition of atoms, current electricity, conductors, insulators, and lightning. Cole and Degen then take Ms. Frizzle and her students on an imaginary trip through a power plant to help readers learn about how steam, turbines, and magnetism produce electricity. As

Ms. Frizzle's class enters the town library through its electric current, readers learn about how a filament in a bulb produces light and how electric current produces heat and runs a motor. At the end of the book is a simple electricity game, as well as a list of further questions generated by Ms. Frizzle's students in order to continue their hands-on approach to the study of electricity. This is an essential book for any classroom study of electricity. (See also **1.41** for another book in this series.)

1.6   Dewey, Jennifer Owings (1998). **Mud Matters.** Photographs by Stephen Trimble. New York: Marshall Cavendish. 72 pp. ISBN: 0-7614-5014-9. Chapter Book.

This is a theme study of mud, filled with the stories of a mud lover. The author grew up in the West, where mud was a central part of her life. She enjoyed stomping through mud in a rainstorm, using it to build a miniature village, and inventing games with it. However, the real strength of this book is that the author weaves together her own personal narrative with interesting stories from science and social studies. For instance, she describes finding a fossil in the mud as a youngster, then gives additional information about life in this part of the United States twenty million years ago. She tells of the nest-building activities of creatures who construct nests of mud, such as mud-daubing wasps, barn swallows, and cliff swallows. She relates the Hopi custom of mudslinging in which in-laws become acquainted by having a big mudslinging bash with each other! The author describes her foolhardy decision at age eleven to step into some quicksand, from which she barely escaped with her life. In this context, she reflects upon the many pioneer wagons that were swallowed up completely in large quicksand beds. The storytelling style of this book would make it an interesting read-aloud for upper-elementary school children.

1.7   English, June, and Thomas D. Jones (1996). **Mission: Earth: Voyage to the Home Planet.** New York: Scholastic. 42 pp. ISBN: 0-590-4871-7. Chapter Book.

June English, scientific writer, and Tom Jones, mission specialist, collaborate to create a unique documentary of two NASA Space Radar Laboratory flights that collected data about Earth's changing environment. Jones' daily journals capture both the wonder of space flight as well as the technology used to gather data. Readers will be amazed to learn how radar can "see" beneath the sands of the Sahara Desert by bouncing waves off deeper bedrock. The information gathered can give scientists clues about Earth's past climates, and perhaps help them better predict future changes in desert areas. Radar also can measure the total leaf area of Appalachian forests in North America, which helps scientists determine the amount of carbon dioxide that these trees can convert to oxygen. The second part of the book gives additional information about the six major environmental issues studied by the space missions and plans for future work. Radar graphics, spectacular photographs, diagrams, and an index add both beauty and clarity to the text. The combination of personal observations and scientific data offers a concerned but hopeful outlook on the environment and our planet's future.

1.8   Ford, Harry (1998). **The Young Astronomer.** New York: Dorling Kindersley. 37 pp. ISBN: 0-7894-2061-9. Picture Book.

This book is a useful introduction to astronomy for the budding young stargazer. It begins with a brief history of astronomy and then devotes a two-page spread to each of the topics discussed, including the moon, the sun, comets, galaxies, and the movement of Earth in space. Each page begins with some background information about the topic and then describes some practical experiments, using everyday materials. Experiments include building tools such as telescopes and quadrants, constructing models of the solar system, and demonstrating scientific concepts such as a lunar eclipse or the expansion of the universe. The text explains how the scientific information of each chapter relates to the suggested experiments. In addition, the text, illustrations, and photographs are silhouetted against a white background, creating a crisp, uncluttered appearance. A strength of the book is the frequent invitations for readers to keep records of their observations, such as the phases of the moon, the location of sunspots, and the position of the planets. Charts with information about the stars and planets, and a list of useful addresses, are included at the end of the book.

1.9   Fradin, Dennis (1997). **The Planet Hunters: The Search for Other Worlds.** New York: Margaret K. McElderry. 148 pp. ISBN: 0-689-81323-6. Chapter Book.

How did people discover the planets of our solar system? How likely is it that life exists somewhere beyond our solar system? The author discusses these two questions in this entertaining and highly readable account. One of the strengths of the book is that it describes the discoveries of planets in their historical context. For instance, the author describes the prevailing religious views of the times, and frequently cites primary sources to convey a real flavor for the beliefs and personalities of the planet hunters. Journal entries, conversations, engravings, and photographs make these planetary adventures enjoyable to read. The fervent battle between the Ptolemaic and Copernican systems for explaining the universe is discussed. The professional jealousy and competitiveness surrounding the discovery of Neptune in the 1840s helps to demonstrate the bitter human side of scientific discoveries. Another highlight of the book is the author's interview with ninety-year-old Clyde Tombaugh about his discovery of Pluto in the 1930s. The book ends with a look to the future and the discovery of one of the first known planets beyond our solar system. This is a fascinating resource that conveys the excitement and challenge of scientific research.

1.10 Gibbons, Gail (1997). **The Moon Book.** New York: Holiday House. Unpaged. ISBN: 0-8234-1297-0. Picture Book.

Gail Gibbons is known for the clarity and simplicity of her beginning science books for children, and this book is no exception. She provides an informative and easy-to-follow introduction to Earth's nearest neighbor, the moon. The book contains basic information on the phases of the moon, solar and lunar eclipses, tides, craters on the moon, and lunar explorations. The large type and bold, bright illustrations work together nicely to explain each scientific concept. The explanation for the phases of the moon is particularly well done. Readers see the changing shape of the moon in a series of nine rectangular blocks. Each block represents the shape of the moon as well as the position of Earth and the moon. Inviting children to keep moon journals is a natural extension to discussing this chart of the moon. Different stories and legends are included in the text and in an appendix at the end of the book. These brief stories might prompt children to investigate other tales about the moon.

1.11 Gillette, J. Lynett (1997). **Dinosaur Ghosts: The Mystery of Coelophysis.** Illustrated by Douglas Henderson. New York: Dial. 32 pp. ISBN: 0-8037-1721-0. Picture Book.

This book highlights one of the great dinosaur discoveries—and mysteries—of all time. Over 225 million years ago in New Mexico, hundreds of speedy dinosaurs known as Coelophysis died quite suddenly. The arrangement of their bones yields some clues to the mystery of how and why these dinosaurs perished. One of the strengths of this book is that it demonstrates the tentative nature of scientific work. Each chapter focuses on a different theory that scientists have proposed to explain this mystery: Did the dinosaurs get stuck in the mud? Were their deaths caused by a volcano or a huge asteroid colliding with the earth? Did they drink some poisoned water? Did they die from a drought or a flood? Readers learn how scientists gathered evidence to support and then refute each of these theories. A current theory is shared at the end of the book, but with a word of warning that "scientists are always ready to change their ideas." The illustrations complement the mystery in an engaging way. Photographs depict the original excavation, and lifelike paintings of the dinosaurs capture their fateful last days.

1.12 Goodman, Susan E. (1998). **Stones, Bones, and Petroglyphs: Digging into Southwest Archaeology.** Photographs by Michael J. Doolittle. New York: Atheneum Books for Young Readers. 48 pp. ISBN: 0-689-81121-7. Chapter Book.

A group of eighth graders from Hannibal, Missouri, travel to the Four Corners region of the Southwest to help archaeologists solve a mystery. Ancestral Puebloans lived in the area for over a thousand years but then suddenly moved away around 1300 C.E. The question is, why? The students spend a week assisting archaeologists in their work and also finding out about this ancient culture. The real attraction of this book is that it allows the voices of the children to tell the story. They learn to grapple with the uncertainty of archaeological work, such as surmising why potters used certain designs or why Puebloans built T-shaped doorways. They learn that "Archaeology isn't just finding stuff, it's finding out what it means." They learn about the pitfalls in interpreting ancient culture through the framework of their own values and customs. They gain a deep respect and appreciation for the hard work, skill, and inventiveness of the ancient Puebloans by engaging in some of the work of these people. The students build their own pithouse by using ancient building techniques, grind corn on a stone slab, start a fire by using friction, and make pottery. This book is an excellent resource for helping students view the world from an archaeologist's perspective.

1.13   Platt, Richard (1997). **Disaster! Catastrophes that Shook the World.** Illustrated by Richard Bonson. New York: Dorling Kindersley. 32 pp. ISBN: 0-7894-2034-1. Picture Book.

This book gives a brief glimpse of twelve major disasters, including the eruption of the volcano on Mt. Vesuvius in 79 C.E., the Black Death of fourteenth-century Europe, the Great Fire of London in the seventeenth century, the disastrous blizzard that struck New York in 1888, the tidal wave that hit Japan in 1896, the earthquake that shook San Francisco in 1906, and the terrible flood of China in 1935. A two-page spread is devoted to each disaster, and each story is enhanced by a wealth of photographs, drawings, and maps. The author effectively describes for readers why and how the disasters occurred without dwelling on the horror of the events. Thus, readers learn about the stages of a volcanic eruption, the birth of a blizzard, the cause of a tsunami, and the movement of tectonic plates. The last chapter points to some possible future disasters, such as rainforest destruction and the depletion of the ozone layer. The book does include one unfortunate comment made by the Lord Mayor of London, who initially was not alarmed by the fire and said "a woman could piss it out." Inclusion of this comment detracts from an otherwise informative text.

1.14   Reid, Struan (1997). **The Children's Atlas of Lost Treasures.** Brookfield, CT: Millbrook. 95 pp. ISBN: 0-7613-0219-0. Chapter Book.

If you are in search of lost treasure, you will enjoy these tales of intrigue. With stunning photographs of some magnificent riches, this atlas chronicles the discovery of lost treasures from around the world. The chapters are organized by topic and cover a wide range of stories. "Offerings to the Gods" tells of royal burials that have been uncovered, such as King Tut's tomb, the treasure of Mycenae, and the golden treasures from the tomb of Philip of Macedon. There are also chapters entitled "War, Piracy and Disasters," as well as "Riches from the Deep" and "Stolen Treasures." All of the stories demonstrate a natural integration of science, history, politics, and religion. Each chapter begins with an introduction and a helpful map so readers are acquainted with the locations of these discoveries. The book concludes with some unsolved mysteries of buried treasure, such as the whereabouts of Captain Kidd's booty or the riches from the lost city of Atlantis. Occasionally there are explanations of the excavation process, such as the method of recovering corpses of people and animals killed during the eruption of Mt. Vesuvius. These brief stories of mystery and adventure are sure to spark some children to do further research.

1.15 Wilkinson, Philip (1998). **Spacebusters: The Race to the Moon.** New York: Dorling Kindersley. 48 pp. ISBN: 0-7894-2961-6. Chapter Book.

Here is a book for young readers that tells the exciting story of Apollo 11 and the United States' first piloted expedition to the moon. One of the strengths of this book is the way it continually highlights the dangers that the astronauts faced throughout the mission. It discusses the dangers involved in navigating the landing craft so that it would avoid setting down in a large crater, the potential of moon dust exploding when it came in contact with oxygen (a theory proposed by some scientists at the time), the possibility of not reconnecting with the space module and being left on the moon, and the dangers of reentry. Color photographs and illustrations work well with the text to demonstrate the peril and adventure of this space expedition. Some of the photographs supplement the text with additional information, such as the labeled diagram of a spacesuit, a slice of a moon rock, and a close-up of the landing craft feet covered in gold foil to protect them from the cold. This is an action-filled tale that is made accessible to young readers without comprising the integrity of the writing.

Secondary Reviews

1.16 Becklake, Sue (1998). **Space: Stars, Planets, and Spacecraft.** Illustrated by Brian Delf and Luciano Corbella. New York: Dorling Kindersley. 64 pp. ISBN: 0-7894-2966-7. Picture Book.

A liberal use of diagrams and illustrations helps reduce the density of this information-packed resource. Many illustrations spread across two pages, adding to the text a sense of the vastness of space. The extensive number of topics covered—from planets, asteroids, and recent technological advances to theories about black holes—prevent in-depth coverage. Highlighted boxes and captions provide some additional details about selected topics. The book has an index, but no glossary.

1.17 Johnson, Rebecca L. (1997). **Braving the Frozen Frontier: Women Working in Antarctica.** Minneapolis: Lerner. 112 pp. ISBN: 0-8225-2855-X. Chapter Book.

How cold is cold? Readers of *Braving the Frozen Frontier* might actually feel cold as they learn about women working in Antarctica. The intense cold seeps into everything these women do, whether they are studying algae, nematodes, Weddell seals, or Adelie penguins. The women range in occupation from biologists, graduate students, and high school teachers to pilots, electricians, heavy equipment operators, and carpenters. Close-up photos show the many layers of protective clothing the women must wear in order to survive the dangerous working conditions. This collection of stories about women scientists and employees of McMurdo Station will inspire readers to dream about nontraditional careers in uncommon places.

1.18   Petty, Kate (1997). **I Didn't Know That Dinosaurs Laid Eggs, and Other Amazing Facts about Prehistoric Reptiles.** Brookfield, CT: Copper Beech. 32 pp. ISBN: 0-7613-0549-1. Picture Book.

This introductory book presents facts about the appearance, size, and behavior of dinosaurs. The book contains a variety of interesting color illustrations, such as close-ups of nests, teeth, and feathers. It also shares with readers some unanswered questions about dinosaurs, for example, the cause of their extinction and their actual colors. The book has several drawbacks: there is no pronunciation key, there is a symbol for "fun projects" to do but only one is suggested, and some pages include too many technical terms for readers to follow.

Another book in this series is:

Petty, Kate (1997). **I Didn't Know That the Sun Is a Star, and Other Amazing Facts about the Universe.** Brookfield, CT: Copper Beech. 32 pp. ISBN: 0-7613-0567-X. Picture Book.

1.19   Wetterer, Margaret (1996). **Clyde Tombaugh and the Search for Planet X.** Illustrated by Laurie A. Caple. Minneapolis: Carolrhoda. 48 pp. ISBN: 0-87614-893-3. Picture Book.

This book tells the story of a farm boy, Clyde Tombaugh, who discovered Pluto. Intended for early readers, the book begins with Clyde using his uncle's telescope for his first view of the moon. His fascination for the starry sky never left him; he later worked for the Lowell Observatory in Arizona, where at age twenty-four he discovered Pluto. The story celebrates Clyde's diligence in making this discovery. The colorful illustrations also convey the persistence and determination of this young scientist, who overcame many obstacles to fulfill his life's dream of becoming an astronomer.

1.20 Wilson, Colin (1997). **The Unexplained: Mysteries of the Universe.** New York: Dorling Kindersley. 37 pp. ISBN: 0-7894-2165-8. Picture Book.

This collection of some of the world's greatest mysteries, ranging from the Loch Ness monster to crop circles, tickles the imagination of the reader. Wilson is careful to expose documented hoaxes as well as to detail more credible work by scientists and researchers. The combination of facts and speculation challenges readers to come to their own conclusions. It seems that some of the accounts and photographs are included only for their sensational appeal, however. The book includes an index for quick reference.

Other books in this series include:

Wilson, Colin (1998). **The Unexplained: Ghosts and the Supernatural.** New York: Dorling Kindersley. 37 pp. ISBN: 0-7894-2819-9. Picture Book.

Wilson, Colin (1998). **The Unexplained: Psychic Powers.** New York: Dorling Kindersley. 37 pp. ISBN: 0-7894-2820-2. Picture Book.

Wilson, Colin (1997). **The Unexplained: UFOs and Aliens.** New York: Dorling Kindersley. 37 pp. ISBN: 0-7894-2166-6. Picture Book.

Health and Medicine

Primary Reviews

1.21 Bauer, Marion Dane (1997). **If You Were Born a Kitten.** Illustrated by JoEllen McAllister Stammen. New York: Simon & Schuster Books for Young Readers. Unpaged. ISBN: 0-689-80111-4. Picture Book. (See **13.1**)

1.22 Brown, Laurie K., and Marc Brown (1996). **When Dinosaurs Die: A Guide to Understanding Death.** Boston: Little Brown. 32 pp. ISBN: 0-316-10917-7. Picture Book.

In simple language the authors explain the feelings that people have about death, and the different ways that people honor the memory of a loved one. Rather than tell a story to express these ideas, this book talks about these issues in a direct yet comforting way. It discusses matter-of-factly that people's lives can be long or short, and can end in many different ways. The dialogue of child-like characters throughout the book expresses common reactions to death, including bad dreams, loss of appetite, and not believing that it really happened. Feelings of anger, worry, frustration, and sadness are all highlighted to show that "when someone dies there is no right or wrong way to feel." The illustrations depict reactions to the death of human friends as well as birds and household pets. The authors do an excellent job of describing a wide range of customs for honoring the deceased. They also share various beliefs about what comes after death, including reincarnation and resurrection. This is a book that treats a delicate subject in a sensitive and respectful manner.

1.23   Ganeri, Anita (1997). **Funny Bones and Other Body Parts**. Illustrated by Steve Fricker and John Holder. New York: Simon & Schuster. 30 pp. ISBN: 0-689-81187-X. Picture Book.

"What am I made of?" is the opening question in this informative and entertaining book about the mechanics of the major human body systems. Supplementing the traditional table of contents is a pictorial guide composed of drawings of systems, such as the skeletal system, and a caption: "Find out about your funny bones on pages 10–11." A two-page spread is devoted to each system. The text has many technical terms, but they are explained in understandable ways. For example, "The bones at a joint are held is place by ligaments that are like elastic bands." The cartoonlike illustrations extend the use of analogies in the text by visually comparing body parts to mechanical devices. The book includes an index and foldout pages that invite the reader to identify the organs described throughout the book. The concluding section, "Amazing Body Parts," gives statistics and records (e.g., longest fingernails) that children also will enjoy.

1.24   Lee, Barbara (1996). **Working in Health Care and Wellness.** Minneapolis: Lerner. 112 pp. ISBN: 0-8225-1760-4. Sophisticated Chapter Book.

Readers of this book will step into the working lives of twelve professionals in the field of health care, ranging from the more traditional careers of registered nurse and paramedic to the less typical acupuncturist. Each interview follows the same format: a description of the daily routine, including hours of work and the variety of daily tasks; a personal history describing the person's interest in the field and education; a discussion of the future of the profession and/or the person's thoughts about future employment opportunities; and recommendations for readers who might aspire to similar careers. The professionals who were interviewed present an honest view of their work. Some describe the emotional stresses of their jobs, or bemoan the long hours of paperwork. On the other hand, they convey a spirit of dedication to their fields and an excitement about technological developments such as diagnostic scanners. The book also includes information boxes on various topics, a bibliography, and an index. It is part of the Exploring Careers series.

1.25 Miller, Brandon Marie (1997). **Just What the Doctor Ordered: The History of American Medicine.** Minneapolis: Lerner. 88 pp. ISBN: 0-8225-1737-X. Chapter Book.

Through the liberal use of primary sources, such as writings by soldiers and explorers, historical drawings, and photographs, this fascinating history comes alive for today's reader. The opening story, documented by French explorer Jacques Cartier in 1535–1536, recounts how sailors suffering from mysterious symptoms were cured by following the advice of a Native American. The disease was scurvy, and the tree bark that cured them was rich in Vitamin C. In the pages that follow, the relationships among diet, basic hygiene, sanitation, and health are recurrent themes. We learn that physicians in the 1840s debated whether it was necessary to wash hands between surgeries on different patients. The author documents the fight against history's major diseases—yellow fever, tuberculosis, cholera, polio, and so forth—and leaves the reader contemplating today's battle with AIDS. A bibliography and index are included as reference tools. This book is part of the People's History series.

1.26 Pringle, Laurence (1997). **Everybody Has a Bellybutton: Your Life before You Were Born.** Illustrated by Clare Wood. Honesdale, PA: Boyds Mills. Unpaged. ISBN: 1-56397-009-0. Picture Book.

A bellybutton is more than a funny-looking mark on the stomach. A bellybutton is a reminder of the miraculous story of human development from a tiny cell to a baby ready to be born. The book says little about the actual birth and even less about how babies are conceived. Instead the author focuses on the amazing story of the development of a baby inside the mother's womb. He describes the function of the umbilical cord as it supplies rich nutrients, water, and oxygen. The book is told in second person so that readers can make a personal connection to the miracle of prenatal development. The gentle pencil and pastel pictures alternate between representations of the growing fetus and the expectant mother and older sibling. The illustrations convey the joy and excitement of pregnancy and the love of a caring family.

1.27   Simon, Seymour (1996). **The Heart.** New York: Scholastic. Unpaged. ISBN: 0-590-12120-0. Picture Book.

The author takes advantage of the new machines that scientists are using to peer inside the human body and uses this technology to create a fascinating view of the heart. The colored images presented in the book, taken with high-powered scanners, show a beating heart in action, red blood cells traveling through a blood vessel, and white blood cells surrounding and destroying germs. Other computer-enhanced images show the branching blood vessels in the lungs, as well as a remarkable illustration of a blood clot that depicts red blood cells and platelets trapped in a web of fibrin (connective tissue that begins to close the wound). Simon writes in his characteristic clear and direct way. He often uses descriptive comparisons that make the ideas accessible to readers, such as that the heart is as big as a fist and weighs as much as a sneaker, or that each person has more red blood cells (25 trillion) than there are stars in the Milky Way galaxy. The text and the photographs work well together to convey a respect and appreciation for the mystery and miracle of the human body.

A related book is:

Simon, Seymour (1997). **The Brain: Our Nervous System.** New York: Morrow. 32 pp. ISBN: 0-688-14641-4. Picture Book.

Secondary Reviews

1.28   Hawcock, David (1997). **The Amazing Pull-out Pop-up Body in a Book.** New York: Dorling Kindersley. Unpaged. ISBN: 0-7894-2052-X. Picture Book.

This is a basic book for young readers on the human body that discusses bones, nerves, muscles, blood, and digestion. It uses helpful comparisons—for example, that nerve messages travel faster than a race car—so that children can better understand the statistical information. It also introduces some simple activities, such as a touch test for the arm and a tendon experiment for the hand. Diagrams of body parts superimposed on photographs effectively convey their location for young children. However, the large foldout of the body is difficult to manage and would have been more useful as a separate poster.

1.29 Quigley, James (1997). **Johnny Germ Head.** Illustrated by JoAnn Adinolfi. New York: Henry Holt. 72 pp. ISBN: 0-8050-5395-6. Chapter Book. (See **7.45**)

1.30 Rosenberg, Maxine (1997). **Mommy's in the Hospital Having a Baby.** Photographs by Robert Maas. New York: Clarion. 28 pp. ISBN: 0-395-71813-9. Picture Book.

The special wonders and worries of a soon-to-be sibling are sensitively addressed in this reassuring book. Through the informative text and numerous photographs, children will better understand their mothers' stay at a hospital, the appearance of newborns, breast and bottle feeding, and their own special privileges as older brothers and sisters. Advice is given gently, such as "to talk softly in the hospital so you won't wake up the babies and other moms who are taking naps." This book would be a helpful resource for parenting centers.

1.31 Sanders, Pete, and Steve Myers (1997). **Drinking Alcohol.** Brookfield, CT: Copper Beech. 32 pp. ISBN: 0-7613-0573-4. Sophisticated Picture Book.

A cartoon-format story about a teen's struggle with alcohol is paired with straightforward text in this comprehensive guide for adolescents. The book is designed for use as a discussion guide or as a resource for individual readers. Issues ranging from peer pressure to fetal alcohol syndrome are addressed in clear, readable language. Advice for parents and other adults is included. Other resources include an index and a list of ten organizations to be consulted for additional support and information.

Inventions, Discoveries, and Statistics

Primary Reviews

1.32   Alphin, Elaine Marie (1997). **Vacuum Cleaners.** Minneapolis: Carolrhoda. 48 pp. ISBN: 1-57505-018-8. Chapter Book.

The dreaded symbol of household chores becomes a star of engineering history in the hands of Elaine Marie Alphin. The text opens with a thorough description of the kinds of dust in the atmosphere—including pollen, dander, and smoke—as well as a discussion of the health dangers of dust and dust mites. Next the mechanics of modern vacuum cleaners are explained, accompanied by clearly drawn and labeled diagrams. The real treat of the book, however, comes in the next two chapters. Humans' battle with dust comes alive with numerous photographs and drawings of brooms, carpet beaters, carpet sweepers, vacuums, and their inventors. The text nicely demonstrates the old maxim, "Necessity is the mother of invention" by stressing how the limitations of one vacuum inspired the development of new technology. A section called "Vacs of the Future" shows how engineers continue to work for improvements in the cleaning field. Technical terms, which are printed in boldface type, are fully explained in the glossary. The book also includes an index and directions to build a small vacuum. Children will enjoy creating their own working vacuum and seeing for themselves the mechanics of this important machine.

1.33   Dunn, Andrew (1997). **The Children's Atlas of Scientific Discoveries and Inventions.** Brookfield, CT: Millbrook. 96 pp. ISBN: 0-7613-0220-4. Picture Book.

From the earliest of times people have been discovering and inventing new things in an effort to understand and control the world around them. This book gives a comprehensive look at some of these major events. It distinguishes between discoveries, which reveal something that already exists (e.g., magnetism), and inventions, which involve creating something for the first time (e.g., bicycles and mousetraps). The book is divided into four main sections: "Technology and the Birth of Ideas," "Communication and Travel," "Learning about Life" (medicine, genetics, disease), and "Astronomy and Cosmology." In all chapters readers are given an historical look at major advances in these areas. For instance, the history of time shows early timekeepers, ancient calendars, and our modern-day time zones. One of the strengths of the book is the use of numerous photographs (especially of artifacts) and historical drawings and paintings. There are clearly explained diagrams throughout to illustrate some of the scientific concepts, such as the movement of the continental plates, the interior of a cell, and the cycles of water and oxygen. This book gives an interesting perspective to the history of thought and ideas.

1.34   Farndon, John (1996). **What Happens When . . . ? You Turn on the TV? Switch on a Light? Mail a Letter? And Much More!** Illustrated by Steve Fricker and Mike Harndon. New York: Scholastic. 45 pp. ISBN: 0-590-84754-6. Picture Book.

If you wanted light, water, or food two hundred years ago, you had to go get it and carry it in yourself. But today it seems all you need to do is flick a switch, turn on a faucet, or call a delivery service. On the opening page of this intriguing book, readers view a cutaway illustration of a house that shows the common daily occurrences that will be described, such as mailing a letter, watching television, ordering flowers, and turning on the heat. Each page begins with an interesting question: How does rain get to your faucet? What happens to garbage? What's the secret of television? The book is well organized; each question is given a two-page spread, and the profuse illustrations and the step-by-step numbered directions make it easier for readers to follow each explanation. Two large foldout sections offer some additional information about mailing letters and making a pizza, such as how the International Date Line works (the letter is going from New York to Australia) and what parts of the world produce certain ingredients for the pizza. This book certainly could serve as a catalyst for further reading about many topics.

1.35   Mugford, Simon (1997). **The Fantastic Cutaway Book of Rescue!** Illustrated by Alex Pang. Brookfield, CT: Copper Beech. 40 pp. ISBN: 0-7613-0616-1. Picture Book.

People are rescued from all kinds of dangerous situations. This book shows cutaway illustrations of various vehicles and equipment, such as rescue helicopters, fire engines, and numerous submersibles. Readers learn what this equipment looks like, and how it is used to rescue people in trouble. It is this diversity of tools that makes this book so appealing; for example, the book discusses vehicles and equipment to rescue a troubled diver deep beneath the ocean as well as a damaged space station high above the earth. The wide range of vehicles helps readers appreciate how these tools are adapted to address a specific need, such as the robot that is designed to dismantle terrorist bombs, or the lifeboat that will right itself if it should be capsized by rough seas. The vehicles are depicted in color illustrations as well as photographs that show the vehicle in operation. Parts of each vehicle are labeled so that readers can follow more easily the technical description in the text. At the end of the book there is a helpful chronology that details important landmarks in the history of rescue vehicles.

Another book in this series is:

> Kirkwood, Jon, and Alex Pang (1997). **The Fantastic Cutaway Book of Giant Buildings.** Brookfield, CT: Copper Beech. 40 pp. ISBN: 0-7613-0615-3. Picture Book.

1.36 Pedersen, Ted, and Francis Moss (1997). **Internet for Kids! A Beginner's Guide to Surfing the Net.** New York: Price Stern Sloan. 219 pp. ISBN: 0-8431-7937-6. Chapter Book.

This well-organized beginner's guide to the Internet will draw children of all ages to the never-ending world of cyberspace. Readers are invited to join students Kate and Zack at Cyberspace Academy, where they are advised by the cartoon character CyberSarge. For example, in the section on e-mail, CyberSarge suggests from the margins: "When telling someone your email address, say the word 'at' for the @, and say 'dot' instead of 'period.'" Through the entertaining medium of story, children learn step-by-step instructions to use the Internet easily, as well as sample projects to try. Computer language is highlighted in boldface type, and these terms are defined more thoroughly in sidebars on the same page and in the glossary. An index is also included. Topics include basic rules for surfing the Internet, recommended Web sites, writing and receiving e-mail, and the technology behind what users see on the screen. Although the book contains a great deal of information, wide margins and illustrations make it manageable for children. Parents and teachers will appreciate the section written especially for them, which addresses issues of safety and responsibility. A sample parent-child contract is included as a guide for wise use of this marvelous tool.

Secondary Reviews

1.37 Hetherington, Tim, and Esther Labi, editors (1996). **Essential Facts.** New York: Dorling Kindersley. 128 pp. ISBN: 0-7894-1020-6. Picture Book.

This pocket-sized resource serves as a mini-encyclopedia packed with tables, charts, maps, and statistics. Information is easy to access from a well-organized table of contents and an index. A two-page guide also aids the reader in using the book effectively. Sections include "The World Around Us" (solar system), "The Political World," "Technology," "Science," "Mathematics," and "People." The book serves as a handy research tool for locating basic information in a variety of areas.

1.38 Kirkwood, Jon (1997). **Cutaway Trucks.** Brookfield, CT: Copper Beech. 32 pp. ISBN: 0-7613-0710-9. Picture Book.

Children who love trucks will enjoy this basic book on these vehicles. It covers a wide variety of trucks, such as tankers, trailers, and dump trucks. It includes trucks for special places, for example, trucks for traversing the desert or a frozen lake. It discusses the different jobs that trucks might perform at a single building site: bringing gravel, dumping cement, or scraping the earth. Colorful photographs and drawings are silhouetted against a white background and enhance the text's clarity. Labeled drawings identify important features of the trucks and are helpful in illustrating the brief text on each page.

Another book in this series is:

Kirkwood, Jon (1997). **Cutaway Firefighters.** Brookfield, CT: Copper Beech. 32 pp. ISBN: 0-7613-0711-7. Picture Book.

1.39 Nichelason, Margery G. (1997). **Shoes.** Minneapolis: Carolrhoda. 48 pp. ISBN: 1-57505-047-1. Chapter Book.

The history of shoes reflects not only fashion but the clever work of inventors who sought to make foot coverings practical and comfortable. This book addresses a wide range of topics, from the development of a *last* (shoe form), to the derivation of the word *sabotage* (peasants sometimes used wooden shoes, or *sabots*, to stomp on crops in vengeance against overbearing landlords). Historical photographs, drawings, and highlighted sidebars add interest to the informative and entertaining text. The book also includes a glossary, index, and suggested art projects with recycled shoes.

This book is part of a series of household history books that also includes:

> Goldstein, Margaret (1997). **Eyeglasses.** Minneapolis: Carolrhoda. 48 pp. ISBN: 1-57505-001-3. Chapter Book.

> Josephson, Judith Pinkerton (1998). **Umbrellas.** Minneapolis: Carolrhoda. 48 pp. ISBN: 1-57505-098-6. Chapter Book.

Forthcoming books in the series will address other common household objects such as toasters, telephones, and doors.

Looking Closely at the Natural World

Primary Reviews

1.40   Cobb, Vicki (1998). **Dirt and Grime.** New York: Scholastic. 32 pp. ISBN: 0-590-92666-7. Picture Book.

This book takes a close look at what many people consider unpleasant, and unhealthy, parts of our world: dirt, grime (dirt stuck to surfaces), cobwebs, mold, germs, and garbage. However, Cobb describes these subjects in an informative way. She often adds mathematical facts that provide interesting detail, such as that the force of a sneeze has been clocked at more than one hundred miles per hour, or the exponential growth rate of bacteria. She points out some of the benefits of this microscopic world, such as the accidental discovery of penicillin in the midst of a study of mold, and the enormous contribution of fruit flies to genetic research. Another strength of this book is that it is filled with photographs taken with a high-powered electron microscope. Beautiful colors, patterns, and textures are revealed in this close-up look at dirt and grime. There are health lessons to be learned here as well, such as cleaning sponges and cutting boards to prevent the growth of bacteria.

Another book in this series is:

> Cobb, Vicki (1997). **Blood and Gore.** New York: Scholastic. 32 pp. ISBN: 0-590-92665-9. Picture Book.

1.41   Cole, Joanna (1996). **The Magic School Bus: Inside a Beehive.** Illustrated by Bruce Degen. New York: Scholastic. 48 pp. ISBN: 0-590-44684-3. Picture Book.

Are you ready for another ride? Ms. Frizzle and her class of young explorers are off again to investigate the hive of honeybees. Throughout their journey, important scientific concepts are conveyed in a whimsical yet informative way. As with the rest of the books in the Magic School Bus series, the author tells two stories at the same time: the story of the students' trip into the hive, and the children's reports of what they are discovering along the way. Thus the children's writing helps move the text along and is a powerful demonstration that children's questions ought to drive authentic scientific research. The children's reports focus on some fascinating aspect of the bees, such as how they communicate (through smells as well as their dances), why they sting, and how they help flowers. The frequent use of drawings helps to convey many of these important ideas. Another appealing part of Cole's book is her sense of humor; there is a section on bee riddles, and there are constant word plays (a queen who lays fifteen hundred eggs per day receives an "eggs-cellent" rating). (See also **1.5** for another book in this series.)

1.42   Esbensen, Barbara Juster (1996). **Echoes for the Eye: Poems to Celebrate Patterns in Nature.** Illustrated by Helen K. Davie. New York: HarperCollins. 32 pp. ISBN: 0-06-024398-8. Picture Book. (See **10.41**)

1.43   Frasier, Debra (1998). **Out of the Ocean.** San Diego: Harcourt Brace. 40 pp. ISBN: 0-15-258849-3. Picture Book.

Here is a story that makes readers look more closely at the beauty of their world. A mother and her daughter walk along the beach, admiring all that they see. The mother says the ocean can grant wishes. She proves her point by asking the ocean for sun and water each day, and each day she is granted these two beautiful gifts. The daughter asks if other treasures can be found. Together they look closely and find pelican feathers, skate egg pouches, and some shark's teeth. They also find human artifacts, such as broken glass, a pile of rope, and a beam from a sunken ship. As the book concludes, the daughter learns her mother's secret: There are treasures everywhere, and it's not the asking, but the remembering to look, that makes the difference. Detailed notes at the end of the book give excellent information about the objects found at the beach, from the life of sea turtles to the story of rafts abandoned by Cuban refugees. The dangers that humans pose to the environment also are discussed. The mixed-media collage illustrations of photographs and paper cutouts convey the splendor of the ocean in a magnificent way.

1.44   Levy, Matthys, and Mario Salvadori (1997). **Earthquake Games.** New York: Margaret K. McElderry. 116 pp. ISBN: 0-689-81367-8. Chapter Book.

The authors discuss the power and nature of earthquakes and volcanoes in this accessible book for upper-elementary school students. The format of the book makes it an inviting resource. Each chapter begins with some scientific background, describes easy-to-follow experiments, and concludes with questions commonly asked by children. The simple black-and-white drawings and diagrams are easy to follow and complement the scientific concepts being discussed in the text. Each chapter addresses different aspects of earthquakes and volcanoes: understanding the interior of the earth, the mystery of the 1811 earthquake in St. Louis, measuring the strength of earthquakes, the formation of tidal waves, engineering techniques to support buildings during earthquakes, and the causes of volcanoes. The experiments use common objects—such as blocks, cereal boxes, and even your hands—to effectively convey the processes described in the text. This is an excellent resource for understanding basic geological processes.

1.45   Malam, John (1996). **Highest Longest Deepest: A Fold-out Guide to the World's Record Breakers.** Illustrated by Gary Hincks. New York: Simon & Schuster. 41 pp. ISBN: 0-689-80951-4. Chapter Book.

If you want to travel the world and explore the highest mountain, the deepest ocean trench, the biggest cave, and the longest coral reef, then this is the book for you! It covers many different aspects of the natural world, from volcanoes to deserts and from lakes to caves. Each brief chapter provides a variety of information in a visually appealing manner. For instance, in the chapter on the highest mountains, readers are treated to a foldout visual that compares the world's highest peaks. There are two helpful diagrams that show how mountains are made and how the shape of mountains reveals their relative age. There are also several illustrations of animals that inhabit these high regions, such as the chamois, the ibex, and the high-flying Andean condor, which can withstand the fierce mountain winds. Throughout the book there are animals depicted to show the diversity of life that exists even in these extreme conditions. Children might want to learn more about these animals and investigate how they have learned to adapt to these particular climates. One of the strengths of this book is that it goes beyond just listing statistical wonders to explain how such things as glaciers, lakes, and coral reefs came to be.

1.46 Mason, Adrienne (1998). **Living Things.** Photographs by Ray Boudreau. Buffalo, NY: Kids Can. 32 pp. ISBN: 1-55074-343-0. Picture Book.

Young scientists will want to roll up their sleeves and gather materials for twelve experiments as soon as they open this bright guide to important ideas in life science. The investigations demonstrate that all living things need air, food, water, and a habitat. The plants and animals needed for the experiments were carefully chosen to show diversity: sow bugs, mealworms, humans, yeast, green plants, and flowers. The layout of the book is easy to follow. Each experiment covers a two-page spread, with a colorful photograph of children in action and sections labeled "You will need," "What to do," and "What's happening?" This third section gives the scientific explanation behind the results of the investigation in an accurate but simple way. Several experiments also feature a highlighted box that provides helpful hints or additional facts. For example, an explanation of metamorphosis accompanies instructions on raising mealworms. Several of the experiments result in a special product, such as baked bread, a book of pressed flowers, or alfalfa sprouts. Parents and teachers will appreciate the section of helpful hints for adults. The book also includes a simple glossary and an index.

Other books in the Starting with Science series include:

The Ontario Science Centre (1998). **Plants.** Photographs by Ray Boudreau. Buffalo, NY: Kids Can. 32 pp. ISBN: 1-55074-193-4. Picture Book.

The Ontario Science Centre (1998). **Solids, Liquids and Gases.** Photographs by Ray Boudreau. Buffalo, NY: Kids Can. 32 pp. ISBN: 1-55074-195-0. Picture Book.

1.47 Older, Jules (1997). **Cow.** Illustrated by Lyn Severance. Watertown, MA: Charlesbridge. Unpaged. ISBN: 0-88106-957-4. Picture Book. (See **13.21**)

1.48 Orr, Katherine (1997). **Discover Hawaii's Freshwater Wildlife.** Aiea, HI: Island Heritage. 44 pp. ISBN: 0-89610-243-2. Chapter Book.

An excellent nonfiction resource, Orr teaches us about Hawaii's freshwater community. Hawaii's unique water cycle allows the islands to flourish amidst its people, plants, and wildlife. As water falls onto the land, it changes the land's shape, giving each island its own distinct streams, valleys, and island formations. She invites readers to explore the world of the wildlife, insects, and waterfowl that thrive in and depend on these tropical freshwater communities. Her illustrations are clear and inviting, and the information she provides is appropriate for older readers investigating water systems and communities throughout the United States. Because Hawaii's freshwater system is also very fragile, Orr challenges her readers to respect Hawaii's water so the islands can maintain a balance with nature. She suggests helpful ideas for children that can help maintain this freshwater ecosystem. This book is part of a series of other discovery books about Hawaii.

1.49 Orr, Katherine, and Mauliola Cook (1997). **Discover Hawaii's Birth by Fire Volcanoes.** Aiea, HI: Island Heritage. 44 pp. ISBN: 0-89610-245-9. Chapter Book.

In her continuing Discover Hawaii series, Katherine Orr and coauthor Mauliola Cook invite readers to discover the wonders of Hawaii's volcanoes. In describing Hawaii's birth, they share both Hawaiian and scientific perspectives. The first Polynesians to discover Hawaii told legends that spoke of its birth and development. Scientists theorize that Hawaii moves with the Pacific plate along a hot spot where molten rock spews out through Earth's crust. After billions of years of volcanic eruptions, the tallest peaks surfaced from the ocean, forming island chains. Over the next billion years, the islands underwent changes; gravity, weathering, and erosion wore away the islands, and plant and animal life thrived. At the end of an island's cycle, only guyots remain when the coral reef and tiny atoll is finally washed away. Bright illustrations enhance the text. Older readers will appreciate the book and become inspired to inquire further.

1.50 Parker, Steve (1997). **The Beginner's Guide to Animal Autopsy: The Hands-on Approach to Zoology.** Illustrated by Rob Shone.

Brookfield, CT: Copper Beech. 48 pp. ISBN: 0-7613-0702-8. Picture Book.

Want to see a close-up of a chameleon from the inside out? Step inside the pages of this book to find detailed descriptions of the anatomy of more than thirty creatures. The book is divided into five chapters that group animals according to scientific classification, such as "Slithery-Slimies" (mollusks and crustaceans). A separate guide to animal classification, a glossary, and an index are also helpful tools for the young researcher. A brief introduction outlines reasons why scientists dissect animals, such as to know more about how the body works and to learn how animals are related to one another. The author carefully points out that no animal was harmed for the book's preparation. To keep from making the illustrations too gory, the animals are portrayed as either plastic toys or stuffed animals. The information is presented in an entertaining yet informative style, describing the crocodile's movement as a "two-speed swim" or the penguin's as "flapstroke, not backstroke." Information boxes further explain how various organs function, or address a common question such as, "Why are elephant ears so huge?" The book combines humor with facts, making it inviting to young readers and adults alike.

1.51 Ross, Michael E. (1997). **Bug Watching with Charles Henry Turner.** Illustrated by Laurie A. Caple. Minneapolis: Carolrhoda. 48 pp. ISBN: 1-57505-003-X. Chapter Book.

Charles Henry Turner was a premier entomologist whose interest in bugs began when he was a small boy. His story is all the more remarkable because he was an African American growing up in the post–Civil War era. The strengths of this engaging biography are that it describes the prejudices that Turner encountered and overcame, but also celebrates his scientific thinking. Turner spent most of his life teaching as a high school science teacher even though he had the qualifications to teach at a university. Most universities at that time did not hire African American professors. Despite these hardships, Turner never lost his curiosity for the natural world and continued to conduct experiments and write about his research throughout his life. The book describes some of his experiments involving the shape of spiders' webs, the homing instinct of ants, the eyesight of bees (Are they color-blind?), and the intelligence of cockroaches (Can they learn by trial and error?). Side boxes describe similar experiments that children can try. This biography wonderfully demonstrates the mind of a scientific thinker who looks closely, inquires, and keeps asking questions.

1.52   Ross, Michael E. (1997). **Flower Watching with Alice Eastwood.** Illustrated by Laurie A. Caple. Minneapolis: Carolrhoda. 148 pp. ISBN: 1-57505-005-6. Chapter Book.

If you want to know how to look at the world through the eyes of a botanist, come along with Alice Eastwood. This book retells the fascinating life of one of America's most well-known botanists, who spent her life documenting the plants and flowers of Colorado and California. The author does an excellent job of detailing significant events in Eastwood's life, including a difficult childhood, a brief teaching career, and her work at the Academy of Sciences in San Francisco. One of the strengths of this book is the inviting way that the text and the illustrations work together. For instance, when readers learn of Eastwood's observation of the showy columbine flower, the two featured illustrations give information about that flower and tips on how to use a magnifying lens. When the text describes the field guides that Eastwood carried with her, the illustration gives an example of the kind of classification key found in these guides and asks readers to test it out. There is a constant interplay between Eastwood's life and what children can do today to become naturalists in their own right. Eastwood remained active throughout her eighties, learning about a whole new group of flowers. Her life is a wonderful demonstration of a life-long learner.

1.53   Ross, Michael E. (1997). **Wildlife Watching with Charles Eastman.** Illustrated by Laurie A. Caple. Minneapolis: Carolrhoda. 48 pp. ISBN: 1-57505-004-8. Chapter Book.

One of the great naturalists of our time was born in 1858. He was born a Sioux, but later converted to Christianity and adopted the name of Charles Eastman. His grandmother introduced him to the wonders of nature and taught him the art of being quiet in the woods. Readers can learn how to be invisible observers themselves by following the accompanying tips in the text. One of the strengths of this book is the correlation of the life of Eastman and appropriate activities for children to pursue. Eastman's uncle taught him to look for the minute details. "Like a wolf," he said, "take a second look at everything." The accompanying box tells readers how to take a "Memory Walk" and learn how to notice. Readers also learn how to make alarm calls to attract curious animals, analyze scats, recognize animal tracks, and read animal trails. These tips help readers feel what it's really like to be a naturalist. In addition, the book also describes the injustices delivered upon the Sioux and other Native American peoples by the federal government. In this way, Eastman's life is viewed in its historical and political context.

1.54 Sauvain, Philip (1996). **Oceans.** Minneapolis: Carolrhoda. 32 pp. ISBN: 1-57505-043-9. Chapter Book.

Did you know that if there were no oceans to warm the earth, the weather would be far too cold for human life to survive? This book provides an interesting introduction to the oceans of the world, explaining its special features, its movement, its creatures, and its hazards and potentials. It starts by distinguishing among oceans, seas, gulfs, and straits. Diagrams are interspersed throughout the text so that scientific ideas can be understood more easily. For instance, there are informative diagrams to show the shape of the ocean floor, the direction of ocean currents, and the location of plants and animals in the sea. Each two-page spread contains photographs and maps, as well as diagrams, to complement the written text. The format of each page also includes a box labeled "Geography Detective," and a box that contains additional information about the current topic. The latter box often has intriguing statistical information, such as the fact that the Pacific Ocean is so big that one could place all the land on the earth's surface there and still have enough room for a second Asia! Occasionally there are case studies that illustrate real-life applications of these ideas, such as the Zuider Zee reclamation project in the Netherlands.

Another book in this series is:

Sauvain, Philip (1996). **Rain Forests.** Minneapolis: Carolrhoda. 32 pp. ISBN: 1-57505-041-2. Chapter Book.

1.55 Wick, Walter (1997). **A Drop of Water.** New York: Scholastic. 40 pp. ISBN: 0-590-22197-3. Picture Book.

Spectacular photographs of water and an informative text make this one of the most compelling science books for students of all ages. Evaporation, condensation, surface tension, and capillary action are all illustrated with clear photographs and a simple text. The photographs capture the many fascinating transformations of water in magnificent detail. For instance, the elastic surface of water, known as surface tension, is shown through a series of six photographs as a drop of water falls from a faucet. A series of time-lapse photographs show the processes of condensation and evaporation through the use of kitchen silverware and glasses. Magnified photographs of snowflakes demonstrate their intricate and unique patterns. The photographs of the glistening drops of water on a spider's web are so sharp that readers can see the reflection of the landscape mirrored in each droplet. There are helpful suggestions at the end of the book for how to conduct some of the experiments shown in the text. Some of these include how to float a needle, make a rainbow with a garden hose, and use salt to show condensation around a particle. This is a book that is sure to fill readers with awe and respect for the earth's most precious resource.

1.56 Winner, Cherie (1996). **The Sunflower Family.** Photographs by Sherry Shahan. Minneapolis: Carolrhoda. 48 pp. ISBN: 1-57505-007-2. Picture Book.

What do thistles, sagebrush, dandelions, and leafy lettuce all have in common? All of these plants belong to the 25,000-member *compositæ* family, which is also known as the sunflower family. Much of the text is devoted to describing the life cycle of plants in this family, including sprouting, growth, reproduction, and seed dispersal. Technical terms are highlighted in boldface type, accompanied by phonetic pronunciation, and are included in the glossary. The index also is helpful. Another main purpose of the book is to document the enormous variety of these fascinating plants through stunning photographs and descriptive narration. Although readers will recognize many common species, they also will marvel at plants as rare as the desert yellowhead, which lives only on a twenty-acre area in central Wyoming. Winner presents convincing arguments for the need to protect rare and endangered plants by explaining their crucial role in ecosystems. She also devotes a section to describing the many uses of members of the *compositæ* family. Leaves from a plant called guaco, for example, can be thrown into a stream to stun fish so that they are easily caught. Readers will come away with a sense of appreciation for the diversity, beauty, and versatility of this family of plants.

Secondary Reviews

1.57 Barlowe, Sy (1997). **101 Questions about the Seashore.** Mineola, NY: Dover. 54 pp. ISBN: 0-486-29914-7. Chapter Book.

The questions addressed in this small volume are best suited to readers already quite familiar with the seashore. Although there is a wealth of information in the book, there is no index and it is difficult to locate specific information from the chapter titles (e.g., "The Upper Seashore"). Some questions follow a form younger children might use (e.g., "What do seagulls eat?"). The primary intent of many others seems to be the introduction of key vocabulary (e.g., "What is an operculum?"). The accompanying black-and-white drawings are detailed. The book is scientifically accurate, but its audience is narrow.

1.58 Fletcher, Ralph (1997). **Ordinary Things: Poems from a Walk in Early Spring.** Illustrated by Walter Lyon Krudop. New York: Atheneum. 48 pp. ISBN: 0-689-81035-0. Chapter Book. (See **10.10**)

1.59 Fletcher, Ralph (1997). **Twilight Comes Twice.** Illustrated by Kate Kiesler. New York: Clarion. 32 pp. ISBN: 0-395-84826-1. Picture Book. (See **10.1**)

1.60 Florian, Douglas (1998). **Insectlopedia: Poems and Paintings.** San Diego: Harcourt Brace. 47 pp. ISBN: 0-15-201306-7. Picture Book. (See **10.32**)

1.61 Godkin, Celia (1998). **What about Ladybugs?** San Francisco: Sierra Club Books for Children. Unpaged. ISBN: 0-87156-549-8. Picture Book.

In this story a gardener learns the lessons of ecological balance. He was fond of ladybugs, but did not know the role they played in maintaining the natural balance in his garden. Consequently, he sprays a pesticide on his garden to control aphids. His garden deteriorates until he finally is informed of the value of ladybugs for keeping aphids in check. He reintroduces ladybugs in his yard and restores the beauty of his garden. The close-up illustrations help readers see the important role that insects play in nature's interdependent system.

1.62 Johnson, Neil (1997). **A Field of Sunflowers.** New York: Scholastic. Unpaged. ISBN: 0-590-96549-2. Picture Book.

Through a series of color photographs and simple text, the reader is told the story of a field of sunflowers from planting to blooming. Parts of the story are explained quite well, such as the movement of the sunflower plants from east to west each day. However, another page on pollination contains too much technical vocabulary for young children. The photographs also are of varied quality; some provide good close-ups of the plant, while many others are too dark. The fact that the farmer never harvests the sunflowers (he leaves them for the birds) seems a bit anticlimactic.

1.63   Loewer, Peter, and Jean Loewer (1997). **The Moonflower.** Atlanta: Peachtree. 27 pp. ISBN: 1-56145-138-X. Picture Book. (See **7.17**)

1.64   Maass, Robert (1998). **Garden.** New York: Henry Holt. 32 pp. ISBN: 0-8050-5477-4. Picture Book.

Lovely photographs and a simple text tell the story of different kinds of gardens. After a brief introduction to gardens in general, the book describes the steps involved in planting a garden. It gives some important tips: tilling the soil, spacing the seeds, the benefits of compost and worms, and the use of poles and trellises. The photographs reflect a wide range of ages and ethnic groups. The overuse of the wide-angle lens, however, creates unnecessary distortions that detract from otherwise appealing compositions.

1.65   Maynard, Christopher (1997). **Why Do Volcanoes Erupt?** New York: Dorling Kindersley. Unpaged. ISBN: 0-7894-1532-1. Picture Book.

This book is part of a series that features questions young children commonly ask about the natural world. This particular book contains eight questions and answers about Earth on two-page spreads. Although the intent of the book is commendable, there are often problems in the way the text is developed. Complex questions are answered in rather simplistic ways. Often other questions on the page are only distantly related to the main question. In other instances, the use of diagrams or the suggestion of some basic experiments would have made these concepts more accessible to younger children.

Other books in this series include:

Martin, Terry (1996). **Why Do Sunflowers Face the Sun?** New York: Dorling Kindersley. Unpaged. ISBN: 0-7894-1120-2. Picture Book.

Martin, Terry (1996). **Why Does Lightning Strike?** New York: Dorling Kindersley. Unpaged. ISBN: 0-7894-1123-7. Picture Book.

Maynard, Christopher (1997). **Why Are Pineapples Prickly?** New York: Dorling Kindersley. Unpaged. ISBN: 0-7894-1530-5. Picture Book.

Maynard, Christopher (1997). **Why Are There Waves?** New York: Dorling Kindersley. Unpaged. ISBN: 0-7894-1531-3. Picture Book.

1.66 Patent, Dorothy Hinshaw (1997). **Apple Trees.** Photographs by William Muñoz. Minneapolis: Lerner. 48 pp. ISBN: 0-8225-3020-1. Chapter Book.

A series of appealing photographs complement a thorough description of apples, from their growth through marketing. Technical vocabulary is accompanied by phonetic pronunciations in the text, and is defined in the glossary. The opening page conveys a didactic tone, however, inviting the reader to be a "word detective" by finding the listed vocabulary while reading. A two-page guide for adults at the end of the book gives instructions for questioning that might detract from the natural curiosity of the young readers for whom the book is intended.

1.67 Sandved, Kjell B. (1996). **The Butterfly Alphabet.** New York: Scholastic. Unpaged. ISBN: 0-590-48003-0. Picture Book. (See **7.28**)

1.68 Speed, Toby (1998). **Water Voices.** Illustrated by Julie Downing. New York: Putnam. Unpaged. ISBN: 0-399-22631-1. Picture Book. (See **7.19**)

1.69 Scheffler, Ursel (1997). **Grandpa's Amazing Computer.** Illustrated by Ruth Scholte van Mast. Translated by Rosemary Lanning. New York: North-South. 48 pp. ISBN: 1-55858-795-0. Chapter Book. (See **7.41**)

1.70 Stroud, Virginia (1996). **The Path of the Quiet Elk.** New York: Dial. 30 pp. ISBN: 0-8037-1717-2. Picture Book. (See **7.35**)

1.71 Yolen, Jane (1996). **Sea Watch: A Book of Poetry.** Illustrated by Ted Lewin. New York: Philomel. 32 pp. ISBN: 0-399-22734-2. Picture Book. (See **10.50**)

A.

B.

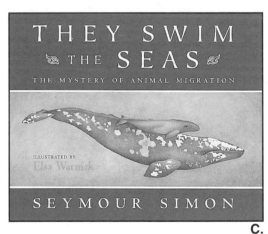

C.

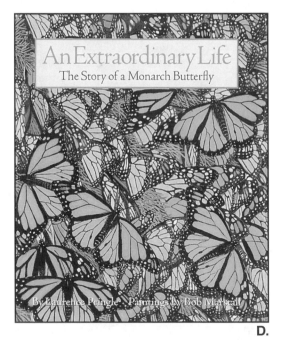

D.

A. *Anthology for the Earth,* Judy Allen (**2.1**). **B.** *Swift as the Wind: The Cheetah,* Barbara Juster Esbensen/Jean Cassels (**2.6**). **C.** *They Swim the Seas: The Mystery of Animal Migration,* Seymour Simon/Elsa Warnick (**2.23**). **D.** *An Extraordinary Life: The Story of a Monarch Butterfly,* Laurence Pringle/Bob Marstall (**2.20**).

2 Our Changing World

Dick Koblitz

Contributing reviewers included Susie Bargiel, Maureen Dietzel, Susan Flynn, Dick Koblitz, and Jane Soelhke.

Earth and everything in the universe beyond our planet is in a constant state of change. Sometimes the changes seem to occur very slowly, as when a desert is formed over hundreds of thousands of years, or animals develop special adaptations that increase their chances for survival in a particular habitat. Sometimes changes occur very rapidly, as when a tornado forms and within seconds changes the face of the landscape, or a sudden change in temperature causes water drops to form ice crystals and blanket a portion of Earth with white. Some changes create great beauty, such as the metamorphosis of a caterpillar into a butterfly, while others cause great destruction, such as the mass extinction of the dinosaurs. Often new life arises out of death and destruction, as when a tree falls in the forest and over time decomposes to enrich the soil where new plants can take root. Change is all around us every second of our lives. Children need to understand change in the world around them in order to better adapt themselves to an ever-increasing rate of human and global change, as well as to respect and appreciate the way nature works to continually recreate Earth and the world beyond.

In this section, we review books that discuss the lives of plants and animals, life cycles, the balance of nature, endangered species and habitats, systems, and physical and earth science. More than two-thirds of the books we selected to include in this section are about mammals, reptiles, birds, and fish. Many of these books, as well as several we chose about plant life, also contain the themes of life cycles, the balance of nature, and endangered species and habitats. This was by far the largest grouping of books we reviewed, which indicates that books about animals continue to hold great interest for children of all ages, and that writers, illustrators, and publishers continue to respond to this interest. We found incredibly beautiful, well-researched, and well-written books about the monarch butterfly, the honeybee, the bald eagle, the bison, the cheetah, snakes, dinosaurs, and other well-known and little-known members of the animal kingdom. Information about species and habitat destruction is a common theme in many of the books we selected. Several tell about the life cycle of a particular animal and its place in the balance of nature. We also found books about the life cycle of trees and the important role they play in our changing world. One unique book we included is an anthology of short stories, poems, and other writings over the past two thousand years that celebrate life in all its forms on our planet Earth.

Around the theme of systems, we found several newly published books about the sky, weather, sun, moon, and stars. Some present factual information while others tell about ancient myths and legends. Several books related to the plants and animals theme also include a systems theme, in particular books about honeybees and trees. New books about electricity, deserts, a lake, and an island will help young readers to understand the concept of change in our physical world as well as how some of these topics fit into a systems way of thinking.

Because of the overlapping of the six themes in many of the books in this section, we decided to organize them into two broad categories— Changes in the Natural World and Changes in the Physical World. Most of the books in this chapter are nonfiction, although a few are fictional or include fictional stories. Several books were written in a storylike, narrative style that will draw children into the topic of the book and sustain their interest. The quality of illustrations, whether original artwork or photographs and diagrams, is extremely high in the books we selected to review. The research of the authors is meticulous, which shows a great deal of respect for their young audiences. Children have an inherent interest in the world around them, and the quality of books in this section will entertain as they teach children about our constantly changing planet.

------

*The titles listed below each subheading are organized into Primary Reviews and Secondary Reviews. The Primary Reviews describe outstanding books in each subheading. The Secondary Reviews provide brief information about other books worthy of consideration. Some titles listed below are **not** reviewed in this chapter; entries for these titles are not annotated and contain only bibliographic information. In such cases, a cross reference to the annotated entry contained elsewhere in this volume is provided in boldface type at the end of the bibliographic information.*

Changes in the Natural World

See also the section entitled Looking Closely at the Natural World in chapter 1, "Stories of the Universe."

Primary Reviews

2.1   Allen, Judy, editor (1998). **Anthology for the Earth.** Cambridge, MA: Candlewick. 96 pp. ISBN: 0-7636-0301-5. Chapter Book.

This is a collection of more than forty writings by both well-known and unknown authors celebrating our planet Earth. The result is an impressive reminder of the complex and often delicate relationships that exist between humans, plants, animals, and Earth itself. Judy Allen has gathered short stories, poems, and other writings of people from many cultures throughout the past two thousand years who have spoken or written in defense of Earth. Joseph Bruchac, a Native American poet and storyteller, writes about an old man who gathers toads blinded by a car's headlights on a highway. Nineteenth-century English novelist Thomas Hardy tells of two executioners carrying axes who fell a two-hundred-year-old tree in less than two hours. Even the Roman poet Ovid implored the world more than two thousand years ago to respect all animal life. The visual images of more than thirty illustrators accompany the various texts. Also included is a table of contents, indexes of authors and illustrators, and short biographies of each author.

2.2   Bateman, Robert, and Rich Archbold (1998). **Safari.** New York: Little Brown. Unpaged. ISBN: 0- 316-08265-1. Picture Book.

Take a safari through the game reserves of subsaharan Africa in this large format picture book for young and old readers alike. Former teacher, naturalist, and painter Robert Bateman has spent years studying, sketching, and painting the wild animals of the African grasslands and jungles. In his latest book, readers learn about the elephant, cheetah, lion, giraffe, wildebeest, gorilla, zebra, and many more of Africa's most endangered mammals. Large detailed paintings that are so realistic they look almost like photographs accompany the lean, easy to read text. The author provides basic information about each animal, as well as a highlighted section on the animal's habitat, height, weight, length, food, and range. The endpapers are filled with Bateman's rough sketches of animals he has included in the book. The author makes a plea at the end for saving the habitats of these special and increasingly rare creatures.

2.3   Bosveld, Jane (1997). **While a Tree Was Growing.** Illustrated by David O'Leary. New York: American Museum of Natural History and Workman. Unpaged. ISBN: 0-7611-0540-9. Picture Book.

The life history from seed to maturity of a giant sequoia in California's Sierra Nevada Mountains is told against major events in human history, from the development of writing in China in 1500 B.C.E. to the discovery of ice on the dark side of the moon in 1996. *Sequoia-dendron giganteum* are the largest and among the oldest living organisms on Earth. The story of the growth of one of these giants is juxtaposed against thirty-five hundred years of human history. Each page describes the growth of the tree, provides information about the animals and insects that live and feed off it, and discusses three historical events that occurred simultaneously, such as Tutankhamen becoming king of Egypt, the Greek poet Homer writing the *Iliad* and the *Odyssey*, the Chinese beginning to make books, Mohammed being born in Mecca, the French Revolution occurring, and astronauts walking on the moon. Full-page paintings by artist David O'Leary illustrate the growth of the giant sequoia. Information about famous giant sequoia trees is provided at the end of the book, as is a pullout poster showing the mature tree with a timeline of historical events. This is an excellent book to help children begin to think about the temporal stability of nature in relation to the ever-changing events of human history.

2.4   Bouchard, David (1996). **Voices from the Wild: An Animal Sensagoria.** Illustrated by Ron Parker. San Francisco: Chronicle. 72 pp. ISBN: 00-8118-1462-9. Chapter Book.

This anthology of twenty-five poems about various wild mammals and birds provides a lyrical and sensory description of these animals generally not found in fiction or nonfiction books. Written from the animals' point of view and in first person, these poems are organized into chapters focusing on the five senses of sight, smell, touch, hearing, and taste. The sense most important to each animal's survival determines in which chapter the poem appears. Each poem is illustrated with a full-page, color, limited-edition art print. This beautifully written and illustrated anthology provides an excellent means for integrating poetry into the study of animals and their characteristics.

2.5   Desimini, Lisa, David Ricceri, Sara Schwartz, and Dan Yaccarino (1997). **All Year Round: A Book to Benefit Children in Need.** New York: Scholastic. Unpaged. ISBN: 0-590-36097-3. Picture Book. (See **13.3**)

2.6   Esbensen, Barbara Juster (1996). **Swift as the Wind: The Cheetah.** Illustrated by Jean Cassels. New York: Orchard. Unpaged. ISBN: 0-531-09497-9. Picture Book.

This narrative about the fastest-running land mammal is full of facts about the cheetah. Information about its speed, physical characteristics, habitat, and behavior are told in an easy-to-read prose style. The cheetah's hunting and reproductive habits are included in great detail. Jean Cassels' watercolor paintings of the cheetah and the African savanna are very detailed and evoke the majesty, speed, and unique feline qualities of this endangered species.

2.7   Galan, Mark (1997). **There's Still Time: The Success of the Endangered Species Act.** Washington, DC: National Geographic. 40 pp. ISBN: 0-7922-7092-4.

Over a quarter of a century ago, the U.S. government took decisive action to protect native American plants and animals that were on the verge of extinction. The Endangered Species Act passed by Congress in 1973 has made possible the survival of many threatened and endangered species for future generations, from the bison and bald eagle to the Louisiana pearlshell mussel and Loch Lomand coyote thistle. Author Mark Galan tells the success stories of these and fourteen other American flora and fauna that have been rescued from extinction because of strict laws that have curtailed hunting and protected natural habitats. An easy-to-read and informative text, accompanied by many full- and double-page color photographs by National Geographic staff photographers, make this an invaluable resource book for any classroom study of American wildlife. A foreword by Secretary of the Interior Bruce Babbitt includes comments by children about the importance of preserving species diversity.

2.8   Gibbons, Gail (1997). **The Honey Makers.** New York: Morrow Junior Books. Unpaged. ISBN: 0-688-11386-9. Picture Book.

This detailed, fact-filled, and richly illustrated picture book narrative tells the story of how honey is made. Beginning with information about the physical characteristics of honeybees and their colonies, author-illustrator Gail Gibbons uses her meticulous research to provide a fascinating look at these very social insects. She describes the different kinds of honeybees, their reproductive habits, and their life cycle, and makes the complex process of collecting nectar to make honey easily understood to the reader. She also provides amazing facts that are sure to interest young readers, such as "to make one pound of honey, it takes nectar from over one million flowers." The book concludes with a description of how beekeepers manage beehives, including a Beekeeper's Yearbook. Special vocabulary is highlighted within the text and illustrations, making this an essential book for any study of bees or insects. Pair this book with Cole (1996), *The Magic School Bus: Inside a Beehive* (see **1.41**).

2.9   Gibbons, Gail (1998). **Soaring with the Wind: The Bald Eagle.** New York: Morrow Junior Books. Unpaged. ISBN: 0-688-13730-X. Picture Book.

The life cycle of the bald eagle is richly described in this informative picture book with beautiful watercolor, colored-pencil, and black-ink illustrations. Readers learn about the physical characteristics, behavior, eating habits, and reproductive cycle of this majestic raptor, as well as Native American beliefs and mythology about the creature. The technique of interweaving special vocabulary into both text and illustrations is characteristic of much of the author's work and makes this book useful for research as well as pleasure reading. Information about the bald eagle's endangered status and efforts to ensure its survival have greatly increased the chances that this "warrior of the sky" will continue to soar with the wind as a symbol of strength, dignity, and freedom for all Americans.

2.10 Hoffman, Mary (1998). **Sun, Moon, and Stars.** Illustrated by Jane Ray. New York: Dutton Children's Books. 74 pp. ISBN: 0-525-46004-7. Chapter Book.

Mary Hoffman has collected twenty-one myths and legends of the sky, sun, moon, and stars from around the world and retold them in simple one- and two-page prose stories. From ancient Greece, Egypt, Japan, and China to aboriginal Australia and the Navajo nation come stories that explain the mysteries of what ancient peoples saw when they looked skyward from their homes on Earth. Included are the stories of the Egyptian twins Nut and Geb who became the sky and the Earth, Phoebus' son Phaeton who wanted to drive his father's golden chariot across the sky, Anancy's gift to his children for saving his life, and the seven beautiful sisters called the Meamei who became the constellation Pleiades. In addition to myths and legends, there are also facts about the sky, navigation, the calendar, and the signs of the zodiac, as well as sunlore, moonlore, and starlore. Each page of text is generously illustrated by Jane Ray's brightly colored, jewel-toned pictures with highlights of silver and gold, including nearly a dozen full-page paintings. A bibliography gives the source of each myth and legend.

2.11   Hoopes, Lyn (1997). **Condor Magic.** Illustrated by Peter C. Stone. Fairfield, CT: Benefactory. Unpaged. ISBN: 1-882728-95-5. Picture Book. (See **10.36**)

2.12   Lesser, Carolyn (1997). **Storm on the Desert.** Illustrated by Ted Rand. San Diego: Harcourt Brace. Unpaged. ISBN: 0-15-272198-3. Picture Book. (See **10.42**)

2.13   Ling, Mary, and Mary Atkinson (1997). **The Snake Book.** Photographs by Frank Greenaway and Dave King. New York: Dorling Kindersley. Unpaged. ISBN: 0-7894-1526-7. Picture Book.

This is an essential book for snake lovers of all ages, or for any child studying or researching these reptiles. Each double-page spread contains a large, close-up photograph of a different snake with accompanying text set in various-sized print. There is a four-page foldout of a reticulated python in the middle of the book. The size and realism of the photographs make the snakes appear real and ready to slither off the pages. Beware if you are not a snake lover! An introduction provides general information on snakes. The last page contains small photographs of each of the one dozen snakes described in the book, with additional information about each one.

2.14   Martin, Bill, Jr. (1998). **The Turning of the Year.** Illustrated by Greg Shed. New York: Harcourt Brace. Unpaged. ISBN: 0-15-201085-8. Picture Book. (See **13.38**)

2.15   Matsumoto, Lisa (1996). **Beyond ʻŌhiʻa Valley: Adventures in a Hawaiian Rainforest.** Illustrated by Michael Furuya. Honolulu: Lehua. 35 pp. ISBN: 0-9647491-2-2. Picture Book. (See **14.32**)

2.16   Mora, Pat (1998). **This Big Sky.** Illustrated by Steve Jenkins. New York: Scholastic. Unpaged. ISBN: 0-590-37120-7. Picture Book. (See **10.44**)

2.17 Pfeffer, Wendy (1997). **A Log's Life.** Illustrated by Robin Brick-man. New York: Simon & Schuster Books for Young Readers. Unpaged. ISBN: 0-689-80636-1. Picture Book.

The cycle of life described in this story ironically begins as a tremendous oak tree nears death. It crashes to the earth in a thunderstorm and becomes a life-giving force to the plants and animals of the forest. As the log decays, it provides shelter for insects, slugs, salamanders, and other creatures. The wood and decaying leaves nourish fungi along with the animals, and in ten years the oak has become "a mound of rich, black earth." When a squirrel buries an acorn in this fertile bed, the cycle of life begins again. What makes the book especially compelling are the poetic language and dramatic illustrations. The reader can almost hear the activity of the insects: "In the spring click beetles snap and click their bodies and flip high in the air . . ." The pictures are vivid and lifelike. Children will be fascinated to find that the illustrator used only watercolor paper, which she cut, painted, sculpted, and glued together. The resulting pieces look three-dimensional, with varying textures to show a bird's feathers, a salamander's wet skin, and spongy fungi. The text is arranged tastefully around the pictures. The result is a unified, harmonious whole, consistent with the theme of the wholeness of an ecosystem.

2.18 Pirotta, Saviour (1997). **Turtle Bay.** Illustrated by Nilesh Mistry. New York: Farrar, Straus and Giroux. Unpaged. ISBN: 0-374-37888-6. Picture Book.

This book is a story of friendship. Jiro-san teaches Taro and Yuko how to fish and prepare for the coming of Jiro-san's dear old friends. They sweep and clean the nearby beach and wait for their arrival. At first, Yuko thinks Jiro-san is crazy because of the strange things he does. But when she sees the loggerhead sea turtles come ashore to lay their eggs in the sand, and then watches the baby turtles hatch and find their way back to sea, Yuko becomes convinced that Jiro-san is a wise man. This inspiring story represents a true respect and love for nature and the bridging of generations. Further information about sea turtles is given at the end of the book.

2.19 Prelutsky, Jack (1997). **The Beauty of the Beast: Poems from the Animal Kingdom.** Illustrated by Meilo So. New York: Knopf. 101 pp. ISBN: 0-679-87058-X. Chapter Book. (See **10.39**)

2.20 Pringle, Laurence (1997). **An Extraordinary Life: The Story of a Monarch Butterfly.** Illustrated by Bob Marstall. New York: Orchard. 64 pp. ISBN: 0-531-30002-1. Chapter Book.

Winner of the Orbis Pictus award for excellence in nonfiction writing for children, *An Extraordinary Life* is the story of the life cycle of a monarch butterfly (*Danaus plexippus*).Written as the story of the birth, development, migration, reproduction, and death of one monarch butterfly named Danaus, author Laurence Pringle has done extensive research on all aspects of the monarch's life and has paid meticulous attention to detail. Information about the monarch's metamorphosis from caterpillar to butterfly and subsequent flight from a Massachusetts hayfield to the oyamel fir forests of central Mexico give the reader an appreciation for the migratory instincts of this beautiful orange-and-black insect. Facts about the physiology of the monarch and threats to its survival make the reader appreciate the unique and special qualities of this apparently fragile, but actually quite resilient, butterfly. The last two chapters of the book tell about efforts to save the monarch's overwintering sites and how to raise monarch butterflies. Bob Marstall's colorful and detailed paintings illustrate the narrative-style text, including sidebars with additional illustrations, captions, labels, and maps. A table of contents, suggestions for further reading, and detailed index are included, as well as an e-mail address and Web site for additional information on the monarch butterfly.

2.21 Rogers, Sally (1998). **Earthsong.** Illustrated by Melissa Bay Mathis. New York: Dutton Children's Books. Unpaged. ISBN: 0-525-45873-5. Picture Book. (See **11.19**)

2.22 Simon, Seymour (1997). **Ride the Wind: Airborne Journeys of Animals and Plants.** Illustrated by Elsa Warnick. Orlando, FL: Harcourt Brace. Unpaged. ISBN: 0-15-292887-1. Picture Book.

The atmosphere that surrounds Earth is part of the natural habitat of many plants and animals. Renowned science writer Seymour Simon explains the migratory habits of numerous birds, bats, and insects and the windborne journeys of seeds and fruits in this first of a trilogy on migration. The life cycles of many airborne travelers are described as they journey through the air and ride the wind. Elsa Warnick's soft watercolor illustrations highlight the easy-to-read text and give a sense of flight and movement to the plants and animals described. In a special section at the end of the book, the author tells about the four main flyways on the North American continent and explains how radar is used to study bird and bat migrations. He explains how scientists recently have discovered that birds use the sun, the stars, and even the magnetic fields as a compass. Although many unanswered questions remain, scientists are learning more about the relationship between life cycles and migration.

2.23 Simon, Seymour (1998). **They Swim the Seas: The Mystery of Animal Migration.** Illustrated by Elsa Warnick. Orlando, FL: Harcourt Brace. Unpaged. ISBN: 0-15-292888-X. Picture Book.

In *Ride the Wind: Airborne Journeys of Animals and Plants,* Seymour Simon looked at the atmosphere that surrounds Earth as a highway for many plants and animals. In this second informational picture book in his trilogy on animal migration, Simon looks at the oceans as highways for various marine flora and fauna. An informative, easy-to-read, and well-researched text tells the reader about tuna that migrate to warmer ocean waters to spawn. Eels from America and Europe migrate from freshwater ponds, lakes, and rivers to the seaweed of the Sargasso Sea near Bermuda every autumn to lay their eggs, yet no adult eel has ever been seen. Some elephant seals migrate thousands of miles each year, using different migration patterns depending on where they live. Elsa Warnick's beautiful watercolor paintings show the movement and diversity of all the travelers on the oceans' highways. Simon has included a special section at the end of the book that tells more about the ocean journeys of the plants and animals in the book.

2.24 Swanson, Diane (l996). **Buffalo Sunrise: The Story of a North American Giant.** San Francisco: Sierra Club Books for Children. 64 pp. ISBN: 0-87156-861-6. Chapter Book. (See **3.102**)

2.25 Tanaka, Shelley (1998). **Graveyards of the Dinosaurs: What It's Like to Discover Prehistoric Creatures.** Illustrated by Alan Barnard. New York: Hyperion Books for Children. 48 pp. ISBN: 0-7868-0375-4. Picture Book.

Shelley Tanaka's newest book in the I Was There series is an essential volume for any dinosaur enthusiast. Richly illustrated with full-color paintings by Alan Barnard and others, as well as diagrams, maps, and photographs of fossils and paleontologists at work, this well-researched account of three expeditions to Canada, Argentina, and the Gobi Desert is filled with some of the latest information from the world's dinosaur graveyards. Each expedition is explained in informative, easy-to-read text that focuses on a paleontologist or paleontological team, their major new discoveries, and how these discoveries have changed long-held theories about dinosaurs and their way of life. Each expository section is followed by a short fictional story that offers an explanation for each dinosaur's death. Although much has been learned about dinosaurs in the past twenty years, there still remain many unanswered questions about these long-extinct creatures. A prologue introduces readers to Ray Chapman Andrews, one of the first paleontologists to discover dinosaur fossils in Asia. An epilogue provides many possible reasons for the dinosaurs' extinction nearly seventy million years ago, and a world map highlights new dinosaur finds around the world. A glossary and suggested further readings also are included.

2.26 Wright-Frierson, Virginia (1996). **A Desert Scrapbook: Dawn to Dusk in the Sonoran Desert.** New York: Simon & Schuster. Unpaged. ISBN: 0-689-80678-7. Picture Book.

Author-illustrator Virginia Wright-Frierson invites the reader into the world of the Sonoran Desert as she watches, sketches, collects feathers and rocks, and writes about the wonders she observes. The author's first-person narrative is intimate and honest: "I sit unseen on the rocks and sketch a herd of javalinas as they eat prickly pear pads and saguaro fruits. They leave a strong musky scent in the air." Richly detailed watercolor illustrations capture the vastness and intricacies of the desert, from expansive sunsets and thunderstorms to tiny quail eggs and cactus spines. Sketches and notes are included throughout the scrapbook. As the author explores and enjoys the desert alone, we find that she is a confident, independent, and talented woman. This scrapbook provides readers of all ages with an excellent demonstration of careful and thorough investigation of nature. It would serve as an inspiration to readers to create their own special scrapbook.

2.27 Wright-Frierson, Virginia (1998). **An Island Scrapbook: Dawn to Dusk on a Barrier Island.** New York: Simon & Schuster. Unpaged. ISBN: 0-689-81563-8. Picture Book.

An artist and her daughter explore and study a barrier island off the North Carolina coast. Together they lead the reader to experience the diverse ecosystems found there, including a salt marsh, a freshwater pond, a maritime forest, and an oceanfront beach. The reader learns about these diverse habitats through the author-artist's sketches, notes, and paintings. This beautiful picture book evokes the unique world of the island through the mother's and daughter's joy of discovery on a perfect summer day. Wright-Frierson's watercolor paintings of the various flora and fauna are luminous, and the sketches with accompanying notes are highly informative.

Secondary Reviews

2.28   Arnold, Caroline (1996). **Bat.** Photographs by Richard Hewett. New York: Morrow Junior Books. 48 pp. ISBN: 0-688-13726-1.

This book is one in a series of baby animal books by award-winning author Caroline Arnold and award-winning photographer Richard Hewett. The author tells about two types of bats—a Mexican free-tail bat and a big, brown bat—both of whom live at a California wildlife center. The day-to-day activities of the bats, Tad and Gus; their endangered habitats; their physical characteristics; and the archeological history of the area are fully described. The full-color photographs make it easy to see every detail of a bat's body.

2.29   Arnosky, Jim (1997). **All about Rattlesnakes.** New York: Scholastic. Unpaged. ISBN: 0-590-46794-8. Picture Book.

Fourteen of the most common rattlesnakes from around the world are described in this introduction to this usually fearsome reptile. The descriptions of the snakes are informational, telling about the many kinds of scales and markings, as well as how rattlesnakes camouflage themselves to blend into their environment. The book is filled with interesting as well as erroneous facts about rattlesnakes. In addition to being informational, the book tells the reader what to do and not to do when confronted by a rattlesnake while out hiking or camping.

2.30   Asch, Frank (1998). **Cactus Poems.** Illustrated by Ted Levin. San Diego: Harcourt Brace. Unpaged. ISBN: 0-15-200676-1. Picture Book. (See **10.47**)

2.31   **Atlas of Animals: A Scholastic First Discovery Book (1996).** New York: Scholastic. 36 pp. ISBN: 0-590-58280-1. Picture Book.

More than fifty different animals are featured in this mini-atlas for young readers, from the bald eagle of North America to the polar bear at the North Pole. Colorful illustrations with see-through acetate pages show children an animal silhouette and allow them to take animals in and out of their habitats. The book is organized by continent, showing the shape of each continent on the globe and describing interesting facts about specific animals of that land mass. This is an outstanding first nature book for young children.

2.32 Curtis, Patricia (1997). **Animals You Never Even Heard Of.** San Francisco: Sierra Club Books for Children. 32 pp. ISBN: 0-87156-594-3. Picture Book.

What do the axolotl, caracal, jabiru, and markhar have in common? All are unusual and little-known animals that scientists have classified as in danger of becoming extinct. Each of the one dozen animals in this collection is described in an easy-to-read text, accompanied by a full-page color photograph. The introduction tells readers about the reasons animal species are becoming endangered, and what scientists are doing to try to protect them. The status of each animal (rare, threatened, endangered) is highlighted, along with efforts to stabilize their populations. An index also is included.

2.33 Dorros, Arthur (1997). **A Tree Is Growing.** Illustrated by S. D. Schindler. New York: Scholastic. Unpaged. ISBN: 0-590-45300-9. Picture Book.

This wonderfully illustrated informational picture book on trees provides readers a look at an oak tree through the seasons. Explanations of the tree's life cycle give the reader a sense of the importance that trees play in the ecology of Earth. Important vocabulary—such as *cambium, photosynthesis, xylem,* and *phloem*—is reinforced in the detailed, colored-pencil illustrations by botanist S. D. Schindler. Facts about oak trees are written on the sides of each double-page illustration. A section on leaf identification of popular trees also is included.

2.34 Gibbons, Gail (1996). **Deserts.** New York: Holiday House. Unpaged. ISBN: 0-8234-1276-8. Picture Book.

This book by well-known author-illustrator Gail Gibbons will entice young readers to learn more about desert ecosystems. Information about how deserts are formed is provided, with beautifully colored and detailed drawings that invite browsing and lingering. Each drawing is labeled with special vocabulary. Deserts of the world are listed and discussed, as well as the plants, animals, and human inhabitants that are found in desert regions. An uncluttered format with easy-to-read typesize lends to the readability of the book. At the end is a page of intriguing facts about deserts.

2.35   Hanna, Jack, and Rick A. Prebeg (1996). **Jungle Jack Hanna's Safari Adventure.** New York: Scholastic. 44 pp. ISBN: 0-590-67322-X. Picture Book.

In this picture book, the authors write about a month-long safari they organized in Kenya and Uganda. Color photographs and a simple text make the reader feel as though he or she is a member of the safari. Numerous animals of the savanna are described. Four pages of text and illustrations are devoted to the Masai, including pictures showing a Masai home, a young girl milking a goat, and the colorful clothing of these indigenous people. Jack Hanna is director emeritus of the Columbus Zoo.

2.36   Hodge, Deborah (1997). **Whales: Killer Whales, Blue Whales and More.** Illustrated by Pat Stephens. Buffalo, NY: Kids Can. 32 pp. ISBN: 1-55074-356-2. Picture Book.

Presentation of numerous facts about whales—such as their different types, how they move, how they sound, how they protect themselves, and where they live—make this an excellent resource for young readers interested in basic information about these gentle giants of the sea. The illustrations are clear and detailed, and the book is organized so that information can be found easily by any young researcher. At various intervals in the book, there are small boxes with a whale fact highlighted (indicated by a small outline of a whale with the words "whale fact" inside). This book is one in a series about different animals, including wild cats, wild dogs, and bears.

2.37   Hopcraft, Carol, and Xan Hopcraft (1997). **How It Was with Dooms.** New York: Margaret K. McElderry. 64 pp. ISBN: 0-689-81091-1. Chapter Book.

This is a true story about an African boy and his family, and how they befriend a cheetah cub named Dooms. The life of a young cheetah on the African plains is described in very accurate detail using dialect appropriate to this part of the world. Readers not only learn about the cheetah, but also about how people live in eastern Africa. The book features photographs from the family album of the cheetah cub. It is an excellent book to read aloud to primary-age children.

2.38 Hunter, Sally M. (1997). **Four Seasons of Corn: A Winnebago Tradition.** Illustrated by Joe Allen. Minneapolis: Lerner. 40 pp. ISBN: 0-8225-2658-1. Picture Book.

This photographic essay tells the history of corn, and depicts a season of corn by illustrating the cycle of planting, harvesting, drying the corn, eating corn soup, and dancing the Green Corn Dance at the powwow. Twelve-year-old Russell learns the traditions of corn from his grandfather. Russell, who lives away from the reservation, learns how the corn connects him to the land and his culture. This essay explains how corn is regarded as a gift and a food with sacred value.

2.39 Johnson, Sylvia (1997). **Ferrets.** Minneapolis: Carolrhoda. 48 pp. ISBN: 1-57505-014-5.

Award winning children's author Sylvia Johnson introduces young readers to the world of ferrets with an easy-to-read text complemented by numerous color photographs. Although most of the book describes the domesticated ferret and how to care for it as a pet, the final chapter talks about the endangered black-footed ferret and its ecological link to the prairie dogs of the North American Plains. The book provides a good descriptive example of the balance of nature, and how human intervention has destroyed that natural harmony.

2.40 London, Jonathan (1998). **Phantom of the Prairie: Year of the Black-footed Ferret.** Illustrated by Barbara Bash. San Francisco: Sierra Club Books for Children. Unpaged. ISBN: 0-87156-387-8. Picture Book.

In this informative and colorful picture book, a litter of black-footed ferrets is born in the springtime. One of the litter is called Phantom, and it is she who will lead her brothers and sisters through the abandoned prairie-dog burrow in which they were born out into the tall—and sometimes dangerous—grasses of the prairie night. It is through the eyes of Phantom that the reader experiences the seasons of the prairie, and the vast world of the creatures that live there and are symbiotically linked in life and in death. Jonathan London's lyrical text flows like poetry, and Barbara Bash's sweeping double-page paintings of Phantom's world are vibrant.

2.41   Macquitty, Miranda (1996). **Amazing Bugs.** Photographs by Andy Crawford and Geoff Brightling. New York: Dorling Kindersley. 44 pp. ISBN: 0-7894-1010-9.

The many fascinating facts about insects presented in this book will delight readers interested in the world of bugs. Three-dimensional models allow the reader to look inside an insect's body to see how its internal organs work. A clearly written text and colorful photographs make this an excellent resource for any classroom or library. A table of contents and index are included.

2.42   McMillan, Bruce (1998). **Salmon Summer.** Boston: Houghton Mifflin. 32 pp. ISBN: 0-395-84544-0. Picture Book.

Bruce McMillan's outstanding photography offers a rarely seen glimpse of Kodiak Island, Alaska. In this photographic essay, we get to know nine-year-old Alex, a native Aleut. Throughout the book, we see Alex's love for the outdoors and for fishing. Up-close photographic views help the reader to understand how salmon fishing is done. Pictures show other local animals that also feed on the salmon, including bears, eagles, foxes, magpies, and gulls. Finally, salmon is used to bait a line in order to catch much larger fish. A glossary of terms is included, as well as a bibliography for additional reading.

2.43   Mercredi, Morningstar (1997). **Fort Chipewyan Homecoming: A Journey to Native Canada.** Illustrated by Darren McNally. Minneapolis: Lerner. Unpaged. ISBN: 0-8225-2659-X. Picture Book.

Morningstar Mercredi (Chipewyan, Cree, and Metis) takes the reader and her twelve-year-old son, Matthew, on a summer journey to the place of his Native American heritage, Fort Chipewyan. It is the oldest settlement in Alberta, Canada, and inaccessible by road. This summer, Matthew will experience the Chipewyan celebration called Treaty Days, a two-day event marking the 1899 signing of Treaty Number 8 between the Chipewyan people and the Canadian government, which gave the Chipewyans reservation land and hunting and fishing rights. On this trip, we take a boat ride on a river, try our hand at fishing, make traditional bannock bread, eat moose meat, see an eagle, and collect traditional medicinal herbs and roots. We also are invited to set fishnets and return the next day to "pull in the catch," and learn how to preserve the fish in the traditional way. We all come home with a better understanding of traditional Chipewyan life.

2.44 Miller, Debbie S. (1997). **Disappearing Lake: Nature's Magic in Denali National Park.** Illustrated by Jon Van Zyle. New York: Walker. Unpaged. ISBN: 0-8027-8474-7. Picture Book.

Nature's ever-changing panorama is the theme of this nonfiction picture book's narrative of a vernal ecosystem in Alaska's Denali National Park. The author describes the formation of Disappearing Lake, a temporary water system formed in the spring of the year as snow melts from the mountains and water drains into a meadow. The new lake provides an inviting and rich habitat for many animals and plants that are part of the web of life. As the seasons change, the lake gradually disappears and turns into a beautiful meadow. As winter approaches, the meadow itself disappears under a heavy blanket of snow. Double-page paintings of the flora and fauna that depend on this fragile ecosystem make this a very inviting book to read aloud, or for younger children to read themselves. A section entitled "Field Notes" and an author's note at the end give additional information about Disappearing Lake and the wildlife to be found in and around it.

2.45 Minor, Wendell (1998). **Grand Canyon: Exploring a Natural Wonder.** New York: Blue Sky. Unpaged. ISBN: 0-590-47968-7. Picture Book.

The simple beauty of the Grand Canyon has come to life for children and adult readers alike, thanks to Wendell Minor's dedication to illustrating nature for children. For twelve days, Minor recorded his daily encounters with the canyon's majesty and splendor in on-the-spot sketches and paintings, much like the artist Thomas Moran (1837–1926). In accompanying notes, Minor records his impressions alongside historical vignettes. "It's a nice journal," remarked Cody, age ten. "His words are like poetry." The book is filled with vibrant images of the canyon, graceful sketches of wildlife, and quiet reflections on the simplicity of nature.

2.46 Moss, Cynthia (1997). **Little Big Ears: The Story of Ely.** Photographs by Martyn Colbeck. New York: Simon & Schuster. 34 pp. ISBN: 0-689-80031-2. Picture Book.

A baby elephant named Ely struggles to walk and survive in this true story of courage and determination. After many attempts at standing, Ely is able to straighten out his crooked legs. With hard work and practice, he slowly learns to walk. He gradually becomes better at walking, climbing, and swimming, but has difficulty using his trunk. Eventually Ely learns that his trunk is important for eating and drinking. Ely is determined to succeed and does so through perseverance.

2.47   Nicoll, David, and Jane Donnelly (1996). **Fearsome Hunters of the Wild.** Illustrated by Ellis Nadler and Derek Matthews. Photographs by Peter Anderson, Geoff Brightling, Frank Greenaway, Dave King, and Jerry Young. New York: Dorling Kindersley. Unpaged. ISBN: 0-7894-1111-3. Picture Book.

Eight animals of the land, sea, and air are featured in this large-print book for young readers, with two full-page labeled illustrations. Amazing facts about the tiger, cheetah, eagle, gray wolf, alligator, lion, shark, and polar bear provide an introductory look at these fearsome predators. Words that might be unfamiliar are defined in context.

2.48   Otto, Carolyn (1996). **What Color Is Camouflage?** Illustrated by Megan Lloyd. New York: HarperCollins. 32 pp. ISBN: 0-06-027094-2. Picture Book.

This picture book for young readers discusses the topic of camouflage in the animal kingdom in an easy-to-read narrative text augmented by colorful, labeled pictures. The author discusses the reasons for camouflage, as well as the difference between those animals whose physical characteristics and coloring help them to blend in with their surroundings and those who can actually change themselves to look like their surroundings. Part of the Let's-Read-and-Find-Out Science series, this book is labeled by the publisher as a Stage Two book that explores "more challenging concepts for children in the primary grades" and includes "hands-on activities that children can do themselves."

2.49   Philip, Neil (1996). **Earth Always Endures: Native American Poems.** Illustrated by Edward S. Curtis. New York: Viking. Unpaged. ISBN: 0-670-86873-6. Chapter Book. (See **10.56**)

2.50   Roop, Peter (1996). **The Buffalo Jump.** Illustrated by Bill Farnsworth. Flagstaff, AZ: Northland. Unpaged. ISBN:0-873-58616-6. Picture Book. (See **3.99**)

2.51   Ryder, Joanne (1997). **Shark in the Sea.** Illustrated by Michael Rothman. New York: Morrow Junior Books. Unpaged. ISBN: 0-688-14909-X. Picture Book.

The combination of Joanne Ryder's descriptive, lyrical text and Michael Rothman's acrylic underwater paintings invites readers to experience the natural habitat of the great white shark. As in the previous animal books in the Just for a Day series, a young child is magically transformed into an animal—in this case a shark—and then allowed to see how this animal lives. Here the reader experiences the underwater world of the ocean's most feared predator as it swims through the waters of the sea. With its keen senses and constant movement, the shark hunts for prey and is finally successful. An author's note at the beginning of the book provides additional information about the great white shark.

2.52 Silverstein, Alvin, and Virginia Silverstein (1997). **The Mustang.** Illustrated by Laura Silverstein Nunn. Rookfield, CT: Millbrook. 64 pp. ISBN: 0-7613-0048-1. Chapter Book.

This fascinating and informative book for upper-elementary students looks at mustangs throughout history, from prehistoric times to the present. It clarifies often misunderstood facts, such as the difference between a wild horse and a mustang, the history of the mustang, and the habitat of the mustang through the ages. The author notes that the future of this endangered species is in jeopardy, and provides a list of names and addresses of several organizations that support the survival of the mustang. A table of contents, index, and a fingertip fact page are included, as well as suggested further readings. This book is from the Endangered in America series.

2.53 Steiner, Barbara A. (1996). **Desert Trip.** Illustrated by Ronald Himler. San Francisco: Sierra Club Books for Children. Unpaged. ISBN: 0-87156-581-1. Picture Book.

The wonders of a desert canyon come alive as a mother takes her young daughter on her first backpacking adventure. As they hike, they discover the unique variety of plants and animals that inhabit the fragile desert environment. The mother tells her child about each thing that she sees, also providing information about how native desert people once used what the desert offers. The strong female roles created by Steiner are impressive. Himler's rich watercolors are evidence of his many years of desert living, and his awareness of the subtle changes of light and color as the sun moves across the brilliant, clear desert skies.

2.54   Stone, Lynn (1997). **Cougars.** Minneapolis: Lerner. 48 pp. ISBN: 0-8225-3013-9. Chapter Book.

This is an easy-to-read, large-print chapter book on cougars. Information about cougars and their habitat show readers how the cougar successfully adapts to its environment and relates to humans. Authentic photographs of cougars in their natural surroundings will capture the attention of young children. A map, table of contents, glossary, and index make this a useful reference book. An added feature is a note to adults at the end of the book on how to share a book with children, including how to ask questions and help children learn vocabulary.

2.55   Swanson, Diane (1996). **Buffalo Sunrise: The Story of a North American Giant.** San Francisco: Sierra Club Books for Children. 58 pp. ISBN: 0-87156-861-6. Chapter Book. (See **3.102**)

2.56   Taylor, Barbara (1997). **Incredible Plants.** Photographs by Geoff Brightling. New York: Dorling Kindersley. 44 pp. ISBN: 0-751-3-54996. Chapter Book.

A clearly written text with annotations, illustrated cross sections, and detailed three-dimensional models provide information on plants from around the world. Readers can look inside the structures of plants and explore how plant anatomy functions. Information on roots, stems, pollination, and plant defenses are clearly labeled and explained in detail. The author tells how all the different parts of a plant operate as a system, and how plants and humans live together and survive as living partners on Earth. A table of contents, glossary, and index are included.

2.57   Van Camp, Richard (1997). **A Man Called Raven.** Illustrated by George Littlechild. San Francisco: Children's Book. Unpaged. ISBN: 0-89239-144-8. Picture Book.

A contemporary story teaching respect for all life. A mysterious man confronts two young brothers after they injure a raven using their hockey sticks. The man tells the boys a story about a mean old man who hurt ravens and was punished by being turned into a raven. The raven can transform into a man again for only a short time in order to teach those who have forgotten that all life is sacred. The aura about this stranger who "smells of pine needles" and has "large, dark, piercing eyes" creates a sense of magic and mystery in this raven tale. Van Camp nicely blends traditional animal legends and folklore with today's Native American culture and lifestyle. George Littlechild draws on his own Native American heritage in creating bold illustrations that complement Van Camp's text. Van Camp and Littlechild have collaborated on another stunning book about the Pacific Northwest, *What's the Most Beautiful Thing You Know about Horses?* (see **20.60**).

2.58 Viera, Linda (1997). **Grand Canyon: A Trail through Time.** Illustrated by Christopher Canyon. New York: Walker. Unpaged. ISBN: 0-8027-8625. Picture Book.

Linda Viera and Christopher Canyon have teamed up to bring the beauty and drama of the canyon to children. Shifting from bird's-eye, to mule's-eye, to lizard's-eye views, the richly colored, acrylic-on-canvas illustrations invite the reader to witness the majesty of the Grand Canyon. Viera's text integrates information about the canyon's history, flora, wildlife, and human inhabitants in descriptions of the day's events. The layers in the geological evolution of the Grand Canyon are discussed at the end of the book, and an appendix contains an illustrated timeline of human interactions with this wonder of the world. An index may help elementary-aged readers use this book as a reference text as well.

2.59 Yee, Tammy (1997). **Baby Honu's Incredible Journey.** Aiea, HI: Island Heritage. 32 pp. ISBN: 0-89610-285-8. Picture Book. (See **5.137**)

2.60 Yolen, Jane (1998). **Snow, Snow: Winter Poems for Children.** Illustrated by Jason Stemple. Honesdale, PA: Boyds Mills. 32 pp. ISBN: 1-56397-721-4. Picture Book. (See **10.51**)

Changes in Our Physical World

Primary Reviews

2.61 Delano, Marfe (1998). **Sky.** Washington, DC: National Geographic. 60 pp. ISBN: 0-7922-7047-9. Reference Book.

An easy-to-read text and beautiful color photographs combine to form a reference book on the sky for young children. Topics include air, weather, clouds, precipitation, storms, sun, planets, and stars. Much of the information is conveyed to the reader through the detailed captions accompanying the photographs, drawings, and diagrams. A wonderful book to be read aloud or used for independent research, *Sky* introduces children to the wonders of the natural world around and above them. A table of contents, glossary, and index are included. Other books in National Geographic's Nature Library series discuss such topics as mammals, birds, fish, amphibians, plants, insects, and Earth.

2.62 Kramer, Stephen (1997). **Eye of the Storm: Chasing Storms with Warren Faidley.** Photographs by Warren Faidley. New York: Putnam. 48 pp. ISBN: 0-399-23029-7.

The author tells the story of prize-winning, severe-weather photographer Warren Faidley as he chases storms with his camera and tripod. Spectacular color photographs of lightning, thunderstorms, and tornadoes illustrate the text. Descriptions of various types of severe weather, as well as chapters on respecting storms and storm safety, make this book a useful reference for any indepth study of weather. It also would be very informative for students interested in photography. A table of contents, glossary, and suggested further readings are included.

2.63 Lauber, Patricia (1996). **Hurricanes: Earth's Mightiest Storms.** New York: Scholastic. 64 pp. ISBN: 0-590-47406-5. Chapter Book.

Award-winning nonfiction writer Patricia Lauber tells readers everything they would want to know about hurricanes. In addition to describing famous hurricanes such as Andrew, Camille, Iniki, Hugo, and the so-called monster storm of 1938, the author also gives a detailed account of how hurricanes are formed, with accompanying colored maps and diagrams. Pictures and descriptions of weather instruments such as the barometer, anemometer, and thermometer are included, as well as world names for hurricanes. There are many photographs of the destruction and devastation caused by hurricanes. A table of contents, index, and a list of books for further reading also are provided.

2.64 Locker, Thomas (1997). **Water Dance.** San Diego: Harcourt Brace. 32 pp. ISBN: 0-15-201284-2. Picture Book. (See **10.43**)

2.65 Yolen, Jane (1997). **Once Upon Ice, and Other Frozen Poems.** Illustrated by Jason Stemple. Honesdale, PA: Boyds Mills. 40 pp. ISBN: 1-56397-408-8. Picture Book. (See **10.46**)

Secondary Reviews

2.66 Bourgeois, Paulette (1997). **The Sun.** Illustrated by Bill Slavin. Buffalo, NY: Kids Can. 40 pp. ISBN: 1-55074-158-6. Chapter Book.

Young readers will enjoy learning facts about the sun in this question-and-answer book that is part of the Starting with Space series. Myths about the sun begin each of the four chapters, and Try It! sections tell about experiments children can do to reinforce concepts and learn more about the sun. A table of contents, index, and glossary are included. Other books in this series tell about the moon and Earth.

2.67 Haddon, Mark (1996). **The Sea of Tranquility.** Illustrated by Christian Birmingham. Orlando, FL: Harcourt Brace. Unpaged. ISBN: 0-15-201285-0. Picture Book.

This picture book is about a young boy and his love for the moon. He is captivated by the wonder of what it would be like to walk on the moon, and the reader sees the historic first landing on the moon through his eyes. Included in the story are the historical facts that led up to the Apollo XI flight by Neil Armstrong, Edwin Aldrin, Jr., and Michael Collins. It reminds adult readers of what we were doing and where we were when astronauts first walked on the moon.

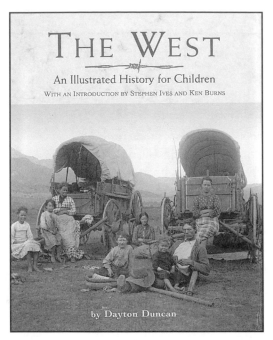

A.

B.

C.

D.

A. *The West: An Illustrated History for Children,* Dayton Duncan (**3.83**). B. *We Have Marched Together: The Working Children's Crusade,* Stephen Currie (**3.80**). C. *Minty: A Story of Young Harriet Tubman,* Alan Schroeder/Jerry Pinkney (**3.14**). D. *The Golden Sandal: A Middle Eastern Cinderella Story,* Rebecca Hickox/ Will Hillenbrand (**3.130**).

3 Exploring Our Past

Beth Berghoff

Contributing reviewers included Beth Berghoff, Pamela Swinford, Denice Haines, Jenay Burck, and Ruby Clayton.

Learners live in the present and know best their own experiences, cultural groups, and social contexts. When teachers attempt to share with children the lessons of the past, they must begin with the children's current personal and social knowledge (Short, Harste, and Burke 1996). Learners who have adopted an inquiry stance never finish asking questions about their own identities and experiences. Each learner asks: Who am I? What matters to me? Why? How did I end up where I am? What is going to happen next? To a large extent, the answers to these questions come to us from the past—from the people who have lived their lives and have asked the same questions. We look to the past to understand the present and to change the future.

The members of the review committee working on this chapter have attempted to assemble books that address questions that matter today as much as they did in the past—questions of identity, of being part of a larger whole, and of being affected by contexts and forces beyond our control. This chapter is filled with books that tell powerful stories that enable readers to learn vicariously. Although we cannot physically visit the past, a compelling narrative colored by a story-teller's moral imagination can enable us to learn by example, and to take to heart the author's gift of grace (Coles 1989).

As the committee members worked on this chapter, we often commented on the richness of the texts available today. What counts as knowledge is changing. When we were in school, we learned about the past by memorizing specific bits of information and important concepts. We learned the same information that our peers did, out of textbooks that reduced history to lists of dates, events, and causes. Today there is a new way of knowing, what Eisner (1998) describes as *productive diversity.* Instead of seeking to transmit a uniform body of knowledge to students, today's educators need to operate on the assumption that there are many ways to see and describe any event or time period. Understanding history depends on having multidimensional knowledge. Facts and dates have to be connected to stories of people's lives and historical accounts from varied perspectives, as well as to the art, music, stories, images, and other cultural artifacts of the past. In contrast to our own education, the members of this committee believe that we should try to teach children that there is never a simple, one-dimensional explanation of the past. Instead we teach so that learners develop a repertoire of questions to ask about the past, and a habit of seeking a variety of perspectives.

When teachers use multiple texts to explore the past, they can teach children to appreciate how writing is influenced by an author's identity and purposes. No two books written by different authors will offer exactly the same perspectives on the past. Writing is a process that forces an author to make decisions about what to present and what to leave out, about what sense to make of the world and how to communicate that perspective. When teachers explore with children the productive diversity among authors, we teach them that any text tells as much about the author as it does about history. We teach them to ask about the cultural and historical frameworks of the authors, and to wonder about the nature of each author's research and sense of purpose in writing. We can do all this because the texts available to us today provide so much more information about these issues. Most of the books in this chapter provide background information about the authors and about their studies of history. There are forewords and endnotes that describe the primary resources used to gather information, or the stance or purpose of the authors. In many cases, we even get information about what the illustrators tried to contribute with their choice of media and images.

As teachers or adults helping young people to locate and read books today, we have more opportunity to impact the ethical development of learners than did teachers of the past, who were locked into a textbook curriculum. As we choose books for a study or for reading with youngsters, we can choose according to our passions (Rief and Barbieri 1995), to what we know about our learners, and to what we know about teaching the foundations of democracy. We have to be inquirers along with our students, learning to ask what we see and know differently from each perspective, and what essential questions need to be answered before we can rest assured that we know enough to act on our knowledge. In this age of information, we have to choose those texts that invite a community of learners to question what has been, what could be, and what each of us must do to make new possibilities become realities.

As a committee, we looked for books that we believed could contribute to a productive diversity of knowledge and to inquiry into particular time periods or cultures. We looked at historical fiction and nonfiction, and at traditional stories and descriptions of cultural traditions of different groups of people. As we read and discussed books, we selected for this chapter those books that

1. *Created a rich vicarious experience.* Because we cannot experience the events of the past in an embodied way, we have to rely on vicarious experiences of the past. Wilhelm and Edmiston (1998) write about how readers can do this by getting inside a book—by adopting its perspectives and imagining that they are the characters. Readers can imagine the parameters of the story's time and place, and step into a story world where they live the experiences of the characters in the story. We judged that a book had this quality when—as readers—we could not put it down, or when the experience of reading it was so compelling that we found ourselves thinking and talking about the book long after closing its pages. We also watched to see if this happened when we gave the book to readers in our classrooms, or read it aloud to our children at home.

2. *Offered a powerful ethical message.* Some books or stories stood out because they delivered important lessons or raised significant questions. For example, *Minty* (Schroeder 1996), a picture book about the early life of Harriet Tubman, conveys the depth of Tubman's desire for freedom and her deliberate plans and actions in pursuit of it. She was only one woman with a dogged determination, but she changed many lives and eventually the course of history. Another such book was *We Have Marched Together: The Working Children's Crusade* (Currie 1997). The photographs in this book make the human rights discussed in it jump off the page. These books start needed conversations and force us to ask how people can live together in more ethical ways.

3. *Presented accurate information.* Whether looking at fiction or nonfiction books, we asked ourselves whether the information presented by the authors was accurate. Some of the books have documentation to support the facts or explain the research that went into writing the book. We found this particularly helpful. Many of the books in this chapter also were selected by other *Adventuring with Books* committees charged with reviewing books about particular cultural groups, and we respect their expertise in choosing books that accurately portray these cultures.

4. *Offered multiple layers of meaning.* Many of our favorite choices in this chapter are books that are rich with layers of meaning. We selected picture books such as *So Far from the Sea* (Bunting 1998) and *Starry Messenger* (Sis 1996) because their stories were complex, and their complexity was further enriched by the art. The illustrations in these books add depth of emotion

and detail to the thought-provoking stories. Other books, such as *Out of the Dust* (Hesse 1997) or *The Indian School* (Whelan 1996), offered stories with many dimensions, including specific time periods, geographical locations, economic hardships, social relationships, government actions, and coming-of-age experiences. These books lend an understanding of the complexity of people's lives in times past, and invite students to think about the many types of information that can contribute to historical analysis.

5. *Provided a unique or connective perspective.* We also included books that provided a fresh or uncommon perspective or seemed likely to help learners bridge the present and the past. We thought Kathryn Lasky's *Hercules* (1997), in which Hercules tells his story in the first person, would appeal to youngsters attracted to superheroes and action stories. We included several stories that highlight African American, Native American, or Hispanic American perspectives, as well as stories in which girls or women are the prominent characters and history makers. In each case, we asked ourselves whether the text was likely to add something significant to our knowledge about a previous time, a past event, or a particular cultural group. We looked for books likely to engage learners in using what they know about the present to think about the past.

This chapter is divided into two major sections. The first section, Histories and Herstories, is filled with stories of the past that give insight into specific time periods, events, and cultural groups. These books are divided into three categories: Historical Fiction, Historical Nonfiction, and Stories of War. In the second section, Cultural Traditions, readers will find texts that give insight into the past and other cultures in less direct ways. These texts contain the stories of different cultural groups, and explanations of the origins of their rituals and ways of life. Books in this section fall into the categories of Traditional Literature and Cultural Practices and Celebrations.

The breadth of books in this chapter is fascinating in and of itself. There is so much to know about the past and its impact on us, and there are so many authors trying to help us understand how we got to be who we are and to think as we do today. We hope these books help readers to relive the past, and to envision and build better tomorrows!

Works Cited

Coles, Robert. 1989. *The Call of Stories.* Boston: Houghton Mifflin.

Eisner, Eliot. 1998. *The Schools We Need.* Portsmouth, NH: Heinemann.

Rief, Linda, and Maureen Barbieri, eds. 1995. *All that Matters: What Is It We Value in School and Beyond?* Portsmouth, NH: Heinemann.

Short, Kathy, Jerome Harste, and Carolyn Burke. 1996. *Creating Classrooms for Authors and Inquirers.* Portsmouth, NH: Heinemann.

Wilhelm, Jeffrey, and Brian Edmiston. 1998. *Imagining to Learn: Inquiry, Ethics, and Drama Integration through Drama.* Portsmouth, NH: Heinemann.

----

*The titles listed below each subheading are organized into Primary Reviews and Secondary Reviews. The Primary Reviews describe outstanding books in each subheading. The Secondary Reviews provide brief information about other books worthy of consideration. Some titles listed below are **not** reviewed in this chapter; entries for these titles are not annotated and contain only bibliographic information. In such cases, a cross reference to the annotated entry contained elsewhere in this volume is provided in boldface type at the end of the bibliographic information.*

Histories and Herstories

See also the section entitled Family Experiences through the Ages in chapter 4, "Families."

Historical Fiction

Primary Reviews

3.1 Benton, Amanda (1997). **Silent Stranger.** New York: Avon. 160 pp. ISBN: 0-380-97486-X. Chapter Book. (See **13.49**)

3.2 Carling, Amelia Lau (1998). **Mama and Papa Have a Store.** New York: Dial. Unpaged. ISBN: 0-8037-2044-0. Picture Book. (See **4.97**)

3.3 Coleman, Evelyn (1996). **White Socks Only.** Illustrated by Tyrone Geter. Morton Grove, IL: Whitman. Unpaged. ISBN: 0-8075-8955-1. Picture Book. (See **20.10**)

3.4 Forrester, Sandra (1997). **My Home Is over Jordan.** New York: Lodestar. 163 pp. ISBN: 0-525-67568-X. Chapter Book. (See **20.11**)

3.5 Hesse, Karen (1997). **Out of the Dust.** New York: Scholastic. 227 pp. ISBN: 0-590-36080-9. Sophisticated Chapter Book. (See **4.48**)

3.6 Holt, Kimberly Willis (1998). **My Louisiana Sky.** New York: Henry Holt. 132 pp. ISBN: 0-8050-5251-8. Chapter Book. (See **4.66**)

3.7   Jiang, Ji-Li (1997). **Red Scarf Girl: A Memoir of the Cultural Revolution.** New York: HarperCollins. 240 pp. ISBN: 0-06-027585-5. Sophisticated Chapter Book. (See **20.47**)

3.8   Lomas Garza, Carmen (1996). **In My Family/En mi familia.** Translated by Francisco X. Alarcón. San Francisco: Children's Book. Unpaged. ISBN: 0-89239-138-3. Picture Book. (See **4.14**)

3.9   Lorbiecki, Marybeth (1998). **Sister Anne's Hands.** Illustrated by K. Wendy Popp. New York: Dial Books for Young Readers. Unpaged. ISBN: 0-8037-2038-6. Picture Book. (See **20.3**)

3.10 McKissack, Patricia C. (1997). **Run Away Home.** New York: Scholastic. 160 pp. ISBN: 0-590-46751-4. Chapter Book. (See **5.79**)

3.11 Miller, William (1998). **The Bus Ride.** Illustrated by John Ward. New York: Lee & Low. Unpaged. ISBN: 1-880000-60-1. Picture Book. (See **20.26**)

3.12 Mitchell, Margaree King (1997). **Granddaddy's Gift.** Illustrated by Larry Johnson. Mahwah, NJ: BridgeWater. Unpaged. ISBN: 0-8167-4010-0. Picture Book. (See **20.27**)

3.13 Paterson, Katherine (1996). **Jip: His Story.** New York: Lodestar. ISBN: 0-52567-543-4. 181 pp. Sophisticated Chapter Book.

As this deeply moving story unfolds, readers meet Jip (short for gypsy), a young orphan who "fell" from a wagon as a two-year-old. As a result, Jip is being raised on a dreary mid-1800s Vermont poor farm along with an assortment of other unfortunate residents. His kind, caring nature is revealed as he gently tends the animals and befriends the other residents. During his brief experience in school, he is captivated by the story Teacher reads—*Oliver Twist*—and wonders whether he too has a loving parent somewhere. Through his friendship with Teacher and her Quaker boyfriend, Jip learns that his mother was a runaway slave who was raped by her owner. Eventually Jip is forced to flee to Canada to escape a slave catcher. Paterson presents difficult and challenging themes—abandonment, slave catching, loyalty, and poverty—through this readable and thought provoking book.

3.14 Schroeder, Alan (1996). **Minty: A Story of Young Harriet Tubman.** Illustrated by Jerry Pinkney. New York: Dial Books for Young Readers. Unpaged. ISBN: 0-8037-1888-8. Picture Book.

"Harriet Tubman is remembered as one of the bravest and most admired women in American history because of her tireless and daring work as a conductor on the Underground Railroad," author Alan Schroeder notes. In this beautiful and touching biography of Tubman's early years, Schroeder explains that Minty (Tubman's childhood name) was considered a "problem" slave. The author has taken basic facts about Tubman's life and created a memorable story of her early determination to be free. Pinkney's beautiful illustrations bring authenticity, realism, and dignity to the spirit of Minty, and to the family who loved her and taught her the skills she needed to survive. The author and illustrator notes add much to the historical perspective of the book, and the story makes a good Readers Theater text because the characters speak in dialect and the story is gripping.

3.15 Stanley, Diane (1996). **Elena.** New York: Hyperion. 55 pp. ISBN: 0-7868-0256-1. Chapter Book.

Diane Stanley recounts the true and remarkable story of a young Mexican girl and her struggle to achieve her dreams. Living an idyllic life in a quiet Mexican village, Elena, the youngest of five daughters, is not content to sing, dance, and sew as girls were expected to do in the early 1900s. She longs for an education, and the longing does not go away. It bothers her like a buzzing bee, always hovering about and coming right back whenever she brushes it away. Finally she talks the village priest into helping her learn to read and write, and she spends her pesos on books. Elena also chooses the person she will marry, contrary to the wishes of her father. Later she saves herself and her children from the revolution. Elena's education, her courage, and her determination make this an unforgettable journey to freedom. When Jessica (age nine) read the book, she commented: "Elena had a good heart, and she made good choices. She was independent and made up her own mind. I think Mrs. Stanley wrote this book to show girls that you can choose for yourself."

3.16 Stewart, Sarah (1997). **The Gardener.** Illustrated by David Small. New York: Farrar, Straus and Giroux. Unpaged. ISBN: 0-374-32517-0. Picture Book.

Stewart has created a gentle and memorable picture book about young Lydia Grace Finch. The year is 1835, and Lydia's parents are out of work. Lydia is sent to live with her ornery uncle, a baker, in the big city. Before she leaves, she fills her suitcase with plants from her grandma's garden. Through the letters she writes home, we find a strong, confident young girl who works to keep her good humor as she explores places she can plant her flowers and vegetables. On July fourth, Uncle Jim is invited to the rooftop, where he is shown everything Lydia Grace has learned about beauty. This lovely story lends itself well to discussions about the virtues of this special young girl. David Small's black-ink, pastel, and watercolor illustrations are appealing. They capture the characters and provide interesting perspectives on the cityscape.

3.17   Turner, Ann (1997). **Mississippi Mud: Three Prairie Journals.** Illustrated by Robert J. Blake. New York: HarperCollins. 44 pp. ISBN: 0-06-024432-1. Picture Book. (See **10.22**)

3.18   Waters, Kate (1996). **Tapenum's Day: A Wampanoag Indian Boy in Pilgrim Times.** Photographs by Russ Kendall. New York: Scholastic. Unpaged. ISBN: 0-590-20237-5. Picture Book.

This book makes history come alive. The meticulous recreation of the Wampanoag's way of life is documented using current photographic technology. Readers follow Tapenum, an eleven-year-old Wampanoag boy, through a day of hunting, fishing, and doing chores. Tapenum's first-person narrative provides insight into his determination to train and work hard so he can be recognized by his people as a *pniese*, a warrior-counselor. He has the support of many important people during his period of coming-of-age, including his parents, his friend Nootimis, and an elder named Waban. The book is the third in a trilogy that includes *Sarah Morton's Day: A Day in the Life of a Pilgrim Girl* and *Samuel Eaton's Day: A Day in the Life of a Pilgrim Boy.* It is an intimate and accurate portrayal of Native American life at the time of European colonization, complete with historical notes and a glossary of Wampanoag words. First graders learned so much from this book that they could dramatize the daily life of the tribe members.

Waters, Kate (1989). **Sarah Morton's Day: A Day in the Life of a Pilgrim Girl.** Photographs by Russ Kendall. New York: Scholastic. ISBN: 0-590-42634-6. Picture Book.

Waters, Kate (1996). **Samuel Eaton's Day: A Day in the Life of a Pilgrim Boy.** Photographs by Russ Kendall. New York: Scholastic. ISBN: 0-590-48053-7. Picture Book.

3.19 Whelan, Gloria (1996). **The Indian School.** Illustrated by Gabriela Delosso. New York: HarperCollins. 89 pp. ISBN: 0-06-027077-2. Chapter Book.

It is autumn 1839, and eleven-year-old Lucy is newly orphaned. She will go to live with Uncle Edward and Aunt Emma, missionaries who run a mission school for Native American children in northern Michigan. Through Lucy, Whelan provides the young reader with some insight into the existence of Indian mission boarding schools as a part of American history and of federal policy to assimilate Native Americans into mainstream society. The experiences of Native American children—many of whom endured and survived traumatic separation from their families when they were as young as five years old—is palpable in the characters of Raven and Matthew. Raven defiantly resists conformity and invisibility during her stay. "I cannot tell who I am if I look like everyone else," she insists, as she refuses to change into school dress. Raven's resistance, and her adherence to her strong Native American identity, intrigue Lucy. Raven's seemingly stubborn behaviors demonstrate to Lucy that there is much value in the Native American way of life.

3.20 Wolff, Virginia E. (1998). **Bat 6.** New York: Scholastic. 230 pp. ISBN: 0-590-89799-3. (See **20.43**)

Secondary Reviews

3.21 Appelbaum, Diana (1997). **Cocoa Ice.** Illustrated by Holly Meade. New York: Orchard. Unpaged. ISBN: 0-531-33040-0. Sophisticated Picture Book.

Two girls, one from Santo Domingo and the other from Maine, tell a cross-cultural story set in the late 1800s, when Yankee schooners brought ice and refined sugar to Santo Domingo in trade for cocoa and coffee beans. The two girls are linked by a sailor-uncle who carries bits of culture back and forth. Contrasting the warm colors of a tropical Caribbean island and the cool colors of a Maine winter, this book invites readers to find something in common among people from very different places.

3.22 Armstrong, Nancy M. (1994). **Navajo Long Walk.** Illustrated by Paulette Livers Lambert. Boulder, CO: Roberts Rinehart. 128 pp. ISBN: 1-879373-56-4. Chapter Book.

A good beginning book that offers an introduction to the Navajo and the Long Walk. This story begins with a young boy named Kee and his family, who live at their ancestral home before the U.S. Cavalry rounds up the Navajo and moves them to Bosque Redondo, a government internment camp. Like many Navajo, Kee's family attempts to avoid captivity but later surrenders. The reader experiences their hardships and confusion on the Long Walk, their four-year stay at the Bosque Redondo, and their strength in overcoming hardships in order to survive. After the return to their ancestral home, Kee feels the best way to help his family is to learn about the white man, so he makes the decision to go to school. This book is part of the Council for Indian Education series.

3.23   Birchman, David F. (1997). **A Green Horn Blowing.** Illustrated by Thomas B. Allen. New York: Lothrop, Lee & Shepard. Unpaged. ISBN: 0-688-12389-9. Picture Book. (See **11.13**)

3.24   Bruchac, Joseph (1998). **The Arrow over the Door.** New York: Dial Books for Young Readers. Illustrated by James Watling. 96 pp. ISBN: 0-8037-2078-5. Chapter Book.

This story is based on a 1777 encounter between Native Americans in Saratoga Springs, New York, and a group of Friends (Quakers) in Easton, New York. The extensive author's note at the end of the book elaborates on this historical event within the framework of the Revolutionary War. Bruchac again writes a coming-of-age story in which Samuel, a Quaker boy, and Stands Straight, a young Abenaki boy, come to understand the meaning of peaceful coexistence—a concept that defies the actions of the Loyalists and Patriots of the day. Through this tale—which is told as only a good storyteller can—the reader gets a chance to look at both Quaker and Native American life from a fresh perspective. To discover more about storytelling, read Bruchac's *Tell Me a Tale.*

> Bruchac, Joseph (1998). **Tell Me a Tale: A Book about Storytelling.** San Diego: Harcourt Brace. 140 pp. ISBN: 0-15-201221-4. Chapter Book.

3.25   Burks, Brian (1998). **Walks Alone.** San Diego: Harcourt Brace. 128 pp. ISBN: 0-15-201612-0. Chapter Book.

This brief but realistic portrayal of the Warm Springs Apache around 1879 captures the physical hardship and loss they endured as they resisted removal to a reservation. Walks Alone is a teenage girl through whose experiences the reader senses the brutality and destruction of the Apache people just before the Battle of Tres Castillos. Although the author uses terse descriptions and easily read text, the tragedy of the story is not sacrificed. As Walks Alone is injured; suffers the death of her brother, grandmother, and fiancé; and finally is captured and led away by Mexican soldiers, the hopelessness of the Native American situation is mirrored through her perspective. The sources cited provide evidence of the author's research, and the information is presented through a courageous female protagonist who is to be revered by readers of both genders.

3.26 Chambers, Veronica (1998). **Amistad Rising: A Story of Freedom.** Edited by Shelly Bowen and Allyn M. Johnston. Illustrated by Paul Lee. San Diego: Harcourt Brace. Unpaged. ISBN: 0-15-201803-4. Picture Book.

This book tells the true story of a man named Joseph Cinque, who was born free and made a slave after being kidnapped from his homeland in Africa and imprisoned on the ship called *Amistad*. The book records Cinque's brutal experiences and documents his bravery throughout his ordeal. During the ensuing landmark trials centering on Cinque's right to freedom, John Quincy Adams, a key figure in American history, served as Cinque's ally. This powerful rendering of a historical occurrence should be used with other resources.

3.27 Crook, Connie Brummel (1998). **Maple Moon.** Illustrated by Scott Cameron. Don Mills, Ontario, Canada: Stoddart Kids. 32 pp. ISBN: 0-7737-3017-6.

Crook has created an appealing tale of how Northeast Woodland Native Americans might have discovered maple syrup. A small boy accidentally discovers that sweet sap is dripping from a tree, but when he shows the elders of the tribe what is happening, the sap stops flowing. As the days become warmer, the sap flows again, and the tribe rejoices in the child's discovery. Cameron's oil-on-canvas illustrations convey a sense of nature and woodland warmth.

3.28 Cushman, Karen (1996). **The Ballad of Lucy Whipple.** New York: Clarion. 195 pp. ISBN: 0-395-72806-1. Sophisticated Chapter Book. (See **5.51**)

3.29   Friedrich, Elizabeth (1996). **Leah's Pony.** Illustrated by Michael Garland. Honesdale, PA: Boyds Mills. Unpaged. ISBN: 1-56397-189-5. Picture Book.

When her family's farm is threatened by foreclosure during the Dust Bowl, Leah decides to sell her pony in hopes of helping her father. Through the ensuing sale, we learn about the penny auctions common during the Depression, in which a neighbor bid low on an item and no one else bid. The neighbor then gave the item back to the owner. This book invites a discussion of community solidarity and problem solving.

3.30   Hall, Donald (1996). **Old Home Day.** Illustrated by Emily Arnold McCully. San Diego: Harcourt Brace. Unpaged. ISBN: 0-15-276896-3. Picture Book

This book tells the story of a New Hampshire pond beginning thousands of years ago when there were only fish and animals in the environment. Eventually people came to live by the pond, and Blackwater Village flourished. Then people began to move away, and the village declined. In 1899, the governor of New Hampshire declared Old Home Week, and many past residents returned to reminisce and share stories of the simpler life. This book would be good as part of a set of change-over-time texts.

3.31   Hamm, Diane Johnston (1997). **Daughter of Sugua.** Illustrated by Paul Micich. Morton Grove, IL: Whitman. 154 pp. ISBN: 0-8075-1477-2. Chapter Book.

Ida is a ten-year-old Suquamish living in a small village on Puget Sound at the turn of the nineteenth century. Changes are occurring very rapidly for Ida, her parents, and her grandmother. Their coastal village is being abandoned as tribal members move to land allotments further inland to which they have been assigned. Ida's father is not a farmer, yet they will be expected to farm their new lands; Mother will have to quit her work because it will be too far for her to commute daily. Then Ida is informed that she will have to attend the boarding school for children who live too far from the village school. Grandmother is a comforting figure to Ida and her parents during this time. Appealing, realistic characters give readers a chance to see, hear, and feel the heartbeat of the Native American people as they adjust and adapt to many of the changes that were imposed on them by treaties and federal mandates during the late nineteenth century.

3.32 Hansen, Joyce (1997). **I Thought My Soul Would Rise and Fly: The Diary of Patsy, a Freed Girl.** New York: Scholastic. 202 pp. ISBN: 0-590-84913-1. Chapter Book.

Patsy, a young kitchen slave, secretly learns to read and write. When the Civil War ends, she keeps a diary detailing the changes that emancipation brings to her and other slaves. Patsy also teaches the plantation children the basic skills they need to exercise their newly-won freedom. Information about Hansen's use of primary historical documents such as diaries, oral histories, notes, photographs, engravings, recipes, songs, and maps helps to make the story authentic.

3.33 Hearne, Betsy G. (1997). **Seven Brave Women.** Illustrated by Bethanne Andersen. New York: Greenwillow. Unpaged. ISBN: 0-688-14503-5. Picture Book. (See **4.47**)

3.34 Hest, Amy (1997). **When Jessie Came across the Sea.** Illustrated by P. J. Lynch. Cambridge, MA: Candlewick. Unpaged. ISBN: 0-7636-0094-6. Picture Book.

This is a simple immigration story with Cinderella-like qualities. A young girl from a village in Eastern Europe is chosen by her rabbi to make the journey to America to live with the rabbi's sister-in-law in New York. Thirteen-year-old Jessie makes the journey alone, earns her living by working in a dress shop, falls in love, sends money to her grandmother to come to America, marries, and lives happily ever after. The illustrations in the book are rich, with authentic detail and warm, memorable images.

3.35 Hobbs, Will (1997). **Ghost Canoe.** New York: Morrow Junior Books. 195 pp. ISBN: 0-688-14193-5. Chapter Book.

In this mystery, fourteen-year-old Nathan fishes for salmon and halibut and hunts seals and gray whales with the Makah, a whaling tribe in the Pacific Northwest. The story takes place in 1874 on the very tip of Washington's Olympic Peninsula, and things heat up when Nathan discovers clues to a lost Spanish treasure. Will Hobbs has researched extensively the geography, natural history, and human history of the Pacific Northwest.

3.36 Howard, Ellen (1996). **The Log Cabin Quilt.** Illustrated by Ronald Himler. New York: Holiday House. Unpaged. ISBN: 0-8234-1247-4. Picture Book.

This is a tender story about the hardships families faced when they moved west during the 1800s. Winter winds blow through the cracks of the cabin, and Pa should have been home hours ago. Elvirey has the good sense to stuff the cracks in the walls with quilt scraps, but this reminds everyone of their deceased mother. Fortunately good memories outweigh the painful, Pa returns home, and the family finds new courage and shared determination.

3.37   Janeczko, Paul B. (1997). **Home on the Range: Cowboy Poetry.** Illustrated by Bernie Fuchs. New York: Clarion. 40 pp. ISBN: 0-8037-1910-8. Sophisticated Picture Book. (See **10.28**)

3.38   Johnston, Tony (1996). **The Wagon.** Illustrated by James E. Ransome. New York: Morrow. Unpaged. ISBN: 0-688-13457-2. Picture Book.

This is the story of a little boy who grows up as a slave in the Carolinas. He quickly learns what slavery means by working for the master from dawn until dusk. He dreams that the wagon built by his father to carry slaves could one day become a gorgeous chariot. His dreams of freedom are inspired by the sun and nature that surround him. His grandmother encourages him to think of positive things to keep from losing hope. The story ends as the slaves are freed at the end of the Civil War.

3.39   Littlesugar, Amy (1997). **A Portrait of Spotted Deer's Grandfather.** Illustrated by Marlowe DeChristopher. Morton Grove, IL: Whitman. 32 pp. ISBN: 0-8075-6622-5. Picture Book.

George Catlin traveled the western frontier and painted portraits of Native Americans during the 1830s. In this story, young Spotted Deer wants his grandfather to sit for a portrait, but Moose Horn is concerned that having his portrait painted might take away his spirit. In this book, readers learn about Catlin and the tools he used in his work. The author's view is not necessarily that of Native Americans' in respect to Catlin and his work, a point teachers may wish to discuss with readers.

3.40   Marrin, Albert (1996). **Plains Warrior: Chief Quanah Parker and the Comanches.** New York: Atheneum Books for Young Readers. 200 pp. ISBN: 0-689-80081-9. Sophisticated Chapter Book.

This book tells the story of Quanah Parker during the dramatic and tragic years in Native American history when tribes went from living free on the Great Plains to containment on reservations. Throughout the narrative, the reader gets a view of the Comanche way of life and the influence of key historical events and people on that life. Marrin supports the text with photographs, maps, quotes from the people involved, newspaper clippings of the times, government documents, journal entries, drawings, and sketches.

3.41   Matcheck, Diane (1998). **The Sacrifice.** New York: Farrar, Straus and Giroux. 224 pp. ISBN: 0-374-36378-1. Sophisticated Chapter Book.

This is a fast-moving, suspenseful story of a young Apsaalooka (Crow) girl. It was prophesied at her birth and that of her twin brother that one of them would become the great leader of their people. Her twin brother is presumed to be the Great One, and even after his death it is not recognized that she might be the Great One. After her father's death leaves her orphaned, the young girl sets out to avenge his death and prove that she is the prophesied Great One. When she is captured by the Pawnee, she receives an unexpected friendly welcome that causes her to be uneasy and distrusting. As her time with the Pawnee increases, so does her knowledge of her role in the Morning Star ceremony, and her fight for survival begins once again. The author's note provides brief background information on the Pawnee and Apsaalooka, the Morning Star ceremony, additional resources, and references.

3.42   McCully, Emily Arnold (1996). **The Bobbin Girl.** New York: Dial Books for Young Readers. 34 pp. ISBN: 0-8037-1827-6. Sophisticated Chapter Book.

Rebecca, the bobbin girl, is a ten-year-old who goes to work in the textile mills of Lowell, Massachusetts, in the 1930s to help her struggling mother. The conditions in the mill are bad—loud machinery, unhealthy air, many injuries, and low wages. When the mill owners threaten to lower wages even more, the women at the mill stage a turnout. Even though the protest fails, Rebecca vows to continue the fight for better working conditions. (See also **20.30**)

3.43   McCully, Emily Arnold (1997). **Starring Mirette and Bellini.** New York: Putnam. 29 pp. ISBN: 0-399-22636-2. Picture Book. (See **5.128**)

3.44   Pfitsch, Patricia Curtis (1997). **Keeper of the Light.** New York: Simon & Schuster Books for Young Readers. 137 pp. ISBN: 0-689-81492-5. Chapter Book.

Following the death of her father, Faith assumes the role of lighthouse keeper on the rocky coast of Lake Superior. Although Faith shows she is capable, her mother decides the family will move into town. Faith is stifled by the role expected of young women in 1872, and fears the lighthouse will not be well tended. Eventually a storm tempts Faith into rescuing passengers from a ship that has run aground, and she comes to understand her father and herself better.

3.45   Pryor, Bonnie (1996). **The Dream Jar.** Illustrated by Mark Graham. New York: Morrow Junior Books. Unpaged. ISBN: 0-688-13062-3. Picture Book.

When Valentina's family emigrates from Russia, everyone works to save coins to help the family purchase a small store. Valentina discovers she can teach English to immigrant adults in her neighborhood and helps to earn pennies for the family's dream jar. The detail found in the warm illustrations provides a realistic portrayal of the immigrant experience for young readers.

3.46   Riggio, Anita (1997). **Secret Signs: Along the Underground Railroad.** Honesdale, PA: Boyds Mills. 32 pp. ISBN: 1-56397-555-6. Picture Book.

This book is based on historical documentation of the struggles and hardships encountered by slaves in their quest for freedom during the Civil War. Told in narrative form, the story focuses on a deaf boy named Luke and his mother, who make sugar eggs to sell at the general store. Communicating in sign language, Luke and his mother formulate a plan to communicate with a little slave girl at the store. The plan is interrupted by a slave catcher, but through quick thinking Luke is able to distract the slave catcher and pass on to the little girl information about the next safe stop on the Underground Railroad. This book could be used with a variety of ages, but some background information on signing and the Underground Railroad would be needed for it to make sense to most children.

3.47   Rumford, James (1998). **The Island-below-the-Star.** Boston: Houghton Mifflin. Unpaged. ISBN: 0-395-85159-9. Picture Book.

This is the story of five brothers who use the stars to guide their voyage to the Hawaiian Islands. Each brother has a special skill, and together the brothers are able to follow a star through treacherous storms and high waves to reach the island below the star. James Rumford's watercolors complement the poetic rhythm of the text, which is written in English and Hawaiian. Readers are enlightened about the historical origins of Polynesian migration more than fifteen hundred years ago.

3.48   Ryan, Pam Muñoz (1998). **Riding Freedom.** Illustrated by Brian Selznick. New York: Scholastic. 138 pp. ISBN: 0-590-95766-X. Chapter Book.

This historical novel is based on the true story of Charlotte Parkhurst, a teenager who discovered she could do the things she wanted if she pretended to be a man. Charlotte, orphaned at an early age, struggles with the limited options open to women. She passes herself off as a boy to get a job working in a horse stable, and becomes an excellent stagecoach driver. In the mid-1800s, she moves to California where—as a man—she can own land and vote. Charlotte lives by the motto "You gotta do what your heart tells you," and her story provides insight into both the times and the spirit that shaped the United States.

3.49   St. George, Judith (1997). **Sacagawea.** New York: Putman. 128 pp. ISBN: 0-399-23161-7. Chapter Book.

Judith St. George provides young readers with a story about the strong and resourceful Shoshone woman, Sacagawea. The primary focus of the book is the Lewis and Clark expedition. Readers will see how Sacagawea's extensive knowledge of the people, land, animals, and plants had a significant and positive impact on the expedition's success. This book is well researched.

3.50   Swain, Gwenyth (1996). **The Road to Seneca Falls: A Story about Elizabeth Cady Stanton.** Illustrated by Mary O'Keefe. Minneapolis: Carolrhoda. 64 pp. ISBN: 0-87614-947-6. Chapter Book.

This well-written, fictionalized biography shows the strength and perseverance of Elizabeth Cady Stanton, a pioneer in obtaining equality for women throughout the country. The historical Stanton grew up in Johnstown, New York, in the 1820s, and accompanied her husband to the World Anti-Slavery Convention in

London. Here Stanton met Lucretia Mott, a Quaker minister who wasn't afraid to speak out. The two became friends, and eventually organized the first Women's Rights Convention held in 1848 in Seneca Falls, New York.

3.51   Tunnell, Michael O. (1997). **Mailing May.** Illustrated by Ted Rand. New York: Greenwillow. 32 pp. ISBN: 0-688-12878-5. Picture Book.

This unbelievable story is based on a real-life adventure in Idaho in the early 1900s. May's folks cannot afford a ticket for her to ride the train seventy-five miles to visit her grandparents, but they work out a deal with her postmaster-uncle that allows her to be "shipped" as a rail package—for fifty-three cents. This delightful story about creative problem solving lends itself to a study of life in this historical time period. The illustrations include many artifacts such as period photographs and train tickets.

3.52   Vick, Helen Hughes (1998). **Shadow.** Boulder, CO: Roberts Rinehart. 128 pp. ISBN: 1-57098-195-7. Chapter Book.

Shadow is the first book in Vick's new Courage of the Stone series, and is based on the prehistoric culture of the Sinagua people who inhabited the area of northern Arizona around 1180 C.E. Shadow, the female protagonist, is thirteen years old and has always taken a subservient role to her twin brother, Sun. Shadow senses danger, injury, and an evil presence pursuing her brother and father, both of whom are long overdue from a quarrying expedition. She packs a few things to take with her, and sets out on a journey filled with danger, mystery, and self-growth in the hope of finding Sun and Stone Gatherer. This well-written, exciting plot provides lots of anthropological imagery as Shadow uses the tools, materials, and plants available to her to search for her father and brother, and eventually to nurse her injured father back to health. Her ultimate confrontation with the Spirit of Fear is one of personal growth, immense courage, and triumph over both evil and the restrictive female code of conduct that is a part of her culture. The book includes a map of Arizona and archaeological insights into the Sinagua.

3.53   Wells, Rosemary (1998). **Mary on Horseback: Three Mountain Stories.** New York: Dial Books For Young Readers. 53 pp. ISBN: 0-803-72154-4. Chapter Book.

Mary Breckenridge changed people's lives by starting the Frontier Nursing Service in rural Appalachian Kentucky. Trained as a nurse in World War I, and faced with the painful loss of her own children, Breckenridge turns her grief into positive action and begins riding into the hills on horseback to provide medical attention to some of the poorest people in America. Three memorable characters tell touching stories of Mary's heroism.

3.54 Williams, Rianna M. (1997). **Mahealani and the King of Hawai'i.** Illustrated by Jackie Black. Honolulu: Ka mea Kakau. 103 pp. ISBN: 0-9658621-0-0. Chapter Book.

A historical account of two significant moments in Hawaiian history—King Kalakaua's coronation and his fiftieth birthday. Although told within a fictive context, the narratives are based on actual events in Hawaiian history carefully researched by the author. These events are told in a storylike format ideal for young readers. The preface and endnotes differentiate the real and fictional characters, and clarify the backgrounds of actual people.

3.55 Yee, Paul (1996). **Ghost Train.** Illustrated by Harvey Chan. Emeryville, CA: Groundwood. Unpaged. ISBN: 0-88899-257-2. Sophisticated Picture Book. (See **4.61**)

Historical Nonfiction

Primary Reviews

3.56 Ancona, George (1997). **Mayeros: A Yucatec Maya Family.** New York: Lothrop, Lee & Shepard. Unpaged. ISBN: 0-688-13465-3. Picture Book.

Ancona gives a splendid historical overview of the blending of Mayan and Spanish traditions in the Yucatec Maya's lifestyle as he chronicles the daily lives of two children, Armando and Gaspar, and their family. Through the lens of his extraordinary camera, readers accompany Ancona on a visit to the Yucatán, the home of his grandparents, where he rediscovers the food, stories, music, and jokes of his childhood and ancestors. An author's note adds more historical details, and a glossary of Spanish and Yucatec words provides translations and pronunciations. This book could be used with *Children of Yucatán* by Frank Staub, also illustrated with full-color photographs, to provide an in-depth look at the Yucatán past and present. (See also **20.51**)

> Staub, Frank J. (1996). **Children of Yucatán.** Minneapolis: Carolrhoda. 48 pp. ISBN: 0-87614-984-0. Picture Book.

3.57   Brook, Donna (1998). **The Journey of English.** Illustrated by Jean Day Zallinger. New York: Clarion. 48 pp. ISBN: 0-395-71211-4. Chapter Book. (See **13.2**)

3.58   Bruchac, Joseph (1997). **Lasting Echoes: An Oral History of Native American People.** Illustrated by Paul Morin. New York: Harcourt Brace. 176 pp. ISBN: 0-15-201327-X. Sophisticated Chapter Book.

Bruchac tells the story of Native Americans in the United States using their own words. Borrowing from speeches, letters, journals, and other source materials, he documents the ideas of many different tribes and famous Native American leaders such as Geronimo and Sitting Bull. The result is a unique view of history from a Native American perspective. This book compresses a lot of history into a few short pages, beginning with the arrival of Europeans on the North American continent and continuing to the present. It also provides a compelling portrait of Native American peoples. This book will be most accessible to older students with some sense of history.

3.59   Cooney, Barbara (1996). **Eleanor.** New York: Viking. Unpaged. ISBN: 0-670-86159-6. Picture Book. (See **5.39**)

3.60   Dash, Joan (1996). **We Shall Not Be Moved: The Women's Factory Strike of 1909.** New York: Scholastic. 165 pp. ISBN: 0-590-48409-5. Sophisticated Chapter Book. (See **20.23**)

3.61   Egan, Ted (1998). **The Drover's Boy.** Illustrated by Robert Ingpen. Melbourne, Australia: Lothian. Unpaged. ISBN: 1-887734-52-X. Sophisticated Picture Book.

This haunting and hard-hitting story, accompanied by music and lyrics, describes the contributions of aboriginal women disguised as men to circumvent a law that forbade employment of aboriginal women as drovers. In some cases, as this story relates, love developed between the aboriginal drover "boys" and their white bosses. Gold-tone illustrations displayed in a scrapbook fashion, and large two-page illustrations of cattle drives, help readers understand the hardships of these courageous women. This book would provide opportunity for conversations about Aborigines, slavery, prejudice, and interracial families.

3.62 Fisher, Leonard Everett (1997). **Anasazi.** New York: Atheneum. Unpaged. ISBN: 0-689-80737-6. Picture Book.

Fisher's first-rate anthropological study of the Anasazi clearly fills a void for intermediate readers. Inhabiting the Four Corners area of the southwestern United States more than two thousand years ago, these "ancient ones" left behind remnants of their culture in the form of cliff dwellings, tools, pottery, baskets, and petroglyphs. From what remains, we can only speculate as to their cultural traditions and beliefs. However we are able to track changes in architecture, diet, artifacts, and tools for daily use, as well as interactions and encounters with other native groups in the area. What remains of their civilization motivates us to ask more questions about their existence, and many questions are posed and answered in this text. Fisher's distinctive art in sepia tones gives readers a sense of time past. Additional information includes a parallel timeline of significant world events that occurred during the time of the Anasazi, as well as an area map of their cultural range.

3.63 Gerstein, Mordicai (1998). **The Wild Boy.** New York: Farrar, Straus and Giroux. 39 pp. ISBN: 0-374-38431-2. Chapter Book.

This poignant tale is based on the true story of Victor, the Wild Child of Aveyron, who was found in southern France in 1800. Through Gerstein's text and paintings, the events unfold as the boy is found by hunters, taken to the Institute for Deaf-Mutes in Paris, probed by doctors, and jeered at by cruel crowds. Those who try to communicate with him finally give up—all except a young doctor named Jean-Marc Itard. Realizing that Victor never learned to be a child, Itard and his empathetic housekeeper take the enigmatic young boy into Itard's home and tenderly care for him. Although he never learns to speak, Victor does learn to discriminate touch, hot, and cold; to wear clothing; and to help with chores like chopping wood. Children will be touched by this moving story of this remarkable boy and his teacher, a story that calls to the wild child in us all.

3.64 Hansen, Joyce (1998). **Women of Hope: African Americans Who Made a Difference.** New York: Scholastic. 32 pp. ISBN: 0-590-93973-4. Picture Book. (See **20.12**)

3.65 Josephson, Judith Pinkerton (1997). **Mother Jones: Fierce Fighter for Workers' Rights.** Minneapolis: Lerner. 144 pp. ISBN: 0-8225-4924-7. Picture Book. (See **5.14**)

3.66 Knight, Margy Burns (1996). **Talking Walls: The Stories Continue.** Illustrated by Anne Sibley O'Brien. Gardiner, ME: Tilbury. Unpaged. ISBN: 0-88448-165-4. Picture Book. (See **7.21**)

3.67 Macy, Sue (1996). **Winning Ways: A Photohistory of American Women in Sports.** New York: Scholastic. 217 pp. ISBN: 0-590-76336-9. Chapter Book. (See **12.21**)

3.68 Meltzer, Milton (1998). **Ten Queens: Portraits of Women of Power.** Illustrated by Bethanne Andersen. New York: Dutton Children's Books. 134 pp. ISBN: 0-525-45643-0. Chapter Book. (See **5.24**)

3.69 Millard, Anne (1998). **A Street through Time: A 12,000-Year Walk through History.** Illustrated by Steve Noon. New York: Dorling Kindersley. 32 pp. ISBN: 0-789-43426-1. Sophisticated Picture Book.

This book is an excellent resource for helping students understand the concept of history. It traces the changes that have taken place on a small stretch of land that borders a waterway, beginning with a Stone Age nomadic village and ending with a modern street. The depth of detail in the full-color illustrations makes this exploration of change over time a visual enterprise. Readers get some information through the print text, but most of what the book has to tell is conveyed through pictures and labels. Rather than tell readers what there is to know about each particular period in history, the author invites investigation with questions and hints about what to look for in each picture.

3.70 Mochizuki, Ken (1997). **Passage to Freedom: The Sugihara Story.** Illustrated by Dom Lee. New York: Lee & Low. Unpaged. ISBN: 1-880000-49-0. Picture Book. (See **20.28**)

3.71 Myers, Walter Dean (1997). **Harlem.** Illustrated by Christopher Myers. New York: Scholastic. Unpaged. ISBN: 0-590-54340-7. Picture Book. (See **10.19**)

3.72 Pinkney, Andrea Davis (1996). **Bill Pickett: Rodeo-Ridin' Cowboy.** Illustrated by Brian Pinkney. San Diego: Harcourt Brace. Unpaged. ISBM: 0-15-200100-X. Picture Book.

Bill Pickett was born to slaves in the 1800s and grew up south of Abilene, Texas. As a young boy, he wanted to learn all about the cowboys who passed by his parents' farm. He loved listening to the stories told by his older cousins, who were trail-driving horse-men. Pickett set out to prove that he had what it took to be a cow-boy. Seeing some men trying to rope a calf, Pickett showed them how he had seen a bulldog bite the lip of a calf and hold it down. His adaptation of this technique became known as *bulldogging*. At fifteen, Pickett learned to lasso and ride, and set out, with great success, to find paying work as a cowboy. News of his skill soon spread throughout the West, and everyone wanted to see him per-form. Pickett was one of the first African American rodeo per-formers, but his fans focused on his skill, rather than on the color of his skin. Pickett made a living as a bulldogger and traveled around the world, performing in all the famous rodeos, until his retirement. This engaging text includes many details and descrip-tions, and the illustrations richly complement the story.

3.73 Pringle, Laurence (1998). **One Room School.** Illustrated by Bar-bara Garrison. Honesdale, PA: Boyds Mills. Unpaged. ISBN: 0-56397-583-1. Picture Book. (See **6.3**)

3.74 Sis, Peter (1996). **Starry Messenger.** New York: Farrar, Straus and Giroux. Unpaged. ISBN: 0-374-37191-1. Sophisticated Picture Book.

This Caldecott Honor Book tells the story of Galileo in words and stunning pictures that capture the essence of his era in history. The author says that Galileo was born with stars in his eyes, and that he was a celebrated scientist until he discovered that the earth cir-cled the sun rather than the other way around. The story tells of Galileo's life from childhood through his final days as a prisoner of the church. Using seventeenth-century symbols and images and quotes from Galileo's own writings, the author allows readers to cross the boundaries of time and space to enter Galileo's world. The story unfolds on many levels simultaneously, making this a book that has appeal for adults as well as children.

3.75 Tillage, Leon Walter (1997). **Leon's Story.** Illustrated by Susan Roth. New York: Farrar, Straus and Giroux. 107 pp. ISBN: 0-374-34379-9. Chapter Book. (See **20.18**)

Secondary Reviews

3.76 Adler, David A. (1997). **A Picture Book of Thurgood Marshall.** Illustrated by Robert Casilla. New York: Dial Books for Young Readers. 48 pp. ISBN: 0-8234-1506-6. Picture Book.

This book is about a well-known individual who fought for equality for all Americans throughout his lifetime, Thurgood Marshall. One of Marshall's significant childhood memories was of having to memorize parts of the U.S. Constitution when he got in trouble at school. Later, this experience would serve Marshall well when he became a lawyer for the National Association for the Advancement of Colored People (NAACP). Marshall became the first African American to sit on the Supreme Court of the United States. This book tells his story in language accessible to young children.

3.77   Arnold, Caroline (1996). **Stories in Stone: Rock Art Pictures by Early Americans.** Photographs by Richard Hewett. New York: Clarion. 48 pp. ISBN: 0-395-72092-3. Picture Book.

The author's insightful text and full-color photographs by Richard Hewett provide an exploration into the ancient art carved into rock walls and painted on stone surfaces. The area highlighted in this book is Ridgecrest, California. Ridgecrest is northeast of Los Angeles in the Coso Range of the Mojave Desert. Native Americans used this site for thousands of years and created many designs, including abstract patterns and both small and life-sized pictures of people and animals. A glossary and a listing of other places to view rock art are included at the end of the book.

3.78   Cha, Dia (1996). **Dia's Story Cloth.** Illustrated by Chue Cha and Nhia Thao Cha. New York: Lee & Low. Unpaged. ISBN: 1-880000-34-2. Sophisticated Picture Book.

The hand-embroidered story cloth shown in the book describes the history of the Hmong people. The illustrations depict the journey of the Hmong, from their origins in China centuries ago, through years of joys and hardships, and ending with the eventual immigration of over 125,000 refugees to the United States after the Vietnam War. Though the story could be enjoyed by all, older audiences will better understand the historical relevance and struggle of the race.

3.79   Ciment, James, with Ronald LaFrance (1996). **Encyclopedia of the North American Indian.** New York: Scholastic. 224 pp. ISBN: 0-590-22790-4. Reference Book.

This resource book includes information on 143 different Native American tribal groups from the Arctic Circle through Central America and the Caribbean. The tribal groups are listed in alphabetical order, and each entry includes important information, people, and events unique to each particular group. This encyclopedia gives both historic and contemporary information.

3.80 Currie, Stephen (1997). **We Have Marched Together: The Working Children's Crusade.** Minneapolis: Lerner. 88 pp. ISBN: 0-8225-1733-7. Chapter Book.

Stephen Currie's chapter book explores the cruel hardships endured by child workers in Philadelphia in the early 1900s, and the courageous crusade of Mother Jones, the fiery labor leader who led an army of men, women, and child laborers all the way from Philadelphia to New York. Through vivid text, illustrated with photographs from the Library of Congress, the reader marches beside the children in their struggle for better working conditions. This book will raise discussions about many human rights issues.

3.81 Czech, Kenneth (1996). **Snapshot: America Discovers the Camera.** Minneapolis: Lerner. 88 pp. ISBN: 0-822-51736-1. Chapter Book.

Photography is taken for granted today, but students may begin to appreciate it more if they study this readable book about the history and impact of cameras. The stories show how the camera not only recorded history, but also impacted people's awareness of issues and conditions. The book is filled with black-and-white photographs spanning the decades between 1839, when the camera was invented, and World War II.

3.82 Dewey, Jennifer Owings (1996). **Stories on Stone: Rock Art: Images from the Ancient Ones.** Boston: Little Brown. 32 pp. ISBN: 0-316-18211-7. Picture Book.

This book introduces young readers to the rock art and petroglyphs of the Anasazi people. Explaining places she visited in New Mexico as a child, Dewey takes the reader on a journey through her childhood and explains how her curiosity about the art symbols began. She uses colored-pencil illustrations to show many of the symbols that have been found, and explains these symbols with historical information about the Anasazi.

3.83 Duncan, Dayton (1996). **The West: An Illustrated History for Children.** New York: Little Brown. 136 pp. ISBN: 0-316-92236-6. Sophisticated Picture Book.

This visual and informative narrative of the discovery and settlement of the American West is based on a PBS television documentary. It contains over 400 photographs that create a gripping journey through the turbulent history of the region. Its stories tell of people coming from all corners of the earth and highlight the tensions between European and native peoples. The book also touches on the experiences of Hispanic/Latino people, the Chinese, and African slaves in the United States. The American Library Association says, "This book is as sprawling, vast, and rich as the history and land it describes."

3.84   Fleming, Candace (1996). **Women of the Lights.** Illustrated by James Watling. Morton Grove, IL: Whitman. 79 pp. ISBN: 0-8075-9165-3. Chapter Book.

Since 1768, at least 250 women have served as lighthouse keepers on America's coasts. This book focuses on four of these courageous women: Ida Lewis, who was famous for her rescues; Kate Walker, who kept an isolated lighthouse for more than thirty years and saved more than fifty people; Hattie Colfax, who retired at age eighty; and Emily Fish, who made her lighthouse on a California peninsula a social and cultural center.

3.85   Ganeri, Anita (1996). **The Young Person's Guide to the Orchestra.** Compact disc narrated by Ben Kingsley. San Diego: Harcourt Brace. 56 pp. ISBN: 0-15-201304-0. Picture Book. (See **11.20**)

3.86   Goodman, Susan E. (1998). **Stones, Bones, and Petroglyphs: Digging into Southwest Archaeology.** Photographs by Michael J. Doolittle. New York: Atheneum Books for Young Readers. 48 pp. ISBN: 0-689-81121-7. Picture Book.

This photographic essay shows eighth graders exploring the Mesa Verde region of Colorado. These students are trying to determine why the ancestral Puebloan people who lived in the area for over one thousand years suddenly moved away. This book is a first-hand account of the science of archaeology, desert ecology, and ancient Native American skills. Numerous close-up photographs add to the information presented. The book ends with a glossary, and suggestions for further reading.

3.87   Hampton, Wilborn (1997). **Kennedy Assassinated! The World Mourns: A Reporter's Story.** New York: Candlewick. 96 pp. ISBN: 1-564-02811-9. Chapter Book.

Hampton was a brand new reporter when President Kennedy was assassinated, and his recollections of the experience are both personal and objective. The reader is carried through the minute-by-minute chronicle of the tragic events by Hampton's engaging narrative and collection of historic photographs. The overall effect of the book is powerful, bringing to life a shocking episode in American history.

3.88 Haskins, James, and Kathleen Benson (1998). **African Beginnings.** Illustrated by Floyd Cooper. New York: Lothrop, Lee & Shepard. 48 pp. ISBN: 0-688-10256-5. Picture Book. (See **3.89** below)

3.89 Haskins, James, and Kathleen Benson (1999). **Bound for America: The Forced Migration of Africans to the New World.** Illustrated by Floyd Cooper. New York: Lothrop, Lee & Shepard. 48 pp. ISBN: 0-688-10258-1. Picture Book.

These two informative historical picture books for children, begin with the history of the empires of Africa prior to 1492 and continue with the history of the Atlantic slave trade. From the coastal regions to the inland regions, from northern to southern Africa, and from the history of conquered regions to what these areas are called today, these books provide a comprehensive overview of the history of the African continent. Floyd Cooper's illustrations, along with historical photographs and portraits, assist in making the book's historical descriptions informative and comprehensible for both children and adults. Both books include special sections entitled "Milestones in African History" and "Bibliography Especially for Young People" to assist young readers in broadening their knowledge of African and African American history.

3.90 Igus, Toyomi (1998). **i see the rhythm.** Illustrated by Michele Wood. San Francisco: Children's Book. 32 pp. ISBN: 0-89239-151-0. Picture Book.

Paintings by Wood and text by Igus unite to create a colorful documentary of the origins of African American music. From the sounds of Africa and the songs sung by slaves in the United States to the imagery of rap and hip hop, *i see the rhythm* is an informative guide with factual timelines for young and old readers to enjoy. The colorful paintings, pages, and layouts all give the reader a feel for the music of each era.

3.91   Johnson, Dinah (1998). **All Around Town: The Photographs of Richard Samuel Roberts.** Photographs by Richard S. Roberts. New York: Henry Holt. 32 pp. ISBN: 0-8050-5456-1. Picture Book.

Memorable experiences are seen through the eyes of self-taught photograher Richard Samuel Roberts in his explorations of the lifestyle and social life of African Americans in South Carolina in the early 1920s. These photographs tell the story of the many different professions that were held by African Americans of this era, even though they were few in number. The black-and-white photographs bring to life the pride and self-worth felt by their subjects. The text complements the images, usually by explaining them. This book, which could be used with a variety of age levels, contributes to readers' understanding of the American dream by bridging the past and the future.

3.92   Johnson, Sylvia A. (1997). **Tomatoes, Potatoes, Corn, and Beans: How the Foods of the Americas Changed Eating Around the World.** New York: Atheneum. 138 pp. ISBN: 0-689-80141-6. Reference Book.

For those interested in both food and history, this book provides a valuable resource for scientific, historical, and cultural studies. Many foods originally grown only in the Americas were taken to other lands by early explorers. Readers learn how Native Americans used these plants, as well as the impact of these vegetables on other parts of the world as they became crucial to nutrition and world cuisine.

3.93   King, Martin Luther Jr., (1997). **I Have a Dream.** New York: Scholastic. 40 pp. ISBN: 0-590-20516-1. Picture Book.

Dr. Martin Luther King's leadership was fundamental to the American Civil Rights movement's success in ending legal segregation in the South and other parts of the United States. In this book, the meaning of Dr. King's famous "I Have a Dream" speech is portrayed by several well-known artists, who use their creative talent to illustrate the thoughts and emotions of the speech. The artwork is done in a variety of forms, and creates a bond of the ideas and feelings of many individuals. Just as Dr. King believed in nonviolence, the illustrations depict warmth, peace, love, and harmony for all people. This book should be used with other supportive and connective activities, and would be particularly appropriate for use at the upper elementary and middle school levels.

3.94 Lavender, David (1998). **Mother Earth, Father Sky.** New York: Holiday House. 117 pp. ISBN: 0-8234-1365-9. Chapter Book.

Through detailed descriptions, black-and-white illustrations, and photographs we learn about Puebloan culture, the interdependency of man and environment, and adaptations made by the Pueblo people over the centuries. Topics covered include crop cultivation, irrigation, home building, spiritual life, the influence of the Spanish in the sixteenth and seventeenth centuries, and the later influences of the Santa Fe Railroad and its threat to traditional ways. This is a well-researched informational resource.

3.95 Morris, Juddi (1997). **Tending the Fire: The Story of Maria Martinez.** Flagstaff, AZ: Rising Moon. 113 pp. ISBN: 0-87358-654-9. Chapter Book.

Maria Martinez, one of the best-known potters of all time, began making pottery as a child by making clay dishes for her playhouse. She took lessons from her aunt, and later collaborated with her husband to perfect black-on-black pottery. Maria helped revive the dying art of pottery making and turned it into one of the enduring art forms of her tribe. During her life, she visited four presidents in the White House and demonstrated at world fairs and exhibitions.

3.96 Parks, Rosa, and Jim Haskins (1997). **I Am Rosa Parks.** Illustrated by Wil Clay. New York: Dial Books for Young Readers. 48 pp. ISBN: 0-8037-1206-5. Chapter Book.

This easy-to-read historical book contains information about the life struggles and hardships of Rosa Parks during her life in Alabama. Traveling home after work, this courageous African American woman refused to give up her seat on the bus to a white man who was standing. Parks was then arrested for defending what she believed was her right to remain seated. Through this book, young children are able to learn about the Civil Rights movement and how it impacted the lives of people then and now.

3.97 Parks, Rosa, with Gregory Reed (1996). **Dear Mrs. Parks: A Dialogue with Today's Youth.** New York: Lee & Low. 112 pp. ISBN: 1-880000-45-8. Chapter Book.

How often do children have a chance to hear from an important figure in history? In this book, Rosa Parks shares the letters she has written to children who wrote to her with questions. She provides consistent, clear-headed thinking about how to be a force for positive change in society. In her life work and stirring messages, readers can find the strength and courage to be leaders.

3.98   Ryan, Pam Muñoz (1996). **The Flag We Love.** Illustrated by Ralph Masiello. Watertown, MA: Charlesbridge. Unpaged. ISBN: 0-88106-846-2. Picture Book. (See **10.14**)

3.99   Roop, Peter (1996). **The Buffalo Jump.** Illustrated by Bill Farnsworth. Flagstaff, AZ: Northland. Unpaged. ISBN: 0-87358-616-6. Picture Book.

The buffalo was essential to all aspects of Native American life among the Plains tribes, and many methods were used to capture them. The setting of this book is the Madison Buffalo Jump on the Blackfeet reservation in Montana. The text concerns who leads the buffalo to the jump, and how a young boy's anger, jealousy, and courage lead to his personal growth and to his new name, Charging Bull. Well-researched and sensitive portrayals of Native Americans by illustrator Bill Farnsworth complement Roop's traditional narrative.

3.100   Sherrow, Victoria (1997). **American Indian Children of the Past.** Brookfield, CT: Millbrook. 96 pp. ISBN: 0-7613-0033-3. Chapter Book.

This very readable text, supported by period black-and-white photographs, explains what life was like for Native children growing up during the eighteenth through the early twentieth centuries. Information presented includes homes, villages, beliefs, food, games, and some coming-of-age rituals. Chapters are divided into five geographical regions: Northeast Woodlands, Southeast, Plains, Southwest, and Northwest Coast. The book includes a table of contents, an index, source notes, a bibliography, and a list of suggested further readings.

3.101   Sneve, Virginia Driving Hawk (1997). **The Apaches: A First Americans Book.** Illustrated by Ronald Himler. New York: Holiday House. 32 pp. ISBN: 0-8234-1287-3. Picture Book.

Sneve, a Dakota Sioux, writes about the Apache in this book that is one in a series about Native American tribes. The Apache nation was divided into six distinct tribes, and although their dialects differed, they were able to understand each other and their lifestyles were similar. Sneve's research spans from creation stories to governing styles and from ceremonies to war and raiding. She also examines everything from encounters with white settlers to the reservation system to Apache life today.

3.102 Swanson, Diane (1996). **Buffalo Sunrise: The Story of a North American Giant.** San Francisco: Sierra Club Books for Children. 64 pp. ISBN: 0-87156-861-6. Chapter Book.

Buffalo Sunrise is an informative book on the history and future of the buffalo. It begins with general data on the buffalo, such as appearance, size, ability, behaviors, and location. Although all Native peoples of the North American Plains were dependent upon the buffalo for their livelihood, Swanson focuses on the Blackfoot from Alberta and Montana during the 1870s. The Great Plains tribes' reverence for the buffalo is shown by its presence within their celebrations, ceremonies, stories, dances, and songs. The hunting techniques of these peoples contrast sharply with the European manner that brought the buffalo close to extinction. Today the buffalo survives on public lands, and laws exist to protect the buffalo for the future. Peter Roop's *The Buffalo Jump* (see **3.99**) makes a nice companion book for students exploring the near-extinction of the buffalo.

3.103 Viola, Herman J. (1996). **North American Indians.** Illustrated by Bryn Barnard. New York: Crown. 128 pp. ISBN: 0-517-59017-4. Chapter Book.

An introduction to the pre-European cultures of Native American tribes from eight regional areas: the Southeast, the Southwest, the West, the Northeast, the Northwest, the Great Plains, the Subarctic, and the Arctic. Native North Americans are grouped together in these common cultural areas because of their proximity to each other and similarities in their languages and ways of life. This is an excellent resource to abolish the stereotypical Great Plains image applied to all Native Americans. It shows distinct cultural differences among the tribes in terms of environment, shelters, diet, ceremonies, language, utensils, clothing, trade routes, etc. Current members of various tribes support the text with maps, photographs of authentic artifacts, paintings, drawings, and essays. A timeline indicates some major events related to Native Americans, from Columbus' arrival in 1492 to the early 1900s.

Stories of War

See also chapter 5, "Struggle and Survival."

Primary Reviews

3.104 Breckler, Rosemary (1996). **Sweet Dried Apples: A Vietnamese Wartime Childhood.** Illustrated by Deborah Kogan Ray. Boston: Houghton Mifflin. Unpaged. ISBN: 0-395-73570-X. Sophisticated Picture Book. (See **3.115**)

3.105 Bunting, Eve (1998). **So Far from the Sea.** Illustrated by Chris K. Soentpiet. New York: Clarion. 30 pp. ISBN: 0-395-72095-8. Sophisticated Picture Book.

With her little brother and parents, Laura walks through the now-deserted Manzanar Relocation Center where her father, grandparents, and ten thousand other Japanese Americans were interned during World War II. Father tells his memories of war—how he wore his Cub Scout uniform to show he was truly American; how the United States took the family's home, possessions, and dignity; and how he believed Grandfather began dying the moment the soldiers came to take them away. Bunting's exquisite writing style is sensitive and gentle, yet vividly captures the harsh realities of war. Striking black-and-white drawings juxtaposed with color illustrations take us between past and present, from the despair of wartime to the healing of moving forward. Readers of all ages will enjoy and appreciate this touching story. An excellent social studies resource for inquiry into different cultural perspectives on war. (See also **20.9**)

3.106 Fox, Robert Barlow (1997). **To Be a Warrior.** Sante Fe, NM: Sunstone. 128 pp. ISBN: 0-86534-253-9. Sophisticated Chapter Book.

Clay Walker, a young Navajo, wanted to be a warrior like the ones in the stories he learned from his grandfather. Like many of his peers, Clay left the reservation as a teenager to join the white world. Although his first experiences were troubling, eventually he was accepted into the U.S. Marines where he became a code talker in the Pacific during World War II. Simple yet emotionally powerful descriptions recount Clay's experiences with pain, destruction, and death. He does become a warrior, but in a world far removed from his pastoral beginnings. This novel is written sensitively and boldly to hold the interest of young readers, without sacrificing the integrity of the book. Use this with Robert Daily's *The Code Talkers: American Indians in World War II* (1995).

> Daily, Robert (1995). **The Code Talkers: American Indians in World War II.** New York: Franklin Watts. 64 pp. ISBN: 0-531-20190-2. Chapter Book.

3.107 Giff, Patricia Reilly (1997). **Lily's Crossing.** New York: Delacorte. 180 pp. ISBN: 0-385-32142-2. Chapter Book.

Lily is relieved to be out of school and packing for the beach. She packs remembrances of her deceased mother, anticipating a wonderful summer with her grandmother and father at Rockaway on the Atlantic Ocean. It's 1944, and this fifth grader's life is about to be completely changed by World War II. Giff's historical fiction novel lets us see World War II through the eyes of a child who makes mistakes and has to live with the consequences. She learns the importance of family and of telling the truth as she finds a way to help a refugee boy from Hungary reunite with his sister. This book would make a nice complement to other World War II fiction such as *Number the Stars* and *So Far from the Sea* (see **3.105**).

> Lowry, Lois (1990). **Number the Stars.** New York: Bantam Doubleday Books for Young Readers. 144 pp. ISBN: 0-440-40327-8. Chapter Book.

3.108 Kaplan, William (1998). **One More Border: The True Story of One Family's Escape from War-Torn Europe.** Illustrated by Stephen Taylor. Toronto, Ontario, Canada: Groundwood. 61 pp. ISBN: 0-88899-332-3. Picture Book. (See **20.14**)

3.109 Lee, Milly (1997). **Nim and the War Effort.** Illustrated by Yangsook Choi. New York: Foster/Farrar, Straus and Giroux. Unpaged. ISBN: 0-374-35523-1. Picture Book.

Lee has created a sensitive and tender story set in San Francisco's Chinatown during World War II. A young Chinese American girl named Nim shows her courage, determination and resourcefulness as she works to win a school paper-drive contest to help the war effort. Nim locates a huge source of newspapers, and must figure out how to get them to the school. Because of this effort, Nim misses Chinese school with her grandfather. This is a very serious offense. Nim explains to her grandfather why the paper drive is so important to her: "I wanted to bring honor to the family. Garland said an American would win the contest, and he was right. An American did win. I was born here. I am the American who won." The colorful artwork in this picture book captures the lifestyles and family traditions of the era.

3.110 Marrin, Albert (1997). **Empires Lost and Won: The Spanish Heritage in the Southwest.** New York: Simon & Schuster. 216 pp. ISBN: 0-689-80414-8. Chapter Book.

Marrin brings a personal flavor to this history of the American Southwest, beginning with Hernán Cortés and the conquest of Mexico and ending with the Mexican War in 1847. The words and deeds of well-known figures such as Cabeza de Vaca and Coronado are balanced with the lives of ordinary, previously unknown people, as Marrin traces the influence of the Spanish heritage in the Southwest. The author's accounts of events such as the conquest of the Pueblos and the Texas war for independence spare none of the often-gruesome details of conquest and life in the brutal desert environment. Carol Cribett-Bell, an intermediate school librarian, found the book to be a very readable nonfiction work that gives a fair summary of both sides of historical events and conveys the passion behind the fighting. The black-and-white illustrations, maps, journal excerpts, bibliography, and index make this volume an outstanding reference for research, as well as enjoyable reading.

3.111 Paulsen, Gary (1997). **Sarny: A Life Remembered.** New York: Delacorte. 97 pp. ISBN: 0-385-32195 -3. Chapter Book.

Sarny is a strong, determined young slave who flees the plantation near the end of the Civil War. She is seeking her two children, who have been stolen from her. An advantage she has as she seeks her children is the schooling she received from Nightjohn. The reader is given a glimpse of skirmishes during the waning weeks of the war, and is shown the terror of battle as seen through Sarny's eyes. Eventually she uses her education to set up schools for newly freed slaves. Once again, she faces difficulty as she is confronted by people determined to destroy her and the schools. This is a fast-paced, straightforward book typical of Paulsen's style. The simple, action-filled text makes it a good choice for many readers.

3.112 Robb, Laura (1997). **Music and Drum: Voices of War and Peace, Hope and Dreams.** Illustrated by Debra Lill. New York: Philomel. 32 pp. ISBN: 0-399-22024-0. Picture Book. (See **10.20**)

3.113 Walker, Sally M. (1998). **The 18 Penny Goose.** Illustrated by Ellen Beier. New York: HarperCollins. 61 pp. ISBN: 0-06-027556-1. Chapter Book. (See **5.35**)

Secondary Reviews

3.114 Balgassi, Haemi (1996). **Peacebound Trains.** Illustrated by Chris K. Soentpiet. New York: Clarion. 48 pp. ISBN: 0-395-72093-1. Sophisticated Picture Book.

As Sumi and her grandmother sit on a hillside overlooking the railroad tracks, Grandmother shares memories of her escape on a train from Seoul during the Korean War. Detailed watercolor illustrations convey many elements of Korean culture, as well as the panic of women and children who often left everything behind while the men stayed to fight the war.

3.115 Breckler, Rosemary (1996). **Sweet Dried Apples: A Vietnamese Wartime Childhood.** Illustrated by Deborah Kogan Ray. Boston: Houghton Mifflin. Unpaged. ISBN: 0-395-73570-X. Sophisticated Picture Book.

Wartime took away their father and grandfather. The children used medicinal herbs and sweet dried apples as their grandfather did before he was called to war. But soon the war was upon them and destroyed their village. They were forced to flee with a few belongings. An important story to help readers understand the struggles many Vietnamese had to endure to survive. Watercolor illustrations bring out the innocence of children, and the harshness of wartime. (See also **20.22**)

3.116 Cornelissan, Cornelia (1998). **Soft Rain: A Story of the Cherokee Trail of Tears.** New York: Delacorte. 115 pp. ISBN: 0-385-32253-4. Sophisticated Chapter Book.

In this story of forced relocation, Soft Rain's Cherokee childhood is traumatically disrupted in 1838 when she and her mother are wrenched from their way of life to begin a walking journey toward the unknown West. Leaving behind all that they know, they endure physical hardship, the stench of sickness and death, and the painful loss of loved ones. Despite such challenges, this is also a story of strength, endurance, and hope.

3.117 English, June, and Thomas D. Jones (1998). **Scholastic Encyclopedia of the United States at War.** New York: Scholastic. 192 pp. ISBN: 0-590-59959-3. Sophisticated Chapter Book.

This chronicle of U.S. involvement in armed conflict explores the lessons of war and the role America has played in the worldwide struggle for justice and freedom. Each chapter is devoted to a specific conflict, spanning from the American Revolution to the Gulf War. The authors are thorough, presenting for each conflict background information, pivotal incidents, campaigns, personalities, the home front, public reaction, and a description of the aftermath of war. The format is lively, including song lyrics, maps, and illustrations throughout.

3.118 Harrah, Madge (1997). **My Brother, My Enemy.** New York: Simon & Schuster Books for Young Readers. 137 pp. ISBN: 0-689-80968-9. Chapter Book.

This story comes from the year 1676, when fourteen-year-old Robert Bradford—determined to avenge the death of his family— joins a volunteer army composed of Virginia plantation owners. Robert, who tells the story in first person, is soon caught up in the action and chaos of Bacon's Rebellion. This book has plenty of action, but also deals with Robert's inner struggle to do what is right.

3.119 Lincoln, Abraham (1998). **The Gettysburg Address.** Illustrated by Michael McCurdy. Boston: Houghton Mifflin. 32 pp. ISBN: 0-395-88397-0. Picture Book.

Michael McCurdy's scratchboard engravings dramatically illustrate scenes from the Civil War, and enhance the power of the text of the Gettysburg Address. This simple black-and-white book demonstrates the power of words to remind us of what we have learned from the past. Its message comes through even though the language is from a different era.

3.120 Mochizuki, Ken (1997). **Passage to Freedom: The Sugihara Story.** Illustrated by Dom Lee. New York: Lee & Low. Unpaged. ISBN: 1-880000-49-0. Picture Book. (See **20.28**)

3.121 Murphy, Jim (1996). **A Young Patriot: The American Revolution as Experienced by One Boy.** New York: Clarion. 101 pp. ISBN: 0-395-60523-7. Sophisticated Chapter Book.

This book offers a perspective on the Revolutionary War that will interest older readers researching the period. The author, Jim Murphy, has based the book on the memoirs of Joseph Plumb Martin, who actually enlisted to fight for the Americans when he was fourteen years old. Murphy skillfully weaves together the details of Joseph's experiences as a soldier and the broader context of historical events. The book is richly illustrated with engravings, paintings, and documents from the period.

3.122 Nivola, Claire A. (1997). **Elisabeth.** New York: Farrar, Straus and Giroux. 32 pp. ISBN: 0-374-32085-3. Sophisticated Picture Book. (See **5.45**)

3.123 Reeder, Carolyn (1997). **Across the Lines.** Illustrated by Robin Moore. New York: Atheneum Books for Young Readers. 220 pp. ISBN: 0-689-81133-0. Chapter Book.

The tension in this story begins in the first chapter, when Edward's family flees their plantation ahead of the Union Army and Simon, Edward's best friend and a slave, takes the opportunity to escape to freedom. During the span of a year, the boys face many hardships brought on by the Civil War, but each continues to learn about freedom and courage. Told alternately from Edward's and Simon's point-of-view, this story makes a good study of different perspectives.

3.124 Viola, Herman J. (1998). **It Is a Good Day to Die: Indian Eyewitnesses Tell the Story of the Battle of the Little Bighorn.** New York: Crown. 101 pp. ISBN: 0-517-70913-9. Chapter Book.

A book of personal narratives regarding Sioux history and participation in Indian wars—specifically the Battle of the Little Bighorn in 1876—this is an excellent reference. The emphasis on Lakota eyewitness accounts allows young readers to see the other side of the picture. Despite that there were no survivors among Custer's men, and therefore no eyewitness accounts from that perspective, the account of this historical event is one-sided. This book illustrates a clash of cultures for survival. Includes many bibliographic references, photographs, and a chronology from 1851 to 1890.

Cultural Traditions

See also the section entitled Family Experiences Around the World in chapter 4, "Families."

Traditional Literature

Primary Reviews

3.125 Aldana, Patricia, editor (1996). **Jade and Iron: Latin American Tales from Two Cultures.** Illustrated by Luis Garay. Translated by Hugh Hazelton. Toronto, Canada: Groundwood. 64 pp. ISBN: 0-88899-256-4. Sophisticated Chapter Book.

This anthology of legends and myths from Latin America is divided into two sections: stories told by the indigenous people of the Americas, and stories of Spanish and Portuguese origin that were brought by the conquistadors but were forever changed by contact with the New World. The stories captivate the reader from beginning to end, portraying the violent suffering of vastly different cultures in conflict with each other and with nature—struggles that are best appreciated by mature readers. Young heroes and heroines, hunters, and volcano spirits populate the legends and creation stories of the New World entries. From Europe come tales of witches and wicked sea captains, tragic lovers, and clever survivors. Luis Garay's characteristically somber pen-and-ink and watercolor illustrations contribute to the emotional impact of these tales.

3.126 Anaya, Rudolfo (1997). **Maya's Children: The Story of La Llorona.** Illustrated by Maria Baca. New York: Hyperion. Unpaged. ISBN: 0-7868-0152-2. Picture Book.

In this story, Anaya recreates the traditional Latin American tale of La Llorona, a weeping woman who wanders the night in search of her children, whom she has killed. For generations, these stories have been used to frighten children to hurry home. However, Anaya's La Llorona does not harm her children, revealing instead her maternal feelings and teaching a lesson about mortality. Maria Baca's double-page, dark-toned gouache paintings create a mysterious atmosphere that supports the text, and prompted Arnold (age eight) to comment, "The pictures are kind of scary." This book might be used in a text-set with other versions of La Llorona, including Gloria Anzaldúa's dual-language book, *Prietita and the Ghost Woman/Prietita y La Llorona*, which is gorgeously illustrated by Mayan artist Christina González. Anzaldúa's text presents a more contemporary version of La Llorona that, together with the powerful imagery of the double-page illustrations, has encouraged critical dialogue among students from first to fifth grade.

> Anzaldúa, Gloria (1995). **Prietita and the Ghost Woman/ Prietita y La Llorona.** Illustrated by Christina González. San Francisco: Children's Book. Unpaged. ISBN: 0-89239-136-7. Picture Book.

3.127 Goble, Paul (1996). **Remaking the Earth: A Creation Story from the Great Plains of North America.** New York: Orchard. Unpaged. ISBN: 0-531-09524-X. Picture Book.

In the author's note at the beginning of the book, Goble explains that the Bible, particularly Genesis, influenced Native American creation stories. Goble researched many versions of native Plains creation stories, searching for the core messages of stories told prior to the influence of missionary teachings. This story comes from the legends of the Algonquin, a language group that includes the Cheyenne, Arapaho, and Blackfeet tribes. Earth Maker was responsible for creating a new world after the crumbling of the old world, which left behind only fishes and animals in the water crying for help. Earth Maker saves the animals and goes on to contour the earth, send down life-giving rain, and people the earth using clay from Grandmother Turtle's back. Earth Maker expects the buffalo and the people to live together in harmony with all the creatures of his creation.

3.128 Goldin, Barbara Diamond (1996). **Coyote and the Firestick: A Pacific Northwest Indian Tale.** Illustrated by Will Hillenbrand. San Diego: Gulliver. Unpaged. ISBN: 0-15-200438-6. Picture Book.

In the time before people had fire, Coyote allows the flattering remarks of his clan to move him to devise a plan to steal fire from the three evil spirits who guard it for themselves. His plan requires a relay race involving the help of Mountain Lion, Deer, Squirrel, and Frog. This humorous *pourquoi* tale offers readers a daring adventure, as well as an explanation of why Coyote's friends look like they do today. Oil and oil-pastel illustrations strongly support the story, and add personality to the characters. The evil spirits are humorously scary, but would not frighten the very young in a read-aloud setting. Author notes provide additional information on coyote tales. The illustrator notes his research of the Native Americans of the Pacific Northwest, who originally told this tale.

3.129 Harper, Jo (1998). **The Legend of Mexicatl/La leyenda de Mexicatl.** Illustrated by Robert Casilla. Spanish edition translated by Tatiana Lans. New York: Turtle. Unpaged. ISBN: 1-890515-05-1 (English)/1-890515-06-X (Spanish). Picture Book.

It will be wonderful news to bilingual teachers that this legend is available in English and Spanish editions. The language is equally expressive and descriptive in both languages. This lovely picture book retells the legend of the origin of the Aztec people of Mexico. Mexicatl, the young hero, has heard since childhood of a valiant leader who will take his people from the harsh desert land to a place of cool waters and peace. After experiencing a wondrous vision, he leads his followers to their promised land. However, life is not harmonious in paradise; Mexicatl discovers that a "true leader" must not only be strong and courageous, but should never place himself above his own people. Lisa, a fourth grader, said, "He really cares about his people . . . and I also like the pictures." Robert Casilla's illustrations in realistic watercolors focus on Mexicatl and his actions, using a warm, earthy palette that emphasizes the primitive and harsh environment of the story's setting. Editions are available in both English and Spanish.

3.130 Hickox, Rebecca (1998). **The Golden Sandal: A Middle Eastern Cinderella Story.** Illustrated by Will Hillenbrand. New York: Holiday House. 32 pp. ISBN: 0-823-413314. Picture Book.

Cinderella is a favorite story in many cultures, and this rich picture book tells the Iraqi version of the tale. Maha, the beloved daughter of a fisherman, saves the life of a red fish who becomes her fairy godmother. Later, Maha loses her golden sandal as she leaves the *henna* (celebration) for a wealthy bride. This retelling is simple but eloquent, and Hillenbrand's illustrations, done on vellum with a variety of media, capture the essence of the unusual setting and the comic characters. Pair this book with *Angkat: The Cambodian Cinderella.*

> Coburn, Jewell Reinhart (1998). **Angkat: The Cambodian Cinderella.** Illustrated by Edmund Flotte. Arcadia, CA: Shen's Books. 32 pp. ISBN: 1-885008-09-0. Picture Book.

3.131 Lester, Julius (1999). **What a Truly Cool World.** Illustrated by Joe Cepeda. New York: Scholastic. 40 pp. ISBN: 0-590-86468-8. Picture Book.

Based on the story "How God Made the Butterflies" from the 1969 collection *Black Folktales, What a Truly Cool World* takes the reader to heaven during the time of creation. While corrections are being made on the world, an angel named Shaniqua has an idea for bringing color into the world. Through hip hop language and colorful illustrations, heaven is portrayed as a pretty casual, down-home place. With the assistance of Joe Cepeda, Lester has brought a modern flavor to an old folktale that can be enjoyed both for the colorful humor in the story and the illustrations on each page.

> Lester, Julius (1992). **Black Folktales.** Illustrated by Tom Feelings. New York: Grove. 110 pp. ISBN: 0-802-132-42-1. Picture Book.

3.132 Moreton, Daniel (1997). **La Cucaracha Martina: A Caribbean Folktale.** New York: Turtle. Unpaged. ISBN: 1-890515-03-5. Picture Book.

This delightful retelling of a Caribbean folktale by Daniel Moreton takes the reader on a quest for the source of the beautiful noise that Cucaracha Martina, a ravishing cockroach, hears one night amidst the unpleasant sounds of the city. Martina scours the city for the source of the melodious sound, and she causes a sensation wherever she appears. A variety of city animals try to woo her with their songs, but Martina remains unmoved by all, rejecting each marriage proposal until she finds the source of the beautiful noise: a cricket. The two insects then live happily ever after. The humorous, computer-generated illustrations invite the reader to participate in the action of the city. Students will quickly join in with the reading of each animal's sound. The lovely cockroach Martina and other popular characters of Caribbean folktales also appear in *Señor Cat's Romance and Other Favorite Stories from Latin America.*

> Gonzalez, Lucia M. (1997). **Señor Cat's Romance and Other Favorite Stories from Latin America.** Illustrated by Lulu Delacre. New York: Scholastic. 48 pp. ISBN: 0-590-48537-7. Picture Book.

3.133 Pollock, Penny (1996). **The Turkey Girl: A Zuni Cinderella Story.** Illustrated by Ed Young. Boston: Little Brown. Unpaged. ISBN: 0-316-71314-7. Picture Book. (See **14.11**)

3.134 Pomerantz, Charlotte (1997). **Mangaboom.** Illustrated by Anita Lobel. New York: Greenwillow. Unpaged. ISBN: 0-688-12957-9. Picture Book. (See **14.12**)

3.135 San Souci, Robert D. (1996). **Pedro and the Monkey.** Illustrated by Michael Hays. New York: Morrow Junior Books. Unpaged. ISBN: 0-688-13743-1. Picture Book.

A poor farmer named Pedro catches in his trap a monkey who is eating all of Pedro's corn. Pedro threatens to sell the monkey as repayment for the money he has lost from the eaten corn. The monkey begs for freedom, and in return promises to set up the poor farmer with the rich landowner's daughter. Although doubtful that the monkey could convince a rich landowner to give his daughter away to a poor farmer, Pedro lets the monkey go. Through many cunning deceptions, the monkey is able to convince the rich landowner that Pedro is wealthy, and thus deserving of his daughter in marriage. Although this story is similar to the various *Puss in Boots* versions told in many cultures, this retelling is based on Fansler's (1921) *Filipino Popular Tales.* Clothing and scenery, beautifully painted on canvas in pastel hues, provide an authentic view of traditional Filipino culture.

> Fansler, Dean Spruill (1921). **Filipino Popular Tales, Collected and Edited, with Comparative Notes by Dean S. Fansler, Ph.D.** Vol. XII of the Memoirs of the American Folklore Society. Lancaster, PA, and New York: American Folklore Society. 473 pp. Chapter Book.

> Perrault, Charles (1990). **Puss in Boots.** Translated by Malcolm Arthur. Illustrated by Fred Marcellino. New York: Farrar, Straus and Giroux. 32 pp. ISBN: 0-374-36160-6.

3.136 San Souci, Robert D. (1998). **A Weave of Words: An Armenian Tale.** Illustrated by Raúl Colón. New York: Orchard. Unpaged. ISBN: 0-531-30053-6. Picture Book. (See **14.34**)

3.137 San Souci, Robert D. (1998). **Cendrillon: A Caribbean Cinderella.** Illustrated by Brian Pinkney. New York: Simon & Schuster. 40 pp. ISBN: 0-689-8066-8-X. Picture Book. (See **14.11**)

3.138 Young, Ed (1997). **Mouse Match: A Chinese Folktale.** San Diego: Silver Whistle. 26 pp. ISBN: 0-152-01453-5. Picture Book.

Although this is a retelling of a Chinese folktale, it is a familiar story told in one version or another in almost every culture. A father and mother mouse want to find the best husband possible for their daughter, and they go to great lengths to find this husband—to the sun, the clouds, the wind, and the mountains. In the end, they realize that what they are seeking is another mouse. They have failed to see the uniqueness and greatness in themselves and their friends. Young has chosen a unique format for this story. The pages of the book are really one long mural that has been folded accordion-style so that each fold brings the readers to a discernible spread. When opened completely, the book depicts the story in one long continuum of color, collage, and mouse silhouettes. The back of the panel has the Chinese text for the story printed white-on-black.

Secondary Reviews

3.139 Ada, Alma Flor (1997). **The Lizard and the Sun/La lagartija y el sol.** Illustrated by Felipe Dávalos. Translated by Rosa Zubizarreta-Ada. New York: Doubleday. Unpaged. ISBN: 0-385-32121-X. Picture Book.

In this dual-language book, Ada recounts in both English and Spanish an old Mexican folktale in which the sun disappears and the days become gloomy. The animals go in search of the sun, and lizard persuades the sleepy sun to arise with promises of the liveliest music and dancing. This explains the importance of the celebration of the sun by many indigenous groups. Dark-chalk illustrations lend a mysterious quality and sense of authenticity to the text.

3.140 Alameida, Roy (1997). **Na Mo'olelo o ka Wa Kahiko: Stories of Old Hawaii.** Honolulu: Best. 124 pp. ISBN: 1-57306-026-7. Sophisticated Chapter Book.

Through a wide array of stories adapted from Dunford's *The Hawaiians of Old*, Alameida informs and entertains readers with forty-five tales of Hawaiian tricksters, voyagers, gods, parents, lovers, and warriors. Written for a fourth-grade level, this book teaches readers myths and legends about earth, fire, and water; beliefs and customs; plants; fish and fishponds; crafts; weapons and warfare; sports and games; and music and dance. Hawaiian translations are provided in the margins. A good social studies resource.

Dunford, Betty (1995). **The Hawaiians of Old.** Illustrated by Aimee A. Kudlak. Honolulu: Best. 220 pp. ISBN: 0-93584-843-6. Chapter Book.

3.141 Behan, Brendan (1997). **The King of Ireland's Son.** Illustrated by P. J. Lynch. New York: Orchard. 40 pp. ISBN: 0-531-09549-5. Picture Book.

Brendan Behan, an acclaimed Irish writer, brings alive this tale from Irish folklore about the adventures of three brothers on a quest for heavenly music and their father's wealth. This book begs to be read aloud, and children will be captivated by Lynch's lavish paintings.

3.142 Ben-Ezer, Ehud (1997). **Hosni the Dreamer: An Arabian Tale.** Illustrated by Uri Shulevitz. New York: Farrar, Straus and Giroux. 32 pp. ISBN: 0-374-33340-8. Picture Book.

Hosni, a shepherd, is fascinated by stories of faraway cities. Finally he has a chance to travel, and he is entranced by the bustling city. Trusting his intuition, he uses his gold dinar to pay a wise man for a bit of wisdom. His friends make fun of him for not buying food or trinkets, but Hosni's wisdom saves his life and changes his fortune. Shulevitz's watercolors echo the muted colors of the desert, and make this a heartwarming storybook.

3.143 Berry, James (1997). **First Palm Trees: An Anancy Spiderman Story.** Illustrated by Greg Couch. New York: Simon & Schuster Books for Young Readers. 40 pp. ISBN: 0-689-81060-1. Picture Book.

The prophet has seen in his dreams a tree that can give both shade and wine. The king wants to know how the tree will be created, and offers a reward to anyone who creates such a tree. Anancy Spiderman hears of the king's reward, and as always plots and schemes in order to get Sky-God to assist him in this creation. Being quite selfish, Anancy cannot see splitting his reward with the Spirits of Sun, Water, Earth, and Air, but agrees to do so, knowing that the tree cannot be created without them. When the palm trees finally emerge, many people from the village present themselves to the king as the rightful winner of the reward besides Anancy. Through the earthtoned illustrations created by Greg Couch, a modern image of Anancy Spiderman is presented in this story of how palm trees were created.

3.144 Demi (1997). **Buddha Stories.** New York: Henry Holt. Illustrated by Demi. Unpaged. ISBN: 0-8050-4886-3. Picture Book.

Beautifully illustrated in traditional Chinese gold ink with pen-and-brush on indigo vellum, this collection of ten Buddha tales originated some twenty-five hundred years ago. Each folktale is one page long, and ends with an explicitly stated lesson. The fate of each villain or triumphant character is clearly conveyed, yet because of the style of both text and illustration, this selection would best be shared with middle elementary and older students.

3.145 Demi (1998). **The Greatest Treasure.** New York: Scholastic. 32 pp. ISBN: 0-590-31339-8. Picture Book.

The simple message of this book comes from a traditional Chinese tale. Li, a poor farmer, enjoys playing his flute for his family while his children sing and dance. When he suddenly becomes wealthy, he almost loses sight of the importance of peace of mind and simple pleasures. Demi's Chinese artwork harmonizes with the story, making the book a delightful visual experience as well as a springboard for interesting discussions about wealth and its importance.

3.146 Goble, Paul (1996). **The Return of the Buffaloes: A Plains Indian Story about Famine and Renewal of the Earth.** Washington, DC: National Geographic. Unpaged. ISBN: 0-7922-2714-X. Picture Book.

In this traditional Lakota tale, the tribe is about to perish because of a lack of buffalo. Goble's illustrations reflect extensive research of various versions of the story and of Lakota Sioux parfleches, which he reproduced in the story from originals. He also visited Wind Cave National Park in Black Hills, South Dakota, to see and study the Breathing Hole, where the wind is said to be the source of breath for yet more buffalo.

3.147 Goble, Paul (1998). **La niña que amaba los caballos salvajes.** Translated by Clarita Kohen. New York: Aladdin Paperbacks (Libros Colibri). Unpaged. ISBN: 0-689-81455-0. Picture Book.

A Spanish translation of Goble's 1978 Caldecott winner, *The Girl Who Loved Wild Horses*. A Plains Indian girl's passion for horses is so great she prefers to live among them rather than stay with her people. Eventually it is believed that she actually turns into a horse herself.

Goble, Paul (1983). **The Girl Who Loved Wild Horses.** New York: Simon & Schuster. 32 pp. ISBN: 0-027-36570-0. Picture Book.

3.148 Goldin, Barbara Diamond (1997). **The Girl Who Lived with the Bears.** Illustrated by Andrew Plewes. San Diego: Harcourt Brace. 40 pp. ISBN: 0-15-200684-2. Picture Book.

Bears, berries, and the Northwest Coast are all present in this retelling of a tale well known to indigenous people living in the Pacific Northwest. A young girl ignores warnings from her girlfriends and defies taboos by talking ill of the bears. Her friends run off, not wanting harm to come to them. The lost girl meets a handsome young man she assumes was sent by her father to rescue her. However the man is really a bear who has the ability to switch between animal and human form. After a series of mysterious events, the young man marries the girl and returns her to her people, although he must die to accomplish this. Humbleness and the importance of listening to elders are the lessons that flow from this skillful retelling. The facial expressions employed in the illustrations add to the effect of the text. The notes at the end of the book provide evidence of extensive research by the author, as well as excellent resource material.

3.149 Hausman, Gerald (1998). **The Story of Blue Elk.** Illustrated by Kristina Rodanas. New York: Clarion. 32 pp. ISBN: 0-395-84512-2. Picture Book.

Rich hues of blue, lavender, and earthtones create a natural setting for this story that celebrates the magic of music and the majesty of wildlife. This Pueblo story is of a boy who was born unable to make a sound. Blue Elk, his elk brother, helps the boy find his voice through a cedar flute.

3.150 Keams, Geri (1998). **Snail Girl Brings Water: A Navajo Story.** Illustrated by Richard Ziehler-Martin. Flagstaff, AZ: Rising Moon. Unpaged. ISBN: 0-87358-662-X. Picture Book.

Keams, a Navajo storyteller, shares a Navajo creation myth in a well-crafted retelling that explains how water came to this world. When a flood forces the People to leave their homes and enter the Fifth World (where we live today), the People discover there is no fresh water in the new world. Someone must go back down and bring up some pure water so First Woman can sing her song of magic and make the rivers grow. Otter, Frog, and Turtle try and fail, and it is Snail Girl who succeeds. From that day forward, the snail has carried the water bottle on its back and leaves bits of moisture on its trail as a reminder of the one who brought water to the earth. The cadence and language of the text is traditional in style, and the colorful illustrations support the text superbly.

3.151 Kellogg, Steven (1997). **The Three Little Pigs.** New York: Morrow Junior Books. 32 pp. ISBN: 0-688-08731-0. Picture Book. (See **14.29**)

3.152 Ketteman, Helen (1997). **Bubba the Cowboy Prince: A Fractured Texas Tale.** Illustrated by James Warhola. New York: Scholastic. 32 pp. ISBN: 0-590-25506-1. Picture Book. (See **14.6**)

3.153 Kurtz, Jane (1996). **Miro in the Kingdom of the Sun.** Illustrated by David Frampton. Boston: Houghton Mifflin. Unpaged. ISBN: 0-395-69181-8. Picture Book.

In this Inca tale from Peru, Kurtz substitutes Miro, an independent heroine, in place of the hero who searches for the healing waters of a mythical lake. The lake is protected by fearsome creatures that have prevented many brave young men from reaching the magic water. The woodcuts by Frampton, striking and bold, convey the terror of the heroine's quest by visually contrasting the diminutive Miro against the immense creatures who guard the lake.

3.154 Lasky, Kathryn (1997). **Hercules: The Man, the Myth, the Hero.** New York: Hyperion Books for Children. 32 pp. ISBN: 0-786-80329-0. Picture Book.

Hercules tells his own story in this book filled with daring adventures, heroics, and tragedies typical of mythology. The paintings that illustrate the story depict action-filled fight scenes and frightening beasts and goddesses. Children who crave superhero action will appreciate this book.

3.155 Lewis, Paul Owen (1997). **Frog Girl.** Hillsboro, OR: Beyond Words. Unpaged. ISBN: 1-582-46003-5. Picture Book.

Lewis, a native of Seattle, Washington, is well versed in the legends and stories of the Haida, Tlingit, and other tribal settlements of the Pacific Northwest. Frog Girl, the heroine of the story, passes through the rites of passage, separation, initiation, and return when she is called to an adventure in a parallel world inhabited by frogs. This tightly woven story is supported by authentically detailed illustrations and large-print text.

3.156 Malotki, Ekkehart (1996). **The Magic Hummingbird.** Illustrated by Michael Lacapa. Santa Fe, NM: Kiva. 40 pp. ISBN: 1-885772-0401. Chapter Book.

This Hopi folktale tells of the people's struggle to survive after four years of drought. A young boy and his sister are abandoned in their village as their parents go elsewhere for food. The boy crafts a hummingbird, and the bird magically comes to life. Lacapa, an Apache, uses designs found in southwestern baskets and pottery. His colors and stylized kachinas fill the pages with geometric shapes and warm southwestern colors. See also Kristina Rodanas' *Dragonfly's Tale* for a related story of two Zuni children left behind but rewarded by the Corn Maidens.

> Rodanas, Kristina (1991). **Dragonfly's Tale.** New York: Clarion. 29 pp. ISBN: 0-395-57003-4. Picture Book.

3.157 Martin, Rafe (1997). **The Eagle's Gift.** Illustrated by Tatsuro Kiuchi. New York: Putnam. 32 pp. ISBN: 0-399-22923-X. Picture Book.

In this retelling of an Inuit tale, Marten agrees to learn what Mother Eagle can teach and joyfully learns to sing, dance, and tell stories. When he is released, he builds a feast hall for his people, and they also learn the joy of celebrating with others through music and story. Rich oil paintings realistically portray both the warm and cool settings of this traditional tale.

3.158 Max, Jill, editor (1997). **Spider Spins a Story: Fourteen Legends from Native America.** Flagstaff, AZ: Rising Moon. 63 pp. ISBN: 0-87358-611-5. Chapter Book.

This collection of legends about Spider includes stories from Kiowa, Tewa, Zuni, Wiyat, Osage, Muskogee, Navajo, Achomawi, Cherokee, Hopi, Cheyenne, and Lakota nations. Spider represents many things, including a mentor, a trickster, a helpful ally, and a worker of miracles. Elders and tribal members tell most of the legends. Each story includes good documentation and biographies of each author and illustrator. Five Native American artists have provided colorful and detailed illustrations for each legend.

3.159 McDonald, Megan (1997). **Tundra Mouse: A Storyknifing Tale.** Illustrated by S. D. Schindler. New York: Orchard. 32 pp. ISBN: 0-531-30047-1. Picture Book.

Yup'ik Eskimo story of two sisters out on the tundra collecting cotton-grass roots. At the urging of her younger sister, Elena tells the tale of Tundra Mouse through the Yup'ik tradition of storyknifing—an oral telling of a story that coincides with a pictorial representation drawn on the ground with an implement. The story provides glimpses of Yup'ik Eskimos' modern life, traditions, family structure, and respect for nature. *Tundra Mouse* is similar in theme to *City Mouse, Country Mouse.*

> Wallner, John (1987). **City Mouse, Country Mouse & Two More Tales from Aesop.** New York: Scholastic. 32 pp. ISBN: 0-590-41155-1. Picture Book.

3.160 Miranda, Anne (1997). **To Market, to Market.** Illustrated by Janet Stevens. New York: Harcourt Brace. 36 pp. ISBN: 0-152-00035-6. Picture Book.

A shopping expedition begins with the nursery rhyme, "To market, to market, to buy a fat pig. Home again, home again, jiggity jig!" This is the story of an endearing older shopper whose house fills with the unruly livestock that she brings from the market. As she and her home succumb to the ensuing chaos, she finally has an idea. She and her new acquisitions return together to the market to buy the ingredients for . . . vegetable soup! While the storyline is worthy and the rhyme fun to read, the real gift of this book is the truly incredible illustrations, which elicit laughter from children and adults alike.

3.161 Nolan, Dennis (1997). **Androcles and the Lion.** New York: Harcourt Brace. 32 pp. ISBN: 0-152-03355-6. Picture Book.

Nolan retells and illustrates this 2,000-year-old tale of unusual friendship between a man and a lion. Androcles is a runaway slave who would rather feel the burn of the sun on his back than the sting of his master's whip. He takes shelter in a cave, where he meets a lion with a thorn in his paw. Androcles helps the lion, and his kindness is repaid years later when he and the lion meet again in the Roman arena. Their happy reunion convinces the spectators that both Androcles and the lion should be free at last. The tawny hues of the illustrations make the handsome lion and desert setting come alive.

3.162 Paterson, Katherine (1998). **Parzival: The Quest for the Grail Knight.** New York: Lodestar. 127 pp. ISBN: 0-525-67579-5. Chapter Book. (See **14.53**)

3.163 Peterson, Julienne (1996). **Caterina, the Clever Farm Girl: A Tale from Italy.** Illustrated by Enzo Giannini. New York: Dial. Unpaged. ISBN: 0-8037-1181-6. Picture Book.

In this refreshing Tuscan folktale, Caterina is invited to be the king's bride. Unfortunately, Caterina's wit and spunkiness pose problems for the king, as she often disagrees with his decisions. Finally the king orders her to "Take from the palace that which is most dear to you." Much to the king's surprise, he awakens in her bed on the farm! This is a satisfying tale with an appealing heroine. Giannini's ink and watercolor illustrations reflect the architecture and landscapes of Tuscany.

3.164 Ramirez, Michael Rose (1998). **The Legend of the Hummingbird.** Illustrated by Margaret Sanfilippo. New York: Mondo. Unpaged. ISBN: 1-57255-232-8. Picture Book.

Ramirez loved to hear his grandmother's stories about Puerto Rico, including the legend about how the hummingbird came to be. Brightly colored watercolor illustrations compliment the text. Older readers may be interested in this story for its parallels to *Romeo and Juliet*. The closing pages include information and photographs about the history and people of Puerto Rico, as well as a brief discussion of transformation tales across indigenous American cultures.

3.165 Rosen, Michael J. (1998). **The Dog Who Walked with God.** Illustrated by Stan Fellows. Cambridge, MA: Candlewick: 40 pp. ISBN: 07636-0470-4. Picture Book.

Based on a creation myth of the Kato (a small group of Athapakan from northern California), this story explains that our world emerged from such a dark, empty, watery place that even the Creator needed a companion before setting foot on it. An author note defines the style of the poetic, repetitive text as similar to traditional tellings recorded by anthropologists in 1906. Exquisite watercolor and pencil illustrations support the text well, and reinforce the importance of and respect for each creature and object on Earth. The disappointingly small size of the illustrations limits the impact of the book.

3.166 Schami, Rafik (1996). **Fatima and the Dream Thief.** Illustrated by Els Cools and Oliver Streich. New York: North-South. Unpaged. ISBN: 1-55858-653-9. Picture Book. (See **14.35**)

3.167 Stanley, Diane (1997). **Rumpelstiltskin's Daughter.** New York: Morrow Junior Books. Unpaged. ISBN: 0-688-14328-8. Picture Book.

Rumpelstiltskin's daughter is definitely not intimidated by the greedy king, who demands that she spin straw into gold. Because she never learned the trick, she must use her intelligence to outsmart the ruler. This folktale emphasizes a clever female protagonist, and is a story with a twist. Children will love comparing this determined daughter to her mother in the original story.

3.168 Taylor, Harriet Peck (1997). **When Bear Stole the Chinook: A Siksika Tale.** New York: Farrar, Straus and Giroux. Unpaged. ISBN: 0-374-10947-8. Picture Book.

Illustrated with beautiful borders and detailed illustrations, this is a tale of how a poor Native American boy and his animal friends journey to the lodge of the Great Bear to release the chinook—the warm wind that melts the snow and brings spring. This tale also explains why bears hibernate. This well-researched tale is adapted from Fraser's *The Bear Who Stole the Chinook: Tales from the Blackfoot.* The Siksika, which means black-footed people, live in what is now southern Alberta.

> Fraser, Frances (1991). **The Bear Who Stole the Chinook: Tales from the Blackfoot.** Seattle: University of Washington Press. 144 pp. ISBN: 0-295-97101-0. Chapter Book. (out of print)

3.169 Van Laan, Nancy (1997). **Shingebiss: An Ojibwe Legend.** Illustrated by Betsy Bowen. New York: Houghton Mifflin. Unpaged. ISBN: 0-395-82745-0. Picture Book.

Shingebiss, a little merganser duck, lived on the banks of Lake Superior. His planning and work enable him always to have plenty to eat in all seasons. One particularly bitter winter, Winter Maker was determined to prove more powerful than the duck. Despite great winds and cold, which froze the lake solid, Shingebiss refused to see winter as an enemy. This Ojibwe legend keeps alive the belief of its people that nature is a teacher, and Shingebiss—the spirit teacher who can change forms at any time—represents the importance of conservation, resourcefulness, and perseverance. The bold woodblock prints add to the animation of Van Laan's narration. A glossary and author's note invite readers to understand the nature of the Ojibwe stories that have been passed down.

3.170 Walking Turtle, Eagle (1997). **Full Moon Stories: Thirteen Native American Legends.** New York: Hyperion Books for Children. 47 pp. ISBN: 0-7868-0225-1. Picture Book.

Eagle Walking Turtle provides a written version of thirteen Northern Arapaho legends that were told to him by his Grandpa Iron. Within each story, he shows the oral traditions of his family as he weaves together family memories, traditional customs, and the legend itself. Each story teaches lessons of the balance that exists in nature, and of the harmony that humans should have with the world around them.

3.171 Young, Ed (1998). **The Lost Horse: A Chinese Folktale.** San Diego: Silver Whistle/Harcourt Brace. Unpaged. ISBN: 0-15-201016-5. Picture Book.

This retelling of Chinese folklore enhances our realization that things always happen for a reason. Events that first appear good may turn out to be bad, and other events that appear bad may turn out to be good. Readers learn they must take every day as it comes, and make the most of every situation without concern for what the future will bring. The pastel-and-watercolor collage help the story come alive. Good for younger readers.

Cultural Practices and Celebrations

See also the section entitled Family Experiences through the Ages in chapter 4, "Families."

Primary Reviews

3.172 Ancona, George (1998). **Fiesta Fireworks.** New York: Lothrop, Lee & Shepard. Unpaged. ISBN: 0-688-14817-4. Picture Book.

Fiesta Fireworks depicts the celebration of San Juan de Dios, the patron saint of Tultepec, Mexico. Readers follow Caren Reyes Urban, whose grandfather is a master fireworks maker, through a day filled with delicious looking food that makes the children hungry, and colorful preparations for the fireworks explosions and parade. This book connects children to celebrations in their own lives. A student named Chris felt that this celebration reminded him of the Fourth of July in the United States, Jacqui was reminded of the local street fair because of the papier mâché and food, and Briana said it reminded her of an art show. Sofia mentioned that she was like Caren because she too covered her ears during fireworks. The photographs are full of rich, cultural details that create good discussion opportunities. There is an author's note at the end of the book explaining more about the history of fireworks and of San Juan de Dios.

3.173 Ancona, George (1998). **Let's Dance!** New York: Morrow Junior Books. Unpaged. ISBN: 0-688-16211-8. Picture Book. (See **11.57**)

3.174 Blue, Rose (1997). **Good Yontif: A Picture Book of the Jewish Year.** Illustrated by Lynne Feldman. Brookfield, CT: Millbrook. 32 pp. ISBN: 0-7613-0142-9. Picture Book.

Good Yontif is a wonderfully rich picture book of a calendar year of Jewish celebrations. Conceived by Blue, the story is actually told through beautiful color illustrations by Lynne Feldman. Through Feldman's eyes, the reader is invited into the home of a Jewish family to enjoy the celebrations and accompanying rituals. From Rosh Hashanah at the beginning of the new year to the last celebration of Shabbat, the illustrator depicts the importance of family, tradition, and celebration in the life of eight-year-old Jacob. Preschool and elementary students who look closely at the paintings are bound to come up with rich similarities to their own families. The endearing role of the grandmother and the birth of a new baby offer much opportunity for discussion. Each holiday page is named in both English and Hebrew. Blue completes this wordless book by giving additional background information on the holidays in the author's notes.

3.175 Carlson, Lori Marie (1998). **Sol a Sol: Bilingual Poems.** Illustrated by Emily Lisker. Translated by Lyda Aponte de Zacklin. New York: Henry Holt. Unpaged. ISBN: 0-8050-4373-X. Picture Book. (See **10.52**)

3.176 Colón-Vilá, Lillian (1998). **Salsa.** Illustrated by Roberta Collier-Morales. Houston, TX: Piñata. Unpaged. ISBN: 1-55885-220-4. Picture Book. (See **11.22**)

3.177 Erlbach, Arlene (1997). **Sidewalk Games around the World.** Illustrated by Sharon Lane Holm. Brookfield, CT: Millbrook. 64 pp. ISBN: 0-7613-0008-2. Picture Book. (See **12.42**)

3.178 Johnston, Tony (1997). **Day of the Dead.** Illustrated by Jeanette Winter. San Diego: Harcourt Brace. 56 pp. ISBN: 0-15-222863-2. Picture Book.

Day of the Dead is a wonderful way to acquaint children with the Mexican custom of El Día de los Muertos, celebrated on November 2. Traditionally in Mexico and many Hispanic/Latino communities in the United States, families visit the cemetery to spend time with the souls of departed loved ones. This petite and colorfully illustrated text takes the reader along as one family prepares for their annual visit to the tombs of deceased relatives. As traditional foods are prepared, anxious children beg for a little taste. "Espérense," they are told by the different family members preparing tasty tamales, mole, empanadas, and *pan de muerto.* "Wait," they are urged by relatives purchasing *calaveras de azúcar* and gathering flowers to take along on the night-long vigil at the graveyard. The brilliant acrylic illustrations rendered on a black background were particularly appealing to students. Each page is widely bordered with images of traditional foods or symbols of the Day of the Dead. "The borders really add a lot to the book," remarked Allison (age eleven).

3.179 King, Elizabeth (1998). **Quinceañera: Celebrating Fifteen.** New York: Dutton. 40 pp. ISBN: 0-525-45638-4. Chapter Book.

Elizabeth King has done an excellent job describing the biggest and most important celebration in the life of Hispanic girls: their fifteenth birthday. The book describes the *quinceañeras* of two girls—one from El Salvador and the other from Mexico—although both celebrations take place in California, against the backdrop of historic Spanish missions. A well-integrated text allows readers to vicariously experience the two *quinceañeras* while learning about the history of the celebration and the various forms it takes in different countries of origin. The presentation of King's vibrant photographs gives the book an albumlike quality, full of remembrances. Even the book jacket resembles a matted portrait. Middle-school girls like Xochitl, an eighth-grade student, enjoyed reading the book and recognized its practical side as well: "I shared the book with my mother and she liked it because it has ideas on how to organize my quinceañera." This book can be used for studies related to the themes of family, celebrations, and religion, among others.

3.180 Kleven, Elisa (1996). **Hooray, a Piñata!/¡Viva! ¡Una piñata!** New York: Dutton Children's Books. Unpaged. ISBN: 0-525-45606-8 (English)/0-525-45606-6 (Spanish). Picture Book. (See **6.22**)

3.181 Kroll, Virginia (1998). **Faraway Drums.** Illustrated by Floyd Cooper. New York: Little Brown. Unpaged. ISBN: 0-316-50449-1. Picture Book. (See **14.8**)

3.182 Lankford, Mary D. (1996). **Jacks around the World.** Illustrated by Karen Dugan. New York: Morrow Junior Books. 40 pp. ISBN: 0-688-13708-3. Picture Book. (See **12.43**)

3.183 Lomas Garza, Carmen (1996). **In My Family/En mi familia.** Translated by Francisco X. Alarcón. San Francisco: Children's Book. Unpaged. ISBN: 0-89239-138-3. Picture Book. (See **4.14**)

3.184 Luenn, Nancy (1998). **A Gift for Abuelita: Celebrating the Day of the Dead/Un regalo para Abuelita: En celebración del Día de los Muertos.** Illustrated by Robert Chapman. Translated by Mario Lamo-Jiménez. Flagstaff, AZ: Northland. Unpaged. ISBN: 0-87358-688-3. Picture Book. (See **4.15**)

3.185 Mora, Pat (1996). **Confetti: Poems for Children.** Illustrated by Enrique Sanchez. New York: Lee & Low. 32 pp. ISBN: 1-880000-25-3. Picture Book. (See **10.53**)

3.186 Normandin, Christine, editor (1997). **Echoes of the Elders: The Stories and Paintings of Chief Lelooska.** New York: DK Ink. 40 pp. ISBN: 0-7894-2455-X. Picture Book.

Stunning illustrations of Northwest Native American art abound in this lavishly illustrated oversized book. Chief Lelooska was a master performer of Kwakiutl oral tradition and storytelling. Five traditional myths and legends are retold here with the intention of preserving their authenticity. Stories incorporate many traditional storytelling elements used in Native American tales, and accurately reflect the mythical traditions of the region. The author/storyteller is an adopted member of the Kwakiutl tribe, and was known as a professional storyteller for over forty years. A compact disc is included so that the reader can hear the author's actual words, cadence, and distinct pronunciations. Retellings on the compact disc do not duplicate the printed text; there are slight variations, serving as a reminder that stories evolve and change in their retellings. This was reviewed favorably in the *School Library Journal* and chosen as one of its Best Books for 1997. The stories revolve around common Northwest Coast themes such as the raven, loon, beaver, and thunderbirds.

3.187 Ross, Kathy (1997). **The Jewish Holiday Craft Book.** Illustrated by Melinda Levine. Brookfield, CT: Millbrook. 96 pp. ISBN: 0-7613-0055-4. Picture Book. (See **12.51**)

3.188 Soto, Gary (1997). **Snapshots from the Wedding.** Illustrated by Stephanie Garcia. New York: Putnam. Unpaged. ISBN: 0-399-22808-X. Picture Book. (See **4.25**)

3.189 Thomassie, Tynia (1996). **Mimi's Tutu.** Illustrated by Jan Spivey Gilchrist. New York: Scholastic. Unpaged. ISBN: 0-590-44020-9. Picture Book. (See **11.60**)

Secondary Reviews

3.190 Adoff, Arnold (1997). **Love Letters.** Illustrated by Lisa Desimini. New York: Scholastic. 32 pp. ISBN: 0-590-48478-8. Picture Book. (See **10.23**)

3.191 Alarcón, Francisco X. (1997). **Laughing Tomatoes and Other Spring Poems/Jitomates risueños y otros poemas de primavera.** Illustrated by Maya Christina González. San Francisco: Children's Book. 32 pp. ISBN: 0-89239-139-1. Picture Book. (See **10.60**)

3.192 Bartone, Elisa (1996). **American Too.** Illustrated by Ted Lewin. New York: Lothrop, Lee & Shepard. Unpaged. ISBN: 0-688-13279-0. Picture Book.

During the time of European immigration to America, Rosie lives on a street in New York that has become much like her native Italy. When she is chosen to be the queen of the feast of San Gennaro, Rosie surprises everyone by dressing as the Statue of Liberty to show she is modern and American too. This break from tradition helps her family and community recognize and celebrate the American dream they have moved across the ocean to find.

3.193 Bateson-Hill, Margaret, (1998). **Shota and the Star Quilt.** Illustrated by Christine Fowler. New York: Zero To Ten. 32 pp. ISBN: 1-84089-021-5. Picture Book.

Interweaving both contemporary and traditional life experiences, this story focuses on the universal theme of goodness, love, and friendship overcoming evil, power, and greed. Shota—a Lakota girl who has moved from the reservation to Minneapolis—and her friend Esther visit Shota's grandmother at Pine Ridge for the annual powwow. Just before departing, a letter comes to Shota's parents saying that their apartment will be destroyed to make way for more office buildings. During the visit, Shota learns of the significance of the star pattern on her own quilt, and her grandmother helps the girls make a quilt symbolizing the love within their neighborhood. A complete Lakota translation accompanies the English text in this dual-language book. Both instructions for creating a star collage and cultural insights about the Lakota people and the star quilt enhance this book.

3.194 Bunting, Eve (1997). **Moonstick: The Seasons of the Sioux.** Illustrated by John Sandford. New York: HarperCollins. Unpaged. ISBN: 0-06-024804-1. Picture Book.

Changes come both in nature and in the life of the Sioux people with each new moon of the Sioux year. Detailed, researched paintings show notches being made in a boy's counting stick, and give a glimpse into the tribe's way of living. Throughout the book, changes of seasons are echoed by changes in a boy as he journeys toward manhood. The book ends with the man reflecting on how his life and that of his tribe have changed.

3.195 Bunting, Eve (1997). **The Pumpkin Fair.** New York: Clarion. 32 pp. ISBN: 0-395-70060-4. Picture Book.

Filled with delightfully bright and humorous illustrations, *The Pumpkin Fair* is a story of beauty showing from the inside out. Tightly hugging the pumpkin she has grown herself, a little girl enters the pumpkin fair where she is awed by the many sights. When she wins the ribbon for "The best-loved pumpkin anywhere!" the child exclaims, "How did they know? How did they see the way I felt inside of me?" This book is a wonderful autumn read-aloud book.

3.196 Chin-Lee, Cynthia (1997). **A Is for Asia.** Illustrated by Yumi Heo. New York: Orchard. Unpaged. ISBN: 0-531-30011-0. Picture Book. (See **7.32**)

3.197 Demi (1997). **Happy New Year! Kung-hsi Fa-ts'ai!** Illustrated by Demi. New York: Crown. Unpaged. ISBN: 0-517-70957-0. Picture Book.

Chinese New Year erupts in celebration from the pages of this information-packed book. All facets of the holiday are described, from the preparations through the Lantern Festival. Demi's characteristic tiny figures illustrate a text that offers definitions and explanations of the history, symbols, and rituals associated with the holiday. Readers of all ages will find this lively, colorful picture book a useful reference tool.

3.198 Dolphin, Laurie (1997). **Our Journey from Tibet: Based on a True Story.** Photographs by Nancy Jo Johnson. New York: Dutton Children's Books. 40 pp. ISBN: 0-525-45577-9. Sophisticated Picture Book.

Three young girls leave their homeland of Tibet to obtain not only religious freedom, but also the freedom to openly celebrate their Tibetan traditions and customs. They travel to nearby India, where they begin life anew. This is an extraordinary story of overcoming ones fears in search for freedom. The book contains a letter from His Holiness the Dalai Lama, as well as an afterword from Rinchen K. Choegyal, Minister-in-Charge of Education. Expressive photography adds richness to this unforgettable story.

3.199 Erlbach, Arlene (1997). **Happy Birthday, Everywhere.** Illustrated by Sharon L. Holm. Brookfield, CT: Millbrook. 48 pp. ISBN: 0-7613-0007-4. Chapter Book.

Birthdays are celebrated differently all over the world, and this book explores the traditions from nineteen countries. Children can learn new games—such as the clothesline game from Russia or the sheep and hyena game from Sudan—and try recipes like fairy bread from Australia and *taartjes* from the Netherlands. Special crafts are sprinkled throughout the book, one that will appeal to children of all ages.

3.200 Goble, Paul (1997). **Love Flute.** New York: Aladdin. Unpaged. ISBN: 0-689-81683-9. Picture Book.

The flute, which appears in love stories in many traditions, is the vehicle for a shy young man in this story to express his feelings to the young girl whom he has adored from afar. The author gives a simple description of the courting ritual practiced by many Native American tribes. The colorful and detailed illustrations are in Goble's traditional style, in which he only shows profiles of the characters' faces out of respect for Native American people.

3.201 Hausman, Gerald (1996). **Eagle Boy: A Traditional Navajo Legend.** Illustrated by Cara Moser and Barry Moser. New York: HarperCollins. 32 pp. ISBN: 0-06-021100-8. Picture Book.

Hausman retells the story of the first Navajo traditional healing ceremony—the Eagle Way. A young boy dreams of flying with the eagles and is taken by Father Eagle to the Eagle Chief to learn the sacred dances and healing songs. After escaping the trickery of coyote and proving worthy of his new name, he returns to his home and grows up to be a great medicine man.

3.202 Hickox, Rebecca (1997). **Zorro and Quwi: Tales of a Trickster Guinea Pig.** Illustrated by Kim Howard. New York: Bantam Doubleday Books for Young Readers. Unpaged. ISBN: 0-440-41183-1. Picture Book.

Zorro and Quwi is a colorful picture book in the tradition of trickster stories from Peru. The central character, a guinea pig named Quwi, continually outsmarts a determined fox named Zorro. Splashy, bold, and vibrant colors fill double page spreads by illustrator Kim Howard, enhancing the silliness and frivolity of the story. Despite the gratuitous use of a few common Spanish words, such as "*Caramba,*" fourth graders loved hearing about Quwi's adventures as they attempted to predict how the guinea pig would get the better of the fox. Young readers enjoyed Zorro's gullibility as well as Quwi's cleverness. They giggled, for example, when Quwi—in order to marry a large (but rich) bride—tricks the fox into taking his place in a cage, and they howled with laughter when Zorro mistakes a bald head for a rock.

3.203 Hobbs, Will (1997). **Beardream.** Illustrated by Jill Kastner. New York: Atheneum Books for Children. Unpaged. ISBN: 0-689-31973-8. Picture Book.

The Bear Dance is still practiced as a spring ritual among the Ute people of Colorado. Will Hobbs pays tribute to the story behind this ritual in the beautifully told and illustrated *Beardream.* Short Tail, a young boy, becomes concerned that the Great Bear, endearingly referred to as "The One Going Around in the Woods," "old Honey Paws," and "Grandfather," has not yet made an appearance to welcome the arrival of spring. Short Tail goes in search of "Grandfather" and rouses him from a deep "beardream" of spring. In coming to awaken "Grandfather," Short Tail has acted respectfully, and he is rewarded with an invitation not only to see the bears dancing but to "dance with us to celebrate the end of winter." Short Tail joins the bear celebration, his own "beardream." He is then instructed to go back and tell his people how to do the bears' dance. Short Tail's people listen and learn, and "Grandfather" is assured that his instructions have been followed.

3.204 Hoyt-Goldsmith, Diane (1997). **Potlatch: A Tsimshian Celebration.** Photographs by Lawrence Migdale. New York: Holiday House. 32 pp. ISBN: 0-8234-1290-3. Picture Book.

Potlatch shows the importance of traditions and family cultures, as well as how the community works together to plan the four-day celebration. A thirteen-year-old boy narrates this story of a potlatch celebrated by the Tsimshian living in Metlakatla, Alaska. Beautiful photographs illustrate pottery, the interior of homes, and gifts being made. Also included in the book are maps of the area, historical photographs, and a glossary of terms.

3.205 Hoyt-Goldsmith, Diane (1998). **Celebrating Chinese New Year.** Illustrated by Lawrence Migdale. New York: Holiday House. 32 pp. ISBN: 0-8234-1393-4. Picture Book.

Chinese Americans celebrate the Chinese New Year by participating in a variety of traditions. Through actual photographs of one Chinese American family, readers learn how the Chinese prepare for the celebration, honor their ancestors, instill Chinese language and culture in their young, and prepare traditional dishes that symbolize prosperity, good luck, and rebirth. A glossary of terms defines and describes each Chinese tradition to help readers understand the significance of the Chinese New Year.

3.206 Johnston, Tony (1996). **The Magic Maguey.** San Diego: Harcourt Brace. Unpaged. ISBN: 0-15-250988-7. Picture Book.

The entire pueblo loves the giant maguey plant that grows near Miguel's Mexican adobe house. Yet the landowner plans to cut it down. Miguel's resourcefulness saves the plant. This story is told in cut paper, watercolors, and pastels. The book's message of love and community is suitable for all ages. This book lends itself to rich discussions of cultural differences and similarities, conservation and recycling, and the needs of community over the needs of the individual.

3.207 Kalman, Bobbie (1997). **Celebrating the Powwow.** New York: Crabtree. Unpaged. ISBN: 0-86505-640-4. Picture Book.

Powwows are a family affair. Dancing regalia are designed for specific dances, and are the products of hours of embroidering, sewing, beading, and gathering. All family members may participate, from the smallest child to the most respected and experienced elders. Most significant is that powwows have blended traditional format with modern ideas, and serve as a means to ensure the preservation and sharing of cultural activities.

3.208 Kudler, David (1997). **The Seven Gods of Luck.** Illustrated by Linda Finch. Boston: Houghton Mifflin. Unpaged. ISBN: 0-395-78830-7. Picture Book. (See **14.9**)

3.209 Lee, Huy Voun (1995). **In the Park.** New York: Henry Holt. Unpaged. ISBN: 0-8050-4128-1. Picture Book. (See **11.42**)

3.210 Moreillon, Judi (1997). **Singing down the Rain.** Illustrated by Michael Chiago. Santa Fe, NM: Kiva. Unpaged. ISBN: 1-885772-07-6. Picture Book.

With rhythmical text, the author captures the sense of oneness and respect for nature that underscores the beliefs of the desert people of southern Arizona. For centuries, the Tohono O'odam (also known as the Papago) have relied on the summer rains to sustain their crops. To ensure that the rains will fall again, the people gather annually to participate in a very special ritual: the saguaro wine ceremony. Instructions for presenting this story in a Reader's Theater format are included.

3.211 Mott, Evelyn Clarke (1996). **Dancing Rainbows: A Pueblo Boy's Story.** New York: Cobblehill. Unpaged. ISBN: 0-525-65216-7. Picture Book.

By focusing on the Tewa celebration of the Feast of San Juan, Mott highlights the tribal preparations and family activities that precede the yearly event. What is particularly pleasing about this text is the glimpse of contemporary family life. Andy Garcia has devoted his life to teaching tribal dances and participating in traditional ceremonies, and the text and photographs show these traditions being passed on to his grandson, Curt. To the Tewa, dances are a form of prayer that give strength and power. Some political and historical background is provided, including U.S. government restrictions placed on Tewa ceremonies. An abundance of color photographs and limited text make this a useable resource for young readers.

3.212 Nichols, Richard (1998). **A Story to Tell: Traditions of a Tlingit Community.** Illustrated by Bambi D. Kraus. Minneapolis: Lerner. 48 pp. ISBN: 0-8225-2661-1. Picture Book.

This beautiful photo essay, written and illustrated by Native Americans, invites readers to learn about the culture and history of the Tlingit people. Marissa, an eleven-year-old Tlingit girl, takes a trip with her grandmother to her family's ancestral home in Kake, a small Alaskan village. The easy-to-read text and extensive research by Nichols about Tlingit customs makes this book an excellent resource for young readers. The book is part of the We Are Still Here: Native Americans Today series (see **3.221** for other titles in the series).

3.213 Philip, Neil (1996). **Earth Always Endures: Native American Poems.** Illustrated by Edward S. Curtis. New York: Viking. Unpaged. ISBN: 0-670-86873-6. Chapter Book. (See **10.56**)

3.214 Rendon, Marcie R. (1996). **Powwow Summer: A Family Celebrates the Circle of Life.** Photographs by Cheryl Walsh Bellville. Minneapolis: Carolrhoda. 48 pp. ISBN: 0-87614-986-7 (hardcover)/1-57505-011-0 (paperback). Chapter Book.

This contemporary book is about the Anishinabe, also known as the Ojibwe or Chippewa. The book is a chronology of several days in the Downwind family. Photographs show the private life of tribe members, and the preparation for a present-day powwow. The significance of family is brought out through discussions of how the family cares for family members, the larger community, and foster children.

3.215 Purdy, Carol (1997). **Nesuya's Basket.** Illustrated by Paulette Livers Lambert. Boulder, CO: Roberts Rinehart. 110 pp. ISBN: 1-57098-087-X. Chapter Book.

Nesuya's Basket informs young readers about the culture of the Maidu, and exposes them to Nesuya's personal struggle to live up to the social expectations of her family and people. The Maidu culture revolves around a cycle of elaborate dance ceremonies, and these are woven into the story. This book is part of a series developed by the Council for Indian Education for use by Native American children. The author's authentic descriptions of village life and cultural ceremonies provide a powerful portrayal of the Maidu in the 1840s.

3.216 Rosales, Melodye (1996). **'Twas the Night B'fore Christmas: An African-American Version.** New York: Scholastic. 32 pp. ISBN: 0-590-73944-1. Picture Book.

This beautifully illustrated book depicts the Christmas holiday on a Southern plantation near the turn of the century. The story takes place on Christmas Eve at the Wetherbys' house as Dad quietly observes St. Nick going about his work. Readers experience the excitement of Christmas through the eyes of children and their father. The Southern dialect adds beauty and charm to this glimpse of American culture.

3.217 Russell, Ching Yeung (1997). **Moon Festival.** Illustrated by Christopher Zhong-Yuan Zhang. Honesdale, PA: Boyds Mills. Unpaged. ISBN: 1-56397-596-3. Picture Book.

A Chinese girl celebrates with her extended family the traditional autumn holiday called the Moon Festival. Although it is a time of reunion, her parents are far away and she prays to Chang O, the mythical beauty who lives in the moon, that they will soon return. The sights, sounds, and smells of the celebration radiate from richly colored oil paintings. The customs of the Moon Festival might inspire young readers to further research this Chinese holiday.

3.218 Silverman, Erica (1997). **The Halloween House.** New York: Farrar, Straus and Giroux. Unpaged. ISBN: 0-374-33270-3. Picture Book.

It's Halloween night, and two escaped convicts running from the police find refuge in what they think is a safe, abandoned house. In actuality, the house is filled with all kinds of scary creatures, including vampires, squirming worms, swooping bats, and chasing monsters. Kindergartner Colin loved this predictable book, which is a takeoff of the popular counting book, *Over in the Meadow.*

> Langstaff, John (1989). **Over in the Meadow.** Illustrated by Feodor Rojankosky. New York: Harcourt Brace. 32 pp. ISBN: 0-1567-0500-1. Picture Book. (Originally published in 1957 by Harcourt Brace with a musical score for voice and piano by Marshall Woodbridge.)

3.219 Walton, Darwin M. (1998). **Kwanzaa.** Austin, TX: Raintree Steck-Vaughn. 21 pp. ISBN: 0-8172-5561-3. Picture Book.

Kwanzaa is written especially for elementary students to enjoy. This book explains why and how this holiday is celebrated, featuring beautiful color photographs of each part of Kwanzaa. Children will learn that Kwanzaa is a very recent nonreligious holiday that began in the United States in 1966, and is celebrated by many people of African heritage who live in America.

3.220 Warren, Scott (1997). **Desert Dwellers: Native People of the American Southwest.** San Francisco: Chronicle. 64 pp. ISBN: 0-8118-0534-4. Chapter Book.

This resource is a useful overview of the Native peoples who inhabit the southwestern region of the United States. Brief historical information introduces each group, and then specific cultural distinctions are discussed. Dances, festivals, and creation myths for some tribes are included, as well as contemporary portraits of the people as they live today. The easy-to-read text is accompanied by color photographs taken by the author.

3.221 Yamane, Linda (1997). **Weaving a California Tradition: A Native American Basketmaker.** Photographs by Dugan Aguilar. Minneapolis: Lerner. 48 pp. ISBN: 0-8225-2660-3. Picture Book.

Yamane focuses on the importance of sustaining Native American culture and beliefs through the teaching and maintaining of traditional cultural arts. This photographic essay chronicles Carly Tex, an eleven-year-old basketweaver and member of the Western Mono tribe of central California, as she learns the traditional steps taken by weavers for gathering and preparing materials, and designing and weaving baskets. Considerable information about the steps in basketmaking is given, and the detailed drawings help readers to understand this portion of the text. Readers not only learn about the Mono culture, but also about how contemporary life is adversely affecting their weaving as pollution and residential development deplete the natural areas where traditionally used bushes and grasses grow. The book is part of the We Are Still Here: Native Americans Today series.

Other books in the series include:

Braine, Susan (1995). **Drumbeat . . . Heartbeat: A Celebration of the Powwow.** Minneapolis: Lerner. 48 pp. ISBN: 0-8225-2656-5. Picture Book.

Roessel, Monty (1993). **Kinaalda: A Navajo Girl Grows Up.** Minneapolis: Lerner. 48 pp. ISBN: 0-8225-9641-5. Picture Book.

Roessel, Monty (1995). **Songs From the Loom: A Navajo Girl Learns to Weave.** Minneapolis: Lerner. 48 pp. ISBN: 0-8225-9712-8. Picture Book.

Swentzell, Rina (1993). **Children of Clay: A Family of Pueblo Potters.** Illustrated by Bill Steen. Minneapolis: Lerner. 40 pp. ISBN: 0-8225-9627-X. Picture Book.

A.

B.

C.

D.

A. *Twins!,* Elaine Scott/Margaret Miller (**4.22**). **B.** *A Pillow for My Mom,* Charissa Sgouros/ Christine Ross (**4.124**). **C.** *A Ride on Mother's Back: A Day of Baby Carrying around the World,* Emery & Durga Bernhard (**4.110**). **D.** *Happy Adoption Day!,* John McCutcheon/Julie Paschkis (**4.69**).

4 Families

Cathy Beck

Anne O'Connor

The archetypal family personified in the school reading materials of years past—which consisted of Mom, Dad, three kids, a dog, and a cat—no longer fits the face of most contemporary families. Today children in our classrooms come from diverse family structures. They don't necessarily live in a home where Father knows best, Mother waxes floors in high heels and pearls as a juicy pot roast simmers in the oven for the evening's meal, and cookies and milk await the children's return from school. Today's children live in single-parent, divorced, blended, or traditional families. Today's children continue to grapple with issues surrounding sibling rivalry and finding one's identity within the family. Many of today's children are fortunate enough to grow up in loving, caring homes, regardless of their economic, social, or racial status. Many more children grow up in fragile family environments in which racism, drugs, violence, abuse, poverty, and neglect play a significant role. Other children grow up in families ravaged by war and political conflicts. These families may be immigrants or refugees, but they are certainly living under challenging circumstances.

Slowly the publishing industry has responded to the changing faces of families and their circumstances by providing books that present more diverse family circumstances. The books in this section present two powerful images of families. Many of these books celebrate the best of what families can provide to young children: security, loving family members, respect for individual differences and talents, and support during important life stages and milestones. Other books help children and adults make sense of the social, political, and personal challenges facing today's families at home and abroad. As we considered the books to be included in this section, the following criteria emerged:

1. *The book had to be well written and offer the best of the writer's craft in the particular genre in which the story is being told.* The books in this section represent contemporary realistic fiction, historical fiction, biography, poetry, fantasy, and nonfiction, and include both picture books and chapter books.

2. *The characters—whether real or fictional—had to be richly developed and believable.* We wanted books about characters that

children would fall in love with, or from whom they would learn or find inspiration. To accomplish this, authors needed to show readers how characters overcame obstacles in their lives, and the role that family played in their lives.

3. *The book needed to represent a diverse view of families and their circumstances.* We attempted to create a balance between contemporary and historical families, and family experiences that reflect the racial, cultural, economic, and social diversity found in our society. In addition, we wanted to include families living in the United States, families emigrating to the United States, and families living elsewhere in the world.

4. *The book needed to represent the diverse family structures reflected in our society.* Many of the books in this chapter show children living in traditional, two-parent families. Other books include single-parent families, blended families, adoptive and foster families, multiracial families, and families with same-sex parents.

5. *Those books that included controversial issues had to deal with these issues in honest ways.* Not all families live happily ever after, and simple solutions to complex problems rarely exist in our world. We wanted to include books in which children grappled in realistic ways with real-life internal issues (e.g., alcoholism, violence, drugs, abuse, or neglect) and external issues (e.g., racism, persecution, war, or natural disaster). We wanted books with believable characters who responded to these issues in believable ways.

6. *Those books that included controversial issues had to offer a sense of hope or options for personal action.* We rejected books that offered simplistic "just say no" solutions (even if they had happy endings) in favor of books that honored the complexity of the challenges encountered (even if everything didn't turn out all right at the end). We looked for books that showed children and families with hope, courage, and determination willing to take social action on behalf of themselves, their families, or others.

7. *Books had to have the potential to inspire children, families, and those who care about them.* We wanted books that included success stories, stories of overcoming all odds, and stories that offered visions of what could be in the future.

Most of the books included in this chapter do not meet all of these criteria. They do, however, meet enough of these criteria that we considered them worthy of inclusion in this chapter on families.

The books in this chapter are organized around several themes or concepts that we often use when studying families and family issues with students. The first—and largest—section, Family Stories: Fiction,

Nonfiction, and Personal Narratives, includes the stories families pass on from one generation to the next and stories about everyday families involved in the business of living together. In Family Experiences through the Ages, readers will find books about families from a broad range of historical time periods. These books provide insights into family life during these periods of history, but also provide demonstrations of how families might respond to today's challenges. The section entitled Changing Family Structures highlights those books that reflect the variety of family structures found in today's society, as well as the changes that families encounter with the arrival of a new sibling or parent. Family stories, because they deal with the most intimate social structure, often deal as well with the most private and controversial topics. In Controversial Issues in Family Life, readers will find books that deal explicitly with the most troubling of family events and circumstances. These are the books that most often require mediation by a caring adult as children attempt to make sense of the characters' lives and their own. Some experiences are common to all families, and others reflect the particular cultural, political, and geographical setting in which the family lives. In the section entitled Family Experiences around the World, readers will find books that highlight the common threads among all families, as well as those that celebrate the differences that make each community and culture unique. In Life Stages and Milestones, readers will find books that show families celebrating and mourning together as the cycle of life plays out. In the final section, Relationships with Others, books stress the importance of appreciating the uniqueness of individual family members who add to the richness of daily lives.

Well-written books that show realistic families dealing with real-life issues—both positive and negative—can help teachers, parents, and children come to understand the changing face of today's families. These books can help children living in supportive environments develop understanding and empathy for those living under harsh circumstances. In addition, these books can help children in fragile families make sense of their experiences, while creating visions of new possibilities. Considering the lives of families from the past can help all of us make sense of what families endure today, and help us to realize the important role that families play in supporting young children. In many of the books reflecting struggle within families, a common thread running through their pages is a striking optimism that love can exist—and even flourish—despite the family milieu. These books show characters growing stronger as they face and overcome their family's issues.

We hope children, and the important adults in their lives, will find joy and inspiration in these books.

---

*The titles listed below each subheading are organized into Primary Reviews and Secondary Reviews. The Primary Reviews describe outstanding books in each subheading. The Secondary Reviews provide brief information about other books worthy of consideration. Some titles listed below are **not** reviewed in this chapter; entries for these titles are not annotated and contain only bibliographic information. In such cases, a cross reference to the annotated entry contained elsewhere in this volume is provided in boldface type at the end of the bibliographic information.*

Family Stories: Fiction, Nonfiction, and Personal Narratives

Primary Reviews

4.1   Ancona, George (1998). **Barrio: José's Neighborhood.** San Diego: Harcourt Brace. Unpaged. ISBN: 0-15-201049-1. Picture Book.

Famed writer-photographer George Ancona provides glimpses of San Francisco's Mission District through photos of a young boy's daily activities. This picture book of colorful, energetic photographs shows a lively, active community that generates wonder and invites the viewer to compare and contrast his or her own community to that of young José Luis. Mission District—"El Barrio" to its residents—has sheltered various immigrants in its long past and now is predominantly Spanish speaking. As José is photographed walking and playing in his neighborhood, brightly colored murals depicting the struggle of its many immigrants can be seen on the walls of an elementary school, a woman's center, churches, and on fences. These works of art illustrate the hardships of immigrants not only in their homeland, but also in this country. Family and neighborhood celebrations occur in the streets and in the schools, with participants from many cultures. Here is a community where José Luis' family can retain their traditions and customs, yet be able to witness the practices of other cultures. Third grader Allison said, "I like it because in our classroom we are studying our barrio and I think it is a great book to read." "It is almost the same as our barrio," said Marina, her classmate. "I like all the photos."

4.2 Brown, Ruth (1997). **Cry Baby.** New York: Dutton Children's Books. Unpaged. ISBN: 0-525-45902-2. Picture Book. (See **11.24**)

4.3 Browne, Anthony (1998). **Voices in the Park.** New York: Dorling Kindersley. 30 pp. ISBN: 0-7894-2522-X. Picture Book. (See **20.52**)

4.4 Bunting, Eve (1996). **Going Home.** Illustrated by David Diaz. New York: HarperCollins. Unpaged. ISBN: 0-06-026296-6. Picture Book.

A family of farm laborers is returning to their hometown in Mexico for the Christmas holidays. The children—Carlos, Nora, and Dolores—are unsure of why they are taking the long trip to La Perla, and why their parents keep saying that they are "going home." Carlos asks his father why they left La Perla, and his father explains that they left for better work opportunities and for their children's futures. The voice of Carlos describes the family's trip through Mexico, and the small towns, people, and animals they see on their way to La Perla. There the family has a joyous reunion with their relatives. The children recognize their parents' happiness on returning to their roots, and begin to understand the significance of their parents' sacrifice. The illustrations by award-winning artist David Diaz use photographs of traditional Mexican clay figures, superimposed with Rivera-like paintings and enclosed within black decorative frames. The artist also has created an original font for the text. Young readers who live in a close-to-the-border community, and who routinely travel to visit with families in northern Mexico, identified with many aspects of this story. This book could be part of a text-set on families, migrant labor, or homecomings. (See also **20.1**)

4.5 Bunting, Eve (1997). **Twinnies.** Illustrated by Nancy Carpenter. New York: Harcourt Brace. Unpaged. ISBN: 0-15-291592-3. Picture Book.

Parents and siblings of multiple-birth children certainly will enjoy Eve Bunting's playful look at twins and their impact on the family. In *Twinnies,* big sister tells us that the worst thing about having twin sisters is that there are two of them. They need two of everything, they take up lots of space, and they're "twice as much work" for Mom. When the family goes out for a walk or goes to the beach, the twinnies get all the attention. Big sister laments the fact that the twins are girls and that she's no longer Daddy's special girl. But she finds out that the twinnies also bring lots of joy and laughter to the family, and that her special place in her parents' hearts is secure. Nancy Carpenter's oil paintings capture both the delights and challenges of raising twins.

4.6   Curtis, Gavin (1998). **The Bat Boy & His Violin.** Illustrated by E. B. Lewis. New York: Simon & Schuster. Unpaged. ISBN: 0-689-80099-1. Picture Book.

Reginald's father manages the team with the worst record in the Negro Baseball Leagues, and he needs a bat boy. However, Reginald wants to play the violin instead of chasing baseballs and picking up bats. Forced to join the team, Reginald learns to appreciate his father's passion for baseball, while his father comes to value Reginald's passion for playing the violin. Lewis' watercolors evoke the 1940s, the Negro Baseball Leagues, and a world in which a boy's "fiddlin'" Schubert sonatas coexists with—and actually fosters—home runs. The use of vernacular dialogue ("'Startin' to get the hang of it, ain't you,' Papa says.") helps the book ring with authenticity. The book presents an expansive vision of what it means to be a male, an African American, a father, and a son.

4.7   Dolphin, Laurie (1997). **Our Journey from Tibet: Based on a True Story.** Photographs by Nancy Jo Johnson. New York: Dutton Children's Books. 40 pp. ISBN: 0-525-45577-9. Picture Book. (See **3.198**)

4.8   Grambling, Lois G. (1998). **Daddy Will Be There.** Illustrated by Walter Gaffney-Kassell. New York: Greenwillow. Unpaged. ISBN: 0-688-14983-9. Picture Book.

The loving relationship between father and daughter is celebrated in this engaging picture book. This nurturing relationship is presented through everyday vignettes that portray the father as insightful and caring. Activities such as playing with blocks, pulling a wagon, watching ladybugs, and going to a boy's birthday party effectively avoid gender stereotyping. The themes of caring, love, and respect are well developed through the father's interactions with his daughter. Young readers will appreciate the airbrush and watercolor illustrations that enhance this poetic book. The book provides a rich contextual background for discussing family members and how they nurture one another.

4.9   Herron, Carolivia (1997). **Nappy Hair.** Illustrated by Joe Cepeda. New York: Random House Books for Young Readers. Unpaged. ISBN: 0-679-87937-4. Picture Book.

When Brenda, a beautiful and proud African American girl, attends her family's backyard picnic, everybody talks about her nappy hair. It's the curliest, nappiest, kinkiest hair that anyone has ever seen. Although the family likes to tease Brenda, they marvel at the true meaning of this curly hair and its relevance to Brenda's African heritage. As the story is told through the words of Uncle Mordicai and other family members, it involves readers through the use of rhythmic chatter and exaggerated conversation. The bold and lively illustrations enhance the text and add to the distinct character of the book. A wonderful lesson in pride and self-worth is taught by Brenda and her family through the text. Although this book has generated considerable controversy in a New York elementary classroom, we believe it can spark many discussions about various types of hair among different cultures, and become a vehicle to better understand the differences as well as the universalities inherent in all kinds of families. See also *I Love My Hair* (**8.61**).

4.10   Hesse, Karen (1996). **The Music of Dolphins.** New York: Scholastic. 181 pp. ISBN: 0-590-89797-7. Chapter Book.

Mila, a feral child raised by dolphins, is picked up off the coast of Florida by researchers. Taken to a research lab, Mila is taught about the human world, including language, loneliness, territory, anger, and aggression. When Mila compares the world of the dolphins to the human world, it is easy to see why she misses her dolphin family. The dolphins are a true family who care for one another unselfishly, appreciate one another's individuality, and depend on each other to sustain their community. Mila longs to return to her dolphin family even though she experiences conflicting feelings about her two worlds. Although Mila recognizes the advantages of a human life, she needs the nurturing environment of the dolphins to thrive and decides to return to the sea.

4.11   Johnson, Angela (1997). **Daddy Calls Me Man.** Illustrated by Rhonda Mitchell. New York: Orchard. Unpaged. ISBN: 0-531-30042-0. Picture Book.

Angela Johnson, a Coretta Scott King Award winner, uses four short verses to communicate a little boy's feelings about his daddy, mama, and sisters. In each successive verse, a painting by his parents inspires Noah to compare his shoes to Daddy's, spin with his older sister, wonder about the moon, or share with his baby sister. Noah tells us that because he is a caring brother, "Mama calls me sweetheart and Daddy calls me man." With just a few words, Johnson conveys the strength and love that abounds in this family of artists. Mitchell's big, bold oil paintings present interesting perspectives as Noah lines up his shoes beside Daddy's or looks down on his baby sister in her playpen.

4.12 Kroll, Virginia L. (1996). **Can You Dance, Dalila?** Illustrated by Nancy Carpenter. New York: Simon & Schuster. 32 pp. ISBN: 0-689-80551-9. Picture Book.

Dalila and her grandmother share many wonderful times and experiences together. With her grandmother's help, Dalila is immersed in dancing, but finds it is not as easy as it seems. As she experiences the different forms of dance, she finally finds one through which she can express herself and her feelings. The warm, inviting illustrations in this picture book help to portray all of Dalila's feelings as she learns about dancing.

4.13 Lachtman, Ofelia Dumas (1997). **Leticia's Secret.** Houston, TX: Piñata. 126 pp. ISBN: 1-55885-209-3. Chapter Book. (See **5.141**)

4.14 Lomas Garza, Carmen (1996). **In My Family/En mi familia.** Translated by Francisco X. Alarcón. San Francisco: Children's Book. Unpaged. ISBN: 0-89239-138-3. Picture Book.

This dual language book, awarded the Children's Book of Distinction from the *Hungry Mind Review* of 1997, is a wonderful visual depiction of healings, celebrations, and family gatherings from Garza's childhood growing up in Kingsville, Texas. Her illustrations are detailed, clear, sharp, and colorful, affecting a folk-art style. A personal narrative explains each event and the people portrayed in her illustrations. This book will evoke vivid memories for young and old, especially those from a Hispanic community. When Amanda, a second grader, saw the home remedy of burning the tip of a rolled-up newspaper inserted in the ear, she responded, "My tía does it when my tío's ear is plugged." In a question-and-answer section at the end of the book, Garza reveals that her work is her motivation—a way of demonstrating pride in her culture and healing the shame she was made to feel toward her culture and language while growing up. After reading her forward and hearing her answer questions pertaining to her art and personal life, children who feel culturally alienated may be able to relate to this artist and her work.

4.15   Luenn, Nancy (1998). **A Gift for Abuelita: Celebrating the Day of the Dead/Un regalo para Abuelita: En celebración del Día de los Muertos.** Illustrated by Robert Chapman. Translated by Mario Lamo-Jiménez. Flagstaff, AZ: Northland. Unpaged. ISBN: 0-87358-688-3. Picture Book.

The special warmth of a grandmother-grandchild relationship and the rituals surrounding the Day of the Dead—a memorial celebration common in many Mexican American communities—are carefully interwoven in this beautifully illustrated book. Rosita and her grandmother enjoy many hours together, filling their days with handicrafts, cooking, and gardening. When Abuelita becomes ill and dies, Rosita is beyond consolation. Her family comforts her and also respects her grieving, assuring her that her participation in the Day of the Dead preparations will ease her suffering and allow her to show how much she misses her grandmother. Like any young child, Rosita misunderstands what her elders mean when they tell her that Abuelita will come back to see her, so she waits for a physical presence. Finally after much waiting, she feels a special warmth and a brush of wings on her cheek that let her know her Abuelita's spirit has received her love. Although this is Robert Chapman's first experience in book illustration, he is widely known as an artist who works with handmade and cast papers. The illustrations provide a richly colored, highly textured celebration that adds even more layers of meaning to this wonderful story. The text is set on bordered pages facing each illustration, with English given privilege in position. Both English and Spanish versions flow easily and naturally. Our young listeners (ages six, sevem, and eight) became noticeably hushed when Abuelita died. "I felt better when her grandmother's spirit kissed her cheek," commented Emmalisa (age seven). Needless to say, the balance of the discussion was filled with grandmother stories.

4.16   McKissack, Patricia C. (1997). **Ma Dear's Apron.** Illustrated by Floyd Cooper. New York: Simon & Schuster. Unpaged. ISBN: 0-689-81051-2. Picture Book.

A young boy learns the days of the week by associating the color of the apron worn by his mother with certain days of the week. Conversations are kept alive between mother and son by the many questions he asks as he learns about life. This story is warm and sensitive, and provides a great experience for young readers.

This award-winning book has splendid illustrations that bring out the life experiences discussed by mother and son, and the feelings shared between the two.

4.17   Melmed, Laura Krauss (1997). **Little Oh.** Illustrated by Jim La-Marche. New York: Lothrop, Lee & Shepard/Morrow. Unpaged. ISBN: 0-688-14208-7. Picture Book.

A gentle blending of acrylics and colored pencils unite with the text of this magical story-within-a-story, in which an origami doll comes to life. Created by a lonely artist, Little Oh surprises the woman when she awakes with the greeting, "Good morning, Mother." The two grow to know and love one another. During a venture to the marketplace, Little Oh becomes separated from her mother, escapes a dog's vicious attack, and befriends a protective swan. After many days, a man and his son find Little Oh, who has formed herself into the shape of a heart. They return the paper child to her mother, where she instantly becomes a real little girl. In this fairytale-like ending, the man, his son, Little Oh, and her mother become one family, living together in harmony. This story will captivate both young and older audiences alike.

4.18   Numeroff, Laura J. (1998). **What Daddies Do Best, What Mommies Do Best.** Illustrated by Lynn Munsinger. New York: Simon & Schuster. Unpaged. ISBN: 0-689-80577-2. Picture Book.

What do daddies and mommies do best? In this clever, predictable language book for young children and their parents, we find out. There are really two stories here, one about what mommies do best, the other about what daddies do best. After finishing one story, the reader must close the book and flip it upside down in order to read the other story. We find in the book lots of simple and fun things both parents can do with their children. It is important to note that the activities are the same in both stories. Both mommies and daddies are seen playing in the park, reading to their child, watching a sunset together, and gardening. Munsinger's bright, colorful watercolor-and-ink illustrations feature a variety of appealing animal characters. This book reminds us all to spend time with the children in our lives.

4.19   Rosa-Casanova, Sylvia (1997). **Mami Provi and the Pot of Rice.** Illustrated by Robert Roth. New York: Atheneum. Unpaged. ISBN: 0-689-31932-0. Picture Book.

A Puerto Rican grandmother called Mami Provi and her grand-daughter, Lucy, live on separate floors of the same apartment building. Lucy falls ill with chicken pox, and Mami Provi decides to make her *arroz con pollo,* or chicken with rice. As the grandmother climbs the stairs to Lucy's apartment, she smells foods from many different cultures cooking. She knocks on doors, offering some of her arroz con pollo in exchange for other delicious dishes. In the end, Mami Provi and Lucy enjoy a magnificent, multicultural meal brought together by the grandmother's encounters with all their friendly neighbors. Robert Roth's distinctive watercolor illustrations provoked many positive comments. "I love painting with watercolors," commented Gabriel (age seven). The characters, portrayed in vibrant watercolor prints against simplified backgrounds, add a special touch of neighborly warmth to the story.

4.20   Sachar, Louis (1998). **Holes.** New York: Farrar, Straus and Giroux. 233 pp. ISBN: 0-374-33265-7. Chapter Book. (See **13.55**)

4.21   Sáenz, Benjamin Alire (1998). **A Gift from Papá Diego/Un regalo de Papá Diego.** Illustrated by Gerónimo García. El Paso, TX: Cinco Puntos. 40 pp. ISBN: 0-938317-33-4. Picture Book.

As Dieguito's birthday approaches, he hopes for a Superman costume so he can fly from his home in El Paso, Texas, to visit his grandfather, Papá Diego, in Chihuahua, Mexico. He even practices his reading by pouring over Superman comics that belonged to his father, in hopes of learning more about how to fly. His parents indulge him, and he receives his birthday wish, only to become frustrated and angry when he realizes the costume can't help him get to Papá Diego. However, Dieguito's parents have arranged for a special surprise visit from Papá Diego, culminating in a wonderful family scene that prompts students to share their own family experiences. The second graders who read this book were intrigued with the painted clay illustrations created by Gerónimo García. Derek (age seven) realized that after shaping the clay into figures, a photographer "took pictures of it." The students were pleased to see both Spanish and English texts on the same page, and were eager to try reading in both languages. The end pages include a brief glossary, and information about both author and illustrator that will help children understand more about how the book came to be.

4.22   Scott, Elaine (1998). **Twins!** Illustrated by Margaret Miller. New York: Simon & Schuster. Unpaged. ISBN: 0-689-80347-8. Picture Book.

Twins! presents a lively look at twins that is informative for adults and children alike. Colorful photographs show the ins-and-outs of daily living with eight sets of preschool twins and their families. Scott points out qualities that are unique to twins, and those that are common to all children. Sharing toys and parents' attention, and getting along with siblings, are issues for twins just as they are for any other child. Although identical and fraternal twins have much in common, it is particularly important to remember that each twin is still a unique individual. Scott's creative use of text highlights special words, and asks questions that invite the child to interact with the text. The "Parent's Note" at the back of the book offers a helpful and frank discussion of how to help young children understand the phenomenon of twins.

4.23   Shaw, Eve (1997). **Grandmother's Alphabet.** Duluth, MN: Pfeifer-Hamilton. Unpaged. ISBN: 1-57025-127-4. Picture Book.

What a delightful, lively, and varied bunch of grandmothers we find in this inspiring book. Gone is the little old lady sitting in a rocker! Here bright pages show us grandmothers who are young and old; grandmothers who are Native American, Asian American, and African American; grandmothers in wheelchairs, in airplanes, under the ocean, and in courtrooms; and grandmothers who are teachers, painters, nurses, and engineers. Predictable language describes a variety of careers on each page. For example, the "F" page reads as follows: "Grandma is a Florist creating lovely gifts from flowers. Grandma can be . . . a firefighter, a forester, or a family counselor . . . and so can I." The illustrations beg to be studied, with their detailed borders often relating to the featured career and a small sketch at the bottom of each page showing tools used. A great book for career exploration.

4.24   Sisalu, Elinor Batezat (1996). **The Day Gogo Went to Vote.** Illustrated by Sharon Wilson. New York: Little Brown. Unpaged. ISBN: 0-316-70267-6. Picture Book. (See **20.32**)

4.25   Soto, Gary (1997). **Snapshots from the Wedding.** Illustrated by Stephanie Garcia. New York: Putnam. Unpaged. ISBN: 0-399-22808-X. Picture Book.

Gary Soto's book *Snapshots from the Wedding* is told from the perspective of the wedding party's flower girl, Maya, using code-switching that alternates the use of English and Spanish in conversations. The text is written almost as if family members are reviewing wedding photographs to put in an album. Stephanie Garcia's unique double-page illustrations, which won her the Pura Belpre Illustrator's Award, enrich the text by combining Sculpy clay characters with real items such as crystal goblets, potato chips, and ribbon, photographed against lace backgrounds. The illustrations prompted one teacher to retell the story of her wedding to her bilingual kindergarten class, and will provide a similarly rich context for telling stories about the celebrations of many cultures. Gary Soto combines his typical code-switching with José Cepeda's richly colored illustrations in another favorite tale of family life, *The Old Man and His Door*.

Soto, Gary (1996). **The Old Man and His Door.** Illustrated by Joe Cepeda. New York: Putnam. Unpaged. ISBN: 0-399-22700-8. Picture Book.

4.26 Steptoe, Javaka, editor (1997). **In Daddy's Arms I Am Tall: African Americans Celebrating Fathers.** Illustrated by Javaka Steptoe. New York: Lee & Low. Unpaged. ISBN: 0-880000-31-8. Picture Book.

The thirteen poems in this collection portray strong, sensitive, proud, hard-working, gentle, talented, and loving fathers and grandfathers. Written by contemporary African American poets, each of the poems depicts in a different way the theme of the opening Ashanti proverb, "When you follow in the path of your father / You learn to walk like him." The influence of a father on a son is portrayed not only through the words of the poems, but also through Steptoe's mixed-media collages. By using found objects such as metal screening, dirt, fabric, and shells, combined with cut and torn paper and strong lines in chalk and ink, Steptoe conveys not only the bond between father and son but also the cultural influence of the African American's heritage. This intergenerational tie is expressed by Sonia Sanchez' closing poem, "I have looked into / My father's eyes and seen an / African sunset."

4.27 Tillage, Leon Walter (1997). **Leon's Story.** New York: Farrar, Straus & Giroux. Illustrated by Susan L. Roth. 107 pp. ISBN: 0-374-34379-9. Chapter Book. (See **20.18**)

4.28 Watts, Jeri Hanel (1997). **Keepers.** Illustrated by Felicia Marshall. New York: Lee & Low. Unpaged. ISBN: 1-880000-58-X. Picture Book.

Kenyon loves baseball, and spends his spare time working on improving his baseball skills. Kenyon also loves hearing the stories his grandmother tells. These are the stories of his people and his family that have been passed on through oral storytelling from generation to generation by the women designated to be the keeper of the stories. Kenyon adores these stories and wants to be the keeper, but is told that only females may pass on the tradition. Kenyon writes down the stories that he has heard so often and, as a special gift, presents them to his grandmother on her ninetieth birthday. The significance of story, the power of literacy, and the importance of who gets to tell the stories are themes that beg to be explored further. This is a lovely picture book done in acrylic and acrylic-oil on watercolor paper by Felicia Marshall.

4.29 Wyeth, Sharon Dennis (1998). **Something Beautiful.** Illustrated by Chris K. Soentpiet. New York: Bantam Doubleday Dell. 30 pp. ISBN: 0-385-32239-9. Picture Book. (See **8.64, 20.8**)

Secondary Reviews

4.30 Antle, Nancy (1997). **Staying Cool.** Illustrated by E. B. Lewis. New York: Dial Books for Young Readers. 32 pp. ISBN: 0-8037-1876-4. Picture Book.

Curtis is working out at his grandfather's gym. He wants to fight in the Golden Gloves boxing tournament to make his grandfather proud of him. Curtis learns valuable lessons about life and self-control while he's in the boxing ring. The beautiful illustrations add warmth to this story about family, friends, and setting goals in life.

4.31 Aylesworth, Jim (1998). **Through the Night.** Illustrated by Pamela Patrick. New York: Atheneum. Unpaged. ISBN: 0-689-80642-6. Picture Book.

Driving north toward home during the early evening, Daddy travels through the quiet countryside and the bustling city thinking of his wife and children who greet him when he arrives. Bright illustrations depicting the 1940s create an idyllic representation of families of the past.

4.32   de Paola, Tomie (1996). **Strega Nona: Her Story.** New York: Putnam. Unpaged. ISBN: 0-399-22818-7. Picture Book. (See **13.41**)

4.33   English, Karen (1998). **Just Right Stew.** Honesdale, PA: Boyds Mills. 32 pp. ISBN: 1-56397-487-8. Picture Book.

To celebrate Big Mama's birthday, the whole family tries to cook her famous oxtail stew, but since no one knows the recipe, something is missing! They try different ingredients but the stew still doesn't taste right. When Big Mama arrives for dinner, she adds the secret ingredient without telling her daughters what it is. Only her granddaughter knows the secret. This family story is funny, and will surely remind readers of special foods shared at family gatherings.

4.34   Hru, Dakari (1996). **The Magic Moonberry Jump Ropes.** Illustrated by E. B. Lewis. New York: Dial Books for Young Readers. Unpaged. ISBN: 0-8037-1754-7. Picture Book.

Two sisters, April and Erica, love to jump rope, especially Double Dutch. When summer arrives, they can't wait to fill their days jumping rope, but they can't find any friends that will turn the rope for them. One afternoon, Uncle Zambegi returns from a trip to East Africa. He brings the girls a pair of beautifully dyed jump ropes as a gift. He tells them the ropes are magic and if they make a wish, it will come true. This is a great book full of traditional jump rope rhymes handed down through generations. The illustrator's beautiful watercolors will make readers yearn for summer!

4.35   Hudson, Wade, and Cheryl Willis Hudson, compilers (1997). **In Praise of Our Fathers and Our Mothers.** East Orange, NJ: Just Us. 131 pp. ISBN: 0-940975-59-9. Picture Book.

This book was created to celebrate those who inspired Black writers and illustrators when they were children. *In Praise of Our Fathers and Our Mothers* explores the personal lives of more than forty Black artists through illustrations and essays that give honor to their caregivers. These stories of childhood memories, with illustrations that reflect the artists' interpretation of family and love, make up a unique book created by Black artists who have dedicated their talents to children's literature. Also included is an article about the Pinkney family, as well as an interview by artist Pat Cummings with the children of writer and author John Steptoe, who died in 1989.

4.36   Igus, Toyomi (1996). **The Two Mrs. Gibsons.** Illustrated by Daryl Wells. San Francisco: Children's Book. 32 pp. ISBN: 0-89239-135-9. Picture Book.

Toyomi Igus recounts her childhood experiences growing up with two women, one African American and the other Japanese, who had their differences but who shared in their love of young Toyomi. Igus describes the experience of playing dress-up with her Japanese mother, who places one of her kimonos on Toyomi, and her grandmother, who tops off her wardrobe by placing a big "Sunday-go-to-meetin'" hat upon her head, and explains how her mother and grandmother each told her how special the item was to them. This book shows how two cultures can meet and blend through the love of a little girl.

4.37   Johnston, Tony (1996). **Fishing Sunday.** Illustrated by Barry Root. New York: Morrow. Unpaged. ISBN: 0-688-13458-0. Picture Book.

A grandson reluctantly goes fishing with his grandfather each Sunday. His grandfather's appearance and actions embarrass the grandson—the way he dresses, talks, and chants to the fishes. But then he notices how much the other fishermen respect him. He soon learns to appreciate his grandfather for his strengths—his wisdom, kindness, and zest for life. The grandson develops pride for his grandfather in this beautiful story that teaches us about valuing our elders.

4.38   Mitchell, Barbara (1996). **Red Bird.** Illustrated by Todd Doney. New York: Lothrop, Lee & Shepard. 31 pp. ISBN: 0-688-10859-8. Picture Book.

Katie and her family live and work in the city. Every September, they pack their car and leave the city to attend the annual Nanticoke powwow in southern Delaware, where they renew friendships and family ties. Author Barbara Mitchell takes young readers through the events of the weekend powwow, where hundreds of Native Americans from more than forty tribes celebrate their heritage through song and dance. Easy-to-read text and colorful illustrations will keep the interest of young readers in this contemporary Native American story.

4.39   Mitchell, Rhonda (1997). **The Talking Cloth.** New York: Orchard. Unpaged. ISBN: 0-531-30004-8. Picture Book.

When young Amber visits her Aunt Phoebe, she knows that she will always find surprises. Aunt Phoebe has a wonderful collection of what some would call "junk," but Amber enjoys listening to the different stories about all the items. She especially likes the story about a piece of cloth that her aunt calls the "talking cloth." The beautifully colored cloth, with its African symbols, fills Amber's mind with a curiosity and longing to know all about the cloth. Aunt Phoebe and Amber share many loving conversations about the cloth. The oil paintings add a special touch to this book about family relationships and the sharing of family stories.

4.40   Wells, Ruth (1996). **The Farmer and the Poor God: A Folktale from Japan.** Illustrated by Yoshi. New York: Simon & Schuster Books for Young Readers. Unpaged. ISBN: 0-689-80214-5. Picture Book.

The textured-silk surface illustrated with colored dyes helps to convey this humorous Japanese folktale, appropriate for any age. A farmer determines his misfortune is caused by the Poor God rather than through any fault of his own. The Poor God cleverly gets the bickering family members to work together to create the beautiful sandals that he has designed. Together the family prospers, questioning the Poor God's existence as they live in harmony.

4.41   Yolen, Jane (1998). **Nocturne.** Illustrated by Anne Hunter. New York: Harcourt Brace. Unpaged. ISBN: 0-15-201458-6. Picture Book.

Another delightful book by Jane Yolen, *Nocturne* presents an inviting bedtime story that children can relate to with ease about exploring the backyard on a summer's night. Anne Hunter's pen-and-ink, watercolor, and colored-pencil illustrations immerse us in the blue velvet of night as Yolen's words take us on this adventure, with parent and child exploring the mysteries of the nocturnal world. With flashlight in hand, they view the star-filled night sky, the moths by the porch light, the lightning bugs blinking in the Queen Anne's lace, and the owl swooping from its perch high in a tree, before climbing into a cozy bed and drifting off to sweet dreams of nighttime creatures. A great way to end the day!

Family Experiences through the Ages

See also the section entitled Histories and Herstories in chapter 3, "Exploring Our Past."

Primary Reviews

4.42 Calvert, Patricia (1998). **Sooner.** New York: Simon & Schuster. 166 pp. ISBN: 0-689-81114-4. Chapter Book.

The Bohannon family shows us a slice of Missouri farm life in the late 1860s. When Black Jack Bohannon abandons his family to follow General Jo Shelby into Mexico after the Civil War, thirteen-year-old Tyler finds himself in charge of the Bohannon farm. The struggles of Tyler, his mother Ellen, and his younger siblings show us what life was like in this time and place; eating raccoon and cornmeal mush fried in bacon grease, stocking the root cellar, and dealing with scalawags are part of everyday life. When Ellen remarries, Tyler takes off for fresh job opportunities and cheap land in the West. Fresh yet folksy dialogue creates images of farm life that will linger in readers' minds.

4.43 Cushman, Karen (1996). **The Ballad of Lucy Whipple.** New York: Clarion. 195 pp. ISBN: 0-395-72806-1. Chapter Book. (See **5.51**)

4.44 Dorris, Michael (1996). **Guests.** Illustrated by Ellen Thompson. New York: Hyperion. 119 pp. ISBN: 0-7868-1108-0. Chapter Book.

Adolescence is the time when questions arise about who we are, what we are supposed to be, and when we will be recognized as an adult. *Guests* is set in a Native American village somewhere in the Northeast during the early period of European colonization. It is a story of two friends, Moss and Trouble, and their struggle with responsibility, coming-of-age, and adjustment to internal and external change. Moss disagrees with his father about inviting strangers to a celebration dinner, and leaves his village. Trouble runs away from an abusive family situation, which she doesn't want anyone to know about, and is seeking some alone time. Oral tradition is used as a vehicle to provide understanding about individual and community responsibility and insights into how one finds himself or herself. The story contains important messages, and sensitively approaches the subject matter.

4.45 Friedrich, Elizabeth (1996). **Leah's Pony.** Illustrated by Michael Garland. Honesdale, PA: Boyds Mills. Unpaged. ISBN: 1-56397-189-5. Picture Book. (See **3.29**)

4.46 Giff, Patricia Reilly (1997). **Lily's Crossing.** New York: Delacorte. 180 pp. ISBN: 0-385-32142-2. Chapter Book. (See **3.107**)

4.47 Hearne, Betsy G. (1997). **Seven Brave Women.** Illustrated by Bethanne Andersen. New York: Greenwillow. Unpaged. ISBN: 0-688-14503-5. Picture Book.

Hearne writes of "all the women in our family who made history by not fighting in wars." Each brief chapter depicts a woman's courage during wartime by immigrating to America, moving in a covered wagon, riding a horse with a regular saddle, establishing a women's hospital in India, working as an architect, and raising two small children alone. Hearne learned these family stories from her mother, a library storyteller, and also learned that for every girl, "there are a million ways to be brave." Andersen's warm oil-paint illustrations enrich the text by depicting treasured family items. A thin pink ribbon carried on each page throughout the book by a dove visually ties the author to her past. This book portrays a feminine, everyday side of the wars that often dominate history books and curriculum.

4.48 Hesse, Karen (1997). **Out of the Dust.** New York: Scholastic. 227 pp. ISBN: 0-590-36080-9. Chapter Book.

In this 1998 Newbery Award winner, the voice of fourteen-year-old Billie Jo Kelby hauntingly tells the story of her family and the Oklahoma Dust Bowl through a series of narrative poems that capture the era. She creates haunting images of her Oklahoma farm and family drowning in dust. These might be overwhelming if not for the lyrical language and the music flowing from Billie Jo's piano throughout the story. Billie Jo struggles with the accidental death of her pregnant mother, which she blames partly on herself and partly on her father Bayard. Billie Jo's hands, which become charred as she tries to save her mother, symbolize the emotional scarring she suffers as well as the scarring of the land by nature's fury. Billie Jo grows as she struggles through her adversity. In the end, this heroine attempts to run away, but realizes as she flees that she has developed the incredible resilience she needs to survive any hardships life could deal her. Hesse skillfully weaves historical data throughout the text of the poems: bank closings, extreme poverty, the scourge of grasshoppers, the Dionne quintuplets, the Kilauea eruption, and the ever-present dust storms. This book is an excellent read-aloud and invites discussion about both historical experiences and coming-of-age issues.

4.49 Kaplan, William (1998). **One More Border: The True Story of One Family's Escape from War-Torn Europe.** Illustrated by Stephen

Taylor. Toronto, Ontario, Canada: Groundwood. 61 pp. ISBN: 0-88899-332-3. Picture Book. (See **20.14**)

4.50 Lee, Milly (1997). **Nim and the War Effort.** Illustrated by Yang-sook Choi. New York: Farrar, Straus and Giroux. Unpaged. ISBN: 0-374-35523-1. Picture Book. (See **3.109**)

4.51 Stanley, Diane (1996). **Elena.** New York: Hyperion. 55 pp. ISBN: 0-7868-0256-1. Chapter Book. (See **3.15**)

4.52 Stewart, Sarah (1997). **The Gardener.** Illustrated by David Small. New York: Farrar, Straus and Giroux. Unpaged. ISBN: 0-374-32517-0. Picture Book. (See **3.16**)

4.53 Woodtor, Dee Parmer (1996). **Big Meeting.** Illustrated by Dolores Johnson. New York: Atheneum. Unpaged. ISBN: 0-689-31933-9. Picture Book.

As the third week of August rolls around each summer, families come from far and wide, by train and car, across Pigeon Creek to arrive Down Home for the Big Meeting. Grandma and Grandpa welcome aunts, uncles, and cousins as they return for this joyous reunion. There's cooking and storytelling and getting ready for the Big Meeting. Dressed in their finest, the visitors head for the Little Bethel A.M.E. Church. Reverend Lomax speaks, the choir sings, and Grandpa leads the worshipers in a soulful rendition of "Amazing Grace." Delores Johnson illustrates the story using etchings and aquatints with watercolor and colored pencils. She captures the closeness of family, the spirit of the church meeting, and the joy of the reunion expressed in Woodtor's warmhearted text.

Secondary Reviews

4.54 Anderson, Leone Castell (1997). **Sean's War.** Forreston, IL: Shadow-Play. 159 pp. ISBN: 0-9638819-5-7. Chapter Book.

In this vivid picture of 1830s Illinois, twelve-year-old Sean Callahan struggles to reconcile the different attitudes of his father Brady and his stepmother Ingrid. Brady's past encounters with Native Americans and the struggle to survive on the Illinois prairie have left him bitter and distrusting. Sigrid, a gentle Norwegian immigrant, is trusting and peaceful. As Brady and Sigrid continue to grow apart, Sean feels caught in the middle.

4.55 Bartone, Elisa (1996). **American Too.** Illustrated by Ted Lewin. New York: Lothrop, Lee & Shepard. Unpaged. ISBN: 0-688-13279-0. Picture Book. (See **3.192**)

4.56 Fleming, Candace (1996). **Women of the Lights.** Illustrated by James Watling. Morton Grove, IL: Whitman. 79 pp. ISBN: 0-8075-9165-3. Chapter Book. (See **3.84**)

4.57 Hest, Amy (1997). **When Jessie Came across the Sea.** Illustrated by P. J. Lynch. Cambridge, MA: Candlewick. Unpaged. ISBN: 0-7636-0094-6. Picture Book. (See **3.34**)

4.58 Johnson, Paul Brett (1997). **Farmers' Market.** New York: Orchard. Unpaged. ISBN: 0-531-30014-5. Picture Book.

On summer Saturdays, Laura and her family load up their pickup truck with vegetables to take to the farmers' market. Laura spends the morning working with her family, and the afternoon exploring the market with her friend Betsy. This book includes rich, vivid, and colorful illustrations with a big center foldout of the market.

4.59 Peck, Richard (1998). **A Long Way from Chicago.** New York: Dial Books. 148 pp. ISBN: 0-8037-2290-7. Chapter Book.

For seven consecutive summers from 1929 to 1935, Joey and his sister Mary Alice leave Chicago in August to spend a week with Grandma Dowdel in a small rural Illinois town. Each trip holds an adventure that over the years endears Joey and Mary Alice to their eccentric, free-spirited, but always loving grandmother.

4.60 Pryor, Bonnie (1996). **The Dream Jar.** Illustrated by Mark Graham. New York: Morrow Junior Books. Unpaged. ISBN: 0-688-13062-3. Picture Book. (See **3.45**)

4.61 Yee, Paul (1996). **Ghost Train.** Illustrated by Harvey Chan. Emeryville, CA: Douglas & McIntyre. Unpaged. ISBN: 0-88899-257-2. Picture Book.

After his accidental death, Choon-yi's father visits Choon-yi in a dream and asks her to draw the train that he helped build. When she meets the ghosts of her father's coworkers who also died in the accident, Choon-yi fully understands his last request. She burns the drawing at the village hilltop so the men's souls can find their way home. This story is based on a tale told by the Chinese people who settled on the West Coast in the early 1900s.

Changing Family Structures

Primary Reviews

4.62   Boyd, Candy Dawson (1995). **Daddy, Daddy, Be There.** Illustrated by Floyd Cooper. New York: Philomel. Unpaged. ISBN: 0-399-22745-8. Sophisticated Picture Book.

Daddy, Daddy, Be There is a beautifully crafted book in which children make a plea to their daddies to be there, not only for the big events but also for the day-to-day happenings that are the building blocks for a meaningful relationship between father and child. The text could serve as a handbook for all fathers. It says, "Be there, be my rock, be there for me when I need guidance." It points to the fact that neglect can have a powerful effect on children, and that neglect can take place in affluent families as well as poor ones. Floyd Cooper's use of soft, earthy colors in his illustrations creates a warm, enveloping aura that surrounds the reader with emotion.

4.63   Dines, Carol (1997). **Talk to Me: Stories and a Novella.** New York: Delacorte. 223 pp. ISBN: 0-385-32271-2. Sophisticated Chapter Book; adult mediation required. (See **20.53**)

4.64   Hausherr, Rosmarie (1997). **Celebrating Families.** New York: Scholastic. Unpaged. ISBN: 0-590-48937-2. Sophisticated Picture Book.

Hausherr presents a photographic gallery of fourteen different children and their families. Among the types of families included are the more common family structures such as a nuclear family, a single-parent family, a foster family, a stepfamily, an adoptive family, and a divorced family. Others that she includes are a biracial family, a homeless family, a family whose father is in prison, a family with a physically disabled mother, a family that lives in a cooperative community, and a family with two mommies. Hausherr tells about the family members with whom each child lives, and describes some of the activities they enjoy in their daily lives. Love is the glue that binds all of these diverse families and gives each child cause to celebrate. Hausherr's large color and black-and-white photographs are filled with vitality, and complement the informative and sensitive text.

4.65   Hines, Anna Grossnickle (1996). **When We Married Gary.** New York: Morrow. Unpaged. ISBN: 0-688-14276-1. Sophisticated Picture Book.

When We Married Gary is an autobiographical account of Hines' marriage to Gary, told through the eyes of her young daughter. This is Mama's second marriage, and Beth is old enough to remember when Daddy still lived with them. Gary brings laughter and kisses to Mama, and welcomes the children into his life while acknowledging that they already have a father. The strong sense of reality comes through in believable dialogue and direct discussions of why Daddy doesn't live with them anymore. The watercolor and colored-pencil illustrations focus on the children and their family experiences during this time of transition, capturing the range of emotions and responses that might be typical of a joyful second marriage.

4.66   Holt, Kimberly Willis (1998). **My Louisiana Sky.** New York: Henry Holt. 132 pp. ISBN: 0-8050-5251-8. Chapter Book.

Twelve-year-old Tiger lives with her Granny and her mentally disabled parents in a small town in Louisiana during the late 1950s. Except for one friend who continues to stay by her, Tiger's peers shun her because of her family. Granny is the one who nurtures her and loves her fiercely. With Granny's love and guidance, she gains confidence that she can handle things "one day at a time." This is a deeply moving novel of poverty, death, inspiration, and learning to live with situations that cannot be changed. It cleverly deals with a "first kiss" and with acceptance. "I never asked Granny about Momma again. But over the years I learned that Momma was like a child—happy when everything was going fine, upset if something stopped her fun."

4.67   Ingold, Jeanette (1996). **The Window.** New York: Harcourt Brace. 179 pp. ISBN: 0-15-201264-8. Chapter Book. (See **5.102**)

4.68   Johnson, Angela (1998). **Heaven.** New York: Simon & Schuster. 138 pp. ISBN: 0-689-82229-4. Sophisticated Chapter Book.

Living in Heaven, Ohio, doesn't mean that one is sheltered by the evils in life, but it is a place where things can heal over time. Ever since she was six, Marley has been going to the Western Union counter to send money to her Uncle Jack, someone she has known only through letters from across the country. Marley has memorized the code words for each day of the week—code words that Uncle Jack created so that, on his travels across the country with his dog Boy, he wouldn't have to show identification when he picked up the money she sent. After a series of bombings of Black churches in the South, Marley learns that her life is not what she thought it was and that Uncle Jack is not who she thought he was. Through the assistance of family and friends, Marley struggles to accept who she really is and begins to heal in *Heaven.*

4.69 McCutcheon, John (1996). **Happy Adoption Day!** Illustrated by Julie Paschkis. Boston: Little Brown. Unpaged. ISBN: 0-316-55455-3. Sophisticated Picture Book.

Songwriter John McCutcheon, two-time Grammy nominee and winner of two Children's Album of the Year Awards, has created an endearing story about adoption. His lively verses express the delight of adoptive parents as they celebrate their child's adoption day and the birth of their family. This mom and dad make a multitude of preparations for baby, and travel abroad to bring their baby home. As baby grows, adoption day becomes a cherished celebration. Bright, colorful illustrations lend a cheerful and festive feeling to this joyful story. Notations for the lyrics are included.

4.70 Rogers, Fred (1997). **Stepfamilies.** Illustrated by Jim Judkis. New York: Putnam. Unpaged. ISBN: 0-399-23145-5. Sophisticated Picture Book.

Stepfamilies is one in a series of Let's Talk About books by Fred Rogers. In his own inimitable style, Mr. Rogers talks to children about being a member of a stepfamily. In today's society, more and more children are dealing with divorce, single-parent families, and stepfamilies. Mr. Rogers discusses some of the changes, both positive and negative, that they may encounter when moms and dads remarry. He talks about the wide range of feelings children may have, and the importance of talking about these feelings with a trusted adult. He reassures children that in time, they can come to enjoy being with the members of their stepfamily and broaden their circle of belonging. Color photographs of several stepfamilies learning to live together complement the text.

4.71 Russo, Marisabina (1998). **When Mama Gets Home.** New York: Morrow. Unpaged. ISBN: 0-688-14985-5. Sophisticated Picture Book.

Waiting for Mama to get home from work can be very hard. Helping big sister and big brother prepare the dinner and watching out the window help the little girl in this story pass the time. Then Mama arrives to finish the dinner and listen to her children take turns telling about their day at school. After a nice warm bath, Mama tucks the girl into bed and reads a story before turning off the lights and saying goodnight to her little "peach." This portrait of a single-parent family presents a caring, cooperative family that works together to get things accomplished, and enjoys spending time together. Young readers will delight in the full-color gouache paintings that Russo uses to illustrate her story.

4.72 Wing, Natasha (1996). **Jalapeño Bagels.** Illustrated by Robert Casilla. New York: Atheneum. Unpaged. ISBN: 0-689-80530-6. Picture Book.

Pablo cannot decide what kind of food to take for the International Day Celebration at his school. The food is supposed to reflect his heritage, but Pablo comes from a multicultural family—his mother is Mexican American and his father is Jewish. Pablo's mother invites him to assist at the family bakery to help him make up his mind. As he and his mother make *empanadas, chango* bars, and *pan dulce,* Pablo debates the merits of takings these foods to school. He helps his father make bagels and *challah.* Finally Pablo decides that jalapeño bagels would be perfect because they are a mixture of both his parents. The watercolor illustrations by Robert Casilla capture the textures of the ingredients so well that readers can almost smell what is baking in the ovens. The Spanish and Yiddish words are defined within the text, as well as in a glossary. Recipes at the end of the book were greeted with shouts of "Yummy!" and demands for a cooking center.

4.73 Winthrop, Elizabeth (1998). **As the Crow Flies.** Illustrated by Joan Sandin. New York: Clarion. 32 pp. ISBN: 0-395-77612-0. Picture Book.

Elizabeth Winthrop's touching picture book poignantly depicts a young boy's love for his father despite a separation of "two thousand miles as the crow flies." Michael, a second grader whose parents are apparently divorced, excitedly awaits the yearly visit of his father to Arizona from Delaware. For one whole week, Michael lives with his father at a hotel. Their brief time together is packed with both special and everyday activities such as perusing picture albums, taking hikes into the desert, and eating out. The depth of feeling between Michael and his dad is evident in their smiling, touching, and hugging, shown on nearly every page. At the same time, conflicting emotions are not avoided when Michael states his love for his parents, but his hate for the fact that they do not talk to one another. With the departure of Michael's father, there is parental agreement that Michael is now old enough to fly alone to Delaware in the summer. Samantha, an insightful fourth grader, said, "Even if someone lives far away, he still loves you." Joan Sandin's watercolor and pencil illustrations are expressive and supportive of the text. Despite the artist's residency in Tucson, Arizona, the community she portrays is a bit stereotypical of the Southwest. However, there are also a few settings that the locals will recognize.

Secondary Reviews

4.74   Bauer, Joan (1998). **Rules of the Road.** New York: Putnam. 201 pp. ISBN: 0-399-23140-4. Chapter Book.

Sixteen-year-old Jenna drives Mrs. Gladstone, the elderly owner of a successful chain of shoe stores, from Chicago to Texas. Jenna runs from her alcoholic father, and Mrs. Gladstone struggles with her son, who attempts a hostile takeover. Jenna's friendship with Harry Bender, the best salesman in the chain, gives her the determination to confront her father and his alcoholism.

4.75   Say, Allen (1997). **Allison.** Boston: Houghton Mifflin. 32 pp. ISBN: 0-395-85895-X. Picture Book.

Illustrated in Say's realistic watercolor technique, this selection presents a story about interracial adoption. When a young Japanese child named Allison receives a kimono from her grandmother, she becomes angry and pushes away her parents because she realizes she is adopted. But through various events, she learns to appreciate their love and accepts them in her heart. Young children who face the same struggles as Allison will find this story empowering.

4.76   Wong, Janet (1996). **A Suitcase of Seaweed and Other Poems.** New York: Margaret K. McElderry Books. 42 pp. ISBN: 0-689-80788-0. Chapter Book.

This collection is based on the author's personal experiences growing up as an American of Korean and Chinese descent. Through Wong's poetry, readers learn of ethnic family traditions, clashes between being Asian and Asian American, and the intersection of cultural boundaries across ethnicities and generations. A delightful and eye-opening experience.

Controversial Issues in Family Life

See also the section entitled Family Hardship in chapter 5, "Struggle and Survival."

Primary Reviews

4.77 Bunting, Eve (1998). **Your Move.** Illustrated by James E. Ransome. New York: Harcourt Brace. Unpaged. ISBN: 0-15-200181-6. Picture Book. (See **5.71, 20.33**)

4.78 Fox, Paula (1997). **Radiance Descending.** New York: Dorling Kindersley. 101 pp. ISBN: 0-7894-2467-3. Chapter Book. (See **20.2**)

4.79 Haddix, Margaret Peterson (1996). **Don't You Dare Read This, Mrs. Dunphrey.** New York: Simon & Schuster. 108 pp. ISBN: 0-689-80087-5. Sophisticated Chapter Book. (See **6.56**)

4.80 Haddix, Margaret Peterson (1998). **Among the Hidden.** New York: Simon & Schuster. 153 pp. ISBN: 0-689-817700-2. Sophisticated Chapter Book.

This is an intriguing yet chilling look at the Garner family, who lives in a future American totalitarian society that allows only two children per family. Famines and drought producing global starvation have resulted in government-controlled food production and population control. Twelve-year-old Luke, the third Garner son, is a "shadow child" hidden from the Population Police. He struggles to understand his life as his family pushes him farther into the shadows when land is cleared behind their house. Luke finally discovers Jennifer, another "shadow child." The Internet links Jen to eight hundred other shadow children, and she plans a rally to demand equal rights. After Jen is killed, Luke gives up his family in order to have a chance at life and to continue Jen's dream of equality.

4.81 Hermes, Patricia (1998). **Cheat the Moon.** Boston: Little Brown. 167 pp. ISBN: 0-316-35929-7. Sophisticated Chapter Book.

The folksy, authentic voice of main character Gabby Blakely tells the story of life with an alcoholic father. Gabby and her brother Will have learned to cope with Dad's inconsistent presence ever since Mother's death three years earlier. Dad leaves on binges that sometimes last a month at a time. Gabby has developed a pragmatic approach to dealing with Dad: buy things they'll need while he's sober and working, and store them up for when he'll leave. Will has been scarred by Dad's temporary abandonment. When Dad is killed in a mill accident, Gabby and Will can no longer hope that their dad eventually will come home. Gabby confronts her fears of being abandoned, of having no one to depend on, and of emotionally connecting with others, and discovers her own inner strength.

4.82 Howe, James (1997). **The Watcher.** New York: Atheneum. 172 pp. ISBN: 0-689-80186-6. Sophisticated Chapter Book.

Each day, thirteen-year-old Margaret goes to the beach near her parents' rented cottage, sits at the top of the steps, watches the people, writes in her journal, and fantasizes a perfect family for herself to replace her physically and emotionally abusive father and her ineffective mother. Most chapters are prefaced with the fairy tale she creates as she tries to escape her life. We learn through four points of view that all our lives come up short when measured against our fantasies. The family Margaret imagines as perfect is falling apart as the parents contemplate divorce. The book ends on a more positive note as Margaret gets the help she so desperately needs. Thirteen-year-old Meredith said, "I think it's fascinating how most people think other people have such wonderful lives," when in fact they don't.

4.83 LaFaye, A. (1998). **The Year of the Sawdust Man.** New York: Simon & Schuster. 220 pp. ISBN: 0-689-81513-1. Sophisticated Chapter Book.

Eleven-year-old Nissa, who is wise beyond her years, tries to cope with the changes in her life after her high-spirited mother abandons Papa and her in a small Louisiana town in 1934. In a voice reminiscent of Scout Finch, Nissa poignantly examines Mama's motives, character, and dreams, and searches for a way to maintain a spiritual connection with a mother who is unpredictable and impulsive. Nissa asks big questions in her quest to understand her relationship with her mother, and struggles with conflicting emotions. This first novel is a powerful look at the impact of abandonment and divorce. References to adultery and "baby making" make the book more appropriate for mature middle-school readers.

4.84   Little, Mimi Otey (1996). **Yoshiko and the Foreigner.** New York: Farrar, Straus and Giroux. Unpaged. ISBN: 0-374-32448-4. Picture Book.

A young Japanese woman goes against her culture's customs by speaking and coming to the aid of a foreign American soldier who is lost in the city. Through their conversations, the foreign American learns about Yoshiko's family values and customs. He gives her special gifts—two fish for her father's fishpond, and the finest rice and wine for the family's ancestral shrine. When Yoshiko's father, Mr. Sasagawa, finally learns of their relationship, he warns Yoshiko of Americans' disregard for Japanese culture. But when he learns of the precious gifts from the foreigner given to the family in honor of their culture, and also that the foreigner has learned the Japanese language in order to ask Mr. Sasagawa's permission to marry Yoshiko, Yoshiko's father becomes convinced that the foreigner is truly sincere. A moving story of love and generosity that teaches us how to give of ourselves, embrace and appreciate cultures other than our own, and promote understanding through difference.

4.85   Mazer, Norma Fox (1997). **When She Was Good.** New York: Scholastic. 234 pp. ISBN: 5-590-13506-6. Sophisticated Chapter Book.

The Thurkill family lives in a run-down trailer outside a small town in the middle of New York State. Pamela has a long history of abuse: putting down her mother, intimidating her father, and physically abusing her sister Em. When their mother dies and their father remarries, Pamela and Em move into the city and Em becomes the focus of Pamela's brutality. After Pamela dies of a stroke during a physical attack on Em, Em's life is haunted by the lingering effects of Pamela's abuse and Pamela's ranting voice inside her head. Em gradually comes to terms with Pamela's death and Em's eternal hope that her life will change for the better becomes a reality.

4.86   Mazer, Harry (1998). **The Wild Kid.** New York: Simon & Schuster. 103 pp. ISBN: 0-689-80751-1. Sophisticated Chapter Book.

Sammy, a twelve-year-old child with Down's Syndrome, runs away from home and gets lost deep in the woods. Here he encounters Kevin, a wild child who escaped an abusive family that once locked him in a car trunk. Kevin has survived in the woods for a long time, eating garbage, stealing from cars in the cemetery, and living in a makeshift lean-to. Afraid he'll be discovered if Sammy goes back to his family, Kevin keeps him captive. Strangely, through a series of twists and turns in their relationship, Sammy and Kevin become like brothers. Kevin teaches Sammy an independence he'd never known before. Sammy wants Kevin to come back to live in his home like real brothers, but Kevin knows he's too far removed from the mainstream to fit in. Mazer gives us a hard look at our most marginalized children.

4.87 Rapp, Adam (1997). **The Buffalo Tree.** Asheville, NC: Front Street. 188 pp. ISBN: 1-886910-19-7. Sophisticated Chapter Book. (See **20.5**)

4.88 Spinelli, Jerry (1997). **Wringer.** New York: HarperCollins. 228 pp. ISBN: 0-06-024913-7. Sophisticated Chapter Book. (See **5.82, 20.41**)

4.89 Thomas, Jane Resh (1996). **Daddy Doesn't Have to Be a Giant Anymore.** Illustrated by Marcia Sewall. New York: Clarion. 46 pp. ISBN: 0-395-69427-2. Sophisticated Picture Book. (See **5.93**)

Secondary Reviews

4.90 Draper, Sharon (1997). **Forged by Fire.** New York: Atheneum. 150 pp. ISBN: 0-689-80699-X. Sophisticated Chapter Book.

Gerald experiences neglect and abuse as his drug-addicted mother uses nontraditional methods to teach Gerald the hard lessons in life. This brutality is softened by Aunt Queen. Living with her, he experiences the strength and power of love and develops the inner core that will see him through the troubled times ahead. Mature themes make this a book more suitable for older middle-school readers.

4.91 Grove, Vicki (1998). **Reaching Dustin.** New York: Putnam. 199 pp. ISBN: 0-399-23008-4. Sophisticated Chapter Book. (See **5.75**)

4.92 Krantz, Hazel (1997). **Walks in Beauty.** Flagstaff, AZ: Northland. 192 pp. ISBN: 0-87358-667-0. Chapter Book.

This story depicts the life of a contemporary Navajo girl, Anita Whiterock, who encounters and works through issues relating to adolescence, school, family, and culture. The characters are representative of the different generations and perspectives that exist in her family. Her grandfather is the firm traditionalist connected to his land and animals, while her grandmother is more accepting of changes due to progress. Her mother is not handling her divorce well. She would not leave the reservation for the large city, and still values family and tradition, but enjoys country dancing. Her father is the urban Native American living in far-away Albuquerque. Her younger sister is very social and, like her father, prefers a modern life. Anita values education and is a good student, and she relies on her family's traditional teachings to help her through difficult situations. An excellent resource to show the dynamics of modern reservation life.

4.93   Wolf, Bernard (1997). **HIV Positive.** New York: Dutton Children's Books. Unpaged. ISBN: 0-525-45459-4. Sophisticated Picture Book. (See **5.121**)

Family Experiences around the World

See also the section entitled Cultural Traditions in chapter 3, "Exploring Our Past."

Primary Reviews

4.94   Abelove, Joan (1998). **Go and Come Back.** New York: Dorling Kindersley. 177 pp. ISBN: 0-7894-2476-2. Sophisticated Chapter Book. (See **20.50**)

4.95   Ancona, George (1997). **Mayeros: A Yucatec Maya Family.** New York: Lothrop, Lee & Shepard. Unpaged. ISBN: 0-688-13465-3. Picture Book. (See **3.56, 20.51**)

4.96   Breckler, Rosemary (1996). **Sweet Dried Apples: A Vietnamese Wartime Childhood.** Illustrated by Deborah Kogan Ray. Boston: Houghton Mifflin. Unpaged. ISBN: 0-395-73570-X. Picture Book. (See **3.115, 20.22**)

4.97   Carling, Amelia Lau (1998). **Mama and Papa Have a Store.** New York: Dial. Unpaged. ISBN: 0-8037-2044-0. Picture Book.

Carling draws on her own experiences as the child of Chinese immigrants growing up in Guatemala to write *Mama and Papa Have a Store,* her first book. Her story describes a day in the life of a young girl in her parents' general store, located in Guatemala City during the 1940s. The day begins with the clip-clop of the milkman's horse, and ends with the clic-clac of her father's abacus. Throughout the day, the reader experiences the comings and goings of the Spanish- and Mayan-speaking customers and the Chinese-speaking family members through the child's eyes.

Indigenous people from the mountains come to purchase thread for weaving, street vendors take their posts along the sidewalks, and family members reminisce about their hometown in China. Mother prepares an array of traditional Chinese food for lunch, served with warm corn tortillas. "It's neat how there are so many different cultures. I'd like to live there," commented Miranda (age ten). Cultures and languages blend together as delightfully as the details and nuances of Carling's meticulous watercolor and gouache illustrations in this engaging book.

4.98   Dabcovich, Lydia (1997). **The Polar Bear Son: An Inuit Tale.** New York: Clarion. 37 pp. ISBN: 0-395-72766-9. Picture Book.

Lydia Dabcovich has adapted and beautifully illustrated a version of the traditional Inuit tale of Kunikdjuaq, the polar bear. A lonely old woman who has been fending for herself for a long time finds a polar bear cub on the ice and takes him home. She names him Kinikdjuaq, which means "my son." As he grows, he learns to hunt for her and becomes friends with the children in the village. Soon the woman has more than enough to eat and begins to share her wealth with the rest of the villagers. Her neighbors are jealous and Kunikdjuaq must leave. In the end, the bond between mother and son is stronger than the retribution of the villagers. Dabcovich gives a short explanation of Inuit life in the harsh Arctic environment of northern Canada and Alaska. She details how the story of Kunikdjuaq has been told and retold over centuries. Young children can read this easy-to-read picture book, but the story will appeal to readers of all ages.

4.99   Egan, Ted (1998). **The Drover's Boy.** Illustrated by Robert Ingpen. Melbourne, Australia: Lothian. Unpaged. ISBN: 1-887734-52-X. Sophisticated Picture Book. (See **3.61**)

4.100 Fleischman, Paul (1997). **Seedfolks.** Illustrated by Judy Pedersen. New York: HarperCollins. 69 pp. ISBN: 0-06-027471-9. Chapter Book. (See **7.66, 20.54**)

4.101 Garay, Luis (1997). **The Long Road.** Plattsburgh, NY: Tundra. Unpaged. ISBN: 0-88776-408-8. Picture Book. (See **5.126**)

4.102 George, Jean Craighead (1997). **Arctic Son.** Illustrated by Wendell Minor. New York: Hyperion. 32 pp. ISBN: 0-7868-0315-0. Picture Book.

When Luke is born in the Arctic, he is given both an Eskimo and English name as is customary in the Inupiat Eskimo culture. Although Luke, or Kupaaq, is not an Eskimo, he learns to love the adventure and beauty of this land where the sun does not set in summer or rise in winter. As seen through the eyes of her grandson, Jean Craighead George shares insights into the daily life and culture of the Arctic inhabitants. Kupaaq discovers the ways of the Arctic land with the caring guidance of his friend Aalak, who named him. The unique lifestyle of the Inupiat people is sensitively portrayed with much substantive information to inform the reader about this geographic area of the world. The watercolor illustrations recreate the beauty of the colorful Arctic landscapes and wildlife.

4.103 Jiménez, Francisco (1998). **The Circuit: Stories from the Life of a Migrant Child.** Albuquerque, NM: University of New Mexico. 134 pp. ISBN: 0-8263-1797-9. Chapter Book. (See **20.36**)

4.104 Luenn, Nancy (1997). **Nessa's Fish.** Illustrated by Neil Waldman. New York: Aladdin. Unpaged. ISBN: 0-689-81465-8. Picture Book.

Nessa and her grandmother go ice fishing and catch more than they can carry. Before resting for the night, they stack the fish and cover them with stones to keep away the foxes. Unfortunately, Nessa's grandmother becomes ill, and the next day Nessa must care for her grandmother and guard the fish from a fox, a pack of wolves, and a bear! Her family's teachings about these animals help her to calmly and bravely protect the fish that will feed the people in her camp. The simple, pastel illustrations appropriately convey Nessa's care for her grandmother, her respect for nature, and the remoteness of the environment. This book was the winner of the 1997 Parents' Choice Award.

4.105 Parker, David (1998). **Stolen Dreams: Portraits of Working Children.** Minneapolis: Lerner. 112 pp. ISBN: 0-8225-2960-2. Chapter Book. (See **20.15**)

4.106 Springer, Jane (1997). **Listen to Us: The World's Working Children.** Toronto, Canada: Groundwood. 96 pp. ISBN: 0-88899-291-2. Chapter Book. (See **20.17**)

4.107 Stevens, Jan Romero (1997). **Carlos and the Skunk/Carlos y el zorrillo.** Illustrated by Jeanne Arnold. Translated by Patricia Hinton Davison. Flagstaff, AZ: Northland. Unpaged. ISBN: 0-87358-591-7. Picture Book.

Jan Romero Stevens has written another engaging bilingual picture book full of family love, laughter, and wisdom in a friendly Hispanic/Latino community. In this third sequel, Carlos is a little older and is concerned about impressing his good friend Gloria. While boasting he can catch a skunk safely by its tail, Carlos is sprayed with the animal's stench. By washing himself in a bath of tomatoes, he believes he has solved his smelly problem. Later while attending church, he realizes that he has overlooked something: his shoes. The odor wafts through the building causing people to sneeze, cover their noses, and end church services early. Once again, Carlos learns a lesson: "No puedes creer todo lo que te dicen; You can't believe everything you hear." Jan Romero Stevens follows her story with a tasty recipe for tomato salsa. The English version is given a privileged position on the page, followed by an excellent, natural sounding Spanish translation. The rich language and homey wisdom is brought to life in the vividly colored oil illustrations of Jeanne Arnold, in her third collaboration with Stevens.

4.108 Torres, Leyla (1998). **Liliana's Grandmothers.** New York: Farrar, Strauss and Giroux. Unpaged. ISBN: 0-374-35105-8. Picture Book.

Leyla Torres' story about Liliana and her visits with her two grandmothers, one down the street of her New England town and the other in faraway Colombia, is a heartwarming celebration of differences. As the pages alternate between the two locales, Torres describes how Liliana spends time with her equally loving, but very different grandmothers. Even the layout of the pages contributes to the contrasts and similarities of life in these two worlds. When Torres wishes to highlight parallel activities, she lays out both scenes on facing pages. When differences are the focus, each scene merits a double-page spread. For example, when Liliana visits her New England grandmother in the afternoon to read stories together, the illustration begins at the left and crosses the gutter, with text placement in the upper right. On the next double-page spread, we see Liliana taking an afternoon siesta with her Colombian grandmother, and the orientation of text and illustration is opposite that of the previous pages. At the same time, the gently hued watercolors lend cohesiveness to the book and an aura of love that Liliana shares with both older women. The role of the illustrations in this tale was not lost on Emmalisa (age seven), who followed even the most subtle details: "She must love her teddy bear. She takes it with her everywhere she goes." Her careful observations prompted students to take a much closer page-by-page look, and share many personal stories about grandmothers.

4.109 Zamorano, Ana (1996). **Let's Eat!** Illustrated by Julie Vivas. New York: Scholastic. Unpaged. ISBN: 0-590-13444-2. Picture Book.

Ana Zamorano and illustrator Julie Vivas tell the story of Mamá preparing meals for her family. Each day of the week, Mamá asks Antonio to call everyone to the table, and to Mamá's dismay, each day someone cannot come to the table because he or she is busy. Ana Zamorano's predictable text in large font is easy for children in the primary grades to read. The recurring context alternates the Spanish names of popular regional cuisine, while Zamorano repeats the expression "¡Ay qué pena!" ("What a pity!") each time. The children joined in quickly and later made use of this phrase as they reenacted the story in the dramatic play area. Julie Vivas' muted watercolor palette is typical of other stories that she has illustrated. She perfectly captures the expressions on the characters' faces, as well as the diverse range of activity during their busy family meal times. This book would make a fine addition to a text-set about families or illustration techniques.

Secondary Reviews

4.110 Bernhard, Emery (1996). **A Ride on Mother's Back, A Day of Baby Carrying around the World.** Illustrated by Durga Bernhard. New York: Harcourt Brace. Unpaged. ISBN: 0-15-200870-5. Picture Book.

From the rainforest of central Africa to the mountains of Guatemala to the highlands of Papua New Guinea, mothers and fathers hold their babies as they go about their daily work. This delightful book, created by the husband-and-wife team of Emery and Durga Bernhard, shows the reader how parents around the world carry their most precious cargo. Some are cradled in shawls as mothers make tortillas, some ride in slings as fathers search for honey in tall fig trees, and some are cradled in the hoods of mothers' parkas. Colorful full-page gouache paintings on watercolor paper transport the reader around the globe. The author includes notes about the various people and cultures included in the book.

4.111 Choi, Sook Nyul (1997). **Yunmi and Halmoni's Trip.** Illustrated by Karen Dugan. Boston: Houghton Mifflin. Unpaged. ISBN: 0-395-81180-5. Picture Book.

Yunmi travels with her grandmother from their home in New York to her Halmoni's homeland in Korea. Although she is excited about meeting family members, Yunmi becomes concerned that her Halmoni will not want to return with her when she sees how much she is loved and respected. As in the precursor to this book, *Halmoni and the Picnic,* Yunmi's insecurities about her grandmother are put to rest. Gentle watercolor illustrations contribute to intergenerational and intercultural understanding.

> Choi, Sook Nyul (1993). **Halmoni and the Picnic.** Illustrated by Karen M. Dugan. Boston: Houghton Mifflin. 31 pp. ISBN: 0-395-61326-3. Picture Book.

4.112 Ho, Minfong (1996). **Hush! A Thai Lullaby.** Illustrated by Holly Meade. New York: Orchard. Unpaged. ISBN: 0-531-09500-2. Picture Book.

A Thai mother lovingly tucks her child into his hammock, but fears animal noises will prevent his sleep. She confronts a mosquito, lizard, pig, water buffalo, and elephant, pleading with each one to "hush," so her baby can rest. Unbeknownst to his mother, her baby climbs, hides, swings from railings, and crawls back to bed while she is gone. Young children are sure to have stories of their own about being the only one awake in the house.

4.113 Hoyt-Goldsmith, Diane (1998). **Celebrating Chinese New Year.** Illustrated by Lawrence Migdale. New York: Holiday House. 32 pp. ISBN: 0-8234-1393-4. Picture Book. (See **3.205**)

4.114 Kudler, David (1997). **The Seven Gods of Luck.** Illustrated by Linda Finch. Boston: Houghton Mifflin. Unpaged. ISBN: 0-395-78830-7. Picture Book. (See **14.9**)

Life Stages and Milestones

See also the sections entitled Cultural Traditions, Cultural Practices, and Celebrations in chapter 3, "Exploring Our Past," and Death Themes in chapter 5, "Struggle and Survival."

Primary Reviews

4.115 Farmer, Nancy (1996). **A Girl Named Disaster.** New York: Orchard. 309 pp. ISBN: 0-531-08889-8. Sophisticated Chapter Book. (See **5.73**)

4.116 Giff, Patricia Reilly (1998). **Rosie's Big City Ballet.** Illustrated by Julie Durrell. New York: Viking. 73 pp. ISBN: 0-670-87792-1. Chapter Book. (See **11.61**)

4.117 Hest, Amy (1998). **Gabby Growing Up.** Illustrated by Amy Schwartz. New York: Simon & Schuster. Unpaged. ISBN: 0-689-80573-X. Picture Book. (See **8.38**)

4.118 High, Linda Oatman (1998). **Beekeepers.** Illustrated by Doug Chayka. Honesdale, PA: Boyds Mills. Unpaged. ISBN: 1-56397-486-X. Picture Book.

What could be more fun than helping Grandpa take care of his beehives? After donning her beekeeper's garb, the young girl in this story follows Grandpa to the bee yard. Together they care for the hives and marvel as colorful, pollen-laden bees return to the hives. The adventure heightens when a swarm of bees approaches and settles on a branch overhead. For the first time ever, Grandpa hands her the swarm-gathering pole. Ever so carefully, she gently pulls and shakes the branch until the bees head for the hives. With their chores accomplished, they head back to the house. A proud Grandpa proclaims his granddaughter "a fine keeper of bees," and promises her the season's first chunk of honey. The golden glow of Doug Chayka's oil paintings captures the warmth of the special relationship shared by these beekeepers.

4.119 Hobbs, Will (1996). **Far North.** New York: Morrow Junior Books. 226 pp. ISBN: 0-688-14192-7. Chapter Book. (See **5.110**)

4.120 Kroll, Virginia L. (1997). **Butterfly Boy.** Illustrated by Gerardo Suzan. Honesdale, PA: Boyds Mills. Unpaged. ISBN: 1-56397-371-5. Picture Book.

Emilio's parents say that grandfather doesn't understand words anymore, but Emilio knows better. While he is reading to his grandfather out in the yard, Abuelo points his good hand at five butterflies fluttering near their white garage. Emilio and grandfather spend the summer watching butterflies. Emilio eventually is able to get within inches of the butterflies, earning him the nickname Butterfly Boy. Emilio finds the butterflies in a book. They are red admirals, and are attracted to bright white surfaces. Emilio and Abuelo anxiously await the arrival of the butterflies the following spring. Children will enjoy the happy ending to this story about the Butterfly Boy. Suzan uses bold watercolors for his imaginative illustrations of this charming story about the special relationship between a boy and his ailing grandfather.

4.121 Martinez, Victor (1996). **Parrot in the Oven: Mi Vida.** New York: HarperCollins. 216 pp. ISBN: 0-06-447186-1. Chapter Book. (See **20.4**)

4.122 Rylant, Cynthia (1998). **The Islander.** New York: Dorling Kindersley. 97 pp. ISBN: 0-7894-92490-8. Chapter Book.

Daniel Jennings records his boyhood life with his beloved grandfather on the island of Coquille off the coast of British Columbia. Daniel lives with his grandfather after his parents die. Daniel's chance encounter with a mermaid makes him the recipient of a magic key that helps him find injured birds and later an injured girl. When Grandfather dies unexpectedly, his Bible leads Daniel to investigate his family's history. Daniel's search hints that the mermaid is the spirit of Grandfather's sister Anna. During a violent illness, Daniel asks Anna for help, and she sends him a puppy that becomes his family. Daniel falls in love with Franny, the little girl he saved as a young boy. Daniel's story reveals the mystical and spiritual nature of life, and the connections we weave to make us feel whole.

4.123 Savageau, Cheryl (1996). **Muskrat Will Be Swimming.** Illustrated by Robert Hynes. Flagstaff, AZ: Northland. 32 pp. ISBN: 0-87358-604-2. Picture Book.

In this story, Cheryl Savageau (Abenaki/French) draws on her own childhood, when the place that she lived and all who lived there were called "Lake Rats." Her story is told through Jeannie, who fills the void in her life and defends the place that she loves with anger and hatred. Grandpa helps her not only to understand the motives of those who see her as different, but also to understand her own identity. By relating his own experience and the story of his people, Grandpa allows Jeannie to see that her Native American heritage provides her with the strength to stand proud and face the challenges of the outside world. Savageau's story is beautifully told, and demonstrates that stories from and of the past still have relevance for contemporary lives and experiences.

4.124 Sgouros, Charissa (1998). **A Pillow for My Mom.** Illustrated by Christine Ross. Boston: Houghton Mifflin. Unpaged. ISBN: 0-395-82280-7. Sophisticated Picture Book.

Charissa Sgouros tells the poignant story of a young girl whose mother has become seriously ill. The girl misses her mother and the time they shared together reading stories, telling jokes, and playing games. The girl uses scraps of fabric to make a soft pillow to comfort her mother in the hospital. After Mother dies, the pillow serves to comfort the girl when she misses her mother the most. The simple text deals with an emotionally charged event in a reassuring and life-affirming manner. Christine Ross has created lovely color illustrations that convey the sense of loss that the girl experiences, while showing that life goes on even in the face of such adversity.

4.125 Yolen, Jane (1997). **Miz Berlin Walks.** Illustrated by Floyd Cooper. New York: Philomel. Unpaged. ISBN: 0-399-22938-8. Picture Book.

In *Miz Berlin Walks,* Jane Yolen tells the story of her own grandmother, Fanny Berlin. Mary Louise, a young girl of six or seven, watches from her porch each evening as old Miz Berlin walks past, talking or singing to herself. When curiosity gets the better of her, Mary Louise leaves the safety of her porch and follows Miz Berlin who, without missing a beat, launches into one of her fantastic stories. Mary Louise continues to join Miz Berlin and is drawn into the tales she hears. When Miz Berlin dies, the reader is left with the notion that Mary Louise will continue the wonderful storytelling legacy of Miz Berlin. Warm and glowing oil-wash paintings by Floyd Cooper add to Yolen's story of intergenerational friendship and the power of storytelling.

Secondary Reviews

4.126 Carter, Dorothy (1997). **Bye, Mis' Lela.** Illustrated by Harvey Stevenson. New York: Farrar, Straus, and Giroux. 32 pp. ISBN: 0-374-31013-0. Picture Book.

Children often learn many lessons in life at a tender age. They learn that many things that happen in life can be final. This picture book shows in a sweet and loving way that after someone dear dies, we gain comfort by sharing memories about them. These memories keep that person in our hearts. This story shares a young girl's memories about Mis' Lela, who took care of her while her parents worked.

4.127 Garland, Sherry (1998). **My Father's Boat.** Illustrated by Ted Rand. New York: Scholastic. Unpaged. ISBN: 0-590-47867-2. Picture Book.

A Vietnamese immigrant takes his young son out in his boat and teaches him to fish in the tradition of his own father. Vibrant seascapes done in watercolor, acrylics, and chalk provide a breathtaking backdrop for the fishing boat, and extend the mood created by the lyrical text. Love of family and one's life's work across three generations underlies this story that will be enjoyed by older as well as younger readers.

4.128 Scheffler, Ursel (1997). **Grandpa's Amazing Computer.** Illustrated by Ruth Scholte van Mast. Translated by Rosemary Lanning. New York: North-South. 48 pp. ISBN: 1-55858-795-0. Chapter Book. (See **7.41**)

4.129 Wells, Rosemary (1996). **The Language of Doves.** Illustrated by Greg Shed. New York: Dial. Unpaged. ISBN: 0-8037-1472-6. Sophisticated Picture Book.

On her sixth birthday, Julietta's grandfather gives her one of his homing pigeons. He also tells her the story of his life in a monastery orphanage, where he first began training homing pigeons, and how he used that training during the Great War. When Grandfather dies, the dove returns to Julietta with a message from him that will connect her to Grandfather forever. Gold-tone illustrations contribute to the warmth of the story.

Relationships with Others

Primary Reviews

4.130 Bash, Barbara (1996). **In the Heart of the Village: The World of the Indian Banyan Tree.** San Francisco: Sierra Club Books for Children. Unpaged. ISBN: 0-87156-575-7. Picture Book.

The social, political, and ecological significance of the banyan tree to the life of a small village in India is made clear in a highly informative, yet lyrical, narrative text. A brief creation story introduces readers to the origins of the banyan tree, often called the Many-Footed One because its aerial roots become trunks and a single tree may eventually resemble a forest. Details about the interrelationship among animals, plants, and people show the daily life of the tree as a place for nesting, worshipping, bartering, conversing, giggling, jumping, sleeping, and imagining. Vivid watercolor paintings in double-page spreads further illuminate the importance of the tree in rural Indian culture. The presentation of the text in calligraphy generated by the author contributes to the visual appeal of a book that will fascinate readers of all ages who marvel at the wonders of our natural world.

4.131 Eyvindson, Peter (1996). **Red Parka Mary.** Winnipeg, Manitoba, Canada: Pemmican. 42 pp. ISBN: 0-921827-50-4. Picture Book.

Canadian author and storyteller Peter Eyvindson brings to life the story of a seven-year-old boy and his older neighbor Mary in this heartwarming tale of friendship, appreciation, and reciprocal giving. At first he is afraid to even walk by her house, but as time goes by and he gets to know her, the boy's opinion of Mary changes. Mary teaches him many traditional skills, and he begins to appreciate her cultural knowledge. As they trade Christmas presents, he comes to cherish the biggest gift of all. The colorful illustrations and easy-to-read text, make this book easily accessible to readers in preschool through third grade.

4.132 Hunter, Sally M. (1997). **Four Seasons of Corn: A Winnebago Tradition.** Illustrated by Joe Allen. Minneapolis: Lerner. 40 pp. ISBN: 0-8225-2658-1. Picture Book. (See **2.38**)

4.133 Pirotta, Saviour (1997). **Turtle Bay.** Illustrated by Nilesh Mistry. New York: Farrar, Straus and Giroux. Unpaged. ISBN: 0-374-37888-6. Picture Book. (See **2.18**)

4.134 Plain, Ferguson (1996). **Rolly's Bear.** Winnipeg, Canada: Pemmican. Unpaged. ISBN: 0-921827-52-0. Picture Book.

Rolly's Bear is an intergenerational story. Day after day, a young boy watches Rolly, an elder in the village, as he sits on the fourth step of the Community Administration Building. One day, he decides to join Rolly. The story continues as Rolly tells about the time that he shot a bear. Illustrations are printed on deer-hide shapes. The illustrations, which contain elements of realism and mysticism, have a reddish-pink background with black-penned drawings. Ferguson was awarded the 1993 Commemorative Medal for his significant contributions to Canada. Ferguson is an Ojibwe author and artist from the Sarnia Indian Reserve in Ontario. His work is based on the Ojibwe culture.

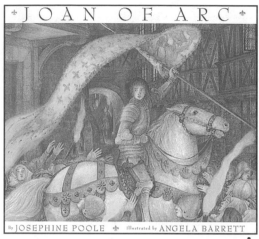

A.

B.

C.

D.

A. *Joan of Arc*, Josephine Poole/Angela Barrett (**5.29**). **B.** *Sarny: A Life Remembered*, Gary Paulsen (**5.114**). **C.** *Sammy's Story*, David Kooharian (**5.140**). **D.** *From Slave Ship to Freedom Road*, Julius Lester/Rod Brown (**5.18**).

5 Struggle and Survival

Jan Keenoy

Joan Von Dras

Susan Wolf

From the beginning of humankind, struggle and survival have been a part of history. The human quest to understand our role on the planet and create an identity has given rise to a diversity of beliefs, cultures, and traditions. These differences have created challenges and struggles within and between groups of people, and within individuals themselves. The collection of books represented in this chapter draws from this diversity, inviting discussion and examination of our mutual relationships, struggles, and survival on this floating sphere we call Earth.

Our review committee discovered that struggle, challenge, and survival have many faces and are present in a variety of scenarios. We decided not to limit ourselves to only the obvious struggles of human versus nature, human versus human, and human versus society, which are so prevalent in elementary-level literature. We sought books that also explored the silent conflicts that involve human versus himself or herself and human versus his or her destiny. We discovered that these conflicts might be experienced by a preschool child as easily as a pre-adolescent or any hero that we might emulate today. We did not, however, abandon the more obvious struggles, for these hardships and challenges play an important role in promoting the strength and survival of the human race.

We selected a variety of books based on the following criteria:

1. *The book had to be well written and easily understood by young readers.* Although the themes of inner struggle that we sought could be obscure and subtle, the words of the author needed to be clear so that they could direct the reader to make inferences and reach conclusions that went beyond the text.

2. *The characters needed to be realistic, authentic, and engaging.* We felt that the theme of struggle and survival could best be tackled if the reader felt a human kinship with the hero or heroine. From this kinship, a relationship of both empathy and sympathy might develop and draw the reader into the story, making the ensuing survival a victory for both the character and the reader.

3. *The book had to have well-paced and efficient action, as well as lively description, that led readers to various high points and mini-climaxes in the story.* We steered away from books with long-winded chapters that did not contain enough turning points to involve the reader. We realized that if the description gets too tedious or no gains are recognizable, the reader can become just an observer and may choose to check out of the struggle altogether.

We maintained an open mind concerning struggle and survival themes, and used a variety of lenses in our exploration of these themes. We discussed the plots, characters, and themes of the books under review, and considered the various ways that teachers and others might categorize books in order to take a critical look at struggle and survival. We chose to organize the books in this chapter around broad topics and themes that we ourselves would use in addressing issues of struggle and survival with our students. Accordingly, the reviews in this chapter have been organized around the following themes: Bigger-than-Life Heroes, Heroines, and Events; Finding One's Own Identity; Rites of Passage; Family Hardship; Making Peace with Family; Catastrophe, Tragedy, and Hardship; Animal Adventures; and Death Themes.

Some of the books reviewed in this chapter contain epic themes of struggle and survival that occur in the context of war, environmental protection, civil rights movements, and enslavement. Other titles relay simple stories of family, neighborhood, friendship, and personal loss that convey equally moving messages about the strength of human courage and the growth that occurs from adversity.

In Bigger-than-Life Heroes, Heroines, and Events, readers will find profiles of individuals who have broken with societal tradition or expectation to pursue what is close to their heart. These role models invite young minds to see the struggles and victories of empowered individuals, and to consider how the lessons learned might influence their own lives.

Many of these individuals discover their own identity in the context of struggling with social, political, personal, or medical issues. Stories of personal growth can be found in the sections entitled Finding One's Own Identity and Rites of Passage. These are stories of breaking away from tradition and establishing a distinct persona, even when the family seems intent on instilling traditional roles and blending characters into the continuum of family history. Each experience proves that the strength to persevere is built upon many small victories—and also that to be saved from the struggle would require being deprived of the victory.

Families provide a strong base of support for individuals struggling with life's challenges, but they also can be a source of contention for individuals. Working together, families often can find the strength necessary to withstand significant hardships such as war, hatred, prejudice, and oppression. Relationships may be either strengthened or severed as the struggle to survive brings clarity to the essence of the human bonds built on trust, respect, and responsibility. Each struggle, whether in the wilderness or in the neighborhood, can lead to enlightenment because the place where courage resides and change takes place is always the same; that place is in the heart. Readers will find stories about family as a source of inspiration and conflict in Family Hardship and Making Peace with Family. In Catastrophe, Tragedy, and Hardship, readers will find individuals, families, and entire communities grappling with some of the worst that life has to offer, including natural disasters, war, and other significant losses.

Some of the most endearing stories of our time capture the incredible journeys and heroic efforts of pets and animals in the wild. These stories of courage, devotion, bravery, and sacrifice offer opportunities for readers to reach inside themselves to find similar qualities. The selections in Animal Adventures contain strong animal characters with the power to touch lives. Many are embroidered with the thread of hope and memory that runs through all stories of struggle. The animal characters are personified with emotions of fear, bravery, love, and dedication that can easily be identified by the young reader. These uncluttered stories invite readers to understand the nature of struggle and survival in simple, direct terms where things almost always end happily ever after.

With many adventures or struggles, death is always one possible outcome. Stories that address the death or near-death of a character allow readers to examine their own feelings and beliefs about death and dying. These feelings and beliefs are grounded in cultural traditions and reflect the diversity of people on our planet. The moving books in Death Themes provide fertile ground for examining the very core of our definitions of life. Death is not treated as defeat in these contexts. Death is a struggle with which each character must reckon. Those who are left behind can conquer the death of a loved one through memories and treasured stories.

Each character in each book has a small story to tell about his or her own struggle for survival. It is through the collective strength demonstrated by these simple struggles for life, peace, happiness, and self-respect that the stories of world-changing heroes and heroines are forged.

In 1945, Franklin D. Roosevelt wrote, "Today we are faced with the preeminent fact that if civilization is to survive we must cultivate the science of human relationships, the abilities of all people of all kinds to live together and work together in the same world at peace" (undelivered speech, on display at the Jefferson National Expansion Museum, St. Louis, Missouri). This statement rings as true today as it has in the past. Literature such as that reviewed in this chapter will keep the past from being forgotten and generate the important conversations, insights, and creative thinking that will enlighten present and future generations of humanity.

---

*The titles listed below each subheading are organized into Primary Reviews and Secondary Reviews. The Primary Reviews describe outstanding books in each subheading. The Secondary Reviews provide brief information about other books worthy of consideration. Some titles listed below are **not** reviewed in this chapter; entries for these titles are not annotated and contain only bibliographic information. In such cases, a cross reference to the annotated entry contained elsewhere in this volume is provided in boldface type at the end of the bibliographic information.*

Bigger-than-Life Heroes, Heroines, and Events

See also the section entitled Histories and Herstories in chapter 3, "Exploring Our Past"; the section entitled Books about Artists in chapter 11, "Fine Arts"; the sections entitled Autobiographies and Biographies in chapter 12, "Sports, Games, and Hobbies"; and the section entitled Biographies and Autobiographies (of Authors, Books, and Characters) in chapter 13, "The Craft of Language."

Primary Reviews

5.1   Antle, Nancy (1998). **Lost in the War.** New York: Dial. 137 pp. ISBN: 0-8037-2299-0. Chapter Book.

Lost in the War is a poignant, often graphic, story of a family trying to find normalcy years after the Vietnam War. Lisa and Jenny's mother is fighting to forget the atrocities and losses from the war. When Lisa's class studies the Vietnam War, the truth about Lisa's parents unfolds and the family transforms as a result. About that same time, the Vietnam Memorial is being dedicated in Washington, D.C. As part of a class art and history project, Lisa also unveils a monument to the war and to her parents. Nancy Antle helps us understand the losses of both those who fought in the war and those who avoided fighting through her well-defined, multi-dimensional characters. This story of love, loss, and going on paints a vivid and historically accurate picture of the Vietnam War and the people who had to deal with its consequences.

5.2 Archer, Jules (1998). **To Save the Earth: The American Environmental Movement.** New York: Viking. 198 pp. ISBN: 0-670-87121-4. Chapter Book.

Archer chronicles the lives, philosophy, and struggles of four prominent environmentalists whose work has impacted the twentieth century. These well-told biographies are followed by a brief history of the environmental movement, a list of current environmental issues, and names and addresses of environmental organizations to join. As readers consider the lives of these four leaders, they can begin to understand how personal conviction and dedication can turn the concerns of individuals into the causes of a generation.

5.3 Cooper, Floyd (1996). **Mandela: From the Life of the South African Statesman.** New York: Philomel. ISBN: 0-399-22942-6. Picture Book.

This gold-toned picture book relates the life of a child named Rolihlahla, who was to be a great leader for his people because he came from a line of great rulers. Although his father was dethroned and his family moved to another village, Rolihlahla was still seen as a child with a promising future. When he started school, he and the other African children were given English names. Rolihlahla's new name was Nelson Mandela. The older Mandela became, the more conscious he became of how unfair the conditions for Blacks were in South Africa. His awareness became so strong that he became active in the African National Congress (ANC). Mandela eventually became a strong voice in the ANC, and because of his stand for justice, he was imprisoned for twenty-seven years. This book takes the reader from the childhood of Rolihlahla and the imprisonment of Nelson Mandela to Mandela's release from prison and his election as president of South Africa.

5.4 Currie, Stephen (1997). **We Have Marched Together: The Working Children's Crusade.** Minneapolis: Lerner. 88 pp. ISBN: 0-8225-I733-7. Chapter Book. (See **3.80**)

5.5   Dash, Joan (1996). **We Shall Not Be Moved: The Women's Factory Strike of 1909.** New York: Scholastic. 165 pp. ISBN: 0-590-48409-5. Sophisticated Chapter Book. (See **20.23**)

5.6   Dillon, Leo, and Diane Dillon (1998). **To Every Thing There Is a Season.** New York: Blue Sky. 34 pp. ISBN: 0-590-47887-7. Picture Book.

Ecclesiastes has never been more beautifully represented than through the timeless art work of Caldecott winners Leo and Diane Dillon. Each turn of the page is a trip through history and culture. The diversity of civilization represented evokes a tapestry of time, from the vessel drawings of Greek civilization to the honor of sacrifice in Aztec culture. This brief yet magnificent march through time is demonstrative of challenges and celebrations that transcend region and time. The simple yet luminous culminating drawing of Earth is supported with the text, "One generation passes away, and another generation comes: but the earth abides for ever." This passage connects humanity's struggle with the cyclic and momentary existence of humans in a parade of time. Hands linked together across the book's end pages show common links through time and the human condition. Ecclesiastes brings an immortal rhythm to the work, a philosophical direction to our lives together, and a sense of what we share as a people across diverse cultures or religions. The Dillons depict ancient cultures and their unique styles of art through varied media, giving authenticity to the time and people they represent. A section at the end presents insight into the origin of each illustration and its meaning.

5.7   Fleming, Candace (1996). **Women of the Lights.** Illustrated by James Watling. Morton Grove, IL: Whitman. 79 pp. ISBN: 0-8075-9165-3. Chapter Book. (See **3.84**)

5.8   Freedman, Russell (1996). **The Life and Death of Crazy Horse.** Photographs by Amos Bad Heart Bull. New York: Holiday House. 144 pp. ISBN: 0-8234-1219-9. Chapter Book.

Using accounts from primary sources and ledger book pictographs that were drawn by a contemporary of Crazy Horse, Freedman has created an intimate portrait of the famous Oglala Sioux warrior. Called "Our Strange One" by his own people, Crazy Horse was indeed a remarkable individual whose greatest achievement was defeating Custer at the Battle of the Little Bighorn in 1876. The author not only tells of Crazy Horse's deeds, but also manages to convey his persona as a boy of dreams and a man of courage. Very few authors today write biographies for young readers with the depth of research that Freedman commits himself to, and his reward to readers is always one of fascinating discoveries and a surprising intimacy with the chosen subject. Included are an annotated bibliography and timeline of events. This book has received numerous awards, including School Library Journal Best Books List for 1997, Booklist's Editors' Choice, NCTBSS, and Teachers' Choice. A must for any school library.

5.9   Gayle, Sharon Shavers (1997). **Kai, A Big Decision, Africa, 1440.** New York: Simon & Schuster. 71 pp. ISBN: 0-689-80990-5. Chapter Book.

The Girlhood Journeys series offers this story of two African sisters who are sent from their village to the king's palace in the big city to seek food for their starving people during a drought. The older sister falls in love with one of the king's young assistants to the court as he helps her prepare the food stores that will be taken to her village. The younger sister discovers the richness of the arts which the big city can provide, helping to develop her talent and interest in sculpture. Both sisters must struggle with their loyalty to their people and their responsibility to family and tradition. They must find a way to be respectful of their background and ties to the village, and also bravely address their own personal needs which the big city and their new acquaintances can best fulfill. The story takes place in 1440, but the theme of struggle and survival is timely today. This book offers a source of discussion for young female readers of the nineties as they plot their own life courses.

5.10 Giff, Patricia Reilly (1997). **Lily's Crossing.** New York: Delacorte. 180 pp. ISBN: 0-385-32142-2. Chapter Book. (See **3.107**)

5.11 Hansen, Joyce (1998). **Women of Hope: African Americans Who Made a Difference.** New York: Scholastic. 32 pp. ISBN: 0-590-93973-4. Picture Book (See **20.12**)

5.12 Hesse, Karen (1997). **Out of the Dust.** New York: Scholastic. 227 pp. ISBN: 0-590-36080-9. Chapter Book. (See **4.48**)

5.13 Hoyt-Goldsmith, Diane (1997). **Buffalo Days.** Illustrated by Lawrence Migdale. New York: Holiday House. 32 pp. ISBN: 0-8234-1327-6. Picture Book.

A terrific photographic portrayal of contemporary Native Americans and their enduring traditional relationship with the American buffalo. Since the nearly endangered buffalo herds were reestablished on the western Plains, native people have become the caretakers and preservers of this animal that has played such a significant role in their culture and lifestyle. Readers are offered a glimpse at how a contemporary, multi-generational Crow family has adapted to technological changes while maintaining family and tribal traditions in their reliance on and care and respect for the buffalo. Hoyt-Goldsmith also gives readers an historical look at the buffalo and its significance to the Crow and other tribes of the region. This author consistently offers her readers an honest and objective look at the individuals about whom she writes, and the quality of this book is comparable to *Pueblo Storyteller, Totem Pole,* and *Day of the Dead: A Mexican-American Celebration.*

> Hoyt-Goldsmith, Diane (1991). **Pueblo Storyteller.** Illustrated by Lawrence Migdale. New York: Holiday House. 30 pp. ISBN: 0-8234-1094-3. Picture Book.

> Hoyt-Goldsmith, Diane (1994). **Day of the Dead: A Mexican-American Celebration.** Illustrated by Lawrence Migdale. New York: Holiday House. 30 pp. ISBN: 0-8234-1094-3. Picture Book.

> Hoyt-Goldsmith, Diane (1994). **Totem Pole.** Illustrated by Lawrence Migdale. New York: Holiday House. 32 pp. ISBN: 08245-1135-4. Picture Book.

5.14 Josephson, Judith Pinkerton (1997). **Mother Jones: Fierce Fighter for Workers' Rights.** Minneapolis: Lerner. 144 pp. ISBN: 0-8225-4924-7. Chapter Book.

Josephson's biography of Mary Harris Jones is a well-researched and documented account of a leading figure in the American labor movement. For six decades, Mother Jones was feisty and unflagging in her efforts to improve conditions among America's poor laborers. Although admired by miners, railroaders, factory workers, and their families, she was also feared and hated by owners. Mother Jones was fiercely devoted to efforts to improve conditions of working families and children. The book includes an author's preface that explains the inclusion of Mother Jones' inconsistent spellings and "peppery words," an index, a list of sources for quotations and historical facts, a bibliography, and photo acknowledgments. Numerous photographs, newspaper headlines, letters, and sketches enhance the narrative. These features of nonfiction writing will help students to grasp the historical context of this intriguing biography of the complex and dynamic Mother Jones.

5.15   Jurmain, Suzanne (1998). **Freedom's Sons: The Story of the *Amistad* Mutiny.** Lothrop, Lee & Shepard. 128 pp. ISBN: 0-688-11072-X. Chapter Book.

Freedom's Sons is the extraordinary story of a successful slave revolt. Fearing for their lives, fifty-three Africans aboard the Cuban slave ship *Amistad* revolted and killed the captain and other captors. Thinking they were headed back to Africa, the inhabitants of the ship—led by the charismatic leader, Cinque—zigzagged across the ocean until they were close to death. Finally in August of 1839, they landed in New York where slavery was illegal. Unfortunately they were apprehended and moved to Connecticut, a slave state, where they were turned over to federal officials. After many court battles, in which they were represented by former president John Quincy Adams, they were finally granted their freedom by the Supreme Court. This is a remarkable story of courage, perseverance, heroism, and victory at a time when most African Americans had no legal rights.

5.16   Katz, William Loren (1997). **Black Indians: A Hidden Heritage.** New York: Simon & Schuster. 198 pp. ISBN: 0-689-80901-8. Chapter Book.

This historical account for young readers gives comprehensive insight into the role of African Native Americans. A group often omitted from the history books, African Native Americans are those who have dual African American and Native American ancestry. Included within this historical overview are fascinating biographies of leaders, army scouts, frontiersmen, and outlaws. The stories of these individuals, which stretch from the earliest European landings to pioneer days, highlight the author's detailed research into the history of various groups and specific individuals. The struggles of African Native Americans during the settling of the West are poignantly told as they search for freedom, land, and identity. Likewise insight is provided into African American slavery, as the book describes situations both before and after the emancipation of slaves. A much-needed perspective is provided in this book, which is illustrated with authentic photographs and early sketches.

5.17   Krull, Kathleen (1996). **Wilma Unlimited: How Wilma Rudolph Became the World's Fastest Woman.** Illustrated by David Diaz. New York: Harcourt Brace. Unpaged. ISBN: 0-15-201267-2. Picture Book.

The life of Wilma Rudolph is an inspiring story of perseverance and inner strength despite overwhelming obstacles. Who could have imagined that the child doctors believed would never walk would become the first woman to win three medals in a single Olympics? Neither the life-threatening childhood illnesses, including polio, nor the crushing oppression of segregation could break Rudolph's will to run and drive to compete. This beautifully illustrated book by David Diaz uses brown-tone photos as borders and acrylics, watercolor, and gouache on watercolor paper to visually carry us back to the childhood of Wilma Rudolph. The author's choice of words serves to make a lasting impression about this young person's journey to succeed despite all odds.

5.18   Lester, Julius (1998). **From Slave Ship to Freedom Road.** Illustrated by Rod Brown. New York: Dial. 37 pp. ISBN: 0-8037-1893-4. Sophisticated Picture Book.

Inspired by the artwork of Rod Brown, Julius Lester has written a unique book about slavery. Intense, almost surreal, Brown chronicles slavery from the departure of a people from Africa to the eventual freedom of an enslaved race. Lester allows the reader to experience the perspective of slave and oppressor through the use of "imagination exercises" that relate first-hand the horror, violence, and humiliation of slavery and the strength, dignity, and honor of an oppressed people. Lester has used the power of Brown's work to discuss honestly and simply a period of history that must be told in order to foster the continued empowerment of a people and teach a lesson about the tragedy of inhumanity to others. As one young reader put it, "It really makes me think and puts me in their place."

5.19   Levy, Marilyn (1996). **Run for Your Life.** Boston: Houghton Mifflin. 217 pp. ISBN: 0-395-74520-9. Sophisticated Chapter Book. (See **20.37**)

5.20 Lorbiecki, Marybeth (1997). **My Palace of Leaves in Sarajevo.** Illustrated by Herbert Tauss. New York: Dial Books. 53 pp. ISBN: 0-8037-2033-5. Chapter Book.

Letters from Nadja to her cousin Alex in Minnesota reveal the story of Nadja's immersion in the terrible war in Bosnia. The letters, based on first-hand accounts of interviews and experiences with Bosnian refugees, chronicle the disintegration of a peaceful city into a war zone filled with hatred and human cruelty. Amidst all of this is young Nadja, who communicates the impact that living amidst warfare has on her life and her family. Writing the letters to Alex is cathartic to her, and in turn the care packages and letters from Alex help Nadja and her family maintain hope through hard times. The book's afterword gives the reader a brief history of the roots of this conflict in the aftermath of World War II. Additionally there is a glossary to aid with pronunciation and meaning, as well as addresses to which to send care packages. This is a book that reminds the reader to recognize that no nation is truly free of the potential for war, and to cherish peace.

5.21 Lorbiecki, Marybeth (1998). **Sister Anne's Hands.** Illustrated by K. Wendy Popp. New York: Dial Books for Young Readers. Unpaged. ISBN: 0-8037-2038-6. Picture Book. (See **20.3**)

5.22 Lowry, Linda (1996). **Wilma Mankiller.** Illustrated by Janice Lee Porter. Minneapolis: Carolrhoda. 56 pp. ISBN: 0-87614-880-1. Chapter Book.

This book conveys the spirit of Wilma Mankiller almost as well as her own autobiography, *Mankiller*, striking at the issues faced by the first woman chief of the Cherokee Nation. Matriarchal tribes don't necessarily encourage women to participate in the political arena, but Mankiller took on the challenge. Her strength and pride in her heritage are reflected in the political decisions she makes and in her sense of oneness with her people. Wilma Mankiller's personal struggles, and her growth as a result of these struggles, serve as an inspiration for all people, native and non-native. The glossary contains a timeline of significant dates in Cherokee history, as well as in the life of Mankiller. The colorful illustrations and easy-to-read text make this book accessible to elementary-level readers.

Mankiller, Wilma, and Michael Wallis (1993). **Mankiller.** New York: St. Martin. 320 pp. ISBN: 0-312-20662-3. Chapter Book.

5.23   McCully, Emily Arnold (1996). **The Bobbin Girl.** New York: Dial Books for Young Readers. 34 pp. ISBN: 0-8037-1827-6. Sophisticated Chapter Book. (See **3.42, 20.30**)

5.24   Meltzer, Milton (1998). **Ten Queens: Portraits of Women of Power.** Illustrated by Bethanne Andersen. New York: Dutton Children's Books. ISBN: 0-525-45643-0. 134 pp. Chapter Book.

Ten courageous women, leaders in their own civilizations over a two-thousand-year span of time, are revealed through the well-researched stories by Meltzer. From Cleopatra to Catherine the Great, the personalities, relationships, and impact of these phenomenally strong individuals help write women back into history and give readers a perspective on leadership and power not dictated by gender, but by intelligence and strength. This would be an empowering book to use in a discussion and comparison of feminism throughout recorded history.

5.25   Mitchell, Margaree King (1997). **Granddaddy's Gift.** Illustrated by Larry Johnson. Mahwah, NJ: BridgeWater. Unpaged. ISBN: 0-8167-4010-0. Picture Book. (See **20.27**)

5.26   Mochizuki, Ken (1997). **Passage to Freedom: The Sugihara Story.** Illustrated by Dom Lee. New York: Lee & Low. Unpaged. ISBN: 1-880000-49-0. Picture Book. (See **20.28**)

5.27   Parks, Rosa, with Gregory Reed (1996). **Dear Mrs. Parks: A Dialogue with Today's Youth.** New York: Lee & Low. 112 pp. ISBN: 1-880000-45-8. Chapter Book. (See **3.97**)

5.28   Pippen, Scottie, with Greg Brown (1996). **Scottie Pippen: Reach Higher.** Illustrated by Doug Keith. Dallas, TX: Taylor. 40 pp. ISBN: 0-87833-981-7. Picture Book. (See **12.2**)

5.29   Poole, Josephine (1998). **Joan of Arc.** Illustrated by Angela Barrett. New York: Knopf. 31 pp. ISBN: 0-679-89041-6. Picture Book.

The miraculous story of Joan of Arc comes to life in a tale written for young readers. The strength and determination of this young woman who courageously departs on a divine mission is an inspiration to young girls, and a confirmation to young boys that the course of history has been influenced by strong individuals of both genders. Joan's selfless mission to liberate Orleans from the English and crown the King of France at Rhiems is supported with artwork that mimics a tapestry from days of old. A map of the region on the end pages provides geographic information about Joan of Arc's struggles. Although it ends in cruel tragedy, Joan's story communicates that the sacrifice of one individual can contribute dramatically to the course of humankind.

5.30 Ryan, Pam Muñoz (1998). **Riding Freedom.** Illustrated by Brian Selznick. New York: Scholastic. 138 pp. ISBN: 0-590-95766-X. Chapter Book. (See **3.48**)

5.31 Schroeder, Alan (1996). **Minty: A Story of Young Harriet Tubman.** Illustrated by Jerry Pinkney. New York: Dial Books for Young Readers. Unpaged. ISBN: 0-8037-1889-6. Picture Book. (See **3.14**)

5.32 Shaughnessy, Diane (1997). **Pocahontas: Powhatan Princess.** New York: PowerKids. Unpaged. ISBN: 0-8239-5106-5. Picture Book.

Diane Shaughnessy's version of the well-known story of Pocahontas expands somewhat on the life of this precocious ten-year-old. Young readers are offered images of the Powhatan people and their way of life before contact with the first early English settlers, including Captain John Smith. They learn that a natural curiosity may have led Pocahontas to become the communication mediator between her people and the English. The author portrays the English desire for land and wealth against the constant possibility of starvation as the backdrop for John Smith's rescue from death by Pocahontas. They also learn that Pocahontas was a victim of captivity. It was during her captivity that Pocahontas became acculturated to the ways of her captors, taking the dress, language, and religion of the English. Her marriage to her English caretaker, John Rolfe, may have worked to improve the relationship between the Powhatans and English. Pocahontas, renamed Lady Rebecca, next traveled to the homeland of the English settlers. Although well-received by the English people, she died of smallpox, a disease unknown among her people. Today she is honored in America for her efforts in helping the English establish permanent settlements in America.

Other PowerKids Press biographies include:

Shaughnessy, Diane (1997). **Sequoyah: Inventor of the Cherokee Written Language.** New York: PowerKids. Unpaged. ISBN: 0-8239-5110-3. Picture Book.

Shaughnessy, Diane (1997). **Sitting Bull: Courageous Sioux Chief.** New York: PowerKids. Unpaged. ISBN: 0-8239-5109-X. Picture Book.

Shaughnessy, Diane, and Jack Carpenter (1997). **Chief Joseph: Nez Perce Peacekeeper.** New York: PowerKids. Unpaged. ISBN: 0-8239-5111-1. Picture Book.

Shaughnessy, Diane, and Jack Carpenter (1997). **Chief Ouray: Ute Peacemaker.** New York: PowerKids. Unpaged. ISBN: 0-8239-5108-1. Picture Book.

Shaughnessy, Diane, and Jack Carpenter (1997). **Sacajawea: Shoshone Trailblazer.** New York: PowerKids. Unpaged. ISBN: 0-8239-5106-5. Picture Book.

5.33 Stanley, Diane (1996). **Elena.** New York: Hyperion. 55 pp. ISBN: 0-7868-0256-1. Chapter Book. (See **3.15**)

5.34 Swain, Gwenyth (1996). **The Road to Seneca Falls: A Story about Elizabeth Cady Stanton.** Illustrated by Mary O'Keefe. Minneapolis: Carolrhoda. 64 pp. ISBN: 0-87614-947-6. Chapter Book. (See **3.50**)

5.35 Walker, Sally M. (1998). **The 18 Penny Goose.** New York: HarperCollins. 61 pp. ISBN: 0-06-027557-X. Chapter Book.

This I Can Read Book tells a true story of the American Revolution that has been handed down by the descendants of young Letty Wright, a New England farmgirl in 1778. Letty and her family are forced to abandon their homestead in rural New Jersey because the British are raiding the local inhabitants to assert their control in the region. Letty is able to leave her belongings, but she cannot bear to think of her gander, Solomon, being harmed by the Redcoats while she is away. She writes the soldiers a note, asking them to spare the gander's life when they come upon Letty's family farm. Letty's family returns after the raids and the damage to Letty's farm is discouraging, but the message the soldiers leave is memorable and warm. This book for young readers is divided into four skillfully sequenced chapters that present an historically accurate scenario that is well told, interesting, and easy to understand.

5.36 Weate, Jeremy (1998). **A Young Person's Guide to Philosophy.** Illustrated by Peter Lawman. New York: Dorling Kindersley. 64 pp. ISBN: 0-7894-3074-6. Sophisticated Picture Book.

"Why are we here? What does it mean to be human?" Humankind has grappled with such questions for over three thousand years. Philosophers such as Thales, Socrates, and De Beauvoir spent their lives puzzling over universal ideas, and in the process influenced societal views, religious ideology, the sciences, and history itself. These individuals challenge our minds and bring about dialogue as we consider the larger questions of humanity. This book engages young readers in learning about these significant individuals and their ideas through well-developed introductions supported by pictures and diagrams. This is a wonderful book to add to a classroom collection.

Secondary Reviews

5.37 Bruchac, Joseph (1998). **The Heart of a Chief.** New York: Dial Books for Young Readers. 153 pp. ISBN: 0-8037-2276-1. Chapter Book.

This story deals with Native American gaming and sports logos that use images of Native American culture. Bruchac, of Abenaki heritage, chose to tell the story on a fictitious reservation so as not to cause conflict with any specific tribe. Chris Nicola, a young Penacook boy, leaves the reservation to attend a public school where the sports logo is the Chiefs. At football games, war cries and tomahawk chants are used to cheer the team to victory. Chris is troubled by this, and seizes the opportunity to take up the issue for a school report and presentation. His leadership skills and agreeable personality are demonstrated by his ability to work with non–Native American children, and he is able to make a difference at school and in his own life. This coming-of-age story is told with a sensitivity that only an insider to Native American culture can deliver.

5.38 Collins, David R. (1996). **Farmworker's Friend: The Story of Cesar Chavez.** Minneapolis: Carolrhoda. 80 pp. ISBN: 0-87614-982-4. Chapter Book.

Intermediate readers who want to know more about the farmworkers' labor movement will enjoy this moving biography of Cesar Chavez. Seven chapters detail specific events in this hero's life, from his early days as a migrant laborer with his family, through the years of community organization and the development of the United Farm Workers union, to his death as a result of his political activism. Black-and-white photographs portray Chavez and his labor movement in journalistic style. Complete with a list of contents, notes, a bibliography, and an index, this book is an excellent biographical source for teachers and older students, and a must for every middle-school library.

5.39   Cooney, Barbara (1996). **Eleanor.** New York: Viking. Unpaged. ISBN: 0-670-86159-6. Picture Book.

Eleanor Roosevelt is one of the "most remarkable and influential women this country has ever known." In this beautiful picture book, Cooney chronicles Roosevelt's triumphs. Always a shy, timid child, she was sent to live with her grandmother after being orphaned at age nine. Although her family was wealthy, it did not provide a happy or congenial setting for children. When Eleanor was sent to boarding school in England, she finally found people who truly cared about her and she began to realize her true potential. Throughout her remarkable life, Eleanor Roosevelt never forgot the poor and disadvantaged. This biography is illustrated in Cooney's colorful style with meticulous attention to detail.

5.40   Fuller, Sarah Betsy (1998). *Hazelwood v. Kuhlmeier:* **Censorship in School Newspapers.** Springfield, NJ: Enslow. 128 pp. ISBN: 0-89490-971-1. Chapter Book.

This book is part of the Landmark Supreme Court Cases series. In this case, students sued the Hazelwood School District on the grounds that their First Amendment rights had been trampled when the principal of their school would not print two pages of articles about the sensitive issue of teen pregnancy. The case was taken to the Supreme Court, where four years later a decision was made in favor of the school district.

5.41   Ganeri, Anita (1996). **The Young Person's Guide to the Orchestra.** Compact disc narrated by Ben Kingsley. San Diego: Harcourt Brace. 56 pp. ISBN: 0-15-201304-0. Picture Book. (See **11.20**)

5.42   Matas, Carol (1997). **The Garden.** New York: Simon & Schuster Books for Young Readers. 102 pp. ISBN: 0-689-80349-4. Chapter Book.

Ruth Mendelson, a survivor of the Buchenwald concentration camp, tells how she dealt with the death of her friends and enemies in bringing about the birth of the state of Israel. Much of the book shows how Mendelson and her friends transform their minds to kill the Arabs who are trying to make them leave their newfound homeland. They look at their sorrowful past where they lost so much of their family to the Nazis, and consider Israel their only hope for the future.

5.43   McCully, Emily Arnold (1998). **Beautiful Warrior: The Legend of the Nun's Kung Fu.** New York: Scholastic. Unpaged. ISBN: 0-590-37487-7. Picture Book.

The title page opens with a dramatic view of a village in China. Within the village, the reader is introduced to an aristocratic family of the Ming Emperor. As the dynasty is attacked, the Emperor's young daughter—who was well educated despite the attitudes toward women at the time—leaves the palace walls to find refuge in a Shaolin monastery. Impressed by her martial art ability, the monks—who are skilled in kung fu—welcome her to the monastery. They name her Wu Mei, which means beautiful warrior. So unfolds the true story of a strong young woman whose legacy is passed on to a young girl in trouble. This wonderful tale of strength and inner-balance discovered through meditation and self-reflection is inspiring. Gentle watercolor illustrations by the author create a sense of the serenity of nature, as well as the drama of peril. This is not only a tale of personal growth, but also a message of control of one's own destiny.

5.44   Morey, Janet Nomura, and Wendy Dunn (1996). **Famous Hispanic Americans.** New York: Cobblehill. 190 pp. ISBN: 0-525-65190-X. Chapter Book.

This collective biography is a good resource for intermediate students who are seeking information on Hispanic Americans who have made positive contributions to our society. The book contains chapters on fourteen different people who represent Hispanic cultures throughout the Americas and an interesting variety of professions including sports, politics, fashion, theater, education, business, science, and entertainment. Fully half of the biographies are about women. Each chapter is approximately twelve to fifteen pages in length, and is written so that the reader has an understanding of the significance of the featured person. The black-and-white photographs and an index enhance this book.

5.45   Nivola, Claire A. (1997). **Elisabeth.** New York: Farrar, Straus and Giroux. 32 pp. ISBN: 0-374-32085-3. Sophisticated Picture Book.

In this beautiful picture book, war is seen through the eyes of a child. A young girl is forced to flee the Nazis during World War II without her special doll, Elisabeth, or any other possessions. Years later through her own daughter, she is miraculously reunited with her doll.

5.46   Philip, Neil, editor (1997). **In a Sacred Manner I Live: Native American Wisdom.** New York: Clarion. 93 pp. ISBN: 0-395-84981-0. Chapter Book.

This edited book is a collection of speeches or portions of speeches that have been made by Native Americans. The speakers or writers range from Chief Powhatan in 1609, to the contemporary Sioux medicine man Leonard Crow Dog in 1995. The editor points out that although there are huge differences among the Native American people represented, they all live in a sacred manner. All Native American nations live with respect for the environment, for the community, and for themselves. Black-and-white photographs accompany each speech. Each has a brief caption describing a Native American tradition or offering information about the speaker. Complete text and picture sources are listed, as well as suggestions for further reading.

5.47   Pryor, Bonnie (1996). **The Dream Jar.** Illustrated by Mark Graham. New York: Morrow Junior Books. Unpaged. ISBN: 0-688-13062-3. Picture Book. (See **3.45**)

5.48   Zaunders, Bo (1998). **Crocodiles, Camels and Dugout Canoes: Eight Adventurous Episodes.** Illustrated by Roxie Munro. New York: Dutton. 48 pages. ISBN: 0-525-45858-1. Chapter Book.

Motivated by the adventures of explorers, Zaunders composed a collection of adventures less commonly known. Each story begins with an interesting experience the explorer had, and then reveals the person's personality and the background that led to the adventure. This is a nice twist on the male-dominated topic of exploration.

Finding One's Own Identity

See also the sections entitled Cultural Traditions: Cultural Practices and Celebrations in chapter 3, "Exploring Our Past," and Learning about Self within a Classroom Context in chapter 6, "School Life."

Primary Reviews

5.49   Bloor, Edward (1997). **Tangerine.** San Diego: Harcourt Brace. 294 pp. ISBN: 0-152-01246-X. Chapter Book. (See **13.50**)

5.50   Bruchac, Joseph (1997). **Eagle Song.** Illustrated by Dan Andreasen. New York: Dial Books for Young Readers. 80 pp. ISBN: 0-8037-1919-1. Chapter Book.

Danny Bigtree's transition from the Mohawk Reservation on the U.S.-Canadian border to Brooklyn, New York, shows the difficulties experienced by a fourth-grade student in bridging the cultural gaps of living in two worlds. Making friends in a new school is never easy, but Danny is plagued by stereotypes of Native Americans because of his long black hair. "Hey, Chief, going home to your teepee?" is the kind of remark this young boy faces on a daily basis. How he deals with this cruel teasing and manages to turn the situation around is a central issue in this book. Joseph Bruchac, of Abenaki/Slovak heritage, illustrates the influence of storytelling through the character of Danny's father. Bruchac also stresses the importance of self-esteem, and he credits his own grandfather with helping him gain his self-esteem in his autobiography, *Bowman's Store.* In *Eagle Song,* all the children are winners.

> Bruchac, Joseph (1997). **Bowman's Store: A Journey to Myself.** New York: Dial. 311 pp. ISBN: 0-8037-1997-3. Chapter Book.

5.51   Cushman, Karen (1996). **The Ballad of Lucy Whipple.** New York: Clarion. 195 pp. ISBN: 0-395-72806-1. Chapter Book.

Arvella Whipple moves from Massachusetts to Lucky Diggins, California, in 1849 and opens a boardinghouse. The widow and her three children—Sierra, Butte, and twelve-year-old California Morning—all struggle to make a new life amidst the harsh realities of the mining camp. Book-loving California Morning longs to return to Massachusetts, and resists her mother's domineering manner by changing her name to Lucy Whipple. This exuberant story told through the eyes of Lucy presents two strong, determined, and independent women and a cast of ragged, rough-hewn characters. The tall tales, yarns, and rich vernacular language that fill the book make it a wonderful read-aloud: "Dag diggety! Git yer carcass off'n my claim afore I bury my shovel in yer yella hair, you diggety dog. Spyin' on me!" The novel reflects much recent historical research that highlights the roles that women played in settling the West.

5.52 Dines, Carol (1997). **Talk to Me: Stories and a Novella.** New York: Delacorte. 223 pp. ISBN: 0-385-32271-2. Sophisticated Chapter Book; adult mediation required. (See **20.53**)

5.53 Egan, Ted (1998). **The Drover's Boy.** Illustrated by Robert Ingpen. Melbourne, Australia: Lothian. Unpaged. ISBN: 1-887734-52-X. Sophisticated Picture Book. (See **3.61**)

5.54 Hesse, Karen (1996). **The Music of Dolphins.** New York: Scholastic. 181 pp. ISBN: 0-590-89797-7. Chapter Book. (See **4.10**)

5.55 Keegan, Marci (1997). **Pueblo Boy.** New York: Viking. Unpaged. ISBN: 0-14-36945-7. Picture Book.

Reprinted in paperback, this contemporary biography gives young readers an intimate portrait of a young boy growing up on the San Ildefonso Pueblo in New Mexico. This photographic essay contains many color photos showing the boy engaged in social, family, and school situations that are typical for most children growing up in the United States today, as well as many activities that are unique to Native Americans living on reservations. A sincere and genuine portrait of a Native American boy growing up and managing the influences of two distinctive cultures in his life.

5.56 Matcheck, Diane (1998). **The Sacrifice.** New York: Farrar, Straus and Giroux. 224 pp. ISBN: 0-374-36378-1. Sophisticated Chapter Book. (See **3.41**)

5.57 Savageau, Cheryl (1996). **Muskrat Will Be Swimming.** Illustrated by Robert Hynes. Flagstaff, AZ: Northland. 32 pp. ISBN: 0-87358-604-2. Picture Book. (See **4.123**)

5.58 Thomassie, Tynia (1996). **Mimi's Tutu.** Illustrated by Jan Spivey Gilchrist. New York: Scholastic. Unpaged. ISBN: 0-590-44020-9. Picture Book. (See **11.60**)

5.59 Voigt, Cynthia (1996). **Bad Girls.** New York: Scholastic. 278 pp. ISBN: 0-590-60134-2. Chapter Book. (See **6.31**)

5.60 Wilson, Nancy Hope (1997). **Old People, Frogs, and Albert.** Illustrated by Marcy D. Ramsey. New York: Farrar, Straus and Giroux. 58 pp. ISBN: 0-374-35625-4. Chapter Book. (See **20.56**)

6.61 Wolff, Virginia E. (1998). **Bat 6.** New York: Scholastic. 256 pp. ISBN: 0-590-89799-3. (See **20.43**)

5.62 Wyeth, Sharon Dennis (1998). **Something Beautiful.** Illustrated by Chris K. Soentpiet. New York: Bantam Doubleday Dell. 30 pp. ISBN: 0-385-32239-9. Picture Book. (See **8.64, 20.8**)

Secondary Reviews

5.63 Bruchac, Joseph (1996). **Children of the Longhouse.** New York: Dial Books for Young Readers. 150 pp. ISBN: 0-8037-1793-8. Chapter Book.

Bruchac captures the essence of adolescent rivalry relevant in today's society. Feelings of insecurity and the need for power and recognition lead a fifteen-year-old Mohawk boy to seek revenge on a younger boy who overheard a conversation that was sure to destroy peace among the neighboring tribes. The younger boy, Ohkwa'ri, and his twin sister go to see their grandmother, who is the Clan Mother and perhaps the most important person in their Iroquois Clan Longhouse. Ohkwa'ti tells his story, and a council meeting soon follows. Quiet confrontation takes place here between the two boys, eventually leading to self-discovery and strength of character. A game of lacrosse, which originated with the Iroquois, is the means by which the boys are tested. Bruchac creates a story historically referenced in Longhouse society, and stresses the importance of oral tradition in teaching values, traditions, and about life in general. The novel also presents a strong picture of women in Iroquois society, source material for an interesting discussion of women's roles today.

5.64 Campbell, Ann Jeanette (1998). **Dora's Box.** Illustrated by Fabian Negrin. New York: Knopf. 30 pp. ISBN: 0-679-87642-1. Picture Book.

"What if you had a box in which you could put everything evil and sad in the world?" So opens this tale of a young couple who want to shield their daughter, Dora, from all the pain in the world. In their attempt to create a world of only happiness and pleasure, they gather into the box all those things that might bring her pain and sadness, such as the sharp thorns from a bush or the sad tears of another child. Dora discovers the box and releases its contents, just as Pandora did. In the end, parents and child appreciate that one cannot know good without knowing evil, or truly appreciate joy without sorrow.

5.65   Curtis, Gavin (1998). **The Bat Boy & His Violin.** Illustrated by E. B. Lewis. New York: Simon & Schuster. 27 pp. ISBN: 0-689-80099-1. Picture Book. (See **4.6**)

5.66   Gerstein, Mordicai (1998). **The Wild Boy.** New York: Farrar, Straus and Giroux. 40 pp. ISBN: 0-374-38431-2. Chapter Book. (See **3.63**)

5.67   Hines, Anna Grossnickle (1998). **My Own Big Bed.** Illustrated by Maru Watson. New York: Greenwillow. 30 pp. ISBN: 0-688-15599-5. Picture Book.

Hines has written a delightful book for young children about the challenge and excitement of moving from crib to bed. Watson's heartwarming illustrations of a beautiful young child make her seem alive within the pages. For each challenge the bed confronts her with she has a remedy that begins with "I can fix that!" The book closes with the advantages of having Daddy read bedtime stories and Mommy tuck in. This is a splendid look at the little struggles young children encounter, and can be used as a point of discussion about what other challenges are encountered as we grow.

5.68   London, Jonathan (1998). **At the Edge of the Forest.** Illustrated by Barbara Firth. Cambridge, MA: Candlewick. Unpaged. ISBN: 0-7636-0014-8. Picture Book.

Snowy illustrations surround a story of a young boy and his family as they contend with life on a farm tending their livestock. When their sheep become threatened by a coyote, the father decides it is time for him to shoot the animal. The young boy discovers a den of coyote pups, and when his father sees that the coyote was just trying to feed its own family, he lowers the barrel of the gun. The message of this story is that all animals have families they need to support and that peaceful alternatives to solving a problem need to be examined.

5.69   Mazer, Harry (1998). **The Wild Kid.** New York: Simon & Schuster. 103 pp. ISBN: 0-689-80751-1. Chapter Book. (See **4.86**)

5.70   Schami, Rafik (1996). **Fatima and the Dream Thief.** Illustrated by Els Cools and Oliver Streich. New York: North-South. Unpaged. ISBN: 1-55858-653-9. Picture Book. (See **14.35**)

Rites of Passage

See also the sections entitled Cultural Traditions: Cultural Practices and Celebrations in chapter 3, "Exploring Our Past," and Life Stages and Milestones in chapter 4, "Families."

Primary Reviews

5.71   Bunting, Eve (1998). **Your Move.** New York: Harcourt Brace. Unpaged. ISBN: 0-15-200181-6. Sophisticated Picture Book.

In this story, a ten-year-old African American boy named Isaac wants to "hang out and do cool stuff" with a group called the K-Bones. Isaac must prove himself by pulling off a risky task that the Bones come up with. When an older gang of boys shows up with a gun, Isaac and his younger brother run. Isaac's decision not to join the group, and the lack of pressure from Kris, the K-Bones representative, leaves the door open to lots of "what if" scenarios that can provide opportunities for classroom discussion. Themes of trust, divorce, being home alone, gangs, vandalism, and guns abound in this beautiful picture book. The phenomenal true-to-life illustrations by James Ransome in oil paint on watercolor paper bring this story to life. (See also **20.33**)

5.72   Dorris, Michael (1996). **Sees Behind Trees.** Illustrated by Linda Benson. New York: Hyperion. 104 pp. ISBN: 0-7868-0224-3. Chapter Book.

A disability is not a handicap but rather an opportunity to find the talents one has to grow, build self-esteem, and become a responsible human being. Dorris, of Modoc heritage, illustrates this message in a coming-of-age story. A young Native American boy named Walnut cannot see like others his age, and fears that he will not pass the shooting test required before he is given his adult name. However his mother discovers his problem and teaches Walnut to develop his sense of hearing, which eventually earns him the name Sees Behind Trees. Experiences with the *weroance*, a revered woman of the village, and her twin brother Gray Fire teach Sees Behind Trees the skills to survive on his own, the values and traditions of his culture, and the responsibilities of adulthood. This is a story to which adolescents of all cultures can relate.

5.73 Farmer, Nancy (1996). **A Girl Named Disaster.** New York: Orchard. 309 pp. ISBN: 0-531-08889-8. Sophisticated Chapter Book.

Nhamo, or "Disaster," is an eleven-year-old Shona girl who escapes her village in Mozambique rather than marry "a diseased man with several wives." She flees alone to Zimbabwe in search of her father. Nhamo's journey is a harrowing and marvelous one during which her physical toughness and emotional strength are severely tested. She is guided by luminous spirits, pilots a crude canoe over long stretches of water, encounters a witch, and lives among a herd of baboons. Nhamo's indomitable spirit and courage make the novel a natural companion to *Julie of the Wolves* and *Island of the Blue Dolphins.* This rite-of-passage adventure ends happily with Nhamo embarking upon a new life. The spirit of her grandmother whispers to her, "We have a long way to go." The list of characters, map, glossary, and historical and cultural notes aid the reader in traversing the foreign territory of the novel.

> George, Jean Craighead (1972). **Julie of the Wolves.** New York: HarperCollins. 192 pp. ISBN: 0-06-021943-2. Chapter Book.

> O'Dell, Scott (1960). **Island of the Blue Dolphins.** New York: Houghton Mifflin. 192 pp. ISBN: 0-395-06962-9. Chapter Book.

5.74 Fields, T. S. (1997). **Danger in the Desert.** Flagstaff, AZ: Northland. 126 pp. ISBN: 0-87358-666-2. Chapter Book.

The terrain of the hot Arizona desert is the focus of much of the action and thrill of the plot in this adventure story. Two brothers, Robbie and Scott, are kidnapped at gunpoint by a frightening man who plans to kill them eventually. Instead he dumps them in the desert, far away from civilization and any help. These two boys learn to use their wits in order to survive the terrible heat, flash floods, poisonous critters, and lack of food and water.

Although Robbie and Scott do not get along at the story's beginning, they realize they must work together to live through this ordeal. Children were highly motivated to read the story because of the book cover, although the snake depicted there and in the interior illustration does not match the description given in the text. This book was chosen by school children as one of the Arizona Young Reader Award books for 1998.

5.75 Grove, Vicki (1998). **Reaching Dustin.** New York: Putnam. 199 pp. ISBN: 0-399-23008-4. Chapter Book.

Carly, set on winning the job of editor of the class newspaper, takes on the task of interviewing Dustin Groat, the class behavior problem. She soon realizes there's a reason Dustin has given up on school, and she makes a concerted effort to reach out to him—especially when she discovers that something she did in third grade contributed to his problems. When Dustin's family takes up arms against the government, Carly's family becomes involved in ways they never dreamed of, trying to help both Dustin and his sister. This is a powerful coming-of-age book that should provoke conversations about bullies, outcasts, and gun control.

5.76 Johnson, Angela (1998). **Songs of Faith.** New York: Orchard. 103 pp. ISBN: 0-531-30023-4. Chapter Book.

Thirteen-year-old Doreen tells her story of life in a divorced family in Ohio during the summer of 1975 from her thoughtful, observant, and often poignant point of view. "Everyone's going when I really need them to just stay put," she says. Eventually she comes to terms with her divorced father in Chicago, her mother who is going to school, her friend Viola who has moved to Connecticut, and her older brother Bobo who stops talking. Her mother, who is working diligently on her master's degree, makes time to teach Doreen to have faith in love. She says, "You can't tear this kind of love away. Love and Faith. That's all it is." This is a story of love, faith, and the strength to keep going.

5.77 Konigsburg, E. L. (1996). **The View from Saturday.** New York: Simon & Schuster. 163 pp. ISBN: 0-689-80993-X. Chapter Book. (See **6.48**)

5.78 Martinez, Victor (1996). **Parrot in the Oven: Mi Vida.** New York: HarperCollins. 216 pp. ISBN: 0-06-447186-1. Chapter Book. (See **20.4**)

5.79 McKissack, Patricia C. (1997). **Run Away Home.** New York: Scholastic. 160 pp. ISBN: 0-590-46751-4. Chapter Book.

This historical novel is set in the 1880s, a time when the Apaches are being relocated and white supremacist groups continue to threaten African Americans in the south. McKissack, a master storyteller, connects these two events in this finely woven book. Sarah Crossman is an eleven-year-old girl who has both African American and Native American ancestry. She spots Sky, an Apache boy, escaping from a train bound for a reservation in Florida. Having heard the horror stories of slavery, Sarah is determined not to turn the boy in. With the help of Sarah's mother, Sky is nursed back to health, and everyone—including her dog Buster—is smitten with him. When the family is about to lose their farm, Sarah comes up with an idea and Sky pulls them through. The closed-mindedness of the nation and the open-mindedness of Sarah's family is a powerful contrast in this exceptional book. McKissack weaves into the narrative a speech given by Booker T. Washington, the famous Black educator, that shows how the members of one community were brought together through their experiences with terrorizing night riders, the un-celebration of the Fourth of July, and the infestation of boll weevils on their farmlands.

5.80 Paterson, Katherine (1998). **Parzival: The Quest for the Grail Knight.** New York: Lodestar. 127 pp. ISBN: 0-525-67579-5. Chapter Book. (See **14.53**)

5.81 Snyder, Zilpha Keatley (1998). **Gib Rides Home.** New York: Delacorte. 247 pp. ISBN: 0-385-32267-4. Chapter Book.

In tribute to the memory of her father who grew up in a Nebraska orphanage and was farmed out to neighboring ranches, Zilpha Keatley Snyder has written a moving account of an orphan boy's story in the early 1900s. Orphaned at age six, Gib Whittaker moves in to the Lovell House Home for Orphaned and Abandoned Boys. Until he's eleven, he hangs on to his "hope dream" of belonging to a real family. He learns that his friend Georgie has been farmed out and might even be dead from the poor treatment he has received. Gib too is farmed out to a family that knew his family, but that has secrets that prevent Gib from belonging and feeling comfortable. His love of horses and Livy keep him going.

This is a heartbreaking story of a determined, bright, caring boy looking for a home and a family to love him.

5.82   Spinelli, Jerry (1997).**Wringer.** New York: HarperCollins. 228 pp. ISBN: 0-06-024913-7. Sophisticated Chapter Book.

What does it take to be a real man? A real boy? In the town of Waymer during the annual Pigeon Day Festival, men shoot thousands of pigeons as a fundraiser, and boys wring the necks of the wounded birds. Boys become wringers when they are ten years old, but nine-year-old Palmer does not want to be a wringer. He is torn between his disgust over the event and peer pressure to conform. His confusion grows greater after he takes in a pigeon as a pet. This rite-of-passage tale explores the courage to resist local norms and societal pressure to do what one believes to be wrong. The moral dilemmas raised will promote intense classroom discussion. (See also **20.41**)

5.83   Swarthout, Glendon, and Kathryn Swarthout (1997). **Whichaway.** Flagstaff, AZ: Northland. 104 pp. ISBN: 0-87358-675-1. Sophisticated Chapter Book.

This coming-of-age adventure story is set in the rough deserts of Arizona during the early half of this century. The main character is a fifteen-year-old boy named Whichaway, whose father is a tough, unemotional rancher who expects the same rugged attitude from his only son. However the boy more closely resembles his mother, an educated pioneer school teacher who had a tenderness for animals and life before her untimely death. Whichaway decides to prove to his father that he is worthy of respect by riding solo out on the ranch to repair the windmills. Unfortunately he is injured by a dust devil while working on the windmill platform, and left stranded there with two broken legs. Trapped on the windmill, he is witness to cattle rustlers and shot at by a crazy prospector. During this time, he decides how to help himself survive and reflects on his relationship with this father. In the end, Whichaway realizes his true inner strengths and comes to terms with his life. Originally published in 1966, this adventure story is an exciting book to read, with an interesting main character who undergoes changes and becomes a young man by the end. There are some colorful western expressions and cowboy lingo that may need clarification for readers, but that add much to the authenticity of the setting.

Secondary Reviews

5.84 Grimes, Nikki (1998). **Jazmin's Notebook.** New York: Dial. 102 pp. ISBN: 0-8037-2224-9. Chapter Book.

Set in the 1960s in Harlem, *Jazmin's Notebook* is rich in both language and plot. Jazmin, a fourteen-year-old African American girl, fills her notebook with her own poetry and tells of her close calls with death, sex, and drugs. Jazmin lives with her sister because her mother is hospitalized in a state mental institution and her father is dead. Jazmin deals in an open-eyed and embracing way with the problems of living with her sister, living in a rough neighborhood, trying not to be too nerdy, and coming-of-age. Nikki Grimes weaves strong figurative language into this beautiful and chaotic story of a girl fighting and succeeding on her way to adulthood.

5.85 Klass, Sheila Solomon (1997). **Uncivil War.** New York: Holiday House. 162 pp. ISBN: 0-8234-1329-2. Chapter Book.

Asa Anderson is challenged by her overweight body, and by the cute new boy in her class who constantly makes fun of her. Asa rises to the occasion and uses her brains to fight back. She learns a lot about why her mother is so overprotective when her baby sister is born premature like she was. This book provides a rich context for discussing peer problems, family issues, and being overweight.

Family Hardship

See also the section entitled Controversial Issues in Family Life in chapter 4, "Families," and Perspectives on Life Inside and Outside of the Classroom Context in chapter 6, "School Life."

Primary Reviews

5.86 Balgassi, Haemi (1996). **Peacebound Trains.** Illustrated by Chris K. Soentpiet. New York: Clarion. 48 pp. ISBN: 0-395-72093-1. Picture Book. (See **3.114**)

5.87 Breckler, Rosemary (1996). **Sweet Dried Apples: A Vietnamese Wartime Childhood.** Illustrated by Deborah Kogan Ray. Boston: Houghton Mifflin. Unpaged. ISBN: 0-395-73570-X. Picture Book. (See **3.115, 20.22**)

5.88 Bunting, Eve (1996). **Going Home.** Illustrated by David Diaz. New York: Cotler. Unpaged. ISBN: 0-06-026296-6. Picture Book. (See **4.4, 20.1**)

5.89 Fleischman, Paul (1997). **Seedfolks.** Illustrated by Judy Pedersen. New York: HarperCollins. 69 pp. ISBN: 0-06-027471-9. Chapter Book. (See **7.66, 20.54**)

5.90 Friedrich, Elizabeth (1996). **Leah's Pony.** Illustrated by Michael Garland. Honesdale, PA: Boyds Mills. Unpaged. ISBN: 1-56397-189-5. Picture Book. (See **3.29**)

5.91 Lachtman, Ofelia Dumas (1997). **Call Me Consuelo.** Houston, TX: Arte Publico. 149 pp. ISBN: 1-55885-187-9. Chapter Book.

When twelve-year-old Consuelo's parents both die in a car accident, she is sent to the United States to live with her American grandmother. Although Consuelo's mother was Mexican and her father American, she has lived her entire life in Mexico. She desperately misses her Mexican friends, warm tortillas, menudo, and her Spanish language. Consuelo resents the attempts of her grandmother to make her feel comfortable, and dreams of returning to live in Mexico. However once Consuelo meets some children her own age, she finds adventure and excitement in her new surroundings as the children try to solve the mysterious disappearance of household items from the neighborhood. By the story's end, they discover the culprit and Consuelo finds a new home for herself in America. This book is nicely formatted with a print size that is appealing to young readers, and simple blackline sketches scattered throughout that add a subtle, friendly feeling to the story. This is a sweet, fun story for children and offers the reader a strong and delightful Mexican American heroine.

5.92 Pryor, Bonnie (1996). **The Dream Jar.** Illustrated by Mark Graham. New York: Morrow Junior Books. Unpaged. ISBN: 0-688-13062-3. Picture Book. (See **3.45**)

5.93 Thomas, Jane Resh (1996). **Daddy Doesn't Have to Be a Giant Anymore.** New York: Houghton Mifflin. 46 pp. ISBN: 0-395-69427-2. Picture Book.

Jane Resh Thomas tells this story from the perspective of a young daughter who is facing the family struggles that result from her father's alcoholism. The little girl tells the reader of the happy times her family has at the beach, and contrasts those with the scary times when her father drinks whisky from a brown bag in the garage and frightens her with accusations that she is spying on him. The story tells of a family intervention where each member of the circle of family and friends confronts the girl's father with the problems that his drinking has caused in their relationships. Finally the little girl is asked to speak and she is fearful she will enrage her father, who has already produced a load of excuses for everyone else for his behavior. She simply tells him that he scares her when he shouts and shakes her, and all she wants is to sit on the porch and count fireflies with him. The story ends on a hopeful note, with her father participating in treatment and returning with the strength and resolve to not drink. This book would be helpful to young readers who are living in similar situations. It also would be beneficial as a literature extension for alcohol awareness programs because it illustrates the power of addiction and the impact that it has on family and friends.

Secondary Reviews

5.94   Hest, Amy (1997). **When Jessie Came across the Sea.** Illustrated by P. J. Lynch. Cambridge, MA: Candlewick. Unpaged. ISBN: 0-7636-0094-6. Picture Book. (See **3.34**)

5.95   Kent, Deborah (1997). **The Only Way Out.** New York: Scholastic. 185 pp. ISBN: 0-590-54081-5. Chapter Book.

Faced with another round of chemotherapy after recovering from a previous battle with Hodgkin's disease, seemingly shy fourteen-year-old Shannon embarks on a journey to find Sister Euprasia, a healer. As she travels to New Orleans, she meets a variety of people and has experiences which help her realize her own determination and inner strength. She comes to terms with her illness when she discovers that sometimes you have to go through struggles in order to become victorious over what challenges you.

5.96   Mora, Pat (1997). **Tomas y la señora de la biblioteca.** Illustrated by Raúl Colón. New York: Dragonfly. Unpaged. ISBN: 0-679-80401-3. (See **20.39**)

5.97   Rodriguez, Luis J. (1997). **América is Her Name.** Illustrated by Carlos Vasquez. Willimantic, CT: Curbstone. Unpaged. ISBN: 1-880684-40-3. Picture Book. (See **20.7**)

Making Peace with Family

See also chapter 4, "Families."

Primary Reviews

5.98 Billingsly, Franny (1997). **Well Wished.** New York: Simon & Schuster. 170 pp. ISBN: 0-689-81210-8. Chapter Book. (See **14.40**)

5.99 Creech, Sharon (1997). **Chasing Redbird.** New York: Harper-Collins. 261 pp. ISBN: 0-06-02698-7. Chapter Book.

Newbery Medal–winner Sharon Creech's book, *Chasing Redbird*, is a beautifully written, thought-provoking story of Zinnia Taylor, an independent thirteen-year-old girl. Zinnia has too many brothers and sisters, and spends a lot of time in the "Quiet Zone" at her Uncle Nate and Aunt Jessie's home. Uncle Nate and Aunt Jessie's daughter, Rose, died when Rose and Zinnia were little. Uncle Nate deals with this terrible loss by spending time in a special place where he can remember little Rose. When Aunt Jessie dies, Uncle Nate and Zinnia must each find their own way of dealing with their grief and of chasing their memories of "Redbird." Zinnia works through her grief by spending ten days alone clearing a mysterious trail—a trail that leads her to a boy named Jake, answers about family mysteries, and a deeper understanding of the love between parents and the love of a parent for a child. Shannon, a fifth-grade student, said she liked the "mystery and romance" in Creech's book.

5.100 Fox, Paula (1997). **Radiance Descending.** New York: Dorling Kindersley. 101 pp. ISBN: 0-7894-2467-3. Chapter Book. (See **20.2**)

5.101 Holt, Kimberly Willis (1998). **My Louisiana Sky.** New York: Henry Holt. 132 pp. ISBN: 0-8050-5251-8. Chapter Book. (See **4.66**)

5.102 Ingold, Jeanette (1996). **The Window.** New York: Harcourt Brace. 179 pp. ISBN: 0-15-201264-8. Chapter Book.

Fifteen-year-old Mandy survives an automobile accident that kills her mother, but she is left blind and without immediate family in the wake of the wreck. Although her own mother had been put up for adoption at birth, the detective work of the social services agency allows Mandy to be placed in the home of her mother's uncles, in the large rural house in which Mandy's maternal grandmother had lived as a girl. Mandy is plagued from the start by the confusion of her identity that resulted from the impulsive and unsettled childhood she experienced with her loving but unstable mother, her recent blindness, and the mystery behind her true family, which she is just beginning to unravel in her new environment. The plot is complicated by "visions" Mandy has as she stands before the attic window of her bedroom. Mandy simultaneously witnesses and experiences the emotions and adolescent crises of her maternal grandmother so that even in the darkness that envelops her, she begins to see the complexity of life, fate, and personal choice. In this story of self-revelation, Ingold incorporates a realistic backdrop with her depiction of the special education modifications for the blind at Mandy's high school, and Mandy's evolving friendship with people who accept her physical challenge and encourage her to move forward to a more enlightened life than she ever embraced as a sighted person. This book is a rich source of discussion for preadolescents and young teens who are struggling with judgmental, shallow evaluations of the family members who have impacted their lives.

5.103 Lee, Milly (1997). **Nim and the War Effort.** Illustrated by Yangsook Choi. New York: Farrar, Straus and Giroux. Unpaged. ISBN: 0-374-35523-1. Picture Book. (See **3.109**)

5.104 Mackel, Kathy (1997). **A Season of Comebacks.** New York: Putnam. 116 pp. ISBN: 0 -399-23026-2. Chapter Book.

In *A Season of Comebacks*, Molly resents the attention her older, talented sister Allie is getting from everyone in Brookdale, but especially from her father. Molly's father, who is Allie's baseball coach, will do just about anything to give Allie the winning season she deserves. When Allie's catcher is incapacitated and no other catcher is willing or able to handle the job, things fall into place and both the family and the team find out what is really important.

Catastrophe, Tragedy, and Hardship

Primary Reviews

5.105 Breckler, Rosemary (1996). **Sweet Dried Apples: A Vietnamese Wartime Childhood.** Illustrated by Deborah Kogan Ray. Boston: Houghton Mifflin. Unpaged. ISBN: 0-395-73570-X. Picture Book. (See **3.115, 20.22**)

5.106 Bunting, Eve (1998). **So Far from the Sea.** Illustrated by Chris K. Soentpiet. New York: Clarion. 30 pp. ISBN: 0-395-72095-8. Picture Book. (See **3.105, 20.9**)

5.107 Cha, Dia (1996). **Dia's Story Cloth.** Illustrated by Chue Cha and Nhia Thao Cha. New York: Lee & Low. Unpaged. ISBN: 1-880000-34-2. Picture Book. (See **3.78**)

5.108 Dolphin, Laurie (1997). **Our Journey from Tibet: Based on a True Story.** Photographs by Nancy Jo Johnson. New York: Dutton Children's Books. 40 pp. ISBN: 0-525-45577-9. Picture Book. (See **3.198**)

5.109 Garner, Alan (1998). **The Well of the Wind.** New York: Dorling Kindersley. 43 pp. ISBN: 0-7894-2519-X. Chapter Book.

This is a simple tale of two infant children who are netted by a fisherman as they float in a crystal box adrift in the sea. The fisherman dies and the two children must fend for themselves, which they do quite well until a wicked witch begins to meddle in their affairs. The witch tempts the boy child with promises of silver springs that offer continuous quenching of the thirst without the continuous fetching of water. She also lures him with reports of acorns of gold that will take care of the children's needs forever. All goes well until the brother goes to the Well of the Wind to fetch the magic white feathers that the witch has promised him. When he does not return, the sister sets out on a perilous adventure to find her brother. Her courage, perseverance, and love help her to rescue her brother and to win the precious diamond from the Well of the Wind. The surprise ending rewards the two of them not just for their courage, but also for their honesty and generosity. This tale is filled with rich visual images and action, and the abstract and poetic illustrations offer a source of discussion for young readers.

5.110 Hobbs, Will (1996). **Far North.** New York: Morrow Junior Books. 226 pp. ISBN: 0-688-14192-7. Chapter Book.

Gabe has relocated himself at a boarding school in the Northwest Territories of Canada to be near his father. Gabe's dad is a speculator who makes his living working the various Canadian booms—oil, gold, and diamonds—while Gabe lives back in Texas with his grandparents. Raymond Providence, a Native Canadian from a remote Dene village, is Gabe's reluctant and emotionally distant roommate. When Gabe's dad arranges for him to tour the scenic highlands of the Northwest Territories with a bush pilot, Gabe feels that he is finally going to see the country that has lured him and his dad away from their home in the United States. Gabe is shocked to discover that Raymond and his elderly uncle Johnny Raven are also scheduled to fly the bush plane, because Raymond is quitting school to return to the Dene village. When the plane experiences engine trouble and the pilot is swept away into Virginia Falls, Gabe, Raymond, and Johnny Raven must survive the brutal "hammer" of cold arctic winds, ice, and snow that grip the Northwest Territories in November. Through their combined struggle, Gabe discovers friendship as Raymond begins to identify with his Dene heritage instead of fighting it. Johnny Raven, aged and feeble, is invigorated by the demands of the wilderness and is rejuvenated as he passes on to the younger generation the Dene culture and survival ethic. This story integrates the development of the characters with the geography and weather conditions of the Canadian Northwest, creating stunning visual images of ice, canyons, rapids, and frozen waterfalls that place the young reader at the scene. The definition of survival is demonstrated on several literal and symbolic levels.

5.111   London, Jonathan (1998). **Hurricane!** Illustrated by Henri Sorensen. New York: Lothrop, Lee & Shepard. Unpaged. ISBN: 0-688-08117-7.

Drawing from his own life experiences as a "navy brat" living in Puerto Rico, London captures the closeness of family and community that can arise from disaster. From the beaches to the mountainous rain forests of El Yunque, we sense the increasing force of the storm as two young boys race from their snorkeling, through their hurricane preparations, to the shelter. Our Puerto Rican reviewer found some problems with this part of the story, noting, "It's almost impossible that these two kids were playing at the beach, diving in pretty weather, and when they got back to the surface, the sky was black, and suddenly the hurricane was over them." She assured us that people of this island country are informed well in advance of such dangerous storms and are safely tucked away in shelters by the time they arrive. Nevertheless, the story is exciting and Sorensen's watercolors heighten the sense of danger. One primary teacher displayed posters of Winslow Homer's Bahamian hurricane scenes during the reading of this book. The children noticed the similarity in style, composition, and subject, and were sure that Sorenson must have been familiar with Homer's work. We also were struck by the diversity of faces among these Caribbean people, reflecting the variety of appearances that is normal among such a racially mixed population.

5.112 Myers, Walter Dean (1999). **Monster.** Illustrated by Christopher Myers. New York: HarperCollins Juvenile. 281 pp. ISBN: 0-06-028077-8. Chapter Book.

This contemporary novel-as-screenplay relates the experiences of sixteen-year-old Steve Harmon, who is incarcerated and on trial for felony murder. The format of the novel is that of a reading movie—literally a visual "replaying" of Harmon's experiences that depicts the atmosphere of the courtroom, his conversations and experiences within the jail cell, the testimony of witnesses, and Harmon's own thoughts. The word *monster* rings out in Harmon's head as he questions his own behavior.

Notes:
I couldn't sleep most of the night after the dream.
The dream took place in the courtroom. I was trying
To ask questions and nobody could hear me. I was
Shouting and shouting but everyone went about their
Business as if I wasn't there. I hope I didn't
Shout out in my sleep.

5.113 Parker, David (1998). **Stolen Dreams: Portraits of Working Children.** Minneapolis: Lerner. 112 pp. ISBN: 0-8225-2960-2. Chapter Book. (See **20.15**)

5.114 Paulsen, Gary (1997). **Sarny: A Life Remembered.** New York: Delacorte. 97 pp. ISBN: 0-385-32195 -3. Chapter Book. (See **3.111**)

5.115 Sachar, Louis (1998). **Holes.** New York: Farrar, Straus and Giroux. 233 pp. ISBN: 0-374-33265-7. Chapter Book. (See **13.55**)

5.116 Shahan, Sherry (1998). **Frozen Stiff.** New York: Delacorte. 151 pp. ISBN: 0-385-32303-4. Chapter Book.

What began as a short camping and kayaking experience in the Alaskan wilderness turns into a survival adventure for two teenage cousins, Cody and Derek. After losing a kayak and part of their supplies, they realize that this is not the worst part. An advancing glacier is flooding the fjord, and although they are paddling, they are getting nowhere. On top of that they sense that something is following them. When Cody is blinded by the sun, Derek goes for help. Cody follows Derek and can't believe what she discovers. Both Derek and Cody are changed forever as a result of this experience outside of their comfort zone. This suspenseful story allows the reader to appreciate this wild, majestic area.

5.117 Shange, Ntozake (1997). **Whitewash.** Illustrated by Michael Sporn. New York: Walker. Unpaged. ISBN: 0-8027-8490-9. Sophisticated Picture Book.

How would it feel to be painted white so you could see what a real "American" was like? Helene-Angel is whitewashed and her older brother Mauricio is beaten up by a white gang in this powerful story by Ntozake Shange. Even after the paint has been washed off, Helene-Angel says, "I could still see it. I could still taste fear in the back of my throat." Embarrassed and broken, Helene-Angel stays in her room until her grandmother demands that she come out. As she opens her bedroom door, her friends coax her to join them and pledge to stick together so "no one will dare bother you or anybody else." This emotion-laden book of trauma and triumph is beautifully illustrated by Michael Sporn, with art from the Carnegie Medal-winning video. (See also **20.16**)

5.118 Springer, Jane (1997). **Listen to Us: The World's Working Children.** Toronto, Canada: Groundwood. 96 pp. ISBN: 0-88899-291-2. Chapter Book. (See **20.17**)

5.119 Tunnell, Michael O., and George W. Chilcoat (1996). **The Children of Topaz: The Story of a Japanese-American Internment Camp, Based on a Classroom Diary.** New York: Holiday House. 74 pp. ISBN: 0-8234-1239-3. Picture Book.

During World War II, a Japanese American teacher and her students kept a diary of their life in a relocation camp in Topaz, Utah. Facsimiles of their actual diary entries are accompanied by black-and-white photographs of the camp as well as background information placing the children's experiences in the context of the times. The children's everyday-life interests and concerns are contrasted with the historical details about families being uprooted, torn apart, and imprisoned. Use this book with Yoshiko Uchida's well-told *Journey to Topaz.*

> Uchida, Yoshiko (1971). **Journey to Topaz: A Story of the Japanese-American Evacuation.** Illustrated by Donald Carrick. New York: Scribner. 149 pp. ISBN: 0-684-12497-1. Chapter Book.

5.120 Walter, Virginia (1998). **Making Up Megaboy.** Illustrated by Katrina Roeckelein. New York: Dorling Kindersley. 64 pp. ISBN: 0-0-7894-2488-6. Sophisticated Chapter Book. (See **20.55**)

5.121 Wolf, Bernard (1997). **HIV Positive.** New York: Dutton Children's Books. Unpaged. ISBN: 0-525-45459-4. Sophisticated Picture Book.

Wolf's remarkable photo essay focuses on the life of Sara, a young single mother who has been diagnosed with AIDS. Sara's ultimate decision to live her life as fully as she can impacts the lives of her two children, Jennifer and Anthony. Through intimate and unflinching photographs that cover a number of months, Wolf realistically captures the disappointments and agonies of AIDS as well as the healing, restorative power of love and family relationships. The book is warmly realistic rather than preachy, drawing a complex and strong picture of Sara and her struggles.

5.122 Yee, Paul (1996). **Ghost Train.** Illustrated by Harvey Chan. Emeryville, CA: Douglas & McIntyre. Unpaged. ISBN: 0-88899-257-2. Picture Book. (See **4.61**)

Secondary Reviews

5.123 Bledsoe, Lucy Jane (1997). **Tracks in the Snow.** New York: Holiday House. 152 pp. ISBN: 0-8234-1309-8. Chapter Book.

Erin's best friends are her pets, so she is particularly attracted to her off-beat, artistic babysitter Amy, who claims all of the creatures in the woods outside of town to be her pets. When Amy fails to appear for a Thursday babysitting job with Erin, Erin is determined to solve the mystery of Amy's disappearance and to disprove her parents' theory of Amy's irresponsibility. She uses an animal footprint project with an unsuspecting work partner from school to gain parental permission to search the woods outside town. An unpredicted blizzard traps the work partners in the maze of the forest, and Erin must trust her intuition, her love of Amy, and her survival skills to bring them through this danger. Erin gains confidence in her convictions and discovers her ability to develop personal relationships with people and not just pets in this story of friendship, problem-solving, and self-development.

5.124 Cornelissan, Cornelia (1998). **Soft Rain: A Story of the Cherokee Trail of Tears.** New York: Delacorte. 115 pp. ISBN: 0-385-32253-4. Sophisticated Chapter Book. (See **3.116**)

5.125 Curlee, Lynn (1998). **Into the Ice.** New York: Houghton Mifflin. 40 pp. ISBN: 0-395-83013-3. Chapter Book.

Into the Ice is a fabulous book about the often treacherous exploration of the Arctic area. From the Inuits who first crossed the Bering landbridge through the first flights into the Arctic, Curlee chronicles those who sought adventure, fame, information, and/or wealth. The book provides a dramatic vision of these explorers and the tremendous obstacles they had to battle every step of the way.

5.126 Garay, Luis (1997). **The Long Road.** Plattsburgh, NY: Tundra. Unpaged. ISBN: 0-88776-408-8. Picture Book.

Drawing on his own experiences since leaving Nicaragua, Garay tells the story of a boy's difficult journey to another country. When civil war disrupts and threatens their lives, José and his mother are forced to flee their home. They walk north in search of refuge from the political unrest plaguing their homeland, taking buses and a plane once they reach the border. When they finally reach their destination in Canada, they encounter many new experiences, both frightening and encouraging. A shelter helps José's mother find work and a place to live. Once José starts school, they settle quickly and happily into their new lives. The heavily textured artwork lends visual authenticity to this warm, but overly optimistic story of the immigrant experience.

5.127 Johnson, Rebecca L. (1997). **Braving the Frozen Frontier: Women Working in Antarctica.** Minneapolis: Lerner. 112 pp. ISBN: 0-8225-2855-X. Chapter Book. (See **1.17**)

5.128 McCully, Emily Arnold (1997). **Starring Mirette and Bellini.** New York: Putnam. Unpaged. ISBN: 0-399-22636-2. Picture Book.

This sequel to the Caldecott Medal winner *Mirette on the High Wire* takes the new high-wire partners, Bellini and Mirette, on tour around the world. In the original story, Mirette helps Bellini overcome his fear of falling as he instructs Mirette on the skills necessary to cross the tightrope. In this sequel, Mirette and Bellini are performing in Russia during the tyrannical rule of the czar. The two performers are saddened and outraged by the hopeless plight of the Russian people. When Bellini is at the height of their high-wire act, he encourages the suffering Russian people by publicly announcing that they will someday be as free as he is above them on the tightrope. Bellini is arrested, and Mirette must make a courageous walk across the high-wire to aid in Bellini's escape from the Russian prison. This story mixes Russian history with the spirit and courage of Bellini and Mirette and their high-wire act. The soft, fuzzy illustrations set against the stark, impoverished background of stony cold Russia will make a lasting impression on young readers who are learning of czarist Russia for the first time.

> McCully, Emily Arnold (1992). **Mirette on the High Wire.** New York: Putnam. Unpaged. ISBN: 0-399-22130-1. Picture Book.

5.129 Napoli, Donna Jo (1996). **Trouble on the Tracks.** New York: Scholastic. 190 pp. ISBN: 0-590-13447-7. Chapter Book.

Thirteen-year-old Zach and his younger sister Eve are traveling an Australian train route called the Legendary Ghan into the central bush country. Their mother, an anthropologist on a research trip to the continent down under, has arranged for the children to travel unaccompanied on the two-day pleasure excursion while she studies the remains of an aboriginal settlement. The siblings find themselves in danger when they discover two men smuggling an endangered cockatoo aboard the train. They are thrown from the train, marooned temporarily in the desert, picked up by a pirated train, and involved in the chase and apprehension of the smugglers all in the same day. This engaging and humorous adventure acquaints young readers with the geography of Australia and the peculiar expressions of Australian English in a conversational and brisk style that moves quickly through this action-packed story.

Animal Adventures

Primary Reviews

5.130 Brenner, Barbara, and Julie Takaya (1996). **Chibi: A True Story from Japan.** Illustrated by June Otani. New York: Clarion. 63 pp. ISBN: 0-395-69623-2. Picture Book.

The bright illustrations of watercolor-and-ink tell the true story of a Spotbill duck who moves into the middle of downtown Tokyo to make a home for her family. She and her ten fluffy ducklings survive the sometimes harsh realities of the urban city with the help of Mr. Sato, an elderly photographer, and the other caring people of Tokyo. This book contains additional information and facts on the pages following the story.

5.131 Hansen, Brooks (1997). **Caesar's Antlers.** New York: Farrar, Strauss and Giroux. 218 pp. ISBN: 0-374-31024-6. Chapter Book.

Caesar's Antlers contains two stories of struggle and survival that demonstrate the universal truths about such experiences, no matter who is involved. Caesar is a Norwegian reindeer who has been entrusted with a special mission by the herdsmen who respect him above all the other reindeer. He is to search for two missing brothers from the tribe who have been on a hunt but have not returned in time for the winter migration—a sure sign that something is wrong. He is harnessed with a sleigh filled with supplies should he find the brothers in peril in the deep woods. The other story is one of love and loss. Two sparrows who have mated for life in the deep woods are separated when the male sparrow dives at a colorful object he wishes to retrieve for his newborn young. The object is on a windowsill of a house, and the sparrow does not realize that the glass will obstruct the dive and injure him. He is rescued by a schoolgirl who is at the house for a visit, and she sneaks him in her baggage and takes him back to her school faraway to recuperate. When the reindeer passes through the woods, the female sparrow enlists Caesar's antlers as a nesting place so that she can travel the same woods on her search, while tending to her newborn young. The story demonstrates the responsibility and passion for life and love that must be factored into any struggle. Interesting characters are met along the way as the male sparrow attempts to learn to fly with the geese in order to wing his way back to the deep woods, and the reindeer must fend off the dangerous natural predators that seek to harm him and his sparrows in their search. In the end, Brooks Hansen employs a magical scene that captures in a metaphorical dream the essence of hope that motivates perseverance in creatures of all shapes and sizes, no matter what the quest. This book offers engaging concepts for literature discussion, both in its realistically portrayed struggles and in its fanciful special effects which lead to its grand climax.

5.132 Johnson, Paul Brett, and Celeste Lewis (1996). **Lost.** Illustrated by Paul Brett Johnson. New York: Orchard. Unpaged. ISBN: 0-531-08851-0. Picture Book.

Get out the tissues and be prepared for tears and lots of lost dog stories when children hear this story about a girl's search in the desert for Flag, her pet beagle. The story opens as the young girl narrator and her father begin their search by following tracks at a water hole. Johnson and Lewis present a text filled with hope and desperation, as the pair of protagonists begin each weekend's quest on an upbeat note and end their search on Sunday afternoons in dejection. The search goes on for a month, and fortunately for all it ends happily, but not without considerable trauma for Flag. As the story unfolds, Johnson shows us the girl's actions, thoughts, and feelings with text and sepia-toned, colored-pencil sketches on the right-hand pages. On the facing pages, full-color acrylic paintings show Flag's adventure and hardships as his condition gradually worsens from exposure to the elements, cactus thorns, and hunger. To those who live in the desert, this is an all-too-familiar tale—one that usually does not turn out this well.

5.133 Yolen, Jane (1997). **The Sea Man.** Illustrated by Christopher Denise. New York: Philomel. 41 pp. ISBN: 0-399-22939-6. Picture Book.

Jane Yolen's beautifully told story is based on her research of mermaids. It is the story of a being—half man, half fish—who is caught in a fisherman's net in the mid-1600s. Although the rest of the crew wants nothing to do with the sea man, Lieutenant Huiskemp and his cabin boy Pieter suspect there is more to this creature. The lieutenant learns of the sea man's family, and "for his own little Jannine," hoists the sea man over the rail and into the water. After learning to communicate with the lieutenant, the sea man eventually returns the favor by saving the crew's lives. We learn that accepting others can open our eyes to truth and understanding. The powerful sketches by Christopher Denise add greatly to this intriguing story of friendship and adventure.

Secondary Reviews

5.134 Naylor, Phyllis Reynolds (1997). **The Healing of Texas Jake.** New York: Simon & Schuster. 115 pp. ISBN: 0-689-81124-1. Chapter Book.

This is story where cats are personified using humor and drama, realistic dialogue, and an action-packed plot. Marco and Polo are two house cats who have discovered the allure of street life in a loft in the market neighborhood near their home. The two house cats must endure danger and threats to their lives by the mean gang of cats that patrol the dump, as well as the insults and taunts of Texas Jake, their leader. The clever interaction from a cat's-eye point-of-view, and the development of the characters' cat personalities, will engage young pet lovers and offer a source for writing ideas that involves talking animals and their adventures.

5.135 Tudor, Tasha (1997). **The Great Corgiville Kidnapping.** New York: Little Brown. 39 pp. ISBN: 0-316-85583-9. Picture Book.

Caleb Corgi is a young dog detective who suspects something is amiss when a large number of raccoons descend upon his town. His suspicions are borne out when the most celebrated rooster in town, Babe, is kidnapped. Caleb sets about finding Babe, which leads to a harrowing hot-air balloon ride that threatens to take both Babe and Caleb out to sea. This story is rich in detail, challenging vocabulary, and structural complexity, but is made understandable because of Tasha Tudor's marvelous illustrations and her storytelling technique. This book is a centerpiece for intermediate-grade lessons on sequencing, the use of context clues, cause and effect, and plot development because of its simple animal story premise and the elaborate, visual unfolding of the tale.

5.136 Waite, Michael P. (1996). **Jojofu.** Illustrated by Yoriko Ito. New York: Lothrop, Lee & Shepard. Unpaged. ISBN: 0-688-13660-5. Picture Book.

Takumi, a young hunter, learns to put his unwavering faith in his brave dog, Jojofu. Jojofu becomes Takumi's eyes and ears, saving his doubting master from a landslide, jagged cliff, and giant serpent. This Japanese folktale, originally told in a Chinese-Japanese hybrid language, was taken from the ancient Ima Mukashi scrolls of 500 B.C.E.–1075 C.E., and is part of the beginnings of the Buddha's birth stories.

5.137 Yee, Tammy (1997). **Baby Honu's Incredible Journey.** Aiea, HI: Island Heritage. 32 pp. ISBN: 0-89610-285-8. Picture Book.

Baby Honu begins his journey from Hawaii's sandy shores to find his ocean home. He faces and escapes the ghost crab, frigatebird, and humpback whale, all factual details about events that threaten endangered green sea turtles today. Yee draws in readers through her bright watercolor and soft pastel paintings of luscious tropical settings, soft baby sea turtles' eyes, and treacherous endangering animal faces. Young readers will enjoy this adventurous tale about Hawaii's sea turtles.

Death Themes

See also the section entitled Life Stages and Milestones in chapter 4, "Families."

Primary Reviews

5.138 Fleischman, Paul (1998). **Whirligig.** New York: Henry Holt. 133 pages. ISBN: 0-8050-5582-7. Chapter Book.

Whirligig by Paul Fleischman weaves music, history, geography, and astronomy into a story about how Brent Bishop's whirligigs changed other people's lives. When Brent's climb to be part of the high school's in-crowd proves disastrous, he decides to end it all on the highway. His life is not lost, but the life of Lea, an eighteen-year-old honor student, is. As retribution, her mother says she wants Brent to build four whirligigs in the corners of the United States in memory of Lea, whose death he caused. Unknown to him, these magical toys bring love to a schoolgirl, comfort to a soon-to-be street sweeper, and relief to a pushed fifth grader and an obsessed teenager. Making them doesn't erase the guilt, but allows him to arise from the ashes ready to begin his life again. Fleischman helps us to see that the world itself is a whirligig, connecting time and place without us realizing it. (See also **20.24**)

5.139 Kimmel, Eric A. (1996). **Billy Lazloe.** New York: Harcourt Brace. 37 pp. ISBN: 0-15-200108-5. Picture Book.

Billy Lazloe was a born sailor. He had survived many hardships on the ocean, and during his many years of seafaring, he had watched good men get eaten by sharks, get washed overboard, and be decapitated by cannibals. Billy was well known among sailors, for he was a fine musician and singer and he entertained the crew on the long ocean journeys. But Billy's favorite place in the world was back at his birth home on the Willamette River in Oregon. Once when he went there, he encountered the magical appearance of Davy Jones. Davy Jones rose from his locker beneath the sea, and he gave Billy a sack of pearls for a promise to come with him and play his concertina to the inhabitants of the watery grave. Billy was able to postpone that performance in Davy Jones's locker for seven years, knowing all the while that his trip to the watery grave would probably be the end of his life on the sea. But this story has a surprise twist at the end, leaving the reader wondering if Billy chose to struggle and survive on the sea or to join his fellow sailors in Davy Jones's locker.

5.140 Kooharian, David (1997). **Sammy's Story.** New York: Dorling Kindersley. 31 pp. ISBN: 0-7894-2466-5. Sophisticated Picture Book.

Sammy's father wrote this tribute to his son, who battled a degenerative disease that slowly and painfully took his young life. Written and illustrated in the form of a comic book, this metaphorical tale tells of Sammy's dreams as he lay on his death bed. He meets people in his dreams who invite him to come away, who assign him the quest of defeating the wicked Zargo, and who offer him support and encouragement in the ensuing struggle. He finally achieves his goals and finds himself in a peaceful environment where he feels confidence, health, strength, and freedom, but he wants to return to his parents. He is told by a gentle man that if he returns, it can only be to say goodbye, and that he will feel the terrible pain in his body again. Sammy agrees to the consequences and returns to the hospital room where his parents are hovering in dismay over his deteriorating condition. He remains just long enough to assure them that he will be all right, and then leaves his parents and the pain. Fifth graders who read this book were engaged and drawn to the colorful, graphic illustrations. They commented that they understood dying better from this book because it showed them that courage is required to die as well as to survive—something that had not occurred to them previously. This book offers food for thought and discussion as students struggle with the terms of mortality and the hope that must be found in the death of those we love.

5.141 Lachtman, Ofelia Dumas (1997). **Leticia's Secret.** Houston, TX: Piñata. 126 pp. ISBN: 1-55885-209-3. Chapter Book.

Rosario, an eleven-year-old girl from the San Fernando Valley, is trying to figure out why everyone in the family gives her cousin Leticia such privileged treatment, and why she visits more and more often. Despite her initial annoyance at the visits, a friendship grows between Rosario and Leticia. The two friends share many things, including a love of reading and writing and a scary nighttime adventure when Rosario learns that her now dear cousin is dying from cancer. Xochitl, an eighth grader, said with joy and emotion, "El libro tiene muchos detalles, muchas historias en una. . . . Como muy latino, habla de que van a hacer tortillas, habla de las niñas, habla de que comían en el patio" ("The book has a lot of details, several stories in one. . . . It is very Latin, it speaks of them making tortillas, it speaks of godmothers, and that they are on the patio"). This excellent chapter book, with some illustrations by Roberta Collier-Morales, is easy to read and touches topics such as jealousy, friendship, death, family, and school life in ways that will strike a note of authenticity in the hearts and minds of middle-school readers.

5.142 Rylant, Cynthia (1996). **The Old Woman Who Named Things.** Illustrated by Kathryn Brown. New York: Harcourt Brace. Unpaged. ISBN: 0-15-257809-9. Picture Book. (See **8.55**)

Secondary Reviews

5.143 McKelvey, Douglas Kaine (1996). **The Angel Knew Papa and the Dog.** New York: Philomel. 89 pp. ISBN: 0-399-23042-4. Chapter Book.

Rich with similes, metaphors, and magical language, this book tells the story of survival on the frontier. It focuses on a seven-year-old girl who must survive a flood without her only living parent, her papa. She forgets her fear of drowning and her worry for her papa when she sees the angel. She is calmed by the stillness with which the angel looks into her eyes, "A stillness without words and a stillness without questions, but a stillness with more meaning than all words that ever were spoken and all questions that were ever asked."

5.144 Schneider, Antoni (1998). **Good-bye, Vivi!** Illustrated by Maja Dusikova. New York: North-South. 26 pp. ISBN: 1-55858-985-6. Picture Book.

A family grows as a result of having Granny move in with her bird Vivi. As she shares the stories of her bird, the family—especially her grandson—begin to incorporate the bird into their own lives. When the bird dies one day, it is Granny who shows how powerful memories and shared stories can be to the healing process that follows a death. This experience later helps the family cope with Granny's death. Dusikova's gently toned artwork supports a warm story of family, loss, and healing.

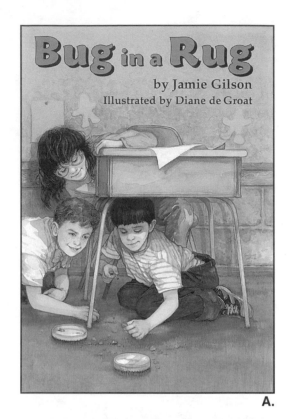

A.

B.

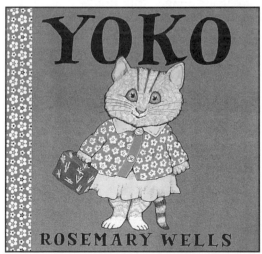

C.

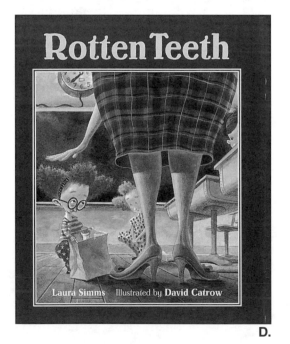

D.

A. *Bug in a Rug,* Jamie Gilson/Diane de Groat (**6.7**). **B.** *Thank You, Mr. Falker,* Patricia Polacco (**6.34**). **C.** *Yoko,* Rosemary Wells (**6.49**). **D.** *Rotten Teeth,* Laura Simms/David Catrow (**6.14**).

6 School Life

Cyndi Giorgis

*Contributing reviewers included Julie Carlton, Pennie Dye,
Cyndi Giorgis, and Dottie Kulesza.*

Most readers can relate to stories about school experiences. Many children value being able to see themselves in the books that they read, and stories about school life provide those connections. Through reading and discussing school stories, students are able to relate to various situations that are presented in the stories and that they encounter in their own lives. These situations and connections may include knowing they are not alone in their desire to gain peer acceptance, understanding they can overcome the challenges that learning can pose, realizing a teacher can make a difference in their life, or discovering that almost everyone has had an embarrassing moment at some point in his or her school life.

The books selected for this chapter are primarily realistic fiction. Many books selected to be reviewed present humorous situations that are generally initiated by the main character in the story. Other books reflect the difficult lives that some students experience both inside and outside of the school context. Some of these stories of challenge and struggle feature real-life heroes and heroines. There are also a few books that present a realistic situation, but use as characters animals that talk and dress like humans. Finally a few poetry anthologies have been included that share schooling experiences through verse.

Stories about school life also are written in a variety of formats. Readers will discover picture book formats that utilize text and illustration to create meaning; easy-to-read chapter books that use a controlled vocabulary to assist emergent readers; transitional chapter books that are generally aimed at students in grades 2 through 4; realistic novels for intermediate-grade readers; and young-adult novels that present experiences appropriate for a middle-school audience. All of these formats are represented in books reviewed within this chapter, and are woven throughout the different categories. In addition, most of the books reviewed in this chapter contain illustrations regardless of whether the story was written in a picture book or chapter book format.

In organizing the chapter, the following categories were used:

- School Environment. This section includes poems, rhyming stories, and informational books that highlight the physical aspects of school.

- Humorous Situations in School. In this section, readers will find contemporary realistic fiction and poetry that share the silly events and experiences students have in school. These books are sure to bring a chuckle to the reader.

- Sharing Experiences and Talents with Others. This section includes stories about show-and-tell, talent shows, and science projects that students can relate to from their own school experiences.

- Friends and Bullies. Here readers will find books about getting along with others. These stories can be found in easy-to-read formats, as well as picture books and chapter books.

- Teachers' Impact on Students' Lives. This section includes both humorous and thought-provoking books that illustrate the role teachers play in students' lives.

- Children Struggling with or Experiencing Academic Success. This section includes books that focus on illiteracy, language differences, Attention Deficit Disorder, and other issues that can impact the learning process.

- Learning about Self within a Classroom Context. Here readers will find several books for older readers in which self-identify plays a key role in students' development.

- Perspectives on Life Inside and Outside of the Classroom Context. This section includes a variety of stories about how family life influences a child's approach to school life.

High-Interest Series Books

There are numerous high-interest series books being published today that appeal to students at all levels of reading ability. The topic of the books may be horror stories, such as those found in the popular Goosebumps series by R. L. Stine, or they may relate experiences familiar to young girls, such as those found in The Baby-Sitters Club series by Ann M. Martin. There are also many high-interest books that are based on television shows, and that usually are adapted from the teleplay.

High-interest books generally rely on a formulaic writing style that adds to the predictability of the plot. Parents and teachers frequently share predictable books with children early in a child's reading development. As children begin reading independently, they are drawn to books that have a predictable plot because there is security in knowing the type of story they will find and the manner in which the plot will unfold. Throughout a series, the characters generally remain the same, although a new character may be introduced in a book for the purpose of conflict with the regular characters. Readers come to know the characters even though there is little character development. Students also understand that even though a character may be bad, he or she may possess some redeeming qualities. Beth (age ten) said, "I like to read series books because you can follow the characters. If you read one book in a series and then another, you know the characters and it's easier to follow the story because the characters are familiar to you."

High-interest series books have a role in children's ongoing literacy development as they provide an opportunity for students to be entertained. These books often do not contain the layers of meaning that warrant discussion among readers. However, as Katina (age twelve) stated, "The reason why I like to read popular books is because everyone is reading them. So if I ask[ed] someone and tried to start a conversation about the book, they [would] know what I am talking about and we could relate to each other and express our feelings about it." These books are enjoyable and encourage independent reading. Fortunately classroom teachers, librarians, and parents can further support children's literacy development by sharing other types of books, such as those reviewed throughout *Adventuring with Books.*

The section entitled High-Interest Series Books contains a sampling of the numerous high-interest series books available for children. In this section, the title refers to the series title rather than one particular book, and readers should keep in mind that there may be as few as five books or as many as one hundred books in the series. Where entries indicate that a series was "created by" a particular author, this does not necessarily mean that the books currently being published in the series were written by that particular individual. The suggested reading level (RL) indicated at the end of the review is provided in order to assist readers in understanding the broad range and readability of these series books. Picture books and young-adult series novels generally do not indicate a reading level.

---

*The titles listed below each subheading are organized into Primary Reviews and Secondary Reviews. The Primary Reviews describe outstanding books in each subheading. The Secondary Reviews provide brief information about other books worthy of consideration. Some titles listed below are **not** reviewed in this chapter; entries for these titles are not annotated and contain only bibliographic* *information. In such cases, a cross reference to the annotated entry contained elsewhere in this volume is provided in boldface type at the end of the bibliographic information.*

School Environment

Primary Reviews

6.1   Hopkins, Lee Bennett (1996). **School Supplies: A Book of Poems.** Illustrated by Renee Flower. New York: Simon & Schuster Books for Young Readers. 37 pp. ISBN: 0-689-80497-0. Picture Book. (See **10.3**)

6.2   Lindbergh, Reeve (1997). **The Awful Aardvarks Go to School.** Illustrated by Tracey Campbell Pearson. New York: Viking. Unpaged. ISBN: 0-670-85920-6. Picture Book.

A fictional school environment is the setting for the chaos created by the aardvarks' visit to the animals' school. Each page cleverly integrates artifacts, activities, signs, pictures, and a list of words that all start with the selected letter of the alphabet. At the end of the book, the aardvarks, with a trail of destruction behind them, leave the reader to wonder what zaniness they will cause when they arrive at the zoo. Cartoon illustrations done in watercolor and pen-and-ink add to the frenzy and hilarity of the situation. This book is great for younger children due to its rhyming text and comical situation, but is appropriate for older readers as well due to the splendid vocabulary used.

6.3   Pringle, Laurence (1998). **One Room School.** Illustrated by Barbara Garrison. Honesdale, PA: Boyds Mills. Unpaged. ISBN: 0-56397-583-1. Picture Book.

Author Laurence Pringle provides a factual account of his days in a one-room schoolhouse in the 1940s. Pringle reminisces about the last year of classes held in School 14 in rural New York before it closed its doors forever. The narration of a typical day helps explain how the teacher, Miss Shackelton, organized instruction to meet the needs of eighteen students from grades one through eight. "This is sort of like our multiage class where there are kids from different grades all in the same room," observed Michael (age nine). The author also provides historical background about the time period by including student activities that helped support the war effort, namely collecting milkweed seedpods for life preservers and scrap iron for tanks and ships. Many of the school's activities weren't much different than those that take place today, which makes this a wonderful book for students to compare and contrast past and present schooling experiences. Garrison's collagraph illustrations are primarily brown and white in appearance, and resemble photographs in an album.

Secondary Reviews

6.4 Lasky, Kathryn (1996). **Lunch Bunnies.** Illustrated by Marylin Hafner. Boston: Little Brown. Unpaged. ISBN: 0-316-51525-6. Picture Book.

It's the night before his first day in school, and Clyde is terrified— terrified of school lunchtime. He has spent time practicing with a tray, but he also has heard the stories of the cross lunch ladies, and he fears their wrath and his probable humiliation should he do even the slightest thing wrong. Hafner's gentle watercolor-and-ink drawings do justice to the young bunny's expressions of fear in an overwhelming situation, and of confidence gained through caring for others.

Humorous Situations in School

Primary Reviews

6.5 Clements, Andrew (1997). **Double Trouble in Walla Walla.** Illustrated by Sal Murdocca. Brookfield, CN: Millbrook. Unpaged. ISBN: 0-7613-0306-5. Picture Book. (See **13.12**)

6.6 Dakos, Kalli (1997). **Get out of the Alphabet, Number 2! Wacky Wednesday Puzzle Poems.** Illustrated by Jenny Graham. New York: Simon & Schuster. 32 pp. ISBN: 0-689-81118-7. Picture Book. (See **10.8**)

6.7 Gilson, Jamie (1998). **Bug in a Rug.** Illustrated by Diane de Groat. New York: Clarion. 69 pp. ISBN: 0-395-86616-2. Chapter Book.

Richard's eccentric Aunt Nannie and Uncle Ken arrive in town for a short visit. Aunt Nannie has made Richard an enormous pair of bright purple pants that Richard must tightly hold onto in order to keep them up. When he is asked to pass out the mealworms in class for a science experiment, readers can predict what embarrassing events might occur. Uncle Ken adds to the situation when he brings a pair of bright red suspenders to school for Richard. Uncle Ken decides to stay awhile in the classroom, sharing his own brand of humor with Richard's classmates. De Groat's warm black-and-white drawings match the text's lighthearted mood. Many students will be able to reflect on a time when they were forced to wear silly clothing to school. This is a good book for reading aloud to students, or for those readers making the transition into longer chapter books.

6.8 Omerod, Jan (1996). **Ms. McDonald Has a Class.** New York: Clarion. Unpaged. ISBN: 0-395-77611-2. Picture Book. (See **10.30**)

Secondary Reviews

6.9 Cox, Judy (1998). **Third Grade Pet.** Illustrated by Cynthia Fisher. New York: Holiday House. 93 pp. ISBN: 0-8234-1379-9. Chapter Book.

This short chapter book provides a lot of laughs centered around the addition of a new classroom pet. Rosemary is horrified when a rat named Cheese becomes the class pet. When it is Rosemary's turn to take care of Cheese, she grows so fond of him that she decides to take him home. Black-and-white illustrations accompany the fast-moving text and add to the humorous situations that Rosemary creates in her efforts to protect Cheese.

6.10 Hurwitz, Johanna (1998). **Starting School.** Illustrated by Karen Dugan. New York: Morrow Junior Books. 102 pp. ISBN: 0-688-15685-1. Chapter Book.

Readers of Hurwitz's Class Clown series will recognize Lucas Cott's twin brothers, Marcus and Marius. The twins are placed in separate kindergartens and although they don't look at all alike, the two teachers are both familiar with their mischievous nature. The age of the twins is younger than the age of the perceived reader, but all children will delight in the antics and chaos created by the brothers.

6.11 Lansky, Bruce, editor (1997). **No More Homework! No More Tests! Kids' Favorite Funny School Poems.** Illustrated by Stephen Carpenter. New York: Scholastic, 74 pp. ISBN: 0-590-58036-1. Picture Book.

Lansky's introduction indicates that he asked over one hundred elementary school teachers to find the fifty funniest poems about school ever written. Poets such as Jack Prelutsky, Shel Silverstein, Colin McNaughton, and Kalli Dakos are included in this collection. This humorous anthology of poems tells about what really happens in school.

6.12 Munsch, Robert (1998). **Get out of Bed!** Illustrated by Alan Daniel and Lea Daniel. New York: Scholastic. 30 pp. ISBN: 0-590-76977-4. Picture Book.

Amy stayed up watching the late show; the late, late show; and even the later show. In the morning, family members cannot seem to wake sleepy Amy, so they decide to take her to school in her bed. The watercolor illustrations add energy to the activity going on, as Amy sleeps peacefully throughout the day. This humorous book is great for reading aloud, especially with small groups who can benefit from a closer look at the illustrations.

Sharing Experiences and Talents with Others

Primary Reviews

6.13 Henkes, Kevin (1996). **Lilly's Purple Plastic Purse.** New York: Greenwillow. Unpaged. ISBN: 0-688-12897-1. Picture Book.

Lilly loves school and her upbeat, positive teacher Mr. Slinger. One day, Lilly proudly brings her new purple plastic purse and flashy sunglasses to school. Because she is unable to contain her excitement about sharing them with her classmates, Mr. Slinger has no choice but to confiscate the items, much to Lilly's dismay. "I knew Lilly was gonna get in trouble when she didn't listen to the teacher and she kept goofing around," said Rachel (age six). Lilly's anger at her teacher turns to happiness again as she learns a thoughtful lesson. Henkes has a wonderful gift of telling a humorous yet realistic story with the right amount of emotional tug. His energetic and expressive watercolor illustrations will captivate readers.

6.14 Simms, Laura (1998). **Rotten Teeth.** Illustrated by David Catrow. Boston: Houghton Mifflin. Unpaged. ISBN: 0-395-82850-3. Picture Book.

Quiet, shy Melissa Hartman seeks her brother Norman's assistance in deciding what to take for show-and-tell. Her quest is to find "something kids would *like*." Norman suggests the bottle of rotten teeth from their father's home dental office. Melissa's classmates are intrigued with the teeth, but her teacher finds them inappropriate for sharing with the class. Catrow's cartoon illustrations are hilarious, and the aerial perspective of small Melissa and the sweating brow of her teacher create a heightened sense of visual humor. "I think rotten teeth would be disgusting but since Melissa made friends then maybe it was a good thing to bring to school after all," commented Danielle (age seven).

Secondary Reviews

6.15 Auch, Mary Jane (1998). **I Was a Third Grade Science Project.** Illustrated by Herm Auch. New York: Holiday House. 96 pp. ISBN: 0-8234-1357-8. Chapter Book.

Brian "Brain" Lewis and his classmates decide to hypnotize a dog for their science project. Unfortunately it is Brian's friend Josh who acquires the hypnotic suggestion of being a cat, as evidenced by his newfound love of sushi and catnip. This hilarious novel is great for readers who are ready to move beyond beginning-to-read books.

6.16 Duffey, Betsy (1998). **Spotlight on Cody.** Illustrated by Ellen Thompson. New York: Viking. 74 pp. ISBN: 0-670-88077-9. Chapter Book.

Cody Michaels is desperate to find something he can do for the rapidly approaching third-grade talent show. He attempts comedy without much success, and juggling is out of the question given the number of eggs he has broken. Cody turns to his parents for help, only to learn that their only talents are yodeling and clogging. When Cody attempts to cheer up his father, who is turning 40, he discovers a talent that he did not realize he possessed. Humorous situations and lively pacing make this a realistic and appealing chapter book for intermediate-grade readers.

6.17 Howe, James (1998). **Pinky and Rex and the School Play: Ready-to-Read Level 3.** Illustrated by Melissa Sweet. New York: Atheneum Books for Young Readers. 40 pp. ISBN: 0-689-31872-3. Chapter Book.

This latest addition to the Pinky and Rex series finds the two friends in direct competition with each other. Pinky wants to be an actor when he grows up, but when he convinces Rex to accompany him to tryouts, she is the one who ends up with the lead in the play. However, Pinky is able to resolve his differences with Rex, and even ends up saving the play from an awkward moment.

6.18   Rockwell, Anne (1997). **Show and Tell Day.** Illustrated by Lizzy Rockwell. New York: HarperCollins. Unpaged. ISBN: 0-06-027300-3. Picture Book.

Bright, colorful illustrations complement this simple story about the joy of show-and-tell. A multicultural group of young children shares various items from home, or items that they have made or collected. The opposite page provides an illustration of where or how the child acquired the object. Rockwell's simple book is appropriate for preschool or kindergarten students.

Friends and Bullies

See also chapter 5, "Struggle and Survival."

Primary Reviews

6.19   Adoff, Arnold (1997). **Love Letters.** Illustrated by Lisa Desimini. New York: Scholastic. 32 pp. ISBN: 0-590-48478-8. Picture Book. (See **10.23**)

6.20   Brisson, Pat (1997). **Hot Fudge Hero.** Illustrated by Diana Cain Bluthenthal. New York: Henry Holt. 72 pp. ISBN: 0-8050-4551-1. Chapter Book. (See **7.44**)

6.21   Glenn, Mel (1996). **Who Killed Mr. Chippendale? A Mystery in Poems.** New York: Dutton. 100 pp. ISBN: 0-525-67530-2. Sophisticated Chapter Book. (See **10.27**)

6.22   Kleven, Elisa (1996). **Hooray, a Piñata!/¡Viva! ¡Una piñata!** New York: Dutton Children's Books. Unpaged. ISBN: 0-525-45606-8 (English)/0-525-45606-6 (Spanish). Picture Book.

In this story, available in separate English and Spanish editions, Clara goes shopping for a birthday piñata. Her friend Samson advises her to buy one in the form of a thundercloud monster. Clara, however, chooses a cute little puppy dog and spends the next several days treating it as a living pet. When party time draws near, Clara has become so attached to her piñata that she is reluctant to break it. Samson proves to be a good friend when he cleverly comes to her rescue with his very special birthday gift—the thundercloud piñata. Our students easily related to Clara's problem. "I remember when I didn't want to break my Batman piñata," said Nico (age nine). The scene with children playing with piñata parts at the conclusion of the story elicited even more piñata tales from listeners. The characters and scenery represent diverse ethnic backgrounds, all created in Kleven's unique collage style.

6.23   Mavor, Salley (1997). **You and Me: Poems of Friendship.** New York: Orchard. 32 pp. ISBN: 0-531-33045-1. Picture Book. (See **10.18**)

6.24   Shange, Ntozake (1997). **Whitewash.** Illustrated by Michael Sporn. New York: Walker. Unpaged. ISBN: 0-8027-8490-9. Picture Book. (See **5.117, 20.16**)

6.25   Shreve, Susan (1997). **Joshua T. Bates in Trouble Again.** New York: Knopf. 90 pp. ISBN: 0-679-98520-4. Chapter Book.

This sequel to *The Flunking of Joshua T. Bates* and *Joshua T. Bates Takes Charge* finds the protagonist ready to go to fourth grade after having spent September through Thanksgiving repeating third grade. Joshua wants to change his hairstyle and clothing in order to be accepted without ridicule from class bully Tommy Wilhelm. Joshua even tempts fate by walking into class with a cigarette over his ear, and is eventually called to the principal's office for bringing a knife to school. This is a believable story about a boy who learns to stand up for himself so that he can be himself.

>   Shreve, Susan (1984). **The Flunking of Joshua T. Bates.** New York: Knopf. 82 pp. ISBN: 0-679-84187-3. Chapter Book.

>   Shreve, Susan (1993). **Joshua T. Bates Takes Charge.** New York: Knopf. 112 pp. ISBN: 0-394-84362-2. Chapter Book.

6.26   Steptoe, John (1997). **Creativity.** Illustrated by E. B. Lewis. New York: Clarion. 32 pp. ISBN: 0-395-68706-3. (See **20.6**)

6.27   Van Leeuwen, Jean (1997). **Amanda Pig, Schoolgirl.** Illustrated by Ann Schweninger. New York: Dial Books for Young Readers. 48 pp. ISBN: 0-8037-1980-9. Chapter Book.

This amusing story of Amanda Pig's first day of school is written in an easy-to-read chapter book format. On the first day of school, Amanda makes a new friend who will not tell anyone her name. Amanda and her other friends entertain and coax Lollipop to tell her real name, but to no avail. Finally, after a fun-filled day at school with a patient and understanding teacher, Lollipop whispers her first name to Amanda. This delightfully told story provides early readers with situations they can relate to, text they can read, illustrations that complement the text, and characters of some depth.

Secondary Reviews

6.28 Brown, Laurie Krasny (1997). **Rex and Lilly Schooltime: A Dino Easy Reader.** Illustrated by Marc Brown. Boston: Little Brown. 32 pp. ISBN: 0-316-10920-7. Chapter Book.

Three short, funny chapters comprise this easy-to-read book featuring dinosaurs Rex and Lilly. Rex shares his new zoo underwear during show-and-tell, trades lunches with classmates, and tries to assist Lilly when she gets stuck on a word. The watercolor illustrations add humor to the controlled-vocabulary text.

6.29 Carbone, Elisa (1998). **Starting School with an Enemy.** New York: Knopf. 103 pp. ISBN: 0-679-88639-7. Chapter Book.

It is bad enough when Sarah has go to a new school for fifth grade, but it gets even worse when she has to confront Eric, an enemy who picks on her and humiliates her in public. Fortunately Sarah also makes a friend, Christina Perez, and they enjoy playing soccer and having fun until Sarah's obsession for getting revenge almost destroys her friendship. Sarah is sarcastic and at times insensitive, but she is portrayed with many redeeming qualities that will provide discussion for intermediate-grade students.

6.30 Kline, Suzy (1998). **Horrible Harry and the Drop of Doom.** Illustrated by Frank Remkiewicz. New York: Viking. 58 pp. ISBN: 0-670-85849-8. Chapter Book.

This book, ninth in the series of stories about the students in Miss Mackle's class, finds Harry invited to Mountainside Amusement Park at the end of the school year. Harry is excited about the day until he is told that the newest ride features a thirteen-story drop inside the elevator of a haunted hotel. Kline's writing is easily accessible and amusing for those readers venturing into chapter books.

6.31 Voigt, Cynthia (1996). **Bad Girls.** New York: Scholastic. 278 pp. ISBN: 0-590-60134-2. Chapter Book.

Mickey Elsinger and Margalo Epps are two fifth graders whose friendship is portrayed through acts of loyalty, kindness, betrayal, and mischief. This perceptive and at times irreverent novel also provides a realistic view of preadolescent girls who are struggling to establish their own self-identity amidst the enormous peer pressure found within this age group. Voigt's sequel, *Bad, Badder, Baddest,* continues the story of the two protagonists.

Voigt, Cynthia (1997). **Bad, Badder, Baddest.** New York: Scholastic. 266 pp. ISBN: 0-590-60136-9. Chapter Book.

Teachers' Impact on Students' Lives

Primary Reviews

6.32 Finchler, Judy (1998). **Miss Malarkey Won't Be in Today.** Illustrated by Kevin O'Malley. New York: Walker. Unpaged. ISBN: 0-8027-8653-7. Picture Book.

This sequel to Finchler and O'Malley's *Miss Malarkey Doesn't Live in Room 10* finds Miss Malarkey with a high fever and too sick to go to school. As she begins to think about the various substitutes the principal might call (all of whom have funny, yet descriptive names), Miss Malarkey feels compelled to drag herself to school. She finds the class is calm rather than in chaos, but Miss Malarkey's fears resurface when she discovers that Ima Berpur was the substitute teacher. O'Malley's lively illustrations depict each character through their facial expressions and humorous traits.

Finchler, Judy (1995). **Miss Malarkey Doesn't Live in Room 10.** Illustrated by Kevin O'Malley. New York: Whitman. Unpaged. ISBN: 0-8027-7498-9. Picture Book.

6.33 Lorbiecki, Marybeth (1998). **Sister Anne's Hands.** Illustrated by K. Wendy Popp. New York: Dial Books for Young Readers. Unpaged. ISBN: 0-8037-2038-6. Picture Book. (See **20.3**)

6.34 Polacco, Patricia (1998). **Thank You, Mr. Falker.** New York: Philomel. Unpaged. ISBN: 0-399-23166-8. Picture Book.

Polacco shares a part of her own life in this fictionalized story about learning to read. Going to school was a challenging task for young Trisha; children made fun of her, called her names, and made her feel dumb. Trisha was not getting the help she needed in order to learn how to read and eventually grew to hate school. Finally, her fifth-grade teacher, Mr. Falker, recognized her artistic gifts and helped her overcome her learning disability. Polacco's bold splashes of color capture Trisha's pursuit of knowledge about herself, the world around her, and the joys of being a reader.

6.35　Seuss, Dr., and Jack Prelutsky (1998). **Hooray for Diffendoofer Day!** Illustrated by Lane Smith. New York: Knopf. Unpaged. ISBN: 0-679-89008-4. Picture Book.

When Dr. Seuss (Theodor Geisel) died in 1991, he left behind fourteen pages of sketches and notes for a story about an unusually creative group of teachers, including Miss Bonkers. Jack Prelutsky and Lane Smith were asked by Seuss's editor to complete the project. The result is a whimsical story that celebrates individuality, in which the students pass a standardized test because they have been taught "how to think." Smith has incorporated many of the original Seuss sketches into his own illustrations, which ties the book together. Sharing with students the afterword, which explains how the book evolved, is helpful before reading the book to students. Students are able to gain an insight into both process and product, which in a sense is what the book is all about.

6.36　Slate, Joseph (1996). **Miss Bindergarten Gets Ready for Kindergarten.** Illustrated by Ashley Wolff. New York: Dutton Children's Books. Unpaged. ISBN: 0-525-45446-2. Picture Book.

It's the first day of school and as Miss Bindergarten arrives to unpack boxes, decorate walls, and ready the kindergarten room for her new class, each of her students prepares for the day as well. Alternating pages focus on the children and the teacher. The rhyming text introduces each student alphabetically by name: "Adam Krupp / wakes up. / Brenda Heath brushes her teeth." Ashley Wolff's bright illustrations in ink and watercolor-wash fill every spread with details that are amusing and, at times, touching. This book has been a favorite not only for preschoolers anticipating their arrival in kindergarten, but also for those students already there.

6.37　Slate, Joseph (1998). **Miss Bindergarten Celebrates the 100th Day.** Illustrated by Ashley Wolff. New York: Dutton Children's Books. Unpaged. ISBN: 0-525-46000-4. Picture Book. (See **9.33**)

Secondary Reviews

6.38　Calmenson, Stephanie (1998). **The Teeny Tiny Teacher: A Teeny Tiny Ghost Story.** Illustrated by Denis Roche. New York: Scholastic. Unpaged. ISBN: 0-590-37123-1. Picture Book.

This English folktale adaptation introduces readers to a teeny tiny teacher who takes her teeny tiny students on a teeny tiny walk, where she finds a teeny tiny bone and puts it into her teeny tiny pocket. Upon returning to the classroom, a loud voice demands the bone back. This story for younger children may be scary given the tone of the reader's voice. The bright illustrations in primary and secondary colors add to the schoolhouse setting.

6.39   Krensky, Stephen (1996). **My Teacher's Secret Life.** Illustrated by JoAnn Adinolfi. New York: Simon & Schuster Books for Young Readers. Unpaged. ISBN: 0-689-80271-4. Picture Book.

A young boy believes his teachers live at school, where together they participate in exercise routines, eat cafeteria leftovers, and listen to stories read by the librarian. When the boy sees his teacher Mrs. Quirk in the supermarket, trying on roller skates at the mall, and in the company of a little girl who closely resembles the teacher, he becomes highly suspicious that his teacher has a secret life. Bright watercolor illustrations show what school looks like after hours.

Children Struggling with or Experiencing Academic Success

Primary Reviews

6.40   Gantos, Jack (1998). **Joey Pigza Swallowed the Key.** New York: Farrar, Straus and Giroux. 154 pp. ISBN: 0-374-33664-4. Chapter Book.

This poignant novel deals with Attention Deficit Disorder (ADD) and the effect it can have, not only on the child who suffers from it, but also on parents, teachers, and classmates. Joey Pigza is wired, and even though he attempts to control his behavior, he still manages to swallow his house key, disrupt the class field trip, and lose a fingernail when he tries to sharpen his finger. Fortunately Joey encounters a caring teacher who realizes that the medication is not working and that Joey needs further medical evaluation. "There's a kid in my class like Joey and sometimes you know he's trying to be good but he just can't," remarked Aaron (age eleven).

6.41   Hesse, Karen (1998). **Just Juice.** Illustrated by Robert A. Parker. New York: Scholastic. 138 pp. ISBN: 0-590-03382-4. Chapter Book. (See **7.76, 20.35**)

6.42 Little, Jean (1998). **Emma's Magic Winter.** Illustrated by Jennifer Plecas. New York: HarperCollins. 64 pp. ISBN: 0-06-025389-4. Chapter Book. (See **7.40**)

6.43 Senisi, Ellen (1998). **Just Kids: Visiting a Class for Children with Special Needs.** New York: Dutton. 40 pp. ISBN: 0-525-45646-5. Picture Book. (See **20.59**)

Secondary Reviews

6.44 Aliki (1998). **Marianthe's Story: Painted Words; Marianthe's Story: Spoken Memories.** New York: Greenwillow. Unpaged. ISBN: 0-688-15661-4. Picture Book. (See **7.74**)

6.45 Jiménez, Francisco (1998). **La Mariposa.** Illustrated by Simón Silva. Boston: Houghton Mifflin. Unpaged. ISBN: 0-395-81663-7. Picture Book.

Francisco is unable to understand most of what his first grade teacher says, as he struggles to learn English in his new classroom. Francisco is intrigued by the caterpillar that is in the jar next to his desk, and begins to do some research into how they turn into butterflies. Unable to read the words, Francisco instead reads the pictures and in turn creates his own story. The rich illustrations by Silva show the transformation of both caterpillar and child.

6.46 Lauture, Denizé (1996). **Running the Road to ABC.** Illustrated by Reynold Ruffins. New York: Simon & Schuster Books for Young Readers. Unpaged. ISBN: 0-689-80507-1. Picture Book.

The desire to learn is told through this lyrical tale. Before the sun is up, a group of Haitian boys and girls run through the countryside and town to the school, where they will learn to read and write. The vibrant Caribbean colors and double-page stylized illustrations provide a beautiful backdrop.

6.47 Rodriguez, Luis J. (1997). **América Is Her Name.** Illustrated by Carlos Vasquez. Willimantic, CT: Curbstone. Unpaged. ISBN: 1-880684-40-3. Picture Book. (See **20.7**)

Learning about Self within a Classroom Context

See also the section entitled Finding One's Own Identity in chapter 5, "Struggle and Survival."

Primary Reviews

6.48 Konigsburg, E. L. (1996). **The View from Saturday.** New York: Atheneum Books for Young Readers. 163 pp. ISBN: 0-689-80993-X. Chapter Book.

In this 1996 Newbery Award winner, E. L. Konigsburg weaves a multilayered story of taking journeys, participating in contests, and finding confidence. A group of four sixth graders, who are intricately linked with one another through interesting circumstances, find themselves on the Academic Bowl team vying with other teams for the championship. As their friendship develops, they begin having Saturday afternoon teas at the home of Julian, a team member from India. Mrs. Olinski, a paraplegic woman who has returned to teaching after a ten-year leave of absence, brings the children together to participate in the competitions. The rest of the students are diverse too, but the focus of the story is on their new understandings of mutual respect and kindness. The intricate plot and the format of the story—four short stories about each student woven into the larger story of the team's rise to fame—keeps readers eagerly turning pages. Kristen (age twelve) reminds readers that the book is told through the perspective of the four kids, and so even though the beginning is somewhat confusing, "hang in there because the way it weaves together is worth it."

6.49 Wells, Rosemary (1998). **Yoko.** New York: Hyperion Books for Children. Unpaged. ISBN: 0-7868-2345-3. Picture Book.

Yoko's classmates make fun of the sushi and red-bean ice cream she brings for lunch each day, prompting her teacher to have International Food Day to learn about different types of food. Unfortunately Yoko's sushi goes untouched until Timothy decides to try the rice and raw fish—and finds it rather tasty. Encouraged by his reaction, Yoko's other classmates soon indulge and realize that sushi and red-bean ice cream are quite good. Wells' expressive watercolor illustrations capture the uniqueness of each character, along with a range of emotions. After reading *Yoko* to with her class, one first-grade teacher commented, "It is important for children to realize that culture extends beyond food to valuing each other for the diversity they bring to our classroom."

Secondary Reviews

6.50   Fletcher, Ralph (1998). **Flying Solo.** New York: Clarion. 138 pp. ISBN: 0-395-87323-1. Chapter Book.

What would happen if the substitute failed to show up to teach a sixth-grade class? The students in Mr. Fabiano's class decide that they will run the class themselves according to the routine already established by their creative and well-liked teacher. Fletcher is able to capture the emotions of realistic characters who work through problems, both on a personal level as well as within the class structure. (See also **20.34**)

6.51   Mills, Claudia (1998). **Standing Up to Mr. O.** New York: Farrar, Straus and Giroux. 166 pp. ISBN: 0-374-34721-2. Sophisticated Chapter Book.

This coming-of-age story set within the school environment focuses on the issue of animal rights. When Maggie McIntosh refuses to dissect worms, fish, and frogs in her seventh-grade biology class, it means receiving a grade of F instead of her usual A. Mills is able to present both sides of the argument in a compelling way that will force readers to make up their own minds as to the decision Maggie has taken against killing any living being.

6.52   Nodelman, Perry (1998). **Behaving Bradley.** New York: Simon & Schuster Books for Young Readers. 232 pp. ISBN: 0-689-81466-6. Chapter Book.

Bradley Gold narrates this tale set in Roblin Memorial High School. A Code of Conduct is to be drafted for the high school students, and Brad unwillingly volunteers to serve on the committee. However he decides that the document should include a code for teachers as well. Brad may appear to go on an endless tirade, but the reality of the politics and hypocrisy of administrators, teachers, and peers will befamiliar to anyone who has ever attended school. (See also **20.40**)

Perspectives on Life Inside and Outside of the Classroom Context

See also chapter 4, "Families," and the section entitled Family Hardship in chapter 5, "Struggle and Survival."

6.53   Creech, Sharon (1998). **Bloomability.** New York: HarperCollins. 273 pp. ISBN: 0-06-026993-6. Chapter Book.

Domenica Santolina Doone, or Dinnie for short, has lived in thirteen states in twelve years as her father sought out new opportunities. Dinnie is given her own exciting opportunity when she is sent to the American School in Lugano, Switzerland, where her Uncle Max is the headmaster. During the year, Dinnie learns to ski and to speak Italian, and in the process begins to broaden her own view of the world and her understanding of others. Dinnie faces a difficult decision at the end of the school year: whether or not to return to her family in the United States. Creech's writing is always thoughtful, and takes the reader on a journey of self-discovery right along with the main character. "I like how the character bloomed during the year which is just what the title of the book says, Bloomability," said Patricia (age twelve).

6.54   Dines, Carol (1997). **Talk to Me: Stories and a Novella.** New York: Delacorte. 223 pp. ISBN: 0-385-32271-2. Sophisticated Chapter Book; adult mediation required. (See **20.53**)

6.55   Grimes, Nikki (1997). **It's Raining Laughter.** Photographs by Myles C. Pinkney. New York: Dial. Unpaged. ISBN: 0-8037-2003-3. Picture Book. (See **13.29**)

6.56   Haddix, Margaret Peterson (1996). **Don't You Dare Read This, Mrs. Dunphrey.** New York: Simon & Schuster Books for Young Readers. 108 pp. ISBN: 0-689-80097-5. Sophisticated Chapter Book.

This young-adult novel offers a realistic view of a young girl whose life is in turmoil. When her English teacher Mrs. Dunphrey requires that each student keep a journal, Tish Bonner reluctantly agrees. Tish soon discovers that her teacher is willing to respect her privacy by not reading entries marked, "DO NOT READ." Tish then begins to write candidly about her abusive father, her severely depressed mother, and the many family responsibilities that have become hers. Finally Tish realizes that Mrs. Dunphrey may be the one person who can truly offer her hope. This brief, moving novel explores how one girl begins to deal with her problems through journal writing. One middle-school teacher stated, "I had a young girl in my eighth-grade English class whom I discovered had some of the same difficulties as Tish. It really opened some doors for her . . . and for me in working with her."

6.57   Kline, Suzy (1998). **Horrible Harry Moves up to Third Grade.** Illustrated by Frank Remkiewicz. New York: Viking. 58 pp. ISBN: 0-670-87873-1. Chapter Book. (See **7.55**)

6.58   Lorbiecki, Marybeth (1996). **Just One Flick of a Finger.** Illustrated by David Diaz. New York: Dial. 30 pp. ISBN: 0-8037-1948-5. Sophisticated Picture Book. (See **8.47, 20.38**)

6.59   Naylor, Phyllis Reynolds (1997). **Outrageously Alice.** New York: Atheneum Books for Young Readers. 133 pp. ISBN: 0-689-80354-0. Sophisticated Chapter Book.

Alice is having a difficult time settling into eighth grade after finding it is not what she thought it would be. Alice livens things up in her personal appearance with a change of hairstyle and makeup, and in her social life by joining the explorer club. When she attends a bridal shower for an older woman, Alice is thrust into the midst of adult discussions about sensuality and making love. Growing up without a mother, who died when Alice was four, forces Alice to turn to her brother and father to answer her most direct and personal questions. This is a must-read for preteens trying to handle the changes that creep into every aspect of their lives. Readers can see themselves through Alice's antics and the problems she and her friends face with family and peer relationships. Naylor's series of Alice books also includes *Achingly Alice* and *Alice in Lace.* "It's nice to read a book that is funny, but really shows how tough it is for girls growing up," noted Rebecca (age eleven).

Naylor, Phyllis Reynolds (1996). **Alice in Lace.** New York: Atheneum Books for Young Readers. 139 pp. ISBN: 0-689-80358-3.

Naylor, Phyllis Reynolds (1998). **Achingly Alice.** New York: Atheneum Books for Young Readers. 121 pp. ISBN: 0-689-80355-9.

6.60   Roberts, Willo Davis (1998). **The Kidnappers: A Mystery.** New York: Atheneum. 137 pp. ISBN: 0-689-81394-5. Chapter Book. (See **13.67**)

6.61   Scott, Ann Herbert (1996). **Brave as a Mountain Lion.** Illustrated by Glo Coalson. New York: Houghton Mifflin. 32 pp. ISBN: 0-395-66760-7. Picture Book.

This is a well-written picture book that incorporates traditional Native American thought and actions in dealing with contemporary issues. Spider, a Shoshone child, has been selected by his teacher to represent his class in the school-wide spelling bee. Spider is afraid to go up on the gymnasium's stage in front of so many people. He seeks wisdom and advice from various family members: Father tells him to pretend to be the bravest animal he can think of; Grandmother tells him to be clever like the coyote; and his older brother tells him to be silent and stay cool like the spider from whom he got his name. Overcoming his apprehensions, Spider participates in the contest and conquers his fears. Especially pleasing are the true-to-life scenes of family life at home, the close-ups of Spider with his father, and the interaction with his grandmother as she works on beadwork. Scott writes a well-told, believable story about a contemporary Native American family with an academically successful male as the main character.

6.62 Thomas, Rob (1997). **Slave Day.** New York: Simon & Schuster Books for Young Readers. 188 pp. ISBN: 0-689-80206-4. Sophisticated Chapter Book. (See **20.42**)

6.63 Walter, Virginia (1998). **Making Up Megaboy.** Illustrated by Katrina Roeckelein. New York: Dorling Kindersley. 64 pp. ISBN: 0-0-7894-2488-6. Sophisticated Chapter Book. (See **20.55**)

6.64 Winslow, Vicki (1997). **Follow the Leader.** New York: Delacorte. 215 pp. ISBN: 0-385-32285-2. Chapter Book. (See **20.29**)

6.65 Wolff, Virginia E. (1998). **Bat 6.** New York: Scholastic. 230 pp. ISBN: 0-590-89799-3. (See **20.43**)

Secondary Reviews

6.66 Adler, David A. (1998). **The Many Troubles of Andy Russell.** Illustrated by Will Hillenbrand. San Diego: Harcourt Brace. 136 pp. ISBN: 0-15-201295-8. Chapter Book.

Andy Russell is a fourth grader who wants to do well in school, but his mind is on a variety of other things: his pet gerbils have escaped, his friend Tamika needs a new foster home, and Andy has just found out that his mother is pregnant. Adler's accessible text works well with Hillenbrand's black-and-white drawings.

6.67 Danziger, Paula (1998). **Amber Brown Is Feeling Blue.** Illustrated by Tony Ross. New York: Putnam. 133 pp. ISBN: 0-399-23179-X. Chapter Book.

Amber Brown is faced with a major dilemma. Max, her mother's boyfriend, has invited them to Walla Walla, Washington, for Thanksgiving. However Amber's father is returning from a lengthy job assignment in Paris, and is anxious to take his daughter to New York City to see the Thanksgiving Day parade. Add to this a new girl at school by the name of Kelly Green, and readers familiar with the series will anticipate Amber's discovery of a positive solution to her problem.

6.68 Haddad, Charles (1998). **Meet Calliope Day.** Illustrated by Steve Pica. New York: Delacorte. 150 pp. ISBN: 0-385-32518-5. Chapter Book.

Calliope's father has died, which forces her mother to get a job and Calliope to go to the after-school program (ASP). Coupled with that, her teacher confiscates Calliope's pink vampire teeth, the police are trying to seize her rabbit Mortimer, and Calliope suspects the cranky neighbor Mrs. Blatherhorn of being a witch. The humorous text is enhanced by Pica's black-and-white cartoon illustrations.

6.69 Moss, Marissa (1996). **Amelia Writes Again!** Berkeley, CA: Tricycle. Unpaged. ISBN: 1-883672-42-2. Picture Book.

Ten-year-old Amelia receives a journal for her birthday, and proceeds to record information and pictures about her life in and out of school. Readers gain insight into Amelia's personal thoughts and perceptions of others through humorous text and well-labeled ink-and-watercolor illustrations. A terrific example of how a journal can become meaningful in a child's life.

Another book about Amelia by this author is:

Moss, Marissa (1998). **Amelia Takes Command.** Middleton, WI: Pleasant. Unpaged. ISBN: 1-56247-789-7. Picture Book.

High-Interest Series Books

See also the section entitled Series Books in chapter 7, "Literacy."

6.70 Applegate, K. A. **Animorphs series.** New York: Scholastic.

Jake, Rachel, Tobias, Cassie, and Marco can't tell you who they are or where they live as it would be too risky, but readers do know that these characters are apt to morph into other life forms. The ending of each book sets up the next book in the series, and if readers flip the pages they will see a small illustration on the right bottom corner morph as well. Peter (age ten) explained, "I like reading Animorphs because it always leaves you waiting for what happens next and they are fun books to read." RL 5.

6.71 Bennett, Cherie. **Pageant series.** New York: Berkley Jam.

Teen Spirit magazine is sponsoring four regional pageants across the nation in order to find a real girl to wear the crown. There are a series of books for each regional area, which includes to date midwestern girls, southern girls, and northeastern girls. RL not indicated.

6.72 Berenstain, Stan, and Jan Berenstain. **The Berenstain Bears series.** New York: Random House.

This series continues to be popular with parents and children. In each book, Sister Bear and Brother Bear learn a lesson related to issues such as sharing, fighting, and getting along with each other. RL not indicated.

6.73 Betancourt, Jeanne. **Pony Pals series.** New York: Scholastic.

There are several series such as this one which are focused on friendships built around the love of riding horses. RL 3.

6.74 Brown, Marc, creator. **Arthur Chapter Book series.** Boston: Little Brown.

Stories about Arthur and his friends are presented in a chapter book format for children ready to read independently. RL 3.

6.75 Bryant, Bonnie. **The Saddle Club series.** New York: Skylark.

Over eighty books in this series focus on Carole the horse lover, Stevie the practical joker, and Lisa who is a straight-A student. The common bond between them all is that they enjoy riding horses that are boarded at Pine Hollows Stables. RL 5.

6.76 Campbell, Joanna. **Thoroughbred series.** New York: HarperCollins.

Another series based on characters' love of horses. The four friends in this series include Ashleigh Griffin, Christine Reese, Samantha McLean, and Cindy McLean. RL 5+.

6.77 Dadey, Debbie, and Marcia Thornton Jones. **The Adventures of the Bailey School Kids series.** New York: Scholastic.

The kids at the Bailey School find adventure and mystery both inside and outside of the classroom. Caprice (age 8) said, "I read Bailey School Kids because they are exciting to read over and over again. They talk about witches and mummies and I like that." RL 3.

6.78 Dubowski, Mark. **Sabrina the Teenage Witch series.** New York: Pocket.

Adapted by Mark Dubowski from the television series, this book series takes readers on further adventures with Sabrina the Teenage Witch and her cat, Salem. RL 2.

6.79 Hughes, Dean. **Scrappers series.** New York: Aladdin.

A series that highlights the world of baseball as a team of nine kids fight for a shot at the championship. Each book includes Official Scrappers Trivia Trading Cards that feature facts about the game of baseball and its players. RL 2–6.

6.80 Martin, Ann M. **Baby-Sitters Little Sister series.** New York: Scholastic.

Martin, Ann M. **The Baby-Sitters Club series.** New York: Scholastic.

These series by Ann M. Martin focus on a multicultural group of friends and their siblings. Martin chooses to bring out issues that are relevant to the age group intended for this series. "I like the Baby-Sitters Club books because they talk about girls my age and what they like to do. It also helps me through my life because they sometimes are going through what I am going through," said Cambria (age ten). RL 3–4.

6.81 Martin, Ann M. **California Diaries series.** New York: Scholastic.

Written in a diary format, this series by Martin focuses on the problems of teenagers such as eating disorders, alcohol, friendship, stepparents, boyfriends, etc. Each book in the series deals with the problems of one of the characters, named Dawn, Sunny, Amalia, Maggie, and Ducky. RL 6+.

6.82 Martin, Ann M. **The Kids in Ms. Colman's Class series.** New York: Scholastic.

This series focuses on the students in Ms. Colman's class, and the various issues they face in their lives such as having to go to day camp during summer vacation. RL 2.

6.83 Metzger, Steve. **Dinofours series.** Illustrated by Hans Wilhelm. New York: Scholastic Cartwheel.

This series for young children combines dinosaur characters, all of whom are four years old, and their preschool experiences. RL not indicated.

6.84 Pascal, Francine, creator. **Sweet Valley High series.** New York: Bantam Doubleday Dell.

Stories of teenage twins, Elizabeth and Jessica Wakefield, who encounter all of the difficulties growing up with parents, teachers, and peers. RL 6.

6.85 Pascal, Francine, creator. **Sweet Valley Kids series.** New York: Bantam Doubleday Dell.

Stories about Elizabeth and Jessica Wakefield that take place in Sweet Valley Elementary. RL 2.

6.86 Pascal, Francine, creator. **Sweet Valley Twins and Friends series.** New York: Bantam Doubleday Dell.

This series provides a middle-school setting for Elizabeth and Jessica Wakefield. Also ties into the television program and web site. RL 4.

6.87 **Positively for Kids series.** Dallas, TX: Taylor. (See **12.2**)

6.88 Rees, Elizabeth M. **Heartbeats series.** New York: Aladdin.

This series for adolescents features artistic and romantic rivalries between the students who attend Dance Tech, a combined ballet and ballroom dancing school. RL not indicated.

6.89 **Rugrats series.** New York: Simon Spotlight/Nickelodeon.

These picture books are based on the popular television series and movie featuring the antics of the Rugrats characters. RL not indicated.

6.90 Stine, R. L. **Fear Street series.** New York: Scholastic.

Stine, R. L. **Ghosts of Fear Street series.** New York: Scholastic.

Stine, R. L. **Fear Street Sagas series.** New York: Scholastic.

Intended for older readers, Stine shares gruesome and terrifying horror stories for readers. Children wanting more information can access the Web site. RL not indicated.

6.91   Stine, R. L. **Goosebumps series.** New York: Scholastic.

Stine, R. L. **Goosebumps 2000 series.** New York: Scholastic.

Stine, R. L. **Goosebumps Find Yourself series.** New York: Scholastic.

This enormously popular series provides horror, chills, thrills, and mysteries for readers. "I like to read books by R. L. Stine because his books are exciting, scary, and funny all at the same time," commented Justin (age eleven). RL 4.

6.92   **Two of a Kind series.** New York: Harper Entertainment.

These books are based on the television series featuring twins Mary-Kate and Ashley Olsen. Illustrated with photographs from the television show. RL not indicated.

6.93   Warner, Gertrude Chandler, creator. **The Adventures of Benny and Watch: A Boxcar Children Early Reader series.** New York: Scholastic.

These brief stories feature the four Alden children solving simple mysteries in a beginning-to-read format for younger readers. RL 1–3.

6.94   Warner, Gertrude Chandler, creator. **The Boxcar Children series.** New York: Scholastic.

The four main characters of the original Boxcar Children book—Henry, Jessie, Violet, and Benny Alden—continue having numerous adventures while solving mysteries. Miss Warner passed away in 1979 after having written well over sixty books in the Boxcar Children series. "I like to read The Boxcar Children series because they are good mystery stories. They don't bore or confuse me," said Courtney (age nine). RL 3.

6.95   **Wishbone Classics series.** New York: HarperCollins.

The television canine takes readers through a variety of classics such as *The Odyssey, Oliver Twist, Romeo and Juliet*, and *Frankenstein.* At various times throughout the book, Wishbone tells readers what has happened in the story or the events that are yet to occur. "I like Wishbone because I like learning about the past and how they lived and what they did," said Abigail (age nine). RL 3.5–4.5.

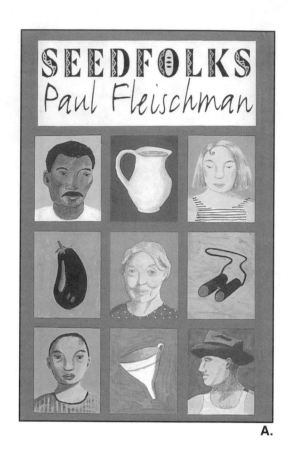

A.

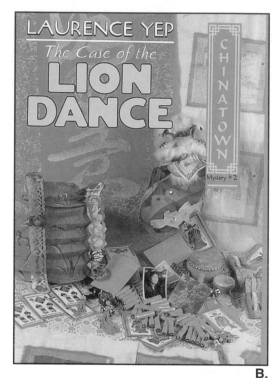

B.

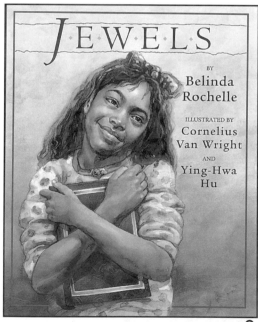

C.

D.

A. *Seedfolks,* Paul Fleischman (**7.66**). **B.** *The Case of the Lion Dance,* Laurence Yep (**7.62**). **C.** *Jewels,* Belinda Rochelle/Cornelius Van Wright and Ying-Hwa Hu (**7.91**). **D.** *The Moonflower,* Peter and Jean Loewer (**7.17**).

7 Literacy

Carol Gilles

Contributing reviewers included Marilyn Andre, Linda Aulgur, Carolyn Dye, Carol Gilles, Janice Henson, Veronica Lee, Jenine Loesing, MariBeth Loesing, Virginia Pfannenstiel, Pam Riggs, Sharon Schneeberger, Sharon Stemmons, and Shelli Thelen.

Frank Smith (1978) once said, "We learn to read by reading" (97). In that sense, all books that children read are literacy books because they help children develop understanding, vocabulary, and fluency while entertaining or informing them. However there are some books that are especially helpful in teaching reading because they are interesting and have been written in ways that are particularly accessible to children. These books include predictable books, concept books, early chapter books, series books, short stories or high-interest books for reticent readers, books about literacy, and books that emphasize the art of storytelling. These are the types of books selected for this chapter.

As our review committee selected outstanding titles, we looked for books that Dorothy Watson (1997) called "supportive texts." Eight-year-old Alvin helped Watson define supportive text when he said, "I can *work* this story." He explained a workable story was one that he liked "enough to try hard" (in Watson 1997, 635). Supportive texts entice readers as they offer the structures necessary to help them create meaning. Supportive texts include those that are predictable in their word patterns, syntax, concepts, or illustrations. They might rhyme or have a rhythm to them. They are also books in which the author gives readers clues to help with difficult concepts or words.

After reading and examining hundreds of books, we decided on the following categorical system for organizing the books reviewed in this chapter:

- Emergent Literacy. This section includes wordless books, highly predictable books where the illustrations tell most of the story, and books with refrains that even young children quickly learn to mimic.
- Rhythm, Rhyme, and Repetition. In this section, we included predictable books that offer a challenge for more mature readers.

- Concept Books. This section includes books that support beginning reading by offering one concept that is developed throughout the book. We chose some concept books for beginning readers, and some for more mature readers.

- ABC Books. In this section, the reader will find books that younger readers can relate to, or books that are conceptual in nature for older readers. Although we examined many ABC books, we chose only a few. Many of the ABC books were attractive, but didn't support readers.

- Beginning Chapter Books. This section includes those books that offer a transition between I-can-read books with few words and many pictures, and more sophisticated literature. The latter still use a simple vocabulary, but the story line carries over into several chapters.

- Series Books. In this section, we included those books in which a character is repeated across many books by the same author. Many of the series books printed today are enjoyable, but are not high-quality literature. We chose for inclusion series that were written by respected authors and in which many of the books in the series were of higher quality. Series books are useful in the reading process because the characters, setting, and plot frequently are similar across the series. Because readers often will read all the books in the series, predicting and confirming is made easier and the student can work on fluency. Books in this section have been subdivided into three categories: Emergent-Reader Books, Beginning Chapter Books, and Books for Mature Readers.

- Books for Reticent Readers. In this section, we have included books that appeal to a broad range of readers, even those who may have difficulty reading. We also have chosen to put outstanding short stories here. Often older at-risk readers are intimidated by long chapter books, but are eager to read good stories. The short-story books listed here contain outstanding stories that can be handled easily by older readers, or used as read-aloud texts. Some of the books in this section have strong subject appeal without sacrificing literary quality, enticing reluctant readers into the world of print.

- Books about Literacy. This section includes books that use a journal or letter format, and it also includes books that deal with the topic of learning how to read.

- Storytelling Books. We have included here books that either include references to storytelling or are composed of an oral story that has been written down. Storytelling is an old and honored tradition, and these books allow children to experience the tradition of storytelling across cultures.

Works Cited

Smith, Frank. 1978. *Reading without Nonsense*. New York: Teachers College.

Watson, Dorothy. 1998. Beyond Decodable Text: Supportive and Workable Literature. *Language Arts* 74, no. 8: 635–643.

---

*The titles listed below each subheading are organized into Primary Reviews and Secondary Reviews. The Primary Reviews describe outstanding books in each subheading. The Secondary Reviews provide brief information about other books worthy of consideration. Some titles listed below are **not** reviewed in this chapter; entries for these titles are not annotated and contain only bibliographic information. In such cases, a cross reference to the annotated entry contained elsewhere in this volume is provided in boldface type at the end of the bibliographic information.*

Emergent Literacy

Primary Reviews

7.1 Harris, Marian (1998). **Tuesday in Arizona.** Illustrated by Jim Harris. Gretna, LA: Pelican. Unpaged. ISBN: 1-56554-233-9. Picture Book. (See **8.37**)

7.2 Hoban, Tana (1997). **Look Book.** New York: Greenwillow. Unpaged. ISBN: 0-688-14971-5. Picture Book.

Tana Hoban has created another wordless book using nature photographs. Readers are challenged to guess what picture will be revealed through the cutout. Beautiful color photographs of sunflowers, cabbages, birds, a dog, pretzels, an ostrich, a lobster, a hippopotamus, and a butterfly help students appreciate nature. Students will naturally want to create their own version of this impressive book. In addition to discovering the photo in its entirety, one reviewer's kindergarten students began a discussion about the animals in various habitats. This book will spark talk in the classroom.

7.3 Inkpen, Mick (1996). **Everyone Hide from Wibbly Pig.** New York: Penguin. Unpaged. ISBN: 0-670-87489-2. Picture Book.

This flap book was a definite first-grade favorite! The pigs play hide-and-seek, and Tiny Pig needs help choosing a good hiding place. Wibbly Pig begins his search and finds pigs under the towel, behind the towel, and in the shower. Soon all the pigs are found, and the troops begin a pig hunt for Tiny Pig. Will he be found? The best flap is saved for last! Children in one reviewer's class made their own flap books. Drawing the objects on the page, and then designing a flap that was part of the environment and large enough to cover the drawing, was a great problem-solving adventure.

7.4 Tafuri, Nancy (1997). **What the Sun Sees.** New York: Greenwillow. Unpaged. ISBN: 0-688-14493-4. Picture Book.

Nancy Tafuri explores the concept of the sun and moon with beautiful full-page colored-pencil, watercolor and black-ink illustrations that support the simple, repetitive text. The first half of the book investigates what the sun sees. Then the reader must turn the book over and upside down to discover what the moon sees. Emergent first-grade readers were intrigued by the layout, and wanted to talk about the book's format after the read-aloud session. The book encourages children to develop illustrations and text that explore their own concept of what the sun and moon see.

Secondary Reviews

7.5 Harter, Debbie (1997). **Walking through the Jungle.** New York: Orchard. Unpaged. ISBN: 0-531-30035-8. Picture Book.

The lush, colorful illustrations brimming with wildlife invite the reader to travel through the desert, the mountains, and the ocean, enjoying the animals and terrain of each habitat. The rhythmic rhymes of the book support the development of early readers. First graders enjoyed chanting along with this read-aloud book and finding animals in the various habitats. The book was a popular choice during sustained silent-reading sessions, as well as a useful resource book for habitat or animal studies.

7.6 Nicholson, Sue (1998). **A Day at Greenhill Farm.** New York: Dorling Kindersley. 32 pp. ISBN: 0-7894-2957-8. Picture Book.

Early in the morning, the rooster at Greenhill Farm starts the day by waking all the farm animals with his cock-a-doodle-doo! This nonfiction picture storybook is an ideal resource for primary teachers to include in their classroom libraries. The simple, informative text describes the various animals on the farm, and allows young readers to use the book as a primary source for research. The book contains real-life photographs, and just the right amount of text. It is an invaluable tool for learning when studying the farm.

Rhythm, Rhyme, and Repetition

See also chapter 10, "Poetry"; and the section entitled Riddles, Chants, and Poems in chapter 13, "The Craft of Language."

Primary Reviews

7.7   Greene, Rhonda Gowler (1997). **Barnyard Song.** Illustrated by Robert Bender. New York: Atheneum. Unpaged. ISBN: 0-689-80758-9. Picture Book.

The barnyard is alive with animal noises and cries until a bee with a contagious sneeze turns the song into sniffles and wheezes. Children love Bender's large colorful illustrations of a sick horse with a water bottle on his head, or the farmer giving medicine to a bee with an eyedropper. This book demands to be read and enjoyed multiple times. First graders chanted the repetitive parts, sang the book, dramatized the story with animal sound effects, put on a musical puppet dramatization, and added other animal characters. When one reviewer put the book out for individuals or groups to revisit, it stayed in constant use.

7.8   Marsh, T. J., and Jennifer Ward (1998). **Way out in the Desert.** Illustrated by Kenneth Spengler. Flagstaff, AZ: Northland. Unpaged. ISBN: 0-87358-687-5. Picture Book.

This book uses the tune of "Over in the Meadow" to introduce readers to different animals in the Sonoran desert. From the beginning lines, "Way out in the desert having fun in the sun, lived a mother horned lizard and her little toady ONE," readers are caught up in the rhyme and the vibrant illustrations. After two readings, this book became the favorite singing book of several groups of children during independent reading time. Kenneth Spengler used gouache on watercolor paper to create bold, double-page spreads that present the desert from animal-eye perspectives and that are often large enough for an entire class to enjoy them together. He hides a number in each illustration that matches the number in the verse, inviting children to revisit this book again and again. A glossary of the desert animals introduced in the book will help children become more familiar with the unique collection of desert animals presented here. Musical notation also is included for teachers and students who may not be familiar with the melody.

7.9   Zamorano, Ana (1996). **Let's Eat!** Illustrated by Julie Vivas. New York: Scholastic. Unpaged. ISBN: 0-590-13444-2. Picture Book. (See **4.109**)

Secondary Reviews

7.10   Hazen, Barbara (1998). **That Toad Is Mine!** Illustrated by Jane Manning. New York: Harper Festival. Unpaged. ISBN: 0-694-01035-9. Picture Book.

This book concerns two boys who are friends and who share everything, until they both decide they want a toad and can't figure out a way to share it. As they're fighting over the toad, it hops away. They resolve their dispute and become friends again. The story is written in rhyme and is easy to read. The pleasing watercolor illustrations emphasize the relationship between the two friends.

7.11   Jessup, Harley (1997). **What's Alice Up To?** New York: Penguin. Unpaged. ISBN: 0-670-87396-9. Picture Book.

Do you like mysteries? As you read this book, use the clues to help the dog figure out what Alice is up to. As Alice's dog watches her gather a variety of items from around the house and yard, the dog and the reader naturally ask questions. Jessup's large, detailed illustrations add to the clues. A delightful, surprise ending tops off this unique mystery.

7.12   Mahy, Margaret (1996). **Boom, Baby, Boom, Boom!** Illustrated by Patricia MacCarthy. New York: Viking. Unpaged. ISBN: 0-670-87314-4. Picture Book.

Mahy uses onomatopoeia and repeated phrases to create a natural read-aloud book. When Mama ignores Baby to play her diddy-dum-drums, the farm animals creep, gallop, scuttle, trot, and amble into the kitchen and eat Baby's lunch. As the drums become silent, the animals retreat and Mama, finding Baby alone with a clean plate, is delighted. First-grade children loved the large, colorful illustrations and enjoyed repeating the phrase "boom-biddy-boom-biddy-boom-boom-boom!"

7.13   Mayer, Marianna (1998). **The Mother Goose Cookbook: Rhymes and Recipes for the Very Young.** Illustrated by Carol Schwartz. New York: Morrow Junior Books. 37 pp. ISBN: 0-688-15242-2. Picture Book. (See **12.56**)

7.14   Reiser, Lynn (1998). **Tortillas and Lullabies/Tortillas y cancionci-tas.** Illustrated by Corazones Valientes. Translated by Rebecca Hart. New York: Greenwillow. 40 pp. ISBN: 0-688-14628-7. Picture Book. (See **13.39**)

Concept Books

See also the section entitled Math Concept Books in chapter 9, "Mathematics."

Primary Reviews

7.15   Harris, Pamela (1998). **Hot, Cold, Shy, Bold: Looking at Opposites.** Toronto, Canada: Kids Can. Unpaged. ISBN: 1-55074-153-5. Picture Book.

This concept book focuses on opposites. The photographs and repetitive language enable many beginning readers to read this book after hearing it a few times. Children's and grown-ups' faces are used to introduce opposites such as hot/cold, shy/bold, hello/goodbye, old/new, and serious/funny. On each page one new word is introduced, supported by picture clues. The photographs, rich in color and texture, appeal to young children and adults. Emergent readers will find they can read this book quickly. Children also will enjoy making their own opposites books using photographs or magazine cutouts.

7.16   Llewellyn, Claire (1997). **Spiders Have Fangs and Other Amazing Facts about Arachnids.** Illustrated by Mike Taylor and Christopher Shield. Brookfield, CT: Millbrook. 32 pp. ISBN: 0-7613-0610-2. Picture Book.

Students will enjoy the bold, bright colors contrasted with a black background, which makes the spiders seem to move off the page of this book. In addition to providing the reader with useful information about arachnids, symbols indicate projects to try and true-false questions children may enjoy answering. Page borders give additional exciting information. The format is intriguing, with each page spread organized around an "I didn't know that" statement, including "I didn't know that some spiders spit," "I didn't know that spiders have eight eyes," and "I didn't know that spiders change color." A table of contents, index, and glossary provide an excellent opportunity to introduce the structure of nonfiction books. Fascinating for fourth graders, younger readers were also captivated by this book.

7.17   Loewer, Peter (1997). **The Moonflower.** Illustrated by Jean Loewer. Atlanta: Peachtree. 27 pp. ISBN: 1-56145-138-X. Picture Book.

This concept book explores nature at night. As the moonflower blooms, crickets chirp, bats glide, fireflies flicker, and hawkmoths appear. The large, bright illustrations cover three-quarters of a page. The book has a melodic narrative line, as well as a column of factual information on each page. For example, the narrative says, "The fireflies of summer will soon begin to send their flashing codes, shining like flying sparklers," while the scientific section states, "Fireflies, or lightning bugs, use a blinking glow to communicate with each other. The male firefly flashes a special code that only female fireflies of the same species understand." The combination of fact, fiction, and lush illustrations appeals to many readers.

7.18   Morton, Christine (1998). **Picnic Farm.** Illustrated by Sarah Barringer. New York: Holiday House. Unpaged. ISBN: 0-8234-1332-2. Picture Book.

Gorgeous and bright pastel illustrations create initial interest in this picture book about children who visit a farm, and then go on a picnic. At the picnic, food is consumed from each of the farm crops or livestock the children saw on the first few pages. The book makes it very clear that the products are from the animals they saw. For example, the texts explains that the farmer spread out "A rug, a rug-of-wool from the sheep. At the picnic people eat, Eggs, eggs—laid by the hen. Honey, honey made by the bees." For early childhood classes studying food or farms, this concept book provides a beautiful resource that young children will return to often.

7.19   Speed, Toby (1998). **Water Voices.** Illustrated by Julie Downing. New York: Putnam. Unpaged. ISBN: 0-399-22631-1. Picture Book.

This book is an inspiring read-aloud full of riddles that are rich in imagery. Each riddle describes a different form of water that children enjoy, such as morningmist, sprinklerspray, and oceanwave.

One riddle asks:

when your fingers wrinkle
and the soap slips
and the waves make little plishings
and all the hard parts of the day
go sailing off in cups and scoops,
I hold you close in my lap
Who am I? (Answer: Bedtime bath.)

Downing's soft, flowing watercolors add to the wet experience. First graders spent a lot of time talking about the words and the pictures that were created in their heads. The discussion then turned to other water voices that weren't included in the book. After naming several, some of the students wrote riddles about them.

Secondary Reviews

7.20 Cabrera, Jane (1997). **Cat's Colors.** New York: Dial Books for Young Readers. Unpaged. ISBN: 0-8037-2090-4. Picture Book.

The simple, bright illustrations in this book intrigued children as they learned about colors. A kitten presents the question, "What is my favorite color? Is it green?" That question is repeated with various colors throughout the story. At the end, the reader finds that the kitten's favorite color is orange because it is the color of her mother. Each page layout displays the background color in simple finger-paint style, with the kitten appearing on every spread. The predictable text is supportive and allowed one reviewer's special needs students to read the question on each page and identify the colors.

7.21 Knight, Margy Burns (1996). **Talking Walls: The Stories Continue.** Illustrated by Anne Sibley O'Brien. Gardiner, ME: Tilbury. Unpaged. ISBN: 0-88448-165-4. Picture Book.

A continuation of the award winning *Talking Walls,* this nonfiction picture book shares stories about walls that have been built to divide, protect, and enhance the lives of people. Readers will develop respect for various cultures by learning the cultural significance of each wall, and the purpose and effort it took to construct it. This selection provides much potential for the investigation of culture and other aspects of social studies throughout the world.

Knight, Margy Burns (1992). **Talking Walls.** Illustrated by Anne Sibley O'Brien. Gardiner, ME: Tilbury. ISBN: 0-88448-102-6. Picture Book

7.22   Yaccarino, Dan (1997). **Good Night, Mr. Night.** San Diego: Harcourt Brace. Unpaged. ISBN: 0-15-201319-9. Picture Book.

This imaginative concept book about night is unusual and promotes discussion. The text describes Mr. Night brushing past the trees, closing the flowers, and quieting the animals. The stylized watercolor illustrations add to the feeling of security. During a study of day and night, one reviewer read this book to her first-grade class. They liked the imaginative view of night, and decided there should be a book about day starring a woman.

ABC Books

Primary Reviews

7.23   Ada, Alma Flor (1997). **Gathering the Sun: An Alphabet in Spanish and English.** Illustrated by Simón Silva. Translated by Rosa Zubizaretta. New York: Lothrop, Lee & Shepard. Unpaged. ISBN: 0-688-13903-5. Picture Book.

Gathering the Sun is an alphabet book of original Spanish poems, accompanied by faithful English translations. The individual poems can stand powerfully by themselves. Each letter of the alphabet is represented by a poem that honors the lives of farm workers and their families. Simón Silvas' vibrant gouache illustrations show the hearts, homes, and cultures of the people who work the fields in scenes that will be recognized by anyone who has crossed the fertile valleys of our country. This book can be used in both primary and intermediate grades for many purposes, including learning the alphabet, studying poetic form in either language, and learning more about migrant workers.

7.24   Dakos, Kalli (1997). **Get out of the Alphabet, Number 2! Wacky Wednesday Puzzle Poems.** Illustrated by Jenny Graham. New York: Simon & Schuster. 32 pp. ISBN: 0-689-81118-7. Picture Book. (See **10.8**)

7.25   Ellwand, David (1996). **Emma's Elephant and Other Favorite Animal Friends.** New York: Dutton Children's Books. Unpaged. ISBN: 0-525-45792-5. Picture Book. (See **11.35**)

7.26 Pandell, Karen (1996). **Animal Action ABC.** Photographs by Art Wolfe and Nancy Sheehan. New York: Dutton. Unpaged. ISBN: 0-525-45486-1. Picture Book. (See **13.22**)

7.27 Rosenberg, Liz (1997). **A Big and Little Alphabet.** Illustrated by Vera Rosenberry. New York: Orchard. Unpaged. ISBN: 0-531-30050-1. Picture Book. (See **13.24**)

7.28 Sandved, Kjell B. (1996). **The Butterfly Alphabet.** New York: Scholastic. Unpaged. ISBN: 0-590-48003-0. Picture Book.

World-renowned nature photographer Kjell B. Sandved once noticed the letter *F* on the wing of a tropical moth. So began his journey to find alphabet letters on butterfly and moth wings. The close-up color photographs in this book are vivid and textured. Each butterfly and moth species is correctly labeled on the bottom of the page, and is pictured in full in the upper-left corner. In addition, the alphabet letter highlighted on each page, and the word in the verse that begins with that letter, are illustrated in the same color. For example, the *C* page states, "The rainbow gave to butterflies / Spots of *color* just their size." Opposite the verse, one can see clearly the magnified *C* on the Christmas swallowtail butterfly. This book will delight both older and younger readers.

7.29 Schnur, Steven (1997). **Autumn: An Alphabet Acrostic.** Illustrated by Leslie Evans. New York: Clarion. Unpaged. ISBN: 0-395-77043-2. Picture Book. (See **13.9**)

7.30 Shannon, George (1996). **Tomorrow's Alphabet.** Illustrated by Donald Crews. New York: Greenwillow. Unpaged. ISBN: 0-688-13504-8. Picture Book.

Instead of creating the traditional alphabet book, which matches picture to letter, Shannon has shown what an object might potentially become. For example, "F is for wheat—tomorrow's flour. T is for bread—tomorrow's toast. V is for paper—tomorrow's Valentine." Several features make this book appealing: simple, repetitive language; the letter and the key word in the same color; a consistent two-page layout; and simple, uncluttered illustrations that support the text. When one reviewer's first-grade students made an alphabet book using the same style, they carefully considered the potential of many objects in the world, such as M is for cows—tomorrow's milk.

7.31   Wilbur, Richard (1997). **The Disappearing Alphabet.** Illustrated by David Díaz. San Diego: Harcourt Brace. Unpaged. ISBN: 0-15-201470-5. Picture Book. (See **13.27**)

Secondary Reviews

7.32   Chin-Lee, Cynthia (1997). **A Is for Asia.** Illustrated by Yumi Heo. New York: Orchard. Unpaged. ISBN: 0-531-30011-0. Picture Book.

Organized as an alphabet book, this text takes readers to various Asian cultures to learn about their traditions, treasures, and symbolic events. These cultural events involve children, and the book explains how they take part in appreciating the uniqueness of their respective cultures by participating in these events. The descriptions on each page also are represented in the native language of the culture represented, maintaining the culture's authenticity and voice. Color and life jump off each page, making this an attractive book for young readers.

7.33   Holtz, Lara Tankel (1997). **Alphabet Book.** Photographs by Dave King. New York: Dorling Kindersley. Unpaged. ISBN: 0-7894-2053-8. Picture Book.

Young children love the adventure and interaction found in search-and-find books, and this book is no exception. In addition to finding many objects starting with the named letter ("Can you see sixteen starfish scattered in the sand?"), readers also are challenged to solve riddles. The bright colors and clever arrangements will attract children of all ages, and based on how one reviewer's kindergarten class reacted, this book will be devoured by all children. The reviewer's kindergarten students talked about this book for weeks, and selected it as a favorite for the entire school year.

7.34   Kusugak, Michael (1996). **My Arctic 1, 2, 3.** New York: Annick. 22 pp. ISBN: 1-55037-505-9. Picture Book. (See **9.4**)

7.35   Stroud, Virginia (1996). **The Path of the Quiet Elk.** New York: Dial. 30 pp. ISBN: 0-8037-1717-2. Picture Book.

Virginia Stroud, a Cherokee-Creek author and illustrator, has created an alphabet book that looks at life's connection with the earth. Looks Within, a young Native American girl living during the

1880s, learns about the interconnectedness of everything on earth through her elder, Wisdom Keeper. Stroud assembles twenty-six ways for Looks Within to search out what the earth has to offer her. Each of the twenty-six letters is illustrated with a nature scene in Stroud's distinct artistic style. This book will hold the interest of students in kindergarten through third grade.

7.36 Tobias, Tobi (1998). **A World of Words: An ABC of Quotations.** Illustrated by Peter Malone. New York: Lothrop, Lee & Shepard Books. Unpaged. ISBN: 0-688-12129-2. Picture Book.

This unusual alphabet book features quotations that fit the whimsical illustrations. Quotations range from Native American Ute sayings to the words of Edna St. Vincent Millay, Shakespeare, and Lucille Cliffton. Children will delight in discovering that Thomas Jefferson said, "I cannot live without books," while Kate Guess mused, "As a child, I had two copies of each of my favorite books: one for the bathtub, and one for dry land." Younger children will enjoy hearing these quotations and marveling at the bright full-color illustrations, while older children will enjoy reading this book independently.

Beginning Chapter Books

Primary Reviews

7.37 Byars, Betsy (1997). **Ant Plays Bear.** Illustrated by Marc Simont. New York: Viking. 32 pp. ISBN: 0-670-86776-4. Chapter Book.

In this companion book to *My Brother Ant,* Anthony and his brother demonstrate the loving relationship they share. For example, when Ant frantically wakes his brother because he hears someone tapping on the window, his brother patiently dispels all his wild imaginings of giants by explaining, "Everyone with very long legs is playing basketball." Finally Ant realizes a tree branch is responsible for the tapping, and both brothers go back to sleep. This Viking Easy-to-Read book (reading level 3) could be used as a bridge to longer chapter books. The vocabulary, amount of text, and story content are appropriate for early primary readers, who could read this book independently.

> Byars, Betsy (1998). **My Brother Ant**. Illustrated by Marc Simont. New York: Viking. 32 pp. ISBN: 0-14-038345-X. Chapter Book.

7.38 Cosby, Bill (1998). **Money Troubles.** Illustrated by Varnette P. Honeywood. New York: Scholastic. 40 pp. ISBN: 0-590-16402-3. Chapter Book.

Little Bill's dreams of purchasing a telescope so that he can become a famous astronomer change once he begins to realize what it will take to earn the remaining money to purchase it. The little jobs around the house and throughout the neighborhood don't raise the money quickly enough. Little Bill begins to collect recyclable cans from the street and bumps into a young boy who is collecting cans to raise enough money to eat. Little Bill stops thinking about himself and turns his attention to establishing a food drive program at his school. He realizes that he will still become famous one day, but for now he is happy simply being recognized for such a good deed. Varnette P. Honeywood's colorful illustrations assist new readers in comprehending the text.

7.39 Lawlor, Laurie (1998). **The Worst Kid Who Ever Lived on Eighth Avenue.** Illustrated by Cynthia Fisher. New York: Holiday House. 48 pp. ISBN: 0-8234-1350-0. Chapter Book.

Leroy, the bad-news kid from Eighth Avenue, is back! The Eighth Street gang watch him bury something (probably money), and they decide to become detectives to solve the crime. In six chapters, Lawlor spins a solid tale. The full-color illustrations and large print make this book accessible to beginning chapter-book readers. Second graders enjoyed reading this book independently, and also enjoyed it as a read-aloud text. They talked about making predictions about people, and about what could happen if one assumes too much about a person.

7.40 Little, Jean (1998). **Emma's Magic Winter.** Illustrated by Jennifer Plecas. New York: HarperCollins. 64 pp. ISBN: 0-06-025389-4. Chapter Book.

This is a simple story of a shy young girl who is embarrassed to read aloud in front of the class, and a new neighbor who is afraid she won't be able to make friends, overcoming their fears. Large, attractive illustrations sprinkled throughout this book make it even more accessible for beginning chapter-book readers. When one reviewer read this book to second-grade girls, they especially appreciated the common fears that the girls conquered and their use of imagination as part of their play. Even within the constraints of a limited vocabulary, the author manages to write with finesse. The characters are believable, and the story is interesting and easy to follow.

7.41 Scheffler, Ursel (1997). **Grandpa's Amazing Computer.** Illustrated by Ruth Scholte van Mast. Translated by Rosemary Lanning. New York: North-South. 48 pp. ISBN: 1-55858-795-0. Chapter Book.

When Ollie has an opportunity to visit his grandfather, he discovers that Grandpa doesn't know anything about computers, even though he could benefit from one because he is so forgetful. Grandpa shows Ollie nature's oldest computer—a seed. Not only does this book provide a look at the generational differences associated with using computers, it also makes a great addition to a text-set about plants. Although it is not a chapter book, it is very similar in format to early chapter books. This appealed to budding first-grade readers eager to read chapter books.

7.42 Walker, Sally M. (1998). **The 18 Penny Goose.** Illustrated by Ellen Beier. New York: HarperCollins. 61 pp. ISBN: 0-06-027556-1. Chapter Book. (See **5.35**)

Secondary Reviews

7.43 Bauer, Marion Dane (1998). **Bear's Hiccups.** Illustrated by Diane Dawson Hearn. New York: Holiday House. 48 pp. ISBN: 0-8234-1339-X. Chapter Book.

First graders ready for beginning chapter books enjoyed this book. They identified with the problem that bear and frog have sharing the pond that each has claimed as his own. The repetitive language in the text, such as "Otter was so hot he quit playing. Frog was so hot he quit croaking," supports beginning readers. Bauer also uses strong similes, such as "The pond lay flat and still, like a scarf dropped in the grass." Hearn's large, comical illustrations add to the humor in the story. The large type and pictures on every page make this a good transitional text into chapter books.

7.44 Brisson, Pat (1997). **Hot Fudge Hero.** Illustrated by Diana Cain Bluthenthal. New York: Henry Holt. 72 pp. ISBN: 0-8050-4551-1. Chapter Book.

Bertie celebrates every personal victory with a hot fudge sundae. The three stories are funny, lifelike, and teach a lesson. In one,

Bertie needs to get his ball back from the yard of Mr. Meckleberg, a mean old man with a dog named Attila and a cat named Screamer. At the library, Bertie finds *How to Make Friends in Five Easy Steps,* and proceeds to try each step until he makes Meckleberg his friend and retrieves his ball. Second graders appreciated how each story involved a hot fudge sundae. They liked the details the pen-and-ink drawings added to the stories.

7.45 Quigley, James (1997). **Johnny Germ Head.** Illustrated by JoAnn Adinolfi. New York: Henry Holt. 72 pp. ISBN: 0-8050-5395-6. Chapter Book.

Johnny Jarvis wants to be a doctor, so his parents buy him a microscope. Looking into the microscope, Johnny discovers that germs are everywhere! Johnny becomes obsessed with germs and needs to cure his phobia. This book complemented a second-grade unit on the human body, during which one reviewer's class talked about the immune system, various germs, and diseases. The black-and-white illustrations add drama to Johnny's phobia about germs.

Series Books

See also the section entitled High-Interest Series Books in chapter 6, "School Life."

Emergent-Reader Books

Primary Reviews

7.46 Brown, Marc (1998). **Arthur's Mystery Envelope.** Boston: Little Brown. 58 pp. ISBN: 0-316-11546-0. Picture Book. (See **13.60**)

7.47 Frith, Margaret (1997). **Mermaid Island.** Illustrated by Julie Durrell. New York: Grosset & Dunlap. 48 pp. ISBN: 0-448-41618-2. Picture Book. (See **14.25**)

7.48 Rylant, Cynthia (1997). **Mr. Putter and Tabby Row the Boat.** Illustrated by Arthur Howard. San Diego: Harcourt Brace. Unpaged. ISBN: 0-15-256257-5. Chapter Book.

On a very warm day during the last few weeks of school, one reviewer read this book to her second and third graders. The children listened intently, and were able to see how each chapter led into the next. The children chimed in as she read similar sentences ("They sweated on the front porch," "They sweated in the kitchen," "They sweated under the oak tree") and lines repeated across text ("It was a hot walk," "It was a sweaty walk," "It was a slow walk"). The children enjoyed the simple story of friendship between Mr. Putter and Mrs. Teasberry, and suggestions for things to do in the summer. Howard's pencil, watercolor, and pastel illustrations add humor to the story. Rylant's series of Mr. Putter and Tabby books concern everyday events with an eye to detail.

7.49 Rylant, Cynthia (1998). **Henry and Mudge and the Sneaky Crackers.** Illustrated by Sucie Stevenson. New York: Simon & Schuster Books for Young Readers. 40 pp. ISBN: 0-689-81176-4. Chapter Book.

This is another popular series by Rylant. Mudge is Henry's 180-pound dog, who is also his best friend. In this book, Henry and Mudge are spying with their new spy kit when they came across a letter in code. They crack the code, leave a message in code, and eventually meet another boy-and-dog spy team. All the books in this series follow the same pattern. They focus on the Henry and Mudge relationship, and concern one specific event or day in their lives. The colorful, cartoonlike drawings support the text, and add even more humor to the series. Sixteen of these warm, humorous books have been published to date. Rylant has found a way to make beginning reading fun.

7.50 Sloan, Peter, and Sheryl Sloan (1998). **Machines in the Home.** Littleton, MA: Sundance. 8 pp. ISBN: 0-7608-3152-1. Picture Book.

This is the first book in the Little Blue Readers series, forty nonfiction books designed for emergent to proficient readers. These informational books are leveled (stages one to four) and use full-color photographs and predictable sentence structure to support readers. For example, in this book, each page follows the structure, "This machine picks up dirt. It is a vacuum cleaner." Books for higher reading levels have more complex sentences and more print on each page. Books throughout the series offer information that enhances science or social studies investigations with clear, bright photographs. This series will be useful for students who gravitate towards nonfiction.

Secondary Reviews

7.51   Kemp, Moira. **Lift-the-Flap series.** New York: Lodestar.

Titles in this series include:

Lift-the-Flap Chick (1998). Unpaged. ISBN: 0-525-67565-5. Picture Book.

Lift-the-Flap Kitten (1998). Unpaged. ISBN: 0-525-67564-7. Picture Book.

Lift-the-Flap Mouse (1998). Unpaged. ISBN: 0-525-67563-9. Picture Book.

Lift-the-Flap Puppy (1998). Unpaged. ISBN: 0-525-67566-3. Picture Book.

This series of interactive peek-a-boo books with sturdy flaps designed to endure many rough readings includes simple and predictable stories. Each book invites the reader to look for an animal hiding in, under, and behind various items. Little eyes will love finally discovering the hidden animal on the last page. These interactive books will engage infants through toddlers. The simple, predictable text quickly becomes familiar to children, so that they can chime in as the adult reads the story.

7.52   Mitchell, Claudette, Gracie Porter, and Patricia Tefft Cousin (1996). **Jump-rope.** San Diego: Arborlake. 8 pp. ISBN: 1-57518-0641-2. Picture Book.

The Visions: African-American Experiences Young Reader series offers simple, predictable stories that highlight African American children. The topics concern daily life, such as playing basketball, getting ready for school, going to the swimming pool, or making sandwiches. *Jump-rope* celebrates the joy of rope jumping with friends: "Jump! Jump! Jump! Jump! You move out and I move in. Twist and turn and do it again." Clear, simple illustrations and predictable sentence structure offer support to emergent readers.

Beginning Chapter Books

Primary Reviews

7.53   Giff, Patricia Reilly (1998). **Rosie's Big City Ballet.** Illustrated by Julie Durrell. New York: Viking. 73 pp. ISBN: 0-670-87792-1. Chapter Book. (See **11.61**)

7.54 Howe, James (1997). **Pinky and Rex and the New Neighbors.** Illustrated by Melissa Sweet. New York: Simon & Schuster. 40 pp. ISBN: 0-689-80022-3. Chapter Book.

In this series, Pinky and Rex have adventures based on childhood events, such as participating in a spelling bee, going to camp, having a new baby, and dealing with a bully. The characters are believable and childlike. In this book, Pinky and Rex are worried that a new boy their age who moves into the neighborhood will break up their special friendship. The events in the story ring true, and children can use Sweet's watercolor paintings, which accompany the text, to support their predictions. Part of the Ready-to-Read series, this is a level 3 reading alone book. It would be appropriate for proficient readers in grades 1 through 3, or a struggling reader in higher grades.

7.55 Kline, Suzy (1998). **Horrible Harry Moves up to Third Grade.** Illustrated by Frank Remkiewicz. New York: Viking. 58 pp. ISBN: 0-670-87873-1. Chapter Book.

This early chapter-book series continues to show how well Suzy Kline knows third graders. Horrible Harry has been featured in at least nine of Kline's books. In this saga, Harry and his best friend Doug, now third graders, face school changes, more trouble from Sidney, and a mine adventure. The theme of school and practical jokes will strike a chord with children in second through fourth grade. Beginning chapter-book readers will enjoy the humor and the lifelike characters.

7.56 Mills, Claudia (1998). **Gus and Grandpa Ride the Train.** Illustrated by Catherine Stock. New York: Farrar, Straus and Giroux. 48 pp. ISBN: 0-374-32826-9. Chapter Book.

Books in the Gus and Grandpa series demonstrate warmth and affection between a boy and his grandpa. Whether they are baking cookies, riding a train, or just thinking, they are a perfect team. The language in this book is simple, and the sentences are short. The line-and-wash illustrations complement the story, offering support to emergent readers. The following is an example of Mills' style that clearly demonstrates the tone of the story: "Gus felt his happy steam bubble over again. He and Grandpa forgot a lot of things. But Gus never forgot that he loved Grandpa. And Grandpa never forgot that he loved Gus."

7.57   Pippen, Scottie, with Greg Brown (1996). **Scottie Pippen: Reach Higher.** Illustrated by Doug Keith. Dallas, TX: Taylor. 40 pp. ISBN: 0-87833-981-7. Picture Book. (See **12.2**)

7.58   Scieszka, John (1996). **Tut, Tut.** Illustrated by Lane Smith. New York: Viking. 74 pp. ISBN: 0-140-36360-2. Chapter Book. (See **14.58**)

Secondary Reviews

7.59   Christopher, Matt (1998). **The Dog That Called the Pitch.** Illustrated by Daniel Vasconcellos. Boston: Little Brown. 38 pp. ISBN: 0-316-14207-7. Chapter Book. (See **12.38**)

7.60   Costello, Emily (1998). **On the Sidelines.** New York: Skylark. 150 pp. ISBN: 0-553-48645-4. Chapter Book. (See **12.39**)

7.61   Perez, Eduardo (1998). **The Young Baseball Player.** New York: Dorling Kindersley. 37 pp. ISBN: 0-7894-2825-3. Picture Book. (See **12.31**)

Books for Mature Readers

Primary Reviews

7.62   Yep, Laurence (1998). **The Case of the Lion Dance: Chinatown Mystery #2.** New York: HarperCollins. 214 pp. ISBN: 0-06-024447-X. Sophisticated Chapter Book.

This series of books has some interesting components that enable the books to rise above the ordinary. The books are set in San Francisco's Chinatown, and use the complex social climate of the community as a backdrop for the mystery stories. In this book for more mature readers, money is stolen at the grand opening of a Chinese restaurant owned by the family of the narrator. The detectives solving the crime are teenage cousins and their eccentric aunt. Aunt Tiger Lily has been a star of martial arts action movies for many years, but the only kung fu she knows is what she learned from watching her male stunt double. The solving of the mystery is less important than the escapades of the young detectives. Good writing and the use of modern-day Chinese and American culture make this an interesting book to read.

Secondary Reviews

7.63   Christopher, Matt (1997). **At the Plate with . . . Ken Griffey, Jr.** Boston: Little Brown. 121 pp. ISBN: 0-316-14233-6. Chapter Book. (See **12.4**)

7.64 Long, Barbara (1997). **Jim Thorpe: Legendary Athlete.** Springfield, NJ: Enslow. 128 pp. ISBN: 0-89490-865-0. Chapter Book. (See **12.11**)

Books for Reticent Readers

Primary Reviews

7.65 Dingle, Derek T. (1998). **First in the Field: Baseball Hero Jackie Robinson.** New York: Hyperion Books for Children. 48 pp. ISBN: 0-7868-0348-7. Picture Book. (See **12.5**)

7.66 Fleischman, Paul (1997). **Seedfolks.** Illustrated by Judy Pedersen. New York: HarperCollins. 69 pp. ISBN: 0-06-027471-9. Sophisticated Chapter Book.

This unusual collection of short stories is tied together by the theme of turning a trash-filled lot in Cleveland into a community garden. Kim, who wants to prove to her dead Vietnamese father that she is a farmer, begins the garden. She scrapes away the debris and plants three lima bean seeds. The garden has a transforming effect on all who choose to plant there: Gonzalo views his father as a worthy man for the first time; Maricela realizes the baby within her is a part of a grand life cycle; and Mr. Myles, an invalid in a wheelchair, is again able to care about living. The Gibb Street Garden creates a community out of strangers. Pederson's pen-and-ink drawings add to the reality of the book. Because each story is complete in itself and is also part of a larger whole, this book generates talk about community, lives in crisis, and what is important in our lives. The quick stories are powerful, yet use simple language. A must read for older students! (See also **20.54**)

7.67 Huynh, Quang Nhuong (1997). **Water Buffalo Days: Growing Up in Vietnam.** New York: HarperCollins. 117 pp. ISBN: 0-06-024957-9. Chapter Book.

In this sequel to *The Land I Lost*, Huynh Quang Nhuong once again takes us to Vietnam before the war. Readers share the adventure and excitement of a young boy growing up in the verdant hills of Vietnam. We hear continuing stories of Tank, the water buffalo, who is strong, a fierce fighter, and a protector of Nhuong. Each story is complete in itself, but part of the larger story about the experience of growing up in a totally different culture. Reticent readers will enjoy the short, complete stories that they are able to read in one sitting. This book is a good read-aloud text as well.

> Huynh, Quang Nhuong (1982). **The Land I Lost: Adventures of a Boy in Vietnam.** Illustrated by Vo-Dinh Mai. New York: Harper & Row., 115 pp. ISBN: 0-06-024592-1. Chapter Book.

7.68 Kramer, S. A. (1998). **Hoop Heroes.** Illustrated by Ken Call. New York: Grosset and Dunlap. 47 pp. ISBN: 0-448-41883-5. Chapter Book.

This book includes biographical sketches of four famous basketball players: Anfernee "Penny" Hardaway, Grant Hill, Stephon Marbury, and Patrick Ewing. The simple text moves as quickly as a basketball game. Kramer has included both the excitement of the NBA and personal information, such as that Marbury was so poor as a child that his family couldn't afford a couch or extra chairs. Readers who have difficulty will be interested in the Ewing section because he was not able to read when he started playing for Georgetown University, and was ridiculed by fans with taunts such as "Ewing Kant Read Dis." There is even a picture of him working with a tutor. This book should be of great interest to students who love basketball.

7.69 Romero, Maritza (1997). **Selena Perez: Queen of Tejano Music.** New York: PowerKids. 24 pp. ISBN: 0-8239-5086-7. Chapter Book.

This book is one of six in the Great Hispanics of Our Time series, and is written for readers in the third to fourth grades. Selena's brief life is explored in an easy-to-read format. This book works better as an informational book than as a story because it does not create much feeling and emotion about the main character. Each book in the series has a message for young people, and in *Selena Perez* the message is to stay in school and reach for your dream. Young girls lined up for this book because they thought the photos were wonderful and because they see Selena as a heroine. Other personalities in this series—Henry Cisneros, Ellen Ochoa, Joan Baez, Jaime Escalante, and Roberto Clemente—were less popular with students. Each book has the same easily understood format and includes a glossary, index, table of contents, large type, and photographs. Some of the more difficult words are printed in bold-face type with a phonetic pronunciation key in parentheses after the word, a feature that some readers may find distracting. Nevertheless this series offers young students a good option for research and reading about influential Hispanic/Latino people.

7.70   Rosen, Michael J. (1997). **The Heart Is Big Enough: Five Stories.** Illustrated by Matthew Valiguette. San Diego: Harcourt Brace. 198 pp. ISBN: 0-15-201402-0. Chapter Book.

Michael J. Rosen has compiled five stories about kids on the verge of adolescence. From Matthew, who has had a hip replacement and learns to swim with the dolphins, to Jonathan, who becomes a caretaker of pets and plants for an elderly lady named Sam, all of these characters discover the importance of caring. As Sam explains, "[W]hen it comes down to it, I'm only an old lady . . . and you're only a young man, and caring is caring because if you do, whatever creature comes into your life becomes a part of that caring, right?" These stories are humorous and filled with lessons about living. The simple style and content about people on the verge of adolescence make them just right for many students who are struggling readers.

Secondary Reviews

7.71   Brooks, Bruce (1997). **Woodsie.** New York: HarperCollins. 116 pp. ISBN: 0-06-027349-6. Chapter Book. (See **12.36**)

7.72   Christopher, Matt (1997). **Penalty Shot.** Boston: Little Brown. 131 pp. ISBN: 0-316-13787-1. Chapter Book. (See **12.37**)

7.73   Gutman, Bill (1996). **Grant Hill: Basketball's High Flier.** Brookfield, CT: Millbrook. 48 pp. ISBN: 0-7613-0038-4. Chapter Book. (See **12.16**)

Books about Literacy

See also the section entitled Children Struggling with or Experiencing Academic Success in chapter 6, "School Life."

Primary Reviews

7.74   Aliki (1998). **Marianthe's Story: Painted Words; Marianthe's Story: Spoken Memories.** New York: Greenwillow. Unpaged. ISBN: 0-688-15661-4. Picture Book.

Marianthe is a young Greek immigrant girl who does not know the language. Aliki portrays her difficulty fitting into the school culture, learning English, and then learning how to read and write.

Aliki uses colored pencil and crayons to produce large, expressive illustrations that extend the text. He not only portrays the difficulty Mari faces with language barriers, but also the intelligence of her teacher, who initially lets her use art to tell her life story, and then words when she has been in the United States longer. Children love the format of the book. Part one of Marianthe's story ends about halfway through the book. For part two, the reader must turn the book over and begin at the back, and then end up in the middle again. Children who are new in the classroom and those who have encountered difficulty learning to read or write will find hope in this book.

7.75   Grimes, Nikki (1998). **Jazmin's Notebook.** New York: Dial. 102 pp. ISBN: 0-8037-2224-9. Chapter Book. (See **5.84**)

7.76   Hesse, Karen (1998). **just Juice.** Illustrated by Robert A. Parker. New York: Scholastic. 138 pp. ISBN: 0-590-03382-4. Chapter Book.

just Juice is the story of nine-year-old Justus (Juice) Faulstitch, who is repeating third grade because she still can't read. Her mother is pregnant with a fifth child, her father cannot find steady work, and the family is about to lose their home. As the story unfolds, a persistent and caring teacher identifies Juice's learning disability and provides the help she needs to begin reading. This is a heartwarming story about a loving family and the power of literacy. Like most of Hesse's books, *just Juice* highlights a caring, real-life family living on the edge of poverty and the fringes of society. The strong family unit provides the supportive backdrop against which Juice demonstrates a growing sense of responsibility, overcomes childhood fears, and develops a greater understanding of and appreciation for members of her family. The book is liberally sprinkled with black-and-white line drawings that further develop the rich characters with memorable images from key events in the story. (See also **20.35**)

7.77   Mora, Pat (1997). **Tomás and the Library Lady/Tomas y la señora de la biblioteca.** Illustrated by Raúl Colón. New York: Knopf (English)/Dragonfly (Spanish). Unpaged. ISBN: 0-679-80401-3. Picture Book. (See **20.39**)

7.78   Moss, Marissa (1996). **Amelia Writes Again!** Berkeley, CA: Tricycle. Unpaged. ISBN: 1-883672-42-2. Picture Book. (See **6.69**)

7.79 Polacco, Patricia (1996). **Aunt Chip and the Great Triple Creek Dam Affair.** New York: Philomel. Unpaged. ISBN: 0-399-22943-4. Picture Book.

Everyone in Triple Creek loves television except Aunt Chip, who has retired to her bed in protest. Books have been relegated to being used "for doorstops, to hold up roofs, to sit on, to eat off, to sleep under, to mend fences, to stuff potholes, to prop up sagging buildings and even to shore up the dam." As a result, the stories have been lost and the children—instead of playing, talking, or laughing—are watching television screens. Aunt Chip decides to rectify this travesty and begins to read to her nephew Eli. Soon Aunt Chip is reading to many children who, in an effort to find more books for her to read, remove the books from their structural positions in town. The resulting miracle causes the town to once again put reading back into the community. Polacco's intense, whimsical illustrations add even more fancy to this mythical tale.

7.80 Polacco, Patricia (1998). **Thank You, Mr. Falker.** New York: Philomel. Unpaged. ISBN: 0-399-23166-8. Picture Book. (See **6.34**)

7.81 Stewart, Sarah (1997). **The Gardener.** Illustrated by David Small. New York: Farrar, Straus and Giroux. Unpaged. ISBN: 0-374-32517-0. Picture Book. (See **3.16**)

7.82 Swanson, Susan Marie, and Peter Catalanotto (1998). **Letter to the Lake.** New York: Dorling Kindersley. Unpaged. ISBN: 0-7894-2483-5. Picture Book.

On a cold, hard day in winter, Rosie begins writing a letter to the lake, a favorite place from last summer. As she thinks about the fun she had at the lake, she can see a hint of summer tucked somewhere in each gray, wintry scene. The contrast between the drab scenes of winter and the brilliant colors of summer remembrances makes it easy for children of all ages to follow the story. One reviewer's first graders were fascinated with the idea of writing a letter to a place. They especially liked the illustration at the end, where the lake seems to be looking at Rosie. Some of the children even decided to write a letter to a favorite place in response to this book.

7.83 Wilson, Nancy Hope (1997). **Old People, Frogs, and Albert.** Illustrated by Marcy D. Ramsey. New York: Farrar, Straus and Giroux. 58 pp. ISBN: 0-374-35625-4. Chapter Book. (See **20.56**)

Secondary Reviews

7.84 Brown, Marc (1996). **Arthur Writes a Story.** Boston: Little Brown. Unpaged. ISBN: 0-316-10916-9. Picture Book.

Arthur's homework assignment to write a story goes awry when he tries to incorporate everyone's ideas into his story. What starts out as a personal experience story about how he got his dog, Pal, ends up as a song-and-dance routine about Planet Shmellafint (it's hard to find words that rhyme with elephant!). The result is a stunned and speechless audience. Mr. Ratburn, his teacher, helps Arthur realize the best stories are the ones that are "important to you." One reviewer used this book to begin a primary writing workshop. The class talked about what made the puppy story the best story, including the fact that the episode happened to Arthur and that he knew about this event. The class also identified authors who write about things that happened when they were children, especially Tomie De Paola and Patricia Polacco.

7.85 Numeroff, Laura J. (1998). **What Daddies Do Best, What Mommies Do Best.** Illustrated by Lynn Munsinger. New York: Simon & Schuster. Unpaged. ISBN: 0-689-80577-2. Picture Book. (See **4.18**)

7.86 Walsh, Ellen Stoll (1997). **Jack's Tale.** San Diego: Harcourt Brace. Unpaged. ISBN: 0-15-200323-1. Picture Book.

Jack, a frog, doesn't want to be in a fairy tale. However the author convinces him, and soon he's dodging trolls and trying to save the princess. This simple story takes readers through the mechanics of story development. The illustrations contain charming multi-colored frogs on a white background. This book appealed to primary children who had struggled to create their own fairy tales. They thought it was a good way to learn the important elements of a fairy tale.

7.87 Williams, Suzanne (1997). **Library Lil.** Illustrated by Steven Kellogg. New York: Dial. Unpaged. ISBN: 0-8037-1698-2. Picture Book.

This tall tale about a librarian strong enough to lift the bookmobile and mean enough to intimidate motorcycle gang members deserves a place next to Pecos Bill or Paul Bunyan. From birth, Lil was a reader, and it was natural for her to become a librarian. But she met her match when she moved to Chesterville, a community of couch potatoes who would rather sit and watch television than read. When a terrible storm cuts off all electricity, Lil has a chance to convince folks that reading is more fun than sitting in the dark. Steven Kellogg's humorous drawings add to the tall-tale nature of this story. This read-aloud book will keep children laughing, and perhaps checking out those books!

Storytelling Books

See also the sections entitled Histories and Herstories and Cultural Traditions: Traditional Literature in chapter 3, "Exploring Our Past."

Primary Reviews

7.88 Mamchur, Carolyn (1997). **The Popcorn Tree.** Illustrated by Laurie McGaw. Toronto, Canada: Stoddart Kids. Unpaged. ISBN: 0-7737-2896-1. Picture Book.

Two simultaneous stories, "Peeps and Sighs" in brown tones, and colorful "Christmas Rains" on the opposing pages, merge in this unusual story. In "Peeps and Sighs," the brown-tone pages illustrate the story of the ornaments lying dormant in Aunt Rosa's basement and wanting a new home, and how they come to be wrapped and sent to the children. In "Christmas Rains," we see Mrs. Finley and her children stringing popcorn for their Christmas tree while she once again tells them her childhood memories about special tree ornaments. After hearing the story, the children write to ask Aunt Rosa to send the ornaments to them to complete their tree. The ornaments arrive just in time to add magic to the tree, and everything is right for Christmas. The ornaments are happy to be in use, for they know the children will continue the tradition. When read aloud, this book encourages adults to be storytellers, and to share our tales as each item is brought out to decorate for the holidays.

7.89 Mitchell, Rhonda (1997). **The Talking Cloth.** New York: Orchard. Unpaged. ISBN: 0-531-30004-8. Picture Book. (See **4.39**)

7.90 Morin, Paul (1998). **Animal Dreaming: An Aboriginal Dreamtime Story.** San Diego: Harcourt Brace. Unpaged. ISBN: 0-15-200054-2. Picture Book.

In *Animal Dreaming,* we join a young boy named Merri as he hears from an elder named Gadurra how the earth was first shaped. The walkabout through aboriginal Australia proceeds through textured, earthy paintings. The storyteller focuses the reader's attention on the pictographs on the stone wall, while relating how land formations were created to make homes for the animals. Readers learn how each animal arrived, until "Before long each of the animals had made their home in the land. The animals were at peace. And from that day on when they dreamed, they lived their dreams." This book is an extraordinary account of how stories help people know who they are and where they came from. From a story told to the author by Bill Neidjie, a Gagadu elder.

7.91   Rochelle, Belinda (1998). **Jewels.** Illustrated by Cornelius Van Wright and Ying-Hwa Hu. New York: Lodestar. Unpaged. ISBN: 0-525-67502-7. Picture Book.

Through Lea Mae's summer visit to her grandparents, students can experience the tradition of storytelling. As Rochelle says, "With each tongue, with each telling, the stories are saved. . . . Like diamonds, sapphires, and rubies, the stories are like jewels to treasure forever." The stories about Lea Mae's family connect students to events of the past, and spark interest and curiosity about the stories of their families. After reading this book, first graders in one reviewer's classroom shared stories their parents told about things that had happened to them or to others in their family. Some of the children talked to grandparents about stories they remember being told as a child. As one of the children shared after a weekend visit to her grandparents, "I didn't know my family had so many jewels. I can't wait to go back and hear some more stories."

Secondary Reviews

7.92   Bertrand, Diane Gonzales (1996). **Sip, Slurp, Soup, Soup/Caldo, caldo, caldo.** Illustrated by Alex Pardo DeLange. Houston, TX: Piñata. Unpaged. ISBN: 1-55885-183-6. Picture Book.

By the time readers finish this dual-language treat, they likely will share Jeffrey's (age seven) opinion: "I can almost smell it cooking!" In a dual-language text that presents English and then Spanish on each page, readers follow the step-by-step preparation of *caldo,* a meat and vegetable soup, and take a trip with the story characters to a *tortillería* where they see how tortillas are made. The English text is sprinkled with Spanish words that readers can interpret easily within the context of the story. The words *caldo, caldo, caldo* are repeated on each page, inviting class participation in the storytelling. The detailed and colorful pictures by Alex Pardo DeLange, using watercolors and ink, depict a loving family with cultural authenticity. After spying the recipe for *caldo* that follows the story, a multiage primary class researched their families' recipes for *caldo*, and then cooked up a pot of their own, each child contributing an ingredient.

7.93 Bouchard, David (1997). **The Great Race.** Illustrated by Zhong-Yang Huang. Brookfield, CT: Millbrook. Unpaged. ISBN: 0-7613-0305-7. Picture Book.

Grandmother unfolds on the little girl's bed the tale of the Chinese zodiac, and gingerly picks up the paper cutouts of the animals. The paintings in this book capture the strength of the dragon, the cockiness of the rooster, and the cunning of the rat as they race with their nine other contenders to reach the Emerald City. A calendar is included in the closing pages, as we are reminded of Grandmother's wise saying, "It is not who wins that matters."

7.94 Melmed, Laura Krauss (1997). **Little Oh.** Illustrated by Jim La-Marche. New York: Lothrop, Lee & Shepard/Morrow. Unpaged. ISBN: 0-688-14208-7. Picture Book. (See **4.17**)

7.95 Van Leeuwen, Jean (1998). **The Tickle Stories.** Illustrated by Mary Whyte. New York: Dial Books for Young Readers. 29 pp. ISBN: 0-8037-2048-3. Picture Book.

Snuggles, tickles, and bedtime giggles abound in this story about a grandpa who tells fanciful stories about when he was a boy as he tries to put his grandchildren to bed. The soft watercolors and Grandpop's stories take the adult reader back to all those family stories told by grandparents, great-aunts, and great-uncles. It reminds moms and dads of the importance of preserving our heritage by sharing those family stories with our children. The book stimulates children to interview grandparents or older adults and hear their stories.

A.

B.

C.

D.

A. *Whoever You Are,* Mem Fox/Leslie Staub (**8.9**). **B.** *The Bootmaker and the Elves,* Susan Lowell/Tom Curry (**8.13**). **C.** *Baboon,* Kate Banks/Georg Hallensleben (**8.1**). **D.** *Squids Will Be Squids: Fresh Morals, Beastly Fables,* Jon Scieszka/Lane Smith (**8.20**).

8 Picture Books

Shari Nelson-Faulkner

Contributing reviewers included Katherine Hawker, Beth Mayberry, Norma Nelson, and Shari Nelson-Faulkner.

Children who love to read usually discover the joy of books early through the exploration of picture books. These books are designated as such because they are graced with illustrations, whether simple or lush, amateurish or masterful. However, one of their greatest values is that they introduce children to the wonder of language. Thus the text often bears primary responsibility for the quality of a picture book. Even in a book with little or no text, the quality of the book resides in the story it tells and the story the reader tells about it. The value of good artwork should not, of course, be dismissed. Beautiful or fascinating art often is what draws a reader to a book, and it can greatly enhance the experience of a story. But sumptuous illustrations cannot rescue lifeless text. In the best picture books, strong illustrations act together with compelling text to create a work of unalloyed pleasure.

During the selection process, the members of our book review committee identified several characteristics shared by what we considered the better-quality picture books. In many respects, our standards for what constitute good picture books coincided with our standards for good adult books. Good stories possess internal logic and characters that are well developed enough that their actions seem to flow naturally from their personality rather than from a preordained plot. These books demonstrate originality, believability, and adept use of language. In the best books, the story transfixes the reader from start to finish, encouraging the reader to invest herself or himself wholly in the act of reading.

Of course, other considerations come into play when evaluating children's books. For example, one hallmark of a great picture book is that adults and children alike can enjoy it. This is important not simply because adults are the primary purchasers of picture books; any parent or teacher knows that a three-year-old child can endlessly pore over a book based on a television series and bought secondhand. But a book that truly *excites* both adults and children is a book more likely to be shared. These books present the best critical opportunity for passing on to children the joy of reading.

Because the best picture books are those most likely to be shared intergenerationally, we believe a good picture book also must lend itself to oral reading. Some prose forces readers into a dull monotone and defies them to vary inflection. The meter of some verse falters or is forced to fit a rhyme scheme, either of which can jar the reader and auditor alike and reduce the pleasure of reading. Good prose may overflow with simple, declarative sentences, or it may challenge the reader with long, complex sentences, but it always pleases the ear. Good verse is easily scannable, and either makes the verbal rhythm evident to all or allows itself to be read appealingly in several different ways.

We did not find ourselves favoring any particular type of narrative or plot, but we did tend to shy away from trite themes or books that revisited ideas found in recently successful books. A few exceptions surprised us—for example, books such as *Whoever You Are* (Fox 1997) and *Rosie's Fiddle* (Root 1997), which built on well-worn themes but brought to those themes either something new or a rare degree of quality that elevated them beyond cliche. These we were pleased to include.

One issue that arose several times during our committee's deliberations was how to handle potentially disturbing texts. If a book is not appropriate for early readers and prereaders, those usually thought of as the market for picture books, can it be considered exemplary of its type? Picture books have never been exclusively the realm of soft, cozy images. So the first question we found that we needed to ask was, "For whom is this book intended?" Not every cartoon or text with pictures is intended for small children; some are not intended for children at all. Quality can be determined only when the age-group targeted by the book has been identified. The next question that we asked of a troubling book was, "What is worthwhile about this book?" Some books we read seemed pointlessly disturbing with no redeeming qualities, except perhaps a vague or misguided moral. Others, such as the controversial *Arlene Sardine* (Raschka 1998), presented excellent opportunities to introduce older elementary readers to literary concepts such as irony. We decided to include such books where merited, and to note in our reviews both the appropriate age group for the books and what we considered to be valuable about them.

This chapter does not include all current picture books of merit. Where appropriate, many were placed in other chapters to better enable librarians and educators to locate books dealing with certain issues or themes. But a simple, gentle story about a young baboon's introduction to the world may not have much to do with the life of real baboons. And not every picture book that features a talking animal fits the traditional genre of fantasy. This chapter provides a place for such books.

---

*The titles listed below each subheading are organized into Primary Reviews and Secondary Reviews. The Primary Reviews describe outstanding books in each subheading. The Secondary Reviews provide brief information about other books worthy of consideration. Some titles listed below are **not** reviewed in this chapter; entries for these titles are not annotated and contain only bibliographic information. In such cases, a cross reference to the annotated entry contained elsewhere in this volume is provided in boldface type at the end of the bibliographic information.*

Primary Reviews

8.1 Banks, Kate (1997). **Baboon.** Illustrated by Georg Hallensleben. New York: Farrar, Straus and Giroux. Unpaged. ISBN: 0-374-30474-2. Picture Book.

Soft, gorgeous paintings highlight this book about a baby baboon learning about the world. When little Baboon wakes up in the morning atop his mother's back, she begins introducing her son to the world. Being new to his environment, Baboon tries to grasp the larger picture by generalizing from his limited experience. So when, near the forest, his mother says, "Look. That is the world," Baboon assumes, "So, the world is green." Mother baboon gently instructs him, "Some of it." At each encounter with his surroundings and the animals that inhabit it, Baboon's mother briefly but lovingly corrects or expands his assumptions, until on the last page she merely affirms Baboon's observation that, "Yes. The world is big." Graced by Georg Hallensleben's densely colored, almost clay-like paintings, *Baboon* is one of those rare picture books in which text and illustrations equal each other in rich and deceptively simple beauty.

8.2 Best, Cari (1997). **Top Banana.** Illustrated by Erika Oller. New York: Orchard. Unpaged. ISBN: 0-531-30009-9. Picture Book.

Flora Dora dotes on her parrot Benny, and he adores her too. One day, Flora spots a beautiful orchid in a store window and brings it home. Now Benny finds he must share everything with the delicate plant—his music, his games, even Flora's devotion. Benny jealously thinks of ways he can get rid of his competition. But when he finds Flora grieving because her beautiful orchid looks sickly, his compassion for Flora overcomes his jealousy, and Benny sets about saving his one-time rival. When he succeeds, Flora celebrates by lavishing attention on Benny—attention that, for once, he does not mind sharing. In Erika Oller's soft, pillowy-looking illustrations, muted colors fill the street scenes, while Flora and Benny and the home they share are suffused with warm, tropical colors that seem to flow from their love for each other.

8.3   Blake, Robert J. (1997). **Akiak: A Tale from the Iditarod.** New York: Philomel. Unpaged. ISBN: 0-399-22798-9. Picture Book.

Akiak, a ten-year-old dog on a team running the Iditarod, is old for a competing sled dog. But Akiak has a talent for picking the best route, and her musher, Mick, would not want to leave her behind. Mick has no choice, however, when Akiak injures her paw and has to be flown back home. Akiak has other plans. Breaking free of her handlers, she heads down the trail many hours behind her team. When Akiak finally catches up with her team five days later, she saves them from running down the wrong trail, thereby enabling them to win the race. In Blake's painterly illustrations, the coolness of the colors convincingly conveys the coolness of the landscape. The story works on both an informational and inspirational level, with the rules and problems associated with sled-dog racing conveyed in a story about success through determination.

8.4   Browne, Anthony (1998). **Voices in the Park.** New York: Dorling Kindersley. Unpaged. ISBN: 0-7894-2522-X. Picture Book. (See **20.52**)

8.5   Buckley, Helen E. (1997). **Moonlight Kite.** Illustrated by Elise Primavera. New York: Lothrop, Lee & Shepard. Unpaged. ISBN: 0-688-10931-4. Picture Book.

Three monks in a crumbling monastery spend their days silently gardening, cooking, and mending, until one day a brother and sister climb up their hill with a bright orange kite. As the hidden monks watch, the children fly their kite all day, until it gets caught in a tall tree. That night, the monks rescue the kite and fly it for hours, fondly remembering childhood. Returning the next day, the children find the kite retrieved and decide to leave it there again, just in case the unseen monks like to fly kites, too. Soon more children ascend the hill with their kites and fill the monastery with their laughter, causing the monks to smile in a shared joy. Elise Primavera portrays the monastery as a dark and crumbling place until the arrival of the orange kite, which practically glows, lighting up the landscape as well as the monks' hearts.

8.6 Conrad, Pam (1996). **The Rooster's Gift.** Illustrated by Eric Beddows. New York: HarperCollins. Unpaged. ISBN: 0-06-023603-5. Picture Book.

Pam Conrad spins a tale of talent, pride, and self-esteem in the daily life of a chicken coop. One night, very, very late, young Rooster wakes with a powerful urge to go outside. Followed outside by his disapproving sisters, he hops up to the top of the coop and crows. When light appears on the horizon shortly thereafter, Rooster's sisters stop scolding and stare in awe at the day they believe he has made. Before long, Rooster grows too proud of himself to take time even to speak to his sisters. But one day Rooster does not wake in time, and the sun rises without him. Devastated by this revelation, Conrad's Rooster attains unprideful self-esteem only when he comes to a realistic self-assessment of his true talent. The expressiveness of the birds' faces, the richness of the colors, and the photographic composition of the paintings are a friendly and captivating complement to the heartwarming text. Pair this book with Chall's *Rupa Raises the Sun* (see **8.26**).

8.7 Coy, John (1996). **Night Driving.** Illustrated by Peter McCarty. New York: Henry Holt. Unpaged. ISBN: 0-8050-2931-1. Picture Book.

McCarty's simple, yet lush black-and-white pencil illustrations reflect the quiet beauty of this story of a father-and-son road trip. Excited to be on his first vacation to the mountains, where he will get to sleep in a tent, the young narrator has no trouble staying awake at the beginning of their all-night drive. The plot contains no momentous events. The text contains no elaborate metaphors. And yet the story conveys the feeling of an unforgettable journey, as the father quietly passes on little pieces of knowledge to his son. Although the soft edges of the illustrations and the 1950s automobiles suggest the adult recollection of a warm childhood memory, the uncomplicated sentence structure and the immediacy of the first-person narration create a believable childlike perspective. This story richly conveys both the wonder of new experience and the confidence built up in a loving parent-child relationship.

8.8   Egan, Tim (1997). **Burnt Toast on Davenport Street.** Boston: Houghton Mifflin. Unpaged. ISBN: 0-395-79618-0. Picture Book.

In this laugh-aloud tale, two vaguely gentrified-looking dogs, Arthur and Stella Crandall, live a fairly ordinary life, spoiled only by the crocodile bullies on the corner. When a fly one day buzzes into the kitchen claiming to be a magic fly who will grant him three wishes, Arthur clearly is not impressed. Still he complies, offhandedly and sardonically, and in a few days forgets all about it. Then the Crandalls begin noticing some odd occurrences, and Arthur realizes that not only is the fly granting his wishes, but also that the fly has gotten his first two wishes mixed up. Wry and witty, *Burnt Toast on Davenport Street* should be read aloud to be fully appreciated. Over and over, Tim Egan demonstrates a humorist's feel for the cadence of dialogue, and his simple but stylized watercolors reemphasize the wry tone of the text.

8.9   Fox, Mem (1997). **Whoever You Are.** Illustrated by Leslie Staub. New York: Harcourt Brace. Unpaged. ISBN: 0-590-20027-5. Picture Book.

Whoever You Are is the familiar and beloved story of how all children are valued despite an array of differences. As the author explains, "Joys are the same, and love is the same. Pain is the same, and blood is the same." Fox reminds us that we share not only happiness but also sadness, and she invokes deeper sensitivity than most in this genre. It is surprising that such a talented author has chosen to return to such common fair, but perhaps this offers testimony to our cultural longing for acceptance amidst our diversity. The incredibly rich illustrations by Staub provide another reason to return to this theme once again. The book itself creates a sense of inclusivity that makes it useful for a variety of settings, whether secular or religious.

8.10   Jackson, Shelley (1998).**The Old Woman and the Wave.** New York: Dorling Kindersley. Unpaged. ISBN: 0-7894-2484-3. Picture Book.

Whimsical collages highlight this tale of an old woman who resents the wave perpetually hanging over her house. The wave loves the woman, dropping kisses on her and throwing her the occasional fish for supper. But the old woman is so afraid of getting dripped on that she goes around hunched over and squinting, never noticing the wave's—or the world's—beauty. One day, she spies her beloved dog swimming at the top of the wave. She angrily rows her boat up the steep slope of water, retrieves her dog, and then looks around her. Much to her astonishment, the world seems a wondrous place from this vantage point. This story might not be quite so impressive if not for Shirley Jackson's fascinating artwork. A reader could study the collages for hours, identifying and analyzing the use of text, maps, sheet music, and so on, over which Jackson paints and draws to create beautiful, interesting illustrations.

8.11 Lee, Milly (1997). **Nim and the War Effort.** Illustrated by Yangsook Choi. New York: Farrar, Straus and Giroux. Unpaged. ISBN: 0-374-35523-1. Picture Book. (See **3.109**)

8.12 Lowell, Susan (1996). **Los tres pequeños jabalíes/The Three Little Javelinas.** Illustrated by Jim Harris. New York: Scholastic. Unpaged. ISBN: 0-590-00319-4. Picture Book.

Fans of Susan Lowell's special brand of humor will be delighted to know that her much-loved *The Three Little Javelinas* has been translated into Spanish and published in a dual-language version. The translators have successfully created a Spanish dialect accessible to Spanish speakers of all regions, while maintaining the spirit of the original version and the story's Southwestern roots. In this hilarious version of "The Three Little Pigs," three javelinas, or wild peccaries, build houses of tumbleweeeds, saguaro ribs, and adobe bricks. The brains of the pig family turns out to be the female javelina, who lights a fire in her wood stove just in the nick of time. The traditional wolf's role is played by the trickster in many of the region's indigenous tales, the coyote, who recalls his suffering at the hands of the javelinas with his every yowl in the desert nights.

8.13 Lowell, Susan (1997). **The Bootmaker and the Elves.** Illustrated by Tom Curry. New York: Orchard. Unpaged. ISBN: 0-531-30044-7. Picture Book.

In typical Susan Lowell cowboy-tale style, the traditional story of "The Shoemaker and the Elves" is transformed into a rollicking Old West version sure to amuse any reader or listener. With all the hyperbole common to this genre, Lowell creates an unsuccessful bootmaker whose boots are "just plain ugly," and poor-fitting to boot. In predictable fashion, help comes from a pair of elves—mistaken for pack rats at first—who leave pair after pair of elaborately and outrageously decorated boots. Although no self-respecting real cowboy would ever be caught dead in a pair of the magically created boots, they appeal to an odd assortment of characters who come through the door of the shop. By the time the elves leave at the end of the tale, they are outfitted with their own tiny boots, embroidered with lucky clovers to complement their outfits of blue jeans, western-style shirts, hats, and socks—all tiny to be sure. Curry's paintings in acrylic drybrush on hardboard are cartoonish and full of whimsy, a perfect complement to this fun story.

8.14   Pilkey, Dav (1996). **God Bless the Gargoyles.** New York: Harcourt Brace. Unpaged. ISBN: 0-15-202104-3. Picture Book.

Dark in color as well as theme, Dav Pilkey's emotionally wrenching book nevertheless has a strong, comforting power. Long ago people carved gargoyles to guard cathedrals, but over the centuries people have forgotten this and begun to fear and detest the stone creatures. Broken-hearted and alone, the gargoyles continue to watch over the churches until passing Chagall-like angels hear their grieving. The angels comfort the gargoyles and bring them to life, taking them along on their nightly flight over the earth and singing songs of healing. This song, from which comes the book's title, begins "god bless the rain, and the stormclouds that bring it" and continues to call down blessings on the dying, the grieving, the dreamers, and the outcasts. Although the song dwells on life's sadness, its acknowledgment and love for those in pain feels tremendously reassuring. It does not produce the facile answers of some other angel books, but respects the complexity—the despair as well as the joy—of life.

8.15   Rael, Elsa Okon (1996). **What Zeesie Saw on Delancey Street.** Illustrated by Marjorie Priceman. New York: Simon & Schuster. Unpaged. ISBN: 0-689-80549-7. Picture Book.

On her seventh birthday, a young Jewish girl learns about the blessing of giving and receiving when she attends her first "package party," where food packages are sold to benefit friends in the old country. Sitting with her family, Zeesie notices men entering and leaving a room one at a time. Her father explains that each man leaves or takes money as he has ability or need, but no one is to know which. When Zeesie sneaks into the forbidden room, she learns a lesson about her responsibility to her community. Marjorie Priceman's gouache illustrations emphasize family and community, and picture people leaning over to share food, kids running through the ballroom holding hands, and parents tending children. The only pictures not filled with the warm colors of a loving community are those of the money room, the one place where need is evident and the expression of love is necessarily private.

8.16 Raschka, Chris (1998). **Arlene Sardine.** New York: Orchard. Unpaged. ISBN: 0-531-30111-7. Picture Book.

This wonderful and disturbing book tells the story of a little fish who lives in a fjord with "ten hundred thousand friends" and wants more than anything to become a sardine. When she dies on a fishing boat less than halfway through the book, Arlene's dream is finally fulfilled. Raschka's beautiful, simple watercolors and hand-lettered text follow Arlene from her watery home to the deck of the fishing boat, and through the factory until she is packed in a can with her picture on it. From the book jacket, which offers the deceptive message "EASY-OPEN BOOK," through the factory, where the narrator speculates about the dead heroine's feelings, this book exudes a gentle and decidedly unheavy-handed irony. Passages such as, "Then she was smoked, delicately. She was delicately smoked. Delicately smoked was she," evoke similar passages in easy-reader books, giving students an opportunity to discuss parody and perhaps providing a springboard for creating their own.

8.17 Rathmann, Peggy (1998). **10 Minutes till Bedtime.** New York: Putnam. Unpaged. ISBN: 0-399-23103-X. Picture Book.

This new bedtime book by the author of *Officer Buckle and Gloria* and *Good Night, Gorilla* is short on text but full of delightful pictures. Before the title page, a uniformed hamster clicks on a Web site for a "10-Minute Bedtime Tour." Then, as the official story pages open, a boy with fuzzy slippers looks out the window while his uniformed hamster announces, "They're coming," and his oblivious father, who is reading the newspaper, informs him, "10 Minutes till Bedtime." The rest of the book follows the boy and the arriving hamsters through various stages of getting ready for bed, punctuated by the boy's father counting down the minutes until bedtime. Although the book tells a simple story, readers of whatever age or reading ability could spend hours poring over the illustrations and following the antics of the many hamsters. A rare visual treat, *10 Minutes till Bedtime* could become a bedtime classic.

> Rathmann, Peggy (1994). **Good Night, Gorilla.** New York: Putnam. Unpaged. ISBN: 0-399-22445-9.

> Rathmann, Peggy (1995). **Officer Buckle and Gloria.** New York: Putnam. Unpaged. ISBN: 0-399-22616-8.

8.18 Root, Phyllis (1997). **Rosie's Fiddle.** Illustrated by Kevin O'Malley. New York: Lothrop, Lee & Shepard. Unpaged. ISBN: 0-688-12852-1. Picture Book.

The devil challenges a talented fiddler to a duel in a well-executed rendition of a familiar formula. Rosie O'Grady's neighbors creep over to her farmhouse and hide behind the bushes just to listen whenever she plays. One day, hearing of her reputation, a well-dressed man with horns and a tail shows up and proposes a contest: Whoever wins two out of three rounds gets to keep one thing that belongs to the other. Knowing what is really at stake, but undaunted, Rosie accepts. In keeping with the formula, each contestant wins one of the first two rounds. But Rosie triumphs at last when she takes up her fiddle a third time and plays a tune to which even the devil must dance. In Kevin O'Malley's masterfully composed paintings, Rosie appears implacable and defiant, and the devil sly and very sinister.

8.19 Rowe, John A. (1997). **Smudge.** New York: North-South. Unpaged. ISBN: 1-55858-788-8. Picture Book.

With dark and often forbidding pictures, this book has the shadowy feel and dry humor of a Dickens novel. Snatched up by a bird while drinking a bottle of milk, the infant Smudge soon finds himself in a nest being used as a beak polisher by baby birds. Before long, they begin to treat him as one of the family, and he learns to chirp and ruffle himself—but not to fly. Smudge can only watch as his new family one day flies off without him. Next a dog grabs him and takes him home, where the cycle starts all over again. Eventually his mother finds him and carries him home, where everyone welcomes him and no one uses him for anything. Although on one level this book can be disturbing, the text and the pictures of Smudge's true family also have a very loving feel to them. It could be useful as an introduction to tone.

8.20 Scieszka, Jon (1998). **Squids Will Be Squids: Fresh Morals, Beastly Fables.** Illustrated by Lane Smith. New York: Viking. Unpaged. ISBN: 0-670-88135-X. Picture Book.

Jon Scieszka presents a series of quirky fables about responsibility, safety, table manners, and self-importance with a humor that will appeal to both elementary students and adults. In Scieszka's fables, a grasshopper puts off his homework until the last minute, Elephant forgets to call home, a pessimistic squid misses out on fun, and Straw learns why it is not a good idea to play with matches. The morals at the end of each tale usually sidestep the issue at hand, thus cleverly avoiding preachiness while delivering extra laughs and presenting to teachers and parents a wonderful opportunity to talk with children about what moral the children might assign to the stories. The misnamed "serious historical foreword" provides a brief, enlightening introduction to fable-writing, while the "very serious historical afterword" throws in a cautionary tale about Aesop that might get students thinking about the power of the pen.

8.21 Shannon, David (1998). **No, David!** New York: Scholastic. Unpaged. ISBN: 0-590-93002-8. Picture Book.

David Shannon presents life from a child's perspective in a remake of a book he wrote as a small boy. Most children will relate to little David, who does not seem to be able to keep out of trouble. Every time he starts having fun, his mother says, "No, David!" He is not allowed to draw on the wall, run naked through the streets, play with his food, or jump on his bed. When he plays ball in the house and breaks a vase, David is sent to sit in the corner. Shannon's sympathetic paintings do justice to the range of childhood feelings: the joy of play, the frustration of being told "no," the vulnerability in reaching to Mommy for comfort, the contentment in a parent's love. The bright illustrations are a visual treat, and the childlike simplicity of the figures and lettering supports the juvenile perspective.

Secondary Reviews

8.22 Asch, Frank (1998). **Good Night, Baby Bear.** New York: Harcourt Brace. Unpaged. ISBN: 0-15-200836-5. Picture Book.

Nature is calling Mother Bear to hibernate. Baby Bear, who has spent the entirety of his short life outside, neither understands nor likes this new situation. When Mother Bear takes Baby Bear into a cave to sleep, Baby Bear makes demands for something to eat, something to drink, and finally for the moon—demands that Mother Bear reacts to with frustration, creativity, and love. Mother Bear's exasperation and Baby Bear's restlessness are easily seen in the simple illustrations.

8.23   Bliss, Corinne Demas (1997). **Electra and the Charlotte Russe.** Illustrated by Michael Garland. Honesdale, PA: Boyds Mills. Unpaged. ISBN: 1-56397-436-3. Picture Book.

Mama is having a tea party and sends her young daughter, Electra, to the bakery to buy charlotte russes. When Electra is almost home, an accident mashes the whipped cream on top of the desserts, a fact she tries to cover up with disastrous results. Feeling guilty, she lies to Mama about what happened. Fortunately, after the guests leave, Electra learns that not only do mothers always know when you lie, but they also forgive. Michael Garland's soft illustrations complement the gentle story.

8.24   Bogacki, Tomek (1997). **Cat and Mouse in the Rain.** New York: Farrar, Straus and Giroux. Unpaged. ISBN: 0-374-31189-7. Picture Book.

Cat and Mouse are friends who venture out on a cloudy day. As the rain begins to fall, Cat and Mouse decide to stay dry by huddling together under a leaf—until a frog tempts the careful animals into the uncharted territory of mud puddles, where they find delight in splashing and water play. This lighthearted story, illustrated with vibrant brush strokes, encourages the reader to entertain risk and try new things.

8.25   Brett, Jan (1997). **The Hat.** New York: Putnam. Unpaged. ISBN: 0-399-23101-3. Picture Book.

As a curious hedgehog examines one of Lisa's woolen stockings, which has blown from her clothesline, the stocking becomes stuck on his prickles. To cover his embarrassment, he tries to convince his animal friends that the stocking is his new hat and that it is they who are lacking. Hedgie is so convincing that Lisa soon finds all of Hedgie's friends with a piece of her woolens on them. Jan Brett's characteristic illustrations grace the text.

8.26   Chall, Marsha Wilson (1998). **Rupa Raises the Sun.** Illustrated by Rosanne Litzinger. New York: Dorling Kindersley. Unpaged. ISBN: 0-7894-2496-7. Picture Book.

Having walked around her campfire every morning for over sixty years in order to raise the sun, Rupa needs a break. Her feet need to heal. When she is granted permission to sleep in one morning by the kind but clueless village elders, Rupa discovers herself finally free of her daily burden as the sun rises on its own. Rosanne Litzinger's quirky gouache illustrations with primitively drawn characters of indeterminate race and culture lend a feeling of universality to the text. Pair this book with Conrad's *The Rooster's Gift* (see **8.6**).

8.27   Denim, Sue (1997). **The Dumb Bunnies Go to the Zoo.** Illustrated by Dav Pilkey. New York: Blue Sky. Unpaged. ISBN: 0-590-84735-X. Picture Book.

Fans of *The Stupids* will delight in the antics of the Dumb Bunnies, Momma, Poppa, and Baby Bunny. On an Octember [sic] morning, the Bunnies go off to the zoo, enjoy upside-down ice cream from Custard's Last Stand, cause a panic when they mistake a fluttering butterfly for an escaped lion, and let all the animals out of their cages. After being kicked out of the zoo, the family returns home to their new waterbed, a standard bed with an oscillating lawn sprinkler attached. Older readers who take the time to explore such items as the copyright page and the jacket flap will be in for a treat. For example, they will learn that illustrator Dav Pilkey collaborated closely with Sue Denim (pseudonym—get it?). Use this title along with *Miss Spider's New Car* (see **8.44**) and *Detective Donut and the Wild Goose Chase* (see **8.62**) to explore visual puns and literary devices. Readers also might be interested in two other related books by Pilkey, *The Dumb Bunnies* and *The Dumb Bunnies' Easter*.

Pilkey, Dav (1998). **The Dumb Bunnies.** New York: Scholastic. Unpaged. ISBN: 0-590-47709-9. Picture Book.

Pilkey, Dav (1998). **The Dumb Bunnies' Easter.** New York: Scholastic. Unpaged. ISBN: 0-590-20242-1. Picture Book.

8.28   English, Karen (1998). **Just Right Stew.** Illustrated by Anna Rich. Honesdale, PA: Boyds Mills. Unpaged. ISBN: 1-56397-487-8. Picture Book. (See **4.33**)

8.29   Ernst, Lisa Campbell (1996). **Duke the Dairy Delight Dog.** New York: Simon & Schuster. Unpaged. ISBN: 0-689-80750-3. Picture Book.

Lisa Campbell Ernst portrays prejudice and acceptance in this tale of a dog striving for a place to call home. Duke has lived on his own all his life, but when he sees the mouthwatering Dairy Delight sign, he decides he will stay here forever. However Darla, the proprietor of Dairy Delight, does not like dogs, and her obsessive efforts to keep him away culminate in an accident that helps her see Duke through new eyes. Ernst's colorful illustrations will be familiar to readers of *Ginger Jumps.*

> Ernst, Lisa Campbell (1990). **Ginger Jumps.** New York: Simon & Schuster. Unpaged. ISBN: 0-689-80652-3.

8.30   Ernst, Lisa Campbell (1997). **Bubba and Trixie.** New York: Simon & Schuster. Unpaged. ISBN: 0-689-81357-0. Picture Book.

Bubba the caterpillar is a nervous Nelly until he meets Trixie, a confident ladybug with a crimped wing. Trixie convinces Bubba to accompany her on a tour of the garden, pointing out interesting sights and teaching him how to have fun. Bubba soon grows content and wishes for everything to stay exactly as it is forever. However when he learns he is to turn into a butterfly, he becomes upset and afraid that he will lose his friend Trixie. Despite her assurances, Bubba settles into his cocoon with the firm conviction never to change. Of course he needn't have worried, for when spring arrives and the two friends awake, Trixie climbs onto Bubba, who is now a butterfly, and off they fly to touch the stars. Ernst's soft pastel illustrations are well-suited to this quiet story. The inclusion of facts about ladybugs and caterpillars makes this a useful supplement to an insect unit. The story line also would support a self-esteem unit in combination with *Mr. Bumble* (see **8.43**), *A Bad Case of the Stripes* (see **14.15**), or *The Very Hungry Caterpillar.*

> Carle, Eric (1987). **The Very Hungry Caterpillar.** New York: Philomel. Unpaged. ISBN: 0-399-20853-4. Picture Book.

8.31   Fleming, Candace (1997). **Gabriella's Song.** Illustrated by Giselle Potter. New York: Atheneum Books for Young Readers. Unpaged. ISBN: 0-689-80973-5. Picture Book.

Along the Grand Canal, a girl named Gabriella hears the song of the morning. She sings the song back to life itself, and the song carries. She sings to the baker, who sings to the widow, who sings to the gondolier. When Gabriella happens by the door of a frustrated composer while singing her morning song, he hears the tune for which he has longed and his symphony pours forth. A delightfully affirming tale.

8.32 Fleming, Denise (1997). **Time to Sleep.** New York: Henry Holt. Unpaged. ISBN: 0-8050-3762-4. Picture Book. (See **11.28**)

8.33 Franklin, Kristine L. (1996). **The Wolfhound.** Illustrated by Kris Waldherr. New York: Lothrop, Lee & Shepard. Unpaged. ISBN: 0-688-13674-5. Picture Book.

Tapestry frames surround engaging illustrations in this story about a boy in Tsarist Russia. Pavel finds a dying wolfhound and brings it home to nurse it back to health. His father tells him that he must drive away the dog for fear someone will think it was stolen. Pavel understands the risk, but has a sense of compassion for the beautiful creature that ultimately is rewarded. Kristine Franklin spins a warm tale about concern for others and the courage to do good.

8.34 Garay, Luis (1997). **Pedrito's Day.** New York: Orchard. Unpaged. ISBN: 0-531-09522-3. Picture Book.

Pedrito longs for a bicycle, both to help his family deliver tamales to the market and for his own play. His family tells him he is too young for a bicycle, so Pedrito begins to save his own money for the bicycle from his shoeshine job. When his aunt sends him on an errand to get change for a bill she gives him, he is distracted by a game of soccer and loses the money. Chagrined, Pedrito returns to his aunt, explains what he has done, and repays her from his bicycle savings. The family, in turn, acknowledges his sense of responsibility by telling him that the entire family will help him save money for the bicycle. The lesson is a powerful one for Pedrito and, vicariously, for readers. Drawing from his Guatemalan origins, Garay's illustrations, done in paint with inked cross-hatching, depict a very poor family. It would be interesting to have children discuss the economic status of Pedrito's family and perhaps contrast this book with others about Hispanic/Latino families from different economic situations.

8.35   Gliori, Debi (1996). **The Snow Lambs.** New York: Scholastic. Unpaged. ISBN: 0-590-20304-5. Picture Book.

Dad, Sam, and Bess the sheepdog are bringing their herd of sheep to the barn one evening when a winter storm hits. After finally reaching the house, Sam becomes frightened for Bess, who is nowhere to be found. As Mom and Dad take care of and comfort Sam in the house, the opposing illustrations show Bess struggling to get a pregnant ewe back to safety. This tender story and its illustrations invite the reader to return many times.

8.36   Grambling, Lois G. (1998). **Daddy Will Be There.** Illustrated by Walter Gaffney-Kessell. New York: Greenwillow. Unpaged. ISBN: 0-688-14983-9. Picture Book. (See **4.8**)

8.37   Harris, Marian (1998). **Tuesday in Arizona.** Illustrated by Jim Harris. Gretna, LA: Pelican. Unpaged. ISBN: 1-56554-233-9. Picture Book.

There's no mistaking the true nature of a pack rat in this fun-loving tale from Marian and Jim Harris, an author-illustrator team. As an old miner's life goes from bad to worse in the space of a week, readers can follow the intricacies of his story by closely examining the illustrations. The text is minimal and full of puns, leaving readers lots of room to enjoy the book on both a literary and visual level. Jim Harris' detailed and textured watercolors convey much of the action, while the text connects each event to the next. The pack rat provides unity, causing mischief on every page but also holding the key to the miner's happiness in the end. Anyone who knows what an adorable nuisance a pack rat can be will examine each spread with anticipation. This book would be wonderful for emerging readers who are learning to use illustrations to support their reading.

8.38   Hest, Amy (1998). **Gabby Growing Up.** Illustrated by Amy Schwartz. New York: Simon & Schuster. Unpaged. ISBN: 0-689-80573-X. Picture Book.

Gabby eagerly looks forward to being more grown-up, but like most children at her stage of life, she is an uncomfortable mixture of adolescent and child. Her mother clearly also feels uncomfortable with Gabby changing, but her tolerance and Grampa's easy acceptance make the transition gentler for Gabby. The simple lines and bright colors of Amy Schwartz's paintings are an appropriate accompaniment to this simple, yet engaging story of a young girl's start down the road to adulthood.

8.39 Hoberman, Mary Ann (1997). **One of Each.** Illustrated by Marjorie Priceman. New York: Little Brown. Unpaged. ISBN: 0-316-36731-1. Picture Book.

Oliver Tolliver values simplicity. The brown dog lives all alone in a house containing only one of each item: one bed, one clock, one book, one chair. But a cat named Peggoty Small clearly disapproves of this arrangement; Oliver's house has room for only one person, too. In this story, Caldecott Honor-winning illustrator Marjorie Priceman's bold, eye-catching pictures capture the cheerful spirit of a dog learning to share.

8.40 Inkpen, Mick (1997). **Nothing.** New York: Orchard. Unpaged. ISBN: 0-531-30076-5. Picture Book.

A tattered and worthless stuffed animal is left behind when a family moves. Alone in the empty attic, the stuffed animal yearns to discover its long-forgotten identity. A long and winding journey culminates when a friendly cat drops the stuffed animal onto the lap of Grandfather. Here the stuffed animal discovers that he is not "nothing"; he is the beloved stuffed animal that once sat in the grandfather's crib.

8.41 Johnson, Angela (1997). **The Rolling Store.** Illustrated by Peter Catalanotto. New York: Orchard. 32 pp. ISBN: 0-531-30015-3. Picture Book.

As a little girl and her friend are about to start out with their wagon loaded with goodies, she is reminded of a story her granddaddy would tell her about the Rolling Store. The Rolling Store would come to the countryside and people would come from miles around to buy things they needed and things they didn't need. This was a time to visit with friends and talk the day away. The warm and inviting pictures take you back to a time "when the world was still young," as granddaddy would say!

8.42 Joosse, Barbara M. (1997). **Nugget and Darling.** Illustrated by Sue Truesdell. New York: Clarion. 32 pp. ISBN: 0-395-64571-9. Picture Book.

Barbara Joosse uses pets to illustrate this sweet story about jealousy. Nell and her scruffy brown dog Nugget are best friends. But Nugget's discovery of an abandoned kitten threatens to jeopardize their close relationship when Nell starts showering affection on the kitten she names Darling, and Nugget feels left out. Sue Truesdell's cartoonlike watercolors ably capture Nugget's emotions as he sulks and mopes and longs for Nell's company and understanding.

8.43   Kennedy, Kim (1998). **Mr. Bumble.** Illustrated by Doug Kennedy. New York: Hyperion. Unpaged. ISBN: 0-7868-0263-4. Picture Book.

This is an inspiring story about Mr. Bumble—"the clumsiest bee that ever buzzed"—whose clumsiness and cowardliness sends him back to the hive empty-handed every time. Saved by thoughtful fairies, Mr. Bumble learns to fly with grace and courage. Applause from his peers and praise from the queen highlight his triumphant return to the hive. This story helps children learn about the process of overcoming obstacles to achieve a goal. The bees, fairies, and flowers have human faces, and their comic expressions are brought to life with the use of soft colors and textures. Readers can relate to Mr. Bumble on many levels and will likely be cheering for him by story's end.
Related books include:

Kraus, Robert (1994). **Leo the Late Bloomer.** Illustrated by Jose Aruego. New York: HarperCollins. 30 pp. ISBN: 0-064-4334-8-X. Picture Book.

Lionni, Leo (1994). **Cornelius.** New York: Knopf. 32 pp. ISBN: 0-679-86040-1. Picture Book.

8.44   Kirk, David (1997). **Miss Spider's New Car.** New York: Scholastic. Unpaged. ISBN: 0-590-30713-4. Picture Book.

David Kirk's familiar, brilliantly hued paintings highlight this latest installment of the Miss Spider saga, in which the friendly arachnid buys a car. Miss Spider knows right away what car she wants, but her husband Holley insists they shop around first. As they go from dealer to dealer, Holley finds most of the vehicles a little too daring. Finally Holley buys the car Miss Spider originally wanted and surprises her with it as an acknowledgment that she was right all along.

8.45 Lodge, Bernard (1997). **Tanglebird.** New York: Houghton Mifflin. Unpaged. ISBN: 0-395-84543-2. Picture Book.

With his muted-color prints, Bernard Lodge evokes an earlier style of picture-book illustrations in this book about a ne'er-do-well bird. Nicknamed Tanglebird because of his inability to build a neat nest, this inept bird finally learns to weave from a young girl, who sends him off with her love and a bunch of colorful string. Back in the woods, Tanglebird amazes the other birds and pleases himself with his artfully woven nest, a tribute to perseverance and friendship.

8.46 Loomis, Christine (1997). **Cowboy Bunnies.** Illustrated by Ora Eitan. New York: Putnam. Unpaged. ISBN: 0-399-22625-7. Picture Book.

Playful paintings on plywood panels highlight fun, easy verse about a day in the life of cowboy bunnies. The meter is simple and a pleasure to read: "Cowboy bunnies / Wake up early / Ride their ponies / Hurly Burly." They are child bunnies, having fun imitating the adult world. In the most endearing part of the book, the sleepy bunnies come home after a long day and get ready for bed: "Cowboy bunnies / In pajamas / Hug and kiss / Their cowboy mamas."

8.47 Lorbiecki, Marybeth (1996). **Just One Flick of a Finger.** Illustrated by David Diaz. New York: Dial. Unpaged. ISBN: 0-8037-1949-3. Sophisticated Picture Book.

Lorbiecki and Diaz are to be commended for tackling a difficult topic with great finesse. The narrator is a youth with whom the audience will identify—a good guy who just wants to be cool. But when he wields his father's weapon and his friend is the accidental victim, cool is changed forever. Although the resolution of the story verges on a happily-ever-after ending, the dangers are not diminished. The text is rhythmic, and the illustrations vivid. (See also **20.38**)

8.48 Machado, Ana Maria (1996). **Nina Bonita.** Illustrated by Rosanna Faria. Brooklyn, NY: Kane/Miller. 24 pp. ISBN: 0-916-29163-4. Picture Book.

The white rabbit wants to know how Nina Bonita became so black. The rabbit wants to know so he can become black too. The adventuresome Nina Bonita gives the rabbit many answers, but none of them is true. The rabbit does not understand that he cannot be turned a color, but can only be born a color. Each time Nina Bonita makes up another explanation for how she became black, the rabbit experiences another mishap. Once Nina Bonita's mother tells the white rabbit the truth, he stops chasing Nina for the answer and settles down happily with his own solution. The light pastel colors in the illustrations are accented by the beautiful tropical landscape, and contrast with the curious white rabbit and the beautiful little Black girl, Nina Bonita.

8.49 McPhail, David (1998). **The Puddle.** New York: Farrar, Straus and Giroux. Unpaged. ISBN: 0-374-36148-7. Picture Book.

On a rainy day, a young boy playing in a puddle exercises his imagination. Enjoined by his mother not to get in any puddles, the boy decks himself out in rain gear and goes out to sail his boat. Once outside, a frog, an alligator, a pig, and an elephant decide to join the fun and make a mess. In his soft ink-and-watercolor paintings, David McPhail gently evokes the world of childhood make-believe.

8.50 Miranda, Anne (1997). **To Market, to Market.** Illustrated by Janet Stevens. New York: Harcourt Brace. Unpaged. ISBN: 0-15-200035-6. Picture Book. (See **11.4**)

8.51 Modarressi, Mitra (1998). **Monster Stew.** New York: Dorling Kindersley. 48 pp. ISBN: 0-7894-2517-3. Picture Book.

Toothy beasts replace familiar characters in these three monstrous renditions of traditional fairy tales, such as "Peas," in which a princess proves herself unworthy to marry green Prince Thugmond after making a fuss about a lumpy mattress. Happily the prince gets to marry his rough-and-tumble, non-royal best friend instead. Modarressi's watercolors manage to create monsters that are simultaneously fearsome and charming, and her tales succeed in being both more humorous and more morally satisfying to a modern audience than the originals.

8.52 Naylor, Phyllis Reynolds (1997). **"I Can't Take You Anywhere."** Illustrated by Jef Kaminsky. New York: Simon & Schuster. Unpaged. ISBN: 0-689-31966-5. Picture Book.

Accident-prone Amy Audrey begs her relatives to take her with them when they go out. But when Amy falls into the fountain at the museum, spills water at the restaurant, or gets on the wrong escalator at the mall, they all say, "Amy Audrey, I declare! I can't take you anywhere!" Jef Kaminsky's brightly colored cartoons and big-eyed characters accompany this humorous story of a hapless girl with whom many children will be able to identify.

8.53 Pinkney, Brian (1997). **The Adventures of Sparrowboy.** New York: Simon & Schuster. 40 pp. ISBN: 0-689-81071-7. Picture Book.

Henry, the neighborhood paperboy, loves to read the headlines and the comics before he delivers the paper. He enjoys reading about his favorite superhero, and he wonders what it would be like to become a superhero himself. He gets that chance when a sparrow lands in his path while he is riding his bike delivering papers. "ZAP"—Henry can fly like the sparrow! Children will enjoy seeing how an ordinary paperboy saves his neighborhood.

8.54 Plourde, Lynn (1997). **Pigs in the Mud in the Middle of the Rud.** Illustrated by John Schoenherr. New York: Scholastic. Unpaged. ISBN: 0-590-56863-9. Picture Book.

The pigs are only the first of a series of animals that find their way into the mud in this rollicking farm tale. The animals cause a traffic problem for the Model-T Ford carrying Grandma and her family. Each family member in his or her turn attempts to move the accumulating tangle of animals. The story is delightfully written with rhythmic text. The concepts of sequence and accumulation are taught through captivating illustrations.

8.55 Rylant, Cynthia (1996). **The Old Woman Who Named Things.** Illustrated by Kathryn Brown. New York: Harcourt Brace. Unpaged. ISBN: 0-15-257809-9. Picture Book.

In this story about the risks of love, an old woman who has outlived all her friends refuses to name anything that will not outlive her. When a stray puppy comes daily to visit her, she feeds it and sends it on its way. It is not until the dog fails to show up for several days that she realizes how attached she has become to the animal. Kathryn Brown's watercolor illustrations ably capture the frailty and resigned contentedness of an old woman afraid of being hurt by her own love, as well as her trepidation over committing to a new friend who might one day leave her.

8.56 Sandoval, Dolores (1996). **Be Patient, Abdul.** New York: Simon & Schuster. Unpaged. ISBN: 0-689-50607-4. Picture Book.

Abdul is a seven-year-old boy from Freetown, Sierra Leone, who loves learning. His simple goal is to earn enough money to pay tuition and attend school. A series of minor challenges frustrates Abdul, and the adults in his family take turns encouraging him to "be patient, Abdul." As he works to learn patience, his minor setbacks are also the source for unexpected successes.

8.57 Shannon, Margaret (1998). **Gullible's Troubles.** New York: Houghton Mifflin. Unpaged. ISBN: 0-395-83933-5. Picture Book.

The title says it all as poor, trustworthy Gullible—who believes everything he hears—is sent for a visit with some rather uncharitable relatives. Gullible tries his best to fit in, asking to help his aunt bake a cake, trying to tidy up for his uncle, but each attempt to help goes awry. Taking advantage of his weakness, his relatives tell him many tales—tall and small—that frighten and confuse the poor little guinea pig into doing things like eating fifty non-moldy carrots (which he was told would make him invisible). Finally Gullible manages to hightail it home to the safety of his mother's embracing arms. A poignant reminder that no matter how far we roam, there is no place like home.

8.58 Soto, Gary (1997). **Chato y su cena.** Illustrated by Susan Guevara. Translated by Alma Flor Ada and F. Isabel Campoy. New York: Putnam and Grosset. Unpaged. ISBN: 0-698-11601-1. Picture Book.

Chato's Kitchen, a popular, humor-filled picture book with bold illustrations, is now available in Spanish. The translation employs rich, colorful language that demonstrates Gary Soto's deft use of code-switching and barrio expressions. Some expressions are not translated and, interestingly, the italicized words are not the same in each version. Chato, a local homeboy cat, invites a new neighbor family of mice over for dinner—dinner being the mice. As Chato and his pal Novio Boy create innumerable tasty dishes, the felines extend the invitation to one of the mice's old friends, Chorizo, from their former neighborhood. After hours of preparation and anticipation of a savory meal of succulent mice, the low-rider cats react in horror when they see their guests enter. Bilingual fourth graders chuckled and cheered when they realized that Chorizo is, in fact, a dog. Garret (age eight) gleefully said, "Those cats were bummed out 'cause they didn't get to eat the mice." Susan Guevara's richly colored, expressive paintings, outlined in black in the Mexican muralist style and spilling across double-page spreads, earned the Pura Belpre Illustrator Award for 1996.

> Soto, Gary (1995). **Chato's Kitchen.** Illustrated by Susan Guevara. New York: Putnam. Unpaged. ISBN: 0-399-22658-3. Picture Book.

8.59 Stanley, Diane (1996). **Saving Sweetness.** Illustrated by G. Brian Karas. New York: Putnam. Unpaged. ISBN: 0-399-22645-1. Picture Book.

Set against a western backdrop with thought-provoking illustrations, this tale follows the sheriff on his quest to save an orphan named Sweetness, who is running away from her evil caretaker. But as he struggles to "save Sweetness," he is repeatedly the recipient of *her* salvation. Here is a story depicting a young girl in the role of courageous and resourceful heroine. The story line may be familiar, but the well-written narrative and lovable characters are delightfully unique.

8.60 Steig, William (1998). **Pete's a Pizza.** New York: HarperCollins. Unpaged. ISBN: 0-06-205157-1. Picture Book.

It is raining, and Pete is upset. In an an effort to lighten his son's mood, Pete's fifty-ish father lays him down on the kitchen table and begins making Pete into a pizza. He kneads and tosses Pete, then covers him with oil, flour, cheese, and tomatoes (really checkers). Along the way comes tickling, giggling, chasing, and hugging. Steig's familiar illustration style highlights the affection of family members for each other in this tribute to creative parenting.

8.61 Tarpley, Natasha Anastasia (1998). **I Love My Hair.** Illustrated by E. B. Lewis. Boston: Little Brown. 32 pp. ISBN: 0-316-52275-9. Picture Book.

Kenyana narrates the bedtime ritual of getting her hair combed. She admits that sometimes it hurts. When the combing becomes too difficult, Mama stops combing to tell Kenyana why she is so fortunate to have the type of hair that she has. Through the well-defined illustrations of E. B. Lewis, each of Kenyana's hairstyles comes to life. From the spinning wheel that weaves a soft puffy bun that sits upon her head, to the pair of wings that are actually two open pigtails, Kenyana's hair is explained and celebrated. Kenyana tells how she feels about each hairstyle, and how some people make fun of her hairstyles while others (like her teacher) make her feel good about how she wears her hair. Pair this book with Herron's *Nappy Hair* (see **4.9**).

8.62   Whatley, Bruce, and Rosie Smith (1997). **Detective Donut and the Wild Goose Chase.** New York: HarperCollins. Unpaged. ISBN: 0-06-026604-X. Picture Book.

The bumbling bear Detective Donut works to solve the case of the missing archeology professor, conveniently overlooking clues not only to the whereabouts of the professor, but also to the nature of the rare statue he's uncovered. Warm, funny illustrations contain visual puns that give the reader clues to the mystery, and to the identity of the nefarious kidnapper. Mouse, the detective's partner, is mentioned in the text only once, but the illustrations chart his assistance in solving the crime. Primary-age readers who catch the not-so-hidden bits of humor will respond well to this comical story. The mystery will also spark young detectives' interest, especially when used in conjunction with other detective tales designed for young readers such as Doug Cushman's *The Mystery of King Karfu*.

> Cushman, Doug (1996). **The Mystery of King Karfu.** New York: HarperCollins. Unpaged. ISBN: 0-060-24796-7. Picture Book.

8.63   Wood, Audrey (1998). **Sweet Dream Pie.** Illustrated by Mark Teague. New York: Scholastic. Unpaged. ISBN: 0-590-96204-3. Picture Book. (See **14.20**)

8.64   Wyeth, Sharon Dennis (1998). **Something Beautiful.** Illustrated by Chris K. Soentpiet. New York: Bantam Doubleday Dell. Unpaged. ISBN: 0-385-32239-9. Picture Book.

This inspirational story follows a little girl's journey to find something beautiful in a neighborhood marred by the many signs of urban blight. She finds signs of hope in the relationships between adults and children in her community, and from each she elicits "something beautiful." In her quest to find beauty, the little girl tells us how she transformed her space to create something beautiful. Rich illustrations bear witness to the challenge of life in urban America. (See also **20.8**)

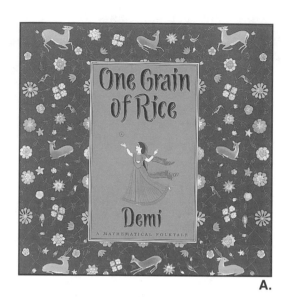

A.

B.

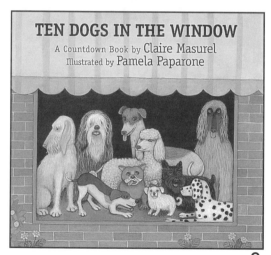

C.

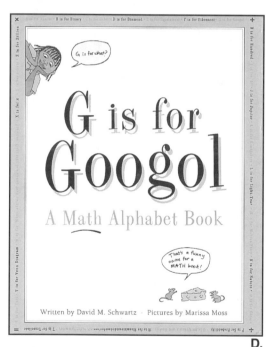

D.

A. *One Grain of Rice: A Mathematical Folktale,* Demi (**9.13**). **B.** *City by Numbers,* Stephen T. Johnson (**9.3**). **C.** *Ten Dogs in the Window,* Claire Masurel/Pamela Paparone (**9.5**). **D.** *G is for Googol: A Math Alphabet Book,* David M. Schwartz/Marissa Moss (**9.26**).

9 Mathematics

Carol Gilles

Contributing reviewers included Marilyn Andre, Carol Gilles,
Jenine Loesing, Marilyn Soucie, Shelli Thelen, and Beverly Vick.

In 1989, the National Council of Teachers of Mathematics published *Curriculum and Evaluation Standards for School Mathematics* for grades K–12. Four of the standards apply to all grade levels: teaching mathematics as problem solving, teaching mathematics as communication, teaching mathematics as reasoning, and teaching mathematical connections. These standards signified a major shift in the way mathematics is viewed and taught in the classroom.

The use of literature can assist children in meeting those goals and developing an appreciation for the power of mathematics in their lives. As Whitin and Wilde (1995) have noted, "Learners let go of rules and algorithms that don't make sense, but they hold on to stories" (xi). Stories brings meaning into our lives, helping children to understand mathematics rather than to memorize rules. Children's love for stories, and the social interaction that occurs when a teacher shares a story with a class, serve to engage children's interest in and build their confidence in their ability to use mathematics. Reading and sharing stories helps children make sense of mathematics as they encounter mathematical problems in a natural context. "Stories help learners see that mathematics is more than numbers on a page" (Whitin and Wilde 1995, 95). Approaching mathematics through literature also can help children make connections among curricular areas. Stories can offer rich problem-solving situations for children to investigate, discuss, and solve, thus developing their ability to reason and communicate. Mathematics is often referred to as a language of its own. Through stories, children learn the vocabulary of mathematics in an authentic context. They hear, read, and write the words that help make sense of and relate mathematics to their daily lives.

In choosing mathematics-related literature, it is important to remember that the book must first be good literature. Each book should be enjoyed as a story first; it should be read and reread, allowing children to respond through observation and prediction. Mathematics should be a part of the story rather than an interruption. The story also should allow for interpretation on several levels. Once the story is enjoyed, the discussion about it that follows can aid in launching experiences that might further conceptual mathematical understanding. With careful guidance, these ideas may be used to supplement basic mathematical thinking. As with all good literature, learners should be encouraged to not only read mathematics-related literature, but also to listen to the ideas of others and to talk and write about their impressions of the story.

The books reviewed in this chapter are organized into three broad categories. The first section includes Counting Books that develop and reinforce counting and number concepts. The second section contains Problem-Solving Storybooks. These books use a folktale, fairy tale, or other narrative to present a mathematical problem experienced by one or more of the characters which children can recognize and solve along with the characters. The third section includes Math Concept Books. These books investigate or present specific information about a mathematical concept.

Works Cited

National Council of Teachers of Mathematics, Commission on Standards for School Mathematics. 1989. *Curriculum and Evaluation Standards for School Mathematics*. Reston, VA: National Council of Teachers of Mathematics.

Whitin, David J., and Sandra Wilde. 1995. *It's the Story That Counts*. Portsmouth, NH: Heinemann.

---

*The titles listed below each subheading are organized into Primary Reviews and Secondary Reviews. The Primary Reviews describe outstanding books in each subheading. The Secondary Reviews provide brief information about other books worthy of consideration. Some titles listed below are **not** reviewed in this chapter; entries for these titles are not annotated and contain only bibliographic information. In such cases, a cross reference to the annotated entry contained elsewhere in this volume is provided in boldface type at the end of the bibliographic information.*

Counting Books

Primary Reviews

9.1   Alda, Arlene (1998). **Arlene Alda's 1 2 3: What Do You See?** Berkeley, CA: Tricycle. Unpaged. ISBN: 1-883672-71-6. Picture Book.

Through the use of photography, Arlene Alda artistically portrays numerals that appear all around us. Children are delighted to discover the various numerals creatively hidden in each full-color photograph. They first count up to ten and then count back again to zero. Each photograph depicts the shape of a numeral in an unexpected location. The numbers one through ten appear on each page of this wordless book, with the appropriate numeral highlighted. This allows children to compare the artists' numeral to the typed numeral on the page. Three appears as a banana peel, two as a swan, and ten is found in the reflection of the arch of a bridge. Using an artist's eye, children will see numbers in a whole new light and be challenged to find their own examples of numbers in nature.

9.2   Carlstrom, Nancy White (1996). **Let's Count It Out, Jesse Bear.** Illustrated by Bruce Degen. New York: Simon & Schuster Books for Young Readers. Unpaged. ISBN: 0-689-80478-4. Picture Book.

Jesse Bear is off for the day, and this time he is counting. From Band-Aids to bubbles, children are invited to count right along with Jesse. Each page shows the number written as a word, the corresponding numeral, and the objects to be counted. The story is told through cheerful rhyme that will have the children chanting. Each page uses the same counting pattern. First, the children count the objects, one, two, three, four. Then they are prompted to say that four and one more is five, thus introducing the concept that the next number in the sequence is one more than the previous number. Young children will have fun helping this playful bear count to twenty.

9.3   Johnson, Stephen T. (1998). **City by Numbers.** New York: Viking. Unpaged. ISBN: 0-670-87251-2. Picture Book.

This striking companion volume to the Caldecott Honor book *Alphabet City* helps readers to see numbers in urban settings. New York City is the setting for these perceptive paintings. Using the ground rules that each number must be "in its natural position, out of doors or in a public space, readily accessible to everyone who looks carefully," Johnson takes readers on a journey to discover the numbers one through twenty. We see the Manhattan bridge as a figure 4, while shadows form a 5 and wastebaskets form an 8. This book appeals to old and young alike, and it could be a companion to *Arlene Alda's 1 2 3: What Do You See?* (see **9.1**).

Johnson, Stephen T. (1995). **Alphabet City.** New York: Viking. Unpaged. ISPN: 0-670-85631-2. Picture Book.

9.4 Kusugak, Michael (1996). **My Arctic 1, 2, 3.** New York: Annick. 22 pp. ISBN: 1-55037-505-9. Picture Book.

In this number book, Inuit storyteller Michael Kusugak tells about the animals and people of Rankin Inlet, located near Hudson Bay in the Arctic region of Canada. Kusagak carries an animal theme through his investigation of the numbers one through ten, describing arctic animals and their activities. At the bottom of each of page, the numbers are also printed in the Inuit alphabet. This easy-to-read, colorful picture book will delight younger children learning to count, and will interest older readers wanting to know more about the arctic habitat.

9.5 Masurel, Claire (1997). **Ten Dogs in the Window.** Illustrated by Pamela Paparone. New York: North-South. Unpaged. ISBN: 1-55858-754-3. Picture Book.

Ten dogs of all kinds and sizes wait in the window hoping for just the perfect home. The countdown begins as, one-by-one, the dogs are chosen because "You're the perfect dog for me!" The language is rhythmic and repetitive, making it supportive for early readers. Children enjoy guessing which dog each customer will choose. A large numeral appears on each page, helping children develop numeracy. The bright illustrations will generate many stories about dogs or other pets readers have known, and children will cheer to find that all the dogs find their special homes. The final illustration shows the shopkeeper and ten cats in the window, providing a perfect opportunity for children to tell or write their own sequel.

9.6 McGrath, Barbara Barbieri (1998). **The Cheerios Counting Book.** Illustrated by Rob Bolster and Frank Mazzola, Jr. New York: Scholastic. Unpaged. ISBN: 0-590-00321-6. Picture Book.

It's time to munch Cheerios and read! In this book, children learn first to count from one to ten, and then to count to one hundred by tens. Each page shows the number written as a word, and the corresponding numeral. Each number is brightly illustrated with Cheerios and pieces of fruit. The arrangement of the Cheerios could lead to the discussion of many mathematical concepts such as number patterns, groupings by tens, and even and odd numbers. The text's strong rhyme invites the children to count along. This book is a great read-aloud. It will be hard to read this book without having a healthy Cheerios snack at hand!

9.7 Appelt, Kathi (1996). **Bat Jamboree.** Illustrated by Melissa Sweet. New York: Morrow Junior Books. Unpaged. ISBN: 0-688-13882-9. Picture Book.

The Bat Jamboree, starring fifty-five bats, has farm animals packing into an old drive-in movie for the bats' program. The children in one reviewer's first-grade class counted along with the ever-increasing number of bats as they came out to perform. The greatest act was building the the Great Bat Pyramid, with ten acrobats on the base. The story ends with a prediction about next year's show, which "won't be over until the bat lady sings." The charming illustrations add to the whimsical nature of the book. Several children in the reviewer's class wanted to see how many bats would be in pyramids with bases of different sizes. This counting book lead to a discussion of addition and patterns that absorbed first graders for days.

9.8 Foglesong Guy, Ginger (1996). **¡Fiesta!** Illustrated by René King Moreno. New York: Greenwillow. Unpaged. ISBN: 0-688-14331-8. Picture Book.

Three young children search the market for toys and candies to fill a piñata for their fiesta. As they shop, they count the objects that go into their basket. In this dual-language counting book for young children, simple and predictable text in a large font invites shared reading experiences. Although Spanish is given preferential placement on the page, beginning readers of any linguistic background will enjoy learning numbers in Spanish and English through the use of this patterned-language book. Artist René King Moreno uses pastels, watercolors, and colored pencil to create illustrations that correspond closely with the text, supporting readers as they count along with the children in the story.

9.9 Rankin, Laura (1998). **The Handmade Counting Book.** New York: Dial. Unpaged. ISBN: 0-8037-2309-1. Picture Book.

This book is both a counting book and an introduction to American Sign Language. Through clear, vivid illustrations, the reader learns the hand signs for the numbers one through twenty, twenty-five, fifty, seventy-five, and one hundred. The illustrations on each page model the hand position required, and provide objects for children to count. An artist's note at the beginning of the book gives the reader information about American Sign Language, and tips for using this book.

Problem-Solving Storybooks

Primary Reviews

9.10 Axelrod, Amy (1997). **Pigs Go to Market: Fun with Math and Shopping.** Illustrated by Sharon McGinley-Nally. New York: Simon & Schuster Books for Young Readers. Unpaged. ISBN: 0-689-81069-5. Picture Book.

This book is one of a series of adventures surrounding the Pig family and their problems. In this story, the Pigs are preparing for Halloween and discover to everyone's dismay that all the candy has been eaten before the big night arrives. The Pigs rush to the market to purchase more treats, and win a surprise shopping spree for being the one-millionth customer. Mrs. Pig dashes through the store grabbing up bags of candy while being cheered on by her family and other customers. The illustrations are bright, and show the pigs cavorting happily from page to page. At the end of the story, drawings of each purchase allow the reader to use multiplication to compute how much candy the pigs collected at the market.

9.11 Bauer, Joan (1996). **Sticks.** New York: Yearling. 182 pp. ISBN: 0-440-41387-7. Sophisticated Chapter Book.

This chapter book examines the world of Mickey Vernon, a ten-year-old boy who has lost his father and who lives to play pool. He wants more than anything to win the ten- to thirteen-year-olds' nine-ball championship, and wear the champion shirt just like his father. In order to do that, he accepts the help of Joseph—an old, lost friend of his father—and learns first-hand about patience, practice, and winning. Mickey's friend Arlen introduces mathematics into the plot. Arlen is a math whiz who figures out how vectors can help Mickey's pool game, how to win the jelly-bean prediction contest, and how Mickey can use math to have an awesome science project. Intermediate-grade students will enjoy both the story and the mathematical concepts inherent in it.

9.12 Burns, Marilyn (1997). **Spaghetti and Meatballs for All.** Illustrated by Debbie Tilley. New York: Scholastic. Unpaged. ISBN: 0-590-94459-2. Picture Book.

Come to the party! Mr. and Mrs. Comfort plan a spaghetti-and-meatball dinner for thirty-two family members and friends. Mr. Comfort takes care of the menu, while Mrs. Comfort arranges for the tables and chairs needed to seat all the guests. As guests start arriving and pushing tables together, the trouble begins. Children quickly make the prediction that there will not be enough chairs for all, and chaos seems imminent. The exchanges become humorous as more and more guests arrive. "'Hey,' Mrs. Comfort's brother's daughter's son said to his twin brother, 'that's my bread you're eating!'" The illustrations helpfully portray the activity of the party. Everyone pitches in to solve the problem. The tables are returned to their original locations, and the dinner is successful. At the end of the book, Burns includes information regarding this problem and additional ideas for mathematical puzzles.

9.13 Demi (1997). **One Grain of Rice: A Mathematical Folktale.** New York: Scholastic. Unpaged. ISBN: 0-590-93998-X. Picture Book.

This mathematical folktale concerns an Indian raja who refuses to share the rice of the kingdom with his people during a time of famine. A village girl does a good deed for the raja, and in return asks for the simple reward of a grain of rice to be doubled each day for thirty days. The raja soon realizes the power of doubling, for on the thirtieth day, over 500 million grains of rice must be delivered to the girl. In all, the girl receives over one billion grains of rice, leaving no rice for the raja. When asked what she will do with the rice, she answers, "I shall give it to all the hungry people." This tale teaches the raja a lesson about fairness. A table at the end of the book helps children appreciate the power of doubling numbers. The rich color and detail of the illustrations reflect the Indian setting.

9.14 Enzensberger, Hans Magnus (1997). **The Number Devil.** Illustrated by Rotraut Susane Berner. Translated by Michael Henry Heim. New York: Metropolitan. 262 pp. ISBN: 0-8050-5770-6. Sophisticated Chapter Book.

The most unfortunate thing about this amusing chapter book is its title. Some teachers and readers will be put off by the word *devil* in the title, and the devil that enters twelve-year-old Robert's dreams. However, this number devil shows Robert what math is really about—zeros and ones, infinite numbers, probability and primes, and the Fibonacci sequence, just to mention a few items. Each chapter is another dream and another lesson presented in an interesting and easy-to-understand way. For example, raising a number to a higher power is referred to as *hopping,* as in $2 \times 2 = 4$, $2 \times 2 \times 2 = 8$, and $2 \times 2 \times 2 \times 2 = 16$. Enzensberger is well known as one of Europe's intellectuals, and he writes with insight and great wit. This book is a good resource both for students, and for teachers looking for novel ways to present information.

9.15 Murphy, Stuart J. (1998). **Lemonade for Sale.** Illustrated by Tricia Tusa. New York: HarperCollins. 31 pp. ISBN: 0-06-446715-5. Picture Book.

The neighborhood clubhouse is falling down, and a group of children decide something must be done to rebuild it. To earn money for the building materials, the children set up the traditional lemonade stand. The concept of graphing is introduced as the children record on a bar graph their profits from each day's sales. Children reading this book did notice that one part of the graph was missing in these illustrations: the title. The children are faced with declining sales on the fourth day, but solve their problem by working with a competing business. This book lends itself to a discussion of many economic concepts and storytelling about lemonade stands or business ventures in which children participated. When one reviewer read this book aloud to her fourth graders, she found "It was a great spark for looking at and making graphs."

Secondary Reviews

9.16 Adler, David A. (1997). **Easy Math Puzzles.** Illustrated by Cynthia Fisher. New York: Holiday House. Unpaged. ISBN: 0-8234-1283-0. Picture Book.

These short math puzzles are interesting to investigate and solve. Every puzzle is presented briefly, and is supported by a black-and-white illustration. For example, the following puzzle is entitled Eggs for Breakfast:

If it takes 3 minutes
To boil 3 eggs for breakfast,
How long would it take
To boil 10 eggs?

One reviewer used these problems as warm-ups during the home-to-school transition in the first grade. Children worked cooperatively or individually to solve these tricky problems. The reviewer encouraged them to examine the language carefully to find out what question was being asked. These problems provided wonderful opportunities for children to exchange ideas, use vocabulary, and critically examine the language of mathematical problems.

9.17   Losi, Carol A. (1997). **The 512 Ants on Sullivan Street.** Illustrated by Patrick Merrell. New York: Scholastic. Unpaged. ISBN: 0-590-30876-9. Picture Book.

This cumulative tale is from the Hello Math Readers series. The books were written with parents and children in mind. The text is very readable for young children, and the illustrations are colorful and bold. In this book, a young girl and her father plan a picnic on Sullivan Street. They are visited by one ant "who carried a crumb," two ants "with some pieces of plum," then four ants, eight ants, and still more ants. The number of ants keeps doubling until finally "512 ants all ready to dine, picked up the cake and got right in line." At the end of the story Marilyn Burns, an expert in elementary mathematics curriculum, includes information and tips for parents to help their child understand the mathematical concepts involved.

9.18   Murphy, Stuart J. (1997). **Divide and Ride.** Illustrated by George Ulrich. New York: HarperCollins. 33 pp. ISBN: 0-06-446710-4. Picture Book.

This book is part of the MathStart series. Eleven friends decide to go to a carnival. Over and over again, they must divide into groups in order to ride the various rides. When they divide by twos, they have one friend who needs a partner. They ask other children to join them for each ride to even out the pairings. The realistic illustrations aid readers in quickly identifying with the problems that arise during a day at the carnival. This book helps children work with the concept of division and remainders. Number sentences are included to show how the problem was solved. There also is a strong friendship theme that children will want to discuss. The end of the book includes extension activities and suggestions for discussing the book with children.

9.19	Murphy, Stuart J. (1998). **A Fair Bear Share.** Illustrated by John Speirs. New York: HarperCollins. 33 pp. ISBN: 0-06-027438-7. Picture Book.

This is the delightful story of four little bears who are sent to collect nuts, berries, and seeds so mother can make her special blue-ribbon blueberry pie. Three of the bears do their fair share of gathering the necessary ingredients. When they return home, mother adds the nuts, berries, and seeds and finds there are not enough for the pie. The fourth bear is sad, and hurries out to collect her fair share so that all can enjoy the pie. The illustrations are alive and bright, capturing children's interest. The story could be read first as a story, skipping the pages showing how the seeds and other items are counted. The computation sections illustrate how objects can be grouped into tens and added easily, but may interrupt the flow of the story.

9.20	Ziefert, Harriet (1998). **Rabbit and Hare Divide an Apple.** Illustrated by Emily Bolam. New York: Viking. Unpaged. ISBN: 0-670-87790-5. Picture Book.

Rabbit and Hare have an apple that both want, and realize that they are going to need to split it. Unfortunately Rabbit and Hare don't split the apple in half, and they begin to fight. Along comes Mr. Raccoon, who seems to think he can help solve their problem. This book introduces the basic concept of the fraction *one-half*. Children will naturally want to try cutting an apple in half after reading this book. This book from the Viking Easy-to-Read series has simple text supported clearly by the illustrations.

Math Concept Books

Primary Reviews

9.21	Barrett, Judi (1998). **Things that Are Most in the World.** Illustrated by John Nickle. New York: Atheneum. Unpaged. ISBN: 0-689-81333-3. Picture Book. (See **13.11**)

9.22	Maganzini, Christy (1997). **Cool Math.** Illustrated by Ruta Daugavietis. New York: Price Stern Sloan. 95 pp. ISBN: 0-8431-7857-4. Chapter Book.

This book contains a wealth of information for the older child. The work of mathematicians such as Fibonacci, Euler, and Pythagoras are introduced to children through intriguing puzzles and problems. The material is presented in an easy-to-find and easy-to-understand format. The presence and importance of mathematics in children's daily lives is uncovered as children learn about math facts and their relationship to items in nature. The material is so engrossing that some children don't believe they are learning mathematics! The pages are even numbered using mathematical equations. The book includes a glossary and index, making it even easier to find information. Adults will also be fascinated by the number patterns and puzzles contained in this book.

9.23 McMillan, Bruce (1996). **Jelly Beans for Sale.** New York: Scholastic. Unpaged. ISBN: 0-590-86584-6. Picture Book.

Jelly Beans for Sale provides a mouthwatering introduction to basic money concepts. McMillan's colorful photographs of children enjoying jelly beans that they have purchased are filled with color and money concepts. The book begins with a young boy who has one strawberry jelly bean and one penny in his hand. Each photograph depicts a natural progression of coins—pennies, nickels, dimes, and quarters. At the end of this counting book, there is a history of jelly beans and a seven-day recipe for making them. There also is a discussion of coins, and a number to call for a free jelly bean kit, video, and jelly beans for teaching.

9.24 Morgan, Rowland (1997). **In the Next Three Seconds.** Illustrated by Rod Josey and Kira Josey. New York: Lodestar. 32 pp. ISBN: 0-525-67551-5. Picture Book.

Did you know that in the next three seconds loggers will cut down 199 trees? Each page of this book is covered with predictions and information about events that will occur in the next three seconds, minutes, hours, days, nights, weeks, months, years, decades, and centuries. Children are amazed and fascinated to read each prediction, and to think about each segment of time. The question inevitably arises: How does the author know this? Fortunately at the beginning of the book, the author describes how he went about making his predictions. This book will lead to many discussions surrounding his environmental predictions and their ramifications. An index and table of contents are included. The bright illustrations lead the reader's eye from one amazing prediction to another.

9.25 Neuschwander, Cindy (1998). **Amanda Bean's Amazing Dream: A Mathematical Story.** Illustrated by Liza Woodruff. New York: Scholastic. Unpaged. ISBN: 0-590-30012-1. Picture Book.

Amanda Bean loves to count, and she counts everything she sees from library books to pickles. One night, Amanda has a dream in which her counting gets out of hand. She dreams of eight bicycles ridden by sheep. As she tries to count the bicycle wheels and then the legs of the sheep, she discovers that for larger numbers, counting just does not work. Finally Amanda wakes up and realizes that multiplication is a faster and easier way of counting. The illustrations provide many opportunities for children to count along with Amanda, and clearly show the concept of multiplication through the groupings of various objects. Marilyn Burns, an expert on elementary mathematics curriculum, has provided multiplication extension activities at the end of the book for teachers and parents.

9.26 Schwartz, David M. (1998). **G Is for Googol: A Math Alphabet Book.** Illustrated by Marissa Moss. Berkeley, CA: Tricycle. 57 pp. ISBN: 1-883672-58-9. Sophisticated Chapter Book.

What's a googol? Read this book, and you'll discover there is both an easy way and a hard way to write this number. This mathematics alphabet book for the older child presents information on many concepts, such as the googolplex, Fibonacci, the Konigsberg Bridge problem, and many more intriguing mathematics-related topics. The text is conversational, and the cartoonlike illustrations clearly demonstrate the concepts. The book presents information in such a way that readers will be eager to explore and test the relationships described. This book sparked many explorations for the fourth- and fifth-grade math clubs under one reviewer's guidance. Activities like the Möbius strip captured the children's curiosity. The students' favorite extension of the book was investigating the appearance of numbers in the Fibonacci sequence in pinecones, pineapples, seashells, and other objects. An easy-to-use glossary is included for reference.

Secondary Reviews

9.27 Cristalsdi, Kathryn (1996). **Even Steven and Odd Todd.** Illustrated by Henry B. Morehouse. New York: Scholastic. Unpaged. ISBN: 0-590-22715-7. Picture Book.

Even Steven carefully organizes his life using safe, even numbers. He has six cats, checks out four books, and even eats six pancakes. He is visited by his cousin Odd Todd, who wakes up at nine o'clock, knocks three times, and eats three pancakes. Children in one reviewer's class quickly noticed the difference between the characters, and began anticipating the problems that would arise. This book led to a discussion of even and odd numbers, but children also were quick to comment on the need to accept people different from themselves. The children loved the emotion captured in the illustrations. This story is from the Hello Math Readers series. The stories are easy-to-read and were written for the parent-and-child audience. Marilyn Burns, an expert in elementary mathematics curriculum, provides parents with activities at the end of the book for extending the mathematical concepts discussed.

9.28   Harper, Dan (1998). **Telling Time with Big Mama Cat.** Illustrated by Barry Moser and Cara Moser. San Diego: Harcourt Brace. Unpaged. ISBN: 0-15-201738-0. Picture Book.

Big Mama Cat's day begins at 6:00 A.M. with a stretch. She must stay on schedule. At seven breakfast is served, and her busy day moves ahead. This delightful story tells about the day in the life of a family who owns a cat. Each page includes inviting text, a sturdy clock showing the current time, and a warm watercolor illustration. Young children will enjoy opportunities to identify and explore the times represented in the story. Time concepts represented in the book include even, half, quarter, and three-quarter hours. Children will be able to see the parallel between their own lives and that of Mama Cat's household.

9.29   McGrath, Barbara Barbieri (1998). **More M&M's Math.** Watertown, MA: Charlesbridge. 32 pp. ISBN: 0-88106-993-0. Picture Book.

More M&M's Math is a follow up to *The M&M's Counting Book.* This counting book extends the concepts presented in its predecessor. Learners are encouraged to graph, sort, and estimate using their candy. Concepts such as regrouping, multiplication, and repeated addition are presented. Problem-solving and critical thinking are encouraged as learners manipulate their M&M's using ordinal numbers (1st, 2nd, etc.). Students love this book, and it provides a wonderful way to launch a lesson introducing any of the above concepts.

McGrath, Barbara Barbieri (1994). **The M&M's Counting Book.** Watertown, MA: Charlesbridge. 32 pp. ISBN: 0-88106-854-3. Picture Book.

9.30   Murphy, Stuart J. (1997). **Just Enough Carrots.** Illustrated by Frank Remkiewicz. New York: HarperCollins. 31 pp. ISBN: 0-06-026778-X. Picture Book.

Murphy's MathStart books are clear, and present information in an easy-to-follow format with supportive, colorful illustrations. *Just Enough Carrots* introduces the basic math concepts of *fewer, same,* and *more.* Rabbit, his mom, Elephant, and Bird are shopping at the grocery story. Rabbit can't understand why his mom is buying so many peanuts and worms, when all he wants is some carrots. After reading the story, one reviewer asked her students to follow the model of the book showing "our set, fewer, same, and more." Students used beans to create their own set, as well as one that had less, the same, and more.

9.31   Murphy, Stuart J. (1998). **The Penny Pot.** New York: HarperCollins. 33 pp. ISBN: 0-06-027606-1. Picture Book.

Another MathStart series book, *The Penny Pot* is about a girl named Jesse who wants to have her face painted at a school fun fair, but does not have the necessary fifty cents. Fran, the art teacher and face-painter, encourages Jessie to wait for the money she needs. As children come to Fran with more than enough money, she encourages them to put extra pennies into the penny pot. Miguel, who wants to be a clown, adds three pennies, while Annie, who wants to be a monster, adds four. Finally Jesse waits long enough to retrieve the extra coins and get her own face painted. The whimsical illustrations show Jessie, Fran, and the children requesting the face painting, and display the coins mentioned in the story. The book can be extended by talking about trading (regrouping) and shopping, or by making a coin game.

9.32   Schlein, Miriam (1996). **More than One.** Illustrated by Donald Crews. New York: Greenwillow. Unpaged. ISBN: 0-688-14102-1. Picture Book.

This book looks at the concept *one.* First the reader sees one sun and one whale. The author then moves the reader to consider one pair of shoes, one team, one week, and other groups to see how "one" can actually be more than one. This book sparks discussion and inspires story writing as children think of other situations where one group is greater than one. The illustrations are bold and bright, and enable the children to count along.

9.33 Slate, Joseph (1998). **Miss Bindergarten Celebrates the 100th Day.** Illustrated by Ashley Wolff. New York: Penguin. Unpaged. ISBN: 0-525-46000-4. Picture Book.

In preparation for the 100th day of school, Miss Bindergarten begins a variety of activities on the first day of school that her students clamor to join. Each student in Miss Bindergarten's class makes a poster that depicts a collection of one hundred, which they hang across the classroom on a clothesline and then share using repetitive language. For example, Gwen makes a poster of one hundred fingers and toes, while Wanda makes a lariat of one hundred rubber bands. Miss Bindergarten even makes a one-hundred-day punch, which of course is made with one hundred cherries. Rich discussions and many ideas for the concept of one hundred are introduced, and can easily be used to launch related lessons.

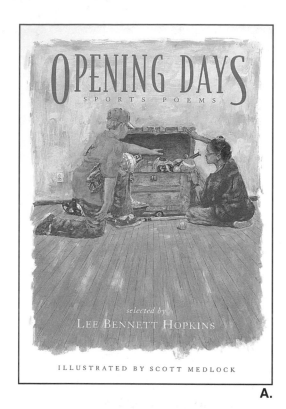

A.

B.

C.

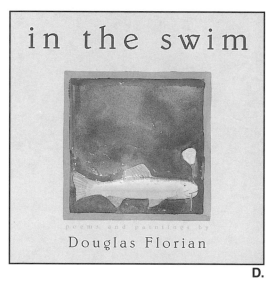

D.

A. *Opening Days: Sports Poems,* Lee Bennett Hopkins/Scott Medlock (**10.17**). **B.** *Confetti: Poems for Children,* Pat Mora/Enrique O. Sanchez (**10.53**). **C.** *The Great Frog Race and Other Poems,* Kristine O'Connell George/Kate Kiesler (**10.2**). **D.** *In the Swim: Poems and Paintings,* Douglas Florian (**10.35**).

10 Poetry

Amy McClure

Contributing reviewers included Joan Bownas, Lisa Dapoz, Karen Hildebrand, Amy McClure, Peggy Oxley, Lillian Webb, and Lynda Weston.

Listening and responding to poetry provides wonderful opportunities for children to appreciate the subtleties of language. Some of our most rewarding moments in teaching have occurred during literature discussions in which poetry is the focus. Over time, the members of our review committee have developed criteria for determining what constitutes high-quality literature in this genre. Good poetry for children doesn't necessarily have to rhyme. However, it should focus on things that interest children, feature imagery that is within their experience, and evoke thoughtful response. It can be humorous, but should respect the boundaries of good taste. We hope this chapter provides you with some resources that meet these criteria.

Our committee examined virtually every poetry book published between 1996 and 1998. We then field-tested the ones we thought would most appeal to children. During our monthly meetings, we discussed which books were instant hits and which ones took some teacher encouragement to capture a group's interest. Thus children's preferences and interests were central to our decisions about what should be included in this chapter. However, we also strongly believed that only collections of well-crafted poetry should be included, so if a book appealed to children but wasn't good poetry, it was eliminated.

We also worked hard to achieve balance and diversity. We searched for books that reflected various cultural perspectives. We included some from both established and emerging poets. We made sure books for different age groups were selected. However, quality of writing always undergirded our choices. For example, if a book featured an interesting cultural perspective but didn't appeal to children or meet our criteria for good poetry, it wasn't included.

After selecting books for inclusion, we agreed upon categories by which to organize the chapter. One of the special delights gained from reading poetry is how it helps us see common, everyday things with new eyes. In the first section, Making the Ordinary Extraordinary, readers will find books that fit this description. In the section entitled People: Past and Present, we have included poetry that clarifies and illuminates our understandings of other people, both contemporary and historical. Because much children's poetry focuses on describing animals and nature, we decided it was important to have sections devoted to these topics. These books can be found in separate sections entitled The Animal World and The Natural World. Finally the section entitled Transcending Cultural Boundaries highlights the poetry from diverse cultures that is now available to children.

We trust that teachers won't use these books to teach formal poetic analysis or solely as an adjunct to other curricular activities. Rather we hope that expanding teachers' awareness of good poetry will help them become skilled at articulating what it is about a poem that makes it so appealing, and that this in turn will bring their students to love the genre. We hope that teachers will not reserve poetry for a special month of the year, but rather infuse the entire curriculum with the insights and perspectives only poetry can provide.

Acknowledgment: We particularly appreciate the additional insights gained from working with the following colleagues: Becky Book, Dublin City Schools; Sarah Goldshall, Ohio Wesleyan University; Judy Markham, Columbus School for Girls; Kathleen Taps, Upper Arlington City Schools; and Joan Smith, Westerville City Schools.

---

*The titles listed below each subheading are organized into Primary Reviews and Secondary Reviews. The Primary Reviews describe outstanding books in each subheading. The Secondary Reviews provide brief information about other books worthy of consideration. Some titles listed below are **not** reviewed in this chapter; entries for these titles are not annotated and contain only bibliographic information. In such cases, a cross reference to the annotated entry contained elsewhere in this volume is provided in boldface type at the end of the bibliographic information.*

For other books that include poetic literature or language—such as songs, chants, and rhyming or rhythmic text—see also the section entitled Rhythm, Rhyme, and Repetition in chapter 7, "Literacy"; the section entitled Music Books: Rhymes, Chants, and Songs in chapter 11, "Fine Arts"; and the section entitled Riddles, Chants, and Poems in chapter 13, "The Craft of Language."

Making the Ordinary Extraordinary

See also the section entitled Looking Closely at the Natural World in chapter 1, "Stories of the Universe."

Primary Reviews

10.1 Fletcher, Ralph (1997). **Twilight Comes Twice.** Illustrated by Kate Kiesler. New York: Clarion. 32 pp. ISBN: 0-395-84826-1. Picture Book.

Kate Kiesler's double-page oil paintings in pink and coral set the mood for this exquisite book of poetic prose that will appeal to all ages. Twilight is described as a crack that opens twice between night and day, while "Dusk gives the signal for night to be born" and "dawn is like a seed that will grow into daylight." Other phrases that will delight both children and teachers are, "Slowly dusk pours its syrup of darkness into the forest" and "Dawn slowly brightens the empty baseball diamond until it shines." Fletcher uses springtime and summertime descriptions of dusk and dawn. Children could try a similar format for fall or winter. Each illustration and accompanying text invite new writings, as well as personal memories of twilight encounters as reflected in the following poems written by upper-elementary students.

Dusk

The sun is falling
The sky turns pink and orange
And the water twinkles.
The fish jump
Just to see the colors

        Heather Shepherd

Dawn

From far out of no place
The sun takes its fingertips
And slides them across nighttime
Like you brush your hair in the morning.

        Collin English

10.2 George, Kristine O'Connell (1997). **The Great Frog Race and Other Poems.** Illustrated by Kate Kiesler. New York: Clarion. 40 pp. ISBN: 0-395-77607-4. Picture Book.

A series of short, reflective poems show a young girl enjoying the seasonal pleasures of country life. The imagery is very child-oriented, and uses easily understood comparisons like a weeping willow that "weeps piles of tears for me to rake" and a wooden swing "pillowed with snow." Kiesler's realistic oil paintings bring to life each poem. Teachers can find in this collection many examples of word-crafting to discuss with children. Polliwogs are described as "Chubby commas" "Huddled in puddles / snuggled in mud." Words are placed artfully to convey the rhythmic flight of Canadian geese: "See them sketching, stretching skyward. / Hear their lonely cry." Evening rain is described as "taking thin silken stitches / with strands of wet thread." Children may need help understanding some of the images. For example, when one reviewer read aloud from the book to her second graders, they were quite interested in events described in the poems but needed support appreciating the subtle aspects of word-crafting. We also thought the book might appeal only to middle-grade children. However we found that it continued to strike a chord with older students, as eighth grader Nate attested: "These poems are brisk and colorful stories about little things that make up the special feelings that surround you."

10.3 Hopkins, Lee Bennett, editor (1996). **School Supplies: A Book of Poems.** Illustrated by Renee Flower. New York: Simon & Schuster. 36 pp. ISBN: 0-689-80497-0. Picture Book.

The best part about beginning a new school year is buying new school supplies! Start your school year with the perfect poetry book that describes those new pencils, erasers, crayons, and more in unique and appealing ways. Lee Bennett Hopkins selected sixteen lively poems that appeal to a wide range of ages, written by children's favorite well-known poets including J. Patrick Lewis, Jane Yolen, and Carl Sandburg. The bold watercolor and colored-pencil illustrations add a new dimension to the poems. A first grader commented on how the supplies "dance and fly through the pages." Another child noticed the personified pens and pencils with smiles on their "faces." Kimberleigh, a third grader, particularly enjoyed how one poet described a paper clip as a monster, and the lines on a notebook page as "telephone wires." "I'll never look at those things the same way again," she declared. Her friend Amanda liked the poem "Ballpoint Pen" because it was graceful, and "Lunch Bag" because of the surprising ending.

Before one reviewer read this book to her students, she filled a tote bag with all of the school supplies mentioned in the book. She asked a child to select a supply from the bag, then read the corresponding poem. The children had fun taking turns guessing which poem would be read next. Their favorite was "The Eraser Poem," by Louis Phillips. They enjoyed listening to their teacher trying to read aloud a poem that actually disappears off the page! A second reviewer did the same activity with her fifth graders with equally positive results.

10.4 Prelutsky, Jack (1996). **A Pizza the Size of the Sun.** Illustrated by James Stevenson. New York: Morrow. 160 pp. ISBN: 0-688-13236-7. Chapter Book.

Once again, Prelutsky unerringly shows he understands children's dreams, concerns, and interests. Poems about trying out new roller skates, contending with an overpopulation of gerbils, and concocting strange mixtures with a chemistry set speak to real children and their lives. Some of the poems play with words ("Mrs. Misinformation," "The Puppy Made Off with My Slippers"), and some play with form ("A Triangular Tale," about a pie, is written in the shape of a pie slice.) Some poems are delightfully gross. Children likely will find this collection on their own due to its topics, predictable rhyme and rhythm, and Prelutsky's reputation. However, it's also a great read-aloud text. One reviewer had her third graders read it on their own, then share requests. They particularly enjoyed those poems that were funny or had a surprise ending. Stephanie, a third grader, seemed to speak for them all when she said, "[This book] is good for kids of all ages because it has no violence in it . . . and it makes you laugh."

10.5 Ridlon, Marci (1996). **Sun through the Window: Poems for Children.** Honesdale, PA: Boyds Mills. 64 pp. ISBN: 1-56397-454-1. Chapter Book.

Selections from Ridlon's superb 1969 collection *That Was Summer* are integrated with new work. The poems focus on simple aspects of children's lives like snow, bad days, happy feelings, and puddle-jumping, making them readily accessible to a wide audience. Some poems—such as "Bad Day," "Angry," "My Brother Johnny," and "Melissa Melinda"—are reminiscent of A. A. Milne in topic and rhythm. Some make you giggle, while others remind you of smells and tastes. These poems speak directly to children, and many would work well for Reader's Theater or dramatic interpretation. All beg to be recited over and over. One reviewer's third graders particularly enjoyed "That Was Summer" and "Catching Quiet." Several wrote their own poems in response to "That Was Summer."

Brian's Spring Poem

Have you ever smelled spring?
Well, I have and
here are my memories.

Have you ever gone out after it rains?
Do you remember the smell of humidity?
That was spring.

Have you ever planted a garden?
Do you remember the smell of dirt?
That was spring.

Have you ever climbed up in a tree house?
Do you remember the smell of fresh wood?
That was spring.
So, do you remember spring now?

Brian Sherman

Summer's Here

One day as I was climbing my friend's tree,
I smelled the fresh air of summer.
I heard the car beeping.
I saw children playing.
I smelled the red roses.
I heard the birds singing.
I heard the bee buzzing, and
I smelled that summer was here.

Heather Smith

That Was Winter

Have you ever tasted winter?
Remember the hot chocolate burning,
Snow melting, icicles falling, and candy breaking?
That was winter.

Have you ever touched winter?
Remember the soft snow, fuzzy sweaters,
hard bark, cold frost, and furry mittens?
That was winter.

Have you ever seen winter?
Remember the snow falling,
Christmas trees growing, and snowplows plowing?
That was winter.

Have you ever heard winter?
Remember the sleds swooshing,
boots scrunching, icicles breaking, and children playing?
That was winter.

Have you ever smelled winter?
Remember the cookies baking,
candy canes crackling, and furnaces burning?
That was winter.

Scott Clouse

This is a collection that, with teacher support, will delight a wide audience of children.

> McGill, Marci (1961). **That Was Summer.** Illustrated by Mia Carpenter. Chicago: Follett. 80 pp. ISBN: 0-695-88510-3. Picture Book.

10.6 Schertle, Alice (1996). **Keepers.** Illustrated by Ted Rand. New York: Lothrop, Lee & Shepard. 32 pp. ISBN: 0-688-11634-5. Picture Book.

Alice Schertle is a crafter of words. Her poems, both humorous and poignant, are subtle, smooth-flowing, and written in a variety of forms and rhyme schemes. They added color and depth to various studies in one reviewer's class. "I really like 'The Better Beetle.' Read it again, please!" begged Bobby. "It's like a story poem," added Nicole, "and it rhymes." The beetle thinks he's better "because he's higher, but higher, the woodpecker can see you," explained Heather. The poem added an entertaining touch to an insect study, while warning against false pride. It was a favorite of the children, as was "Skeleton Key," a quizzical addition to the class' Halloween poetry collection. To begin a collection of dog poems and to introduce a book like *Along Came A Dog*, teachers can use "My Old Dog" who "doesn't move much anymore. / . . . Now he likes it best / to rest / here on the floor . . ." Complemented by Ted Rand's drawings, this book is a keeper!

> DeJong, Meindert (1958). **Along Came a Dog.** Illustrated by Maurice Sendak. New York: Harper. 192 pp. ISBN: 0-06-440114-6. Chapter Book.

10.7 Young, Ed (1997). **Voices of the Heart.** New York: Scholastic. Unpaged. ISBN: 0-590-50199-2. Picture Book. (See **11.40**)

10.8 Dakos, Kalli (1997). **Get out of the Alphabet, Number 2! Wacky Wednesday Puzzle Poems.** Illustrated by Jenny Graham. New York: Simon & Schuster. 32 pp. ISBN: 0-689-81118-7. Picture Book.

It's wacky Wednesday, and the students in this book are having a wild time with the ABCs! There are letters on the clock and the number 2 sneaks into the alphabet. The letter *I* wants a perm so it will look more like an *S*. The letter *Z* shoves in line ahead of *B*. The bright, childlike gouache paintings offer clues to the riddles. Celebrate wacky Wednesday in your own classroom. Your students will have fun finding all the crazy, mixed-up letters and numbers. What a wild, wacky way for young children to learn about the alphabet and numbers through poetry.

10.9 Dotlich, Rebecca Kai (1998). **Lemonade Sun and Other Summer Poems.** Honesdale, PA: Boyds Mills. 32 pp. ISBN: 1-56397-660-9. Picture Book.

From the taste of lemonade "splashing sunshine on frosty squares" to the feel of feet "touching the tickle of new grass," this collection celebrates the pleasures of summer. The images are fresh and original yet childlike, making the book appealing to many ages. We found it evoked much discussion and writing about children's favorite summer experiences. Fourth grader Abby particularly enjoyed "Jump Rope Rhyme" because of the catchy rhyme and rhythm, as well as how the names of various states are incorporated into the poem. She also liked "Sunflower" because of the description of these flowers as "garden kings with chocolate eyes."

10.10 Fletcher, Ralph (1997). **Ordinary Things: Poems from a Walk in Early Spring.** Illustrated by Walter Lyon Krudop. New York: Atheneum. 48 pp. ISBN: 0-689-81035-0. Chapter Book.

A quiet, solitary walk in spring takes the reader through the woods and home again, observing small, often unnoticed objects—some in nature, and some not. This small book with pencil-sketch artwork and thoughtful metaphorical poetry could be shared with students before taking a "poetry walk" and looking for images in their own neighborhoods and forests in spring . . . or summer, or fall, or winter.

10.11 Hopkins, Lee Bennett, editor (1997). **Song and Dance: Poems.** Illustrated by Cheryl Munro Taylor. New York: Simon & Schuster. 32 pp. ISBN: 0-689-80159-9. Picture Book.

Hopkins blends the music of contemporary poets with more traditional voices, creating a collection of poems full of joyful rhythms that make you want to dance and shout to the sky. Many of the images are very unusual and will expand children's thinking about what can be called music and dance. The handcut and colored papers used in the illustrations are positioned so as to convey movement, effectively complementing the rhythmic feel of the poems.

10.12 Katz, Bobbi (1997). **Truck Talk: Rhymes on Wheels.** New York: Scholastic. 32 pp. ISBN: 0590-69328-X. Picture Book.

Many poems for younger children are story rhymes. This book is written in the form of individual poems about different kinds of trucks, such as ambulances, moving trucks, delivery trucks, and cement mixers. Accompanying each poem are several photographs of the truck being described. Children love this book, and clamor for it to be read over and over. It is a good introduction to the poetic genre for young ones.

10.13 Liatsos, Sandra Olson (1997). **Bicycle Riding and Other Poems.** Illustrated by Karen Dugan. Honesdale, PA: Boyds Mills. 30 pp. ISBN: 1-56397235-2. Picture Book.

With poems rhymed and unrhymed, this book reminded children in one reviewer's class of events in their own lives, such as backyard camping, playing in autumn leaves, and climbing trees. They enjoyed clapping a jump-rope rhythm to "Pumpkin Picking," and singing "Sea Wave" to the tune of "Do Your Ears Hang Low?" They agreed that "Eating Blueberries" would make a nice introduction to *Blueberries for Sal.* Fourth graders also enjoyed this collection. Kelly liked "Bicycle Riding" because she thought "this poem expresses a child's feelings." Katie enjoyed "The Hero of Our Street" because "it leaves us in suspense." In addition to identifying with these lilting poems, the children also deepened their appreciation for poetry.

 McCloskey, Robert (1948). **Blueberries for Sal.** New York: Viking. Unpaged. ISBN: 0-670-17591-9. Picture Book.

10.14 Ryan, Pam Muñoz (1996). **The Flag We Love.** Illustrated by Ralph Masiello. Watertown, MA: Charlesbridge. 32 pp. ISBN: 0-88106-846-2. Picture Book.

This beautifully illustrated, patriotic poem presents the history and symbolism of our nation's flag. Pam Muñoz Ryan writes factual information at the bottom of each page to elaborate on the ideas presented in each poem. Find out who really sewed the first flag, who wrote the "Pledge of Allegiance," where the "Star-Spangled Banner" is displayed, and how many flags have been planted on the moon. Ralph Masiello's extraordinary oil paintings include Jesse Owens at the 1936 Olympics, the Abraham Lincoln funeral train, the Vietnam Veterans Memorial in Washington, D.C., and the bombing of Ft. McHenry during the War of 1812. This book belongs in classrooms all across America!

People: Past and Present

See also chapter 3, "Exploring Our Past."

Primary Reviews

10.15 Barnwell, Ysaye M. (1998). **No Mirrors in My Nana's House.** Illustrated by Synthia Saint James. San Diego: Harcourt Brace. 32 pp. ISBN: 0-15-201825-5. Picture Book.

This stunning picture book portrays what it is like to see beauty through the eyes of a loved one and to grow up only seeing the positive aspects of life. From one of the songs sung by the popular a cappella quintet Sweet Honey in the Rock, and written by one of the members of the group, this story explains how not having a mirror in the house changed the way one person thought of the environment around her. *No Mirrors in My Nana's House* is brought to life through the brightly colored paintings of Synthia Saint James. This book includes a compact disc of the song sung by Sweet Honey in the Rock, along with a reading of the book by the author.

10.16 Holbrook, Sara (1996). **Am I Naturally This Crazy?** Honesdale, PA: Boyds Mills. 48 pp. ISBN:1-56397-640-4. Chapter Book.

Sara Holbrook's poems are funny, feisty, and full of the frustrating problems and exhilarating joys of children's lives. This book focuses particularly on the roller coaster ride of emotions that kids experience growing up. Rejection, family squabbles, first love, making friends, and taking risks are all topics she addresses sensitively and with a strong dose of humor. Her work helps children define who they are, and provides some guidance as they navigate their way through the world. One reviewer has watched Holbrook, who is a gifted performer, share her poetry with students of all ages. They invariably respond with enthusiasm, clamoring for more. Teachers can use this collection along with *I Never Said I Wasn't Difficult* and *Walking on the Boundaries of Change* to stimulate discussion about feelings and issues in their students' lives.

> Holbrook, Sara (1996). **I Never Said I Wasn't Difficult: Poems.** Honesdale, PA: Boyds Mills. 48 pp. ISBN: 1-56397-390-2. Chapter Book.

> Holbrook, Sara (1998). **Walking on the Boundaries of Change: Poems of Transition.** Honesdale, PA: Boyds Mills. 64 pp. ISBN: 1-56397-737-0. Chapter Book.

10.17 Hopkins, Lee Bennett, editor (1996). **Opening Days: Sports Poems.** Illustrated by Scott Medlock. San Diego: Harcourt Brace. 35 pp. ISBN: 0-15-200270-7. Picture Book.

This collection features poems about kids playing various sports, from karate to ice-skating to tennis. There is a nice balance between poems about boys and girls as well as diverse styles from free verse to rhymed quatrains. One reviewer read this book aloud to her third graders. Jane Yolen's "The Karate Kid" was particularly intriguing to them. Tiffany found the last stanza with its series of single words ("Chop. / Kick. / Peace. / Power.") "awesome," and declared "she put in the perfect words to end it." When the reviewer asked if their favorites were the poems about their own preferred sports, the group responded with a resounding "no." John further commented, "I liked ones about my sport but I liked others too—like the 'Speed' one because it really captures your ears because of the words she picked." Adam liked the poem "Skiing" because of the line "I am the mountain and the mountain is me." "The poem just makes you want to go out and do it," he added. This would be a good book to read aloud and get children interested in poetry. The subject matter appeals to both genders, and the poetic styles are easily accessible to children. We found only a few poems—like "Boyhood Baseball" and "Tomorrow"—that were a bit nostalgic, and that might require some explanation before they could be appreciated by most children. The reviewer's students thought the book would be a good model for children to write their own poems about sports.

10.18 Mavor, Salley, editor (1997). **You and Me: Poems of Friendship.** New York: Orchard. 32 pp. ISBN: 0-531-33045-1. Picture Book.

Mavor has selected work from Jack Prelutsky, Judith Viorst, Langston Hughes, Lucille Clifton, and others to explore the joys of friendship—including shared lemonade stands, red tennis shoes, favorite secret places, and playing in the snow. The full-color reproductions of fabric sculptures provide wonderful texture, and add a note of whimsical realism to the poems. One reviewer found that students particularly enjoyed the poems "Since Hanna Moved Away" by Judith Viorst, and "My Natural Mama" by Lucille Clifton. Students also made spontaneous connections to the many other books and poems about friendship. This book would be a fine addition to any elementary classroom collection.

10.19 Myers, Walter Dean (1997). **Harlem.** Illustrated by Christopher Myers. New York: Scholastic. Unpaged. ISBN: 0-590-54340-7. Picture Book.

A journey into the very heart and soul of Harlem. Walter Dean Myers' poetic words and his son Christopher's bold, collage gouache-and-ink illustrations make this book jump off the page with life. Myers relates the journey to Harlem "that started on the banks of the Niger / And has not ended"—much like the journey of his foster parents (to whom the book is dedicated), whose journey began in West Virginia before they moved to Harlem with three-year-old Walter. With historical references to Langston Hughes, Joe Louis, Malcolm X, and other great African Americans, the community of Harlem unfolds as "a place where a man didn't have to know his place simply because he was Black." The music, art, sports, literature, and people of Harlem through the years come alive in this 1998 Coretta Scott King award winner. Older students will enjoy this poem not only as a biographical peek into the author's childhood, but also to experience the rhythm and art that comprise the heartbeat of Harlem.

10.20 Robb, Laura, editor (1997). **Music and Drum: Voices of War and Peace, Hope and Dreams.** Illustrated by Debra Lill. New York: Philomel. 32 pp. ISBN: 0-399-22024-0. Picture Book.

Fifth graders were unanimous in their expressions of identification with the emotion-packed words, images, and ideas evoked by the poems Robb chose to include in this anthology. They appreciated the various ages, backgrounds, and levels of experience with war represented by the poets whose works are included. Although the group of students concerned is almost too young to know about the last war in which the United States was involved, they were saddened by Matti Yosef's plaintive "I Don't Like Wars," and by the losses described in Amit Tal's "Father and Son." The unreal and numbing nature of distant wars described in "War Games" seemed like a "Calvin and Hobbes" comic strip to several of them. Robb provides relief by juxtaposing poems of hope and peace with those of sadness and loss. For example, "Birdsong," written by a child from the Terezin concentration camp, describes beauty in the world and says there is joy to be derived from knowing one is alive, while Mary O'Neill says "Hope is the light in the awful dark." Students both young and old will benefit from this unique look at the effects of war, and the uplifting words of hope expressed by this rich variety of poets.

10.21 Steptoe, Javaka (1997). **In Daddy's Arms I Am Tall.** New York: Lee & Low. Unpaged. ISBN: 1-880000-31-8. Picture Book. (See **4.26**)

10.22 Turner, Ann (1997). **Mississippi Mud: Three Prairie Journals.** Illustrated by Robert J. Blake. New York: HarperCollins. 44 pp. ISBN: 0-06-024432-1. Picture Book.

Amanda, Caleb, and Lonnie journey in a covered wagon with their mother and father across the breadth of America from Kentucky to the rich and promising land of western Oregon. Each describes his or her thoughts and observations in a series of free verse poems that create a multifaceted memoir in diary form. Amanda writes, we "sat in the back / looking out the puckered hole, / and I thought our wishes rose / to the sky like smoke." Through her eyes, we see disappointment and fear when the town they have all been waiting for is there and gone in a flash. "It's gone already, like a peppermint sliver / swallowed up whole." There are good times too—around the campfire after the day's journey is behind; when Columbia, their new sister, is born; and when a photographer takes a family portrait. There is fear when small sister Nell becomes ill, and sadness when Jake the dog "just wore out." Once they have arrived at their destination and settled in, Lonnie dreams of the time when the "forest will come down. / Soon we'll start the orchard." Third graders with whom we shared this book appreciated the variety of voices describing the trip, and the hopes and dreams wrapped within each poem. We think this is a book that, with teacher assistance, can be appreciated by many ages, particularly if used during a study of pioneers and westward expansion.

Secondary Reviews

10.23 Adoff, Arnold (1997). **Love Letters.** Illustrated by Lisa Desimini. New York: Scholastic. 32 pp. ISBN: 0-590-48478-8. Picture Book.

Love letters can be too sentimental for elementary age children, but we found that Adoff's *Love Letters* were just right for the young listener or reader. Written in his well-known free verse style, the letters are addressed to a variety of people including Gram, Playground Snow Girl, Ms. Back Row, Teacher, Mom, and Hard Working Dad. In a group of third graders, the writers among them quickly turned to composing letters after *Love Letters* was shared with them. The children's letter-poems were written most frequently to pets! Fifth graders also were intrigued by the idea of writing love letters to different kinds of people, and repeatedly asked to reread the book. Desimini's illustrations play well with Adoff's shape poems. Upon closer examination, the illustrations are a combination of unusual objects including yellow jackets, puzzle pieces, a Band-Aid, and pen springs. There is much to love in this book of poetry, and not only at Valentine's time.

10.24 Aylesworth, Jim (1996). **My Sister's Rusty Bike.** Illustrated by Richard Hull. New York: Atheneum. 32 pp. ISBN: 0-689-31798-0. Picture Book.

Imagine riding your sister's rusty bike all across the country, and the unusual people you might meet along the way. This book of rollicking verses was a favorite with one reviewer's class. "Oh, good, we love that book!" exclaimed Laura. "May we help you on the parts?" "I've read that book about one thousand times!" added Kailey. The children noticed the boy-girl sequential pattern, the narrator hidden in each picture, and the book's geographical implications. They loved joining in on the rhyming refrain. With infectious rhythm and fun, this book draws children to poetry.

10.25 Belafonte, Harry, and Lord Burgess (1999). **Island in the Sun.** Illustrated by Alex Ayliffe. New York: Dial Books for Young Readers. ISBN: 0-8037-2387-3. Picture Book.

The 1950s song by Harry Belafonte has been transformed into a colorful children's picture book celebrating the memory of Belafonte's love for Jamaica. The bright, colorful island illustrations that display both work and recreation on the island of the sun bring to life the imagery that is portrayed in the text. The illustrations and text counter many of the stereotypical images of Caribbean life.

Oh, island in the sun,
Willed to me by my father's hand,
All my days I will sing in praise
Of your forests, waters, your shining sand.

10.26 Gerber, Carole (1997). **Hush! A Gaelic Lullaby.** Illustrated by Marty Husted. Danvers, MA: Whispering Coyote. 32 pp. ISBN: 1-879085-57-7. Picture Book.

Flowing words and luminous seascapes brought immediate response from one reviewer's class as they followed the patterns and repeated refrains in *Hush!* Bobby commented on the cold feeling evoked by the words as the family prepared for a storm. All felt warmed by the final scene: family gathered by the firelight, and baby finally sleeping. Interesting to compare with Minfong Ho's *Hush! A Thai Lullaby* (see **4.112**), this Irish lullaby is a beautiful marriage of artwork and poetry.

10.27 Glenn, Mel (1996). **Who Killed Mr. Chippendale? A Mystery in Poems.** New York: Dutton. 100 pp. ISBN: 0-525-67530-2. Sophisticated Chapter Book.

A startling book of poetry from acclaimed poet Mel Glenn that presents not only an accurate look at high school life told through free-form poetry vignettes, but also weaves a murder mystery into the voices behind each poem. The reader gets a glimpse of the innermost thoughts and feelings of students, teachers, counselors, the police, and even the murderer as they deal with the crime. This book already has become a favorite with young adolescents. As eighth grader Vicki commented, "I think it was well written. It was real easy to read . . . and I like how the end of each poem leaves me hanging."

10.28 Janeczko, Paul B., editor (1997). **Home on the Range: Cowboy Poetry.** Illustrated by Bernie Fuchs. New York: Clarion. 40 pp. ISBN: 0-8037-1910-8. Sophisticated Picture Book.

This collection is a new kind of book for the children's poetry market. Janeczko has selected nineteen poems that celebrate cowboy poets and their lifestyles. Pencil-and-oil illustrations on colored paper enhance the mood of the poems, often portraying the solitary life of cowboys. This book is most appealing to middle-school and upper-elementary students.

10.29 Medearis, Angela Shelf (1997). **Rum-A-Tum-Tum.** Illustrated by James E. Ransome. New York: Holiday House. 32 pp. ISBN: 0-8234-1123-5. Picture Book.

This entertaining book depicts the daily activities of the French market in New Orleans. We hear the chants of the street vendors as they peddle their fruits, vegetables, and other wares. Market-goers listen to the rhymes of Creole women in red bandannas selling baskets of pears and yellow bananas. The book is written from the perspective of one little girl as she listens to the vibrant beating of the drum and the playing of the horns as a band marches past. She is encouraged to join in the fun, and the excitement continues as everyone claps their hands, stomps their feet, and snaps their fingers to the beat.

10.30 Omerod, Jan (1996). **Ms. McDonald Has a Class.** New York: Clarion. Unpaged. ISBN: 0-395-77611-2. Picture Book.

A primary class trip to the farm, using the well-known song's pattern and tune, allows Jan Ormerod to showcase her humor, artistic skill, and knowledge of children. Twenty-four children are pictured at the farm and in the classroom, and the illustrations tell as much of the story as the words. We found ourselves giggling at the students' ever-so-typical antics, and the teacher is right in the middle of all of the fun. This is a wonderful book to help kids recall their own class trips, and to introduce lyric writing for well-known tunes. We used this successfully with first through third graders.

The Animal World

See also chapter 1, "Stories of the Universe"; and chapter 2, "Our Changing World."

Primary Reviews

10.31 Dotlich, Rebecca Kai (1996). **Sweet Dreams of the Wild: Poems for Bedtime.** Illustrated by Katharine Dodge. Honesdale, PA: Boyds Mills. 32 pp. ISBN: 1-36397-180-1. Picture Book.

Bedtime, with all its accompanying rituals, is a special time of day. This book is in the form of imagined conversations between a sleepy child and a series of gentle creatures, in which the child asks each animal where it sleeps. Nuggets of factual information about each animal are tucked into the poems. The soft pastel-pencil illustrations help extend the cozy feel of the poetry. One reviewer used this book with a group of kindergarten and first-grade students, and found that they particularly enjoyed the rhymed, repetitive text and often joined in on the refrain, "I cuddle up tight / with sweet dreams of the wild, / and THAT'S where I sleep, / sleepy child." Haileigh commented that she liked the book because "it makes you feel warm and cuddly." She also enjoyed the interesting phrases, such as a cat "curled half-moon" and a mountain goat "wrapped in a shawl / of warm, wooly hair." This would be an excellent book to read with other collections of nighttime poetry, such as *When the Dark Comes Dancing*.

> Larrick, Nancy (1983). **When the Dark Comes Dancing: A Bedtime Poetry Book.** Illustrated by John Wallner. New York: Putnam. 79 pp. ISBN: 0-399-20807-0. Chapter Book.

10.32 Florian, Douglas (1998). **Insectlopedia: Poems and Paintings.** San Diego: Harcourt Brace. 47 pp. ISBN: 0-15-201306-7. Picture Book.

We think this is the best of Florian's animal poetry collections. Students in many classrooms delighted in the humorous verses, which combine playful humor and rhyme with subtle word play as they describe a range of creatures that creep, swoop, sting, and fly. Fourth grader Marc, for example, commented on how the words in "The Dragonfly" "give action so you can see in your mind what the dragonfly is doing." His classmates Kim and Megan particularly liked the way the words rhymed in several places, and how Florian portrayed the insects so it "sounded like the truth." Florian's watercolor illustrations, done on brown paper bags, provide a fitting accompaniment to the lighthearted tone of the poems. Children can use Florian's descriptions to write their own bug poems. Teachers can help them appreciate his playful use of form in "The Inchworm," as well as how he plays with the sounds of words in many of the other poems. This is an excellent complement to other insect poetry collections such as Fleischman's *Joyful Noise* and Hoberman's *Bugs*.

Fleischman, Paul (1988). **Joyful Noise: Poems for Two Voices.** Illustrated by Eric Beddows. New York: Harper & Row. 44 pp. ISBN: 0-06-021852-5. Picture Book.

Hoberman, Mary Ann (1976). **Bugs: Poems.** Illustrated by Victoria Chess. New York: Viking. Unpaged. ISBN: 0-670-19454-9. Picture Book.

10.33 Rylant, Cynthia (1996). **The Whales.** New York: Scholastic. 36 pp. ISBN: 0-590-58285-2. Picture Books.

The most popular poetry book in one reviewer's first-grade classroom was *The Whales.* When the reviewer first read this book aloud to the class, they had just begun researching whales. The children marveled at the vibrant acrylic illustrations, and enjoyed the sophisticated yet simple verse, which presents information from an aesthetic perspective. They reacted to this book with as much enthusiasm as if they were on a real whale watch! Rylant wonders what the whales may be thinking or dreaming, and what their personalities are like. From the large fluke (tail) on the cover to the spattered whale silhouettes on the end pages, the whimsical artwork throughout the book is appealing to children and extends the contemplative mood of the poetry. Rylant's awesome tribute to these gentle giants of the sea will complement any classroom study of whales.

10.34 Sierra, Judy (1998). **Antarctic Antics: A Book of Penguin Poems.** Illustrated by Jose Aruego and Ariane Dewey. San Diego: Harcourt Brace. Unpaged. ISBN: 0-15-201006-8. Picture Book.

Squeals of delight erupted when one reviewer introduced *Antarctic Antics: A Book of Penguin Poems* to a group of third and fourth graders. They were fascinated by penguins, and this book drew them in with its bright, colorful pictures by Jose Aruego and Arianne Dewey and its lively poetry. The children particularly enjoyed the visual and aural images of little penguins leaping into icy water for their first swim, belly-sliding on glaciers, and waiting patiently to be fed by Dad with regurgitated food. Fourth grader Katie, author of an in-depth penguin report, was particularly interested in this book, and enjoyed reading some of the penguin predator poems to her classmates and making them guess the animal. Her favorite poem was "Antarctic Anthem" because "[It] was beautiful . . . and ended the book good." This is an excellent book to provide a more aesthetic perspective on the study of the Antarctic region.

10.35 Florian, Douglas (1997). **In the Swim: Poems and Paintings.** San Diego: Harcourt Brace. 47 pp. ISBN: 0-15-201307-5. Picture Book.

This humorous collection features twenty-one poems about various sea creatures. Some of the animals are shown realistically, while others are depicted whimsically or, in some cases, absurdly. For example, a hummingbird is compared to a helicopter that hovers and hums. The picture that accompanies this poem portrays the bird with blades for feet and helicopter wings. Children will enjoy the humorous descriptions, and can use them as a basis for creating their own whimsical animal poems and pictures.

10.36 Hoopes, Lyn (1997). **Condor Magic.** Illustrated by Peter C. Stone. Fairfield, CT: Benefactory. Unpaged. ISBN: 1-882728-95-5. Picture Book.

This beautiful book celebrates the ten-year project to increase the population of the endangered California Condor. Lyn Littlefield Hoopes' dynamic poem is factual, rhythmic, and filled with fascinating language. First-grade students enjoyed listening to her descriptions of the condor: "You eat sticky innards, and gutsy mush. / Your neck feathers bristle like a toilet brush." Hoopes chooses descriptive words and phrases a child can relate to: "Your wings open wide as a soccer goal." Stone's earthy illustrations have a textured quality to emphasize the California and Arizona canyon habitats of the condor. He also incorporates subtle Native American symbols into his paintings. The end of the story leaves one feeling hopeful about this endangered species.

10.37 Levy, Constance (1996). **When Whales Exhale and Other Poems.** Illustrated by Judy La Braca. New York: Simon & Schuster. 42 pp. ISBN: 0-689-80946-8. Chapter Book.

Using patterned, occasional, and irregular rhyme schemes, Levy examines interesting events in these appealing poems. "Suppose / you're in a forest place / . . . and find that you / are face to face / with two fresh / bear prints . . ." To one reviewer's class, this was a reminder of Teddy Bear Day. "Worm Out" reminded Angela that when you save worms, "You're also saving the earth." Nicole noticed that the words ending each verse of "Wild Blueberries" "all rhyme and they're all the ends of the lines." Cassandra compared the line, "the spinning mix that tricks the eye" in "On Rolling

Down Grassy Hills" with opening your eyes while underwater, saying, "it's all blurry!" With assonance, metaphor, and lovely language, Levy captures the imaginations of all who share these fresh new poems.

10.38 Livingston, Myra Cohn (1997). **Cricket Never Does: A Collection of Haiku and Tanka.** Illustrated by Kees de Kiefte. New York: Simon & Schuster. 42 pp. ISBN: 0-689-81123-3. Chapter Book.

Not wishing to stop
his chirping the whole night long
Cricket never does

More than fifty original haiku and tanka selections grace this little book. The undersized book lends itself well to the short verses within its pages. One pen-and-ink illustration begins each chapter. The poetry selections are divided into four sections by the seasons of the year, providing a thoughtful glimpse of a year in verse. These tiny verses are engaging to older students, and offer a subtle invitation to try writing some of their own poetry using these forms.

10.39 Prelutsky, Jack, editor (1997). **The Beauty of the Beast: Poems from the Animal Kingdom.** Illustrated by Meilo So. New York: Knopf. 101 pp. ISBN: 0-679-87058-X. Chapter Book.

Over two hundred poems arranged by zoological category celebrate the animal kingdom. Although some are humorous, many are serious and complex and provide a more introspective look at this topic. The images often are lush and vivid. Captured fireflies are described as "imprisoned fire," whales are said to have "hot, wild, white breath," and giraffes are "built silent and high; / ornaments against the sky." Meilo So's soft, double-page watercolor illustrations teem with life. This is a book teachers can dip into for poems on a particular animal, pairing them with poems about the same animal from other collections.

The Natural World

See also chapter 1, "Stories of the Universe"; and chapter 2, "Our Changing World."

Primary Reviews

10.40 Baylor, Byrd (1997). **The Way to Make Perfect Mountains: Native American Legends of Sacred Mountains.** Illustrated by Leonard

Chana. El Paso, TX: Cinco Puntos. 62 pp. ISBN: 0-938317-26-1. Chapter Book.

This collection of poems includes creation stories gathered from various southwestern Native American groups. The author's vivid descriptions transport the reader to the mysterious mountains of the Southwest. They tell of the importance the mountains have, and the role they continue to play in the cultural traditions of the Apache, Yaqui, Tohono O'odam, Navajo, Hopi, Jicarella Apache, and Pima in Arizona; the Mohave in California; and the Zuni and other Pueblo groups in New Mexico. The black-and-white illustrations by Leonard F. Chana, a Tohono O'odam artist, complement the magic of Baylor's words. The author's note is followed by an excellent list of references. This is a book for people of all ages.

10.41 Esbensen, Barbara Juster (1996). **Echoes for the Eye: Poems to Celebrate Patterns in Nature.** Illustrated by Helen K. Davie. New York: HarperCollins. 32 pp. ISBN: 0-06-024398-8. Picture Book.

The author and illustrator combined their love of nature's repeating patterns to create this book, which is a visual and auditory delight to the senses. Free verse, simile, assonance, and exquisite language are used to describe spirals, branches, polygons, meanders, and circles. For example, hurricanes "spin their terrible winds," a glacier is "a heavy unfolding / ribbon of snow and ice," and "musk oxen . . . spokes of a dark muscular / wheel . . . a watchful compass rose." In one reviewer's class, Laura pointed out the images on facing pages: branches in trees and branches in the leaves, veins in hands and veins in lightning, etc. Many of her classmates made connections to patterns they'd noticed in nature and those they'd studied in a unit on sound and the ear. Inspired by "Circles"—in which the author writes of ripples of water, "wider and wider they grow / out and out and out / from the quick splash to the shore"—Katie wrote the following poem:

Song of the Water

The Song of water is very swift.
The song of water is a gift.
When it's sprayed up, it does a brilliant dance.
When the waves rise up, it speaks of a war.
But then the water all washes up on shore.

Katie Lambrecht

We think children will need some introduction to appreciate the subtle message of this book. But with teacher support, it can generate rich discussion and delight with the many "echoes for the eye" that surround us.

10.42 Lesser, Carolyn (1997). **Storm on the Desert.** Illustrated by Ted Rand. San Diego: Harcourt Brace. Unpaged. ISBN: 0-15-272198-3. Picture Book.

This book provides a poetic picture of how desert plants and animals respond to a rainstorm. It opens with a vivid description of a typical Sonoran desert landscape: a coyote "stretches and howls / to the wisp of a moon / . . . Startled bats swoosh into caves. / Scorpions scuttle under sticks." A storm is brewing, however, and using realistic imagery, Lesser describes how it erupts with cracking thunder and "pelting, piercing / slashing screaming / streaming / rain." Then just as quickly as it began, the storm subsides and lightning becomes "an elusive flicker, / Thunder a murmur." The animals return to drink from newly formed pools, and to feast on the fresh flowers and leaves that emerge. Ted Rand uses bright pastels, chalks, and watercolors to show the changing desert landscape. Double-page spreads and strong lines that slash across the pages give a feeling of the enormous power of the storm and the vastness of the landscape. Some of the pages have no words, allowing the beauty of nature to speak for itself. Tucson-area readers took issue, however, with a couple of the illustrations that depicted landscapes much more like the Painted Desert regions of northern Arizona or the Red Rock country near Sedona, regions that differ vastly from the Sonoran Desert. This is an excellent book to use in a desert unit to provide a more aesthetic perspective. Teachers can discuss how Lesser uses the rhythm of language to show the phases of the storm. Third grader Amanda wrote, "I liked this book because it had good pictures and it was realistic. . . . The words are tense when it gets to the storm part. The words in the beginning and end are soothing."

10.43 Locker, Thomas (1997). **Water Dance.** San Diego: Harcourt Brace. 32 pp. ISBN: 0-15-201284-2. Picture Book.

Thomas Locker once again brings his talent as an oil painter to the picture-book format in *Water Dance.* The spare poetry describes various aspects of the water cycle, providing descriptions that culminate in a natural guessing game. After reading each page, the reader can guess which form of water has been described: stream, waterfall, river, sea, mist, storm front, and so on. The closing pages of the book show each illustration in miniature, with scientific descriptions identifying the different aspects of the water cycle. This book fills several needs in a classroom by combining the literary and scientific genres quite beautifully. We found that teachers are drawn to this book. We also were pleasantly surprised that students could barely conceal their delight with the beautiful illustrations, although they may need help appreciating the poetic imagery. Several reviewers helped their children create a beautiful choral reading of the poem, complete with sound effects and costumes.

10.44 Mora, Pat (1998). **This Big Sky.** Illustrated by Steve Jenkins. New York: Scholastic. Unpaged. ISBN: 0-590-37120-7. Picture Book.

Well-known Latina poet Pat Mora brings readers fourteen spare but lyrical poems about the desert Southwest. The combination of Mora's poems and Steve Jenkins's boldly colored, richly textured, cut-paper collages bring to life the landscapes, animals, and people of the desert. A sense of the desert's heat, vastness, and delicate balance of life inhabits the pages, conveyed by both the poetry and the illustrations, which bleed off the edges of the pages. A group of first and second graders chose "Suspense" as their favorite poem in the book. "That's just what it's like when it rains here in the summer," remarked Ricardo in response to both the text and the illustration. Because this class had been involved in nature sketching at the time, they were particularly appreciative of the amount of detail Jenkins was able to capture with his collage techniques. In some of the poems, Mora includes Spanish words that drop into the poetry quite naturally. Although it's not difficult to gather a sense of the meaning of these words within the context of the poems, a brief glossary of the Spanish words is included at the end of the book.

10.45 Rylant, Cynthia (1998). **Bless Us All: A Child's Yearbook of Blessings.** New York: Simon & Schuster. Unpaged. ISBN: 0-689-82370-3. Picture Book. (See **13.8**)

10.46 Yolen, Jane, editor (1997). **Once upon Ice, and Other Frozen Poems.** Photographs by Jason Stemple. Honesdale, PA: Boyds Mills. 40 pp. ISBN: 1-56397-408-8. Picture Book.

Jane Yolen and sixteen other poets respond in verse to the frozen photographs taken by Jane Yolen's son, Jason Stemple. The sounds, feel, strange roughness, and "smooooth" of ice are but a few of the images captured by writers such as J. Patrick Lewis, Mary Ann Hoberman, X. J. Kennedy, Lee Bennett Hopkins, and Nancy Willard. These poets were prompted to describe ice in its natural forms along rivers, in ice pyramids, or melting during the change of seasons. Artistically designed, this book joins Yolen's *Water Music* as a companion volume to be used alone in its own poetic spotlight, or as a complement to any science unit on water or changing seasons. One middle-school student included one of the poems in her science fair project, adding an aesthetic touch to the scientific investigation. The beauty of ice brought out in the photographs provides tempting lead-ins for student poetry writing.

> Yolen, Jane (1995). **Water Music.** Photographs by Jason Stemple. Hornesdale, PA: Boyds Mills Press. 40 pp. ISBN: 1-56397-336-7. Picture Book.

Secondary Reviews

10.47 Asch, Frank (1998). **Cactus Poems.** Illustrated by Ted Levin. San Diego: Harcourt Brace. Unpaged. ISBN: 0-15-200676-1. Picture Book.

Ted Levin's marvelous full-color photos celebrate the beauty and life forms of four North American deserts, while Frank Asch's poetry gives each image soul. Together they "break down the walls we've placed between ourselves and nature" to bring facts and feelings together. Scientific information on the featured plants and animals is included in an appendix. We found this book appealed to our older elementary students. Fourth graders Marc and K. C. particularly liked how Asch used slow, languid phrasing in "Slow and Steady," while their classmate Brad strongly identified with the wolf in "Howl." A student of one reviewer wrote the following poem in response to the book:

Desert Rain

The land is dry
washed up, lifeless
and deserted.

Then rain pours down
The dryness is gone so fast
Beautiful flowers
And animals come out

The desert is full of life
It looks like a prairie.

by Jordan Norris

10.48 Johnston, Tony (1996). **Once in the Country: Poems of the Farm.** Illustrated by Thomas B. Allen. New York: Putnam. 32 pp. ISBN: 0-399-22644-3. Picture Book.

Each poem in this book is a quiet celebration of the beauty and uniqueness of individual moments experienced on a family farm. Johnston mines each memory to reach its essence, which she communicates using a pleasant variety of poetic forms. The reader need not be a resident of a farming community to appreciate the simple pleasures revealed in *Once in the Country.* Even inner-city children will relate easily to "My Overalls," with its catalogue of positive attributes found in a well-worn pair of overalls. The poems call out to be read and reread silently and aloud, as the beauty of their figurative language is revealed in peaceful contemplation.

10.49 Moore, Lilian (1997). **Poems Have Roots.** Illustrated by Tad Hills. New York: Atheneum. 48 pp. ISBN: 0-689-80029-0. Chapter Book.

In carefully selected words, Moore describes nature as viewed from both east-coast and west-coast sites. Using both rhyme and free verse, she focuses on scenes explained in notes at the back of the book. One reviewer's class chose "Pilgrim Flower" and "Waterfall" as favorite poems that were connected to class studies. Best of all, they liked "The Automated Bird Watcher," which they read in choral fashion, in parts. Rooted in beauty, this book will feed children's love of poetry.

10.50 Yolen, Jane (1996). **Sea Watch: A Book of Poetry.** Illustrated by Ted Lewin. New York: Philomel. 32 pp. ISBN: 0-399-22734-2. Picture Book.

Both benign and malevolent creatures of the sea appear here in cameo roles. Each creature has a moment in the limelight as Yolen and Lewin expose its most basic qualities through razor-sharp figurative language and lively watercolor illustrations. The poetry informs as well as entertains. Readers will laugh at the incongruity of papa seahorse incubating his young, and draw their collective breaths at the menacing behavior of the orca. Children and teachers will return again and again to this collection for enjoyment and enlightenment.

10.51 Yolen, Jane (1998). **Snow, Snow: Winter Poems for Children.** Illustrated by Jason Stemple. Honesdale, PA: Boyds Mills. 32 pp. ISBN: 1-56397-721-4. Picture Book.

Who hasn't grumbled about the inconveniences caused by wet, icy, cold snow? In this book, Yolen incorporates stunning photographs by her son Jason Stemple with both free verse and rhymed poetry to present diverse images of this natural occurrence. From fall leaves covered with icy crystals described as "crisp leaf litter / under snowy glitter" to a tree branch pointing the way to spring with a "mittenless . . . long finger," there is much to think about in this collection.

Transcending Cultural Boundaries

See also the section entitled Cultural Practices and Celebrations in chapter 3, "Exploring Our Past," and the chapters in this volume devoted to the literature of specific cultural groups.

Primary Reviews

10.52 Carlson, Lori Marie (1998). **Sol a sol: Bilingual Poems.** Illustrated by Emily Lisker. Translated by Lyda Aponte de Zacklin. New York: Henry Holt. Unpaged. ISBN: 0-8050-4373-X. Picture Book.

Sol a sol contains fifteen fun and nostalgic poems in English and Spanish about family members, foods, cultural activities, and play. Although each poem selected or written by Lori Marie Carlson is a separate entity, together they tell the story of family life from sunup to sundown. Ivan (age seven) noticed how the structure of the book contributed to its effect: "Es de *Sol a sol* porque va de la mañana a la noche. Pero debe ir a la mañana otra vez porque se va a ver el sol otra vez por la mañana." ("It's *Sol a sol* because it goes from the morning to the night. But it should go to the morning again because you see the sun again on the next morning.") Although the focus is on Hispanic/Latino families, all children will find some personal connection—if not to the mother who smells like "the freshness of the morning," then with the tribute to chocolate or the "leaves that blur into green air" as the bicyclist coasts by. Most pages privilege English in the positioning of text. However, both English and Spanish versions contain rich, lyrical language that maintains the music of the poetry so well that it's difficult to tell which version is the original without reading the notes about translations. The English-to-Spanish translations are beautifully crafted by Lyda Aponte de Zacklin, while Lori Carlson has provided her typically excellent Spanish-to-English translations. Emily Lisker's vibrant acrylic-on-canvas illustrations bring each page to life, with extensive use of contrasting colors bleeding off the edges of many double-page spreads. The visibility of the canvas texture through the paint further contributes to the familiar, touchable quality of this book.

10.53 Mora, Pat, editor (1996). **Confetti: Poems for Children.** Illustrated by Enrique Sanchez. New York: Lee & Low. 32 pp. ISBN: 1-880000-25-3. Picture Book.

This lively anthology celebrates the experiences of daily life within a Mexican American context. Although the poems evoke a strong sense of this unique culture with references to fiestas, clicking castanets, and woodcutters, they also touch on things all children can relate to: trying to catch the wind, sitting on Grandma's lap to talk, and finding dragons in the clouds. Bold, colorful paintings with scatterings of confetti complement the text. Spanish words interspersed throughout the text generally can be understood through context or illustration. If not, a glossary is provided in the back. This collection honors all children who wish to be "free as confetti." We found our children needed teacher support to appreciate these poems. Starting with those that are universal in theme, teachers can contrast the poems in this collection with poems on the same topic from other cultures. For example, Mora's "Leaf Soup" can be compared to Eve Merriam's "Fall Leaves." Then teachers can read and discuss the poems that capture the special aspects of Mexican American life. Teachers also can share other poetry collections from this culture, such as Gary Soto's *Canto familiar* or Tony Johnston's *My Mexico/México mío.*

> Johnston, Tony (1996). **My Mexico/México mío.** Illustrated by F. John Sierra. New York: Putnam. 36 pp. ISBN: 0-399-22275-8. Picture Book.

> Soto, Gary (1997). **Canto familiar.** Illustrated by Annika Nelson. San Diego: Harcourt Brace. 79 pp. ISBN: 0-15-200067-4. Picture Book.

10.54 Nye, Naomi Shihab, editor (1998). **The Space between Our Footsteps: Poems and Paintings from the Middle East.** New York: Simon & Schuster. 143 pp. ISBN: 0-689-81233-7. Chapter Book.

Few children's books have the Middle East as their setting. Even less poetry about this region is available. Naomi Nye's anthology *The Space between Our Footsteps* helps to fill this void by featuring over one hundred poems by poets from nineteen Middle Eastern countries, resulting in an interesting medley of "voices and visions." Nye invites her readers to move beyond the stereotypes they may have about this region and discover universal human connections that transcend a particular culture, such as family love, passion for one's homeland, dreams of peace, and hopes for the future. As she states in the introduction, "I can't stop believing human beings everywhere hunger for deeper-than-headline news about one another. Poetry and art are some of the best ways this heartfelt 'news' may be exchanged." Since the poems are rather sophisticated, we think teachers would find it most useful to select a few to read aloud to fit a theme study or evoke thinking about an issue. Discussing some of the imagery and showing children how the poets are expressing feelings similar to their own will help deepen their appreciation. There is much that will shake complacency and alter thinking in this collection.

10.55 Orozco, José-Luis, editor (1997). **Diez deditos/Ten Little Fingers and Other Play Rhymes and Action Songs from Latin America.** Illustrated by Elisa Kleven. New York: Dutton Children's Books. 56 pp. ISBN: 0-525-45736-4. Picture Book.

José-Luis Orozco, a popular performer and songwriter, has assembled a collection of his own original songs, Spanish adaptations of popular English songs, and traditional action songs and finger rhymes from Spanish-speaking countries. Each song or rhyme is accompanied by an English translation, and preceded by information about its origin and directions for the accompanying hand movements or dance. Orozco also includes musical notation and chords for the guitar and piano for all of the songs. Elisa Kleven's illustrations and borders use combined painting and collage techniques to bring each song and rhyme to life. Teachers will turn to this book frequently as a resource, and children will pore over the illustrations time and time again, singing their way from front cover to back cover. This book makes a fine addition to Orozco's previous collection of songs, *De Colores and Other Latin-American Folk Songs for Children.*

Orozco, José-Luis, editor. (1994). **De colores and Other Latin-American Folk Songs for Children.** Illustrated by

Elisa Kleven. New York: Dutton Children's Books. 56 pp. ISBN: 0-525-45260-5.

10.56 Philip, Neil, editor (1996). **Earth Always Endures: Native American Poems.** Illustrated by Edward S. Curtis. New York: Viking. Unpaged. ISBN: 0-670-86873-6. Chapter Book.

An anthology of selected Native American songs, chants, prayers, and lullabies translated to let readers gain an understanding of Native American cultures and worldviews. The reader also comes to understand the Native American belief that words hold the power to bring about changes in the world, and more specifically that the use of particular combinations of words can bring about desired changes for the benefit of all. Therefore there is purpose to the repetition and limited number of words within the Native American songs, chants, and prayers represented here. These translations illustrate that the language of songs, prayers, and chants is distinguishable from the language of poetry. The former are not purely forms of entertainment, but rather celebrations of and appeals for a good life. These words of power are set against poetic images created by the photographs of Edward S. Curtis.

10.57 Reiser, Lynn W. (1998). **Tortillas and Lullabies/Tortillas y cancioncitas.** Illustrated by Corazones Valientes. Translated by Rebecca Hart. New York: Greenwillow. 40 pp. ISBN: 0-688-14628-7. Picture Book. (See **13.39**)

10.58 Swann, Brian (1998). **Touching the Distance: Native American Riddle-Poems.** Illustrated by Maria Rendon. San Diego: Browndeer. 32 pp. ISBN: 0-15-200804-7. Picture Book.

Puzzle and riddle poems are particularly effective in helping children see how poets use words to describe things in unusual ways. We've found that discussions about imagery and word-crafting emerge as children try to puzzle out the meaning of a riddle. This book can be a wonderful catalyst for this sort of response. The fifteen riddle poems, drawn from Native American sources, are graceful and subtle, and challenge middle-grade children to think divergently. Even we found solving the riddles no easy task. For example, try this one: "There is a place / I know and love well. / It is cut into gullies / where much water fell." (Answer: Grandmother's face.) Or "I can touch something / far off / in the distance." (Answer: eyesight.) Rendon's striking mixed-media illustrations employ wood carvings, stone, fabric, metal, eggshells, paint, and other unusual materials to create an almost three-dimensional effect. They simultaneously depict the riddle while providing hints to the answer. We found it most effective to first read the poem without showing the picture, then let children speculate about the answer, and finally show the picture and discuss the art.

Secondary Reviews

10.59 Ada, Alma Flor (1997). **Gathering the Sun: An Alphabet in Spanish and English.** Illustrated by Simón Silva. Translated by Rosa Zubizaretta. New York: Lothrop, Lee & Shepard. Unpaged. ISBN: 0-688-13903-5. Picture Book. (See **7.23**)

10.60 Alarcón, Francisco X. (1997). **Laughing Tomatoes and Other Spring Poems/Jitomates risueños y otros poemas de primavera.** Illustrated by Maya Christina González. San Francisco: Children's Book. 32 pp. ISBN: 0-89239-139-1. Picture Book.

In this dual-language book, Alarcón, the award-winning Chicano author of seven books of poetry, alternates humorous and serious poems about Mexican culture, family, nature, food, life, and traditional celebrations. In an afterword, the poet explains that some poems were written first in Spanish, others in English, and some simultaneously. Therefore Spanish and English text alternate positions on the pages, equally highlighting both languages. Both language versions rhythmically convey the lyrical imagery, making it impossible to identify which language is the translation. Maya Christina Gonzalez's vivid gouache illustrations and hand-lettered titles support the joy for living and belonging that the poems communicate, as well as the magic of poetry and the playfulness of the words.

10.61 Ho, Minfong, editor (1996). **Maples in the Mist: Children's Poems from the Tang Dynasty.** Illustrated by Jean Tseng and Mou-sien Tseng. New York: Lothrop, Lee & Shepard Books. Unpaged. ISBN: 0-688-12044-X. Picture Book.

A collection of sixteen poems from various Chinese poets. The subject matter of the poems ranges from nature appreciation to special people. Although each poem is translated into English, the original poem written in Chinese is printed along the margins of each page. The poet's red-stamped signature appears on each page, bringing authenticity and authorship to each poem. The watercolor designs lend a softness to the illustrations, and capture the beauty of nature and the details of human expression. Because poetry is an integral part of Chinese culture, the poems in this book often are memorized by Chinese children at a very young age. A biography of each poet at the end of the book provides for the older reader additional information about the poets during the Tang Dynasty, from whence these poems originated.

10.62 Hucko, Bruce (1996). **A Rainbow at Night: The World in Words and Pictures by Navajo Children.** San Francisco: Chronicle. Unpaged. ISBN: 0-8118-1294-4. Picture Book. (See **11.41**)

10.63 Spivak, Dawnine (1997). **Grass Sandals: The Travels of Basho.** Illustrated by Demi. New York: Atheneum. Unpaged. ISBN: 0-689-80776-7. Picture Book.

The journeys across Japan of seventeenth-century haiku poet Basho are outlined in this unique biographical picture book. The text describes his travels—what he did, what he saw, friends he made along the way. Double-page spreads feature Demi's characteristic delicate illustrations of colored inks applied with brushes on textured paper. A haiku by Basho (and one by Issa) appropriate to an event in his travels also appears in each spread, along with a Japanese character, its transliteration, and the word in English. The spacious layout of words and illustrations contributes to the gentle reverence created by Basho's haiku. This lovely and thoughtful work will help students understand the significance of haiku rather than merely copy its structure.

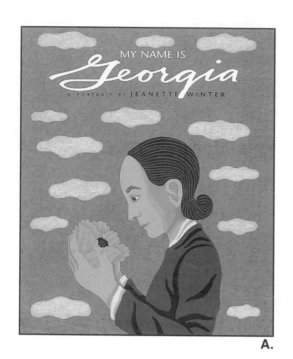

A.

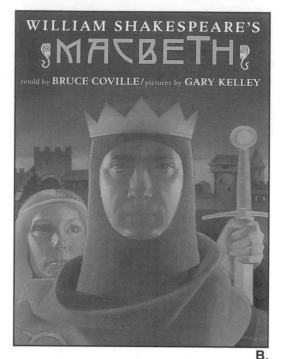

B.

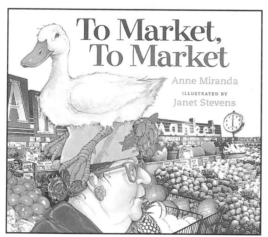

C.

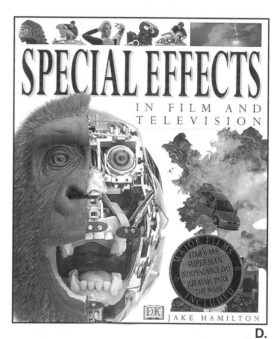

D.

A. *My Name Is Georgia: A Portrait,* Jeanette Winter (**11.50**). **B.** *William Shakespeare's Macbeth,* Bruce Coville/Gary Kelley (**11.27**). **C.** *To Market, To Market,* Anne Miranda/ Janet Stevens (**11.4**). **D.** *Special Effects in Film and Television,* Jake Hamilton (**11.33**).

11 Fine Arts

Carol Gilles

Contributing reviewers included Janet Alsup, Marilyn Andre, Linda Aulgur, Carolyn Dye, Carol Gilles, Janice Henson, Veronica Lee, Jenine Loesing, Virginia Pfannenstiel, Charles Robb, Stephanie Shafer, and Shelli Thelen.

Great books provide children with enjoyment and information while transporting them to higher levels of understanding. Children often connect with great literature in such a way that they are motivated to express their enjoyment and knowledge construction through culturally accepted, alternative sign systems. These alternative ways of knowing about the world help readers mediate or organize their thinking (Bodrova and Leong 1996; Dixon-Krauss 1996; Eisner 1997; Fosnot 1996; Vygotsky 1962; Vygotsky 1978). Using universal symbolic systems such as music, art, dance, or drama, readers can experience and then share with others their interpretation of a superb reading adventure. Some authors and illustrators present their stories in a musical or dance setting. Others might include beautiful or unique visual art to enhance the meaning of the written text. Sometimes the story in the text will inspire readers to perform music, drama, or dance, or to create other forms of expressive art. Books about the makers of art, music, and dance also are intriguing to children as they learn to appreciate the expressive arts.

As educators, we know the importance of presenting learning experiences to our students using a multimodal array of different intelligences (Gardner 1993). Well-written books always have been the mainstay of teachers wanting to reach children's linguistic, interpersonal, and intrapersonal intelligences, but other modes of intelligence—such as musical-rhythmic, bodily-kinesthetic, logical-mathematical, and visual-spatial—also can be embraced in children's literature.

Publishing companies, recognizing the trend to include fine arts in the general curriculum, have flooded the market in recent years with books about music or art. Some are wonderful, others merely mediocre. In this chapter, we present some of the outstanding literary offerings that can enhance children's reading and learning through alternative sign systems such as music, drama, art, and dance. By using or encouraging the use of the expressive arts, these books can unlock meaning and enjoyment for many children who have not previously connected to written texts. Children can become avid readers as they sing their experiences, illustrate their poetry, and dance their stories.

There are many categories that might be included under the umbrella of expressive arts, but the criteria for inclusion in this chapter is that books guide readers to be musicians, dramatists, artists, and dancers. Within each of the four categories that we have used to organize the literature in this chapter, readers will find both books that inspire children to engage in the fine arts and books that help children to appreciate the fine arts. The categories include the following:

- Music Books. This section includes three subcategories of books: Rhymes, Chants, and Songs; Books That Inspire Music; and Music Appreciation.

- Drama Books. In this section, readers will find two subcategories: Books That Inspire Drama, and How-To Drama Books.

- Art Books. This section includes three subcategories of literature: Books That Inspire Art, Books about Artists, and Art Appreciation.

- Dance Books. Here readers will find two subcategories of books: Books That Inspire Dance, and Dance Appreciation.

Works Cited

Bodrova, Elena, and Deborah J. Leong. 1996. *Tools of the Mind: The Vygotskian Approach to Early Childhood Education.* Upper Saddle River, NJ: Prentice Hall.

Dixon-Krauss, Lisbeth. 1996. *Vygotsky in the Classroom: Mediated Literacy Instruction and Assessment.* White Plains, NY: Longman.

Eisner, Eliott. 1997. Cognition and Representation: A Way to Pursue the American Dream? *Phi Delta Kappan* 78, no. 5: 348–353.

Fosnot, Catherine Twomey. 1996. Constructivism: A Psychological Theory of Learning. In *Constructivism: Theory, Perspectives, and Practice,* ed. C. T. Fosnot. New York: Teachers College.

Gardner, Howard. 1993. *Multiple Intelligences: The Theory in Practice, a Reader.* New York: Basic.

Vygotsky, Lev. 1962. *Thought and Language.* Cambridge, MA: MIT.

Vygotsky, Lev. 1978. *Mind in Society: The Development of Higher Psychological Processes.* Cambridge, MA: Harvard University.

---

*The titles listed below each subheading are organized into Primary Reviews and Secondary Reviews. The Primary Reviews describe outstanding books in each subheading. The Secondary Reviews provide brief information about other books worthy of consideration. Some titles listed below are **not** reviewed in this chapter;*

entries for these titles are not annotated and contain only bibliographic information. In such cases, a cross reference to the annotated entry contained elsewhere in this volume is provided in boldface type at the end of the bibliographic information.

Music Books

See also the section entitled Riddles, Chants, and Poems in chapter 13, "The Craft of Language."

Rhymes, Chants, and Songs

Primary Reviews

11.1 Gerber, Carole (1997). **Hush! A Gaelic Lullaby.** Illustrated by Marty Husted. Danvers, MA: Whispering Coyote. 32 pp. ISBN: 1-879085-57-7. Picture Book. (See **10.26**)

11.2 Hoberman, Mary Ann (1998). **Miss Mary Mack: A Hand-Clapping Rhyme.** Illustrated by Nadine Bernard Westcott. Boston: Little Brown. Unpaged. ISBN: 0-316-93118-7. Picture Book. (See **13.36**)

11.3 Jackson, Alison (1997). **I Know an Old Lady Who Swallowed a Pie.** Illustrated by Judith Byron Schachner. New York: Dutton Children's Books. Unpaged. ISBN: 0-525-45645-7. Picture Book.

Here is the much-loved and familiar song "I Know an Old Lady" with a modern twist. The whimsical watercolor illustrations portray the Old Lady as she swallows an entire Thanksgiving feast. She begins with a pie and proceeds to eat the rest of the dinner—"and her future looked murky after she swallowed that turkey." After hearing the first pages, kindergartners and first graders chimed in and helped with the predictable but hilarious lyrics. They were eager to illustrate their own versions of the story afterwards.

11.4 Miranda, Anne (1997). **To Market, to Market.** Illustrated by Janet Stevens. San Diego: Harcourt Brace. Unpaged. ISBN: 0-15-200035-6. Picture Book.

This book is an adaptation of the nursery rhyme, "To market, to market, to buy a fat pig." The author's choice of mixed media, photographs, and drawings, in both black-and-white and color produces an interesting contrast in the book. The rhythmic language supports early readers, and makes this a natural chanting book for large groups, small groups, or with an individual student. The illustrations are a springboard for discussion and promote language development. One reviewer shared this book with Brock, a first grader, who said, "She kept going home again. The pig keeps aggravating her!"

11.5 Orozco, José-Luis, editor (1997). **Diez deditos/Ten Little Fingers and Other Play Rhymes and Action Songs from Latin-America.** Illustrated by Elisa Kleven. New York: Dutton Children's Books. 56 pp. ISBN: 0-525-45736-4. Picture Book. (See **10.55**)

11.6 Sloat, Teri (1998). **There Was an Old Lady Who Swallowed a Trout!** Illustrated by Reynold Ruffins. New York: Henry Holt. Unpaged. ISBN: 0-8050-4294-6.

A rollicking remake of the classic song, *There Was an Old Lady Who Swallowed a Trout!* introduces readers to animals commonly found in Alaska, as the Old Lady swallows one after another to handle the trout that "splished and splashed and thrashed about. It wanted *out!*" When the old lady swallows a whale, young readers are certain they know what will happen to the old lady, but she surprises them by swallowing the ocean. Then "The old lady started to wriggle and jiggle; / The swirling inside made her hiccup and giggle." Finally all the animals come washing out in reverse order. Reynold Ruffins's bold illustrations with lots of reds and blues are reminiscent of the Russian artwork common in parts of Alaska, and capture subtle elements of the habitat for each animal included.

Secondary Reviews

11.7 Catalano, Dominic (1998). **Frog Went A-Courting: A Musical Play in Six Acts.** Honesdale, PA: Boyds Mills. Unpaged. ISBN: 1-56397-637-4. Picture Book. (See **11.31**)

11.8 Halpern, Shari (1997). **Hush, Little Baby.** New York: North-South. Unpaged. ISBN: 1-55858-807-8. Picture Book.

Beautiful collage illustrations with borders made up of quilt pieces give this book a feeling of texture. The text is the exact lullaby many people heard in their childhood. The pictures inspire children to sing along, and also to create their own illustrations with fabric, wrapping paper, string, etc., in collage fashion. These collages could be joined together in a class quilt wallhanging. The sheet music to the lullaby is provided at the end of the book.

11.9 Mahy, Margaret (1998). **A Summery Saturday Morning.** Illustrated by Selina Young. New York: Viking. Unpaged. ISBN: 0-670-87943-6. Picture Book.

Repetitive language, rhythm, and rhyme invite the audience to come along on an exciting Saturday morning adventure. Mahy finds the exact words to portray dogs chasing a cat, a boy, and finally some geese. Her simple verse, which can be sung to the tune of "This is the way we wash our clothes" is well matched to the winsome, descriptive illustrations. This book leaves children chanting, singing, laughing, and telling adventures of their own.

11.10 Omerod, Jan (1996). **Ms. McDonald Has a Class.** New York: Clarion. Unpaged. ISBN: 0-395-77611-2. Picture Book. (See **10.30**)

11.11 Scott, Steve (1998). **Teddy Bear, Teddy Bear.** New York: Harper Festival. Unpaged. ISBN: 0-694-01162-2. Picture Book.

Steve Scott illustrates with bright, simple pictures this book based on the traditional rhyme. The book begins just like the rhyme— "Teddy bear, teddy bear turn around"—but adds new phrases like "jump up now" and "dance on your toes." The large, white printing contrasts with the bright background colors, and naturally draws the eye of the reader. After this book was introduced to first-grade children during a nursery rhyme read-aloud time, they often chanted it in pairs or independently. It was not uncommon to observe one child reading and another "following the directions" during shared reading times.

Books That Inspire Music

Primary Reviews

11.12 Bartlett, T. C. (1997). **Tuba Lessons.** Illustrated by Monique Felix. San Diego: Harcourt Brace. Unpaged. ISBN: 0-15-201643-0. Picture Book.

This nearly wordless book explores the adventures of a young boy on his way to a tuba lesson. Chalk-on-gray illustrations are used imaginatively and whimsically. The illustrations depict a musical staff that becomes the boy's road, a tree he climbs, and finally animals that seem to emerge from the staff. As the boy plays his tuba, huge notes float out and the animals kick, hold, or balance them. The boy meets a bear, who at first becomes tangled in the notes and the staff, but eventually is soothed. Finally all the animals follow the boy to his lesson. Primary students selected notes to wear around their necks, created a movement for the note, and then played it on an instrument. Then the children created patterns on various instruments to match the badger, the bear, the fox, and so on. Using the instruments, they reenacted the story.

11.13 Birchman, David F. (1997). **A Green Horn Blowing.** Illustrated by Thomas B. Allen. New York: Lothrop, Lee & Shepard. Unpaged. ISBN: 0-688-12388-0. Picture Book.

This story, set in the Depression, examines the richness and power of music and friendship. A wandering worker who plays the trumpet stirs in a young boy a yearning to play a horn. While walking home from town, the two discover a green gourd called a trombolia that the man says is for blowing, not eating. This becomes the boy's horn until it goes to seed the next fall. Allen's pastel and colored-pencil illustrations enable readers to step back into the 1930s. This book stimulated discussion among primary children about what they wanted but couldn't have. When asked to listen for a special part of the book, many of the children chose the phrase, "You're a horn player now and for life. And that's something you can hold on to." The children then made connections to other things they could hold on to, including books, songs, learnings, friends, love, dreams, imagination, and God.

11.14 Egan, Ted (1998). **The Drover's Boy.** Illustrated by Robert Ingpen. Melbourne, Australia: Lothian. Unpaged. ISBN: 1-887734-52-X. Sophisticated Picture Book. (See **3.61**)

11.15 Shaik, Fatima (1998). **The Jazz of Our Street.** Illustrated by E. B. Lewis. New York: Penguin. Unpaged. ISBN: 0-8037-1885-3. Picture Book.

Just as the children in this story are called by the beat of the jazz band, the reader is called by the vivid watercolor illustrations and the rhythmic, descriptive language. One feels the connection of the present to the past and the importance of "listening real hard when another has something to say, because all must play along— not just with the songs." Jazz begins to come alive as the beat and rhythm of the language begins to pulse and sway. Readers join a parade of music makers, and "We follow their paths as we dance and walk. We shimmy. We shake like a rumbling train, remembering the times before." Children love to move to the rhythm and the rhyme of this story.

11.16 Takao, Yuko (1997). **Winter Concert.** Brookfield, CT: Millbrook. Unpaged. ISBN: 0-7613-0301-4. Picture Book.

This charming picture storybook explores the lasting effects of a concert. Black pen-and-ink mice fill a theater to listen to a piano concert. Once the concert begins, small dots of color emerge from the piano and begin to cover the black-and-white mice with color. As the mice emerge from the theater, the text reads, "The concert ended but the music did not. It paved their pathways home. It colored their world." Later one mouse records the experience in a journal and a dot of color remains on the page, reminding readers that a special musical performance does become part of ourselves. This book evokes pointillism art projects and profound discussions. One of the most troubled students in one reviewer's first grade class explained, "Like the story, music is always with you."

Secondary Reviews

11.17 Fleming, Candace (1997). **Gabriella's Song.** Illustrated by Giselle Potter. New York: Atheneum Books for Young Readers. Unpaged. ISBN: 0-689-80973-5. Picture Book.

On a walk through Venice, Gabriella hears the sounds of boats, the street traders, pigeons, and church bells; she composes a little city song and hums it to herself. Her song, a compilation of the sounds of Venice, delights the townsfolk, from the baker to the gondolier. Potter's illustrations capture the charm of Venice. First graders in one reviewer's class begged to go on a "music walk" after hearing the story, and they found ways to represent the "music" they had heard. Students even pointed out the song they heard in the sounds in the classroom. This book also sparked discussion about how the same song brings out different feelings for different people because each of us has had different things happen to us.

11.18 Hopkins, Lee Bennett (1997). **Song and Dance: Poems.** Illustrated by Cheryl Munro Taylor. New York: Simon & Schuster. 32 pp. ISBN: 0-689-80159-9. Picture Book. (See **10.11**)

11.19 Rogers, Sally (1998). **Earthsong.** Illustrated by Melissa Bay Mathis. New York: Dutton Children's Books. Unpaged. ISBN: 0-525-45873-5. Picture Book.

We suggest that teachers practice singing the text of this book to the tune of "Over in the Meadow" before presenting it to children.

When the children in one reviewer's classroom heard about each endangered animal (panda, Bengal tiger, Indian lion, etc.) and its habitat in the musical setting, their attention was rapt, and they immediately wanted to "do something with endangered animals." The second and third graders in particular were enthusiastic about using the book as a resource for further research about endangered species. Dark, brilliant color illustrations bring each setting to life; readers can almost feel the heat of the desert or the arctic cold.

Music Appreciation

Primary Reviews

11.20 Ganeri, Anita (1996). **The Young Person's Guide to the Orchestra.** Compact disc narrated by Ben Kingsley. San Diego: Harcourt Brace. 56 pp. ISBN: 0-15-201304-0. Picture Book.

The book and compact disc complement each other as good resources to introduce the orchestra to elementary students. The book provides information about the history of orchestras, sections of the orchestra, and what it is like to play in the great orchestras of the world. Full-color photographs enhance the information for students who do not have experience with real instruments, and are helpful to use when listening to the compact disc. There also is a brief introduction to famous composers from the 1600s through the present. The book includes an index; the compact disc is tucked safely inside the front cover. The book can be used in its entirety, or used a section at a time.

11.21 Pinkney, Andrea Davis (1998). **Duke Ellington: The Piano Prince and His Orchestra.** Illustrated by Brian Pinkney. New York: Hyperion. ISBN: 0-7868-0178-6. Picture Book.

The musical words and textured illustrations in this biography of Duke Ellington jump off the page. This detailed picture book describes the life of Edward Kennedy "Duke" Ellington in a style that gives the reader the feel of the music that he created. The scratchboard illustrations create movement on each page, and the rhythmic words that accompany them are a great dedication to the creative artistry of Ellington.

Secondary Reviews

11.22 Colón-Vilá, Lillian (1998). **Salsa.** Illustrated by Roberta Collier-Morales. Houston, TX: Piñata. Unpaged. ISBN: 1-55885-220-4. Picture Book.

This colorful dual-language edition describes one of the most enjoyable activities for many Latino and Caribbean families—dancing to salsa music—through the eyes of a young girl who pretends to be the various musicians and dancers she knows. Colón-Vilá carefully places the music within the culture and traditions of el barrio families, while also connecting this dance music to its Afro-Caribbean roots. Although the text is rather simplistic, it serves to highlight the intergenerational link of salsa among aunts, uncles, grandparents, and grandchildren. Each boldly colored illustration is surrounded by a musically themed border, and the English and Spanish texts are separated by a series of musical notes.

11.23 Igus, Toyomi. **i see the rhythm.** Illustrated by Michele Wood. San Francisco: Children's Book. 32 pp. ISBN: 0-89239-151-0. Picture Book. (See **3.90**)

Drama Books

Books That Inspire Drama

Primary Reviews

11.24 Brown, Ruth (1997). **Cry Baby.** New York: Dutton Children's Books. Unpaged. ISBN: 0-525-45902-2. Picture Book.

In this picture storybook, no one ever likes to walk with the little sister. She drags her old blanket, which is nearly in shreds; she is afraid of cows and high fences; and she is always crying out "Baba! Baba!" When the walk is nearly complete, the siblings find the little sister is holding one end of a completely unraveled blanket. Retracing her steps to wind up the thread, little sister finds she can willingly do all the things she has whined about earlier. Brown's bright watercolors depicting the English countryside, and the realistic features of the little girl, remind children of their little brothers and sisters or their own experiences. Primary children retold this simple story through movement, music, and art. Using the ball of yarn to connect the episodes in the story, the children acted it out silently, with the dramatic music in the background. They could retell the story in detail days afterwards, and made lasting connections to the action and characters.

11.25 Christopher, Matt (1996). **Great Moments in Baseball History.** Boston: Little Brown. 104 pp. ISBN: 0-316-14130-5. Chapter Book. (See **12.12**)

11.26 Christopher, Matt (1997). **Great Moments in Football History.** Boston: Little Brown. 89 pp. ISBN: 0-316-14196-8. Chapter Book. (See **12.13**)

11.27 Coville, Bruce (1997). **William Shakespeare's** *Macbeth.* Illustrated by Gary Kelley. New York: Dial. Unpaged. ISBN: 0-8037-1899-3. Sophisticated Picture Book.

In this retelling of *Macbeth,* Coville combines modern-day language with some of Shakespeare's most famous lines to create an unforgettable drama. Macbeth is portrayed as a man tormented by the witches' words, a man both heroic and evil. Kelley's illustrations add to the dark and mysterious nature of the story. This book can be shared with intermediate youngsters as their first introduction to Shakespeare, or used with older students before they read the actual book to build up their prior knowledge. One reviewer reported that she read this story to her fourth-grade boys, and they immediately suggested dramatizing the book and looking for more books by Shakespeare.

11.28 Fleming, Denise (1997). **Time to Sleep.** New York: Henry Holt. Unpaged. ISBN: 0-8050-3762-4. Picture Book.

This vivid picture storybook has illustrations that were created by pouring colored cotton pulp through handcut stencils. The result is handmade paper with large, bright, textured images of animals in their habitats. The story concerns a community of animals that warn one another to hibernate as winter approaches. When Bear smells winter in the air, he hurries off to tell Snail that it is time to sleep. Snail tells Skunk, who tells Turtle. Yet each animal tries to put off sleep for just a little longer. The predictable and repetitious structures make this story perfect for bedtime and dramatizing. The father of two small boys in one reviewer's class shared that one of his boys dramatized the story spontaneously as he read it aloud.

11.29 Vail, Rachel (1998). **Over the Moon.** Illustrated by Scott Nash. New York: Orchard. Unpaged. ISBN: 0-531-33068-0. Picture Book. (See **13.26**)

Secondary Reviews

11.30 Casey, Moe (1997). **The Most Excellent Book of Dress Up.** Brookfield, CT: Copper Beech. 32 pp. ISBN: 0-7613-0550-5. Picture Book. (See **12.50**)

11.31 Catalano, Dominic (1998). **Frog Went A-Courting: A Musical Play in Six Acts.** Honesdale, PA: Boyds Mills. Unpaged. ISBN: 1-56397-637-4. Picture Book.

This retelling of the old classic folk song "Frog Went A-Courting" is unique in its presentation as a play. The list of characters appears as a real playbill, and brilliant full-page chalk-pastel illustrations are interspersed with charcoal stage sketches. The characters are whimsically portrayed with great detail, down to the orange-and-green plaid Scottish kilt the frog wears, and the dainty pearl earrings in Miss Mouse's ears. The familiar rhyme appears in large text with a single phrase on each page. The song and directions for simplifying the accompaniment also are included. This book inspired children to write and produce their own plays, including costumes and stage directions.

11.32 Lavis, Steve (1997). **Jump! It's Fun!** New York: Dutton. Unpaged. ISBN: 0-525-67578-7. Picture Book.

Lavis uses simple, lively illustrations to depict the personalities of the animal characters. Whether the frog is jumping, the teddy is soaring, or the elephant is marching, readers will be engaged by the book. One reviewer, a special education teacher, used drama to help children read independently and remember the story. She explained, "My students decided to perform a play from the book. We made individual animal puppets to depict the characters (a tiger, a lion, a snake, a toucan, etc.). I read and reread the book to the children to help them determine the sequence of the characters' appearance. In the dramatization, as I read the book aloud again, each child held up the puppet portrayed in the action. Through this experience, many of the children could later pick up and read this book independently."

How-to Drama Books

Primary Reviews

11.33 Hamilton, Jake (1998). **Special Effects in Film and Television.** New York: Dorling Kindersley. 63 pp. ISBN: 0-7894-2813-X. Picture Book.

This is a complete, easy-to-understand, and fascinating look at special effects. The special effects are divided into categories, such as Camera Effects, Larger than Life, Natural Disasters, Digital Dragons, etc., with color photographs to make the explanations clear. There are many different types of movies discussed, ranging from classics like *Clash of the Titans* to the newest releases. Two students in one reviewer's class gravitated to the book immediately, and started an animated conversation about different movies and techniques used to achieve various effects. This would be an excellent resource book for almost any classroom.

11.34 Wilkes, Angela (1996). **Dazzling Disguises and Clever Costumes: More than 50 Step-by-Step Projects to Make, Paint, Sew, Prepare, and Wear.** New York: Dorling Kindersley. 48 pp. ISBN: 0-7894-1001-X. Picture Book.

Dazzling Disguises and Clever Costumes shows children how to create fabulous costumes and props that are simple and do not require any sewing. Young children are able to make most of these costumes with little help from an adult. Each page has clear, step-by-step directions that are easy to understand. The vibrant colors attract the eye, and children can create many of these disguises by just looking at the pictures. This book is a must in any classroom that uses props, costumes, and disguises when role-playing. One reviewer's kindergartners made medieval hats and crowns to retell the rhyme "The Queen of Hearts." Children had to problem-solve, compare sizes, measure, and talk about shapes to successfully create the hats.

Art Books

Books That Inspire Art

Primary Reviews

11.35 Ellwand, David (1996). **Emma's Elephant and Other Favorite Animal Friends.** New York: Dutton Children's Books. Unpaged. ISBN: 0-525-45792-5. Picture Book.

David Ellwand's *Emma's Elephant* features full-page, black-and-white photos of young children with their chosen animal. Each page introduces in alphabetical order a new animal, its name, and something about it. For example, on the page with the dalmatian, the text states, "David's dotted dog." The children on each page are captured with their animals at just the right moment to convey the child's joy and personality. The animal in each picture represents the feelings of the child it is with. For example, Catherine is shown with her cat. The cat looks calm and gentle, just as Catherine appears to be very timid and delicate. The simple, alliterative text makes it easy for beginning readers to share in the fun of this book.

11.36 Gilchrist, Jan Spivey (1997). **Madelia.** New York: Dial Books for Young Readers. Unpaged. ISBN: 0-8037-2052-1. Picture Book.

Madelia has just received her first set of watercolor paints. She can't wait to paint the Bible stories she has heard in her father's church. Because it is Sunday, Madelia has to leave the paints and go to church. She expects that she can daydream and ignore the sermon, but her father draws her into the sermon and into a place of swirling colors, fragrant smells, and wonderful sounds. This book not only inspires children to use their creativity to express their experiences and view of the world, but it also provides a glimpse into the life of Ms. Gilchrist, whose father was a preacher. Gilchrist's gouache paintings, highlighted with pastels, are warm, expressive, and inspiring. The book touches a chord with primary children who, like Madelia, are experimenting with art.

11.37 Nicholson, Nicholas B. A. (1998). **Little Girl in a Red Dress with Cat and Dog.** Illustrated by Cynthia Von Buhler. New York: Viking. Unpaged. ISBN: 0-670-87183-4. Picture Book.

In the 1830s, traveling portrait painters like Ammi Phillips roamed the countryside searching for work. In this story, the littlest girl in the family is always ignored. She is too small to cut wood with the boys in the family, and the needlework her sisters do is too complex for her. When Mr. Phillips offers to paint a portrait of the family, the little girl is the only one who has the time and patience to be painted. However in the days she sits for the paintings, she begins to be accepted by her family. The finished portrait of her in her red dress is placed above the mantle. In the author's notes we find that Ammi Phillips did use the same composition frequently. The illustrations in this book give us a real sense of the grainy oils that were used and the simple, stilted pictures of that time. Children could use this book as a springboard to study more American folk art, compose their own art in that style, or dramatize this story.

11.38 Solá, Michéle (1997). **Angela Weaves a Dream: The Story of a Young Maya Artist.** Photographs by Jeffrey Jay Foxx. New York: Hyperion Books for Children. 47 pp. ISBN: 0-7868-0073-9. Picture Book.

This look at the Maya culture gives readers an opportunity to share in Angela's pursuit of her dream: winning the local weaving contest. In Chiapas, a town in southern Mexico, the women and girls of the village traditionally participate in a weaving contest. Solá follows Angela daily as she practices creating the "seven sacred designs of San Andrés" in her weaving. Each design is represented and interpreted with inset diagrams, opposite Jeffrey Jay Foxx's full-page, close-up color photographs of the weaving, making it possible for the young reader to experience Angela's growth as a young weaver and her eventual success. Jonathan (age 10) said, "I feel happy because I love to learn about indigenous groups like the Maya. I thought the book was fantastic!" Captions, a glossary, a bibliography, maps, and notes from the photographer and author contribute to this informative piece of literature. The step-by-step instructions and patterns for weaving and other art projects found in Florence Temko's *Traditional Crafts from Mexico and Central America* gave our students their own first-hand experiences as part of a study of indigenous peoples.

> Temko, Florence (1996). **Traditional Crafts from Mexico and Central America.** Illustrated by Randall Gooch. Photographs by Robert L. Wolfe and Diane Wolfe. Minneapolis: Lerner. 64 pp. ISBN: 0-8225-2935-1. Chapter Book.

11.39 Wright-Frierson, Virginia (1996). **A Desert Scrapbook: Dawn to Dusk in the Sonoran Desert.** New York: Simon & Schuster. Unpaged. ISBN: 0-689-80678-7. Picture Book. (See **2.26**)

11.40 Young, Ed (1997). **Voices of the Heart.** New York: Scholastic. Unpaged. ISBN: 0-590-50199-2. Picture Book.

In twenty-six collages composed from a variety of papers (including handmade), Young defines twenty-six feelings or emotions in terms of their relationship to the human heart. The concepts are abstract (e.g., virtue, realization, grace, constancy, wrath, and loyalty), but each concept is taken apart with a Chinese character assigned to each part, accompanied by an explanation in English. The concepts are then reassembled into an ideogram in the seal style of ancient Chinese calligraphy. The collages depict the interaction of the Chinese characters, and incorporate an image of a heart to complete the definition. The overall effect is a stunning work that is appropriate for art, language, and culture studies. It is a picture book for older students who have the sophistication to discuss Young's interpretation of the concepts.

11.41 Hucko, Bruce (1996). **A Rainbow at Night: The World in Words and Pictures by Navajo Children.** San Francisco: Chronicle. Unpaged. ISBN: 0-8118-1294-4. Picture Book.

The impetus for this beautiful book of stories was a child's question: "Have you ever seen a rainbow at night?" For Navajo children, the answer is evident in the world around them. Bruce Hucko allows the children, whose art and youthful wisdom are embodied within the covers of this book, to tell and show the reader how very possible this is. Theirs is a world seen differently, a world that is inclusive of all that has life and spirit. As children, they are able to blend traditional Navajo life and beliefs with modern ideas.

11.42 Lee, Huy Voun (1995). **In the Park.** New York: Henry Holt. Unpaged. ISBN: 0-8050-4128-1. Picture Book.

Xiao Ming, a small Chinese boy, enjoys the pleasures of a spring day in the park with his mother. With cut-paper illustrations that create a colorful three-dimensional effect, this simplistic picture book incorporates the writing of Chinese characters within the story. Young readers will relate to the familiar setting of this contemporary tale, while observing the natural relationship between images, words, and Chinese characters presented.

11.43 Minor, Wendell (1998). **Grand Canyon: Exploring a Natural Wonder.** New York: Blue Sky. Unpaged. ISBN: 0-590-47968-7. Picture Book. (See **2.45**)

11.44 Rumford, James (1996). **Cloudmakers.** Illustrated by James Rumford. New York: Houghton Mifflin. Unpaged. ISBN: 0-395-76505-6. Picture Book.

Captured by the Arabs, Young Wu and Grandfather Wu are given seven days to make a cloud. In the next seven days, grandfather is seen using hemp rope, collecting ashes, beating shoes, and bleaching fibers. By the seventh day, they produce special paper that looks like clouds, and the sultan frees them. A story to intrigue children about the art of papermaking.

11.45 Say, Allen (1996). **Emma's Rug.** Boston: Houghton Mifflin. 32 pp. ISBN: 0-395-74294-3. Picture Book.

Emma stared at her unwashed, ragged rug each day, creating pictures in her mind that she could draw. One day, her mother washed Emma's rug. Emma was devastated; she felt she could no longer create art. But once she sat quietly and explored the recesses of her mind, the images came back to her, and she was able to create again. *Emma's Rug* teaches children how to search within for inspiration and creativity.

11.46 Wood, Nancy, editor (1997). **The Serpent's Tongue.** New York: Dutton. 214 pp. ISBN: 0525-45514-0. Chapter Book.

A collection of stories and artwork presented by many well-known Native American writers, as well as non-native authors who have done extensive research about and work with Native Americans. Photographs of Native American people taken many years after the historical period they record serve to perpetuate stereotypical representations of Native peoples. In the same volume is Paula Gunn Allen's work, which challenges such representations. Most of the artwork by Native American artists displays scenes from everyday life or from tribal legends and myths. The prose and poetry cover all aspects of Pueblo culture and daily life, and the format of the text is very inviting. The contributor's notes and bibliography indicate the level of research done in preparation for editing this text.

Books about Artists

Primary Reviews

11.47 Dionetti, Michelle (1996). **Painting the Wind: A Story of Vincent van Gogh.** Illustrated by Kevin Hawkes. Boston: Little Brown. Unpaged. ISBN: 0-316-18602-3. Picture Book.

The reader sees the light and dark side of Vincent van Gogh through the eyes of Claudine, a child who helps to clean his house. Claudine is mesmerized by van Gogh's paintings, which "do not look like other paintings, neat and perfect. They were thick and wild. Bright suns curled in spangled light. Sunflowers blared like little trumpets." Kevin Hawkes' bright and bold illustrations are reminiscent of van Gogh's paintings. When van Gogh's rage and temper get him thrown out of his house, it is Claudine who tells him that she likes his paintings. One elementary art teacher darkened the room and spotlighted her print of *The Starry Night* before reading the book to children. Another first-grade teacher exclaimed, "As we came into the darkened room, with the bright light on *The Starry Night,* I felt like I was entering the painting, and so did the children." Children immediately wanted to imitate van Gogh's unusual painting style.

11.48 Goldstein, Ernest (1996). **The Journey of Diego Rivera.** Minneapolis: Lerner. 104 pp. ISBN: 0-8225-2066-4. Chapter Book.

In the early 1900s, the brilliant young Mexican painter Diego Rivera traveled to Paris to join the ranks of artists such as Matisse and Picasso, and to participate in the revolutionary modern art movement. His wildly unpredictable behavior shocked the bourgeois and created almost as much notoriety as his sophisticated paintings. The text weaves together his early influences, including El Greco, Monet, the cubists, and later the Italian Renaissance painters and the pre-Columbian art of his beloved Mexico. This lavishly illustrated volume relates in great detail the many turbulent, poignant journeys in Rivera's personal and artistic life. We see the life and mastery of one of this century's most revered muralists. For more mature readers, this book offers a thorough historical context, an accessible discussion of features of his art, and glimpses into Rivera's daily life. Many details of his murals are richly examined, from the peasants of his homeland to his celebration of the age of science and industry. A must for any student of Mexican art history.

11.49 Greenberg, Jane, and Sandra Jordan (1998). **Chuck Close Up Close.** New York: Dorling Kindersley. 47 pp. ISBN: 0-7894-2486-X. Sophisticated Chapter Book.

Chuck Close Up Close is a striking biography of an artist who received recognition in the 1960s by painting enormous, photographically realistic portraits. He uses a grid system and enlarged photographs to produce the meticulous details. He believes his system is a result of his struggle to overcome learning disorders as a boy. In 1988, he experienced what he calls "the event"—a spinal artery collapse that left him with only partial use of his arms and legs. During his rehabilitation, the faces of his visitors reconnected him to his paintings. He continues to paint portraits that are really "hundreds of little abstract paintings—multicolored ovals and gaudy squares, amoebas swimming before your eyes." When one moves back from these enormous pieces, the portrait is clear. This book will interest students of all ages. They will be fascinated by Close's grid system, and many will be interested to see his paintings in museums.

11.50 Winter, Jeanette (1998). **My Name Is Georgia: A Portrait.** San Diego: Harcourt Brace. Unpaged. ISBN: 0-15-201649-X. Picture Book.

This illustrated picture book biography of Georgia O'Keefe will appeal to all ages. As a young girl, O'Keefe did things other girls didn't: She went barefoot, let her hair fly in the wind instead of having it braided, and was always satisfied to be by herself. She also saw the world differently. She carefully examined flowers, sunsets, and deserts. As an artist, she gathered bones and rocks to paint so others would see them the way she did. Winter's illustrations have been "done in homage to [O'Keefe's] art and include many of the images she often used." When paired with Georgia O'Keefe prints, this book calls children to gather items around them and paint them clearly and with emphasis as they see them, just as O'Keefe did.

Secondary Reviews

11.51 Carle, Eric (1996). **The Art of Eric Carle.** Illustrated by Eric Carle. New York: Philomel. 125 pp. ISBN: 0-399-22937-X. Sophisticated Chapter Book.

The Art of Eric Carle is a retrospective of Eric Carle's life and work, with personal photographs and illustrations from his books. It contains an autobiographical chapter; chapters by editors and authorities from America, Germany, and Japan; a photo-essay on Carle's collage technique; some of Carle's sketches; and a list of books Carle has created. The illustrations consist of a wide variety of photographs, some of which span a two-page spread. Others are small, personal photographs of Carle as a small boy. The illustrations from his books include *A Week with Willi Worm*, which became *The Very Hungry Caterpillar*. This is a complete and fascinating resource book for intermediate students and teachers interested in knowing more about the life, times, and art of Eric Carle.

> Carle, Eric. **The Very Hungry Caterpillar.** (1987). New York: Philomel. Unpaged. ISBN: 0-399-20853-4. Picture Book.

11.52 Littlesugar, Amy (1996). **Marie in Fourth Position.** Illustrated by Ian Schoenherr. New York: Philomel. Unpaged. ISBN: 0-399-22794-6. Picture Book.

This compelling tale examines what it may have been like to pose for the artist Edward Degas. In an author's note, Littlesugar reminds us that Marie van Goethem, a poor ballet girl, posed for Degas sometime between 1879 and 1880. Ian Schoenherr's realistic illustrations help readers to understand the difficulty of holding a pose, and the frustration Degas might have experienced trying to get Marie to stretch and stretch "High. Higher. As though you wish to fly." After Degas made several drawings, he actually sculpted the model, and then went a step further by adding hair, slippers, and a real silk tutu. After reading this book, children would enjoy seeing Degas' *The Little Dancer* (located at the Metropolitan Museum of Art) or a replica, or perhaps creating their own pieces, first in two dimensions on paper and later in three dimensions in clay. Other children may wish to use music to imagine what movement would be made prior to a pose.

11.53 Parillo, Tony (1998). **Michelangelo's Surprise.** New York: Farrar, Straus and Giroux. Unpaged. ISBN: 0-374-34961-4. Picture Book.

This story is based on an actual event that occurred in the life of one of Italy's most famous artists. It has snowed in Florence overnight and Sandro, the youngest page in the palazzo, is summoned by a Medici to find Michelangelo. He searches everywhere, from the palazzo to the kitchen to the chapel, and still can't find him. He finally finds Michelangelo sculpting a gorgeous snow sculpture, a surprise for the Medici. The illustrations present a clear idea of how life may have looked during the late 1400s, and include many details about the people and the buildings of Italy. The book presents enough background information about Michelangelo and Italy that it could be used as an introduction to study Italy.

Art Appreciation

Primary Reviews

11.54 King, Penny, and Clare Roundhill (1996). **Artists' Workshop Landscapes.** New York: Crabtree. 32 pp. ISBN: 0-86505-853-9. Picture Book.

Day after day, children pored over the pages of this landscape book, one in a series along with *Artists' Workshop Portraits* and *Artists' Workshop Stories.* They would then head to the art center to respond. This is a great resource book that presents six artists (Hokusai, Klimt, Monet, O'Keefe, Burchfield, and Hundertwasser) and their work, as well as information on the decisions they had to make as artists. The reader can see full paintings as well as detailed close-ups. Following the artist study, the authors provide instructions to create landscapes in that artist's style. The reproductions of all the artists' professional and childhood works are vivid in style and color.

> **Artists' Workshop Portraits.** (1996). 32 pp. ISBN: 0-86505-850-4. Picture Book.

> **Artists' Workshop Stories.** (1996). 32 pp. ISBN: 0-86505-852-0. Picture Book.

11.55 Micklethwait, Lucy (1996). **A Child's Book of Play in Art: Great Pictures Great Fun.** New York: Dorling Kindersley. 45 pp. ISBN: 0-7894-1003-6. Picture Book.

This large-format, colorful book offers children an introduction to great art by using many famous paintings as the basis for activities, from inventing a pattern in modern art to telling a story about paintings from the 1500s. The activities are fun and easy, and children of all ages can access this book. One reviewer's first graders wanted to take it with them on the next museum trip to see if they could find any of the artwork depicted, or to look at the artwork and figure out which section of the book it would fit in. The children recognized the picture *Vincent's Bedroom in Arles* as a Van Gogh from a previous study of his works in *Painting the Wind* (see **11.47**).

Secondary Reviews

11.56 Presilla, Maricel E. (1996). **Mola: Cuna Life Stories and Art.** New York: Henry Holt. Unpaged. ISBN: 0-8050-3801-9. Picture Book.

The Cuna women of the San Blas Islands, located off the northern coast of Panama, create a unique form of art called *mola*. Molas are intricate fabric designs of different colors and textures sewn together in layers. Each mola tells a story, and Presilla presents and interprets the ancient and modern stories depicted in the molas she displays, revealing the culture of the artists' community. In *Life around the Lake*, Presilla and Soto introduce the reader to embroideries by the Tarascan women of Lake Pátzcuaro in Central Mexico. It is a simple yet thoughtful picture book that shows the lives of the Tarascan people through their creative art forms. Together these books provide a glimpse of some of Latin America's creative and resilient artists.

> Presilla, Maricel E. (1996). **Life around the Lake.** Illustrated by Gloria Soto. New York: Henry Holt. Unpaged. ISBN: 0-8050-3800-0. Picture Book.

Dance Books

Books That Inspire Dance

Primary Reviews

11.57 Ancona, George (1998). **Let's Dance!** New York: Morrow Junior Books. Unpaged. ISBN: 0-688-16211-8. Picture Book.

Ancona invites readers with the following observations: "If you can speak, you can sing. If you can walk, you can dance. All you have to do is kick, step, turn, hop, jump, leap, reach and wiggle." In this lively book, readers see full-color photographs of people all over the world dancing, either alone, with a partner, or in a large group. Each page features a dance from a different country, while the small caption gives a more detailed explanation. Traditional dances of particular countries or cultures, such as flamenco dancing or the Jarana from the Yucatan, are featured here, as well as dances that are no longer associated with just one country, such as clog dancing and tap dancing. This joyous book offers an introduction to dance for all ages.

11.58 Gray, Libba Moore (1995). **My Mama Had a Dancing Heart.** Illustrated by Raúl Colón. Unpaged. New York: Orchard. ISBN: 0-531-08770-0. Picture Book. (See **13.6**)

11.59 Rohmann, Eric (1997). **The Cinder-Eyed Cats.** New York: Crown. Unpaged. ISBN: 0-517-70896-5. Picture Book. (See **14.14**)

11.60 Thomassie, Tynia (1996). **Mimi's Tutu.** Illustrated by Jan Spivey Gilchrist. New York: Scholastic. Unpaged. ISBN: 0-590-44020-9. Picture Book.

Mimi loves to go with her momma to her dance classes, and dance with momma at the end. One day another little girl appears at the studio with black leotards and a tutu, and Mimi realizes that she wants one too. Her family helps her connect to her African heritage by making her a *lapa,* a "belt of beige cowrie shells, and beads of black, orange and dark green." The blending of the pastel watercolors in the background add a feeling of warmth to the story and seem to represent the blending of cultures in Mimi's life. The strong colors used to depict Mimi's family add to the strength of family and tradition in the story. After hearing the book, one first grader at Lee School named Ajai said, "I think I need to be like the Lee School song says, unique. I shouldn't have to be exactly like everyone else. That's what Mimi's grandmothers, aunts, and mother helped her find out when they gave her a different kind of tutu."

Secondary Reviews

11.61 Giff, Patricia Reilly (1998). **Rosie's Big City Ballet.** Illustrated by Julie Durrell. New York: Viking. 73 pp. ISBN: 0-670-87792-1. Chapter Book.

Rosie's Big City Ballet touches all those who have a dream while taking ballet. This chapter book helps children who have to deal with the emotion of auditioning and not always being selected. Rosie wonders if her time spent making a special treehouse is a factor when she does not get a part in the ballet. Eventually Rosie learns that even famous dancers are not always selected, and also that other opportunities will come about. First grader Maddy wrote, "I liked it. It changed my mind about going to the ballet." This is one title in a series of six books on dance.

11.62 Hampshire, Susan (1998). **Rosie's Ballet Slippers.** Illustrated by Maria Teresa Meloni. New York: HarperCollins. Unpaged ISBN: 0-06-443488-5. Picture Book.

This picture storybook depicts a young girl in her first ballet lesson with her new pink slippers. Meloni's soft illustrations show the boys and girls learning pliés, sautés, and pointing toes. We feel the joy and jumps as the story brings out the first-day excitement experienced by dancers. Readers simply must get up and dance throughout the story. We see the children in the story with their slippers and dance bags over their shoulders for all the world to see, saying goodbye to each other at the end of their lesson. As one dancer said, "I remember when I got my first ballet shoes and carried them just like that."

11.63 Hopkins, Lee Bennett (1997). **Song and Dance: Poems.** Illustrated by Cheryl Munro Taylor. New York: Simon & Schuster. 32 pp. ISBN: 0-689-80159-9. Picture Book. (See **10.11**)

Dance Appreciation

Primary Reviews

11.64 Isadora, Rachel (1997). **Lili Backstage.** New York: Putnam. Unpaged. ISBN: 0-399-23025-4. Picture Book.

This book provides a view of the backstage world of ballet through the eyes of a child. Readers follow Lili into the orchestra rehearsal studio, the ballet studio, and the theater. Backstage we see the makeup, costumes, and props that are used for plays. When the performance begins, Lili can see how each part comes together in a grand transformation. This book gives readers an intimate glimpse of the world of ballet. The information gained from Isadora's book helped primary students understand all the jobs necessary for the third graders at the school to write, produce, and perform their own opera in the spring.

11.65 Newman, Barbara (1997). **The Illustrated Book of Ballet Stories.** Illustrated by Gill Tomblin. New York: Dorling Kindersley. 64 pp. ISBN: 0-7894-2024-4. Picture Book.

This book combines photographs of ballet stars with illustrations of dance scenes from five well-known ballets, including *The Sleeping Beauty, Giselle, Coppelia, Swan Lake,* and *The Nutcracker.* Young dancers will be fascinated to learn more about the stories and the music that have made these ballets such classics over time. As a resource, the book provides background information, depicts ballet steps and dance positions, and explains terms most children would want to know. The text accurately conveys the story of the ballet and sparks the interest of children. An added benefit is the compact disc, which allows readers to hear musical excerpts from the ballets. This book is a valuable resource for children who are interested in the movement of dance, and also for children who want to learn more about the art of dance.

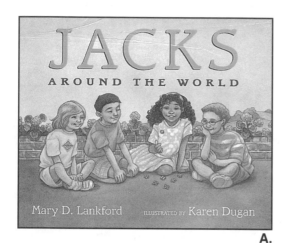

A.

B.

C.

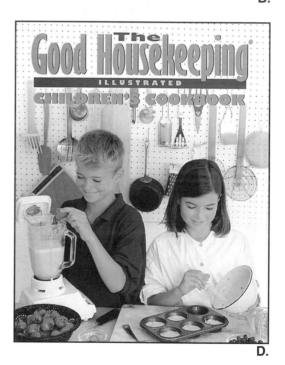

D.

A. *Jacks around the World,* Mary D. Lankford/Karen Dugan (**12.43**). **B.** *First in the Field: Baseball Hero Jackie Robinson,* Derek T. Dingle (**12.5**). **C.** *The Story of Chess,* Horacio Cardo (**12.41**). **D.** *The Good Housekeeping Illustrated Children's Cookbook,* Marianne Zanzarella/Tom Eckerle (**12.55**).

12 Sports, Games, and Hobbies

Lauren Freedman

Contributing reviewers included Lauren Freedman, Penny O'Shaunessey, Sandra Schmidt, Jean Williams, and Allison Young.

The books we have chosen for inclusion in this chapter are often the kinds of books that students choose for voluntary reading, or use when they have free choice for a research project or book share. These are the books that can pique interest and engage students who otherwise may find reading objectionable or difficult, because they are about things that these students hear and see in the world around them outside of school. The subjects are real and offer immediate connections. Through these books, students may be drawn to learn more, and may find themselves looking for books that go beyond their immediate experiences.

The majority of the books in this chapter are nonfiction, and rarely appear within most schools' curricula. While there are a number of fiction books about sports, for the most part they are written by two authors, Matt Christopher and Bruce Brooks, and tend to be formula novels. As with all books, the ones in this chapter provide both mirrors and windows for students to explore the world and their place in it. One of the major benefits to the books in this section is the use of visuals. The authors and illustrators make tremendous use not only of illustration, but also of photography, graphs, maps, charts, and diagrams. The authors also make ample use of supporting material such as indices, glossaries, and lists that increase the books' usefulness as texts for inquiry projects.

The members of the review committee for this section unanimously feel that more use could be made of these books within the framework of the core curriculum, especially as teachers move to a more integrated thematic and inquiry-based curriculum. Many of the books reviewed could fit into text-sets developed around various broad concepts or themes. They could be used as individual reference books or as read-aloud texts for classroom units on topics as wide-ranging as the human body, courage and perseverance, playing by the rules, developing self-esteem and self-discipline, or understanding various math concepts. Many of the books we reviewed could be used by older children as models for writing their own texts.

The reviews in this chapter are organized into three major categories: Sports, Games, and Hobbies. The section on Sports is further divided into five subsections: Autobiographies, Biographies, Information Books, How-to Books, and Fiction and Poetry.

The criteria we used as we reviewed books for inclusion in this chapter were appeal to children, clarity of writing, clarity of illustrations, connection and integration between illustrations and the text, appropriateness for classroom use, representation of diverse groups, and level of complexity. Appeal to children refers not only to visual appeal, but also to such things as content and the amount of white space on a page. It was important that pages not be cluttered or present an overwhelming amount of information. So too, it was extremely important that the author's style be straightforward and simple without being simplistic. The illustrations needed to be clear and uncluttered, and the integration of illustration and text was essential, particularly in the books that described how to play a sport, play a game, or follow a recipe. We also felt that the books we included needed to be ones that could be used by both students and teachers within a classroom or library context. Thus activities described in the books on hobbies and games needed to use materials that could be found and used in schools. Finally, but perhaps most importantly, was the issue of diversity and the representation of as many groups of people as possible. We found, not surprisingly, that many of the sports books leaned toward boys, but that there also was more material about and representation of girls than we had imagined.

As we reviewed the myriad books available for inclusion in our chapter, we also realized that there were some rather glaring omissions, and some areas in which books did not seem to be available. Hispanic/Latino people are severely underrepresented, except in the area of baseball. The representation of Native Americans is almost nonexistent, except for a biography of Jim Thorpe and a book on lacrosse. This is especially disturbing as Native American cultures have shared a number of games with the wider culture. In general we did not find enough books about games, and none that offered the history of many games. We found a few books that took an international approach, but again, not nearly enough. Furthermore, the sports books mostly were limited to mainstream and professional sports. We hope authors, illustrators, and publishers will provide more books on recreational sports such as watersports and winter sports. We were surprised to find next to nothing on horseback riding or roller skating. Finally we feel authors, illustrators, and publishers need to provide more picture books for young children that focus on simple games that can be played in pairs or small groups.

---

*The titles listed below each subheading are organized into Primary Reviews and Secondary Reviews. The Primary Reviews describe outstanding books in each subheading. The Secondary Reviews provide brief information about other books worthy of consideration. Some titles listed below are **not** reviewed in this chapter; entries for these titles are not annotated and contain only bibliographic information. In such cases, a cross reference to the annotated entry contained elsewhere in this volume is provided in boldface type at the end of the bibliographic information.*

Sports

Autobiographies

Primary Reviews

12.1 Lipinski, Tara, and Emily Costello (1997). **Tara Lipinski: Triumph on Ice: An Autobiography.** New York: Bantam. 116 pp. ISBN: 0-553-09775-X. Chapter Book.

This is a wonderful book written by a teenager particularly for teens. The collection of color photographs from Lipinski's infancy to her winning a world championship gold medal is not only fascinating, but has the potential to connect with the reader in ways that the text alone cannot. The story traces Lipinski's figure-skating career through a number of personal anecdotes. It also includes an introduction by Todd Eldredge, a list of important dates, a list of Lipinski's favorite things, a guide to scoring in figure skating, and a glossary of skating terms. One sixth grader commented, "I liked it very much because it told everything in her life and how she was nervous at the competition."

12.2 **Positively for Kids series.** Dallas, TX: Taylor.

Titles in this series include:

Pippen, Scottie, with Greg Brown (1996). **Scottie Pippen: Reach Higher.** Illustrated by Doug Keith. 40 pp. ISBN: 0-87833-981-7. Picture Book.

Rodriguez, Alex, with Greg Brown (1998). **Alex Rodriguez: Hit a Grand Slam!** Illustrated by Doug Keith. 40 pp. ISBN: 0-87833-997-3. Picture Book.

These are two of the books in one of the best sports autobiography or biography series available. These books contain the life stories of Scottie Pippen and Alex Rodriguez as told from their perspectives, along with anecdotes about them from family members, teammates, and friends. The stories are enhanced by photographs and wonderfully realistic paintings. Rodriguez's story is inspirational as well as informative. There are other athletes' life stories in this series, including Troy Aikman, Bonnie Blair, John Elway, Dan Marino, Cal Ripken, Kerri Strug, Sheryl Swoopes, Mo Vaughn, Kristi Yamaguchi, and Steve Young. These books would be excellent for students to use as models for their own autobiographies.

Biographies

Primary Reviews

12.3   Adler, David A. (1997). **Lou Gehrig: The Luckiest Man.** Illustrated by Terry Widener. San Diego: Gulliver. 32 pp. ISBN: 0-15-200523-4. Picture Book.

This is a stunningly told biography. The beautiful, golden acrylic paintings and the narrative are interwoven to present the essence of this real American hero. The book is an extraordinarily moving and inspiring biography that will have readers enthralled with Lou Gehrig and his spirit. This book could be used in many ways with students of all ages. For example, it would make an excellent read-aloud text as an introduction to a study of heroes.

12.4   Christopher, Matt. **Sports Biography series.** Boston: Little Brown.

Titles in this series include:

On the Court with . . . Andre Agassi (1997). 120 pp. ISBN: 0-316-14202-6. Chapter Book.

On the Field with . . . Emmitt Smith (1997). 118 pp. ISBN: 0-316-13722-7. Chapter Book.

On the Court with . . . Grant Hill (1996). 110 pp. ISBN: 0-316-13790-1. Chapter Book.

On the Mound with . . . Greg Maddux (1997). 121 pp. ISBN: 0-316-14191-7. Chapter Book.

On the Court with . . . Hakeem Olajuwon (1997). 111 pp. ISBN: 0-316-13721-9. Chapter Book.

At the Plate with . . . Ken Griffey, Jr. (1997). 121 pp. ISBN: 0-316-14233-6. Chapter Book.

At the Plate with . . . Mo Vaughn (1997). 113 pp. ISBN: 0-316-14192-5. Chapter Book.

On the Mound with . . . Randy Johnson (1998). 116 pp. ISBN: 0-316-14221-2. Chapter Book.

In the Huddle with . . . Steve Young (1996). 131 pp. ISBN: 0-316-13793-6. Chapter Book.

On the Course with . . . Tiger Woods (1998). 117 pp. ISBN: 0-316-13445-7. Chapter Book.

Christopher has a wealth of knowledge and experience when it comes to writing about sports. His most recent endeavor is a series of high-quality sports biographies in a market flooded with inferior-quality literature. These clearly written titles delve into the life of an athlete, starting with childhood. The short chapters center around a particular incident or issue in the athlete's life, reveal how they became interested in the sport, and show how hard work and perseverance made them stars. Descriptive highlights of key games add to the interest of the books. A series of photographs in the center of each book offers visual information to enhance the text.

12.5   Dingle, Derek T. (1998). **First in the Field: Baseball Hero Jackie Robinson.** New York: Hyperion Books for Children. 48 pp. ISBN: 0-7868-0348-7. Picture Book.

This book is written in chronological order and places Jackie Robinson squarely within a historical context that includes both the discrimination all African Americans faced during this time and the outbreak of World War II. Each chapter in the book describes a time in Jackie Robinson's life that coincides with a historical event. The story not only shares Robinson's life, but also describes those people he held as role models. The book contains a list of Milestones in Black Sports, and a selected bibliography of books, films and newsreels, and articles for further investigation. This is an excellent book for reluctant older readers as it has enough text to give interesting information and sufficient supporting material.

12.6 Engel, Trudie (1996). **We'll Never Forget You, Roberto Clemente.** New York: Scholastic. 108 pp. ISBN: 0-590-68881-2. Chapter Book.

A chapter book for young readers, this tribute to Roberto Clemente will captivate and inform. It includes a number of photographs as it follows Clemente from his childhood in Puerto Rico to his rise to prominence in the world of baseball with the Pittsburgh Pirates. The importance of his success is underscored by details such as the fact that, due to the poverty in which he lived, his first bat was a broomstick. The book includes a section entitled Baseball Basics, which defines many of the terms used in the book; a glossary for the Spanish words incorporated into the text; and a chart of Clemente's lifetime statistics.

12.7 Greenfield, Eloise (1997). **For the Love of the Game: Michael Jordan and Me.** Illustrated by Jan Spivey Gilchrist. New York: Harper-Collins. Unpaged. ISBN: 0-06-027298-8. Picture Book.

The boy and girl who narrate this story speak of Michael Jordan's desire to play basketball, as well as his seemingly innate abilities as an athlete. They then look to their own lives and consider what may lie ahead for them. Children are able to understand the poignant message that Greenfield and Gilchrist have communicated in this beautiful tribute to one of the most famous athletes of our time. Greenfield describes how Jordan would go up for a shot, and appear to be suspended in air. "He dreams he can fly, that he is an eagle," said Genell (age eight). A clear message is conveyed through simple prose and vibrant watercolor illustrations. "This book is telling us you have to believe in yourself. Don't believe in anything else. That's what Michael Jordan does," explained Connor (age six).

12.8 Krull, Kathleen (1996). **Wilma Unlimited: How Wilma Rudolph Became the World's Fastest Woman.** Illustrated by David Diaz. San Diego: Harcourt Brace. 32 pp. ISBN: 0-15-201267-2. Picture Book. (See **5.17**)

12.9 Krull, Kathleen (1997). **Lives of the Athletes: Thrills, Spills (and What the Neighbors Thought).** Illustrated by Kathryn Hewitt. San Diego: Harcourt Brace. 96 pp. ISBN: 0-15-200806-3. Chapter Book.

This book profiles twenty great athletes representing a variety of sports. The biographies are presented in chronological order by the birth of the fourteen men and six women who are included. These athletes are representative of a number of ethnic groups. Each story is told by detailing the pivotal events in the athlete's life. The biographies are each about three pages long, and may interest the reader enough to want to learn more about the athlete. The watercolor and colored-pencil illustrations are well-drawn caricatures that include details about aspects of the athlete's life. This would be a great book for upper-elementary students and beyond. It includes a selected bibliography of books for readers who want to find more information.

12.10 Leder, Jane (1996). **Grace and Glory: A Century of Women in the Olympics.** Chicago: Triumph. 102 pp. ISBN: 1-572443-116-4. Chapter Book.

A wonderful tribute to women who made great inroads and advancements in Olympic sports. This important book is arranged in chronological order, beginning with ancient times when women were excluded from sports and continuing to the present. It is fascinating to read about the myths and stereotypes about women who enjoyed participating in athletics and sports. These obscure heroines deserve much credit, for they confronted almost insurmountable prejudices and odds with courage and logic. These brave women led the way for the female athletes of today. We can now look back and find at last that their "grace and glory under pressure are valued and respected." The book is effectively illustrated with photographs, and is a book students may enjoy browsing through while picking and choosing from among the short, readable biographies.

12.11 Long, Barbara (1997). **Jim Thorpe: Legendary Athlete.** Springfield, NJ: Enslow. 128 pp. ISBN: 0-89490-865-0. Chapter Book.

This book is one of six titles in the Native American Biographies series. Jim Thorpe was a member of the Sac and Fox nations. Filled with photographs, the book portrays the life of Jim Thorpe from his birth in 1888 in Prague, Oklahoma, to his Olympic success in 1912. His life story is firmly located within a historical context, including a discussion of Thorpe's experiences at the Carlisle School, where in 1907 he was coached in football by "Pop" Warner. Many students will be able to identify with this name, as "Pop" Warner is the namesake of numerous local youth football leagues. This is a highly readable biography, and should raise a number of questions for the reader to pursue. As one sixth-grade student put it, "I liked it because it is about a legendary athlete."

Secondary Reviews

12.12 Christopher, Matt (1996). **Great Moments in Baseball History.** Boston: Little Brown. 104 pp. ISBN: 0-316-14130-5. Chapter Book.

This book is organized into nine chapters, each one focusing on the accomplishments of a particular player on a particular day during his career. Each chapter describes the event using a play-by-play style. For example, May 25, 1935, was the day that Babe Ruth hit a ball out of Forbes Field. No one had ever done that before. This book lends itself to dramatic renderings.

12.13 Christopher, Matt (1997). **Great Moments in Football History.** Boston: Little Brown. 89 pp. ISBN: 0-316-14196-8. Chapter Book.

This book consists of nine chapters, each focusing on a particular player at a particular moment in his career. Written in a play-by-play style, the book describes events in the careers of such players as Joe Namath, Walter Payton, Joe Montana, and Emmitt Smith. This book lends itself to dramatic renderings.

12.14 DuPlacey, James. **Hockey Superstars (NHL) series.** New York: Morrow Junior Books.

Titles in this series include:

Amazing Forwards (1996). 40 pp. ISBN: 0-688-15024-1. Picture Book.

Champion Defensemen (1997). 40 pp. ISBN: 0-688-15688-6. Picture Book.

Great Goalies (1996). 40 pp. ISBN: 0-688-15020-9. Picture Book.

Top Rookies (1996). 40 pp. ISBN: 0-688-15022-5. Picture Book.

Photographs abound in these books, and the text is biographical in nature and uses a basic and concise style. The biographies range in length from one paragraph to four or five, and highlight the history of and innovations in the respective positions presented in each text. These books glamorize the roughness of professional hockey to some degree. Appropriate for upper-elementary readers and beyond. This series is not very substantive, but might be used to hook reluctant readers and generate beginning interest.

12.15 Egan, Terry, Stan Friedman, and Mike Levine (1997). **The Good Guys of Baseball: Sixteen True Sports Stories.** New York: Simon & Schuster Books for Young Readers. 111 pp. ISBN: 0-689-80212-9. Chapter Book.

Although slim on illustrations and photographs, this book presents substantive biographies of baseball players who exemplify virtuosity and a strong work ethic. Some of the players depicted are not among the most famous or those with the most name recognition, which is what makes this book unique. The players were chosen for their contributions as role models. A wide range of ethnic groups is represented in the biographies, which run approximately ten pages in length. At the end of the book, there are references for further reading.

12.16 Gutman, Bill. **Millbrook Sports World series.** Brookfield, CT: Millbrook.

Titles in this series include:

Alonzo Mourning: Center of Attention (1997). 48 pp. ISBN: 0-7613-0061-9. Chapter Book.

Anfernee Hardaway: Super Guard (1997). 48 pp. ISBN: 0-7613-0062-7. Chapter Book.

Deion Sanders: Mr. Prime Time (1997). 48 pp. ISBN: 0-7613-0224-7. Chapter Book.

Grant Hill: Basketball's High Flier (1996). 48 pp. ISBN: 0-7613-0038-4. Chapter Book.

Scottie Pippen: The Do-Everything Superstar (1997). 48 pp. ISBN: 0-7613-0223-9. Chapter Book.

Steve Young: NFL Passing Wizard (1996). 48 pp. ISBN: 1-56294-184-4. Chapter Book.

This series would be very attractive to younger readers interested in famous athletes. One drawback to the series is that only one female athlete, tennis star Jennifer Capriati, is included in the twenty-one athletes profiled. The series as a whole highlights the accomplishments of numerous professional basketball, football, baseball, and hockey players. Although this series glorifies professional sports, the biographical nature of these books delves into the obstacles that the athletes had to overcome. The writing is engaging for readers with some prior knowledge of athletes and sports. The text is supported by captioned photographs. Each book ends with a list of career highlights, a Find out More section with a list of references and an address for writing to each athlete, and an index.

12.17 Lerner Sports Biographies series. Minneapolis: Lerner.

Titles in this series include:

Fehr, Kristin Smith (1997). **Monica Seles: Returning Champion.** 64 pp. ISBN: 0-8225-2899-1. Chapter Book.

Kramer, Barbara (1996). **Ken Griffey, Junior: All-Around All-Star.** 64 pp. ISBN: 08225-2887-8. Chapter Book.

Morgan, Terri (1997). **Junior Seau: High Voltage Linebacker.** 64 pp. ISBN: 0-8225-2896-7. Chapter Book.

Olney, Ross R. (1997). **Lyn St. James: Driven to be First.** 64 pp. ISBN: 0-8225-2890-8. Chapter Book.

Raber, Thomas R. (1997). **Michael Jordan: Basketball Skywalker.** 64 pp. ISBN: 0-8225-3654-4. Chapter Book.

Savage, Jeff (1997). **Andre Agassi: Reaching the Top—Again.** 64 pp. ISBN: 0-8225-2894-0. Chapter Book.

Savage, Jeff (1997). **Barry Bonds: Mr. Excitement.** 64 pp. ISBN: 0-225-2889-4. Chapter Book.

Savage, Jeff (1997). **Grant Hill: Humble Hotshot.** 64 pp. ISBN: 0-8225-2893-2. Chapter Book.

Savage, Jeff (1997). **Mike Piazza: Hard Hitting Catcher.** 64 pp. ISBN: 0-8225-2895-9. Chapter Book.

Savage, Jeff (1998). **Tiger Woods: King of the Course.** 64 pp. ISBN: 0-8225-3655-2. Chapter Book.

Schnakenberg, Robert (1997). **Scottie Pippen: Reluctant Super-star.** 64 pp. ISBN: 0-8225-3653-6. Chapter Book.

Thornley, Stew (1997). **Deion Sanders: Primetime Player.** 64 pp. ISBN: 0-8225-3658-7. Chapter Book.

Thornley, Stew (1997). **Emmitt Smith: Relentless Rusher.** 64 pp. ISBN: 0-8225-2897-5. Chapter Book.

Thornley, Stew (1997). **Frank Thomas: Baseball's Big Hurt.** 64 pp. ISBN: 0-8225-3651-X. Chapter Book.

Townsend, Brad (1997). **Anfernee Hardaway: Basketball's Lucky Penny.** 64 pp. ISBN: 0-8225-3652-8. Chapter Book.

This series highlights the lives and careers of notable male and female athletes in a variety of sports, from racing and tennis to football and basketball. The books provide interesting and intimate insights into the athletes profiled. For example, in *Monica Seles: Returning Champion,* we learn about the milestones in Seles' career as a young tennis star, as well as the views of her critics and supporters. The career decisions and professionalism of Junior Seau, one of the few great Samoan American football players, are highlighted in *Junior Seau: High Voltage Linebacker,* as are the problems Seau experienced with the SAT, his decision to leave college early, and the personal importance he places on his wife and child. *Lyn St. James: Driven to be First* investigates the life of this female pioneer in the sport of auto racing, and documents her struggles to overcome the traditional demands placed on her to be a lady. *Andre Agassi: Reaching the Top—Again* highlights the ups and downs of Agassi's career, from teen star to professional elite tennis player. It includes a discussion of his outcast image, and his banishment from Wimbledon for his wild hairstyle and colorful clothing. *Tiger Woods: King of the Course* describes the complexities of being an African American golf professional. Statements from his parents highlight his competitive spirit and drive at a young age. The books in the series include photographs, glossaries of sports-related terminology, career highlights, tables of contents, and indices, and some contain reference information for further research.

Information Books

Primary Reviews

12.18 Anderson, Dave. **The Story of . . . Sports series.** New York: Morrow Junior Books.

Titles in this series include:

The Story of Baseball (1997). 150 pp. ISBN: 0-688-143-164. Chapter Book.

The Story of Basketball (1997). 144 pp. ISBN: 0-688-14317-2. Chapter Book.

The Story of Football (1997). 160 pp. ISBN: 0-688-14315-6. Chapter Book.

The Story of Golf (1998). 159 pp. ISBN: 0-688-15797-1. Chapter Book.

Three sports of great interest and one of growing interest to most young Americans are well presented in these books. The information is divided into two parts. The first part covers the history of the sport; the second part covers specific skills and strategies of each sport. The text is lively, and one or two black-and-white photos appear on almost every double-page spread. Most of the photos are action shots. A glossary and index are included in each book. The revised editions of each of the first three titles listed provide up-to-date coverage of specific players and games. These books would be excellent resources for students who are working on an in-depth investigation of one of these sports.

12.19　Horenstein, Henry (1997). **Baseball in the Barrios.** San Diego: Gulliver. 36 pp. ISBN: 0-15-200499-8. Picture Book.

This book is a photo-essay narrated by a fifth-grade Venezuelan boy who loves to play baseball. He talks about his team, and how the game is played in the barrio. He also tells us what a barrio is, and talks about his daily life. The reader meets the members of his family as well. The text makes use of Spanish words and names. It should be of interest to and, at the same time broaden the scope of interest of, young baseball fans; it will be especially welcomed by Hispanic/Latino students. The color photographs are abundant and sharp. At the end of the book is a world map that shows the location of Venezuela. There is also a double-page spread of four categories of baseball terms in English and Spanish, with Spanish pronunciation in parentheses.

12.20　Hoyt-Goldsmith, Diane (1998). **Lacrosse: The National Game of the Iroquois.** Photographs by Lawrence Migdale. New York: Holiday House. 32 pp. ISBN: 0-8234-1360-8. Picture Book.

The gorgeous color photographs, along with two reprints of George Catlin pieces, support this narrative of a middle-school lacrosse player who plays for the Iroquois nation. The narrative includes the history of the game from its Native American origins to the present, the basic rules of the sport, and the skills involved in playing the game. This is a fantastic book for upper-elementary students and beyond, although the pictures and diagrams provide access for younger children as well. The book provides a strong multicultural emphasis. It is clearly written, and the information is easily accessible. The book includes an index and a glossary for easy reference.

12.21 Macy, Sue (1996). **Winning Ways: A Photohistory of American Women in Sports.** New York: Scholastic. 217 pp. ISBN: 0-590-76336-9. Chapter Book.

This is a chronological summary of women's accomplishments in athletics from the nineteenth century through 1995. The book traces the opportunities and obstacles women faced in becoming involved in various sports, including bicycling, horseracing, bodybuilding, soccer, and baseball. Filled with captioned individual and team photographs of the times, the book offers ready access to all students who are interested in this material. It includes reproductions of advertisements and postcards that demonstrate women's changing roles in sports. The author addresses society's views toward women in athletics, and highlights the individual accomplishments of standout female athletes. The book includes a chronology of firsts, records, and noteworthy events; resources for finding further information by topic; and an index.

12.22 Rafkin, Louise (1997). **The Tiger's Eye, the Bird's Fist: A Beginner's Guide to the Martial Arts.** Illustrated by Leslie McGrath. Boston: Little Brown. 133 pp. ISBN: 0-316-73464-0. Chapter Book.

Although there are a few photographs of people doing the martial arts, and there are drawings to support the historical narrative of the book, this is a text-based book. It describes the history, philosophy, legends, and stories of the martial arts, and shares the biographies of famous martial artists. With an emphasis on the philosophy (and in some instances, spirituality) of the martial arts, this book dispels popular misconceptions drawn from media and video games. The biographies help the reader to develop a contemporary context in which to explore the ancient histories of the marital arts. Probably appropriate for upper-elementary students and beyond, this book provides important background information for readers interested in the martial arts. This is an excellent guide and presents some interesting multicultural perspectives on Asian and Indonesian cultures. It includes a bibliography, references for further reading, a list of magazines for martial arts enthusiasts, a list of foundations and associations, and an index.

Secondary Reviews

12.23 Baddiel, Ivor (1998). **Soccer: The Ultimate World Cup Companion.** New York: Dorling Kindersley. 96 pp. ISBN: 0-7894-2795-8. Reference Book.

This book is an encyclopedia of soccer. With numerous photographs supporting the text, the book covers such topics as the history, rules, and techniques of the game; great stadiums; great teams; great players; and the history of the FIFA World Cup. The table of contents and the index offer easy reference for students who are looking for particular information. It is a very appealing and engaging text.

12.24 Brooks, Bruce (1997). **NBA by the Numbers.** Photographs by National Basketball Association. New York: Scholastic. 31 pp. ISBN: 0-590-97578-1. Picture Book.

Organized around flashy photos of NBA stars based on the numbers they wore, this book might be enjoyable for younger readers who have some knowledge of the game. The book discusses basic skills and plays in basketball, as well as highlighting major players both past and present. Although light on text, the text is fairly technical with respect to the game, and it is clear that the author expects prior knowledge on the part of the reader. The book is probably more interesting for the pictures than the text.

12.25 Cooper, Elisha (1998). **Ballpark.** New York: Greenwillow. 40 pp. ISBN: 0-688-15755-6. Picture Book.

This picture book details the behind-the-scenes happenings of a major league baseball stadium, from the laundry room to the groundskeeping. The author uses sparse text and a series of cartoonlike watercolor-and-pencil illustrations to describe the activities that occur in a baseball stadium in preparation for and during the game. The text is printed on the pages in ways that enhance, and almost become part of, the illustrations.

12.26 **Fundamental Sports series.** Minneapolis: Lerner.

Titles in this series include:

Klinzing, James, and Michael Klinzing (1996). **Fundamental Basketball.** Photographs by David Kyle and Andy King. 63 pp. ISBN: 0-8225-3458-4. Chapter Book.

Nitz, Kristin Wolden (1997). **Fundamental Softball.** Photographs by Andy King. 63 pp. ISBN: 0-8225-3460-6. Chapter book.

The two titles listed above are representative of the books in this series. The books are divided into six chapters, followed by a glossary, a bibliography for further reading, and an index. Photographs of athletes who participate in each sport help to demonstrate what is being explained or described in the text. The texts are equitable in relation to gender, with photos of both boys and girls throughout. There are eleven titles in this series, including books on baseball, golf, gymnastics, hockey, mountain biking, snowboarding, soccer, tennis, and volleyball. Julie Jensen has written a Beginning Sports series which she adapted from the books in the Fundamental Sports series. Both series use the same format.

> Jensen, Julie. **Beginning Sports series.** Minneapolis: Lerner.

12.27 Lee, Barbara (1996). **Working in Sports and Recreation.** Minneapolis: Lerner. 112 pp. ISBN: 0-8225-1762-0. Chapter Book.

This book profiles twelve people who are in careers related to sports and recreation, such as a college basketball coach, an athletic trainer, an activities director, and a sportswriter. A wide range of careers is portrayed, with supporting color photographs. This would make a great reference text for a survey of careers in sports and recreation. Anecdotal statements are the basis for the narrative about each career. The section on professional sports is particularly realistic in its focus. Boxed sections in each chapter describe the requirements that are needed to attain the career under discussion. Also included are a table of contents and an index.

12.28 Osborn, Kevin (1997). **Scholastic Encyclopedia of Sports in the United States.** New York: Scholastic. 220 pp. ISBN: 0-590-69264-X. Reference Book.

This book contains easy-to-read entries on a variety of athletes and athletic events in U.S. history from 1770 to 1996. It is organized chronologically. The index provides a handy reference for locating topics of interest. This book could provide students with an excellent resource for looking at sports happenings in relation to other historical events.

How-to Books

Primary Reviews

12.29 Blackstone, Margaret (1998). **This Is Figure Skating.** Illustrated by John O'Brien. New York: Henry Holt. 32 pp. ISBN: 0-8050-3706-3. Picture Book.

The cartoonlike illustrations demonstrate the simple, straightforward descriptions provided in the text. The book follows two girls as they walk to the ice-skating rink in the park, where they see experts doing the moves that are talked about in the text. For several of the moves, the reader also sees one or both of the girls trying the technique. Although the text is limited, it might be an excellent book for developing a beginning interest in ice-skating. As one sixth grader said, "I liked this book because I want to learn how to figure skate."

12.30 McFarlane, Brian (1996). **Hockey for Kids: Heroes, Tips, and Facts.** Illustrated by Bill Slavin. New York: Morrow Junior Books. 64 pp. ISBN: 0-688-15026-8. Picture Book.

Engaging photographs and illustrations support the descriptions of the basics of hockey—skills, rules, equipment, player biographies, and history. Packed with detailed facts about this game, which is enjoying a recent resurgence in popularity, this book is appropriate for upper-elementary students and beyond. This book even features a few pages on women's involvement in the sport, and several girls are depicted in the illustrations throughout the book. A great overview of the sport, this book would be a terrific place to start an inquiry into hockey. The book contains an index for easy reference.

12.31 **Young Enthusiast series.** New York: Dorling Kindersley.

Titles in this series include:

Edwards, Chris (1996). **The Young In-Line Skater.** 37 pp. ISBN: 0-7894-1124-5. Picture Book.

Iguchi, Bryan (1997). **The Young Snowboarder.** 37 pp. ISBN: 0-7894-2062-7. Picture Book.

Mitchell, David (1997). **The Young Martial Arts Enthusiast.** 65 pp. ISBN: 0-7894-1508-9. Picture Book.

Morrissey, Peter (1998). **The Young Ice Skater.** 37 pp. ISBN: 0-7894-2825-3. Picture Book.

Perez, Eduardo (1998). **The Young Baseball Player.** 37 pp. ISBN: 0-7894-2825-3. Picture Book.

The five books listed above are several of the titles in this excellent series aimed at the sports interests of elementary children. Each book in the series is written by a professional athlete in the sport being described. Each title combines high-quality, full-color photo-graphs and a supportive text that outlines the preparation for and execution of moves for each sport. The descriptions are clear and accurate, with step-by-step diagrams of children performing the skills. The children shown represent a variety of ethnic groups. An index, glossary, and useful addresses appear at the end of each book. One sixth grader who read *The Young Snowboarder* com-mented, "I liked the book because it was interesting and it teaches moves." Other subjects in the series include: basketball, dancing, gymnastics, horseback riding, soccer, swimming, tennis, and track and field.

Fiction and Poetry

Primary Reviews

12.32 Bruchac, Joseph (1996). **Children of the Longhouse.** New York: Dial Books for Young Readers. 150 pp. ISBN: 0-8037-1793-8. Chap-ter Book. (See **5.63**)

12.33 Bruchac, Joseph (1998). **The Heart of a Chief.** New York: Dial Books for Young Readers. 153 pp. ISBN: 0-8037-2276-1. Chapter Book. (See **5.37**)

12.34 Curtis, Gavin (1998). **The Bat Boy & His Violin.** Illustrated by E. B. Lewis. New York: Simon & Schuster. Unpaged. ISBN: 0-689-80099-1. Picture Book. (See **4.6**)

12.35 Hopkins, Lee Bennett, editor (1996). **Opening Days: Sports Poems.** Illustrated by Scott Medlock. San Diego: Harcourt Brace. 35 pp. ISBN: 0-15-200270-7. Picture Book. (See **10.17**)

Secondary Reviews

12.36 Brooks, Bruce. **The Wolfbay Wings series.** New York: Harper Trophy.

Titles in this series include:

#1 Woodsie (1997). 116 pp. ISBN: 0-06-027349-6. Chapter Book.

#2 Zip (1997). 106 pp. ISBN: 0-06-027350-X. Chapter Book.

#3 Cody (1997). 117 pp. ISBN: 0-06-027541-3. Chapter Book.

#4 Boot (1998). 122 pp. ISBN: 0-06-027569-3. Chapter Book.

#5 Prince (1998). 122 pp. ISBN: 0-06-027542-1. Chapter Book.

#6 Shark (1998). 118 pp. ISBN: 0-06-027570-7. Chapter Book.

#7 Billy (1998). 94 pp. ISBN: 0-06-027899-4. Chapter Book.

Each of these books centers around one player on the Wolfbay Wings hockey team. Using hockey as the focal point, each book in the series deals realistically with the problem of the title character and takes on a different issue and perspective. Play-by-play hockey action is included in each book, and the last few pages preview the next book in the series. This series is for upper-elementary and middle-school students.

12.37   Christopher, Matt. **Matt Christopher Sports Classics Series.** Boston: Little Brown.

Titles in this series include:

Baseball Turnaround (1997). 122 pp. ISBN: 0-316-14275-1. Chapter Book.

Penalty Shot (1997). 131 pp. ISBN: 0-316-13787-1. Chapter Book.

These books are representative of the stories in a series of sports novels for upper-elementary children written by Matt Christopher. Throughout the series, the protagonists are white males in grades 4 through 8. Usually the stories are set in a small town. The stories are well written for their genre, and while the focus is on the sport, there is always another issue involved, and the main character has learned a life lesson by book's end. Plenty of play-by-play sports action and emotion, along with sports talk and lingo, can be found in each story. These books have all the right ingredients to entice reluctant readers, including straightforward sentence structure, simple vocabulary, well-developed story, and a popular topic.

12.38   Christopher, Matt (1998). **The Dog That Called the Pitch.** Illustrated by Daniel Vasconcellos. New York: Little Brown. 38 pp. ISBN: 0-316-14207-7. Chapter Book.

This is one of a series of books by Matt Christopher that have The Dog as a main character. In this title, Mike and his dog Harry can read each other's minds. Mike is going to pitch at the Little League game that day, and wants his dad to help him practice. As they start to warm up, along comes Mr. Grimley, who is going to be the home-plate umpire for the game. Mr. Grimley, it turns out, can also read Mike's and Harry's thoughts. In the bottom of the eighth inning, Mike accidentally bumps into Mr. Grimley, whose glasses fall off and get stepped on. Harry saves the day by calling the pitches for Mr. Grimley. Much of the book reads like a play-by-play of the game, complemented by the pen-and-ink cartoon drawings. This early reader is another one of Matt Christopher's well-told sports stories, and will be of great interest to baseball fans. The team is made up of both boys and girls.

Other titles in this series include:

The Dog That Stole Home. (1996). 48 pp. ISBN: 0-316-14187-9. Chapter Book.

The Dog That Pitched a No-Hitter. (1993). 48 pp. ISBN: 0-316-14103-8. Chapter Book.

The Dog That Stole Football Plays. (1997). 48 pp. ISBN: 0-316-13423-6. Chapter Book.

The Dog That Called the Signals. (1982). 48 pp. ISBN: 0-316-13980-7. Chapter Book.

12.39 Costello, Emily (1998). **On the Sidelines.** New York: Skylark. 150 pp. ISBN: 0-553-48645-4. Chapter Book.

This book is the second title in Emily Costello's Soccer Stars series. It tells the story of eleven-year-old Fiona who loves soccer, but struggles with asthma and her parents' overprotectiveness. She is an excellent player who is important to her team. With the help of her coach and teammates, she works to figure out how to solve her health and family dilemmas. These books are endorsed by the American Youth Soccer Organization. At the end of each book, readers will find a list of AYSO soccer tips and a glossary of soccer terms.

Other titles in this series include:

#1 Foul Play. (1998). 144 pp. ISBN: 0-553-48644-6. Chapter Book.

#3 Against the Rules. (1998). ISBN: 0-553-48647-0. Chapter Book.

#4 Best Friend Face-off. (1998). 152 pp. ISBN: 0-553-48648-9. Chapter Book.

#5 Tournament Trouble. (1998). ISBN: 0-553-48649-7. Chapter Book.

#6 Lottery Blues. (1998). ISBN: 0-553-48648-9. Chapter Book.

12.40 Mackel, Kathy (1997). **A Season of Comebacks.** New York: Putnam. 116 pp. ISBN: 0-399-23026-2. Chapter Book. (See **5.104**)

Games

Primary Reviews

12.41 Cardo, Horacio (1998). **The Story of Chess.** New York: Abbeville. 48 pp. ISBN: 0-7892-0250-6. Picture Book.

This illustrated book offers a mythical look at the derivation of the game of chess. In so doing, it explains the pieces, the board, and some of the moves. It is a compelling introduction to chess that clearly exemplifies the complex strategies involved in playing the game. The full-color paintings, although fanciful and consistent with the mythological nature of the text, are also representative of the information presented. Cardo achieves a brilliant balance between the myth and the reality of the game. Many students who might not otherwise have shown an interest in chess may well be intrigued by this book and want to experiment with the game.

12.42 Erlbach, Arlene (1997). **Sidewalk Games around the World.** Illustrated by Sharon Lane Holm. Brookfield, CT: Millbrook. 64 pp. ISBN: 0-7613-0008-2. Picture Book.

Using an attractive, inviting, and easy-to-use format, this book introduces popular children's games from twenty-six different countries. Each game is described on a double-page spread introduced with a brief paragraph about the country. A world map on each double-page spread also shows the location of the country. Occasionally there is a language box with a pronunciation key of the terms (usually numbers) used by the children as they play the game. Each set of directions begins with the number of players, what they will need, and how to play. Directions for play are clear and easy-to-understand, and include useful illustrations. There is a broad representation of countries. Games are indexed by continent, age, indoors-outdoors, and number of players required. An extensive bibliography is included at the end. This would be an excellent book to use in a study of diversity.

12.43 Lankford, Mary D. (1996). **Jacks around the World.** Illustrated by Karen Dugan. New York: Morrow Junior Books. 40 pp. ISBN: 0-688-13708-3. Picture Book.

This book includes jacks games from fourteen countries. The book is organized into double-page spreads. The opening spread contains a map of the world with the continents in green and water in blue. The countries with jacks games that are represented in the text are numbered and shown in yellow. A corresponding list of the countries is given on the left-hand side of the double-page spread. The rest of the book has the text on the left-hand page, and a painting of children playing the game on the right. There are details in each illustration pertinent to the country being shown. The name of the game in the country being shown is also presented. For example, in South Korea the game is called *kong-keui,* and in Israel it is called *hamesh avanim.* The text gives a bit of history and background for each game, and then a numbered list of rules for play.

Secondary Reviews

12.44 Cole, Joanna, and Stephanie Calmenson (1998). **Marbles: 101 Ways to Play.** Illustrated by Alan Tiegreen. New York: Morrow Junior Books. 127 pp. ISBN: 0-688-12205-1. Chapter Book.

This book gives the history of the game of marbles, as well as basic how-to information and a myriad of games kids can play with marbles. One sixth grader said, "I bet a lot of kids would take it out and have a fun time with the marbles book." At the end of the book, there is a page listing other things that can be done with marbles, suggestions for starting a marble collection, and a glossary of the different kinds of marbles. The cartoonlike pen-and-ink drawings offer visual support for the directions and descriptions of both the marbles and how to play the various games.

12.45 Diagram Group (1998). **The Little Giant Encyclopedia of Games for One or Two.** New York: Sterling. 510 pp. ISBN: 0-8069-0981-1. Reference Book.

This book offers directions and supportive illustrations for over 130 games that can be played either alone or with one other person. It is divided into three sections. The first section contains games for one; the second section describes games for two; and the third section provides an index to all of the games discussed, organized by type of game (e.g., board games, card games, etc.). There is also an alphabetical index to all of the games.

12.46 Drake, Jane, and Ann Love (1998). **The Kids Campfire Book.** Illustrated by Heather Collins. Buffalo, NY: Kids Can. 128 pp. ISBN: 1-55074-454-2. Chapter Book.

This book offers information about a number of outdoor games and recreation activities. The writing is descriptive and detailed. Musical text and information for campers on nature and conservation techniques also are included. There are also recipes and directions for meals, as well as other things to make and do. This text would be excellent for supporting kids' preparations for a camping trip. The illustrations are pencil drawings. An index is included.

12.47 Drake, Jane, and Ann Love (1998). **The Kids Summer Games Book.** Illustrated by Heather Collins. Buffalo, NY: Kids Can. 176 pp. ISBN: 1-55074-469-0. Chapter Book.

A good reference book of card games and tricks, land and water outdoor activities, and games that simply require paper and pencil. This book would be a great resource for parents as well as teachers and students. The writing is descriptive and technical, but accessible to the interested reader.

Hobbies

Primary Reviews

12.48 Cole, Joanna, and Stephanie Calmenson (1997). **The Rain or Shine Activity Book: Fun Things to Make and Do.** Illustrated by Alan Tiegreen. New York: Morrow Junior Books. 192 pp. ISBN: 0-688-12131-4. Chapter Book.

This attractive and well-organized treasure trove of things to do will be useful to children, teachers, and parents. It has thirteen categories of activities, including card games, paper crafts, jump-rope rhymes, word games, magic tricks, and paper-and-pencil games, and lists ninety activities in all. The format is inviting, and the instructions are easy-to-follow. The illustrations include cartoonlike line drawings that add to the fun, and diagram drawings that support the directions. The book is entirely in black-and-white except for the titles, which are in red. This is a book that students easily could use independently.

12.49 Micklethwait, Lucy (1996). **A Child's Book of Play in Art: Great Pictures Great Fun.** New York: Dorling Kindersley. 45 pp. ISBN: 0-7894-1003-6. Picture Book. (See **11.55**)

12.50 The Most Excellent Book of . . . series. Brookfield, CT: Copper Beech.

Casey, Moe (1997). **The Most Excellent Book of Dress Up.** 32 pp. ISBN: 0-7613-0550-5. Picture Book.

Lincoln, Margaret (1997). **The Most Excellent Book of Face Painting.** 32 pp. ISBN: 0-7613-0551-3. Picture Book.

In each of the two books reviewed, clear step-by-step instructions are offered for creating the costumes and faces depicted in both drawings and photographs. These are books that upper-elementary children could use independently. Both books offer a table of contents and an index for easy reference. As one sixth grader explained, "I like the book because it has nice costumes and you can learn to make them." The first few pages of each book offer information about the origin of costumes and face painting, discussion of different materials to be used, safety tips, and general instructions. Each costume or face is then given in a double-page spread with instructions and accompanying illustrations and photographs.

12.51 Ross, Kathy (1997). **The Jewish Holiday Craft Book.** Illustrated by Melinda Levine. Brookfield, CT: Millbrook. 96 pp. ISBN: 0-7613-0055-4. Picture Book.

This book is organized by holidays. In the table of contents, each holiday is given with two to eight items to make listed underneath. The first page of each section explains the holiday, and then the purpose of each activity in relation to the celebration is explained. The illustrations offer clear support for the directions given in the text, and each craft item is depicted as it will look when fully constructed. The crafts range from very simple to fairly complex. This book invites an exploration of Judaism in a way that provides information and leads to many new questions as well.

12.52 Solá, Michéle (1997). **Angela Weaves a Dream: The Story of a Young Maya Artist.** Photographs by Jeffrey Jay Foxx. New York: Hyperion Books for Children. 47 pp. ISBN: 0-7868-0073-9. Picture Book. (See **11.38**)

12.53 Temko, Florence (1996). **Traditional Crafts from Mexico and Central America.** Illustrated by Randall Gooch. Photographs by Robert L. Wolfe and Diane Wolfe. Minneapolis: Lerner. 64 pp. ISBN: 0-8225-2935-1. Chapter Book. (See **11.38**)

12.54 Wilkes, Angela (1996). **Dazzling Disguises and Clever Costumes: More than 50 Step-by-Step Projects to Make, Paint, Sew, Prepare, and Wear.** New York: Dorling Kindersley. 48 pp. ISBN: 0-7894-1001-X. Picture Book. (See **11.34**)

12.55 Zanzarella, Marianne (1997). **The Good Housekeeping Illustrated Children's Cookbook.** Photographs by Tom Eckerle. New York: Morrow. 176 pp. ISBN: 0-688-13375-4. Reference Book.

This is a traditional recipe book for children. Some of the recipes are creative, but most are standard fare with common names. The directions are clear and attractively arranged. Most of the recipes will need adult supervision. Preparation time, degree of difficulty, number of servings, utensils, and ingredients are given first. Most recipes have only one photograph of the finished product, but the directions are detailed, clear, and easy-to-follow. There are photographs of children representing several ethnic groups throughout the book, but not in abundance. A chapter on the general aspects of cooking begins the book. The recipes are divided into standard but useful groupings: breakfasts, lunches, dinners, snacks, salads, side dishes, drinks, and desserts. At the end of the book, there is a glossary of cooking terms with thorough descriptions for each; an extensive picture-glossary of utensils; and an index. For easy reference, each section is color-coded. For instance, cooking basics and general information are coded in light blue, and breakfast in orange.

Secondary Reviews

12.56 Mayer, Marianna (1998). **The Mother Goose Cookbook: Rhymes and Recipes for the Very Young.** Illustrated by Carol Schwartz. New York: Morrow Junior Books. 37 pp. ISBN: 0-688-15242-2. Picture Book.

The rhyme is on the left-hand page surrounded by a full-color illustration done in gouache and airbrush, and the recipe is on the right. The recipe directions are written in a way that includes rebus-like drawings between the sentences to reinforce the ingredients needed for each step. This is a book that would be fun for young children to use to choose recipes, but the actual preparation would need adult assistance and supervision.

12.57 Ross, Kathy. **Crafts for Kids Who Are Wild About . . . series.** Illustrated by Sharon Lane Holm. Brookfield, CT: Millbrook.

Titles in this series include:

Crafts for Kids Who Are Wild About Dinosaurs (1997). 48 pp. ISBN: 0-7613-0053-8. Picture Book.

Crafts for Kids Who Are Wild About Outer Space (1997). 48 pp. ISBN: 0-7613-0054-6. Picture Book.

Crafts for Kids Who Are Wild About Rainforests (1997). 48 pp. ISBN: 0-7613-0117-8. Picture Book.

These attractive books could be used as much by teachers as by students. The format is inviting and well organized, but the directions for most of the projects are lengthy and detailed. Kids will enjoy making most of the items, but they will need adult or teacher guidance. The topics all have child appeal and could be incorporated easily into units on the topic. Twenty projects are included in . . . *Dinosaurs* and . . . *Outer Space;* thirteen projects are included in . . . *Rainforests.*

12.58 Temko, Florence. **Paper Magic series.** Brookfield, CT: Millbrook.

Titles in this series include:

Animals and Birds (1996). 48 pp. ISBN: 0-7613-0070-6. Picture Book.

Planes and Other Things (1996). 48 pp. ISBN: 0-7613-0041-4. Picture Book.

Paper Gifts and Jewelry (1997). 48 pp. ISBN: 0-7613-0209-3. Picture Book.

Paper Tags and Cards (1997). 48 pp. ISBN: 0-7613-0210-7. Picture Book.

In each book, the full-color illustrations show clearly how to follow the concise and straightforward directions. Each activity is labeled in the table of contents as to its level of difficulty. Three levels are included: easy, you-can-do-it, and expert. Also included are an introduction, a key to the symbols used in the illustrations, and an explanation of the paper and supplies needed to complete each project.

A.

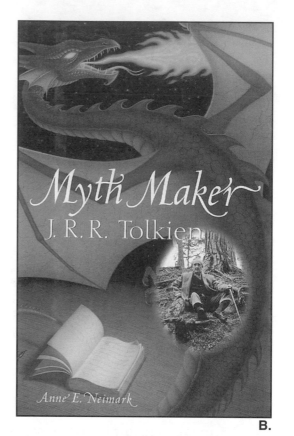

B.

C.

A. *Bless Us All: A Child's Yearbook of Blessings,* Cynthia Rylant (**13.8**). **B.** *Myth Maker: J. R. R. Tolkien,* Anne E. Neimark (**13.47**). **C.** *To Every Thing There Is a Season,* Leo & Diane Dillon (**13.28**).

13 The Craft of Language: Passages, Profiles, and Puzzles

Kathleen Marie Crawford

M. Ruth Davenport

Contributing reviewers included Kathleen Marie Crawford, M. Ruth Davenport, Mary L. Diener, Jill M. Hartke, Lynda S. Hootman, Angela Humphrey, Joyce Madsen, Elizabeth Mena, Pat Pearman, Laurie Reddy, and Jennifer L. Wilson.

The craft of language is important because it draws children into the shared cultural bond that unites us all as people. We support children by helping them become literate and helping them learn the stories that make us who we are. As readers, children can learn to appreciate an exciting beginning, an intriguing tale, a surprising twist of plot, and an unexpected ending. A poignant scene can be relived again and again, just as an unforgettable character stays in our hearts forever. A well-written caper can still make us chuckle, long after the book has been closed. As writers, children can develop a critical eye for the literary craft. They can come to appreciate how a single word can change the reader's mental image, or a single phrase can make the difference between a ho-hum story and a memorable plot. Guided by strong writing mentors, children can learn to fall in love with language, and gain the skill to use the right amount of detail, create dynamic tension, and develop memorable characters.

This chapter reviews books in five major categories: Lovely Language; Language Play; Riddles, Chants, and Poems; Biographies and Autobiographies (of Authors, Books, and Characters); and Mysteries. The books we selected for the section entitled Lovely Language include those in which the author presented "beautiful writing, truly original language, images that make you sit up straight when you're reading" (Fletcher 1993, 139). Lovely Language includes books such as *Daddy Calls Me Man* (Johnson 1997), in which the words of the story playfully dance across the pages. We wanted to share books in which the language would be so memorable that when children read them, the books would "simply take their breath away" (Harwayne 1992, 13). Through a beautiful text such as *My Mama Had a Dancing Heart* (Gray 1995), we see that one way of connecting to books is to find ourselves in passages that present stunning, startling language that gives "the reader a dazzling jolt of recognition" (Fletcher 1993, 147). We wanted to share with children "books that highlight the richness of the English language and . . . celebrate unusual words" (Harwayne 1992, 12).

Books in the section entitled Language Play look at the light-hearted side of the literary craft, such as the use of alliteration and the mischievous joy of simply toying with words. Not only will children learn that language is something malleable and pliant, but also that it is something that can bring great joy. By manipulating and playing with words and phrases, children gain control over language in a way that empowers them to take risks and become inventive. Children enjoy reading these playful texts, and trying out new possibilities by combining the different meanings and sounds of words. Like the girl in *Double Trouble in Walla Walla* (Clements 1997), they get carried away with linguistic pranks. Harwayne (1992) recognizes that "playfulness with words, ideas, and design will come in handy when these young writers begin to generate topics, shape texts, and revise drafts" (12).

The third section is Riddles, Chants, and Poems. Each of these styles of writing uses the craft of language to illuminate an everyday occurrence in a unique manner. Here we review the beautiful words of Nikki Grimes telling us about the love of children's laughter, and Steptoe's artistic celebration of African American fathers through the eyes of several poets. In addition to the hand-clapping rhymes, tongue-twisters, and ridiculous riddles, we share the timeless *To Every Thing There Is a Season* (Dillon and Dillon 1998), accompanied by the Dillons' sumptuous illustrations in a variety of styles. We chose books in this area that would give children the enjoyment of solving brain-teasers, the amusement of skipping to childhood chants, and the delight of reflecting on their lives through exquisite poetry. We agree with Huck et al. (1997), who state, "There is an elusiveness about poetry that makes it defy precise definition. It is not so much what it is that is important, as how it makes us feel" (390).

In the section entitled Biographies and Autobiographies, we explore a wide range of noted writers. Vignettes of George Ella Lyon's life as a child are compared to her life today to create a sense of autobiography in *A Sign* (Lyon 1998). By exploring the lives of authors such as Stevenson, London, and Tolkien, we examine the craft of language and learn how they came to love words themselves. One book in this section is the "biography" of a much-loved children's book, *Goodnight Moon* (Brown 1947). while another presents the autobiography of a famed book character, Strega Nona.

Authors of mysteries and detective stories deliberately use language to "play" with readers' predictions and their inclination to seek patterns and explanations. By leaving a part of the story untold until the end, these writers invite readers to draw on their own life experiences and the clues in the text to propose a story that can explain all the pieces.

In the section entitled Mysteries, there is something for readers of every age. From an *Arthur* story to books for more mature students, there is a mystery here that will capture readers' imaginations. With young main characters who face issues as diverse as witnessing a kidnapping, losing a parent, living with a Native American tribe, and discovering a mute stranger in the barn, readers will be captivated by these intriguing mysteries.

We want children to attend to the craft of language in order to appreciate and honor lovely language and the masterful wielding of the literary craft. We want them to value having fun with language and to "know that people play with language" (Harwayne 1992, 12). We share books filled with riddles, chants, and poems to communicate our enjoyment and enthusiasm for rhythm and the lilt of language. Through biographies, children can appreciate a particular talent with language as writers tell the story of a life well lived. Mystery writers display a unique mastery of the skill of weaving together specific detail, charismatic characters, and tension through unforgettable language (Fletcher 1993). Join us now as we adventure with words and lovely language, explore interesting lives through biographies, and are spellbound by these irresistible mysteries!

Works Cited

Fletcher, Ralph. 1993. *What a Writer Needs*. Portsmouth, NH: Heinemann.

Harwayne, Shelley. 1992. *Lasting Impressions: Weaving Literature into the Writing Workshop*. Portsmouth, NH: Heinemann.

Huck, Charlotte, Susan Hepler, Janet Hickman, and Barbara Z. Kiefer. 1997. *Children's Literature in the Elementary School*. 6th ed. Madison, WI: Brown & Benchmark.

---

*The titles listed below each subheading are organized into Primary Reviews and Secondary Reviews. The Primary Reviews describe outstanding books in each subheading. The Secondary Reviews provide brief information about other books worthy of consideration. Some titles listed below are **not** reviewed in this chapter;*

entries for these titles are not annotated and contain only bibliographic informa-
tion. In such cases, a cross reference to the annotated entry contained elsewhere
in this volume is provided in boldface type at the end of the bibliographic infor-
mation.

Lovely Language

Primary Reviews

13.1   Bauer, Marion Dane (1997). **If You Were Born a Kitten.** Illustrated by JoEllen McAllister Stammen. New York: Simon & Schuster Books for Young Readers. Unpaged. ISBN: 0-689-80111-4. Picture Book.

With a gently flowing text, Bauer celebrates the miracle of birth. By sharing in the experiences of twelve different animals nuzzling their caring mothers (or seahorse father!), we see how each is nurtured as a newborn. The lovely language delights the reader through alliteration and repeated words. Bauer captures the movements, sounds, and features of these varied creatures, showing a common bond of universal love between parent and offspring. There is a tenderness here children will be drawn to, from the furry sleeping mama bear to the baby elephant sucking his trunk. Stammen's illustrations in dry pastel evoke the warmth and cuddling of each family in exquisite detail. This is a delightful text that ends with the welcome of a newborn child after he has been floating in a salty sea, "waiting for us who were waiting for you." Join Bauer and Stammen as they commemorate the fascination and wonder of bearing young.

13.2   Brook, Donna (1998). **The Journey of English.** Illustrated by Jean Day Zallinger. New York: Clarion. 48 pp. ISBN: 0-395-71211-4. Chapter Book.

This is a fascinating, informative history of English. The book begins with an explanation of the extent to which English is used throughout the world, and continues with a look at the language's origins. Beginning with the year 2000 B.C.E. and continuing to modern times, the evolutions and journeys of the English language are traced through wars, conquered empires, slavery, marriages between countries, and much more to show the trading of words and meanings. The discussions of changes and additions are followed by examples of words and phrases currently used in modern English. The book ends with an interesting look at dialect and the speculation that one day England's English and the

United States' English may become two completely different languages. Included at the end is a page about the origin of dictionaries, as well as a resource page on Clues to Word Origin. These pages offer references for additional independent word study.

13.3 Desimini, Lisa, David Ricceri, Sara Schwartz, and Dan Yaccarino (1997). **All Year Round: A Book to Benefit Children in Need.** New York: Scholastic. Unpaged. ISBN: 0-590-36097-3. Picture Book.

In this rhyming picture book, four artists combine their creative talents to illustrate and playfully sprinkle words to depict the passing of time through four seasons. Rainbow-colored snowmen welcome winter with a "frosty party" for their winter friends. Signalled by a patch of green grass peeking through the snow, spring is introduced with a gentle rain shower as birds sing and flowering meadows reappear along a muddy, puddled path. Cleverly chosen rhyming words transport the reader to summer, as the authors show readers a dazzling orange sun shining on beaches filled with children enjoying ice-cream treats, and high waves splashing against the sandy shores. Gray clouds, along with the call of a large black crow flying across the wind-swept sky, usher in fall. Huge piles of brightly colored leaves cover two boys so just their eyes peer above their leafy hiding place. A bright harvest moon reveals scarecrows on hills, waiting patiently "for the seasons to come around again." Through response writings, this story evoked in seven- and eight-year-old children memories about the fun times they spent with their families through the passing seasons of their lives. The Robin Hood Foundation, which serves children in need, will receive a portion of the proceeds of this book to distribute to nonprofit organizations that help families all year round.

13.4 Faulkner, Keith (1996). **The Wide-Mouthed Frog.** Illustrated by Jonathan Lambert. New York: Dial. Unpaged. ISBN: 0-8037-1875-6. Picture Book.

Young children will be amused by this playful tale of a curious frog who keeps asking other creatures he encounters what they like to eat—that is, until he stumbles upon an alligator who eats wide-mouthed frogs! In this silly repetitive story, the mouths of all the animals pop up at the reader and invite interaction with the text. Readers will delight in imitating the shapes of the different mouths as they follow the frog through his escapades in different animals' habitats.

13.5 Fox, Mem (1997). **Whoever You Are.** Illustrated by Leslie Straub. San Diego: Harcourt Brace. Unpaged. ISBN: 0-15-200-787-3. Picture Book. (See **8.9**)

13.6 Gray, Libba Moore (1995). **My Mama Had a Dancing Heart.** Illustrated by Raúl Colón. Unpaged. New York: Orchard. ISBN: 0-531-08770-0. Picture Book.

In this tribute to the beauties of nature and to each other's company, mother and daughter take delight in the sights, sounds, tastes, and ballets of each season. Celebrating a "tip-tapping, song-singing, finger-snapping kind of day," they dance a welcome to the spring rain, summer waves, autumn winds, and winter snows. With a masterful hand, Gray crafts a playful dance with words that portrays the magical encounter with each season these two characters share. Colón's soft, distinctive style perfectly echoes the ethereal, luscious, joyful text. The inspiration of these "hello" ballets stays with the daughter as she feather-floats down on stage as a professional ballerina. An unforgettable lovely language book.

13.7 Johnson, Angela (1997). **Daddy Calls Me Man.** Illustrated by Rhonda Mitchell. New York: Orchard. Unpaged. ISBN: 0-531-30042-0. Picture Book. (See **4.11**)

13.8 Rylant, Cynthia (1998). **Bless Us All: A Child's Yearbook of Blessings.** New York: Simon & Schuster. Unpaged. ISBN: 0-689-82370-3. Picture Book.

Rylant has done it again! With each unique book, she surprises and delights us with her diversity of styles and talents as a weaver of words. In this book of monthly devotions, we also are treated to her folk art: illustrations that show the passing of time, surrounded by quilt squares. The rolling text gives us all gentle reminders of the simple wonders that surround us through the rhythm of the year. This lovely language book offers new insights into Rylant's love of animals, appreciation of family, and awareness of common beauty. Her craft as an author is unmistakable as each word, carefully selected and placed, allows her tribute to unfold across each month.

13.9 Schnur, Steven (1997). **Autumn: An Alphabet Acrostic.** Illustrated by Leslie Evans. New York: Clarion. Unpaged. ISBN: 0-395-77043-2. Picture Book.

In this lovely language text, Schnur cleverly embraces the harvest season with delightful wordplay that presents the serenity and subtle wonders of fall. Each page dances the reader through the alphabet with familiar words that depict the memories of family gatherings, the coziness of fireplaces, the warmth of stacked-high quilts, the bounty of the harvest, the crisp cold air, and frost on window panes. The flawless craftship of Evans' linoleum-cut illustrations helps to extend and illuminate the fullness of autumn. "Oooh," exclaimed Brett (age seven), "I wish I could write a book like that. It makes me feel warm and cozy. Fall is my favorite season of the year." Readers of all ages will appreciate the warm words that build the traditional relationships that autumn brings to Earth. An added delight is the acrostic poem that results from the first letter of each line.

13.10 Young, Ed (1997). **Voices of the Heart.** New York: Scholastic. Unpaged. ISBN: 0-590-50199-2. Picture Book. (See **11.40**)

Language Play

Primary Reviews

13.11 Barrett, Judi (1998). **Things That Are Most in the World.** Illustrated by John Nickle. New York: Antheneum. Unpaged. ISBN: 0-689-81333-3. Picture Book.

Children often ask, "What is a superlative?" The answer to this question can be found in this brilliantly colorful and imaginative book. Each page is dedicated to a superlative, taking the reader from what are the silliest to the smelliest to the wiggliest things in the world. Children of all ages will be inspired to create their own renditions of what is the most in the world.

13.12 Clements, Andrew (1997). **Double Trouble in Walla Walla.** Illustrated by Sal Murdocca. Brookfield, CT: Millbrook. Unpaged. ISBN: 0-7613-0306-5. Picture Book.

Everyone has had a day when they have been tongue-tied and the words just won't come out right. In Clements' delightful text, little Lulu finds herself in exactly this situation in her school classroom. Realizing her homework is a mess, she raises her hand in class and says, "Mrs. Bell, I feel like a nit-wit. My homework is all higgledy-piggledy. Last night it was in tip-top shape, but now it's a big mish-mash." From that point on, Lulu infects the whole school, including the principal, with her rhyming lingo. Just when Walla Walla school thinks it can no longer speak English, the school nurse comes to the rescue and puts everything straight again. Large, brilliant illustrations bring to life the hysterical situations. Michael and Courtney shared that reading this funny book is like reading pages of tongue-twisters. Readers of all ages surely will read this story several times, as those tongue-twisters are truly tricky!

13.13 Edwards, Pamela Duncan (1996). **Some Smug Slug.** Illustrated by Henry Cole. New York: HarperCollins. 32 pp. ISBN: 0-06-024789-4. Picture Book.

With a swagger, a slug slithers up a highly sinister slope. The sparrow, the spider, and the swallowtail are simply trying to save him by screaming at this slug. But the smug slug shambles on. It showed no suspicion "until something shifted, and shuddered and shook." This creative alliteration talk will have children snorting themselves silly at the surprise ending for this very smug slug! The realistic paintings on each page give you a "slug's-eye view" of life at ground level.

13.14 Heller, Ruth (1997). **Mine, All Mine: A Book about Pronouns.** New York: Grosset & Dunlap. Unpaged. ISBN: 0-448-41606-9. Picture Book.

Heller has colorfully added to her collection of acclaimed books about the English language. *Mine, All Mine* highlights pronouns and what our whimsical language would be like without them. Melanie (age eight) commented after her teacher shared the book during Writing Workshop, "I love the illustrations so much I want to take them home with me and keep them forever." As always, Heller provides the reader with gay and richly colored illustrations that capture the imagination and remind us how much fun language really can be.

Secondary Reviews

13.15 Cyrus, Kurt (1997). **Tangle Town.** New York: Farrar, Straus and Giroux. Unpaged. ISBN: 0-374-37384-1. Picture Book.

This story plays on children's love of all things silly. After the first few pages Genell (age eight) said, "Teacher, this is a silly, flip-flop story." The story begins when the mayor gets locked in his office.

He says "I'm getting blisters!" to a passing policeman, who tells a man "We need blasters!" and the pandemonium begins. "This whole town forgot to listen" said Angie (age six). A young girl named Roxy goes to town looking for her escaped cow, and sees the tangled-up mess. She takes charge and sets things right again. After hearing this story, Filemon (age seven) said, "This sure was a tangled tale."

13.16 Falwell, Cathryn (1998). **Word Wizard.** New York: Clarion. 32 pp. ISBN: 0-395-85580-2. Picture Book.

Anna is eating her cereal one morning when she notices the letters on her spoon spell "DAWN." These letters float around and become the word "WAND." Anna begins to find many words and rearranges their letters to make new words. She meets a sad boy named Zack, and with her magic wand helps him find his home, changing words along the way. Each time the two encounter a problem on their journey, Anna waves her wand and changes the problem into a solution. The illustrations are bright and inviting, made from a mixture of cut-paper collage, rubber-stamp prints, and watercolors. The final page of the book is an idea page that suggests ways readers can become word wizards. "This book makes me think of words" said Angie (age six). "There were tons of words in this book" said Clint (age six).

13.17 Grover, Max (1997). **Max's Wacky Taxi Day.** San Diego: Harcourt Brace. Unpaged. ISBN: 0-15-20098-9-2. Picture Book.

This delightful book is a must for the teacher who is exploring the multiple meanings of words in our language. Grover, an artist since childhood, has used brilliant acrylic colors to create illustrations that stimulate the eyes as well as the mind. Children will be amused by the verbal and visual puns as Max, the taxi driver, takes them along in his wacky taxi. Lily (age seven) giggled when she noticed that in order to "train" Hector the dog to be a better passenger in the taxi, Max put him on a train! Another group of children observed that the train was already filled with a menagerie of other animals in need of obedience training. The reader encounters these and similar absurdities created by the literal interpretations of language. Caleb (age eight) thought "the book was so funny that it reminded me of the silly times that I have with my best friend." The entertaining use of language is combined with wacky illustrations, such as the one depicting the harried Ms. Hastings. Fearing she will be late for a meeting, she laments that everyone else has a car phone (a car shaped like a phone). Students will enjoy composing their own visual and verbal puns as they explore language.

13.18 Most, Bernard (1998). **A Pair of Protoceratops.** San Diego: Harcourt Brace. Unpaged. ISBN: 0-15-201443-8. Picture Book.

Author Bernard Most toys with alliteration and delights the imagination of every child in this charming story about two mischievous protoceratop youngsters. Students will identify with the "pair of protoceratops" as they paste paper, practice their penship, ponder over puzzles, pack plastic pails, party in the park, plunge into pools, and play ping-pong. A group of second graders were reminded of their own experiences as they read about the protoceratop pair "pestering papa." Derek (age eight) stated that the protoceratops remind him of his twin cousins, who often get into trouble. Travis (age eight) remembered a time he was punished for "pestering" someone. Like the characters in the story, he had to do some extra chores to atone for his misbehavior. Most's enchanting illustrations and tantalizing text make this book a model of alliteration and a platform for a discussion about the consequences of misbehavior.

13.19 Most, Bernard (1998). **A Trio of Triceratops.** San Diego: Harcourt Brace. Unpaged. ISBN: 0-15-201448-9. Picture Book.

In this companion book to *A Pair of Protoceratops,* an adorable trio of triceratops youngsters try on trousers, taste tangerines, tangle tails, take turns on the teeter-totter, and toot trumpets. Matthew (age eight) thought the book was funny and liked the playful trio. Second grader Brian (age eight) noticed that the trio were troublemakers as they tickled turkeys, terrified turtles, and teased a tyrannosaurus. Andrew (age eight) liked the way Most illustrated the trio. Most's pictures are delightful, and Whitney (age eight) noticed that the numbers *1, 2,* and *3* always are included. Her favorite illustration was the trio of triceratops tanning in the tropics. The intricacies of the illustrations and the alliteration in the text invite the reader to linger and appreciate this charming book.

13.20 Nikola-Lisa, W. (1997). **Tangle Talk.** Illustrated by Jessica Clerk. New York: Dutton. Unpaged. ISBN: 0-525-45399-7. Picture Book.

This humorous book tells of strange events in a topsy-turvy world, while having fun with language. Nikola-Lisa uses simple but tickling language to unfold a story based on an old children's verse from England. It is the story of a gentleman who goes for a stroll through the "wonderful city of May in the month of Boston" and soon realizes that things are "upside down." Most interesting is the way the story ends—just as it begins. Clerk depicts the whimsical rhyming text in a way that immediately draws the attention of the reader. Young readers will surely find this story to be a great way of inventing their own topsy-turvy language!

13.21 Older, Jules (1997). **Cow.** Illustrated by Lyn Severance. Watertown, MA: Charlesbridge. Unpaged. ISBN: 0-88106-957-4. Picture Book.

If you are curious about cows, this is the book for you! Numerous cow facts are revealed throughout this book in a very humorous way. Where do various types of cows come from? What do cows provide for us? How do they survive? The author has a unique way of presenting this information, and in the end makes this non-fiction piece very entertaining. "I loved it because the book was sarcastic and factual at the same time," said Kristin (age eleven). This book also opens up many topics for discussion. "Nobody cares what color a cow is. Why do some care about people's colors?" questioned Tim (age eleven). Not only do students learn facts about cows, but they also are entertained by the pictures on every page. There are many inquiries within science, history, and language arts in this book, which makes it a wonderful teaching tool.

13.22 Pandell, Karen (1996). **Animal Action ABC.** Photographs by Art Wolfe and Nancy Sheehan. New York: Dutton. Unpaged. ISBN: 0-525-45486-1. Picture Book.

This gorgeous alphabet story will hold the interest of even the youngest children. Wolfe has taken close-up photographs of animals in their natural habitat, and Sheehan has taken photographs of children acting like the animals in the photographs. Children feel compelled to identify and mimic the animals' actions. "They want us to act this story out. Let me show you how," said Genell (age eight). Pandell has written a poem to accompany each set of photographs. The alphabet is woven throughout, not by naming the animals, but by identifying the actions in the photographs. A great book to launch a discussion of the language of verbs!

13.23 Root, Phyllis (1996). **Aunt Nancy and Old Man Trouble.** Illustrated by David Parkins. Cambridge, MA: Candlewick. Unpaged. ISBN: 1-56402-3478. Picture Book.

Aunt Nancy doesn't like it when Old Man Trouble shows up because things just don't seem to go her way. Old Man Trouble loves to visit Aunt Nancy, and takes delight in the accidents he causes her. Finally, Aunt Nancy decides to give Old Man Trouble a taste of his own medicine by pretending she likes it when Old Man Trouble smirks at her wrongdoings. Aunt Nancy finally gets even with Old Man Trouble. Children enjoy the irony of the two different perspectives on the same event. The use of dialect makes the language interesting. "I like it when Aunt Nancy would stay happy and act like everything bad was good. She sure tricked him," said Adam (age eight).

13.24 Rosenberg, Liz (1997). **A Big and Little Alphabet.** Illustrated by Vera Rosenberry. New York: Orchard. Unpaged. ISBN: 0-531-30050-1. Picture Book.

This elegantly illustrated alphabet book is tailor-made for lovers of picture books. The antics of the wild collection of creatures invite the reader to explore each page to discover their actions as they romp through the alphabet. The alliteration explosions will delight the reader. Krystal (age eight) noticed that the big and little alphabet letters were illustrated by "a zoo" of creatures that were doing things that began with the letter on the page. Rosenberg's fanciful illustrations encourage prediction and discussion as readers make their way from armadillos aiming arrows to zebras with zippers catching zzz's. This book is an excellent resource to help students become aware of the sounds of letters, as well as discover the use of verbs. Students will delight in choosing an alphabet letter and creating their own playful possibilities.

13.25 Speed, Toby (1995). **Two Cool Cows.** Illustrated by Barry Root. New York: Putnam. Unpaged. ISBN: 0-399-22647-8. Picture Book.

Readers will howl at the antics of these "two cool, too cool cows," as they steal boots from the Huckabuck kids, travel to the mountaintop of Hillimadoon, and (in search of greener pastures) venture to the far side of the moon. After a rollicking picnic in the craters with their cousins, the wayward cool cows return to earth, give back the boots, and head for the Huckabuck farm. Through rhyming, lilting text, Speed takes us on a roller coaster ride of fun language and cow capers. See what really happened when the cow jumped over the moon!

13.26 Vail, Rachel (1998). **Over the Moon.** Illustrated by Scott Nash. New York: Orchard. Unpaged. ISBN: 0-531-33068-0. Picture Book.

Get ready for a rollicking ride through repeated takes at a theater rehearsal as animals attempt to enact the familiar nursery rhyme. The set includes backdrops, prop assistants, stagehands, makeup artists and reviewers with notebooks. This whimsical rendition will split your seams as Broadway-style director Mr. Hi Diddle Diddle tries to direct the cow, little dog, and cat (playing a Stradivarius, of course!) in the infamous jumping-over-the-moon scene. Kids will be tickled by Vail's playful toying with prepositions as the cow just can't seem to get OVER the moon, but succeeds in going under, next to, and through the moon backdrop! Here is great fun through language play, as we get an alternative perspective on these familiar characters, including a cameo appearance by the dish and spoon. Nash's illustrations give the book a cartoonlike feel that adds a comical touch to the hysterical rapid-fire dialogue. Enjoy!

13.27 Wilbur, Richard (1998). **The Disappearing Alphabet.** Illustrated by David Diaz. San Diego: Harcourt Brace. Unpaged. ISBN: 0-15-201470-5. Picture Book.

What would we do without a *Q?* Could we get by without a *Y?* Wilbur's poetic questions and humorous speculations are delightfully portrayed in Díaz's stylized silhouettes. Students will have great fun thinking of their own potential linguistic dilemmas as they play with this fun look at the important role of each letter in the alphabet. Different fonts and words in capital letters help the reader find Wilbur's zany examples of life without each letter. A wonderful addition to any collection of ABC books that helps us appreciate the letters and wonder what we might do without them!

Riddles, Chants, and Poems

See also the section entitled Rhythm, Rhyme, and Repetition in chapter 7, "Literacy"; chapter 10, "Poetry"; and the section entitled Music Books: Rhymes, Chants, and Songs in chapter 11, "Fine Arts."

Primary Reviews

13.28 Dillon, Leo, and Diane Dillon (1998). **To Every Thing There Is a Season.** New York: Scholastic. Unpaged. ISBN: 0-590-47887-7. Picture Book.

For thousands of years, the words of this picture book have served as inspiration, hope, and comfort to millions around the world. With the Biblical text adapted slightly for younger readers, this timeless message is accessible to all. These famous verses encompass a range of emotion and purpose to celebrate the seasons of human experience. Truly doing justice to the universality of these words, the Dillons have drawn on fourteen different styles in their artistic repertoire to lavishly bring to life these poignant lines. Using techniques as diverse as Egyptian murals, Greek vases, Japanese woodblocks, and Australian bark paintings, the Dillons demonstrate their undisputed mastery as artisans. A beautiful text through which to examine myriad art styles, the book offers an excellent explanation and description of each technique used.

13.29 Grimes, Nikki (1997). **It's Raining Laughter.** Photographs by Myles C. Pinkney. New York: Dial. Unpaged. ISBN: 0-8037-2003-3. Picture Book.

The playful language and photographs burst with life in this collection of poems about growing up. Grimes touches on subjects from uncontrollable giggles to being teased, from playing in the garden to playing the piano, from making up with friends to listening to life. The laughing bug that runs through this brilliant collection is a treasure. The photographs are portraits of children at play.

13.30 Jackson, Alison (1997). **I Know an Old Lady Who Swallowed a Pie.** Illustrated by Judith Byron Schachner. New York: Dutton Children's Books. Unpaged. ISBN: 0-525-45645-7. Picture Book. (See **11.3**)

13.31 Steptoe, Javaka (1997). **In Daddy's Arms I Am Tall.** New York: Lee & Low. Unpaged. ISBN: 1-880000-31-8. Picture Book. (See **4.26**)

13.32 Swann, Brian (1998). **Touching the Distance: Native American Riddle-Poems.** Illustrated by Maria Rendon. San Diego: Browndeer. 32 pp. ISBN: 0-15-200804-7. Picture Book. (See **10.58**)

Secondary Reviews

13.33 Cole, Joanna, and Stephanie Calmenson (1996). **Give a Dog a Bone: Stories, Poems, Jokes, and Riddles about Dogs.** Illustrated by John Speirs. New York: Scholastic. 90 pp. ISBN: 0-590-46374-8. Picture Book.

Poems, jokes, and riddles are a great way to get young children involved in reading. This book has all of those and more! Lighthearted, funny, rhyming poems; easy-to-understand jokes and riddles; and a selection of short stories by well-known authors give youngsters a collection of readings all about dogs. Bright and bold illustrations give the book that something extra to enjoy. A rebus story and interesting facts help to lend even more variety for all dog lovers.

13.34 Corwin, Judith Hoffman (1998). **My First Riddles.** New York: Harper Festival. Unpaged. ISBN: 0-694-01109-6. Picture Book.

This brightly colored book is a great primary teaching tool. With every turn of the page, there is a surprise. A riddle is asked, and on the page next to it, clues to the answer are provided in the pictures. Then when the page is turned, the answer is obvious. This book provides illustrations through photographs of fabric appliqué. What a great way to get students making predictions based on picture cues!

13.35 Elya, Susan Middleton (1997). **Say Hola to Spanish, Otra Vez (Again!).** Illustrated by Loretta Lopez. New York: Lee & Low. Unpaged. ISBN: 1-880000-59-8. Picture Book.

Elya and Lopez have teamed up again to create a lively, colorful sequel to their first creation, *Say Hola to Spanish*. Both books aim to teach Spanish in an entertaining manner by using Spanish words within English phrases and sentences. Middleton uses spirited rhythm and rhyme to define over seventy common Spanish words in each book. The colorful illustrations rendered in gouache and colored pencil support the text in a whimsical fashion that is sure to tickle readers of all ages. "It teaches you Spanish in a fun way," said Alexis (age nine). The Spanish-speaking children in our primary classrooms pointed out that these books could also teach them some English, and we observed students teaming up with each other and these books during independent reading time, taking turns with the Spanish and English portions of the text.

Elya, Susan Middleton (1996). **Say Hola to Spanish.** Illustrated by Loretta Lopez. New York: Lee & Low. Unpaged. ISBN: 1-880000-29-6. Picture Book.

13.36 Hoberman, Mary Ann (1998). **Miss Mary Mack: A Hand-Clapping Rhyme.** Illustrated by Nadine Bernard Westcott. Boston: Little Brown. Unpaged. ISBN: 0-316-93118-7. Picture Book.

This is a delightful chant many elementary school children learn to love. Whether it is introduced in music class or the classroom, it must be shared. Students take delight in learning rhymes or chants at an early age. However, putting this story with the wonderful illustrations leaves a child in awe. There is a hand-clapping pattern that children can perform while singing Miss Mary Mack. Westcott does a fabulous job of matching the pictures with the words. Students will get a chance to actually see what they have always been visualizing. Elephants do jump the fence, can touch the sky, and do make really good friends. The illustrations allow the story to come true!

13.37 Marsh, T. J., and Jennifer Ward (1998). **Way out in the Desert.** Illustrated by Kenneth Spengler. Flagstaff, AZ: Northland. Unpaged. ISBN: 0-87358-687-5. Picture Book. (See **7.8**)

13.38 Martin, Bill, Jr. (1998). **The Turning of the Year.** Illustrated by Greg Shed. New York: Harcourt Brace. Unpaged. ISBN: 0-15-201085-8. Picture Book.

Through lilting, poetic text, Martin invites the reader to welcome winter's icy blow, splash through puddles recklessly, and run through fields that praise the sun. Come along on this glorious celebration of the passing of the months. Each page offers an action, a taste, a feel, or a rich experience that fills our senses and helps us recall the sights and sounds of the carefree days of childhood. Taking delight in the simple pleasures of each season, the children in the book savor each moment captured in Shed's ethereal paintings. The rhyming text is poetry in its finest, simplest form.

13.39 Reiser, Lynn (1998). **Tortillas and Lullabies/Tortillas y cancioncitas.** Illustrated by Corazones Valientes. Translated by Rebecca Hart. New York: Greenwillow Books. 40 pp. ISBN: 0-688-14628-7. Picture Book.

This dual-language book reveals how a family from El Salvador passes traditions from the great-grandmother, to the grandmother, to the mother, and finally to the young daughter. "Every time it was the same but different," is the predictable text that concludes each of four sections—Tortillas, Flowers, Washing, and Lullabies. The story closes with a traditional lullaby, in Spanish and English versions, with musical notation. In a somewhat abstract style, the bold, acrylic illustrations depict the generations of a family making tortillas, growing gardens, washing, and singing. The art is a celebration of heritage and change, created by a group of Costa Rican women who call themselves the *Corazones Valientes* (Valiant Hearts). They began their artistic endeavors under the encouragement of translator Rebecca Hart, then a Peace Corp Volunteer in their village. Both Spanish- and English-speaking kindergartners enjoyed this book. It would be a good addition to a text-set about families or lullabies.

Biographies and Autobiographies (of Authors, Books, and Characters)

See also the section entitled Histories and Herstories in chapter 3, "Exploring Our Past"; the section entitled Bigger than Life Heroes, Heroines, and Events in chapter 5, "Struggle and Survival"; and the section entitled Art Books: Books about Artists in chapter 11, "Fine Arts."

Primary Reviews

13.40 Carpenter, Angelica Shirley, and Jean Shirley (1997). **Robert Louis Stevenson: Finding Treasure Island.** Minneapolis: Lerner. 144 pp. ISBN: 0-8225-4955-7. Chapter Book.

Robert Louis Stevenson's biography gives a vivid description of his life and the many experiences that can be found in his books *Treasure Island, Kidnapped, The Strange Case of Dr. Jekyll and Mr. Hyde,* and *A Child's Garden of Verses.* Although he was very ill throughout his childhood, at age six Stevenson won his first writing contest with a dictated story. From this point on, he knew he was destined to become an author. He preferred writing biographies to fiction because it was like fitting a puzzle together. Stevenson's diary is quoted frequently in the biography to provide a realistic sense of his writing style and life history. Pictures from his personal life, as well as illustrations from his books, are woven throughout the story to provide yet another insight into the life of Robert Louis Stevenson.

13.41 de Paola, Tomie (1996). **Strega Nona: Her Story.** New York: Putnam. Unpaged. ISBN: 0-399-22818-7. Picture Book.

The much-beloved Strega Nona returns in this tale to tell us her story. We find that Strega Nona was born into a family of women healers known for their remedies and advice. Nona is left the magic pasta pot, and the secrets that accompany it. This folktale heroine displays cleverness and intelligence along with her magic. Strong, capable women are shown as respected members of their community. Unfortunately this respect is often lacking in classic folktales. Children will enjoy hearing Strega Nona's story, and will be delighted by the colorful de Paola artwork featuring his familiar hearts, doves, and cats.

13.42 Dyer, Daniel (1997). **Jack London: A Biography.** New York: Scholastic. 228 pp. ISBN: 0-590-22216-3. Chapter Book.

Dyer retells John Griffith Chaney's ("Jack London's") life history through an intriguing recounting of many of the adventures in London's short life. From his experiences as an oyster pirate and a fish patrol officer to his time spent in Erie County Penitentiary for vagrancy, and from the time he enrolled as a high school freshman at the age of nineteen to his Gold Rush fever, we get a glimpse of some of his adventures. We also witness his many rejections by publishers before finally receiving the recognition he has achieved today. He wrote his stories in order to honestly relate his experiences, and through this blunt style readers know that what they read in London's books is a true description of various times and places. It is this honesty that has attracted readers of all ages. This biography includes pictures and quotes from Jack London, and shows how one child can rise above a dysfunctional childhood to become one of the most well-known authors of the twentieth century.

13.43 Heller, Ruth (1996). **Fine Lines.** Photographs by Michael Emery. New York: Owen. 32 pp. ISBN: 1-878450-76-X. Picture Book.

Fine Lines is one of many autobiographies published by Richard C. Owen that introduce children to the lives of authors and illustrators. Through this collection, children can discover more about the authors and illustrators they know and love. Often it is difficult for children to realize that these special people are just like someone they know—or even like themselves. The simple text and photographs focus on different aspects of the authors' and illustrators' lives, and give the reader an enjoyable journey as they follow these people through their accomplishments. Wesley (age eight) says it all: "If they can do it, I can too!" Other authors and illustrators who have written in this series include Verna Aardema, Eve Bunting, Lois Ehlert, Paul Goble, George Ella Lyon, Patricia Polacco, Cynthia Rylant, and Jane Yolen.

13.44 Lester, Helen (1997). **Author: A True Story.** Boston: Houghton Mifflin. 32 pp. ISBN: 0-395-82744-2. Picture Book.

In this autobiography, Lester tells children how she came to be a writer, beginning with the story of how she wrote grocery lists for her mother when she was a little girl. She speaks candidly of her learning disability (mirror writing), as well as the process that all writers go through when they write stories. Her sense of humor is present throughout the story, and children feel as if they know her because they know the stories she has written. She also tells readers why she works with an illustrator, noting, "This talented person draws what I would if I could." This book is a must when teaching children about writing, editing, and publishing their own work.

13.45 Lyon, George Ella (1998). **A Sign.** Illustrated by Chris K. Soentpiet. New York: Orchard. Unpaged. ISBN: 0-531-30073-0. Picture Book.

Tracing her dreams of making neon signs, walking a tightrope, and blasting into space, Lyon uses lovely metaphors to bring us into her present life as an author. Abandoning these dreams to become one who can make "words glow," who puts "one word in front of the other, hoping the story won't fall," and who sends words to our hearts, Lyon brilliantly shares the lovely childhood aspirations that evolved into her mature literary endeavors. In his daring watercolors, Soentpeit captures the nuances of shadow and shade and of tension and poise as few others can. A book to give us pause to reflect on how dreams take flight and lead us to become who we are.

13.46 Marcus, Leonard S. (1997). **The Making of Goodnight Moon: A 50th Anniversary Retrospective.** New York: Harper Trophy. Unpaged. ISBN: 0-06-446-192-0. Sophisticated Picture Book.

This is a remarkable tribute to one of the most notable children's books of the century. The book gives background information about the lives of Margaret Wise Brown and her collaborator and illustrator Clement Hurd. Brown's education in early childhood teaching allowed her to explore children's literature in a new and fresh way for the era. Hurd's time in France studying art gave him the ability to focus on a new style of painting. From these two contemporary minds came *Goodnight Moon*, a favorite among families with young children. This tribute includes pictures from the author's and illustrator's lives, rough drafts of the original book, and examples from the popular press that show the extent to which *Goodnight Moon* affected the children's literature industry.

> Brown, Margaret Wise (1947). **Goodnight Moon.** Illustrated by Clement Hurd. New York: Harper. 31 pp. Picture Book.

13.47 Neimark, Anne E. (1996). **Myth Maker: J. R. R. Tolkien.** San Diego: Harcourt Brace. 118 pp. ISBN: 0-15-298847-5. Chapter Book.

Neimark does an excellent job recounting John Ronald Reuel (J. R. R.) Tolkien's life history. She begins with the young Tolkien's life in Africa. Although he was ill as a child, once Tolkien moved to England with his mother and younger brother, the cooler weather found him healthier. Tolkien's love was fairy tales. As soon as he learned to read, dragons and evil fairies played in his head. He loved the outdoors, and his mother encouraged this love with a strong education in botany before he began his studies at King Edward VI School in Birmingham. He married a woman three years his senior during leave from his military duty in World War I. It was creating tales for his children that developed Tolkien's storytelling ability. His stories always included good triumphing over dragons and other evil beings. Tolkien's love of words and word origins showed in his brilliant lectures as a professor of philology at Oxford University. Tolkien created his own language and, through myths and legends, an extensive heritage for this made-up language.

13.48 Rylant, Cynthia (1996). **Margaret, Frank, and Andy: Three Writers' Stories.** San Diego: Harcourt Brace. 48 pp. ISBN: 0-15-201083-1. Chapter Book.

This charming book insightfully portrays the personal lives of Margaret Wise Brown, L. Frank Baum, and E. B. White. Rylant captures the private lives of these familiar authors in three short stories. Each story presents brief anecdotes about the author that show rather than tell the reader about the personality and life history of the writer. Pictures from the authors' lives are added to create a sense of true understanding of their history. In addition to the wonderful primary sources, including pictures and quotes from books written by the authors, Rylant captures each author's successes and failures in relation to writing and his or her personal life.

Mysteries

Primary Reviews

13.49 Benton, Amanda (1997). **Silent Stranger.** New York: Avon. 160 pp. ISBN: 0-380-97486-X. Chapter Book.

One night during the War of 1812, fourteen-year-old Jessica finds a very frightened young man in the family's barn in New York state. Although the young man, named Daniel by Jessica's family, is unwilling or unable to speak, he becomes part of the family and works on the farm for his keep. The sinister Stillwater family, influential local storekeepers, use the political intrigue of war to foster an atmosphere of suspicion in the community. Rumors generated by the Stillwaters raise suspicions about Daniel's identity by suggesting he may be crazy and dangerous, and put the family's farm in jeopardy. Despite pressure from neighbors, Jessica remains drawn to Daniel and sets about discovering the truth about him. Benton's development of this engaging mystery is enhanced by accurate details of frontier life. The ending will surprise everybody.

13.50 Bloor, Edward (1997). **Tangerine.** San Diego: Harcourt Brace. 294 pp. ISBN: 0-152-01246-X. Chapter Book.

Legally blind or not, Paul Fisher clearly sees the world around him. Threatened and dwarfed in all aspects of his life by an egocentric, psychotic, football hero older brother, Paul wonders where he belongs. After his family moves to Tangerine, Florida, where thunderstorms happen daily and a school disappears down a sinkhole, Paul's life begins to change. He gains self-esteem through friendships, success as a soccer goalie, and confidence by helping his teammates save their tangerine grove when it is threatened by a killer frost. He finds the courage to confront the shadowy memories of the event that caused his blindness, and with his newfound strength, Paul breaks free of the fear that has bound him for so long. In the city of Tangerine anything can happen.

13.51 Crowe, Carole (1998). **Sharp Horns on the Moon.** Honesdale, PA: Boyds Mills. 112 pp. ISBN: 1-563-97671-4. Chapter Book. (See **14.51**)

13.52 Paterson, Katherine (1998). **Parzival: The Quest for the Grail Knight.** New York: Lodestar. 127 pp. ISBN: 0-525-67579-5. Chapter Book (See **14.53**)

13.53 Paulsen, Gary (1998). **The Transall Saga.** New York: Delacorte. 248 pp. ISBN: 0-385-32196-1. Sophisticated Chapter Book. (See **14.45**)

13.54 Pullman, Philip (1998). **Clockwork.** Illustrated by Diana Bryan. Brooklyn, NY: Levine. 113 pp. ISBN: 0-590-12999-6. Chapter Book.

In this mystery set in an inn in historic Germany, Fritz the storyteller begins to unravel a story he has not yet completed. With his telling of the tale, he sets the story into motion, and it cannot be stopped until it has run its course. Fritz becomes frightened when, after reading a description of the evil Dr. Kalmenius, the character bursts through the door. Like a good fairy tale, this deceivingly simple but multilayered story will engage both young and old readers and listeners as they become caught up in the story's pleasant mixture of love, intrigue, sorcery, clockwork, and the ultimate triumph of good over evil. Bryan's enchanting but scary illustrations curry the imagination.

13.55 Sachar, Louis (1998). **Holes.** Austin, TX: Foster. 233 pp. ISBN: 0-374-33265-7. Sophisticated Chapter Book.

Accused criminal Stanley Yelnats is sent to Camp Green Lake to serve out his sentence, all the while asserting his innocence. Digging holes was not in his plan, but is part of the routine prescribed by the warden. Mystery builds as Stanley's and fellow inmate Zero's lives and family histories become entangled. Why are they digging these five-foot deep, five-foot across holes every day? What does the situation Stanley finds himself in now have to do with the curse his "no-good-dirty-rotten-pig-stealing-great-great-grandfather" caused to be put on the Yelnats family? A fanciful approach by Sachar lets us follow life in the camp, the building of friendships, and the ever-entertaining endeavors of both the inmates and staff. This amazingly well-written mystery, with information dispensed slowly but with precise timing, will consume the reader until the very last page.

13.56 Skurzynski, Gloria, and Alane Ferguson (1997). **Wolf Stalker.** Washington, DC: National Geographic. 147 pp. ISBN: 0-792-27034-7. Chapter Book.

Set in Yellowstone National Park, this fast-paced mystery involves all the members of a family: father, mother, son Jack, daughter Ashley, and foster child Troy. Mother is bent on solving the riddle of a wolf attack and saving the wolf. Troy is keen to find his mother and return to his home. Troy's rebelliousness is exacerbated by Jack's impatience. Outdoor enthusiasts and animal lovers will find this book hard to put down. The authors introduce considerable detail of life in Yellowstone National Park while tracking a poacher and solving both animal and human mysteries. The accuracy of the geographical information adds an authentic tone to this well-written mystery.

13.57 Wallace, Barbara Brooks (1997). **Sparrows in the Scullery.** New York: Antheneum. 160 pp. ISBN: 0-689-81585-9. Chapter Book.

Nineteenth-century England saw orphans sold to charitable homes, where they were clothed, fed, and then sent off to gloomy factories where they were worked to death. Wealthy eleven-year-old Colley Trevelyn finds himself at Broggin's Home for Boys after being kidnapped a few nights after the accidental death of his parents. Survival becomes the driving force for Colley, generating a need for friendship and collaboration with other inmates. The story of life at Broggin's and the mystery of why he was kidnapped builds to a most happy ending. Andrew (age ten) remarked, "I felt like I was with Colley as he sat in the 'Hole,' ate his daily grey gruel and stale bread, and struggled with his five friends to survive by making a secret home and family." Benton has written a believable story that captures the deprivations of the era.

13.58 White, Ruth (1996). **Belle Prater's Boy.** New York: Farrar, Straus and Giroux. 196 pp. ISBN: 0-374-30668-0. Chapter Book.

After the disappearance of his mother from their home in the hills of Appalachia, Woodrow moves in with his grandparents in the nearby town of Coal Station, Virginia. There a unique friendship blooms between cross-eyed, unattractive Woodrow and his beautiful cousin Gypsy. Both sixth graders have hidden secrets that in the end bind them together despite their differences. White brings you into the life of this community and the lives of these two captivating cousins through the painful mysteries they must face. Readers will find these two characters unforgettable. The story's exploration of the concept of beauty and its impact in the lives of this 1950s community will inspire parallel discussions in today's classrooms.

13.59 Yep, Laurence (1998). **The Case of the Lion Dance: Chinatown Mystery #2.** New York: HarperCollins. 214 pp. ISBN: 0-06-024447-X. Sophisticated Chapter Book. (See **7.62**)

Secondary Reviews

13.60 Brown, Marc (1998). **Arthur's Mystery Envelope.** Boston: Little Brown. 58 pp. ISBN: 0-316-11546-0. Picture Book.

The first in the new Arthur mystery series proves to be a hit. Principal Haney gives Arthur an envelope marked "Private and Confidential" to take home. Arthur and his friends try to guess what kind of trouble could be waiting for Arthur inside the envelope. Could it be information on summer school? After discussing what to do with his friends, Arthur takes the envelope home, only to have it accidentally fall into the trash. What should Arthur do? In this story, Brown addresses a big issue for young readers: how to face consequences. This book also raises for class discussion the issues of honesty and responsibility. After reading the story, a classroom of third graders all agreed that Arthur did the right thing.

13.61 Cushman, Doug (1996). **The Mystery of King Karfu.** New York: HarperCollins. Unpaged. ISBN: 0-060-24796-7. Picture Book.

Wombat detective Seymour Sleuth's engaging casebook takes the reader to Egypt to find ancient pharaoh King Karfu's missing stone chicken. The casebook, complete with coffee stains and fingerprints, leads to four suspects. Photographs, ticket stubs, footprints, letters, and other fascinating clues make this a good read-aloud text as well as a hit with newly independent readers. Solve the secret code to get to the tasty end of this unique picture book. Stephanie (age eight) said, "It is just like a real casebook."

13.62 DeFelice, Cynthia (1998). **The Ghost of Fossil Glen.** New York: Farrar, Straus and Giroux. 167 pp. ISBN: 0-374-31787-9. Chapter Book.

While hunting for fossils in the glen, imaginative and creative sixth grader Allie Nicholas is averted from a near-fatal fall with the guidance of a mysterious voice. This encounter connects her with the ghost of a girl her age named Lucy, who died four years earlier in the glen. The elements that draw readers into this intriguing mystery are a ghost seeking revenge, a sinister real-estate deal, and two red leather-bound journals whose entries bring the past and present together. With the help of her friend Dub, a sympathetic teacher, and clues from the ghost of the murdered Lucy, Allie strives to bring Lucy's killer to justice and save the glen from being made into a housing development. Elena (age ten) said, "I couldn't put the book down. I especially loved following the two journals and the way Allie stood up to her critical disbelieving friends."

13.63 Glenn, Mel (1996). **Who Killed Mr. Chippendale? A Mystery in Poems.** New York: Dutton. 100 pp. ISBN: 0-525-67530-2. Sophisticated Chapter Book. (See **10.27**)

13.64 Hobbs, Will (1997). **Ghost Canoe.** New York: Morrow. 195 pp. ISBN: 0-688-14193-5. Chapter Book.

Cape Flattery in Washington State is the setting for this 1874 murder mystery. Fourteen-year-old Nathan MacAllister works as an assistant lighthouse keeper with his father Zackary, while taking care of his ill mother. In an attempt to improve her failing health, he moves with his mother to a Makah village on the mainland. Their quiet life in this Native American community is interrupted by the wreck of a small ship. The discovery of the captain's murdered body and the eerie footprints leading away from the bodies of the drowned crew sends Nathan off on a search to find the culprits. Filled with hidden treasure, many ghostly overtures, and considerable danger to Nathan, this is an engaging and intriguing story supported by accurate historical and cultural information.

13.65 Marzollo, Jean (1996). **I Spy Spooky Night.** Photographs by Walter Wick. New York: Scholastic. 34 pp. ISBN: 0-590-48137-1. Picture Book.

Wick's theme-oriented photographs are stunning and will instantly grab the attention of youngsters as they read to find out what mysterious real-life objects to look for. Young readers will spend a great amount of time searching for the objects suggested by the riddles on each page. At the end of the book, Marzollo provides extra riddles for the reader to solve. In case children don't get enough in this volume, Marzollo has several other books available, including *I Spy Gold Challenger* and *I Spy Super Challenger.*

Marzollo, Jean (1997). **I Spy Super Challenger.** Photographs by Walter Wick. New York: Scholastic. 32 pp. ISBN: 0-590-34128-6. Picture Book.

Marzollo, Jean (1998). **I Spy Gold Challenger.** Photographs by Walter Wick. New York: Scholastic. 32 pp. ISBN: 0-590-04296-3. Picture Book.

13.66 Miller, Dorothy Reynolds (1996). **The Clearing.** New York: Atheneum. 119 pp. ISBN: 0-689-80997-2. Chapter Book.

Eleven-year-old Amanda spends the summer with relatives in rural Pennsylvania while her parents check out a job possibility in Minneapolis. Cousin Elinore, with her bossy ways, leaves Amanda no alternative but to seek other friends. Her relationships with her cousin Nelson and fourteen-year-old neighbor Cynthia draw her into a maze of events that mysteriously keep leading back to the unsolved disappearance of five-year-old Bucky Meade. Is the long-suspected Spook Wade responsible for Bucky's disappearance, or has someone else been withholding the truth for ten years? Miller's subtle disclosure of the details maintains suspense to the end.

13.67 Roberts, Willo Davis (1998). **The Kidnappers: A Mystery.** New York: Atheneum. 137 pp. ISBN: 0-689-81394-5. Chapter Book.

Eleven-year-old Joey has the misfortune of being the sole witness to the kidnapping of one of his classmates in Willey Groves. When he tries to tell others about what he saw, he is not believed because of his reputation for telling tall stories. Realizing that he is unable to convince adults that there is real trouble, Joey must set about solving the mystery himself. The appearance of the local police vindicates Joey, but leaves him vulnerable to several dangerous contacts with the kidnappers. Suspense builds throughout this thoroughly engaging mystery. Drew (age thirteen) said, "I could identify with Joey's frustration when no one would believe him. The fear he felt when he was kidnapped just jumped off the pages and grabbed me too."

13.68 Roberts, Willo Davis (1998). **Secrets at Hidden Valley.** New York: Atheneum. 150 pp. ISBN: 0-689-81166-7. Chapter Book.

When her actress-mother decides to go on a shoot alone, eleven-year-old Steffi, who has recently lost her dad in an accident, faces a summer with a distant and disagreeable grandfather whom she has never met and who has been estranged from her family since before she was born. Despite the cold welcome to her grandfather's remote Michigan trailer park, Steffi makes a place for herself by cooking; undertaking a project that will benefit the park; and establishing relationships with the local residents, especially Casey. Mysterious threads of this story include why her grandfather appears to dislike her deceased father, why some park residents are fearful of any new people who come to stay, and why an FBI agent is "vacationing" at Hidden Valley. Following an untimely accident, Steffi finds herself running the Hidden Valley Trailer Park, checking in new guests, managing the small store, and cleaning and repairing the grounds. As the mysteries are solved, she and Casey learn that most people have a secret—some are just bigger than others.

13.69 Sharmat, Marjorie Weinman (1998). **Nate the Great and Me: The Case of the Fleeing Fang.** New York: Delacorte. 64 pp. ISBN: 0-385-32601-7. Chapter Book.

This new twenty-fifth anniversary special-edition Nate the Great mystery will be loved by new and old fans alike. In this interactive book, the reader follows clues to help Nate the Great solve his newest mystery. When Nate's friends and their pets decide to give him a surprise Happy Detective Day party, he also gets a new case. He has to find Annie's dog Fang, who ran away on the way to the party. Read along to find out if Nate is able to solve the mystery before the strawberry ice cream melts! Detective tips, a detective certificate, and recipes give a new twist to this series. Bryan (age nine) said, "The tips on how to be a detective are great."

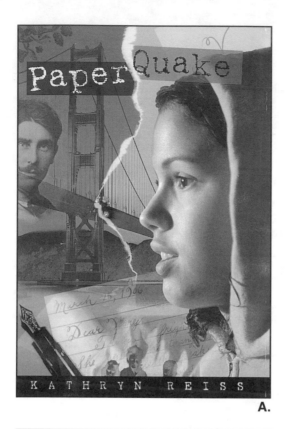

A.

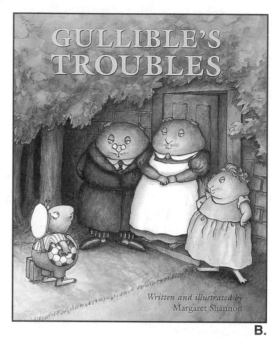

B.

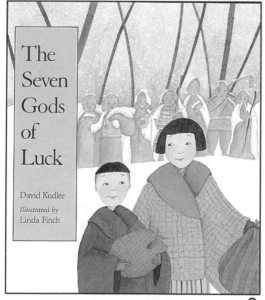

C.

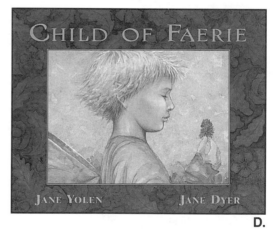

D.

A. *Paper Quake: A Puzzle,* Kathryn Reiss (**14.57**). **B.** *Gullible's Troubles,* Margaret Shannon (**14.16**). **C.** *The Seven Gods of Luck,* David Kudler/Linda Finch (**14.9**). **D.** *Child of Faerie, Child of Earth,* Jane Yolen/Jane Dyer (**14.21**).

14 Fantasy Literature: Making the Impossible Possible

Karen Smith

Contributing reviewers included Cheryl Alley, Kathy Bennett, Laura Burch, Sally Burgett, Diane Elliott, Carol Jones, and Karen Smith

Reading fantasy is demanding work. It requires readers to give themselves over to worlds unlike any they have known. At first these worlds may appear ordinary, but with a slight twist of a character's action, a shift in some detail of the setting, or a curious turn of events, these everyday worlds become unfamiliar. Authors of fantasy literature succeed when readers help to render these unfamiliar worlds believable by suspending disbelief and accepting the possibility of their existence. Consistency is the key to developing a successful fantasy story. In these stories, characters' motives, actions, and language are consistent within the framework developed by the author. Details of the setting also must be consistent within this framework, and developed so thoroughly that readers can see, hear, and feel them. Eleanor Cameron believes that authors of fantasy must establish a premise and an inner logic for their story, and draw boundary lines outside which the fantasy may not wander. "Without ever having to think about it, a reader must feel that the author is working consistently within a frame of reference" (Cameron 1983, 23–24).

As our review committee selected the books for this chapter, we looked for those with well-developed characters, intriguing plots, and familiar themes. To sharpen our focus within the fantasy genre, we adapted the following evaluation criteria from Norton (1994, 335):

1. Are characters' actions consistent with the story parameters developed by the author?

2. How does the author's characterization allow children to suspend disbelief? Do characters begin in a world of fantasy? Do characters begin in a real world before they travel to the world of fantasy? Does a believable character accept a fanciful world, characters, or happenings? Does the author use an appropriate language consistent with the story?

3. Does the author pay careful attention to the details in the setting? If the author develops several timeperiods, are the settings authentic and integral to the story?

4. Are the themes worthwhile for children?

5. Does the author encourage readers to suspend disbelief by developing a point of view that is consistent in every detail, including sights, feelings, and physical reactions?

As we read, discussed, deliberated, and finally selected the books for this chapter, we were pleased by what we found. We were surprised to find so many books like *Lucy Dove* (Del Negro 1998) with strong female protagonists who counter the traditional fairy tale heroine by demonstrating courage and strong will. We were amused by *Bubba the Cowboy Prince* (Ketteman 1997) who, like his predecessor Cinderella, is mistreated by his wicked stepfamily. Our final selection of books was guided mainly by how well we and our students liked the books. The books we selected caused us to imagine other possibilities. They evoked rich discussions and made us question, explore, and argue with others' ways of thinking and behaving. Through careful, critical reading, these books also caused us to envision new theories, make new discoveries, and conceive new worlds.

Our group's greatest challenge was deciding which books fit within the genre of fantasy. We purposely chose not to include many traditional folktales, fables, myths, and legends. These books are highlighted in the Traditional Literature section of chapter 3, "Exploring Our Past." We did, however, include modern stories written in fairy-tale and tall-tale style. We elected not to include collections of short stories. At first, we also ruled out books that were part of a series, but then we reconsidered. We think the series books we chose are compelling enough to stand on their own, and hopefully they will incite readers to seek out other books in the series.

We also tried to balance our selection. For example, we chose books that would be of interest to younger and older children alike. We selected lighthearted fantasy books with whimsical events—such as *A Bad Case of the Stripes* (Shannon 1998), in which a young girl finds herself covered in stripes—as well as more serious fantasies that probe unknown dimensions—such as *The Transall Saga* (Paulsen 1998). In addition, we picked books that require different reading abilities so that all readers, regardless of age or skill, can enjoy reading fantasy.

Fantasy in the Schools

Although fantasy is often the genre of choice for very young readers, older readers often voice their dislike of it. Therefore many students will need support entering these complex worlds and finding relevance and enjoyment in them. The good news is that once students experience success with fantasy, they usually ask for more. With the availability of many wonderful fantasy books and with supportive classroom practices, it is easy for librarians and teachers to foster a love of fantasy in students, but we must be deliberate in our efforts. Reading aloud and discussing a range of fantasy books is a good place to begin. Students need experience with animal fantasies, quests, time-slip tales, and magic; they need to meet fantastic yet believable characters, and frightening spirits; and they need to be introduced to stories with themes that make them consider the emotional and psychological effects of futuristic ideas and conflicts. These experiences will give students footing in fanciful worlds and prepare them to read and respond on their own.

Students need opportunities to read independently and to respond to the impact these experiences will have on them. One form of response—small group discussions—allows students to share personal responses, clarify questions, and explore alternate interpretations. This is especially important with fantasy literature that puts high demands on the imagination. Drama also helps students recapture the impact of their experience by allowing them to assume roles in the story and explore their thoughts and wonderings. Art experiences such as murals and dioramas provide means for recreating settings so readers can better envision and experience these worlds.

Organization of This Chapter

We organized the books in this chapter into two sections: Picture Books and Chapter Books. This organizational scheme is not meant to imply that picture books are for younger children and chapter books are for older children. As you will see, the suggested age ranges reveal that some picture books may not be appropriate for the very young, nor are all chapter books written exclusively for older students. How a particular book and a particular child find each other is often beyond reasonable explanation. However, with caring, passionate adults to support them, we're convinced that many children will find pleasure in the fantasy books that follow.

Within each of our two categories, we have suggested text-sets (Rhodes 1987) in order to help teachers extend their students' experiences with a particular book. We grouped the books according to themes or topics (see figure 1 and figure 2) so teachers can invite students to read all the books within a set and then discuss their similarities, differences, and other connections. This process not only draws out elements

PICTURE BOOKS

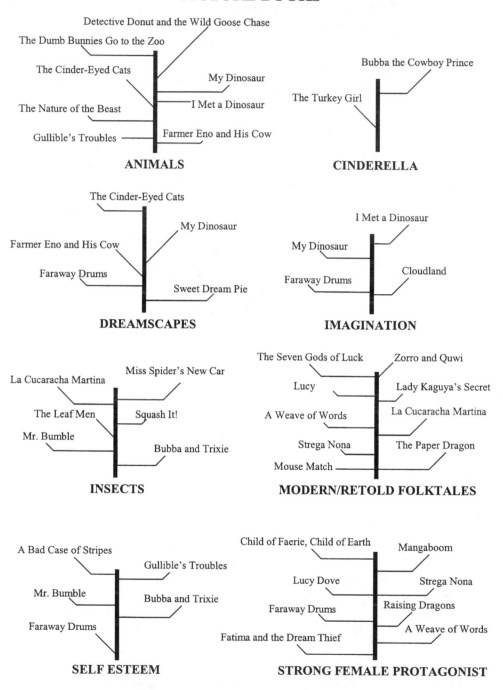

Figure 1

CHAPTER BOOKS

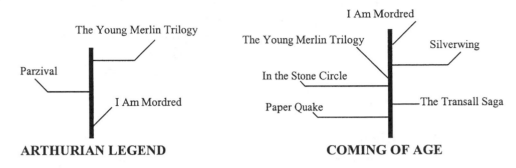

ARTHURIAN LEGEND

The Young Merlin Trilogy
Parzival
I Am Mordred

COMING OF AGE

I Am Mordred
The Young Merlin Trilogy
Silverwing
In the Stone Circle
Paper Quake
The Transall Saga

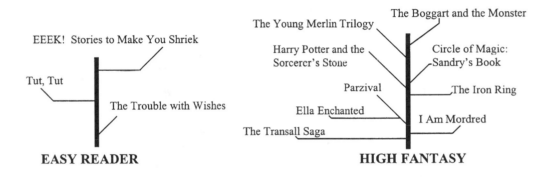

EASY READER

EEEK! Stories to Make You Shriek
Tut, Tut
The Trouble with Wishes

HIGH FANTASY

The Young Merlin Trilogy
The Boggart and the Monster
Harry Potter and the Sorcerer's Stone
Circle of Magic: Sandry's Book
Parzival
The Iron Ring
Ella Enchanted
I Am Mordred
The Transall Saga

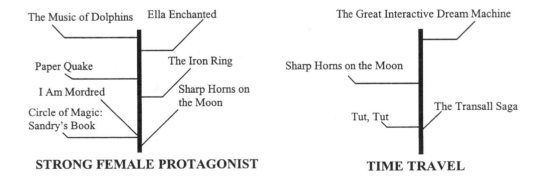

STRONG FEMALE PROTAGONIST

The Music of Dolphins
Ella Enchanted
Paper Quake
The Iron Ring
I Am Mordred
Sharp Horns on the Moon
Circle of Magic: Sandry's Book

TIME TRAVEL

The Great Interactive Dream Machine
Sharp Horns on the Moon
Tut, Tut
The Transall Saga

Figure 2

that make fantasy a unique genre, it also helps students connect to larger ideas that are revealed across texts such as how magic works or how heroes and heroines rise to impossible challenges.

We hope this chapter will serve as a useful guide to literature that will capture the imaginations of even the most reluctant fantasy readers. As we noted above, reading fantasy is indeed demanding work. However given a talented author and a supportive literary environment, reading fantasy is also a thrilling, and often magical, experience.

Works Cited

Cameron, Eleanor. 1983. The Inmost Secret. *Hornbook Magazine* 59, no. 1: 17–24.

Norton, Donna E. 1994. *Through the Eyes of a Child: An Introduction to Children's Literature.* Englewood Cliffs, NJ: Merrill.

Rhodes, Lynn K. 1987. Text Sets. In *Ideas and Insights: Language Arts in the Elementary School,* ed. Dorothy J. Watson. Urbana, IL: National Council of Teachers of English.

*The titles listed below each subheading are organized into Primary Reviews and Secondary Reviews. The Primary Reviews describe outstanding books in each subheading. The Secondary Reviews provide brief information about other books worthy of consideration. Some titles listed below are **not** reviewed in this chapter; entries for these titles are not annotated and contain only bibliographic information. In such cases, a cross reference to the annotated entry contained elsewhere in this volume is provided in boldface type at the end of the bibliographic information.*

Picture Books

Primary Reviews

14.1   Burningham, John (1996). **Cloudland.** New York: Crown. Unpaged. ISBN: 0-517-70928-7. Picture Book.

Kate Greenaway Award winner John Burningham delivers a wonderfully illustrated childhood adventure about a small boy who falls off a cliff while hiking in the mountains. To his amazement, the children who live in the clouds rescue him. After enjoying his time dancing and jumping with his newfound friends, the small boy becomes homesick. Sympathetic to the young boy's feelings, the queen of the cloud children returns him to his parents. This magical tale is full of attractive cutouts of children displayed on top of vibrant, full-colored photos of sky scenes. This touching story of friendship will mesmerize children and set their imaginations afloat. See also Burningham's *Hey! Get off Our Train.*

Burningham, John (1994). **Hey! Get off Our Train.** New York: Crown. 48 pages. ISBN: 0-517-88204-3. Picture Book.

14.2 Davol, Marguerite W. (1997). **The Paper Dragon.** Illustrated by Robert Sabuda. New York: Simon & Schuster. Unpaged. ISBN: 0-689-31992-4. Picture Book.

Mi Fei, a humble scroll painter and historian for his Chinese village, is sent to confront Sui Jen, a vicious dragon intent upon wreaking havoc in the land. To save his life, Mi Fei must perform the dragon's three tasks: wrap fire in paper (he fashions a lantern), capture wind in paper (he makes a fan), and carry the strongest thing in the world in paper. Struggling with the last task, Mi Fei recalls the villagers' faces and paints a magnificent scroll depicting them. When Sui Jen sees the scroll, he realizes that nothing is stronger and disappears. Elaborately detailed cut-tissue papers, created and painted by the artist and affixed to Japanese paper, cover the pages in a series of gatefold illustrations that open to form triple-page spreads. This story will appeal to even the youngest readers. Its sumptuous art and timeless message are for everyone.

14.3 Del Negro, Janice (1998). **Lucy Dove.** Illustrated by Leonid Gore. New York: Dorling Kindersley. 32 pp. ISBN: 0789-42514-9. Sophisticated Picture Book.

In search of a strong female protagonist to counter the traditional fairy-tale heroine, librarian and storyteller Janice Del Negro created her own version of a classic Scottish tale. A rich but superstitious laird offers a sack of gold to the person who can sew him a pair of lucky trousers by moonlight in the confines of St. Andrew's cemetery. Out of all the villagers only Lucy Dove, the poor and elderly tailor recently sacked from the household of the laird in question, has the courage and the will to accept the challenge. With her sights set on "her own bit of shore," Lucy Dove sets off to brave the deadly claws and sickening stench of the vicious cemetery boggle. Del Negro uses her storytelling prowess to weave a text filled with suspense, horror, and humor among Leonid Gore's dark, haunting, but often comical paintings.

14.4 Joyce, William (1996). **The Leaf Men and the Brave Good Bugs.** New York: HarperCollins. Unpaged. ISBN: 0-06-027237-6. Picture Book.

The old, old lady knows her garden is a magical place, but she is unaware of how that magic happens. As both she and her garden begin to fail, readers experience the wonder of this magic when the wisdom of a mysterious toy, the valor of a troop of doodle-bugs, and the courage of Leaf Man come together on a stormy, moonlit night to bring life and hope back to the old lady and the garden. Although the story's conflict will keep the pages turning for its young readers, its themes of love, valor, and the power of memory will linger with them long after they turn the last page.

14.5   Kennedy, Kim (1998). **Mr. Bumble.** Illustrated by Doug Kennedy. New York: Hyperion. Unpaged. ISBN: 0-7868-0263-4. Picture Book. (See **8.43**)

14.6   Ketteman, Helen (1997). **Bubba the Cowboy Prince: A Fractured Texas Tale.** Illustrated by James Warhola. New York: Scholastic. 32 pp. ISBN: 0-590-25506-1. Picture Book.

Helen Ketteman transforms the classic Cinderella story into a classic Texan tall tale, with a hero worthy enough to ride with the likes of John Wayne . . . well, maybe Pecos Bill. Bubba, like his feminine predecessor, is mistreated by his wicked stepfamily (a stepdaddy and two stepbrothers). But with the help of his fairy godcow, he makes it to Miz Lurleen's ball in time to rope her heart and lose his high-heeled boot (cowboys don't two-step in glass slippers). Warhola's bright, magical oil paintings give a kick to the funny, although sometimes stilted, text. The facial expressions of his cartoonish characters, as well as the artist's attention to detail, humorously depict the emotion, action, and setting of the story. Younger readers also will enjoy locating the fairy godcow hidden on almost every page. And of course, the cleverly worded happy ending may prompt a hearty "Yeehaw!" from young and old readers alike.

14.7   Kirk, David (1997). **Miss Spider's New Car.** New York: Scholastic. Unpaged. ISBN: 0-439-04675-0. Picture Book. (See **8.44**)

14.8   Kroll, Virginia L. (1998). **Faraway Drums.** Illustrated by Floyd Cooper. New York: Little Brown. Unpaged. ISBN: 0-316-50449-1. Picture Book.

Inspired by her students, former teacher Virginia Kroll composed this story of two African American girls, Jamila and her younger sister Zakiya, who await their mother's return from her night job. Aided by their active imaginations and the stories their great-gramma told them, they comfort themselves against the city sounds outside their small apartment with thoughts of faraway Africa. Through the eyes of these two girls, Kroll cleverly links images of the urban setting with that of the African one: people's angry voices in the street become hyenas "bickerin' over the scraps they found"; car horns are really "elephants come to the waterin' hole"; and the quick beating of their hearts is surely the echo of the "faraway drums" across the savanna. Moreover, Floyd Cooper's soft oil-wash paintings—reminiscent of Chris Sheban's artwork in Jan Wahl's *I Met a Dinosaur*—offer the reader a visual key to the girls' soothing fantasy world and gently blur the lines between reality and imagination. This book would serve as an excellent springboard for a discussion of the history and traditions of cultures.

> Wahl, Jan (1997). **I Met a Dinosaur.** Illustrated by Chris Sheban. San Diego: Harcourt Brace. 32 pp. ISBN: 0-15-201644-9. Picture Book.

14.9 Kudler, David (1997). **The Seven Gods of Luck.** Illustrated by Linda Finch. Boston: Houghton Mifflin. Unpaged. ISBN: 0-395-78830-7. Picture Book.

Because mother is unable to afford a New Year's feast this year, she instructs Kenji and Sachiko to sell their homemade goods at the local market in hopes of making money. Instead they trade their goods for six bamboo hats, which they place on the snow-covered shrine of the seven gods. In return for their kindness and generosity in keeping the gods warm and happy, the gods give Kenji and Sachiko a very special New Year's feast.

14.10 Nolen, Jerdine (1998). **Raising Dragons.** Illustrated by Elise Primavera. New York: Harcourt Brace. Unpaged. ISBN: 0-15-201288-5. Picture Book.

Jerdine Nolen has written a fantasy about an endearing young girl who finds an unusual egg, waits for it to hatch, and sets out to raise the resulting baby dragon. Ma and Pa don't have any time for dragons, what with their farm work and all, but the girl and the dragon find creative and bigger-than-life ways to help. They also have time for grand adventures. How great to find a female lead in a book about dragons. This bright and stunning picture book features acrylic paints and pastels on gessoed illustration board. The language will excite young people as Nolen describes the dragon food, "Eel pot pies, frog leg pudding, and fish-and-insect stew." This is a story about overcoming challenges, developing trust, and most of all about love. "As I touched skin to scale, I knew I was his girl and he was my dragon."

14.11 Pollock, Penny (1996). **The Turkey Girl: A Zuni Cinderella Story.** Illustrated by Ed Young. New York: Little Brown. Unpaged. ISBN: 0-316-71314-7. Picture Book.

Children will readily see the parallels to traditional European tales in this Zuni Cinderella story. The Turkey Girl, an outcast, is magically readied for the Dance of the Sacred Bird by the turkeys under her care. Fairy godmother-like, the turkeys require her to return by sundown or suffer consequences. Unfortunately by the time she remembers her promise to return before the sun sets, it is too late. She returns to find the turkeys have gone, leaving her empty-handed. The story illustrates that we pay a price when we break our trust with Mother Earth. In the Turkey Girl's case, and in contrast to Cinderella stories in which the heroine captures the prince's heart, she is left with nothing. The book is an excellent vehicle for teachers to use in concert with Western versions of the Cinderella story because the starkness of the ending contrasts strongly with that of the traditional Western tale. Soft oil, crayon, and pastel illustrations by Caldecott Award winner Ed Young offer tender, gentle images to accompany the text. Teachers may want to use this book in combination with other Cinderella story variations, such as *Bubba the Cowboy Prince* (see **14.6**), *The Golden Sandal: A Middle Eastern Cinderella Story* (see **3.130**), and *Cendrillon: A Caribbean Cinderella.*

> San Souci, Robert D. (1998). **Cendrillon: A Caribbean Cinderella.** Illustrated by Brian Pinkney. New York: Simon & Schuster. 40 pp. ISBN: 0-689-8066-8-X. Picture Book.

14.12 Pomerantz, Charlotte (1997). **Mangaboom.** Illustrated by Anita Lobel. New York: Greenwillow. Unpaged. ISBN: 0-688-12957-9. Picture Book.

In this unusual adaptation of "Jack and the Beanstalk," Mangaboom is a gorgeous female Latina giant, effervescent and content in her gargantuan self. Rather unconventional in her ways, Mangaboom loves to climb trees, turn cartwheels, and in general challenge not only the traditional view of giants, but also stereotypes of females. Daniel, a young boy who climbs her beanstalk, has the opportunity to get involved in Mangaboom's search for the perfect companion, one who will accept her—high heels, flamboyant ways, and all. Mangaboom's matchmaking aunt tries to help too, but in the end, Mangaboom's own resourcefulness leads her to the perfect companion. Colorful gouache and watercolor paintings by Anita Lobel artfully give life to this story. Teachers can use this story in the classroom in conjunction with other books, such as Jon Scieszka's *The True Story of the Three Little Pigs* or Stephen Kellogg's *The Three Little Pigs* (see **14.29**), to help students explore alternate versions of traditional fairy tales.

> Scieszka, Jon (1991). **The True Story of the Three Little Pigs.** Illustrated by Lane Smith. New York: Viking. Unpaged. ISBN: 0-670-84162-5. Picture Book.

14.13 Ringgold, Faith (1999). **The Invisible Princess.** New York: Crown. ISBN: 0-517-80024-1. Picture Book.

In the Village of Visible lived Mama and Papa Love. They loved children and wanted to have children of their own, but were afraid to because they were slaves and knew that the horrible plantation owner, Captain Pepper, would probably take their children away and sell them. Their love of children was so strong that once Mama Love gave birth to their first child, their prayers of having a child who only knew freedom is magically granted by the Lady of Peace, who takes the young child away. The little girl grows up in a beautiful world where the elements of nature raise her as a princess. This is one of the first originally created African American fairy tales. Faith Ringgold ironically creates a tale that has never been visible before, and uses the theme of an African American princess who is invisible.

14.14 Rohmann, Eric (1997). **The Cinder-Eyed Cats.** New York: Crown. Unpaged. ISBN: 0-517-70896-5. Picture Book.

On a beautiful sunlit day, a young boy climbs into his sailboat and sets sail—or more exact, sets flight—across the deep blue sea. After dropping anchor on a faraway shore, the young boy ambitiously sculpts a giant fish from the shore's sand as hints of cats and other creatures watch from nearby sites. All is peaceful until twilight time when the sand fish awakens, cats emerge from the woods, and fishes rise from the deep. Together this unlikely cast of characters twirl, weave, wiggle, and dance their way through the night. As in most dream stories, the sun signals that it's time for the frolicking to stop. Although the fishes return to the sea and the boy and cats return to shore, it is clear from the look of contentment on the boy's and cats' faces that this is not a one-time event. Rather the boy will return and the dance will start again once twilight falls "and the moon comes round once more." Rohmann's illustrations add unique perspectives and complexity to a deceptively simple story line.

14.15 Shannon, David (1998). **A Bad Case of the Stripes.** New York: Scholastic. Unpaged. ISBN: 0-590-92997-6. Picture Book.

Camilla Cream loves to please everyone . . . except herself. For example, she loves lima beans, yet refuses to eat them because none of the other children will. Imagine our heroine's surprise when, after trying on forty-two outfits for the first day of school, she looks in the mirror to find herself covered in stripes from head to toe! Her parents are flabbergasted, and none of the doctors or specialists they summon can cure her sickness. In fact, all of their efforts to help her out of her dilemma make her symptoms worse! Not to mention the fact that all of the children at school make fun of her. In the end, Camilla learns an important lesson: just be yourself. This wonderful book is instructive to children, who must deal with pressures from peers, parents, and teachers everyday. The magnificent and colorful illustrations are especially attractive to the younger eye.

14.16 Shannon, Margaret (1998). **Gullible's Troubles.** Boston: Houghton Mifflin. Unpaged. ISBN: 0-395-83933-5. Picture Book. (See **8.57**)

14.17 Teague, Mark (1998). **The Lost and Found.** New York: Scholastic. Unpaged. ISBN: 0-590-84619-1. Picture Book.

Wendell and Floyd's school adventures, which began in *The Secret Shortcut,* continue in this book as the unlucky duo is sent to the principal's office because they were late for class. When Mona Tudburn, the new girl in school, walks into the office looking for her missing lucky hat, she mysteriously disappears into the lost-and-found box. The boys jump in after her and their adventure begins. They journey through various tunnels and rooms until they reach the hat room, where Mona finds her hat. The boys each choose a lucky hat for themselves, and they all return to the principal's office before anyone notices their absence. Teague's characteristic cartoon illustrations are suggestive of animation, which suits the story well.

> Teague, Mark (1996). **The Secret Shortcut.** New York: Scholastic. 32 pp. ISBN: 0-590-67714-4. Picture Book.

14.18 Weatherby, Mark Alan (1997). **My Dinosaur.** New York: Scholastic. Unpaged. ISBN: 0-590-97203-0. Picture Book.

Have you ever dreamed of having a dinosaur as a friend? It seems impossible, but when Sophie, a young girl with a vivid imagination, finds a dinosaur hiding among trees in her backyard, she befriends the gentle giant. Together Sophie and her new friend take readers on a magical nighttime adventure where they explore the world around them while playing hide-and-seek, swimming in moonlit water, and soaring so far above the trees they almost touch the stars. When the sun comes up, Sophie sings goodbye to her new friend: "Good night, my Dinosaur. Sleep tight, my dinosaur. Soon I'll see you again, my very best friend. Good night, sleep tight, my dinosaur . . ." Readers who think the story is only a dream will give pause at the story's end, when the illustrator shows Sophie waking to the morning sun with leaves clinging loosely to her hair. Weatherby's simple text and realistic illustrations (rendered, according to the artist, in acrylics, metallic paints, and fairy dust) create an understated magic that makes this journey one that all readers, young and old alike, will want to take again and again.

14.19 Whatley, Bruce, and Rosie Smith (1997). **Detective Donut and the Wild Goose Chase.** New York: HarperCollins. Unpaged. ISBN: 0-06-026604-X. Picture Book. (See **8.62**)

14.20 Wood, Audrey (1998). **Sweet Dream Pie.** Illustrated by Mark Teague. New York: Blue Sky. Unpaged. ISBN: 0-590-96204-3. Picture Book.

When Pa Brindle has a restless night, he begs Ma to make a sweet dream pie, as she did long ago. Ma agrees, but warns that if things get out of hand, she is not to blame. Ma tosses marshmallows, candy corn, cinnamon hots, chocolate drops, sugar cubes, and the like into the giant pie. When the pie comes out of the oven, the entire neighborhood stops by for a piece. Despite Ma's warning—"Only one piece, or you'll be sorry"—they all help themselves to thirds and fourths. Feeling sleepy, everyone heads home to a night of wild dreams. Ma stays awake to sweep away the unruly dreams with her broom, and only then can all the dreamers settle in for a good night's sleep. The quirky perspectives of Mark Teague's vividly colored double-page spreads might be coupled with Wood's *The Napping House* for a discussion of artistic point of view.

> Wood, Audrey (1944). **The Napping House.** Illustrated by Don Wood. New York: Harcourt Brace. 32 pp. ISBN: 0-1525-6708-9. Picture Book.

14.21 Yolen, Jane (1997). **Child of Faerie, Child of Earth.** Illustrated by Jane Dyer. New York: Little Brown. Unpaged. ISBN: 0-316-96897-8. Picture Book.

One magical Hallow's Eve, a child of Faerie and a child of Earth meet in a woodland clearing by the light of the full moon. The Faerie child leads his newfound human friend on a grand tour of the enchanted faerie realm, complete with "brownies and boggles and sprites / And elven folk and all," and pleads with her to stay. Hesitant to leave her home, the Earth child then takes her gossamer-winged companion through her own world of "colors pure and bright / Of open sight" and "Of warm sunlight," and extends to him the same invitation. Jane Yolen's rhythmic poetry lilts and tumbles through every page, while Jane Dyer's brilliant, highly detailed watercolors highlight at once the vivid contrasts and subtle harmonies between the magical realms of Faerie and Earth.

Secondary Reviews

14.22 Carr, Jan (1996). **The Nature of the Beast.** Illustrated by G. Brian Karas. New York: Morrow. Unpaged. ISBN: 0-688-13596-X. Picture Book.

Isabelle finds a dollar bill and uses it to buy a beast. Isabelle's father thinks the beast will make an interesting scientific experiment, and encourages her to keep a journal documenting the beast's behavior. Her mother, however, says the beast will have to go, despite its uncanny ability to imitate her French lessons. The parental conflict continues until the beast falls ill, bringing compassion and a new awareness to the mother's heart. Finally she concedes that as long as the beast is quiet, he may stay. Any child who has longed for a pet over parental objections will empathize with Isabelle and her struggles to meet the demands of caring for the beast while attempting to placate an unconvinced parent. Whimsical illustrations will aid in engaging young listeners in this comic tale.

14.23 de Paola, Tomie (1996). **Strega Nona: Her Story.** New York: Putnam. Unpaged. ISBN: 0-399-22818-7. Picture Book. (See **13.41**)

14.24 Denim, Sue (1997). **The Dumb Bunnies Go to the Zoo.** Illustrated by Dav Pilkey. New York: Blue Sky. Unpaged. ISBN: 0-590-84735-X. Picture Book. (See **8.27**)

14.25 **EEK! Stories to Make You Shriek series.** Grosset & Dunlap, New York.

Frith, Margaret (1997). **Mermaid Island.** Illustrated by Julie Durrell. 48 pp. ISBN: 0-448-41618-2.

McMullan, Kate (1996). **The Mummy's Gold.** Illustrated by Jeff Spackman. 48 pp. ISBN: 0-448-41310-8.

Dussling, Jennifer (1996). **A Very Strange Dollhouse.** Illustrated by Sonja Lamut. 48 pp. ISBN: 0-448-41311-6.

These books are excellent for beginning or struggling readers, and one reviewer noted that the high-interest nature of the EEK! Stories to Make You Shriek series books made them compelling even to her fifth-grade students.

Jane vacations with her mother and father every summer. This year they stay for a week at Mermaid Island, in the book by the same title. Jane soon befriends Molly, a young girl who has a wonderful shell necklace, can build fantastic sandcastles, won't eat fish, leaves funny silvery things behind in the bathtub, and has a bedroom painted like the underwater world of the sea. Jane is bewildered by all of Molly's eccentricities, but everything makes perfect sense when she finally learns Molly's secret: her mother is a mermaid! The many clues to Molly's secret will keep readers on their toes, and provide an excellent introduction to an author's use of foreshadowing to tell her story.

Jake's brother Henry loves to play tricks on him in *The Mummy's Gold.* So Jake is suspicious when Henry and his friend

Max invite him to a movie—their treat. The movie is about a mummy who searches for his lost treasure and scares people out of their skin by moaning, "I want my Gold!" Afterwards Henry and Max run off, leaving Jake to walk home alone. All of a sudden, Jake finds himself being chased by a real mummy! This story with its many twists and turns will leave readers still wondering at the end.

In *A Very Strange Dollhouse*, Lucy is new in school and everyone thinks she's a little weird. When one of her classmates visits Lucy's house, she thinks it even more odd that Lucy's parents are nowhere to be found. When she plays with Lucy's dollhouse, she notices something even stranger: the dolls seem to change places by themselves, they feel warm, and they even blink! Before long, it is evident that the dolls in Lucy's dollhouse are really her parents, and that Lucy intends to shrink her classmate, too. Her would-be victim just makes it to the door before being caught forever in Lucy's spell. The next day, Lucy's house is for sale, and she is not in school . . .

14.26 Ernst, Lisa Campbell (1997). **Bubba and Trixie.** New York: Simon & Schuster. Unpaged. ISBN: 0-689-81357-0. Picture Book. (See **8.30**)

14.27 Hickox, Rebecca (1997). **Zorro and Quwi: Tales of a Trickster Guinea Pig.** Illustrated by Kim Howard. New York: Bantam Doubleday Books for Young Readers. Unpaged. ISBN: 0-440-41183-1. Picture Book. (See **3.202**)

14.28 Jernigan, E. Wesley (1997). **Cloudcatcher.** Auckland, New Zealand: Shortland. 48 pp. ISBN: 1-57257-668-5. Picture Book.

Manytracks is a curious little boy who is easily distracted from his chores and who constantly gets into mischief. There is concern that his behavior will anger the Kachinas and cause problems for the people of his pueblo. Manytracks tries to behave, but when he discovers a small vaporous form stuck in a pinion pine tree, his curiosity overwhelms him. He frees the little cloud from the tree, but then captures it in a basket, takes it back to his cliff-dwelling home, and hides it from the rest of his family. Eventually Manytracks realizes that the little cloud is growing weaker, and he seeks his father's counsel. His father charges him with nurturing the little cloud until it is strong enough to survive the wind, otherwise his actions may anger the Cloud People and bring drought to his pueblo. In the end, Manytracks accepts responsibility for his actions and nurtures the little cloud until it is strong enough to leave. A gentle story, *Cloudcatcher* emphasizes the importance of taking responsibility for one's actions.

14.29 Kellogg, Steven (1997). **The Three Little Pigs.** New York: Morrow Junior Books. 32 pp. ISBN: 0-688-08731-0. Picture Book.

Everyone knows the story of the Three Little Pigs, but Kellogg's retelling gives it a new twist. Perry, Pete, and Prudence are successful entrepreneurs. They are happy with their waffle franchises until Tempesto the wolf shows up and starts huffing and puffing. Sarafina Sow has to come out of retirement to save the day. Kellogg's clever, full-color illustrations are irresistible.

14.30 Kimmel, Eric A. (1997). **Squash It! A True and Ridiculous Tale.** Illustrated by Robert Rayevsky. New York: Holiday House. Unpaged. ISBN: 0-8234-1299-7. Picture Book.

Author Eric A. Kimmel has adapted a well-known story from Spain and made it outrageous. In this exaggerated tale, made even more hilarious by Robert Rayevsky's bold and cartoonish illustrations, the King of Spain keeps a pet louse that grows to enormous size, and is then carved into a musical instrument after its death. The proud king promises the hand of one of his daughters to anyone who can guess the origin of the instrument. A poor, grubby peasant, wanting riches but (much to the relief of the haughty princess) not a bride, correctly answers the riddle with the help of three insects. Young readers and listeners agreed this folktale is among their favorites. Joey said *Squash It!* is "excellent!"

14.31 Marton, Jirina (1997). **Lady Kaguya's Secret: A Japanese Tale.** New York: Annick. Unpaged. ISBN: 1-55037-441-9. Picture Book.

Kaguya-hima, the Moon King's daughter, falls in love with the Emperor. But because she is not mortal, they are unable to marry. When Kaguya-hima's father comes to take her home, Kaguya-hima gives the Emperor a bottle filled with the elixir of eternal life. Unable to live without her, the Emperor pours the contents atop the highest mountain, hoping the smoke will reach his beloved. Based on an ancient Japanese tale about the Moon Princess, this story offers another perspective on classic themes in fantasy and traditional literature, themes such as lovers giving up worldly goods or eternal life in order to be with their chosen mates. Marton traveled to Japan to complete the research for the stunning oil-and-pastel illustrations that add a mystical quality to the story.

14.32 Matsumoto, Lisa (1996). **Beyond 'Ōhi'a Valley: Adventures in a Hawaiian Rainforest.** Illustrated by Michael Furuya. Honolulu: Lehua. 55 pp. ISBN: 0-9647491-2-2. Picture Book.

Lisa Matsumoto and artist Michael Furuya give the plight of Hawaii's rainforests a friendly, personable face in the form of Kahuli, an endangered tree snail whose wish for adventure is granted as he "surfs the wind" on a leaf blown free from his home in the Great 'Ōhi'a Tree. Kahuli lands in the next valley and befriends Hau'oli, a happy-faced spider. Together they escape predators, fall into a mountain stream, and plunge over a waterfall. Finally a Hawaiian owl airlifts them back to 'Ōhi'a Valley. Relieved and happy, Kahuli now knows where he belongs. Matsumoto authenticates the story with photos and facts about the animals. Young readers will enjoy this well-crafted and beautifully illustrated book, both for the story and for its historical and ecological significance. Nobody can read this book without a renewed reverence for the beauty and balance in nature.

14.33 Rassmus, Jens (1998). **Farmer Eno and His Cow.** New York: Orchard. Unpaged. ISBN: 0-531-30081-1. Picture Book.

Farmer Eno is dreaming of ships, and the ships in his head are appearing on his farm each morning! What begins with one small vessel in the middle of his bedroom leads to quite a large shipyard in his once green fields. When Farmer Eno and his talking cow Africa head to the city for help, the dreams (and the ships) follow . . . until Farmer Eno learns to follow his dreams instead. The bright, fantastic illustrations in this oversized picture book are a lovely complement to this delightful translation of Jens Rassmus' German tale about a dream in search of its farmer.

14.34 San Souci, Robert D. (1998). **A Weave of Words: An Armenian Tale.** Illustrated by Raúl Colón. New York: Orchard. Unpaged. ISBN: 0-531-30053-6. Picture Book.

A master storyteller, Robert San Souci combines several Armenian folktales to create this intriguing story. We find Prince Vachagan out hunting when he meets Anait. Vachagan finds delight in Anait's quick wit, easy laugh, and good sense. When he asks her to marry him, Anait explains that she cannot marry a man who "doesn't know how to read or write, and who can't earn a living by his own hands." Determined to marry the woman he loves, Vachagan teaches himself to read, write, and weave. He and Anait marry and govern together until Vachagan leaves to investigate reported trouble in the eastern part of the kingdom and is captured by the dreaded three-headed devil. Ultimately it is Vachagan's ability to read, write, and weave that allows him to let Anait know of his predicament. Anait battles bravely, and together they overcome the evil devil. Colón's rich, detailed illustrations bring this tale to life. A gripping adventure with a confident, capable heroine.

14.35 Schami, Rafik (1996). **Fatima and the Dream Thief.** Illustrated by Els Cools and Oliver Streich. New York: North-South. Unpaged. ISBN: 1-55858-653-9. Picture Book.

Fatima is worried. Her mother is ill from exhaustion, and her brother Hassan has had his dreams stolen by the evil lord of the castle outside their city. With only enough food left to last them one week, Fatima knows it is up to her to save her family. Despite her mother's warning—"Oh daughter, you're only twelve, and so small and weak!"—Fatima sets off for the evil lord's castle armed only with her courage, confidence, and wit, but manages to win back more than just her brother's dreams. Although the translation of this Swiss-German tale is often imprecise—one has the feeling that brevity was too often favored over clarity and artistry—the overall story flows well. Cools' and Streich's bright watercolor paintings add a comic element to the tale, and help the reader to bring to life the author's fantasy world.

14.36 Stanley, Diane (1997). **Rumpelstiltskin's Daughter.** New York: Morrow Junior Books. Unpaged. ISBN: 0-688-14328-8. Picture Book. (See **3.167**)

14.37 Soto, Gary (1997). **Chato y su cena.** Illustrated by Susan Guevara. Translated by Alma Flor Ada and F. Isabel Campoy. New York: Putnam and Grosset. Unpaged. ISBN: 0-698-11601-1. Picture Book. (See **8.58**)

14.38 Whal, Jan (1997). **I Met a Dinosaur.** Illustrated by Chris Sheban. New York: Harcourt Brace. 31 pp. ISBN: 0-152-01644-9. Picture Book.

After a visit to a museum, a young girl spends the next week seeing dinosaurs wherever she looks. Rhymed text on each page complements the story. Misty, dreamlike illustrations, similar to Floyd Cooper's illustrations in Virginia Kroll's *Faraway Drums* (see **14.8**), are either set within small frames, fill full-page frames, or spill gently off the page. Although a fantasy, this beautifully designed book could be used to supplement a dinosaur unit because the dinosaurs are labeled and a glossary of dinosaur names is included. See also *Patrick's Dinosaurs.*

> Carrick, Carol (1983). **Patrick's Dinosaurs.** New York: Houghton Mifflin. 32 pp. ISBN: 0-599-19189-4. Picture Book.

14.39 Young, Ed (1997). **Mouse Match: A Chinese Folktale.** San Diego: Silver Whistle. Unpaged. ISBN: 0-15-201453-5. Picture Book. (See **3.138**)

Chapter Books

Primary Reviews

14.40 Billingsley, Franny (1997). **Well Wished.** New York: Simon & Schuster. 170 pp. ISBN: 0-689-81210-8. Chapter Book.

Eleven-year-old Nuria, an orphan, wants two things she's never had: someone to love her just the way she is, and a special friend. Her first wish is answered when she comes to live with her kind grandfather, the Aya, in the mysterious town of Bishop Mayne. However the children in her new town have disappeared because someone's wish went wrong at the town's temperamental wishing well. Nuria is pleased to find a friend when she meets up with eleven-year-old Catty, crippled and confined to a wheelchair. Then another wish goes wrong, and Nuria finds herself in Catty's body. Although it is possible to undo a wish, it must be carefully constructed because each person can make only one wish each lifetime. The need to wish carefully suggests a possible link to *Half Magic* and *The Trouble with Wishes* (see **14.55**).

> Eager, Edward (1999). **Half Magic.** New York: Harcourt Brace. 208 pp. ISBN: 0-152-02068-3. Chapter Book.

14.41 Coville, Bruce (1997). **The Skull of Truth.** Illustrated by Gary A. Lippincott. San Diego: Harcourt Brace. 176 pp. ISBN: 0-15-275457-1. Chapter Book.

Charlie has a chronic lying problem. He lies when his mother asks him where he has been for the afternoon, he lies when his teachers ask simple questions. Even he doesn't know why he makes up these stories, and consequently he spends most of his time alone wandering through the swamp behind his house. Then while running away from a bully one afternoon, Charlie takes a wrong turn in the swamp. He finds a shop deep in the cover of the swamp that he does not remember seeing before. It turns out to be Mr. Elives' magic shop. When he thinks he hears a skull named Yorick say, "Take me home," he accidentally steals it from the shop. Mr. Elives sends a message to warn him of the skull's curse, and admits that he is relieved that the skull is gone. Almost immediately, Charlie discovers Yorick's curse: the truth. From then on, Charlie is forced to tell the truth about everything. To his surprise, he finds that people believe him even less when he tells the whole truth. This dilemma brings Charlie trouble, and things get worse until he capitalizes on the curse to save something that he loves dearly.

14.42 Hesse, Karen (1996). **The Music of Dolphins.** New York: Scholastic. 181 pp. ISBN: 0-590-89797-7. Chapter Book. (See **4.10**)

14.43 Levine, Gail Carson (1997). **Ella Enchanted.** New York: HarperCollins. 232 pp. ISBN: 0-06-440405-5. Chapter Book.

This 1998 Newbery Honor book captures the Cinderella story in a new way that will delight and charm readers. Cursed at birth by a fairy's gift of obedience, Ella spends her life trying to outwit, outsmart, and break the curse's hold over her, only to find the power to do so lies within herself. Living in a fairy wonderland peopled by a colorful cast of elves, ogres, giants, princes, and fairies, Ella surmounts many obstacles (including the traditional evil stepmother and self-centered stepsisters) and successfully meets numerous challenges in her quest. This strong, clever, and feisty heroine reminds us all of the central truth: the power to change our lives lies within. *Ella Enchanted* is an excellent vehicle for teachers of intermediate-grade children to use in conjunction with other versions of the Cinderella story. Encouraging students to write alternate versions of Cinderella or other fairy tales is one natural outcome of using this book in the classroom.

14.44 Oppel, Kenneth (1997). **Silverwing.** New York: Simon & Schuster. 217 pp. ISBN: 0-689-81529-8. Chapter Book.

Shade, the runt of his bat colony, becomes separated during a storm as the group makes its winter migration to the warmer Hibernaculum. Alone he struggles through a series of adventures to rejoin his kind. The young bat grows and changes, learning to flee from owls, pigeons, and the evil vampire bats Goth and Throbb. In the process, he learns to trust Marina, a brightwing bat, and Zephyr, an albino. Readers will easily become engrossed in Oppel's fantasy world and enjoy the factual notes at the end of the book.

14.45 Paulsen, Gary (1998). **The Transall Saga.** New York: Delacorte. 248 pp. ISBN: 0-385-32196-1. Sophisticated Chapter Book.

Thirteen-year-old Mark Harrison finds himself in a primitive world where the trees and grass are red, he can't see any stars at night, and the animal life is strange—and dangerous. Monkey–teddy bear mutants throw rocks at him from the trees above, buffalo creatures with sharp tusks charge at him, and scorpion-like insects bite him all over his body. Gary Paulsen's heroic narrative follows Mark through Transall as he tries to find the mysterious blue light, which transported him there, to help him get back home. Sophisticated concepts such as bigotry, war, and slavery are presented in accessible vocabulary and short, action-packed chapters. Paulsen returns to a favorite theme of survival on one's own. Mark's coming-of-age in Transall can only be accomplished by overcoming the challenges of this eerie land, and the strange people who inhabit it.

14.46 Rowling, J. K. (1998). **Harry Potter and the Sorcerer's Stone.** Illustrated by Mary GrandPré. New York: Scholastic. 320 pp. ISBN: 0-590-35340-3. Chapter Book.

Following the death of his mother and father at the hands of the evil sorcerer Voldemort, the baby Harry Potter is sent to live with his cruel aunt and uncle and their rotten son Dudley (three of the biggest "muggles" you'll ever meet). There, for the first eleven years of his life, Harry is forced to live in a cupboard under the stairs and eat nothing but the family's leftovers. He is not even allowed to celebrate his own birthday. On his eleventh birthday, however, with the arrival of a mysterious letter from Hogwart's School of Witchcraft and Wizardry, Harry's life takes a magical turn for the better. He has been accepted into the school without ever applying, and once he gets there, not only does he begin to study the secrets of Herbology, Transfiguration, and the like, he also discovers that his past has already made him something of a celebrity. Moreover with the help of his newfound magical talent and some unlikely friends, Harry must face Voldemort and keep him from stealing the powerful Sorcerer's Stone. Rowling's writing brings fresh style and wit to the traditional high-fantasy genre, and her superb storytelling abilities set this tale on its way to becoming a classic. Adults and children alike are sure to find this book as riveting, magical, and lovable as its hero. See also the sequels *Harry Potter and the Chamber of Secrets* and *Harry Potter and the Prisoner of Azkaban.*

Rowling, J. K. (1999). **Harry Potter and the Chamber of Secrets**. Illustrated by Mary GrandPré. New York: Scholastic. 320 pp. ISBN: 0-439-06486-4. Chapter Book.

Rowling, J. K. (1999). **Harry Potter and the Prisoner of Azkaban**. Illustrated by Mary GrandPré. New York: Scholastic. 435 pp. ISBN: 0-439-13635-0. Chapter Book.

14.47 Spinger, Nancy (1998). **I Am Mordred: A Tale from Camelot**. New York: Philomel. 184 pp. ISBN: 0-399-23143-9. Sophisticated Chapter Book.

This compelling revision of Arthurian lore turns Mordred—the odious bastard son who Merlin prophesied would kill his own father, King Arthur—into a complex young man who has been mislabeled and misunderstood. Seeking to tell his own story and to live nobly, Springer's Mordred faces questions that loom over any coming-of-age: Is my life determined by fate, society, or myself? Is human nature good or bad, and how far can I trust those with experience and power? These considerations are interwoven deftly with a feminist thread as Mordred is aided by the sorceress Nyneve, who rejects Camelot's definition of woman as a lady in need of a knight and who urges Mordred to contend in like fashion with others' attempts to determine his life. Readers will find much to identify with and to ponder as Mordred tries to understand his situation, live with his choices, and find positive meaning in the midst of it all. Another Arthurian revision can be found in Jane Yolen's The Young Merlin series (see **14.48**).

14.48 Yolen, Jane. **The Young Merlin series.**

Passager (1996). San Diego: Harcourt Brace. 76 pp. ISBN: 0-15-200391-6. Chapter Book.

Hobby (1996). San Diego: Harcourt Brace. 90 pp. ISBN: 0-15-200815-2. Chapter Book.

Merlin (1996). San Diego: Harcourt Brace. 91 pp. ISBN: 0-15-200814-4. Chapter Book.

In *Passager*, Yolen introduces us to a wild eight-year-old boy who has been left in the woods to fend for himself. How he came to be there is a mystery, although the boy does recall bits and pieces of the home he once knew. Master Robin, an expert hawker, happens upon the boy one day while hunting in the same tree in which the boy sits. Curious, the boy follows the hunter home. Using patience and gentleness, Master Robin soon gains the boy's confidence, and he quietly becomes part of the household. The story ends as the boy's true name is discovered: Merlin.

In *Hobby*, Merlin is now twelve and part of Master Robin's family. One night, he dreams of a bird with a fiery red breast, but does not know that his dream forebodes disaster. One night soon after, he wakes to find the house where he lives with Master Robin, Mag, and Nell on fire. Merlin himself has time to escape, but is unable to save his family. Alone once more, he wanders into the forest he once called home with a cow and a horse that also managed to survive the blaze. Then he is captured by an evil man named Fowler, and his terrible dog Ranger, who steal his horse and cow and take him to town hoping to sell him. There Merlin is rescued by a magician and his mistress who use his prophetic dreams as a means to draw crowds and earn money. As they travel, a king requests their presence, but the magician becomes nervous about the nature of the boy's dreams and leaves town without him. Once again, Merlin finds himself alone.

In *Merlin*, young Merlin meets a troupe of wodewose who allow the boy to accompany them. At first the wodewose take in Merlin and feed him, but when the wodewose women discover that the boy is a prophetic dreamer, they cage him and put hallucinogenic herbs in his food. Knowing that he does not need the herbs to dream, he refuses to eat. Then one night, he dreams of blood filling the clearing where they are camped. Without waiting for Merlin's interpretation of the dream, the wodewose decide they must break camp and leave. In the confusion, Merlin escapes with Cub, a small wodewose (and the future King Arthur) who insists on running away with him. Soon after their departure, soldiers attack the camp and kill all of the inhabitants. Thus Merlin and the small boy are left to make a life for themselves. Readers who enjoy this trilogy may also want to discover the stories in Yolen's *Camelot* for more Arthurian legend interpretations.

> Yolen, Jane (1995). **Camelot.** New York: Philomel. 198 pp. ISBN: 0-399-22540-4. Chapter Book.

Secondary Reviews

14.49 Alexander, Lloyd (1997). **The Iron Ring.** New York: Dutton Children's Books. 283 pp. ISBN: 0-525-45597-3. Sophisticated Chapter Book.

Long ago in what is now India, an ill-fated game of dice causes Tamar, the young King of Sundari, to lose his freedom to the mysterious Jaya, King of Mahapura. Since Tamar is not just a king, but also a member of the noble warrior caste called the *kshatriyas*, to which honor or *darhma* is everything, he must leave the comfort and safety of his palace and go in search of his destiny—a journey which may or may not end in his death. Tamar and his companions (including his timid teacher, a mischievous monkey-king, a whiny eagle, and an intrepid milkmaid) must brave a world of sharply delineated social castes, belligerent kshatriyas, powerful kings, and evil *rakshasas* (spirits). Their experiences lead them through difficult journeys of the heart, mind, and soul, causing them each to question and challenge traditional ideas of caste, gender, honor, loyalty, and love. Alexander is able to weave multiple complex ideas into a single literary thread with unusual deftness and artistry. Moreover his skillfully developed characters live and breathe on every page, lending themselves well to in-depth comparative analysis.

14.50 Cooper, Susan (1997). **The Boggart and the Monster.** New York: Margaret K. McElderry. 185 pp. ISBN: 0-689-81330-9. Chapter Book.

In this sequel to *The Boggart*, Canadian brother and sister Jessup and Emily Volnik return to Scotland and Castle Keep, where they are reunited with their old friend the Boggart, a nearly invisible, mischievous, shape-changing sprite. On a camping trip to Loch Ness with some friends, the children and the Boggart discover that the legendary creature of the lake is really the Boggart's long-lost cousin, stuck in his monstrous form for centuries. When a high-tech scientific expedition tries to prove the monster's existence, the children must help the two boggarts escape the ensuing media circus. Cooper keeps the action moving by frequently shifting point of view, presenting the story from the perspectives of the children, the scientists, and the fun-loving boggarts themselves, and she convincingly blends ancient magic and modern science. The boggarts provide both comic and poignant moments in a story that stresses the importance of loyalty, family ties, and the power of belief in oneself and one's friends.

Cooper, Susan (1993). **The Boggart.** New York: Simon & Schuster Children's. 208 pp. ISBN: 0-689-80173-4. Chapter Book.

14.51 Crowe, Carole (1998). **Sharp Horns on the Moon.** Honesdale, PA: Boyds Mills. 112 pp. ISBN: 1-563-97671-4. Chapter Book.

Sharp Horns on the Moon tells of the timeless bounds of friendship, the pain of sacrifice, and the connections between past and present. Ivy Marie Bell has spent her whole life with her father and unmarried aunt in the house where her mother grew up. Her mother died soon after Ivy's birth. Since they live outside of town, Ivy is schooled at home by her aunt, but longs to attend the high school in town so she can make friends her own age. As usual, she spends her lonely summers swimming and fishing. One day as she is out swimming, she feels something holding her under the water as she fights to get back to the surface. Soon Ivy learns that the "something" is a ghost named Eleanor, who wants to be her friend. Eleanor turns out to be the same friend her mother had as a child—the ghost of a young girl from a shipwreck long ago. In this suspense-filled time overlap, Ivy risks her life and her friendship to protect Eleanor's family.

14.52 Kimmel, Elizabeth Cody (1998). **In the Stone Circle.** New York: Scholastic. 225 pp. ISBN: 0-590-21308-3. Chapter Book.

Fourteen-year-old Cristyn reacts with typical teenage dismay when her father informs her they will spend the summer in Wales. Once there, they stay with another family in a sixteenth-century house inhabited by a ghost interested in making contact with Cristyn. Eventually they find that the ghost is a young girl from the 1200s, trapped in the house. Cristyn and the other children in the story have repeated encounters with the ghost, until finally they are able to execute a plan that allows the ghost to rest in peace. Riveting text written in a lively, engaging style will capture the reader's interest. Readers who enjoy this story might also try *Sharp Horns on the Moon* (see **14.51**).

14.53 Paterson, Katherine (1998). **Parzival: The Quest for the Grail Knight.** New York: Lodestar. 127 pp. ISBN: 0-525-67579-5.

This story is a retelling of a thirteenth-century Arthurian legend. Raised in the wilderness, Parzival is unaware of his noble birth. One day, after a chance meeting with three men in armor, Parzival decides to go to King Arthur's court to become a knight. His many adventures teach him chivalry and honor, and he comes of age through his quest for the Holy Grail. Readers will appreciate the brief biographical information about the characters at the beginning of the book, as well as source notes about the original epic poem by Wolfram von Eschenbach.

14.54 Peck, Richard (1996). **The Great Interactive Dream Machine: Another Adventure in Cyberspace.** New York: Dial. 149 pp. ISBN: 0-8037-1989-2. Chapter Book.

When computer whiz Aaron Zimmer develops a program that grants wishes, his best friend Josh Lewis accompanies him on adventures through time and space. Each journey begins with cellular reorganization, then personal disintegration, and finally interactivity—but the program has a few bugs and the boys aren't sure exactly when and with whom the computer will interact next. The cast of characters includes the school bullies Stink Stuyvesant and Hulk Hotchkiss; their neighbor's dog Ophelia; their history teacher Mr. Thaw; and the mysterious Watcher, who seems to know all their computer secrets. Aaron and Josh continue the successful combination of humor and science fiction they established in *Lost in Cyberspace.*

> Peck, Richard (1997). **Lost in Cyberspace.** New York: Puffin. 160 pp. ISBN: 0-140-37856-1. Chapter Book.

14.55 Pfeffer, Susan Beth (1996). **The Trouble with Wishes.** Illustrated by Jennifer Plecas. New York: Henry Holt. 71 pp. ISBN: 0-8050-3826-4. Chapter Book.

The day Katie Logan finds a magic wish-granting lamp in the park, she thinks she's died and gone to heaven. She now has three whole wishes to spend however she pleases! She soon realizes, however, that wishing is not all it's cracked up to be. What if she wishes to be rich, only to find out she is the long-lost daughter of a wealthy family and not really the daughter of the parents she loves? Or if she wishes for world peace only to watch the world become overrun by an evil dictator capitalizing on the impossibility of war? Finally Katie settles on what she thinks is a small-scale wish: to have the lead in the class play. She soon discovers, however, that even the smallest of wishes can have dire consequences. This light, easy-reader book could be used to inspire writing projects about wishes, "what if" scenarios, and the like.

14.56   Pierce, Tamora (1997). **Circle of Magic: Sandry's Book.** New York: Scholastic. 252 pg. ISBN: 0-590-55356-9. Chapter Book.

The stories of four young characters are braided together in this tale of elemental magic. Sandry, a noble, is imprisoned in a dark, windowless storeroom. Daja, a trader, is adrift at sea, the lone survivor of a shipwreck. Briar, a thief, stands before the judge, caught nicking others' goods for a third time. And Tris, whose budding, uncontrollable magic powers wreak havoc around her, has just been banished—again—from the children's dormitory in Mnver. Each is rescued by the mysterious Niklaren Goldeye (Niko), and together they are taken to the Winding Circle Temple in Emelan. Drawn together by fate, they come to Discipline Cottage, where they learn new crafts, develop powerful arts of meditation under Master Niko's instruction, and discover unexpected friendships blossoming out of their differences in race and gender. The stories of these four adventurers are continued in three other Circle of Magic books by fantasy author Tamora Pierce.

> Pierce, Tamora (1998). **Circle of Magic: Tris's Book.** New York: Scholastic. 256 pp. ISBN: 0-590-55357-7. Chapter Book.
>
> Pierce, Tamora (1998). **Circle of Magic: Daja's Book.** New York: Scholastic. 288 pp. ISBN: 0-590-55358-5. Chapter Book.
>
> Pierce, Tamora (1999). **Circle of Magic: Briar's Book.** New York: Scholastic. 288 pp. ISBN: 0-590-55359-3. Chapter Book.

14.57   Reiss, Kathryn (1998). **Paper Quake: A Puzzle.** New York: Harcourt Brace. 264 pp. ISBN: 0-15-201183-8. Chapter Book.

Eighth-grader Violet Jackstone's world is a bit shaky. One of a set of triplets, her dark, frizzy hair, brown eyes, and small stature contrast sharply with her two sisters' blond, svelte appearances. Nicknamed "Baby" by her family, Violet struggles between fitting in and asserting her individuality. Recurring earthquake tremors and the accompanying visions Violet has only serve to complicate matters. When one of the tremors exposes a letter hidden in the wall almost a century ago, she marvels at the eerie connections between its contents and the events in her own life. An engaging and creative metaphor (noticeably free of cliched language or action) for the journey through adolescence, the ensuing adventure leads Violet on a tumultuous, often dangerous trip through time, history, and her own identity.

14.58 Scieszka, Jon (1996). **Tut, Tut.** Illustrated by Lane Smith. New York: Viking. 74 pp. ISBN: 0-140-36360-2. Chapter Book.

Joe and his friends Sam and Fred have promised never again to open *The Book*, because the volume causes the time travel that seems always to get the trio into trouble. But when Joe's sister Anna unwittingly opens the book, they land in ancient Egypt, where they are pursued by a mean little priest named the Great Hatsnat, who thwarts their every attempt to reach home. Eventually they find an ally in the boy king Thutmose III, who loves their basketball sneakers. They manage to outwit Hatsnat with a simple physics trick: they ask one of his strongest guards to lean with his head against a wall, and pick up a small footstool. When the guard is unable to, but Anna is magically able to do so, they win a wager with Hatsnat and are able to escape. After some scary but comical adventures, the trio is able to find *The Book,* which allows them all to return home. Those children who enjoy *Tut, Tut* should be sure to check out the other titles in The Time Warp Trio series. These high-interest books make them an excellent choice for reluctant readers.

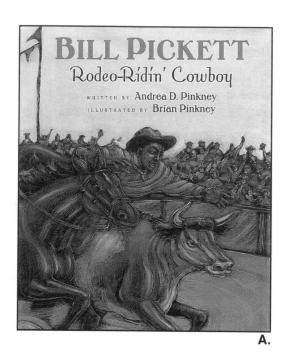

A.

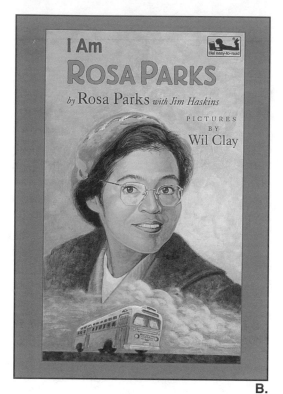

B.

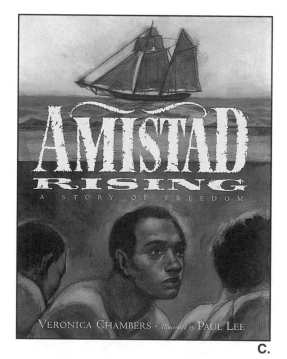

C.

A. *Bill Pickett: Rodeo-Ridin' Cowboy,* Andrea D. Pinkney/Brian Pinkney (**15.25**). **B.** *I Am Rosa Parks,* Rosa Parks with Jim Haskins/Wil Clay (**15.24**). **C.** *Amistad Rising: A Story of Freedom,* Veronica Chambers/Paul Lee (**15.44**).

15 African and African American Voices and Experiences

Patricia Tefft Cousin

Dale Allender

Nancy Tolson

Contributing reviewers included Patricia Tefft Cousin, Claudette Mitchell, Gracie Porter, and Nancy Tolson.

As teachers, we never really think about books without considering their instructional possibilities. This is true whether the instruction is direct or indirect, aesthetic or didactic. That is why we have chosen to introduce this chapter on African and African American children's and young-adult literature by highlighting *authorship* and *context* as two of the most important selection and instruction considerations.

Our first observation about authorship is best summarized by the title of Cornel West's collection of essays: race matters. Often readers and writers privilege the author's imagination over his or her race. They presume that it is enough for a writer to imagine racial positioning in order to convey accurately the experiences of others, or that a writer can rise above his or her social institutions and write about race without being affected by race. This is a particularly troubling position when it is adopted by White European American writers who write about people of color—in this case African Americans. Given the unequal status in the United States between African Americans and White European Americans, African Americans have less power and often are either held under a microscope or completely ignored. It is more often the case that White writers choose to write about people of color than the reverse. Authenticity and exploitation suggest that race should be a far more significant factor than imagination when evaluating literature about African and African American voices and experiences.

Although relaying an authentic experience through children's and young-adult literature is admittedly difficult for any writer, history demonstrates that it is especially difficult for mainstream writers writing about African Americans. In the United States and throughout much of the world, Black cultural expression and contributions to society always have been devalued. Traditional African religion is demonized, even though it provides the basis for many contemporary forms of mainstream religious expression; Black dialect is considered inferior, even though linguists have demonstrated its syntactic integrity and widespread influence on American and European speech; hip hop music is criticized for being antisocial and misogynist, while at the same time it has grown into an international art form. This schizophrenic treatment of Black cultural expression by mainstream society demonstrates the importance of the Black author's authentic reflection from inside the Black experience. What should be highlighted? What should be celebrated? What should be stated matter-of-factly? When mainstream culture demonizes or idolizes Black cultural expression, an authentic and realistic rendering of Black voices and experiences by a mainstream writer is difficult at best.

Authenticity is achieved by moving from inside African American culture and experience outward into the world—evolving internally and influencing externally, and occasionally being influenced from the outside. Too often, writers outside of African American culture and experience write an African American children's or young-adult book that contains subtle or overt inaccuracies and offenses. A writer such as Arnold Adoff occasionally disproves the rule, but such writers are rare. Nonetheless the Arnold Adoffs of the world compel us not to dismiss all writers who write about African Americans but are not themselves African American. Rather, we want to promote African American authors while carefully scrutinizing authors who seek to write about African Americans from outside of African American culture and experience. Such a posture promotes authenticity while combating exploitation.

When sharing African American children's and young-adult literature, teachers should always be attentive to context. In thinking about context, we offer some suggestions and a few cautions. It is crucial that teachers assist students in building a rich context for the reading material. The books reviewed below should not be read in isolation from each other or from other African American and young-adult literature. African American books for children and young adults should be seen as part of the rich and diverse African American literary tradition. Virginia Hamilton or Julius Lester may write about slavery and the Civil War, or retell tales of High John and other tricksters from African and African American mythology, but they also write mysteries, science fiction, fantasy, and realistic fiction. Therefore a good reading list will include a wide range of genres and subject matter. Otherwise we restrict our students' view of the world and of themselves.

African American children's and young-adult books should be paired or grouped in conversation with each other, in order to both offer complementary perspectives and reveal contradiction or divergence within the tradition. For example, Andrea Davis Pinkney's *Bill Pickett: Rodo-Ridin' Cowboy* (1996) might be paired with Joyce Hansen's *I Thought My Soul Would Rise and Fly* (1997) in order to explore different but related experiences within African American history. Pinkney's book also can be paired with her book on Duke Ellington to explore African American biography. The depth of empathy, understanding, and critical insight that readers develop will be influenced by the degree to which teachers build and facilitate the creation of a literary context for their students.

For theme study and literature circles, teachers also may be inclined to pair or group African American books for children and young adults with books about other cultural traditions or experiences. Theme study can widen the reader's experience, but it also can foster color blindness and naive notions of similarity, and decrease the reader's awareness of the critical subtleties of human culture. We suggest that teachers carefully plan out a theme-study unit and encourage students to think beyond simplistic notions of culture and ethnicity in order to explore the ideas of *similarity* and *difference* as social, political, or geographic phenomena, and not as universal truths that underlie all things.

The books in this chapter are organized around six broad topics: Poetry and the Arts, Biographies and Heroes, Family Life and Relationships, Celebrations, Inner Triumphs and Finding One's Identity, and Exploring Our Heritage. Many of the books included in this chapter would fit easily into more than one broad topic. Teachers interested in grouping African American books for theme study or literature circles may find these topics useful starting points. Several of these broad topics overlap with other chapters in *Adventuring with Books*; combining books listed in this chapter with titles from related chapters invites readers to consider multiple perspectives on a particular genre, event, motif, or theme.

In the section on Poetry and the Arts we have included a sampling of books about art, music, photography, dance, and poetry. These books may be starting points for in-depth inquiries into individual arts or the important contributions of African Americans to the arts in this country.

For many individuals, finding one's identity is closely linked to reflection on the inner triumphs that are part of the personal growth process. Inner Triumphs and Finding One's Identity includes books that highlight individual growth and personal acceptance. In Biographies and Heroes we have included those books that present positive and realistic images of important individuals by showing how these individuals set goals and persevered even in the face of disappointment and discrimination.

The section titled Family Life and Relationships includes books about families and books that highlight powerful relationships between individuals who may not necessarily be part of the same family. Celebrations includes books about traditional cultural celebrations as well as some of the reasons people celebrate. The largest set of books in this collection relates broadly to Exploring Our Heritage. These fiction and nonfiction books highlight the people, events, places, and cultural practices that shape African American heritage in this country. While we were pleased to find a significant number of books written by African Americans about African Americans in history, we continue to be concerned about the small number of books that address periods in history other than slavery and the Civil War. We hope the groupings that follow will help to create spaces in all children's lives for the study and celebration of the diverse African and African American experiences and voices.

---

*The titles listed below each subheading are organized into Primary Reviews and Secondary Reviews. The Primary Reviews describe outstanding books in each subheading. The Secondary Reviews provide brief information about other books worthy of consideration. The titles listed below are **not** reviewed in this chapter; entries contain only bibliographic information. A cross reference to the annotated entry contained elsewhere in this volume is provided in boldface type at the end of the bibliographic information.*

Poetry and the Arts

Primary Reviews

15.1 Barnwell, Ysaye M. (1998). **No Mirrors in My Nana's House.** Illustrated by Synthia Saint James. San Diego: Harcourt Brace. 32 pp. ISBN: 0-15-201825-5. Picture Book. (See **10.15**)

15.2 Belafonte, Harry, and Lord Burgess (1999). **Island in the Sun.** Illustrated by Alex Ayliffe. New York: Dial Books for Young Readers. 32 pp. ISBN: 0-8037-2387-3. Picture Book. (See **10.25**)

15.3 Igus, Toyomi (1998). **i see the rhythm.** Illustrated by Michele Wood. San Francisco: Children's Book. 32 pp. ISBN: 0-89239-151-0. Picture Book. (See **3.90**)

15.4 Johnson, Dinah (1998). **All Around Town: The Photographs of Richard Samuel Roberts.** Photographs by Richard S. Roberts. New York: Henry Holt. 32 pp. ISBN: 0-8050-5456-1. Picture Book. (See **3.91**)

15.5 Kroll, Virginia L. (1996). **Can You Dance, Dalila?** Illustrated by Nancy Carpenter. New York: Simon & Schuster. 32 pp. ISBN: 0-689-80551-9. Picture Book. (See **4.12**)

15.6 Medearis, Angela Shelf (1997). **Rum-A-Tum-Tum.** Illustrated by James E. Ransome. New York: Holiday House. 32 pp. ISBN: 0-8234-1123-5. Picture Book. (See **10.29**)

15.7 Pinkney, Andrea Davis (1998). **Duke Ellington: The Piano Prince and His Orchestra.** Illustrated by Brian Pinkney. New York: Hyperion. ISBN: 0-7868-0178-6. Picture Book. (See **11.21**)

15.8 Steptoe, Javaka, editor (1997). **In Daddy's Arms I Am Tall: African Americans Celebrating Fathers.** Illustrated by Javaka Steptoe. New York: Lee & Low. 32 pp. ISBN: 0-880000-31-8. Picture Book. (See **4.26**)

Inner Triumphs and Finding One's Identity

Primary Reviews

15.9 Bunting, Eve (1998). **Your Move.** Illustrated by James Ransome. New York: Harcourt Brace. Unpaged. ISBN: 0-15-200181-6. Picture Book. (See **5.71, 20.33**)

5.10 Curtis, Gavin (1998). **The Bat Boy & His Violin.** Illustrated by E. B. Lewis. New York: Simon & Schuster. Unpaged. ISBN: 0-689-80099-1. Picture Book. (See **4.6**)

15.11 Farmer, Nancy (1996). **A Girl Named Disaster.** New York: Orchard. 309 pp. ISBN: 0-531-08889-8. Sophisticated Chapter Book. (See **5.73**)

15.12 Grimes, Nikki (1998). **Jazmin's Notebook.** New York: Dial. 102 pp. ISBN: 0-8037-2224-9. Chapter Book. (See **5.84**)

15.13 Herron, Carolivia (1997). **Nappy Hair.** Illustrated by Joe Cepeda. New York: Random House Books for Young Readers. Unpaged. ISBN: 0-679-87937-4. Picture Book. (See **4.9**)

15.14 Myers, Walter Dean (1999). **Monster.** Illustrated by Christopher Myers. New York: HarperCollins Juvenile. 281 pp. ISBN: 0-06-028077-8. Chapter Book. (See **5.112**)

15.15 Shange, Ntozake (1997). **Whitewash.** Illustrated by Michael Sporn. New York: Walker. Unpaged. ISBN: 0-8027-8490-9. Sophisticated Picture Book. (See **5.117, 20.16**)

15.16 Tarpley, Natasha Anastasia (1998). **I Love My Hair.** Illustrated by E. B. Lewis. Boston: Little Brown. 32 pp. ISBN: 0-316-52275-9. Picture Book. (See **8.61**)

Secondary Reviews

15.17 Antle, Nancy (1997). **Staying Cool.** Illustrated by E. B. Lewis. New York: Dial Books for Young Readers. 32 pp. ISBN: 0-8037-1876-4. Picture Book. (See **4.30**)

15.18 Cosby, Bill (1998). **Money Troubles.** Illustrated by Varnette P. Honeywood. New York: Scholastic. 40 pp. ISBN: 0-590-16402-3. Chapter Book. (See **7.38**)

15.19 Machado, Ana Maria (1996). **Nina Bonita.** Illustrated by Rosanna Faria. Brooklyn, NY: Kane/Miller. 24 pp. ISBN: 0-916291-63-4. Picture Book. (See **8.48**)

15.20 Pinkney, Brian (1997). **The Adventures of Sparrowboy.** New York: Simon & Schuster. 40 pp. ISBN: 0-689-81071-7. Picture Book. (See **8.53**)

Biographies and Heroes

Primary Reviews

15.21 Adler, David A. (1997). **A Picture Book of Thurgood Marshall.** Illustrated by Robert Casilla. New York: Dial Books for Young Readers. 48 pp. ISBN: 0-8234-1506-6. Picture Book. (See **3.76**)

15.22 Dingle, Derek T. (1998). **First in the Field: Baseball Hero Jackie Robinson.** New York: Hyperion Books for Children. 48 pp. ISBN: 0-7868-0348-7. Picture Book. (See **12.5**)

15.23 Greenfield, Eloise (1997). **For the Love of the Game: Michael Jordan and Me.** Illustrated by Jan Spivey Gilchrist. New York: HarperCollins. 32 pp. ISBN: 0-06-027298-8. Picture Book. (See **12.7**)

15.24 Parks, Rosa, and Jim Haskins (1997). **I Am Rosa Parks.** Illustrated by Wil Clay. New York: Dial Books for Young Readers. 48 pp. ISBN: 0-8037-1206-5. Chapter Book. (See **3.96**)

15.25 Pinkney, Andrea Davis (1996). **Bill Pickett: Rodeo-Ridin' Cowboy.** Illustrated by Brian Pinkney. San Diego: Harcourt Brace. Unpaged. ISBM: 0-15-200100-X. Picture Book. (See **3.72**)

Secondary Reviews

15.26 Cooper, Floyd (1996). **Mandela: From the Life of the South African Statesman.** New York: Philomel. 40 pp. ISBN: 0-399-22942-6. Picture Book. (See **5.3**)

15.27 Hudson, Wade, and Cheryl Willis Hudson, compilers (1997). **In Praise of Our Fathers and Our Mothers.** East Orange, New Jersey: Just Us. 131 pp. ISBN: 0-940975-59-9. Picture Book. (See **4.35**)

15.28 Krull, Kathleen (1996). **Wilma Unlimited: How Wilma Rudolph Became the World's Fastest Woman.** Illustrated by David Diaz. New York: Harcourt Brace. Unpaged. ISBN: 0-15-201267- 2. Picture Book. (See **5.17**)

15.29 Pippen, Scottie, with Greg Brown (1996). **Scottie Pippen: Reach Higher.** Illustrated by Doug Keith. 40 pp. ISBN: 0-87833-981-7. Picture Book. (See **12.2**)

15.30 Rodriguez, Alex, with Greg Brown (1998). **Alex Rodriguez: Hit a Grand Slam!** Illustrated by Doug Keith. 40 pp. ISBN: 0-87833-997-3. Picture Book. (See **12.2**)

Family Life and Relationships

Primary Reviews

15.31 Johnson, Angela (1997). **Daddy Calls Me Man.** Illustrated by Rhonda Mitchell. New York: Orchard. Unpaged. ISBN: 0-531-30042-0. Picture Book. (See **4.11**)

15.32 Johnson, Angela (1998). **Heaven.** New York: Simon & Schuster Books for Young Readers. 138 pp. ISBN: 0-689-82229-4. Chapter Book. (See **4.68**)

15.33 McKissack, Patricia C. (1997). **Ma Dear's Apron.** Illustrated by Floyd Cooper. New York: Simon & Schuster. Unpaged. ISBN: 0-689-81051-2. Picture Book. (See **4.16**)

Secondary Reviews

15.34 Carter, Dorothy (1997). **Bye, Mis' Lela.** Illustrated by Harvey Stevenson. New York: Farrar, Straus and Giroux. 32 pp. ISBN: 0-374-31013-0. Picture Book. (See **4.126**)

15.35 English, Karen (1998). **Just Right Stew.** Honesdale, PA: Boyds Mills. 32 pp. ISBN: 1-56397-487-8. Picture Book. (See **4.33**)

15.36 Hru, Dakari (1996). **The Magic Moonberry Jump Ropes.** Illustrated by E. B. Lewis. New York: Dial Books for Young Readers. Unpaged. ISBN: 0-8037-1754-7. Picture Book. (See **4.34**)

15.37 Igus, Toyomi (1996). **The Two Mrs. Gibsons.** Illustrated by Daryl Wells. San Francisco: Children's Book. 32 pp. ISBN: 0-89239-135-9. Picture Book. (See **4.36**)

15.38 Johnson, Angela (1998). **Songs of Faith.** New York: Orchard. 103 pp. ISBN: 0-531-30023-4. Chapter Book. (See **5.76**)

15.39 Mitchell, Claudette, Gracie Porter, and Patricia Tefft Cousin (1996). **Jump-rope.** San Diego: Arborlake. 8 pp. ISBN: 1-57518-0641-2. Picture Book. (See **7.52**)

Celebrations

Primary Reviews

15.40 King, Jr., Martin Luther (1997). **I Have a Dream.** New York: Scholastic. 40 pp. ISBN: 0-590-20516-1. Picture Book. (See **3.93**)

15.41 Ringgold, Faith (1999). **The Invisible Princess.** New York: Crown. 32 pp. ISBN: 0-517-80024-1. Picture Book. (See **14.13**)

15.42 Rosales, Melodye (1996). **'Twas the Night B'fore Christmas: An African-American Version.** New York: Scholastic. 32 pp. ISBN: 0-590-73944-1. Picture Book. (See **3.216**)

15.43 Woodtor, Dee Parmer (1996). **Big Meeting.** Illustrated by Dolores Johnson. New York: Atheneum. Unpaged. ISBN: 0-689-31933-9. Picture Book. (See **4.53**)

Exploring Our Heritage

Primary Reviews

15.44 Chambers, Veronica (1998). **Amistad Rising: A Story of Freedom.** Edited by Shelly Bowen and Allyn M. Johnston. Illustrated by Paul Lee. San Diego: Harcourt Brace. Unpaged. ISBN: 0-15-201803-4. Picture Book. (See **3.26**)

15.45 Fleming, Candace (1996). **Women of the Lights.** Illustrated by James Watling. Morton Grove, IL: Whitman. 79 pp. ISBN: 0-8075-9165-3. Chapter Book. (See **3.84**)

15.46 Johnston, Tony (1996). **The Wagon.** Illustrated by James E. Ransome. New York: Morrow. Unpaged. ISBN: 0-688-13457-2. Picture Book. (See **3.38**)

15.47 Lester, Julius (1998). **From Slave Ship to Freedom Road.** Illustrated by Rod Brown. New York: Dial. 37 pp. ISBN: 0-8037-1893-4. Sophisticated Picture Book. (See **5.18**)

15.48 Lester, Julius (1999). **What a Truly Cool World.** Illustrated by Joe Cepeda. New York: Scholastic. 40 pp. ISBN: 0-590-86468-8. Picture Book. (See **3.131**)

15.49 McKissack, Patricia C. (1997). **Run Away Home.** New York: Scholastic. 160 pp. ISBN: 0-590-46751-4. Chapter Book. (See **5.79**)

15.50 Mitchell, Rhonda (1997). **The Talking Cloth.** New York: Orchard. Unpaged. ISBN: 0-531-30004-8. Picture Book. (See **4.39**)

15.51 Myers, Walter Dean (1997). **Harlem.** Illustrated by Christopher Myers. New York: Scholastic. 32 pp. ISBN: 0-590-54340-7. Picture Book. (See **10.19**)

15.52 Paulsen, Gary (1997). **Sarny: A Life Remembered.** New York: Delacorte. 97 pp. ISBN: 0-385-32195-3. Chapter Book. (See **3.111**)

15.53 Robb, Laura (1997). **Music and Drum: Voices of War and Peace, Hope and Dreams.** Illustrated by Debra Lill. New York: Philomel. 32 pp. ISBN: 0-399-22024-0. Picture Book. (See **10.20**)

Secondary Reviews

15.54 Berry, James (1997). **First Palm Trees: An Anancy Spiderman Story.** Illustrated by Greg Couch. New York: Simon & Schuster Books for Young Readers. 40 pp. ISBN: 0-689-81060-1. Picture Book. (See **3.143**)

15.55 Duncan, Dayton (1996). **The West: An Illustrated History for Children.** New York: Little Brown. 136 pp. ISBN: 0-316-92236-6. Sophisticated Picture Book. (See **3.83**)

15.56 Hansen, Joyce (1997). **I Thought My Soul Would Rise and Fly: The Diary of Patsy, a Freed Girl.** New York: Scholastic. 202 pp. ISBN: 0-590-84913-1. Chapter Book. (See **3.32**)

15.57 Haskins, James, and Kathleen Benson (1998). **African Beginnings.** Illustrated by Floyd Cooper. New York: Lothrop, Lee & Shepard. 48 pp. ISBN: 0-688-10256-5. Picture Book. (See **3.88**)

15.58 Haskins, James, and Kathleen Benson (1999). **Bound for America: The Forced Migration of Africans to the New World.** Illustrated by Floyd Cooper. New York: Lothrop, Lee & Shepard. 48 pp. ISBN: 0-688-10258-1. Picture Book. (See **3.89**)

15.59 Johnson, Angela (1997). **The Rolling Store.** Illustrated by Peter Catalanotto. New York: Orchard. 32 pp. ISBN: 0-531-30076-5. Picture Book. (See **8.41**)

15.60 Jurmain, Suzanne (1998). **Freedom's Sons: The Story of the *Amistad* Mutiny.** Lothrop, Lee & Shepard. 128 pp. ISBN: 0-688-11072-X. Chapter Book. (See **5.15**)

15.61 Katz, William Loren (1997). **Black Indians: A Hidden Heritage.** New York: Simon & Schuster. 198 pp. ISBN: 0-689-80901-8. Chapter Book. (See **5.16**)

15.62 Kroll, Virginia L. (1998). **Faraway Drums.** Illustrated by Floyd Cooper. New York: Little Brown. Unpaged. ISBN: 0-316-50449-1. Picture Book. (See **14.8**)

15.63 Reeder, Carolyn (1997). **Across the Lines.** Illustrated by Robin Moore. New York: Atheneum Books for Young Readers. 220 pp. ISBN: 0-689-81133-0. Chapter Book. (See **3.123**)

15.64 Riggio, Anita (1997). **Secret Signs: Along the Underground Railroad.** Honesdale, PA: Boyds Mills. 32 pp. ISBN: 1-56397-555-6. Picture Book. (See **3.46**)

A.

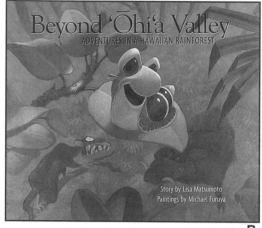

B.

C.

D.

A. *Pedro and the Monkey,* Robert D. San Souci/Michael Hays (**16.11**). **B.** *Behind ʻŌhiʻa Valley: Adventures in a Hawaiian Rainforest,* Lisa Matsumoto/Michael Furuya (**16.9**). **C.** *Beautiful Warrior: The Legend of the Nun's Kung Fu,* Emily Arnold McCully (**16.42**). **D.** *The Great Race,* David Bouchard/Zhong-Yang Huang (**16.46**).

16 Asian, Asian American, and Hawaii Pacific Voices and Experiences

Jann Pataray-Ching

Contributing reviewers included Trina Crawford, Alice Kimura, Patty Leahey, Miki Maeshiro, Jocelyn Mokulehua, Sally Omalza, Marcia Omura, Jann Pataray-Ching, Kathy Phillips, Anna Sumida, and Karla Hawkins Wendelin.

Asian, Asian American, and Hawaii Pacific children's literature are among a growing number of multicultural voices being published today. As we make greater efforts to learn about and embrace diverse cultures, both domestic and international, the need for more fiction and nonfiction literature that represents these cultures and cultural perspectives becomes greater.

This chapter on Asian, Asian American, and Hawaii Pacific children's literature represents three broad cultural traditions. Asians and Asian Americans often are viewed as one homogenous group of people; however their histories and cultures are quite diverse. For example, within the broad Asian cultural tradition, we find that Filipino culture differs greatly from Korean culture, which differs greatly from Indian culture. Even within one culture, there are differences stemming from place and time. Being Japanese in Japan, for example, is different from being Japanese American or from being Japanese in the United States. As Fischer (1986) noted, although each cultural group may find commonality with others through connections to the past and intergenerational lineage, culture is dynamic and evolving. In other words, Asian Americans have no cultural template. Instead each generation must "reinvent and reinterpret" itself while still, in some sense, remaining connected to the past (195).

Good quality children's literature that is both authentic and representative of the diversity among Asian and Asian American cultures and ethnic groups is difficult to find. We were successful at locating a rich collection of literature about Japanese Americans and Chinese Americans (such as Bunting's *So Far from the Sea*, Tunnell's *The Children of Topaz*, and Lee's *Nim and the War Effort*) and Japanese and Chinese culture (for example, McCully's *Beautiful Warrior: The Legend of the Nun's Kung Fu*, Melmed's *Little Oh*, and Bouchard's *The Great Race*). In addition, authors such as Allen Say and Ed Young have been successful at bringing Japanese American and Chinese American voices into the mainstream with books such as *Emma's Rug, Allison, Mouse Match*, and *The Lost Horse*. However, our search has made us aware of the need for more writing that represents the lives of other Asian and Asian American cultural and ethnic groups.

Locating children's literature about these other cultural and ethnic groups is difficult for two reasons. First most major publishing houses do not have an extensive list of cultural and ethnic literature that represents these various groups. Second the literature currently available is often produced by small publishing houses, making the literature difficult to find and therefore less accessible to children, parents, and teachers. We hope that the books we have included here will both celebrate the rich collection of Asian and Asian American voices currently in print, and signal the need to write and publish more literature representing the voices that are absent.

The third broad cultural tradition represented in this chapter is what we have called Hawaii Pacific children's literature. Although the Hawaiian monarchy was overthrown by the U.S. government in 1893, and despite the fact that the island chain became the fiftieth state in the union in 1959, Hawaii still has maintained a distinct identity—perhaps because of the rightful desire of native Hawaiians to reclaim their sovereignty, and because of the influx of foreigners who have arrived and settled on Hawaii's shores. An ethnically diverse population from predominantly Polynesian, Asian, and White European backgrounds makes Hawaii unique. Naturally then, its stories capture the cultural interrelationships born out of harmony and conflict between ethnic groups, and the shared cultural experiences of people living together on a group of islands heavily influenced by a rich cultural history but governed by a dominant western culture.

Stephen Sumida (1986) noted that Hawaii has been traditionally stereotyped in literature either as an island paradise where people enjoy a carefree and indolent lifestyle, or as a place of fantastic adventure. Much of Hawaii Pacific children's literature—even those books written locally—bear traces of these stereotypes, whether they are conveyed through human characters or animal characters. In selecting Hawaii Pacific literature (and the literature of other ethnic groups) for this chapter, we looked for the authors' ability to distinguish between cultural myth and cultural reality.

Cultural and gender stereotypes may be present not only in written text, but also in illustrations. Semiotics has taught us that both written and visual texts construct meaning (Peirce 1960). For example, illustrations in Hawaii Pacific children's literature often contribute to misperceptions of Hawaiians or local residents. Some books include illustrations of Hawaiian characters that are superficial and inaccurate, and that give readers the impression that little girls run around daily in *mu'umu'u* (flowered dresses) and *haku lei* (a string of flowers worn as a crown), or that menehune women (the legendary little people of old Hawaii) have Barbie-doll figures and are rescued by strong menehune men. Therefore it became our challenge to find a variety of fiction and nonfiction children's literature that demystified these stereotypes in both the text and illustrations, accurately educated readers about Hawaii's historical events, and portrayed Hawaii's people with affirmation and dignity. Not surprisingly, many stories selected for inclusion in this section pay tribute to the land, the early Polynesians, and the Hawaiian monarchy.

The books in this chapter have been organized around seven broad themes: Conflict and Memory, Crossing Boundaries, Relationships, Celebrations, Creation and Preservation, Inner Triumphs, and Voices of the Past. We have made our best effort to include a range of entertaining stories and culturally and politically empowering narratives about Asian, Asian American, and Hawaii Pacific racial and ethnic groups. James Clifford (1997) has reminded us that museums are more than storehouses of art; they are places of "contestation," where cultural memory is produced (188–219). In this chapter, we have tried to be sensitive to the political function of literature, and to select works that are both aesthetically exciting and culturally enabling.

Drawing on the ideas of Gramsci, Victor Villanueva (1993) envisions national memory as a mosaic of folklores. We believe this diversity of folklores, joined through a sense of the common good and a recognition of difference, embodies a democratic vision of society and the classroom; and that such a concept of national memory envisions a national consciousness woven out of voices rooted in local spaces. We have tried in this chapter to foreground those voices we find most invigorating and empowering, and that we hope will move students and teachers toward a greater appreciation for culture and diversity in the nation.

Works Cited

Clifford, James. 1997. *Routes: Travel and Translation in the Late Twentieth Century.* Cambridge, MA: Harvard University.

Fischer, Michael M. J. 1986. Ethnicity and the Post-modern Arts of Memory. In *Writing Culture,* eds. James Clifford and George E. Marcus. Berkeley, CA: University of California.

Peirce, C. S. 1960. Division of Signs. In *Collected Papers of Charles Sanders Peirce.* Vol. 2. Cambridge, MA: Harvard University.

Sumida, Stephan H. 1986. Waiting for the Big Fish: Recent Research in the Asian American Literature of Hawaii. In *The Best of Bamboo Ridge,* eds. Eric E. Chock and Darrell H. Y. Lum. Honolulu: Bamboo Ridge.

Villanueva, Victor, Jr. 1993. *Bootstraps: From an American Academic of Color.* Urbana, IL: National Council of Teachers of English.

---

*The titles listed below each subheading are organized into Primary Reviews and Secondary Reviews. The Primary Reviews describe outstanding books in each subheading. The Secondary Reviews provide brief information about other books worthy of consideration. The titles listed below are **not** reviewed in this chapter; entries contain only bibliographic information. A cross reference to the annotated entry contained elsewhere in this volume is provided in boldface type at the end of the bibliographic information.*

Conflict and Memory

Primary Reviews

16.1 Balgassi, Haemi (1996). **Peacebound Trains.** Illustrated by Chris K. Soentpiet. New York: Houghton Mifflin. 48 pp. ISBN: 0-395-72093-1. Picture Book. (See **3.114**)

16.2 Bunting, Eve (1998). **So Far from the Sea.** Illustrated by Chris K. Soentpiet. New York: Clarion. 30 pp. ISBN: 0-395-72095-8. Picture Book. (See **3.105, 20.9**)

16.3 Cha, Dia (1996). **Dia's Story Cloth.** Illustrated by Chue Cha and Nhia Thao Cha. New York: Lee & Low. Unpaged. ISBN: 1-880000-34-2. Sophisticated Picture Book. (See **3.78**)

16.4 Mochizuki, Ken (1997). **Passage to Freedom: The Sugihara Story.** Illustrated by Dom Lee. New York: Lee & Low. Unpaged. ISBN: 1-880000-49-0. Picture Book. (See **20.28**)

16.5 Tunnell, Michael O., and George W. Chilcoat (1997). **The Children of Topaz: The Story of a Japanese-American Internment Camp, Based on a Classroom Diary.** New York: Holiday House. 74 pp. ISBN: 0-8234-1239-3. Picture Book. (See **5.119**)

Secondary Reviews

16.6 Breckler, Rosemary (1996). **Sweet Dried Apples: A Vietnamese Wartime Childhood.** Illustrated by Deborah Kogan Ray. Boston: Houghton Mifflin. Unpaged. ISBN: 0-395-73570-X. Sophisticated Picture Book. (See **3.115, 20.22**)

16.7 Dolphin, Laurie (1997). **Our Journey from Tibet: Based on a True Story.** Photographs by Nancy Jo Johnson. New York: Dutton Children's Books. 40 pp. ISBN: 0-525-45577-9. Sophisticated Picture Book. (See **3.198**)

Crossing Boundaries

Primary Reviews

16.8 Little, Mimi Otey (1996). **Yoshiko and the Foreigner.** New York: Farrar, Straus and Giroux. Unpaged. ISBN: 0-374-32448-4. Picture Book. (See **4.84**)

16.9 Matsumoto, Lisa (1996). **Beyond 'Ōhi'a Valley: Adventures in a Hawaiian Rainforest.** Illustrated by Michael Furuya. Honolulu: Lehua. 55 pp. ISBN: 0-9647491-2-2. Picture Book. (See **14.32**)

16.10 Rumford, James (1998). **The Island-below-the-Star.** Boston: Houghton Mifflin. Unpaged. ISBN: 0-395-85159-9. Picture Book. (See **3.47**)

16.11 San Souci, Robert D. (1996). **Pedro and the Monkey.** Illustrated by Michael Hays. New York: Morrow Junior Books. Unpaged. ISBN: 0-688-13743-1. Picture Book. (See **3.135**)

Secondary Reviews

16.12 Choi, Sook Nyul (1997). **Yunmi and Halmoni's Trip.** Illustrated by Karen Dugan. Boston: Houghton Mifflin. Unpaged. ISBN: 0-395-81180-5. Picture Book. (See **4.111**)

16.13 Marton, Firina (1997). **Lady Kaguya's Secret: A Japanese Tale.** New York: Annick. Unpaged. ISBN: 1-55037-441-9. Picture Book. (See **14.31**)

16.14 Say, Allen (1997). **Allison.** Illustrated by Allen Say. Boston: Houghton Mifflin. 32 pp. ISBN: 0-395-85895-X. Picture Book. (See **4.75**)

16.15 Wong, Janet (1996). **A Suitcase of Seaweed and Other Poems.** New York: Simon & Schuster. 42 pp. ISBN: 0-689-80788-0. Chapter Book. (See **4.76**)

16.16 Yee, Tammy (1997). **Baby Honu's Incredible Journey.** Aiea, HI: Island Heritage. 32 pp. ISBN: 0-89610-285-8. Picture Book. (See **5.137**)

Relationships

Primary Reviews

16.17 Bash, Barbara (1996). **In the Heart of the Village.** San Francisco: Sierra Club Books for Children. Unpaged. ISBN: 0-87156-575-7. Picture Book. (See **4.130**)

16.18 Melmed, Laura Krauss (1997). **Little Oh.** Illustrated by Jim LaMarche. New York: Lothrop, Lee & Shepard. Unpaged. ISBN: 0-688-14208-7. Picture Book. (See **4.17**)

16.19 Pirotta, Saviour (1997). **Turtle Bay.** Illustrated by Nilesh Mistry. New York: Farrar, Straus and Giroux. Unpaged. ISBN: 0-374-37888-6. Picture Book. (See **2.18**)

Secondary Reviews

16.20 Brenner, Barbara, and Julie Takaya (1996). **Chibi: A True Story from Japan.** Illustrated by June Otani. New York: Clarion. 63 pp. ISBN: 0-395-69623-2. Picture Book. (See **5.130**)

16.21 Garland, Sherry (1998). **My Father's Boat.** Illustrated by Ted Rand. New York: Scholastic. Unpaged. ISBN: 0-590-47867-2. Picture Book. (See **4.127**)

16.22 Ho, Minfong (1996). **Hush! A Thai Lullaby.** Illustrated by Holly Meade. New York: Orchard. Unpaged. ISBN: 0-531-09500-2. Picture Book. (See **4.112**)

16.23 Johnston, Tony (1996). **Fishing Sunday.** Illustrated by Barrett V. Root. New York: Morrow. Unpaged. ISBN: 0-688-13458-0. Picture Book. (See **4.37**)

16.24 Kudler, David (1997). **The Seven Gods of Luck.** Illustrated by Linda Finch. Boston: Houghton Mifflin. Unpaged. ISBN: 0-395-78830-7. Picture Book. (See **14.9**)

16.25 Waite, Michael P. (1996). **Jojofu.** Illustrated by Yoriko Ito. New York: Lothrop, Lee & Shepard. Unpaged. ISBN: 0-688-13660-5. Picture Book. (See **5.136**)

16.26 Yee, Paul (1996). **Ghost Train.** Illustrated by Harvey Chan. Emeryville, CA: Douglas & McIntyre. Unpaged. ISBN: 0-88899-257-2. Sophisticated Picture Book. (See **4.61**)

16.27 Young, Ed (1997). **Mouse Match: A Chinese Folktale.** Orlando, FL: Harcourt Brace. Unpaged. ISBN: 0-15-201453-5. Picture Book. (See **3.138**)

Celebrations

Secondary Reviews

16.28 Chin-Lee, Cynthia (1997). **A Is for Asia.** Illustrated by Yumi Heo. New York: Orchard. Unpaged. ISBN: 0-531-30011-0. Picture Book. (See **7.32**)

16.29 Demi (1997). **Happy New Year! Kung-hsi fa-ts'ai!** New York: Crown. Unpaged. ISBN: 0-517-70957-0. Picture Book. (See **3.197**)

16.30 Hoyt-Goldsmith, Diane (1998). **Celebrating Chinese New Year.** Illustrated by Lawrence Migdale. New York: Holiday House. 32 pp. ISBN: 0-8234-1393-4. Picture Book. (See **3.205**)

16.31 Russell, Ching Yeung (1997). **Moon Festival.** Illustrated by Christopher Zhong-Yuan Zhang. Honesdale, PA: Boyds Mills. Unpaged. ISBN: 1-56397-596-3. Picture Book. (See **3.217**)

16.32 Williams, Rianna M. (1997). **Mahealani and the King of Hawai'i.** Illustrated by Jackie Black. Honolulu: Ka mea Kakau. 103 pp. ISBN: 0-9658621-0-0. Chapter Book. (See **3.54**)

Creation and Preservation

Primary Reviews

16.33 Davol, Marguerite W. (1997). **The Paper Dragon.** Illustrated by Robert Sabuda. New York: Atheneum. Unpaged. ISBN: 0-689-31992-4. Picture Book. (See **14.2**)

16.34 Orr, Katherine (1997). **Discover Hawaii's Freshwater Wildlife.** Aiea, HI: Island Heritage. 44 pp. ISBN: 0-89610-243-2. Sophisticated Chapter Book. (See **1.48**)

16.35 Orr, Katherine, and Mauliola Cook (1997). **Discover Hawaii's Birth by Fire Volcanoes.** Aiea, HI: Island Heritage. 44 pp. ISBN: 0-89610-245-9. Sophisticated Chapter Book. (See **1.49**)

16.36 Young, Ed (1997). **Voices of the Heart.** New York: Scholastic. Unpaged. ISBN: 0-590-50199-2. Picture Book. (See **11.40**)

Secondary Reviews

16.37 Knight, Margy Burns (1996). **Talking Walls: The Stories Continue.** Illustrated by Anne Sibley O'Brien. Gardiner, ME: Tilbury. Unpaged. ISBN: 0-88448-165-4. Picture Book. (See **7.21**)

16.38 Lee, Huy Voun (1995). **In the Park.** New York: Henry Holt. Unpaged. ISBN: 0-8050-4128-1. Picture Book. (See **11.42**)

16.39 Rumford, James (1996). **Cloudmakers.** New York: Houghton Mifflin. Unpaged. ISBN: 0-395-76505-6. Picture Book. (See **11.44**)

Inner Triumphs

Primary Reviews

16.40 Demi (1997). **One Grain of Rice: A Mathematical Folktale.** New York: Scholastic. Unpaged. ISBN: 0-590-93998-X. Picture Book. (See **9.13**)

16.41 Lee, Milly (1997). **Nim and the War Effort.** Illustrated by Yangsook Choi. New York: Farrar, Straus and Giroux. Unpaged. ISBN: 0-374-35523-1. Picture Book. (See **3.109**)

16.42 McCully, Emily Arnold (1998). **Beautiful Warrior: The Legend of the Nun's Kung Fu.** New York: Scholastic. Unpaged. ISBN: 0-590-37487-7. Picture Book. (See **5.43**)

Secondary Reviews

16.43 Say, Allen (1996). **Emma's Rug.** New York: Houghton Mifflin. 32 pp. ISBN: 0-395-74294-3. Picture Book. (See **11.45**)

16.44 Wells, Ruth (1996). **The Farmer and the Poor God: A Folktale from Japan.** Illustrated by Yoshi. New York: Simon & Schuster Books for Young Readers. Unpaged. ISBN: 0-689-80214-5. Picture Book. (See **4.40**)

16.45 Young, Ed (1998). **The Lost Horse: A Chinese Folktale.** San Diego: Silver Whistle/Harcourt Brace. Unpaged. ISBN: 0-15-201016-5. Picture Book. (See **3.171**)

Voices of the Past

Primary Reviews

16.46 Bouchard, David (1997). **The Great Race.** Illustrated by Zhong-Yang Huang. Brookfield, CT: Millbrook. Unpaged. ISBN: 0-7613-0305-7. Picture Book. (See **7.93**)

16.47 Ho, Mingfong (1996). **Maples in the Mist: Children's Poems from the Tang Dynasty.** Illustrated by Jean Tseng and Mou-sien Tseng. New York: Lothrop, Lee & Shepard. Unpaged. ISBN: 0-688-12044-X. Picture Book. (See **10.61**)

16.48 Spivak, Dawnine (1997). **Grass Sandals: The Travels of Basho.** Illustrated by Demi. New York: Atheneum. Unpaged. ISBN: 0-689-80776-7. Picture Book. (See **10.63**)

Secondary Reviews

16.49 Alameida, Roy (1997). **Na Mo'olelo o ka Wa Kahiko: Stories of Old Hawaii.** Honolulu: Best. 124 pp. ISBN: 1-57306-026-7. Sophisticated Chapter Book. (See **3.140**)

16.50 Demi (1997). **Buddha Stories.** New York: Henry Holt. Unpaged. ISBN: 0-8050-4886-3. Picture Book. (See **3.144**)

A.

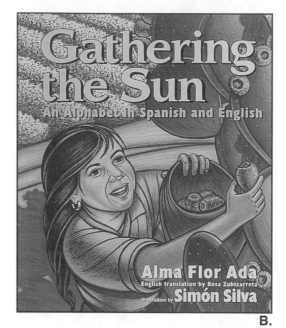

B.

C.

D.

A. *Mama and Papa Have a Store,* Amelia Lau Carling (**17.7**). **B.** *Gathering the Sun: An Alphabet in English and Spanish,* Alma Flor Ada/Simón Silva (**17.44**). **C.** *Sol a Sol: Bilingual Poems,* Lori Marie Carlson/Emily Lisker (**17.2**). **D.** *Mola: Cuna Life Stories and Art,* Maricel E. Presilla (**17.9**).

17 Hispanic/Latino, Hispanic American, and Latino American Voices and Experiences

Caryl Gottlieb Crowell

Contributing reviewers included Carol Cribett-Bell, Caryl Gottlieb Crowell, Kathy Lohse, Carmen M. Martínez-Roldán, Sandra Montiel-Costell, Elizabeth M. Redondo, Betsy Shepard, Kathy G. Short, and Katrina Smits.

In deciding to include books about Hispanics/Latinos throughout this edition of *Adventuring with Books*, rather than reviewing them all in a single chapter, the members of our review committee hope that teachers will include in their language arts curriculum the literature of communities that may not be represented in their school populations. In this way, they can offer children a vision of a world where language and cultural differences are resources, not obstacles. At the same time, we want teachers whose classes may include Hispanic/Latino children to be able to easily access books that may be of particular interest to their students. To this end, we have decided to group the books we reviewed in this chapter into text-sets that teachers may find useful in representing the diversity of Hispanic/Latino culture and language use throughout the world.

In choosing among the many books presented to us for review, we looked for books that provided authentic images of different Hispanic/Latino cultures and language users. Where the author or illustrator was a member of the community he or she was representing, we could be reasonably assured that the portrayal was accurate, and such was the case with almost two-thirds of the books we reviewed. For example, Luis Garay draws heavily upon his own Nicaraguan background in his stories and illustrations. However, if the author was not Hispanic/Latino, we looked for strong ties to the community and culture being depicted or some evidence of extensive research, such as the story of two quinceañeras presented by Elizabeth King.

Although we have included books that deal with such surface-level elements of culture as food and holidays, we also looked for books that moved beyond stereotypes to show these activities embedded in the daily family and community life of Hispanics/Latinos from different areas of the world. This was a particular challenge for our group's members because we are most familiar with the language and culture of our Arizona border community and nearby northern Mexico. We relied on Carmen Martínez, the Puerto Rican member of our group, and other colleagues from Central America, South America, and the Caribbean, to advise us in reviewing books about cultures in their countries.

Language use was of particular interest to us in reviewing books. Hispanic/Latino culture is not monolithic, and neither is the use of Spanish across these distinct communities. In the case of dual-language texts and books simultaneously released in both English and Spanish, we carefully examined books for language that is accessible to all readers, and interpretations that honor the meaning and significance of the story and the richness and rhythm of words in both languages. Some of us have been teaching long enough to remember early translation efforts that were riddled with grammatical and lexical errors. We also considered which language was given privileged position on the page, and have commented on this feature in our reviews.

Often the books we read were written in English with just a few words of Spanish embedded in the texts. In these situations, it is important to acknowledge the purpose of such language use. Where the intent is to teach Spanish as a second language, the insertion of Spanish words does not always sound natural. Many of these books contain glossaries to help readers pronounce the foreign words. In contrast are books that include very authentic code-switching—alternating the use of two languages at the word, phrase, clause, or sentence level—which is a distinctive characteristic of bilingual communities. Code-switching occurs between friends and family members, and is used to help tell stories, identify speakers as members of the same language community, and define the social roles of the speakers. Gary Soto's books are excellent examples of code-switching done well, and readers of his books usually can figure out the meaning of the words from the context.

In reviewing traditional stories from different Hispanic/Latino origins, we paid attention to books that were carefully researched and that offered respectful portrayals of cultures and history. The children who listened to these tales were enchanted with the stories, most of which are enriched by a smattering of indigenous words. In discussions that followed these readings, we reminded children that ways of living change over time, even though a culture's long-standing stories may not. We wanted them to understand that the depictions of early Hispanic/Latino or Native American cultures in folktales is not what they would likely encounter upon visiting these countries today.

Almost all of the books we reviewed were used in classrooms and school libraries with children, in the context of larger theme-based inquiries or literature studies. We want to share these classroom applications with teachers, who may want to focus on the diversity of Hispanic culture by grouping books in the text-sets we've suggested in this chapter, rather than following the themes in the chapters in which the reviews can be found. In the same way that the intensity of colors varies when the background is changed, the focus of these books can shift when they are placed in different text-sets. We have organized the books in this chapter into the following sections: Poetry and Song, Comparing Diverse Cultures, Folktales and Legends, Cultural Foods, The Power of Language and Literacy, Concept Books, A Sense of Community, Heroes and History, and Life Passages.

The books in some of these sections offer a look at past and present cultures in Mexico, the Caribbean, Colombia, Central America, and Hispanic/Latino communities in the United States. The section entitled Comparing Diverse Cultures includes mostly nonfiction works that present traditional ways of life in differing locales. The section A Sense of Community focuses on how families and communities support each other, and Life Passages celebrates the life cycle events that are important to all cultures—birth, birthdays, coming-of-age ceremonies, weddings, and death. The books listed under Cultural Foods give readers an opportunity to discover that not all Hispanics/Latinos eat tacos. The sections Poetry and Song, Concept Books, and Folktales and Legends are thematically similar to the *Adventuring with Books* chapter headings. In Heroes and History, we grouped together books about important historical figures and events from Hispanic/Latino communities, including both famous people and more personal voices from the past. Finally, The Power of Language and Literacy section includes books that consider how access to oral and written language, in both first and second languages, is essential to the personal and communal success of Hispanics/Latinos in the United States.

---

*The titles listed below are **not** reviewed in this chapter; entries contain only bibliographic information. A cross reference to the annotated entry contained elsewhere in this volume is provided in boldface type at the end of the bibliographic information.*

Poetry and Song

17.1 Alarcón, Francisco X. (1997). **Laughing Tomatoes and Other Spring Poems/Jitomates risueños y otros poemas de primavera.** Illustrated by Maya Christina González. San Francisco: Children's Book. 32 pp. ISBN: 0-89239-139-1. Picture Book. (See **10.60**)

17.2 Carlson, Lori Marie (1998). **Sol a sol: Bilingual Poems.** Illustrated by Emily Lisker. Translated by Lyda Aponte de Zacklin. New York: Henry Holt. Unpaged. ISBN: 0-8050-4373-X. Picture Book. (See **10.52**)

17.3 Orozco, José-Luis (1997). **Diez deditos/Ten Little Fingers and Other Play Rhymes and Action Songs from Latin America.** Illustrated by Elisa Kleven. New York: Dutton Children's Books. 56 pp. ISBN: 0-525-45736-4. Picture Book. (See **10.55**)

Comparing Diverse Cultures

17.4 Ancona, George (1997). **Mayeros: A Yucatec Maya Family.** New York: Lothrop, Lee & Shepard. Unpaged. ISBN: 0-688-13465-3. Picture Book. (See **3.56, 20.51**)

17.5 Ancona, George (1998). **Fiesta Fireworks.** New York: Lothrop, Lee & Shepard. Unpaged. ISBN: 0-688-14817-4. Picture Book. (See **3.172**)

17.6 Applebaum, Diana (1997). **Cocoa Ice.** Illustrated by Holly Meade. New York: Orchard. Unpaged. ISBN: 0-531-30040-4. Picture Book. (See **3.21**)

17.7 Carling, Amelia Lau (1998). **Mama and Papa Have a Store.** New York: Dial. Unpaged. ISBN: 0-8037-2044-0. Picture Book. (See **4.97**)

17.8 Presilla, Maricel E. (1996). **Life around the Lake.** Illustrated by Gloria Soto. New York: Henry Holt. Unpaged. ISBN: 0-8050-3800-0. Picture Book. (See **11.56**)

17.9 Presilla, Maricel E. (1996). **Mola: Cuna Life Stories and Art.** New York: Henry Holt. Unpaged. ISBN: 0-8050-3801-9. Picture Book. (See **11.56**)

17.10 Solá, Michéle (1997). **Angela Weaves a Dream: The Story of a Young Maya Artist.** Photographs by Jeffrey Jay Foxx. New York:

Hyperion Books for Children. 47 pp. ISBN: 0-7868-0073-9. Picture Book. (See **11.38**)

17.11 Staub, Frank J. (1996). **Children of Yucatán.** Minneapolis: Carolrhoda. 48 pp. ISBN: 0-87614-984-0. Picture Book. (See **3.56**)

17.12 Temko, Florence (1996). **Traditional Crafts from Mexico and Central America.** Illustrated by Randall Gooch. Photographs by Robert L. Wolfe and Diane Wolfe. Minneapolis: Lerner. 64 pp. ISBN: 0-8225-2935-1. Chapter Book. (See **12.38**)

17.13 Torres, Leyla (1998). **Liliana's Grandmothers.** New York: Farrar, Straus and Giroux. Unpaged. ISBN: 0-374-35105-8. Picture Book. (See **4.108**)

Folktales and Legends

17.14 Ada, Alma Flor (1997). **The Lizard and the Sun: La lagartija y el sol.** New York: Doubleday. Unpaged. ISBN: 0-385-32121-X. Picture Book. (See **3.139**)

17.15 Anaya, Rudolfo (1997). **Maya's Children: The Story of La Llorona.** Illustrated by Maria Baca. New York: Hyperion. Unpaged. ISBN: 0-7868-0152-2. Picture Book. (See **3.126**)

17.16 González, Lucía M. (1997). **Señor Cat's Romance and Other Favorite Stories from Latin America.** Illustrated by Lulu Delacre. New York: Scholastic. 48 pp. ISBN: 0-590-48537-7. Chapter Book. (See **3.132**)

17.17 Harper, Jo (1998). **The Legend of Mexicatl/La leyenda de Mexicatl.** Illustrated by Robert Casilla. Spanish-language edition translated by Tatiana Lans. New York: Turtle. Unpaged. ISBN: 1-890515-05-1 (English)/1-890515-06-X (Spanish). Picture Book. (See **3.129**)

17.18 Hickox, Rebecca (1997). **Zorro and Quwi.** Illustrated by Kim Howard. New York: Delacorte. Unpaged. ISBN: 0-385-32122-8. Picture Book. (See **3.202**)

17.19 Kimmel, Eric A. (1997). **Squash It! A True and Ridiculous Tale.** Illustrated by Robert Rayevsky. New York: Holiday House. Unpaged. ISBN: 0-8234-1299-7. Picture Book. (See **14.30**)

17.20 Kurtz, Jane (1996). **Miro in the Kingdom of the Sun.** Illustrated by David Frampton. Boston: Houghton Mifflin. Unpaged. ISBN: 0-395-69181-8. Picture Book. (See **3.153**)

17.21 Moreton, Daniel (1997). **La Cucaracha Martina: A Caribbean Folktale.** New York: Turtle. Unpaged. ISBN: 1-890515-03-5. Picture Book. (See **3.132**)

17.22 Ramirez, Michael Rose (1998). **The Legend of the Hummingbird.** Illustrated by Margaret Sanfilippo. New York: Mondo. Unpaged. ISBN: 1-57255-232-8. Picture Book. (See **3.164**)

Cultural Foods

17.23 Bertrand, Diane Gonzales (1996). **Sip, Slurp, Soup, Soup/Caldo, caldo, caldo.** Illustrated by Alex Pardo DeLange. Houston, TX: Piñata. Unpaged. ISBN: 1-55885-183-6. Picture Book. (See **7.92**)

17.24 Rosa-Casanova, Sylvia (1997). **Mami Provi and the Pot of Rice.** Illustrated by Robert Roth. New York: Atheneum. Unpaged. ISBN: 0-689-31932-0. Picture Book. (See **4.19**)

17.25 Soto, Gary (1997). **Chato y su cena.** Illustrated by Susan Guevara. Translated by Alma Flor Ada and F. Isabel Campoy. New York: Putnam and Grosset. Unpaged. ISBN: 0-689-11601-1. Picture Book. (See **8.58**)

17.26 Wing, Natasha (1996). **Jalapeño Bagels.** Illustrated by Robert Casilla. New York: Atheneum. Unpaged. ISBN: 0-689-80530-6. Picture Book. (See **4.72**)

17.27 Zamorano, Ana (1996). **Let's Eat!** Illustrated by Julie Vivas. New York: Scholastic. Unpaged. ISBN: 0-590-13444-2. Picture Book. (See **4.109**)

The Power of Language and Literacy

17.28 Lachtman, Ofelia Dumas (1997). **Call Me Consuelo.** Houston, TX: Arte Publico. 149 pp. ISBN: 1-55885-187-9. Chapter Book. (See **5.91**)

17.29 Mora, Pat (1997). **Tomás and the Library Lady/Tomas y la señora de la biblioteca.** Illustrated by Raúl Colón. New York: Knopf

(English)/Dragonfly (Spanish). Unpaged. ISBN: 0-679-80401-3. Picture Book. (See **20.39**)

17.30 Rodriguez, Luis J. (1997). **América Is Her Name.** Illustrated by Carlos Vasquez. Willimantic, CT: Curbstone. Unpaged. ISBN: 1-880684-40-3. Sophisticated Picture Book. (See **20.7**)

Concept Books

17.31 Elya, Susan Middleton (1996). **Say Hola to Spanish.** Illustrated by Loretta Lopez. New York: Lee & Low. Unpaged. ISBN: 1-880000-29-6. Picture Book. (See **13.35**)

17.32 Elya, Susan Middleton (1997). **Say Hola to Spanish, Otra Vez (Again!).** Illustrated by Loretta Lopez. New York: Lee & Low. Unpaged. ISBN: 1-880000-59-8. Picture Book. (See **13.35**)

A Sense of Community

17.33 Ancona, George (1998). **Barrio: José's Neighborhood.** San Diego: Harcourt Brace. Unpaged. ISBN: 0-15-201049-1. Picture Book. (See **4.1**)

17.34 Bunting, Eve (1996). **Going Home.** Illustrated by David Diaz. New York: Cotler. Unpaged. ISBN: 0-06-026296-6. Picture Book. (See **4.4, 20.1**)

17.35 Colón-Vilá, Lillian (1998). **Salsa.** Illustrated by Roberta Collier-Morales. Houston, TX: Piñata. Unpaged. ISBN: 1-55885-220-4. Picture Book. (See **11.22**)

17.36 Garay, Luis (1997). **The Long Road.** Plattsburgh, NY: Tundra. Unpaged. ISBN: 0-88776-408-8. Picture Book. (See **5.126**)

17.37 Garay, Luis (1997). **Pedrito's Day.** New York: Orchard. Unpaged. ISBN: 0-531-09522-3. Picture Book. (See **8.34**)

17.38 Lomas Garza, Carmen (1996). **In My Family/En mi familia.** Translated by Francisco X. Alarcón. San Francisco: Children's Book. Unpaged. ISBN: 0-89239-138-3. Picture Book. (See **4.14**)

17.39 London, Jonathan (1998). **Hurricane!** Illustrated by Henri Sorensen. New York: Lothrop, Lee & Shepard. Unpaged. ISBN: 0-688-12977-3. Picture Book. (See **5.111**)

17.40 Martinez, Victor (1996). **Parrot in the Oven: Mi vida.** New York: Cotler. 216 pp. ISBN: 0-06-026704-6. Sophisticated Chapter Book. (See **20.4**)

17.41 Soto, Gary (1996). **The Old Man and His Door.** Illustrated by Joe Cepeda. New York: Putnam. Unpaged. ISBN: 0-399-22700-8. Picture Book. (See **4.25**)

17.42 Steptoe, John (1997). **Creativity.** Illustrated by E. B. Lewis. New York: Clarion. 32 pp. ISBN: 0-395-68706-3. Picture Book. (See **20.6**)

17.43 Stevens, Jan Romero (1997). **Carlos and the Skunk/Carlos y el zorrillo.** Illustrated by Jeanne Arnold. Translated by Patricia Hinton Davison. Flagstaff, AZ: Northland. Unpaged. ISBN: 0-87358-591-7. Picture Book. (See **4.107**)

Heroes and History

17.44 Ada, Alma Flor (1997). **Gathering the Sun: An Alphabet in Spanish and English.** Illustrated by Simón Silva. Translated by Rosa Zubizaretta. New York: Lothrop, Lee & Shepard. Unpaged. ISBN: 0-688-13903-5. Picture Book. (See **7.23**)

17.45 Aldana, Patricia, editor (1996). **Jade and Iron: Latin American Tales from Two Cultures.** Illustrated by Luis Garay. Translated by Hugh Hazelton. Toronto, Canada: Groundwood. 64 pp. ISBN: 0-88899-256-4. Sophisticated Chapter Book. (See **3.125**)

17.46 Collins, David R. (1996). **Farmworker's Friend: The Story of Cesar Chavez.** Minneapolis: Carolrhoda. 80 pp. ISBN: 0-87614-982-4. Chapter Book. (See **5.38**)

17.47 Marrin, Albert (1997). **Empires Lost and Won: The Spanish Heritage in the Southwest.** New York: Atheneum. 216 pp. ISBN: 0-689-80414-8. Chapter Book. (See **3.110**)

17.48 Morey, Janet Nomura, and Wendy Dunn (1996). **Famous Hispanic Americans.** New York: Cobblehill. 190 pp. ISBN: 0-525-65190-X. Chapter Book. (See **5.44**)

17.49 Romero, Maritza (1997). **Selena Perez: Queen of Tejano Music.** New York: PowerKids. 24 pp. ISBN: 0-8239-5086-7. Picture Book. (See **7.69**)

17.50 Stanley, Diane (1996). **Elena.** New York: Hyperion Books for Children. 55 pp. ISBN: 0-7868-0256-1. Chapter Book. (See **3.15**)

Life Passages

17.51 Guy, Ginger Foglesong (1996). **¡Fiesta!** Illustrated by René King Moreno. New York: Greenwillow. Unpaged. ISBN: 0-688-14331-8. Picture Book. (See **9.8**)

17.52 Johnston, Tony (1998). **Day of the Dead.** Illustrated by Jeanette Winter. San Diego: Harcourt Brace. 56 pp. ISBN: 0-15-222863-2. Picture Book. (See **3.178**)

17.53 King, Elizabeth (1998). **Quinceañera: Celebrating Fifteen.** New York: Dutton Children's Books. 40 pp. ISBN: 0-525-45638-4. Chapter Book. (See **3.179**)

17.54 Kleven, Elisa (1996). **Hooray, a Piñata!/¡Viva! ¡Una piñata!** New York: Dutton Children's Books. Unpaged. ISBN: 0-525-45606-8 (English)/0-525-45606-6 (Spanish). Picture Book. (See **6.22**)

17.55 Lachtman, Ofelia Dumas (1997). **Leticia's Secret.** Houston, TX: Piñata. 126 pp. ISBN: 1-55885-209-3. Chapter Book. (See **5.141**)

17.56 Luenn, Nancy (1998). **A Gift for Abuelita: Celebrating the Day of the Dead/Un regalo para Abuelita: En celebración del día de los muertos.** Illustrated by Robert Chapman. Translated by Mario Lamo-Jiménez. Flagstaff, AZ: Rising Moon. Unpaged. ISBN: 0-87358-688-3. Picture Book. (See **4.15**)

17.57 Reiser, Lynn (1998). **Tortillas and Lullabies/Tortillas y cancioncitas.** Illustrated by Corazones Valientes. Translated by Rebecca Hart. New York: Greenwillow. 40 pp. ISBN: 0-688-14628-7. Picture Book. (See **13.39**)

17.58 Sáenz, Benjamin Alire (1998). **A Gift from Papá Diego/Un regalo de Papá Diego.** Illustrated by Gerónimo García. El Paso, TX: Cinco Puntos. 40 pp. ISBN: 0-938317-33-4. Picture Book. (See **4.21**)

17.59 Soto, Gary (1997). **Snapshots from the Wedding.** Illustrated by Stephanie Garcia. New York: Putman. Unpaged. ISBN: 0-399-22808-X. Picture Book. (See **3.188**)

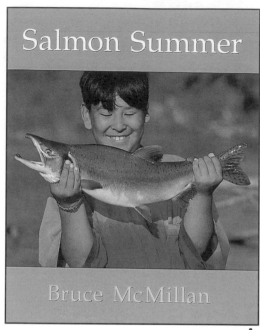

A. **B.**

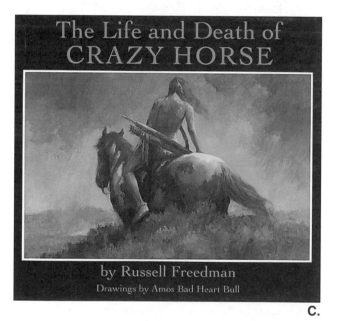

C.

A. *Salmon Summer,* Bruce McMillan (**18.2**). **B.** *Spider Spins a Story: Fourteen Legends from Native America,* Jill Max/various illustrators (**18.37**). **C.** *The Life and Death of Crazy Horse,* Russell Freedman/Amos Bad Heart Bull (**18.73**).

18 Native American Voices and Experiences

Stacie Cook Emert

Contributing reviewers included Sandra Beecher, Caroline Carlson, Stacie Cook Emert, Barbara Greenberg, Janelle Mathis, Bea Nez, and Sheilah Nicholas.

Our committee reviewed the current literature related to Native American people and their experiences. As individuals, we brought diverse experiences and multiple perspectives to the group. These perspectives were important to our conversations as we selected the best Native American literature published between 1996 and 1998. In addition to our varied work experiences as librarians, teachers, curriculum resource staff, and university professors, we each have had varying experiences with children's literature, Native American literature, and Native American people. Some members shared with the committee their Navajo or Hopi heritage and culture. Some had taught undergraduate or graduate children's literature courses, while others shared their experiences working in a school setting with children ages five to fourteen. All members of the committee had taken several graduate courses related to children's literature and had explored multicultural issues. Our combined experiences helped us determine whether the literature we reviewed would be appropriate for classroom use. We initially read and discussed several professional articles to help guide our decisions about selection criteria for the books that we would be reviewing (Caldwell-Wood and Mitten 1991; Kuipers 1991; Slapin and Seale 1992; Slapin, Seale, and Gonzales 1992). A primary concern about past literature related to Native Americans was that the books were not authentic from the Native American point of view (Bader 1997; Harris 1997; Reimer 1992). Accounts of Native American people and their experiences often were written from a European perspective. We wanted to make sure that in the books we reviewed, cultural traditions were honored and Native Americans were recognized for their individual and societal contributions (Ledford and Peel 1998). Using Slapin, Seale, and Gonzales' (1992) criteria as a guide, we noted whether the language in the book was demeaning or condescending. We looked to see whether terms such as *squaw, chief, redskin,* or *savage* were used. We examined how Native American people were portrayed in the illustrations, and paid particular attention to clothing and symbols reflected in traditions and stories to ensure that they were accurate representations of a particular group of people and did not fall prey to stereotypes. Finally we checked the historical accuracy of the literature.

Our interest in authenticity also led us to note whether the authors or illustrators were native people. In addition, we recorded the type of research that the author had done to familiarize himself or herself with the specific group being written about or the area of the country in which the story took place. We recorded the same information about the illustrators. We thought that this additional information would help support how these books were used in the classroom.

The content of the texts also was an important consideration. We wanted to provide a set of materials that could be used across the curriculum in a variety of ways. To help us determine how each book might best be utilized in the classroom, we asked ourselves these questions: Can it be used as a reference book? For what ages is the book appropriate? Is the lesson or moral of the book told from a Native American point of view? What issues are brought out in the book? Who would read this book?

Although we did find some unfavorable materials, overall we found a substantial amount of high-quality literature related to Native Americans. Our experiences reminded us how important it is to take a critical stance as we review and share books with others. Among our favorite selections were contemporary stories and essays about native people. The photo essays were rated highly because of their accurate information and the use of photography. These books showed images of how many Native Americans live today, while still practicing their cultural traditions from the past. Unfortunately much of the literature we reviewed tended to focus on legends and traditional stories. Although these are important, we feel that it is equally important to provide modern images of Native Americans in order to help students relate to current issues. In addition, students need to see how our past influences our present.

Another concern we had was a tendency in the literature to generalize across all Native American groups. Some books tended to attribute information from one tribe to all native people. Because of this, we were careful to select materials that observed the uniqueness of each group and that emphasized the diversity among the various tribes.

Thinking about the diversity issue led us to speculate about the writers and illustrators of the literature we reviewed. We wondered why more Native American authors and illustrators did not participate in the publishing process, and asked ourselves, "What can be done to encourage native people to tell their stories and share their artwork?" Although we have no specific answer to this question, we hope that the issue continues to be discussed as more literature related to Native American voices and experiences is published.

In order to help readers locate the particular type of book needed for a specific text-set, project, or curriculum-related inquiry, we have chosen to organize this chapter around the chapter headings used in this edition of *Adventuring with Books*. Accordingly, the books we reviewed are grouped into the following sections: Our Changing World; Exploring Our Past; Families; Struggle and Survival; School Life; Poetry; Fine Arts; Sports, Games, and Hobbies; Fantasy; and Critical Conversations.

Works Cited

Bader, Barbara. 1997. "They Shall Not Wither": John Bierhorst's Quiet Crusade for Native American Literature. *The Horn Book Magazine* 73, no. 3: 268–281.

Caldwell-Wood, Naomi, and Lisa A. Mitten. 1991. Selective Bibliography and Guide for *"I" Is Not for Indian: The Portrayal of Native Americans in Books for Young People*. Paper presented to the ALA/OLOS Subcommittee for Library Services to American Indian People, American Indian Library Association. Annual meeting of the American Library Association, June, Atlanta, Georgia.

Harris, Violet., ed. 1997. *Using Multiethnic Literature in the K–8 Classroom*. Norwood, MA: Christopher-Gordon.

Kuipers, Barbara J. 1991. *American Indian Reference Books for Children and Young Adults*. Englewood, CO: Libraries Unlimited.

Ledford, Carolyn, and Betty B. Peel. 1998. Images of Native American Cultures: The Works of Paul Goble. *Book Links* 7, no. 6: 32–4.

Reimer, Kathryn Meyer. 1992. Multiethnic Literature: Holding Fast to Dreams. *Language Arts* 69, no. 1: 14–21.

Slapin, Beverly, and Doris Seale, eds. 1992. *Through Indian Eyes: The Native Experience in Books for Children*. 3rd ed. Philadelphia, PA: New Society.

Slapin, Beverly, Doris Seale, and Rosemary Gonzales. 1992. *How to Tell the Difference: A Guide for Evaluating Children's Books for Anti-Indian Bias*. Philadelphia, PA: New Society.

---

*The titles listed below are **not** reviewed in this chapter; entries contain only bibliographic information. A cross reference to the annotated entry contained elsewhere in this volume is provided in boldface type at the end of the bibliographic information.*

Our Changing World

18.1 Hunter, Sally M. (1997). **Four Seasons of Corn: A Winnebago Tradition.** Illustrated by Joe Allen. Minneapolis: Lerner. 40 pp. ISBN: 0-8225-2658-1. Picture Book. (See **2.38**)

18.2 McMillan, Bruce (1998). **Salmon Summer.** Boston: Houghton Mifflin. 32 pp. ISBN: 0-395-84544-0. Picture Book. (See **2.42**)

18.3 Mercredi, Morningstar (1997). **Fort Chipewyan Homecoming: A Journey to Native Canada.** Illustrated by Darren McNally. Minneapolis: Lerner. Unpaged. ISBN: 0-8225-2659-X. Picture Book. (See **2.43**)

18.4 Van Camp, Richard (1997). **A Man Called Raven.** Illustrated by George Littlechild. San Francisco: Children's Book. Unpaged. ISBN: 0-89239-144-8. Picture Book. (See **2.57**)

Exploring Our Past

18.5 Armstrong, Nancy M. (1994). **Navajo Long Walk.** Illustrated by Paulette Livers Lambert. Niwot, CO: Roberts Rinehart. 128 pp. ISBN: 1-879373-56-4. Chapter Book. (See **3.22**)

18.6 Arnold, Caroline (1996). **Stories in Stone: Rock Pictures by Early Americans.** Photographs by Richard Hewitt. New York: Clarion. 48 pp. ISBN: 0-395-72092-3. Picture Book. (See **3.77**)

18.7 Bateson-Hill, Margaret, and Philomine Lakota (1998). **Shota and the Star Quilt.** Illustrated by Christine Fowler. New York: Zero To Ten. 32 pp. ISBN: 1-84089-021-5. Picture Book. (See **3.193**)

18.8 Bruchac, Joseph (1998). **The Arrow over the Door.** Illustrated by James Watling. New York: Dial Books for Young Readers. 96 pp. ISBN: 0-8037-2078-5. Chapter Book. (See **3.24**)

18.9 Bunting, Eve (1997). **Moonstick: The Seasons of the Sioux.** Illustrated by John Sandford. New York: HarperCollins. Unpaged. ISBN: 0-06-024804-1. Picture Book. (See **3.194**)

18.10 Burks, Brian (1998). **Walks Alone.** San Diego: Harcourt Brace. 128 pp. ISBN: 0-15-201612-0. Chapter Book. (See **3.25**)

18.11 Ciment, James, and Ronald LaFrance (1996). **Encyclopedia of the North American Indian.** New York: Scholastic. 224 pp. ISBN: 0-590-22790-4. Reference Book. (See **3.79**)

18.12 Cornelissan, Cornelia (1998). **Soft Rain: A Story of the Cherokee Trail of Tears.** New York: Delacorte. 115 pp. ISBN: 0-385-32253-4. Sophisticated Chapter Book. (See **3.116**)

18.13 Crook, Connie Brummel (1998). **Maple Moon.** Illustrated by Scott Cameron. Don Mills, Ontario, Canada: Stoddart Kids. 32 pp. ISBN: 0-7737-3017-6. Picture Book. (See **3.27**)

18.14 Dewey, Jennifer O. (1996). **Stories on Stone: Rock Art: Images from the Ancient Ones.** Boston: Little Brown. 32 pp. ISBN: 0-316-18211-7. Picture Book. (See **3.82**)

18.15 Fox, Robert Barlow (1997). **To Be a Warrior.** Sante Fe, NM: Sunstone. 128 pp. ISBN: 0-86534-253-9. Sophisticated Chapter Book. (See **3.106**)

18.16 Goble, Paul (1996). **Remaking the Earth: A Creation Story from the Great Plains of North America.** New York: Orchard. Unpaged. ISBN: 0-531-09524-X. Picture Book. (See **3.127**)

18.17 Goble, Paul (1996). **The Return of the Buffaloes: A Plains Indian Story about Famine and Renewal of the Earth.** Washington, DC: National Geographic. Unpaged. ISBN: 0-7922-2714-X. Picture Books. (See **3.146**)

18.18 Goble, Paul (1997). **Love Flute.** New York: Aladdin. Unpaged. ISBN: 0-689-81683-9. Picture Book. (See **3.200**)

18.19 Goble, Paul (1998). **La niña que amaba los caballos salvajes.** New York: Aladdin Paperbacks (Libros Colibri). Unpaged. ISBN: 0-689-81455-0. Picture Book. (See **3.147**)

18.20 Goldin, Barbara Diamond (1996). **Coyote and the Firestick: A Pacific Northwest Indian Tale.** Illustrated by Will Hillenbrand. San Diego: Gulliver. Unpaged. ISBN: 0-15-200438-6. Picture Book. (See **3.128**)

18.21 Goldin, Barbara Diamond (1997). **The Girl Who Lived with the Bears.** Illustrated by Andrew Plewes. San Diego: Harcourt Brace. 40 pp. ISBN: 0-15-200684-2. Picture Book. (See **3.148**)

18.22 Goodman, Susan E. (1998). **Stones, Bones, and Petroglyphs: Digging into Southwest Archaeology.** Illustrated by Michael J. Doolittle. New York: Atheneum Books for Young Readers. 48 pp. ISBN: 0-689-81121-7. Picture Book. (See **1.12, 3.86**)

18.23 Hamm, Diane Johnston (1997). **Daughter of Sugua.** Illustrated by Paul Micich. Morton Grove, IL: Whitman. 154 pp. ISBN: 0-8075-1477-2. Chapter Book. (See **3.31**)

18.24 Hausman, Gerald (1996). **Eagle Boy: A Traditional Navajo Legend.** Illustrated by Barry Moser and Cara Moser. New York: Harper-Collins. Unpaged. ISBN: 0-06-021100-8. Picture Book. (See **3.201**)

18.25 Hausman, Gerald (1998). **The Story of Blue Elk.** Illustrated by Kristina Rodanas. New York: Clarion. 32 pp. ISBN: 0-395-84512-2. Picture Book. (See **3.149**)

18.26 Hobbs, Will (1997). **Beardream.** Illustrated by Jill Kastner. New York: Atheneum Books for Children. Unpaged. ISBN: 0-689-31973-8. Picture Book. (See **3.203**)

18.27 Hobbs, Will (1997). **Ghost Canoe.** New York: Morrow Junior Books. 195 pp. ISBN: 0-688-14193-5. Chapter Book. (See **3.35, 13.64**)

18.28 Hoyt-Goldsmith, Diane (1997). **Potlatch: A Tsimshian Celebration.** Illustrated by Lawrence Migdale. New York: Holiday House. 32 pp. ISBN: 0-8234-1290-3. Picture Book. (See **3.204**)

18.29 Johnson, Sylvia A. (1997). **Tomatoes, Potatoes, Corn, and Beans: How the Foods of the Americas Changed Eating Around the World.** New York: Atheneum. 138 pp. ISBN: 0-689-80141-6. Sophisticated Chapter Book. (See **3.92**)

18.30 Kalman, Bobbie (1997). **Celebrating the Powwow.** New York: Crabtree. Unpaged. ISBN: 0-86505-640-4. Picture Book. (See **3.207**)

18.31 Keams, Geri (1998). **Snail Girl Brings Water: A Navajo Story.** Illustrated by Richard Ziehler-Martin. Flagstaff, AZ: Rising Moon. Unpaged. ISBN: 0-87358-662-X. Picture Book. (See **3.150**)

18.32 Lavender, David (1998). **Mother Earth, Father Sky.** New York: Holiday House. 117 pp. ISBN: 0-8234-1365-9. Chapter Book. (See **3.94**)

18.33 Lewis, Paul Owen (1997). **Frog Girl.** Hillsboro, OR: Beyond Words. Unpaged. ISBN: 1-582-46003-5. Picture Book. (See **3.155**)

18.34 Marrin, Albert (1996). **Plains Warrior: Chief Quanah Parker and the Comanches.** New York: Atheneum Books for Young Readers. 200 pp. ISBN: 0-689-80081-9. Chapter Book. (See **3.40**)

18.35 Martin, Rafe (1997). **The Eagle's Gift.** Illustrated by Tatsuro Kiuchi. New York: Putnam. Unpaged. ISBN: 0-399-22923-X. Picture Book. (See **3.157**)

18.36 Matcheck, Diane (1998). **The Sacrifice.** New York: Farrar, Straus and Giroux. 224 pp. ISBN: 0-374-36378-1. Chapter Book. (See **3.41**)

18.37 Max, Jill, editor (1997). **Spider Spins a Story.** Flagstaff, AZ: Rising Moon. 63 pp. ISBN: 0-87358-611-5. Chapter Book. (See **3.158**)

18.38 McDonald, Megan (1997). **Tundra Mouse: A Storyknifing Tale.** Illustrated by S. D. Schindler. New York: Orchard. Unpaged. ISBN: 0-531-30047-1. Picture Book. (See **3.159**)

18.39 Morris, Juddi (1997). **Tending the Fire: The Story of Maria Martinez.** Flagstaff, AZ: Rising Moon. 113 pp. ISBN: 0-87358-654-9. Chapter Book. (See **3.95**)

18.40 Nichols, Richard (1998). **A Story to Tell: Traditions of a Tlingit Community.** Illustrated by Bambi D. Kraus. Minneapolis: Lerner. 48 pp. ISBN: 0-8225-2661-1. Picture Book. (See **3.212**)

18.41 Normandin, Christine, editor (1997). **Echoes of the Elders: The Stories and Paintings of Chief Lelooska.** New York: Dorling Kindersley. 38 pp. ISBN: 0-7894-2455-X. Picture Book. (See **3.186**)

18.42 Purdy, Carol (1997). **Nesuya's Basket.** Illustrated by Paulette Livers Lambert. Boulder, CO: Roberts Rinehart. 110 pp. ISBN:1-57098-087-X. Chapter Book. (See **3.215**)

18.43 Rendon, Marcie R. (1996). **Powwow Summer: A Family Celebrates the Circle of Life.** Illustrated by Cheryl Walsh Bellville. Minneapolis: Carolrhoda. 48 pp. ISBN: 0-87614-986-7 (paperback)/1-57505-011-0 (hardcover). Picture Book. (See **3.214**)

18.44 Roop, Peter (1996). **The Buffalo Jump.** Illustrated by Bill Farnsworth. Flagstaff, AZ: Northland. Unpaged. ISBN: 0-87358-616-6. Picture Book. (See **3.99**)

18.45 Rosen, Michael (1998). **The Dog Who Walked with God.** Illustrated by Stan Fellows. Cambridge, MA: Candlewick. 40 pp. ISBN: 0-7636-0470-4. Picture Book. (See **3.165**)

18.46 Sherrow, Victoria (1997). **American Indian Children of the Past.** Brookfield, CT: Millbrook. 96 pp. ISBN: 0-7613-0033-3. Chapter Book. (See **3.100**)

18.47 Sneve, Virginia Driving Hawk (1997). **The Apaches: A First Americans Book.** Illustrated by Ronald Himler. New York: Holiday House. 32 pp. ISBN: 0-8234-1287-3. Picture Book. (See **3.101**)

18.48 St. George, Judith (1997). **Sacagawea.** New York: Putman. 115 pp. ISBN: 0-399-23161-7. Chapter Book. (See **3.49**)

18.49 Swanson, Diane (l996). **Buffalo Sunrise: The Story of a North American Giant.** San Francisco: Sierra Club Books for Children. 64 pp. ISBN: 0-87156-861-6. Chapter Book. (See **3.102**)

18.50 Taylor, Harriet Peck (1997). **When Bear Stole the Chinook: A Siksika Tale.** New York: Farrar, Straus and Giroux. Unpaged. ISBN: 0-374-30589-7. Picture Book. (See **3.168**)

18.51 Van Laan, Nancy (1997). **Shingebiss: An Ojibwe Legend.** Illustrated by Betsy Bowen. New York: Houghton Mifflin. Unpaged. ISBN: 0-395-82745-0. Picture Book. (See **3.169**)

18.52 Vick, Helen Hughes (1998). **Shadow.** Boulder, CO: Roberts Rinehart. 128 pp. ISBN: 1-57098-195-7. Chapter Book. (See **3.52**)

18.53 Viola, Herman J. (1996). **North American Indians.** Illustrated by Bryn Barnard. New York: Crown. 128 pp. ISBN: 0-517-59017-4. Chapter Book. (See **3.103**)

18.54 Viola, Herman J. (1998). **It Is a Good Day to Die: Indian Eyewitnesses Tell the Story of the Battle of the Little Bighorn.** New York: Crown. 101 pp. ISBN: 0-517-70913-9. Chapter Book. (See **3.124**)

18.55 Walking Turtle, Eagle (1997). **Full Moon Stories: Thirteen Native American Legends.** New York: Hyperion Books for Children. 47 pp. ISBN: 0-7868-0225-1. Picture Book. (See **3.170**)

18.56 Warren, Scott (1997). **Desert Dwellers: Native People of the American Southwest.** San Francisco: Chronicle. 55 pp. ISBN: 0-8118-0534-4. Chapter Book. (See **3.220**)

18.57 Waters, Kate (1996). **Tapenum's Day: A Wampanoag Indian Boy in Pilgrim Times.** Photographs by Russ Kendall. New York: Scholastic. Unpaged. ISBN: 0-590-20237-5. Picture Book. (See **3.18**)

18.58 Whelan, Gloria (1996). **The Indian School.** Illustrated by Gabriela Dellosso. New York: HarperCollins. 86 pp. ISBN: 0-06-027077-2. Chapter Book. (See **3.19**)

Families

18.59 Dabcovich, Lydia (1997). **The Polar Bear Son: An Inuit Tale.** New York: Clarion. 37 pp. ISBN: 0-395-72766-9. Picture Book. (See **4.98**)

18.60 Dorris, Michael (1996). **Guests.** Illustrated by Ellen Thompson. New York: Hyperion. 119 pp. ISBN: 0-7868-1108-0. Chapter Book. (See **4.44**)

18.61 Eyvindson, Peter (1996). **Red Parka Mary.** Winnipeg, Manitoba, Canada: Pemmican. 42 pp. ISBN: 0-9218-2750-4. Picture Book. (See **4.131**)

18.62 George, Jean Craighead (1997). **Arctic Son.** Illustrated by Wendell Minor. New York: Hyperion. Unpaged. ISBN: 0-7868-0315-0. Picture Book. (See **4.102**)

18.63 Ingold, Jeanette (1997). **The Window.** New York: Hyperion. 106 pp. ISBN: 0-7868-0301-0. Chapter Book. (See **5.102**)

18.64 Krantz, Hazel (1997). **Walks in Beauty.** Flagstaff, AZ: Northland. 192 pp. ISBN: 0-87358-667-0. Chapter Book. (See **4.92**)

18.65 Luenn, Nancy (1997). **Nessa's Fish.** Illustrated by Neil Waldman. New York: Aladdin. Unpaged. ISBN: 0-689-81465-8. Picture Book. (See **4.104**)

18.66 Mitchell, Barbara (1996). **Red Bird.** Illustrated by Todd Doney. New York: Lothrop, Lee & Shepard. 31 pp. ISBN: 0-688-10859-8. Picture Book. (See **4.38**)

18.67 Plain, Ferguson (1996). **Rolly's Bear.** Winnipeg, Manitoba, Canada: Pemmican. Unpaged. ISBN: 0-921827-52-0. Picture Book. (See **4.134**)

18.68 Savageau, Cheryl (1996). **Muskrat Will Be Swimming.** Illustrated by Robert Hynes. Flagstaff, AZ: Northland. Unpaged. ISBN: 0-87358-604-2. Picture Book. (See **4.123**)

Struggle and Survival

18.69 Bruchac, Joseph (1996). **Children of the Longhouse.** New York: Dial Books for Young Readers. 150 pp. ISBN: 0-8037-1793-8. Chapter Book. (See **5.63**)

18.70 Bruchac, Joseph (1997). **Eagle Song.** Illustrated by Dan Andreasen. New York: Dial Books for Young Readers. 80 pp. ISBN: 0-8037-1919-1. Chapter Book. (See **5.50**)

18.71 Bruchac, Joseph (1998).**The Heart of a Chief.** New York: Dial Books for Young Readers. 153 pp. ISBN: 0-8037-2276-1. Chapter Book. (See **5.37**)

18.72 Dorris, Michael (1996). **Sees behind Trees.** Illustrated by Linda Benson. New York: Hyperion. 104 pp. ISBN: 0-7868-0224-3. Chapter Book. (See **5.72**)

18.73 Freedman, Russell (1996). **The Life and Death of Crazy Horse.** Photographs by Amos Bad Heart Bull. New York: Holiday House. 144 pp. ISBN: 0-8234-1219-9. Chapter Book. (See **5.8**)

18.74 Hoyt-Goldsmith, Diane (1997). **Buffalo Days.** Illustrated by Lawrence Migdale. New York: Holiday House. 32 pp. ISBN: 0-8234-1327-6. Picture Book. (See **5.13**)

18.75 Katz, William Loren (1997). **Black Indians: A Hidden Heritage.** New York: Aladdin. 198 pp. ISBN: 0-689-80901-8. Chapter Book. (See **5.16**)

18.76 Keegan, Marci (1997). **Pueblo Boy.** New York: Viking. Unpaged. ISBN: 0-14-36945-7. Picture Book. (See **5.55**)

18.77 Lowry, Linda (1996). **Wilma Mankiller.** Illustrated by Janice Lee Porter. Minneapolis: Carolrhoda. 56 pp. ISBN: 0-87614-880-1. Chapter Book. (See **5.22**)

18.78 Mott, Evelyn Clarke (1996). **Dancing Rainbows: A Pueblo Boy's Story.** New York: Cobblehill. Unpaged. ISBN: 0-525-65216-7. Picture Book. (See **3.211**)

18.79 Philip, Neil, editor (1997). **In a Sacred Manner I Live: Native American Wisdom.** New York: Clarion. 93 pp. ISBN: 0-395-84981-0. Chapter Book. (See **5.46**)

18.80 Shaughnessy, Diane (1997). **Pocahontas: Powhatan Princess.** New York: PowerKids. Unpaged. ISBN: 0-8239-5106-5. Picture Book. (See **5.32**)

18.81 Yamane, Linda (1997). **Weaving a California Tradition: A Native American Basketmaker.** Photographs by Dugan Aguilar. Minneapolis: Lerner. 48 pp. ISBN: 0-8225-2660-3. Picture Book. (See **3.221**)

School Life

18.82 Scott, Ann Herbert (1996). **Brave as a Mountain Lion.** Illustrated by Glo Coalson. New York: Houghton Mifflin. 32 pp. ISBN: 0-395-66760-7. Picture Book. (See **6.61**)

Poetry

18.83 Baylor, Byrd (1997). **The Way to Make Perfect Mountain: Native American Legends of Sacred Mountains.** Illustrated by Leonard Chana. El Paso, TX: Cinco Puntos. 59 pp. ISBN: 0-938317-26-1. Chapter Book. (See **10.40**)

18.84 Philip, Neil (1996). **Earth Always Endures: Native American Poems.** Illustrated by Edward S. Curtis. New York: Viking. Unpaged. ISBN: 0-670-86873-6. Chapter Book. (See **10.56**)

18.85 Swann, Brian (1998). **Touching the Distance: Native American Riddle Poems.** Illustrated by Maria Rendon. San Diego: Harcourt Brace. Unpaged. ISBN: 0-15-200804-7. Picture Book. (See **10.58**)

Fine Arts

18.86 Hucko, Bruce (1996). **A Rainbow at Night: The World in Words and Pictures by Navajo Children.** San Francisco: Chronicle. Unpaged. ISBN: 0-8118-1294-4. Picture Book. (See **11.41**)

18.87 Wood, Nancy, editor (1997). **The Serpent's Tongue.** New York: Dutton. 256 pp. ISBN: 0-525-45514-0. Chapter Book. (See **11.46**)

Sports, Games, and Hobbies

18.88 Hoyt-Goldsmith, Diane (1998). **Lacrosse: The National Game of the Iroquois.** Illustrated by Lawrence Migdale. New York: Holiday House. Unpaged. ISBN: 0-8234-1360-8. Picture Book. (See **12.20**)

Fantasy

18.89 Jernigan, E. Wesley (1997). **Cloudcatcher.** Auckland, New Zealand: Shortland. 48 pp. ISBN: 1-57257-668-5. Picture Book. (See **14.28**)

Critical Conversations

18.90 Hirschi, Ron (1996). **People of Salmon and Cedar.** Illustrated by Deborah Cooper. New York: Cobblehill. 42 pp. ISBN: 0-525-65183-7. Picture Book. (See **20.13**)

A.

B.

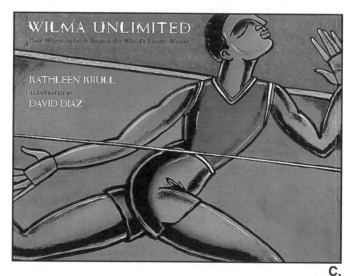

C.

A. *Red Scarf Girl: A Memoir of the Cultural Revolution,* Ji Li Jiang (**19.24**). **B.** *The Bat Boy & His Violin,* Gavin Curtis/E. B. Lewis (**19.2**). **C.** *Wilma Unlimited: How Wilma Rudolph Became the World's Fastest Woman,* Kathleen Krull/David Diaz (**19.41**).

19 Gender Issues: Spunky, Clever, Caring, and Endearing Girls and Boys in Children's Literature

Patricia Heine and David Heine

Contributing reviewers included: Chris Inkster, Frank Kazemek, Sylvia Raschke, Della Stevens, and Sandra Williams.

In this chapter, readers will find some of the best role models available today for our elementary girls and boys: California Morning (Lucy) Whipple, who went to gold mining country with her mother and siblings; Wilma Rudolph, who, despite having polio, won three Olympic gold medals; and Palmer, who is torn between his own beliefs and pressure from peers and townspeople as he makes his decision whether or not to wring the pigeons' necks.

What makes these main characters so special? That is the question our review committee wrestled with for several months. We know that positive role models are important for our children, and that television, advertisements, movies, and much of the literature for children reinforces limiting and often negative stereotypes for both girls and boys. It was our desire, therefore, to find the best books available today that portrayed positive images of boys and girls.

We began this process with the definition of a high-quality gender book as one that provides a positive role model for children today. As we read and rejected hundreds of books and placed a few books in the keeper pile, we realized we were developing a more finely tuned set of criteria. We knew that first and foremost, our recommended books needed to be high-quality literature—literature with a believable and interesting plot, complex characters, worthwhile themes, powerful language, and high-quality illustrations. Only then did we consider the strength of the gender representation.

As we worked with and refined our criteria, we found helpful the material developed by the Council on Interracial Books for Children, "Ten Quick Ways to Analyze Books for Racism and Sexism" (1980) and "Evaluating Books for Bias" (1997). Eventually we developed and applied the criteria below to the books we were reviewing. No single book exemplifies all of the characteristics listed below, but each meets enough of these criteria to create characters who are rich in texture and, we believe, are worthy of being called role models for our children. We were delighted to find such a varied, positive group of male and female characters to share with our students. The following criteria guided our evaluation of the books included in this chapter:

1. *Personal traits of the character.* Does the character display a variety of emotions, abilities, and concerns? Does the character change and grow throughout the book? Is the character persistent, courageous, feisty, intelligent, spirited, humane, resourceful, capable, or independent? Does the character wrestle with significant problems or issues?

2. *Issues important to the character.* Is the character struggling with gender images, including what actions, attitudes, and roles are appropriate for females and males? Does the character approach body-image issues in a positive, accepting way? Is the character facing experiences that help in growing up and reaching maturity? Is the character concerned with issues that make a difference in the world?

3. *How the character solves problems.* Does the character use personal qualities such as humor, strength, intelligence, or cleverness to solve problems as appropriate to the situation? Does the character initiate solving problems rather than waiting for someone else? Does the character find strength and answers from within? Does the character use a wide range of strategies, including seeking help from others, discussing problems with family or friends, or exploring solutions through writing and reading?

4. *The character's relationships with others.* Does the character put forth effort and value establishing healthy relationships with others? Are the character's relationships with others based on or working toward admirable traits such as mutual respect, equality, loyalty, honesty, friendship, commitment, or trust?

5. *How the character departs from traditional stereotypes.* Is the character moving away from the following traits: typical female stereotypes such as being passive, frightened, weak, gentle, easily discouraged, unoriginal, silly, confused, inept, depend-

ent, a follower, a conformist, emotional, concerned about appearance, needful of marriage and motherhood, or passive in language and behavior; or typical male stereotypes such as being active, strong, brave, rough, competitive, logical, unemotional, messy, decisive, a leader, adventurous, or aggressive in language and behavior?

6. *Whether the character provides a voice for those who are often unheard in children's literature.* Is the character in a role not usually found in literature, such as male nurses, female inventors, or females during the gold rush? Does the character represent a cultural, religious, ethnic, ability, or socioeconomic group found infrequently in children's literature?

We found that by using these criteria, we had the tools to justify and articulate our reasons for choosing the books contained in this chapter. These criteria may prove useful as readers examine additional titles for inclusion in classrooms and libraries.

Rather than reviewing them in a single chapter, the members of our committee chose to disperse books with positive role models for boys and girls throughout *Adventuring with Books*. Although we encourage educators to use the titles listed in this chapter as part of a special unit on gender issues, we did not want to limit the books to that use. Instead we recommend that these books be woven into many units throughout the school curriculum. When we are studying the depression era with our students, they need to encounter the character of Leah in *Leah's Pony* (Friedrich 1996). When we look at the labor movement in the United States, students need to find Rebecca Putney in *The Bobbin Girl* (McCully 1996). When studying families, they need to celebrate fathers through the book *In Daddy's Arms I Am Tall* (Steptoe 1997). When we want an exciting read-aloud text for our young children featuring a spunky, confident girl, we can share *Raising Dragons* (Nolen 1998). By both creating a separate index chapter and integrating them throughout the chapters, we felt these books would find their widest use.

We have organized this chapter into three sections: Positive Role Models in History, Positive Role Models in Contemporary Times, and Positive Role Models in Fantasy. The first two sections also are subdivided into Fiction and Nonfiction.

---

*The titles listed below are **not** reviewed in this chapter; entries contain only bibliographic information. A cross reference to the annotated entry contained elsewhere in this volume is provided in boldface type at the end of the bibliographic information.*

Positive Role Models in History

Fiction

19.1   Bartone, Elisa (1996). **American Too.** Illustrated by Ted Lewin. New York: Lothrop, Lee & Shepard. Unpaged. ISBN: 0-688-13279-0. Picture Book. (See **3.192**)

19.2   Curtis, Gavin (1998). **The Bat Boy & His Violin.** Illustrated by E. B. Lewis. New York: Simon & Schuster. Unpaged. ISBN: 0-689-80099-1. Picture Book. (See **4.6**)

19.3   Cushman, Karen (1996). **The Ballad of Lucy Whipple.** New York: Clarion. 195 pp. ISBN: 0-395-72806-1. Chapter Book. (See **5.51**)

19.4   Friedrich, Elizabeth (1996). **Leah's Pony.** Illustrated by Michael Garland. Honesdale, PA: Boyds Mills. Unpaged. ISBN: 1-56397-189-S. Picture Book. (See **3.29**)

19.5   Giff, Patricia Reilly (1997). **Lily's Crossing.** New York: Delacorte. 180 pp. ISBN: 0-385-32142-2. Chapter Book. (See **3.107**)

19.6   Hansen, Joyce (1997). **I Thought My Soul Would Rise and Fly: The Diary of Patsy, a Freed Girl.** New York: Scholastic. 202 pp. ISBN: 0-590-84913-1. Chapter Book. (See **3.32**)

19.7   Hearne, Betsy G. (1997). **Seven Brave Women.** Illustrated by Bethanne Andersen. New York: Greenwillow. Unpaged. ISBN: 0-688-14503-5. Picture Book. (See **4.47**)

19.8   Hest, Amy (1997). **When Jessie Came across the Sea.** Illustrated by P. J. Lynch. Cambridge, MA: Candlewick. Unpaged. ISBN: 0-7696-0094-6. Picture Book. (See **3.34**)

19.9   Lee, Milly (1997). **Nim and the War Effort.** Illustrated by Yangsook Choi. New York: Farrar, Straus and Giroux. Unpaged. ISBN: 0-374-35523-1. Picture Book. (See **3.109**)

19.10 McCully, Emily Arnold (1996). **The Bobbin Girl.** New York: Dial Books for Young Readers. Unpaged. ISBN: 0-8037-1827-6. Picture Book. (See **3.42, 20.30**)

19.11 McCully, Emily Arnold (1997). **Starring Mirette and Bellini.** New York: Putnam. Unpaged. ISBN: 0-399-22636-2. Picture Book. (See **5.128**)

19.12 McCully, Emily Arnold (1998). **Beautiful Warrior: The Legend of the Nun's Kung Fu.** New York: Scholastic. Unpaged. ISBN: 0-590-37487-7. Picture Book. (See **5.43**)

19.13 Paterson, Katherine (1996). **Jip: His Story.** New York: Lodestar. 181 pp. ISBN: 0-525617-543-4. Chapter Book. (See **3.13**)

19.14 Paulsen, Gary (1997). **Sarny: A Life Remembered.** New York: Delacorte. 97 pp. ISBN: 0-385-32195-3. Chapter Book. (See **3.111**)

19.15 Pfitsch, Patricia Curtis (1997). **Keeper of the Light.** New York: Simon & Schuster Books for Young Readers. 137 pp. ISBN: 0-689-81492-5. Chapter Book. (See **3.44**)

19.16 Pryor, Bonnie (1996). **The Dream Jar.** Illustrated by Mark Graham. New York: Morrow Junior Books. Unpaged. ISBN: 0-688-13062-3. Picture Book. (See **3.45**)

19.17 Schroeder, Alan (1996). **Minty: A Story of Young Harriet Tubman.** Illustrated by Jerry Pinkney. New York: Dial Books for Young Readers. Unpaged. ISBN: 0-8037-1889-6. Picture Book. (See **3.14**)

19.18 Stanley, Diane (1996). **Elena.** New York: Hyperion. 55 pp. ISBN: 0-7868-0256-1. Chapter Book. (See **3.15**)

19.19 Stewart, Sarah (1997). **The Gardener.** Illustrated by David Small. New York: Farrar, Straus and Giroux. Unpaged. ISBN: 0-374-32517-0. Picture Book. (See **3.16**)

Nonfiction

19.20 Cooney, Barbara (1996). **Eleanor.** New York: Viking. Unpaged. ISBN: 0-670-86159-6. Picture Book. (See **5.39**)

19.21 Egan, Ted (1998). **The Drover's Boy.** Illustrated by Robert Ingpen. Melbourne, Australia: Lothian. Unpaged. ISBN: 1-887734-52-X. Sophisticated Picture Book. (See **3.61**)

19.22 Fleming, Candace (1996). **Women of the Lights.** Illustrated by James Watling. Morton Grove, IL: Whitman. 79 pp. ISBN: 0-8075-9165-3. Chapter Book. (See **3.84**)

19.23 Hansen, Joyce (1998). **Women of Hope: African Americans Who Made a Difference.** New York: Scholastic. 32 pp. ISBN: 0-590-93973-4. Picture Book. (See **20.12**)

19.24   Jiang, Ji-Li (1997). **Red Scarf Girl: A Memoir of the Cultural Revolution.** New York: HarperCollins. 240 pp. ISBN: 0-06-027585-5. Sophisticated Chapter Book. (See **20.47**)

19.25   Josephson, Judith Pinkerton (1997). **Mother Jones: Fierce Fighter for Workers' Rights.** Minneapolis: Lerner. Unpaged. ISBN: 0-8225-4924-7. Picture Book. (See **5.14**)

19.26   Leder, Jane (1996). **Grace and Glory: A Century of Women in the Olympics.** Chicago: Triumph. 102 pp. ISBN: 1-572443-116-4. Chapter Book. (See **12.10**)

19.27   Macy, Sue (1996). **Winning Ways: A Photohistory of American Women in Sports.** New York: Henry Holt. 217 pp. ISBN: 0-8050-4147-8. Chapter Book. (See **12.21**)

19.28   Meltzer, Milton (1998). **Ten Queens: Portraits of Women of Power.** Illustrated by Bethanne Andersen. New York: Dutton Children's Books. 134 pp. ISBN: 0-525-45643-0. Chapter Book. (See **5.24**)

19.29   Ryan, Pam Muñoz (1998). **Riding Freedom.** Illustrated by Brian Selznick. New York: Scholastic. 138 pp. ISBN: 0-590-95766-X. Chapter Book. (See **3.48**)

19.30   Swain, Gwenyth (1996). **The Road to Seneca Falls: A Story about Elizabeth Cady Stanton.** Illustrated by Mary O'Keefe. Minneapolis: Carolrhoda. 64 pp. ISBN: 0-87614-947-6. Chapter Book. (See **3.50**)

Positive Role Models in Contemporary Times

Fiction

19.31   Farmer, Nancy (1996). **A Girl Named Disaster.** New York: Orchard. 309 pp. ISBN: 0-531-08889-8. Sophisticated Chapter Book. (See **5.73**)

19.32   Grambling, Lois G. (1998). **Daddy Will Be There.** Illustrated by Walter Gaffney-Kassell. New York: Greenwillow. Unpaged. ISBN: 0-688-14983-9. Picture Book. (See **4.8**)

19.33   Holt, Kimberly Willis (1998). **My Louisiana Sky.** New York: Henry Holt. 132 pp. ISBN: 0-8050-5251-8. Chapter Book. (See **4.67**)

19.34   Numeroff, Laura J. (1998). **What Daddies Do Best, What Mommies Do Best.** Illustrated by Lynn Munsinger. New York: Simon & Schuster. Unpaged. ISBN: 0-689-80577-2. Picture Book. (See **4.18**)

19.35 Shaw, Eve (1997). **Grandmother's Alphabet.** Duluth, MN: Pfeifer-Hamilton. Unpaged. ISBN: 1-57025-127-4. Picture Book. (See **4.23**)

19.36 Sisalu, Elinor Batezat (1996). **The Day Gogo Went to Vote.** Illustrated by Sharon Wilson. New York: Little Brown. Unpaged. ISBN: 0-316-70267-6. Picture Book. (See **20.32**)

19.37 Spinelli, Jerry (1997). **Wringer.** New York: HarperCollins. 229 pp. ISBN: 0-06-024913-7. Sophisticated Chapter Book. (See **5.82, 20.41**)

19.38 Steptoe, Javaka, editor (1997). **In Daddy's Arms I Am Tall: African Americans Celebrating Fathers.** New York: Lee & Low. Unpaged. ISBN: 0-880000-31-8. Picture Book. (See **4.26**)

19.39 Watts, Jeri Hanel (1997). **Keepers.** Illustrated by Felicia Marshall. New York: Lee & Low. Unpaged. ISBN: 1-880000-58-X. Picture Book. (See **4.28**)

Nonfiction

19.40 Johnson, Rebecca L. (1997). **Braving the Frozen Frontier: Women Working in Antarctica.** Minneapolis: Lerner. 112 pp. ISBN: 0-8225-2855-X. Chapter Book. (See **1.17**)

19.41 Krull, Kathleen (1996). **Wilma Unlimited: How Wilma Rudolph Became the World's Fastest Woman.** Illustrated by David Diaz. New York: Harcourt Brace. Unpaged. ISBN: 0-15-201267-2. Picture Book. (See **5.17**)

19.42 Wolf, Bernard (1997). **HIV Positive.** New York: Dutton Children's Books. Unpaged. ISBN: 0-525-45459-4. Sophisticated Picture Book. (See **5.121**)

19.43 Wright-Frierson, Virginia (1996). **A Desert Scrapbook: Dawn to Dusk in the Sonoran Desert.** New York: Simon & Schuster. Unpaged. ISBN: 0-689-80678-7. Picture Book. (See **2.26**)

Positive Role Models in Fantasy

19.44 Demi (1997). **One Grain of Rice: A Mathematical Folktale.** New York: Scholastic. Unpaged. ISBN: 0-590-93998-X. Picture Book. (See **9.13**)

19.45 de Paola, Tomie (1996). **Strega Nona: Her Story.** New York: Putnam. Unpaged. ISBN: 0-399-22818-7. Picture Book. (See **13.41**)

19.46 Hesse, Karen (1996). **The Music of Dolphins.** New York: Scholastic. 181 pp. ISBN: 0-590-98797-7. Chapter Book. (See **4.10**)

19.47 Levine, Gail Carson (1997). **Ella Enchanted.** New York: HarperCollins. 232 pp. ISBN: 0-06-027511-1. Chapter Book. (See **14.43**)

19.48 Nolen, Jerdine (1998). **Raising Dragons.** Illustrated by Elise Primavera. New York: Harcourt Brace. Unpaged. ISBN: 0-15-201288-5. Picture Book. (See **14.10**)

19.49 Peterson, Julienne (1996). **Caterina the Clever Farm Girl: A Tale from Italy.** Illustrated by Enzo Giannini. New York: Dial. Unpaged. ISBN: 0-8037-1181-6. Picture Book. (See **3.163**)

19.50 San Souci, Robert D. (1998). **A Weave of Words.** Illustrated by Raúl Colón. New York: Orchard. Unpaged. ISBN: 0-531-30053-6. Picture Book. (See **14.34**)

19.51 Stanley, Diane (1997). **Rumpelstiltskin's Daughter.** New York: Morrow Junior Books. Unpaged. ISBN: 0-688-14328-8. Picture Book. (See **3.167**)

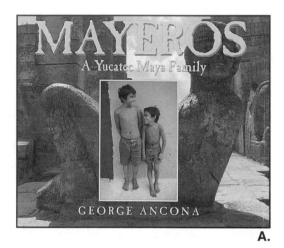

A.

B.

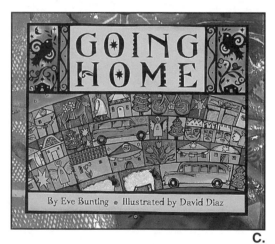

C.

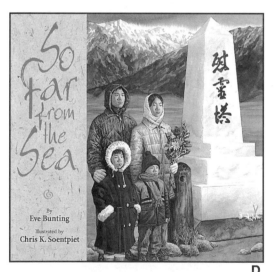

D.

A. *Mayeros: A Yucatec Maya Family,* George Ancona (**20.51**). **B.** *The Circuit: Stories from the Life of a Migrant Child,* Francisco Jiménez (**20.36**). **C.** *Going Home,* Eve Bunting/ David Diaz (**20.1**). **D.** *So Far from the Sea,* Eve Bunting/ Chris K. Soentpiet (**20.9**).

20 Supporting Critical Conversations in Classrooms

Jerome C. Harste

Contributing reviewers included Amy Breau, Jerome C. Harste, Christine Leland, Mitzi Lewison, Anne Ociepka, and Vivian Vasquez.

C ritical conversations are important because they highlight diversity and difference while calling attention to the nature and role of literacy in our society. We have found that some books are particularly useful for starting and sustaining critical conversations in classrooms. These books provide the framework for a new kind of critical-literacy curriculum that focuses on building students' awareness of how systems of meaning and power affect people and the lives they lead. We are interested in studying the conversations that follow the reading of these books, and observing how children become new literate beings as a result of having participated in these conversations.

According to the definition developed by our review committee, books that can help to build a critical-literacy curriculum are those that meet one or more of the following criteria:

1. They don't make difference invisible, but rather explore what differences make a difference.
2. They enrich our understanding of history and life by giving voice to those who traditionally have been silenced or marginalized—those we call "the indignant ones."
3. They show how people can begin to take action on important social issues.
4. They explore dominant systems of meaning that operate in our society to position people and groups of people.
5. They help us question why certain groups are positioned as "others."

Some books in the critical-literacy category focus more on historical issues such as slavery or the industrial revolution and show how large groups of people were marginalized and stripped of their human rights. Others are more contemporary in nature and encourage readers to interrogate current practices that are generally accepted because they are traditional or conventional in nature. For example, if a present-day high school uses a "slave day" theme to raise money for student activities, is it acceptable simply because it's traditional, or do we need to consider that this practice might be seen as sustaining the degrading treatment of African Americans? Other critical-literacy books focus on the issue of "otherness," and how our perceptions of people of different ethnic, cultural, or social groups can change after we get to know them better. Engaging children in conversations about the pernicious effects of otherness can help them begin to see and understand the world in new ways.

In primary classrooms, we have introduced critical-literacy books by reading them aloud. We note the key conversations that are generated by each book, and plan subsequent curricular activities that will help to extend these conversations over time. To foreground children's thinking in regard to critical literacy issues, we select related artifacts to post on the classroom wall. Artifacts might be something as simple as a copy of a page in the book and key conversational interchanges between class members written on three-by-five-inch cards with arrows mapping the flow of conversation over time. The result is what we call an "audit trail" (Harste and Vasquez 1998), or what the three- and four-year-olds in Vivian Vasquez' classroom called "the learning wall" (see Figure 1).

In upper-elementary and middle-school classrooms, we have used multiple copies of four or five critical adolescent novels to create text-sets that students self-select to read and discuss in groups. Members of each group work together to identify themes, after which the whole class comes together to share findings, artifacts, and insights that are then posted on a classroom wall.

Conceptually this approach is anchored in Luke and Freebody's (1997) model of reading as social practice. Arguing that literacy is never neutral, Luke and Freebody lay out a grid showing four different constructions or views of literacy. They argue that historically, reading has been seen as decoding and the function of reading instruction was the development of children's ability to break the code. During the 1970s and 1980s, psycholinguistic and schema-theoretical notions of reading emphasized reader-text interactions and drew attention to "text-meaning practices," or more specifically, the development of a reader who understands how to use the textual and personal resources at hand to coproduce a meaningful reading. In the late 1980s and early 1990s, social-linguistic and social-semiotic theory focused our attention on language in use. During this period, reading was viewed in terms of what it did or could accomplish pragmatically in the real world. More recently,

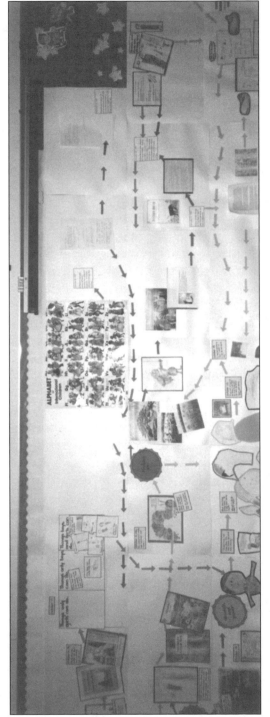

Figure 1. Photograph of Audit Trail in Vivian Vasquez' 3 & 4 year-old room.

Luke and Freebody have suggested that reading should be seen as a non-neutral form of cultural practice, one that positions readers and obliterates as much as it illuminates. Readers for the twenty-first century, they argue, need to be able to interrogate the assumptions that are embedded in a text, as well as the assumptions which they, as culturally indoctrinated beings, bring to the text. Questions such as "Whose story is this?" "Who benefits?" and "What voices are not being heard?" invite children to interrogate the systems of meaning that operate both consciously and unconsciously in a text as well as in society.

Although critical literacy involves critical thinking, it also entails more. Part of that "more" is social action built upon an understanding that literacy positions individuals and, in so doing, serves some more than others. As literate beings, it behooves us not only to know how to decode and make meaning, but also to understand how language works and to what ends, so that we can better see ourselves in light of the kind of world we wish to create and the kind of people we wish to become.

From several perspectives, then, the books we review in this chapter are of critical importance to educators. Although they invite specific conversations around specific topics, they function as a whole to create a curriculum that honors diversity and invites students and teachers alike to explore a new kind of literacy curriculum—one built upon the premise that a model of difference is a model of learning, for individuals as well as for society. One of the implicit arguments being tested by our use of these books in classrooms is that a diversity-and-difference model of education better serves a multilingual and multicultural society such as ours than does the conformity-and-consensus model of learning that currently permeates our educational system.

Given such possibilities, the book reviews that follow are somewhat different from the reviews that are included in other sections of this volume. Although we summarize the text, we also highlight potential conversations that the reading of these texts can make possible. In this way, teachers who wish to invite students to engage in particular conversations about events that have transpired in their community can easily locate texts that fit the bill. Others who have started particular conversations and wish to have them continue will find the thoroughness of our reviews useful as they identify themes and alternative perspectives on issues. Of necessity, therefore, the reviews in this chapter are longer than those found throughout the rest of *Adventuring with Books*.

To expedite organization and planning for teachers, the titles in this chapter were organized into the following five sections, which correspond to the five criteria for critical literacy books discussed above: Understanding Differences that Make a Difference; Giving Voice to the

Indignant Ones; Taking Social Action; Understanding How Systems of Meaning in Society Position Us; and Examining Distance, Difference, and "Otherness." A sixth section entitled Other Ideas for Text-Sets includes three categories of books that teachers might find helpful for putting together additional text-sets. The first category focuses on Child Labor and Children's Rights, and includes books that address these issues from both historical and contemporary perspectives. This text-set provides a wide lens for seeing how working children in a variety of national and international settings have been, and continue to be, marginalized and exploited. The second category, Literacy as Power, pulls together books that demonstrate the power of literacy to allow new voices to be heard. Characters in these books discover how their acquisition or use of literacy allows them to write a new identity, or to interact with others in powerful new ways. The third category is called Multiple Perspectives. Books in this group rely on the use of several different characters to tell the story. Seen through the eyes of these different people, the same events look very different and far more complex than they did at first glance. By highlighting these discrepancies in perception, teachers might find this text-set useful for beginning philosophical conversations about the nature of reality and how our backgrounds and beliefs influence what we see.

Our committee designated as Primary books those that we thought had the most potential for generating the kinds of critical conversations that we want our students to experience. Books designated as Secondary are worthy of consideration, but are not as outstanding as those in the Primary sections. For example, we found that some of these books were not as obviously critical in their approach. Although critical issues and possibilities were present, too much was left unsaid and too much had to be dug out before the critical implications of the book could be realized. In other cases, our committee felt the books were more valuable as references or resource materials for supporting critical conversations rather than as vehicles for beginning them. Finally some of these books we considered too sophisticated for most elementary and middle-school readers.

Arthur Applebee (1997) found that the best teachers thought about curriculum in terms of what conversations they wanted their students to be engaged in, not in terms of what concepts they wanted to introduce through reading or through direct instruction. Concepts, he argues, will come as learners engage in conversations that keep them at the forefront of the discipline they are studying and the world in which they are living. Although many of the books we reviewed can be seen as controversial, they reflect life in a way that most school curricula do not.

It is this relevancy and the potential to explore new curricular possibilities that make this chapter, the books we reviewed, and the topic of critical literacy itself conversations we simply can't afford not to have.

Works Cited

Applebee, Arthur N. 1997. Rethinking Curriculum in the English Language Arts. *English Journal* 86, no. 3: 25–31.

Luke, Allan, and Peter Freebody. 1997. Shaping the Social Practices of Reading. In *Construction of Critical Literacies,* ed. Sandy Muspratt, Allan Luke, and Peter Freebody. Cresskill, NJ: Hampton.

Harste, Jerome C., and Vivian Vasquez. 1998. The Work We Do: Journal as Audit Trail. *Language Arts* 75, no. 4: 266–276.

---

*The titles listed below each subheading are organized into Primary Reviews and Secondary Reviews. The Primary Reviews describe outstanding books in each subheading. The Secondary Reviews provide brief information about other books worthy of consideration. Some titles listed below are **not** reviewed in this chapter; entries for these titles are not annotated and contain only bibliographic information. In such cases, a cross reference to the annotated entry contained elsewhere in this volume is provided in boldface type at the end of the bibliographic information. In other instances, because of the specific nature of the reviews provided in this chapter, titles reviewed below also are reviewed in another chapter in this volume. In such cases, a cross-reference to the other annotated entry is provided in boldface type at the end of the annotation.*

Understanding Differences That Make a Difference

Primary Reviews

20.1   Bunting, Eve (1996). **Going Home.** Illustrated by David Diaz. New York: HarperCollins. Unpaged. ISBN: 0-06-026296-6. Picture Book.

When Carlos' mother says the family is going home to Mexico for Christmas, Carlos isn't sure what to think. What about the house they've lived in for five years, and the crops they've worked for Mr. Culloden? And if Mexico is home, why did his parents ever leave? His father's answer is always the same: "There is no work in La Perla. We are here for the opportunities." But Carlos knows what it's like to work in the hot strawberry fields, and he sees his parents come home tired and sore every night. He wonders what those mysterious "opportunities" might be. When they arrive in La Perla, his parents are more excited and lively than he's ever seen them. It's as if they've forgotten about their sore shoulders and bad knees. Welcoming relatives "don't feel like strangers," and Carlos begins to see why, as his sister tells him, their parents are working to save money to come back to Mexico someday "after our opportunities."

The brightly colored illustrations by David Diaz capture the warmth and festivity of homecoming and holiday celebration in a Mexican town. Although lovely, the colorful photographs of folk art that frame Diaz' work detract from the beautiful illustrations. At the same time that this story dazzles and welcomes, it raises crucial questions about economic disparity, the hard working conditions of farm laborers in the United States, differences in language and culture that can exist within families, and the painful choices and sacrifices facing families who live in poverty. (See also **4.4**)

20.2 Fox, Paula (1997). **Radiance Descending.** New York: Dorling Kindersley. 101 pp. ISBN: 0-7894-2467-3. Chapter Book.

Radiance Descending is a novel about an older brother named Paul who is learning to accept a younger sibling named Jacob, who was born with Down's Syndrome. The unfortunate thing is that readers learn very little about Jacob's condition, but much about Paul's egotism. For example, we learn that Paul doesn't want to take Jacob to the doctor's office.

The real consequence of his taking Jacob to Dr. Brill for his appointments would be that he wouldn't be able to practice not thinking about him. Jacob would haunt him all day long. Paul was being drawn into the life of the family. It felt like the inside of the school bus when it was filled with kids—warm, crowded, humid.

On the positive side, *Radiance Descending* is filled with food for thought.

There's something good about having a brother like Jacob, even though you won't understand it for a few years . . . when you're grown up. People don't like to think about trouble until it slams into them. You'll be more ready for it. It always comes—in one form or another.

Jacob is an eerie child at times. He's irritating. You've explained him to yourself. It's the explanation you think you understand—not Jacob. That's true about other things as well. We're very familiar with our own explanations.

Like Paul, we've all tried to avoid being drawn into the problems we face in life. Although there is no happy ending here, there is value in learning the importance of multiple perspectives. Paul seems to see Jacob as an other. He'd be quite happy if Jacob didn't exist at all. Although Paul doesn't make much progress, near the end of the novel he begins to see the world through less egotistical eyes.

Creating opportunities to talk with children about issues of this sort is what makes this novel worthwhile. *Radiance Descending* is an easy read that invites children to reflect on their own attitudes and behaviors towards others. After reading this book, we found children exploring their feelings and reactions to handicapped children, old people, and members of nondominant minority groups in their community.

20.3   Lorbiecki, Marybeth (1998). **Sister Anne's Hands.** Illustrated by K. Wendy Popp. New York: Dial. Unpaged. ISBN: 0-8037-2038-6. Picture Book.

Set within the context of the racially torn 1960s, this is the story of Anna Zabrocky and her first encounter with an African American. Anna's new second-grade teacher Sister Anne believes in story, the power of example, and hands-on learning. Anna never loved school so much, nor were Sister Anne's lessons ever more meaningful, than the day when a paper airplane crashed into the blackboard with a note that read:

Roses are Red
Violets are Blue
Don't let Sister Anne
Get any black on you!

Like good teachers everywhere, Sister Anne transforms this incident into an opportunity to learn about Black Americans and understand the systems of oppression and opposition in our society. Hands become the metaphor for what we can give and learn across the racial divide.

Sister Anne's Hands is a gentle story, and a gentle way to invite conversations about difference. Teachers in both public and private school settings will find the story uplifting. K. Wendy Popp's illustrations successfully evoke the period in which the story is set as well as the mood of the story. Second grader Robert said of the story, "It's important. You learn to be fair and get along with people."

20.4   Martinez, Victor (1996). **Parrot in the Oven: Mi Vida.** New York: HarperCollins. 216 pp. ISBN: 0-06-447186-1. Chapter Book.

Winner of the 1996 National Book Award for Young People's Literature, *Parrot in the Oven* is a powerfully written account of a Mexican American boy's coming-of-age, and how hard it is for members of underrepresented groups to outgrow the circumstances of their birth. In Mexico there is a saying about a parrot who complains how hot it is in the shade, while all along he is sitting in an oven. In this novel, the protagonist is known as Perico ("parrot" in Spanish), and the more one reads, the more one comes to appreciate the appropriateness of the book's title. Perico is growing up in an oven where his sister dates one of the roughest characters in the barrio, where gang membership is assumed, and where participation in what the gang does, even if it involves robbery, is considered common practice. Fourteen-year-old Manny Hernandez wants to make something of his life, but it's not easy when you have an abusive father; your brother is a member of a gang and can't hold a job; and your mother faces reality by scrubbing the house, physically and metaphorically trying to scrub her troubles away. "Start on the bottom and work your way up," his father tells him. Drop out of school and become a dishwasher. From dishwasher you can become bus boy and finally waiter. Perico thinks otherwise, observing that "most of the people he knew started on the bottom and worked their way sideways."

Parrot in the Oven is an excellent book for literature study. No one can walk away from this book without having a better understanding of home culture—both as a negative and positive tie that binds—as well as a better understanding of the systems of meaning that operate in the larger society to maintain the status quo and ensure that the poor stay poor and the vast inequities never get examined. The chapters entitled "Boxing Match," "Going Home," and "Dying of Love" are particularly excellent in demonstrating the yin and yang of cultures, cruelties, and clashes.

20.5   Rapp, Adam (1997). **The Buffalo Tree.** Asheville, NC: Front Street. 188 pp. ISBN: 1-886910-19-7. Sophisticated Chapter Book.

Each of us knows or has known a juvenile who is out of control. It seems like these young people not only reject the dominant social values, but also are destructive and dangerous to themselves and to society. Told from the perspective of Sura, a juvenile who is doing six months in the Hartford Juvenile Home for "clipping" hood ornaments, *The Buffalo Tree* is a haunting tale of how the juvenile and adult residents of this detention center seem to be doing all that they can to make their collective experience there a living hell. Author Adam Rapp uses "juve talk" to give readers a glimpse of how these troubled adolescents think, and the heavy burdens they carry.

Although this book may not be for everyone, both because of its focus and its language, it is eye-opening and does invite conversations about young people who most adults dismiss as anchorless. Although there is no happy ending in this tale of institutional child abuse, readers are encouraged to reflect on how society positions some of its young people, and who benefits from this positioning. Left unanswered is the question of what we should do. This is a much-needed conversation, for clearly there should be better alternatives than the one portrayed in the book. Although this story is disturbing, then, this also is its virtue.

20.6 Steptoe, John (1997). **Creativity.** Illustrated by E. B. Lewis. New York: Clarion. 32 pp. ISBN: 0-395-68706-3. Picture Book.

Charles is surprised to learn that Hector, the new kid, is Puerto Rican. After all, both boys have the same brown skin and the same black hair, although Hector's is straight and Charlie's is curly. What separates them is their language. In exploring these issues, Charlie begins to see difference as creative rather than problematic.

Although the book focuses on surface issues such as having the right shoes and T-shirt to fit into the group, bigger issues await discussion: how different languages can camouflage a common culture; how pop cultures are created to sell merchandise and define who is "in" and who is "out"; and how language and issues of multiculturalism are related to power in our society. Watercolor pictures by E. B. Lewis capture the kind of transparent role that color in our society should play, but in many ways seem prosaic given the importance that difference and culture make in a book entitled *Creativity*.

Secondary Reviews

20.7 Rodríguez, Luis (1997). **América Is Her Name.** Illustrated by Carlos Vásquez. Willimantic, CT: Curbstone. Unpaged. ISBN: 1-880684-40-3. Picture Book.

In school, nine-year-old América Soliz passes some teachers in the hallway and hears her teacher Miss Gable whisper:

"She's an illegal." How can that be? How can anyone be illegal? She is Mixteco, from an ancient tribe that was here before the Spanish, before the blue-eyed, even before this government that now calls her "illegal." How can a girl called América not belong in America?

Miss Gable finds América's Spanish-speaking class "difficult," but when a Puerto Rican poet named Mr. Aponte comes to visit, América rises to recite Spanish poetry and the whole class listens and applauds. Encouraged by this response, América begins to write poetry, remembering the strong and open voice she had in Oaxaca, the mountainous area in Mexico where she was born. Her father says writing is a waste of time because it won't pay the bills or clean the house. But América continues to write, despite the disheartening gray world of the Chicago ghetto, the violence she sees on the street, and her father's loss of his job. Her stories and poems evoke the mountains in Oaxaca, and even encourage her mother and siblings to write as well. América creates an imaginative and expressive space where she belongs, regaining her own strong and open voice.

Although the ending is rather neat and América often seems more like a grown woman than a nine-year-old girl, this book raises complex and important issues for discussion: urban poverty and lack of opportunity; inequities in education; how schools position students whose primary language is not English; and how the U.S. economy relies on the labor of low-paid workers declared illegal by immigration policy. The illustrations are bright and beautiful, and vividly depict the characters' imaginations.

20.8 Wyeth, Sharon Dennis (1998). **Something Beautiful.** Illustrated by Chris K. Soentpiet. New York: Bantam Doubleday Dell. 30 pp. ISBN: 0-385-32239-9. Picture Book.

The young girl in this book pursues a quest for beauty in her inner-city neighborhood. She initially is discouraged by the blighted areas around her, including the letters "DIE" on her own front door and the trash that is strewn around the yard. But she soon discovers that beauty can be found in a beautiful tasting fish sandwich or the beautiful sound of a baby's laugh, or simply the beauty inside each individual. In the end, the girl takes her own positive action to enhance the beauty of her neighborhood. For her efforts, she receives the approval and appreciation of her mother, who reminds the girl of her own beauty and self-worth.

In the author's note to this book, the reader is informed that the idea for this story sprang from an event in Sharon Wyeth's own childhood as she searched for the beauty in her world. This book offers an opportunity to take a critical look at the places people inhabit, as well as initiate discussions around the multiple meanings of the word *beautiful.* The book itself is made beautiful by the illustrations, which reflect both the joy and despair of living in an inner-city neighborhood. The realistically painted pictures are drawn with serious attention to the details that distinguish the characters and the community. This detailed artwork, along with the well-crafted text, enables the reader to visualize clearly the people who inhabit this cityscape, and appreciate the beauty that does exist here. (See also **8.64**)

Giving Voice to the Indignant Ones

Primary Reviews

20.9 Bunting, Eve (1998). **So Far from the Sea.** Illustrated by Chris K. Soentpiet. New York: Clarion. 32 pp. ISBN: 0-395-72095-8. Picture Book.

In 1942, the Japanese bombed Pearl Harbor. Two months later, President Franklin D. Roosevelt signed Executive Order 9066, which decreed that all people of Japanese ancestry living on the West Coast of the United States must be relocated to internment camps. Many of those interned were American citizens. Set in 1972, *So Far from the Sea* is a story of the Iwasaki family and their visit to the internment camp in California where their father was interned for three and one-half years.

The story raises important issues about the segregation of the Japanese during the war, and offers a demonstration of how easily people can be othered. Questions regarding citizenship, who decides what a good citizen is, and who qualifies to be a citizen can be raised. The story allows space for conversations regarding segregation that exists today, and the systems that maintain its existence. The illustrations by Soentpiet alternate between black-and-white and color, effectively supporting Bunting's description of the sensitive journey. (See also **3.105**).

20.10 Coleman, Evelyn (1996). **White Socks Only.** Illustrated by Tyrone Geter. Morton Grove, IL: Whitman. Unpaged. ISBN: 0-8075-8955-1. Picture Book.

When the little girl in white socks started walking to town, she had no idea of the role she would play in rewriting history. This is a story of a young African American girl who goes to town to find out if it's possible to fry an egg on the sidewalk, and decides to take a drink from a water fountain in segregated Mississippi. Thinking that she understands the "Whites Only" sign on the fountain, she sits down in the grass, takes off her patent-leather shoes, and climbs up on the stool to take a drink with only her clean white socks on her feet. When some of the town's White residents attempt to chastise and humiliate the child, fellow African Americans who witnessed the event decide to take action. The story ends with "And from then on, the 'Whites Only' sign was gone from that water fountain forever."

Although the signs may be gone from water fountains, issues of inequity continue to be played out across the nation. Inspired by childhood memories of places she could not go and things she could not do because of her skin color, Evelyn Coleman presents a thought-provoking story that can provide much needed conversations about segregation, marginalization, the inequitable distribution of power and control, and finding ways to take social action in what can appear to be the least likely places.

20.11 Forrester, Sandra (1997). **My Home Is over Jordan.** New York: Lodestar. 163 pp. ISBN: 0-525-67568-X. Chapter Book.

Life was not easy for newly freed slaves at the end of the Civil War. Caught between the ruined economy and overt racism of the South, former slaves were often homeless and without means. Maddie Henry's family is better off than most because they have the money that her Papa earned working as a soldier for the Union Army. But he ended up giving his life to the war, and now the family is on the road, looking for a place to settle down. Along the way, Maddie befriends Tibby, the child of a master and slave who has neither home nor family. Tibby is a victim who has been so silenced that she literally cannot speak.

This is a story about voice—how Tibby, Maddie, and other family members began to gain new voices that refuse to be drowned out by the waves of hatred around them. This book raises questions about the meaning of freedom, and how racist beliefs cause some groups to deny real freedom to others. It invites conversations about racist attitudes that still exist today and continue to silence people of color.

20.12 Hansen, Joyce (1998). **Women of Hope: African Americans Who Made a Difference.** New York: Scholastic. 32 pp. ISBN: 0-590-93973-4. Picture Book.

A teacher for twenty-two years in New York City, Hansen describes her combined message of self-empowerment and community service in this way: "By reaching their goals, these women helped someone else." Hansen's page-length, inspiring biographies depict the lives of thirteen African American women, arranged chronologically. We meet celebrity authors Maya Angelou and Toni Morrison. We also meet lesser-known women like Ida Wells-Barnet, a teacher and journalist at the turn of the century who exposed inequities in education for Black students and the brutality of lynching in the South, and Dr. Mae C. Jemison, who was not only the first African American woman astronaut, but who also worked as a physician in West Africa. These artists, educators, health care providers, and activists provide role models and inspiration in the integrity, passion, and struggle of their life work as well as in their own words.

Critical questions could explore the obstacles each of these women faced, the resources they called upon to overcome them, and the ways they redefined cultural notions of courage, strength, and heroism. What is perhaps most important is how these stories invite exploration of the unique and individual journeys each of us makes toward finding meaning in our lives. For the upper-elementary school level, this book would work beautifully as a read-aloud text. The striking black-and-white photographs were drawn from the Bread and Roses Cultural Project poster series, *Women of Hope.*

20.13 Hirschi, Ron. (1996). **People of Salmon and Cedar.** Illustrated by Deborah Cooper. New York: Cobblehill. 42 pp. ISBN: 0-525-65183-7. Picture Book.

Although this is a nonfiction text about the Native American tribes that populate the Northwest region of the United States, it is told like a story that invites the reader into these cultures to learn about their history and traditions. The text traces the history of the tribes of the Northwest, such as the Suquamish, S'Klallam, and Lummi, and provides a realistic account of their struggles since Europeans invaded their land. According to this account, it was feared at the end of the 1800s that Native American cultures and traditions would not survive. Thankfully these dire predictions proved untrue, and the author goes on to describe how today "the People" continue their traditional cultural practices and beliefs and "live in harmony with the earth." The author confronts the critical issue of conservation, and exposes the abuses of land and water in the Northwest region. He contends that more and more, modern society is coming to realize the ancient Native American wisdom of replenishing natural resources and taking care not to overuse the land or the rivers.

This text provides the reader with the opportunity to reflect on the local and global repercussions of being careless with consumable resources. At the same time, the book offers ways that this wasteful attitude can be reversed by observing the traditions and practices of an earlier culture. In addition to its thought-provoking and informative text, this book is peppered with beautifully drawn pictures that coincide with the story. In contrast to the colored drawings that reflect an earlier culture, a number of black-and-white photos are included to show a modern view of this region. The combination of drawings and photos in the book presents the reader with visual images of the conflicts in this region that hopefully will be resolved for the next generation.

20.14 Kaplan, William (1998). **One More Border: The True Story of One Family's Escape from War-Torn Europe.** Illustrated by Stephen Taylor. Toronto, Ontario, Canada: Groundwood. 61 pp. ISBN: 0-88899-332-3. Picture Book.

In this powerful example of historical nonfiction, William Kaplan shares the story of the struggle experienced by his father's family as they escaped war-torn Europe during the late 1930s to avoid persecution for being Jewish. The story reveals the social repositioning of the Kaplan family from living in comfort and luxury to being penniless. Through the story of the Kaplan family's escape, the reader learns about the oppression and marginalization of the Jews during the war. Inclusion of authentic artifacts such as photographs, maps, and the visa that allowed Bernard, Igor, and Nomi Kaplan to leave Europe provide a sense of realism.

This book raises thought-provoking questions about how systems of meaning can oppress certain groups or individuals: Who stands to gain from the oppression of others? What do they gain? What are some ways of interrogating persecution in order to take social action and effect change? When paired with *Passage to Freedom: The Sugihara Story* (see **20.28**) this text-set offers a rich demonstration of how people taking social action can make a difference in the lives of the oppressed. Through the support of others, the Kaplans were able to rewrite their lives into existence, and readers are offered a glimpse of their new home in Cornwall, Ontario, Canada. But not all Jewish families who experienced persecution were able to start anew as the Kaplans did. Thus the book can generate further inquiries into what happened to those who were not able to escape. Further the book can offer space for conversations regarding the different ways that some groups and individuals continue to be persecuted and oppressed.

20.15 Parker, David (1998). **Stolen Dreams: Portraits of Working Children.** Minneapolis: Lerner. 112 pp. ISBN: 0-8225-2960-2. Chapter Book.

It is impossible to read this book on the exploitation of children throughout the world and not feel the need to act on their behalf. Although the subject matter is difficult to read about, it is important to be aware of the injustices of child exploitation and labor. The book immediately draws the reader into this timely topic by opening with the story of one exploited child who had the courage to raise his voice against the industry that was oppressing him and many others like him. Although his individual struggle is only one small piece of this pervasive problem, it serves to emphasize how much more needs to be done on behalf of all mistreated children.

Subsequent chapters describe how some children end up in this situation, and what happens to them as a result. There is also a very important chapter with ideas for helping exploited children in the fight for establishing their human rights. The final pages of the book are devoted to poignant letters and genuine questions from children speaking out eloquently against the exploitation of their peers. Throughout the book, stunning and disturbing black-and-white photographs of exploited children reveal their suffering and despair. The pictures speak volumes about these children, and greatly add to the power of the text.

20.16 Shange, Ntozake (1997). **Whitewash.** Illustrated by Michael Sporn. New York: Walker. Unpaged. ISBN: 0-8027-8490-9. Picture Book.

An African American preschooler named Helene-Angel walks home from school with her brother, who doesn't particularly enjoy the task of walking his little sister home. One day, a gang of White kids surround them, blackening Mauricio's eye and painting Helene-Angel's face white as they show her how to be a "true

American" and "how to be White." Helene-Angel is traumatized; she hides in her room until her grandmother forces her to come out. As she emerges from the house, her classmates greet her and promise to stick together so that events like this won't happen again.

Based on a series of true incidents, *Whitewash* is a powerful story written in narrative style by the poet Ntozake Shange, with illustrations from a Carnegie Medal–winning video. The book gives voice to a little-known racial incident that became a lesson in tolerance and a child's triumph. Children need to understand why stories such as this one should never be forgotten. They also should be encouraged to explore how they might transform the bad things in their own lives into triumphs. We found it easy to extend conversations to the topics of diversity and difference, and the role that each must play in a multilingual and multicultural society that seeks to be democratic. (See also **5.117**)

20.17 Springer, Jane (1997). **Listen to Us: The World's Working Children.** Toronto, Canada: Groundwood. 96 pp. ISBN: 0-88899-291-2. Chapter Book.

As the book jacket advertises, *Listen to Us* explores, in a complex and multifaceted fashion, "the difficult questions that surround child labor, including globalization, consumerism, and attitudes toward girls and women." Springer takes seriously the working children who are her subjects, as well as those in her intended audience. She justly describes children as resistors and activists. Some, like Iqbal Masih, are even shapers of history. This Pakistani child worker was killed at the age of twelve as a result of his international efforts to raise consciousness and free children from forced labor. Other child activists and workers speak for themselves in this volume: ten-year-old Nirmala, a Nepalese carpet weaver; sixteen-year-old Christine, a Canadian sex worker; and eighteen-year-old Naftal, kidnapped to be a soldier in the Mozambique National Resistance when he was twelve years old.

This book leaves readers to explore critical questions about the economic and social systems that support the exploitation of children, and what might be done to help them. Springer discusses the potential harm poorly planned boycotts can inflict on working children, who may lose their livelihood and end up working in even worse conditions or on the street. She also describes well-organized, sustained campaigns that are helping to reduce child labor and to provide schooling and basic necessities for former child workers. These include the "Foul Ball" soccer ball campaign and "Free the Children," started by twelve-year-old Craig Kielburger. The only drawbacks to the volume are the inclusion of too many charts and boxed sections that interrupt the text, and the fact that Springer glosses over the poverty and struggle for survival of children within industrialized countries. Overall, however, this is a truly outstanding book, with color and black-and-white photos that take a compassionate look into the difficult, varied lives of working children worldwide.

20.18 Tillage, Leon Walter (1997). **Leon's Story.** Illustrated by Susan Roth. New York: Farrar, Straus and Giroux. 107 pp. ISBN: 0-374-34379-9. Chapter Book.

Every year, Tillage tells the story of his life to the children in the Baltimore school where he works as custodian. We're lucky to have his amazing story in print. Remembering his childhood as the son of a sharecropper in North Carolina, Tillage describes his personal experiences of—and profound insights into—segregation, racial violence, and the economic disenfranchisement of Black Americans in the South as he was growing up. He tells of joining marches for civil rights as a high school student:

Our parents would say to us, "We don't understand. Don't you know you're going to get killed for listening to those people? You're going to get beat up. What's wrong with you?" Then we would say to them, "We're getting beat up now. We're getting killed now. So I'd rather get beat up for doing something or trying to change things. I mean, why get beat up for nothing?"

When he was fifteen, Tillage witnessed the violent murder of his father by some White boys who were drunk, "just out to have some fun," and who never faced any consequences for their crime. And yet his voice, as he shares his story, is often spirited and gentle, rich with wisdom, humor, anger, and pain.

The book covers so much personal, political, and historical ground that critical questions abound. This is truly a book for all ages. Readers can explore American slavery's legacy of racism, racial violence, and economic injustice, as it was when Tillage was growing up and as it persists today. The book also generates discussion about the power of literacy and storytelling. Roth's collage art, although evocative, is an odd choice for the book. Tillage's story is so powerful that Roth's feeling "that even one picture would be too many for Leon Walter Tillage's words" seems wholly unfounded. One returns again and again to the single photo of young Tillage on the cover, wishing for more.

Secondary Reviews

20.19 Egan, Ted (1998). **The Drover's Boy.** Illustrated by Robert Ingpen. Melbourne, Australia: Lothian. Unpaged. ISBN: 1-887734-52-X. Sophisticated Picture Book. (See **3.61**)

20.20 Hurmence, Belinda (1997). **Slavery Time: When I Was Chillun.** New York: Putnam. 96 pp. ISBN: 0-399-23048-3. Chapter Book.

In these twelve stories selected from *Slave Narratives,* the 1930s Works Progress Administration interviewing project, we hear the voices and stories of African American men and women who lived under slavery. These are voices that have been largely erased or ignored by American history and culture. The stories range from nostalgic recollections of childhood games and plantation cuisine, to painful memories of deprivation and abuse. This book truly invites interdisciplinary conversation.

Although the brief introduction makes passing reference to the historical and social context, one disappointing aspect of the book is that some of the stories and photos deserve or require immediate comment, rather than simply leaving it to chance that these conversations will take place. Consequently *Slavery Time* may best be read by students in a group setting, where discussions can explore the crucial and often troubling questions that arise. How can we make sense of the way a former slave recalls the days of slavery as a better time? What did freedom mean in 1865? What does freedom mean today? Finally these narratives are a profound testament to the power of literacy and self-expression, which so threatened the structures of slavery that slave owners strove at all costs—and often by violent means—to keep slaves from reading, writing, and speaking for themselves, as these men and women do so eloquently.

20.21 Stanley, Jerry (1997). **Digger: The Tragic Fate of the California Indians from the Missions to the Gold Rush.** New York: Crown. 104 pp. ISBN: 0-517-70951-1.

Stanley has created a well-researched, highly readable portrait of the destruction of many of the Native American tribes that inhabited what is now California at the time of the first Spanish, and then the European, occupation. Because the Native Americans gathered their food and used sticks to dig vegetables, the forty-niners called them "Diggers," and saw them as "uncivilized creatures that were to be shot on sight." Stanley organizes his account chronologically, first telling readers about what life was like for the Native Americans prior to the coming of the Spanish and Europeans, and then what life was life during the period of the missions and the Gold Rush.

At times *Digger* reads like a social studies text, but few readers will walk away not having learned several interesting facts or having their romanticized notions of the missions and the Gold Rush shattered. Although many events are glossed, the text is full of historical facts and quotations, including the fact that "When Europeans arrived in North America, 10 million people were living there. By 1910, only 230,000 Native Americans were left." Stanley gives voice to a people who have been marginalized by current accounts of history and political policy. Sprinkled throughout the volume are maps, original photographs, drawings, and quotations from an interview with Ishi, a Yahi man believed to be the last Native Californian to live according to the customs of his people. The author provides an extensive index so that students studying this period can locate information. Anyone studying California history or Native American culture at the upper-elementary level and beyond should consider using this book as a read-aloud or as part of a text-set for literature discussion. Who gets to write history, to what effect, and for whose benefit are only a few of the issues raised. When we briefly introduced this book in a multi-age classroom of fifth and sixth graders, one of the questions that arose focused on the responsibility we have today for correcting the sins of our forebearers. This is the kind of question that makes history come alive.

Taking Social Action

Primary Reviews

20.22 Breckler, Rosemary (1996). **Sweet Dried Apples: A Vietnamese Wartime Childhood.** Illustrated by Deborah Kogan Ray. Boston: Houghton Mifflin. Unpaged. ISBN: 0-395-73570-X. Picture Book.

This story is told from the point of view of a young Vietnamese girl whose life is changed by the encroaching war that surrounds her.

What starts out as a distant threat gradually comes to encompass her family and her life. A major figure in the book is Ong Noi, the girl's grandfather, a "revered elder" who has been the herb doctor in his village for many years. When his son becomes a soldier, he comes to help look after his two grandchildren. With him Ong Noi brings baskets of medicinal herbs, and sweet dried apples to cover their bitter taste. When their grandfather leaves to tend wounded soldiers in a distant area, the children continue to gather herbs as he has taught them to do. In the end, Ong Noi uses his position as the herb doctor to sacrifice his own life so that others can have relief from pain and suffering. He gives all of his medicines to others and saves nothing to heal his own wounds. This book invites conversations about the different forms that social action can take and how this action affects people's lives. (See also **3.115**)

20.23 Dash, Joan (1996). **We Shall Not Be Moved: The Women's Factory Strike of 1909.** New York: Scholastic. 165 pp. ISBN: 0-590-48409-5. Sophisticated Chapter Book.

This historical account of the events leading up to a massive women's factory strike almost a century ago shows how taking social action and working together can help to improve conditions for those who lack power. In this case, there was social action on the part of three groups. First, the shirtwaist factory workers themselves, mostly poor young women between the ages of sixteen and eighteen, had the courage to stand up to the powerful factory owners and demand better pay and better working conditions. Starving and without warm clothing, they picketed in the cold and continued their strike for months. When they were terrorized and brutally beaten by hired thugs and hauled off to jail by corrupt police, two other groups of women became involved. Both "the mink brigade" (wealthy women) and "the college girls" had power and were ready to use it to fight for their progressive beliefs. When the strike ended, conditions for the factory workers had improved only slightly, but other gains had been made, including raising public consciousness and establishing a labor union that would ultimately protect the workers who followed.

This book would be appropriate in a historical text-set focusing on civil rights and suffrage issues, as well as in one dealing with current and past labor practices that reward some workers while abusing others. It could provide a starting point for conversations about domestic and foreign sweatshops that still exist to make cheap garments at the expense of the workers who make them.

20.24 Fleischman, Paul (1998). **Whirligig.** New York: Henry Holt. 133 pp. ISBN: 0-8050-5582-7. Chapter Book.

The premise of this book is deceptively simple: The thoughtless act of an unhappy teenager has tragic results that set in motion a series of surprising events. Certainly this theme is a staple of young-adult chapter books. Here, however, Fleischman has cleverly added concurrent storylines to this conventional format in order to make a point about the effect one individual can have on the larger society. As the story opens, the main character, Brent, is charged with the task of designing, constructing, and placing four memorial whirligigs at various locations throughout the United States. We then follow Brent on his journey to various regions of the country in search of appropriate locales for the colorful, wind-driven whirligigs, and witness his growth from a self-centered, careless teenager to a thoughtful young man.

Although Brent's story is engaging in its own right, Fleischman subtly inserts into the story four completely independent narratives about other characters from varying backgrounds and social positions. The single connection between these stories and lives is the whirligigs Brent places throughout the country. In each of these parallel stories, a character has a unique encounter with one of the whirligigs, in some cases years after they were created. As a result of their encounter, each character has to rethink his or her own life. These concurrent narratives provide the reader with a broader perspective of the impact that Brent and the whirligigs have on very different individuals. Just as the wind sets the whirligigs in motion, so Fleischman sets in motion a superb collection of stories with a single common thread. This ingenious literary device offers a wider vision of the effect one individual can have on the larger society, and demonstrates the consequences that a single thoughtless action can have as it ripples over time. (See also **5.138**)

20.25 McGuffee, Michael (1996). **The Day the Earth Was Silent.** Illustrated by Edward Sullivan. Bloomington, IN: Inquiring Voices. Unpaged. ISBN: 0-9634637-1-3. Picture Book.

The class makes a beautiful new flag, which they want to share with all the earth. The principal asks, "Why try?" But one child insists, *"Why not try?"* So the principal tells them to ask the mayor, since she might know. This exchange continues through several permutations as the children keep asking, and keep hearing from weary adults all the reasons for giving up on their plan: it involves too much work, it's too expensive, and on and on, until finally, at a meeting of all the nations, they unveil their flag, and the people of earth finally see—Why not!

In this story, children continue to cooperate, ask insightful questions, and insist on a unity among all people, until the whole world is awed and healed by their vision. But this isn't simply a story of visionary optimism—it's also about the importance of persistence and cherishing small yet significant moments of social change. Edward Sullivan's illustrations radiate the bright energy of kids engaged in creative expression and social action. Possible topics for conversation abound, including the potential of imagining, creating, questioning, and working together to change our world for the better (not to mention the importance of listening to children!). And what better way to initiate this conversation than this story about kids choosing and implementing their own dreams to share with their community and world.

20.26 Miller, William (1998). **The Bus Ride.** Illustrated by John Ward. New York: Lee & Low. Unpaged. ISBN: 1-880000-60-1. Picture Book.

"It's always been this way," Sara's mother replies when Sara asks why she and the other African Americans have to ride in the back of the bus. Curious as to what could possibly justify such a law, Sara heads off to the front of the bus. Once up front she takes a seat and realizes that the only difference is that White people sit there. Regardless, Sara decides to take a seat.

Based on the Montgomery bus boycott, and framed through the experience of Rosa Parks, *The Bus Ride* can be used as a vehicle for conversations about how particular systems of meaning can result in the "othering" of certain groups of people. Other questions that can be raised include: Who does the law support? Who benefits most from certain laws? What role can the media play in raising consciousness or maintaining inequities? Most importantly, *The Bus Ride* demonstrates the possibility of effecting social change through individual or group action.

20.27 Mitchell, Margaree King (1997). **Granddaddy's Gift.** Illustrated by Larry Johnson. Mahwah, NJ: BridgeWater. Unpaged. ISBN: 0-8167-4010-0. Picture Book.

Little Joe lives with her grandparents on a farm in segregated Mississippi. One day when she misses the school bus, Granddaddy drives her all the way to school, insisting that she go and learn as much as she can even though "they're not teaching you everything they should." Little Joe begins to understand this better when her grandfather tries to register to vote. Granddaddy bravely persists in defending his rights even after the town clerk tries to dissuade him, the owner of the town co-op refuses to do business with him anymore, and an arsonist sets fire to the church he attends. On her eighteenth birthday, Little Joe is able to register to vote herself, simply by filling out a voter registration card. She does this while remembering her granddaddy's gift—his example of standing up for things he believed in and being proud, even when he was afraid.

This book celebrates the gift given to us by preceding generations, who made a difference in the struggle for human dignity and civil rights for all. It both honors their achievements and reminds us of the importance of education, pride, and vigilance in the ongoing struggle for social justice. *Granddaddy's Gift* invites students to experience the complex social milieu of segregated Mississippi, and to witness the racism and violence that was encountered by Black citizens who had the courage to stand up for their rights.

20.28 Mochizuki, Ken (1997). **Passage to Freedom: The Sugihara Story.** Illustrated by Dom Lee. New York: Lee & Low. Unpaged. ISBN: 1-880000-49-0. Picture Book.

In July of 1940, young Hiroki Sugihara, son of the Japanese consul to Lithuania, sees hundreds of Jewish refugees from Poland gathered at the gate of his family's house. These people want the consul to give them travel visas so that they can escape from imminent persecution. After Consul Sugihara is denied his government's permission to give out visas to the refugees, he asks his family whether he should help the refugees anyway—by writing visas allowing them to travel through the Soviet Union to Japan, and from there on to safety—and thereby risk punishment by the Nazi, Japanese, and Russian governments. The family's collective decision to help the refugees sets the wheels in motion for the next month, during which Consul Sugihara hand writes thousands of visas while Hiroki plays with the refugee children in the park.

Finally when the Soviets take over Lithuania, they order Consul Sugihara to leave. But as the fascinating afterward notes, the actions of the Sugihara family saved thousands of people.

Dom Lee's sepia-toned illustrations beautifully convey the intense emotion of the Sugihara and refugee families, and are also reminiscent of stark, black-and-white Holocaust photographs. The tone seems just right for this story, which raises important conversations about human rights; the relationships between compassion, courage, and sacrifice; nonviolent resistance; and the power of the pen as an instrument of social justice.

20.29 Winslow, Vicki (1997). **Follow the Leader.** New York: Delacorte. 215 pp. ISBN: 0-385-32285-2. Chapter Book.

Set in 1971 in North Carolina, this is the story of a family that's trying to make a difference. Mrs. Adams remembers segregation laws from her childhood, and now votes only for "people who want to make things better for everybody." Mr. Adams hires subcontractors according to their bids and not who they are, and refuses to join a segregated country club, even though it would help him with business contacts and is "the most beautiful golf course this side of Myrtle Beach." Both Mr. and Mrs. Adams support desegregation of the local schools, even though this means that their daughter Amanda will be bused out of their neighborhood to a downtown school. Resistant at first, Amanda eventually comes to appreciate the teachers and students in her new school, and realizes that the friend she missed so much at first was not the kind of friend she wanted to keep.

Follow the Leader invites conversations about racist attitudes that continue to lurk just below the surface in contemporary life. The book encourages adolescents to interrogate their often tacit acceptance of questionable peer-group ethics, and to rethink their own beliefs. Another important conversation that might come out of this book relates to how the burden of carrying out policy decisions often falls on people who did not make the decisions in the first place. In this case, adult citizens made the decision to desegregate the public schools, but the onus of working through the problems that came with implementation of this order fell on the children and teachers. Because one group elected to think globally in voting for integration, another group had to act locally in terms of figuring out how to make integration work.

Secondary Reviews

20.30 McCully, Emily Arnold (1996). **The Bobbin Girl.** New York: Dial. Unpaged. ISBN: 0-8037-1827-6. Picture Book.

Rebecca Putney is a ten-year-old bobbin girl in nineteenth century Lowell, Massachusetts, who works thirteen-hour days under unhealthy working conditions in order to help support her family. The story, however, is not as much about Rebecca as it is about the social and industrial milieu of the times. More specifically, the story provides much needed space in which to encourage conversation about issues of child labor and child abuse, as well as issues of labor control, enslavement, and the marginalization of women. In the story, Rebecca befriends Judith, another mill worker who puts up with the conditions at the mill in order to finance her studies. It is Judith who rises to the occasion, standing up for the rights of the female factory workers when the mill owner decides to reduce already low wages. At first it appears as though the group of female workers may stand united against management. But in the end, many of them abandon the protest and return to work, driven by the illusion that working in the mill represents their independence.

The Bobbin Girl does not explicitly present itself as a story of triumph for women. However it does raise a number of questions regarding the difficulties involved in any struggle for equity and social justice. It also points to the need for ongoing social action. With regard to gender issues, the book easily lends itself to discussions of what happens when women break the crust of convention and move into positions that challenge the ingrained gender biases in our society. McCully's use of a dark palette and shadows conveys quite effectively the feeling of the poor working conditions in the mill. (See also **3.42**)

20.31 McCully, Emily Arnold (1998). **The Ballot Box.** New York: Knopf. Unpaged. ISBN: 0-679-87938-2. Picture Book.

"All the summer of 1880, Cordelia's job was to go next door, feed Mrs. Stanton's horse and clean out the stall. Every afternoon, Mrs. Stanton put aside her work on *The History of Woman Suffrage* and gave Cornelia a riding lesson." *The Ballot Box,* set in the late 1800s, is a weaving of history and fiction that shares the parallel stories of two females and their attempts to challenge social norms and expectations. Cordelia is a young girl and neighbor to suffragist Elizabeth Cady Stanton. As the book unfolds, we learn of Cordelia's desire to jump a four-foot fence on horseback. This is a feat that her brother is sure she cannot accomplish.

Paralleled with Stanton's story of going to the polls to attempt to vote and fight for women's suffrage, Cordelia's story takes a backseat when she accompanies Stanton to cast a ballot. However the Stanton story is one that is not currently told or made visible in picture-book form. As such, the book is an important demonstration of what it means to take up the plight of women as a marginalized group. The book also clearly reminds us of the position of men, especially White men, as dominant decisionmakers, thus opening up the possibility for a discussion of ways that women can redefine their position in society.

20.32 Sisalu, Elinor Batezat (1996). **The Day Gogo Went to Vote.** Illustrated by Sharon Wilson. New York: Little Brown. Unpaged. ISBN: 0-316-70267-6. Picture Book.

This story of the historic 1994 election in South Africa is told through the eyes of young Thembi. Thembi's grandmother Gogo is determined to cast a ballot in the first election in which native people are allowed to vote. Although she has not been out of the family's yard for years, the elderly Gogo makes the long journey to the balloting place, accompanied by her granddaughter and assisted by numerous community members. Thembi sees how much voting means to Gogo, the oldest voter in the township.

Reading aloud Gogo and Thembi's story could provoke interesting discussion about the importance of democracy during political campaigns and election times. Although the issue of apartheid is not directly discussed in this book, its effects are demonstrated by Gogo's determination to create her own destiny by voting. Paired with *Granddaddy's Gift* by Margaree King Mitchell (see **20.27**), this book raises parallel issues about worldwide struggles for Black suffrage and social justice, and the important contribution our elders have played and continue to play in this struggle.

Understanding How Systems of Meaning in Society Position Us

Primary Reviews

20.33 Bunting, Eve (1998). **Your Move.** Illustrated by James Ransome. New York: Harcourt Brace. Unpaged. ISBN: 0-15-200181-6. Picture Book.

James is ten, and his six-year-old brother Isaac likes to do what-ever he does. One evening after their mother goes to work, James sneaks out to meet the K-Bones, bringing Isaac with him because he can't exactly leave his little brother home alone. The K-Bones, lead by Kris and Bones, claim that they aren't a gang or a crew, just guys who hang out together. James thinks he wants to join them, so they give him a task: Spray paint the K-Bones' name over the Snakes' name, way up on a sign over the highway. "You mean tagging?" James asks. But Bones replies, "Crews tag. We write." James is nervous and scared, wishing he could leave. But how can he? He's there just "to prove I'm tough enough to be in K-Bones." When he's back on the ground with his mission accomplished, James feels "suddenly so cool." But the feeling is short lived. As they flee the scene, James pulls Isaac by the hand and thinks:

> I'm not feeling too great about getting him mixed up in this. I should have known the kind of stuff the K-Bones do. I'm not that dumb. Maybe I did know. But I wanted to be in with them.

And that's when they run into the Snakes, who have a gun. The K-Bones take off. James hears a shot, and little Isaac drops to his knees.

In the end, Isaac ends up with just two skinned knees, but *Your Move* does much more than scratch the surface of the issues it raises. Bunting explores the reasons why James and six-year-old Isaac are attracted to the K-Bones—both seek not only to connect with peers, but also to find older males to look up to, especially since their dad left. The reasons why they both decide not to join the K-Bones when Kris offers them the chance are even more com-pelling. Critical discussion could begin with the choices James and Isaac make. What attracts them to the K-Bones? Why do they each decide to turn down the offer to join? Are there differences between the way ten-year-old James and six-year-old Isaac make their decisions? Exploring with kids what they think is at stake and how they have faced or would face similar decisions is crucial, especially because—as the book reminds us—even very young kids may need to make such difficult and important decisions. *Your Move* also encourages discussion of the challenges single mothers face, particularly in finding safe and affordable childcare, and the way families and communities try to deal with violence. Ransome's fine oil paintings dramatize the complex relationships between characters and the boys' excitement and fear on the street. (See also **5.71**)

20.34 Fletcher, Ralph (1998). **Flying Solo.** New York: Clarion. 144 pp. ISBN: 0-395-87323-1. Chapter Book.

Told from the perspective of different students in Mr. Fabiano's sixth-grade class, this is the story of what happens when a substitute teacher doesn't show up and the class decides they'll run things by themselves for the day. No one discovers their secret as they more or less maintain the usual routine, bringing the attendance sheet to the office, filing to music class in straight rows, and so on. But there's a lot else going on, even as they stick to most of Mr. Fab's lesson plan. Rachel, who hasn't spoken since the death of their classmate Tommy six months ago, confronts Bastian about his cruelty to Tommy while he was alive. The conflict and emotions that ensue make Karen, who masterminded a few lies to keep their day of self-governance secret, wish that Mr. Fab were there after all. But at the same time, the class talks and writes about things they probably wouldn't have with him there. It's only at the end of the day, at the school assembly, that the principal discovers the deception. When Mr. Fab does appear at the end, it's easy to see why the class loves him and his structured routines. Like the other adults, he's concerned and dead serious when he brings up what the class did. But he also wants to know what each of them thinks, and asks each student to write to him with his or her version of what happened that day. The varying responses allow for great discussions on taking responsibility versus being irresponsible, and on how school practices can both inhibit and empower kids. (See also **6.50**)

20.35 Hesse, Karen (1998). **Just Juice.** Illustrated by Robert Andrew Parker. New York: Scholastic. 138 pp. ISBN: 0-590-03382-4. Chapter Book.

This multilayered story is told from the point of view of nine-year-old Juice Faulstich, a chronically truant child who is happier at home with her unsuccessful father and pregnant mother than at school where she is constantly reminded of her inability to read. As the story unfolds, Juice comes to realize that her father is also a nonreader and that his lack of reading proficiency has brought the family to the brink of disaster in the form of eviction from their home. Juice begins to understand that although both she and her father are skilled in many ways, their acceptance by society and even by other family members is greatly affected by their status as illiterate. The book ends on a hopeful note as the family finds a way to avert the eviction and makes literacy a goal for all of them.

The critical issues embedded in this story begin to surface as the reader considers how learning and literacy position individuals as successes or failures both personally and socially, in school and in everyday life. The story of the Faulstich family shows how other ways of knowing are seldom valued as highly as literacy skills. In addition, the story illustrates how the efforts of well-meaning social service professionals can impact negatively on the people they are attempting to help if the voices of those individuals are not being heard. When extended to these critical levels, the story of Juice and the Faulstich family invites readers to consider how some people are marginalized not only by their poverty, but also by their illiteracy. (See also **7.76**, and Patricia Polacco's *Thank You, Mr. Falker* (**7.80**), for another example of how literacy positions individuals.)

20.36 Jiménez, Francisco (1998). **The Circuit: Stories from the Life of a Migrant Child.** Albuquerque, NM: University of New Mexico. 134 pp. ISBN: 0-8263-1797-9. Chapter Book.

In this powerful collection of short stories that flow together like a novel, Franciso Jiménez presents a brilliant, up-close view into the lives of the Mexican immigrant farm workers who harvest produce in the fields of California. We see the humanity of this usually faceless group that brings food to our tables while continually being the object of political and media degradation. The book begins with Jiménez' parents risking everything to come across *la frontera* to the promised land of California in order to escape the poverty of their lives in Mexico. What they find instead of good jobs and a better life is the back-breaking life of migrant workers. As they continually move from place to place on "the circuit" following the ripening of the crops, they live in tents and shacks with no electricity or running water, don't earn enough money to feed their eight children or provide them with medical care, and constantly worry about being deported to Mexico. The twelve stories in this book are told from the perspective of young Panchito, whose authentic voice lets us feel both the joy and despair of migrant life. Jiménez's memoirs of school experiences and the frustration his father feels when he is unable to feed or protect his family are especially poignant.

This book would be a marvelous way to begin class discussions on a variety of critical issues, including poverty in the United

States, the working conditions of farm laborers, labor-management issues, how schools position students whose primary language is not English, healthcare and who's entitled to it, and transient lifestyles. The book is also an inspirational tale of personal courage and growth, despite the last scene of the book in which Panchito is taken out of school by an immigration officer and led into a border-patrol car. The book is the winner of the 1997 John and Patricia Beatty Award from the California Library Association, and the 1997 Américas Award.

20.37 Levy, Marilyn (1996). **Run for Your Life.** Boston: Houghton Mifflin. 217 pp. ISBN: 0-395-74520-9. Sophisticated Chapter Book.

Run for Your Life is based on a true story about the recreation director of a community center in a drug-infested housing project in Oakland, California, and how he impacts positively the lives of a group of teenage girls. Darren, the new center director, enlists the help of thirteen-year-old Kisha and her friend Natonia in convincing other girls in the project to join a newly organized track club. This is not just the story of the rocky and often traumatic road to success for the track club, but also the story of the remarkable growth that takes place in the lives of some of the club's members. The girls spend hours a day working out in the Walt Whitman project, surrounded by crime, drugs, and domestic violence. There is so much unrest in the neighborhood that Kisha's younger brother is afraid to leave the house unless he's with his parents. This book provides an opportunity for students to see the harmful effects of poverty and unemployment, and how hopelessness can lead to domestic violence. Both teenage pregnancy and sexual abuse are briefly dealt with in the book in nongraphic ways.

20.38 Lorbiecki, Marybeth (1996). **Just One Flick of a Finger.** Illustrated by David Diaz. New York: Dial. 30 pp. ISBN: 0-8037-1948-5. Sophisticated Picture Book.

From the first stanza of this story-poem, the reader is drawn into the urban tale of two boys trying to cope with the violence that handguns bring into their lives. The boys know well enough the dangers of handguns, and can articulate the reasons to avoid using these weapons. Yet when one of the boys feels threatened by an older peer, he decides to ignore what good sense tells him and brings his father's gun to school. In the end, the handgun discharges accidentally, wounding the boy and his friend. Although it is a hard lesson, the boy comes to see the folly of carrying a loaded handgun for protection, and vows to rely on his friends and his own intellect to solve his problems in the future.

Life in an urban setting is closely scrutinized in this story. The issues of handguns, personal responsibility, handling conflicts, and making choices can all be interrogated using the context of this story. The use of street language and rhyme gives the story the feel of a rap song. The author's choice to write this story in the form of a poem using urban dialect is both appropriate and intriguing. The illustrations are a combination of vivid, abstract background drawings and individually framed pictures of the characters. The abstract background drawings look somewhat like graffiti, while the framed pictures are like snapshots that record the action as the story progresses. The use of bold colors in the artwork adds to the intense feelings and drama inherent in this all-too-realistic narrative. (See also **8.47**)

20.39 Mora, Pat (1997). **Tomás and the Library Lady/Tomas y la señora de la biblioteca.** Illustrated by Raúl Colón. New York: Knopf (English)/Dragonfly (Spanish). Unpaged. ISBN: 0-679-80401-3 (English and Spanish). Picture Book.

Based on the life of Tomás Rivera, a migrant farm worker who became a national education leader and University of California chancellor, this story shows how literacy and access to good books can work together to give a voice to people who historically have been marginalized. With the help of a caring librarian and lots of books, Tomás is able to forge a new identity as the next-generation storyteller in his family. This book shows how libraries and literacy have the power to help all of us escape the mundane and explore new worlds. The seemingly textured illustrations add an almost surrealistic quality to the story. On another level, *Tomás and the Library Lady* is a story that can help raise children's consciousness about migrant workers and what they and their families endure to survive. This book would be a good addition to a text-set dealing with inequities and harsh working conditions in the workplace.

20.40 Nodelman, Perry (1998). **Behaving Bradley.** New York: Simon & Schuster Books for Young Readers. 232 pp. ISBN: 0-689-81466-6. Chapter Book.

Brad Gold steps into a quagmire when he agrees to provide student input into the Code of Student Conduct at Roblin High

School. After being humiliated by administrators and parents at a parent meeting, he becomes committed to reforming not only the language of the Code, but the way students, teachers, and administrators interact at Roblin High. The fact that Brad is after nothing less than mutual respect is so threatening to the status quo that he is beaten up by school bullies Mandy and Candy, threatened by a midnight caller, and lambasted by teachers for his efforts. In the process, Brad discovers that power in the school resides in some surprising places, that his teachers are humans with heartbreaking problems, and that everything is more bewildering than he ever thought possible. Although the School Board adopts his rewritten version of the Code, perhaps nothing has changed more than Brad himself, who muses:

> If this were a TV show or a movie, I'd know exactly what happened and why it happened and I'd do something about it . . . But it isn't a TV show. It's life. Stuff like that happens to you, or to other people, and you don't know why exactly, or even what did happen, exactly, and it may or may not have a happy ending and it may or may not even be over yet and your best friend won't even tell you about it. It's just plain bewildering.

Nodelman's satirical look at high school life raises some important issues for discussion. Brad's explorations prompt questions of how the social systems in schools position students, teachers, and administrators. A real strength of the book is how Brad's perceptions of people at Roblin change as a result of his growing understanding of the social and institutional dynamics that connect them. Although his depictions of classmates start out as rather cartoonlike, they become increasingly complex. The book also invites discussions on dissent and the process of working toward social change. (See also **6.52**)

20.41 Spinelli, Jerry (1997). **Wringer.** New York: HarperCollins. 229 pp. ISBN: 0-06-440578-8. Chapter Book.

If you grow up as a boy in American society, you generally are expected to endure "the treatment" on your birthday, participate in hunting at a particular age, and be moderately ugly to girls even if they were your best friends a year earlier. Although these behaviors might delight your male peers, amuse your father, puzzle your mother, annoy your female friends, and emotionally traumatize you, they are "what men do." Palmer LaRue is going to be ten, and he is going through his own rite of passage in a town that annually holds a pigeon shoot. In this town, it is the ten-year-olds who get to wring the necks of all the pigeons who are wounded but do not die outright. Not only does Palmer question why he should be expected to do this, but as luck would have it, he also is befriended by a pigeon he calls Nipper, who becomes his pet. Palmer's resulting inner turmoil, the social pressure he endures, and the inevitability of an approaching birthday drive the story forward.

Understanding that "common sense is always just cultural sense," Jerry Spinelli spins a tale that merits unpacking. Boys may just be boys, but that is not accidental. The rituals of male initiation—smoking behind the barn, drinking beer to be part of the gang, learning to hunt—position young boys to be certain kinds of human beings. *Wringer* invites the kinds of conversations that we cannot afford to miss having with children. It invites them to explore the forces that operate in society to make them into certain kinds of people. Perhaps even more important, the book might help them to become more consciously aware of their alternatives. In the end, even Palmer learns to stop being afraid and to stand up for what he believes. His decision to be himself is redeemed in a particularly hopeful scene: as Palmer rushes out of the shooting arena with his wounded bird Nipper, a little boy in the audience asks his father if he too can have a pigeon for a pet. A brilliant, must-read, Newbery Honor Book from the author of the Newbery Award book *Maniac Magee*. (See also **5.82**)

Spinelli, Jerry (1990). **Maniac Magee.** Boston: Little Brown. 184 pp. ISBN: 0-316-80722-2. Chapter Book.

20.42 Thomas, Rob (1997). **Slave Day.** New York: Simon & Schuster Books for Young Readers. 188 pp. ISBN: 0-689-80206-4. Sophisticated Chapter Book.

This book explores how dominant systems of meaning position people and groups in certain ways. Through short, first-person narratives, the reader is able to follow the thoughts and actions of seven students and a teacher as they live through "Slave Day," an annual tradition at Robert E. Lee High School. Although the official purpose for the activity is to raise money for student activities, an African American student named Keene challenges the activity as racist and demeaning. He writes in the school paper that this event is "not perceived as racist simply because it has always existed without comment from those it should chiefly offend—African-American students." Keene calls for social action in the form of a boycott of school on Slave Day by all Black students. This suggestion is rejected by Shawn, a basketball star and the first African American President of the Student Council. For Shawn, "the civil rights movement ended twenty years ago" and has nothing to do with him. When the boycott fails to materialize, Keene decides to "buy" Shawn and raise his—and others'—awareness of racial issues. Other characters in the book interrogate systems of meaning relating to gender, social status, and institutional power. The book encourages readers to rethink the kinds of roles they choose for themselves and assign to others.

20.43 Wolff, Virginia E. (1998). **Bat 6.** New York: Scholastic. 256 pp. ISBN: 0-590-89799-3. Chapter Book.

World War II has recently ended, and everyone in the Oregon towns of Barlow and Bear Creek is gearing up for the yearly "Bat 6," the annual softball game between sixth-grade girls from each town. Both teams have one great new player: Shazam, whose father was killed at Pearl Harbor and who has just come to live with her grandmother; and Aki, a Japanese American girl who has just returned home with her family after years in an internment camp. From the perspectives of twenty-one different characters, we hear first of the excitement and preparation leading up to the game, and then how the game is cut short by a terrible incident of racial violence: Shazam knocks Aki in the head forcefully and intentionally, causing serious injury. What follows is the town's struggle to make sense of what happened that day—a search that brings many to question their acceptance of the war's racism and violence, and their own complicity and silence.

Critical conversations might focus on how social systems of meaning position various characters, including Shazam, Aki, their families, the returning soldier, and the conscientious objector. The technique of using twenty-one voices also provides fertile ground for a discussion of diversity, difference, and dissent, especially in the context of this war, which so often is portrayed as uniting all Americans in moral consensus.

Secondary Reviews

20.44 Haskins, Jim (1998). **Separate but Not Equal: The Dream and the Struggle.** New York: Scholastic. 184 pp. ISBN: 0-590-45910-4. Sophisticated Chapter Book.

Perhaps no event better dramatizes the institutional weight, violence, and injustice of segregated and inequitable education than when young Elizabeth Eckhart tried to pass through the line of armed National Guardsmen called out by Governor Orval Faubus to prevent Black students from entering Central High in 1957. Haskins moves from this starting point to examine the history of Black schooling in America, from violence against slaves who learned to read to the issues behind landmark legal decisions such as *Brown v. Board of Education.* Haskins interrogates subsequent rulings that undermined this stand, including the 1973 Supreme Court ruling that upheld the funding of public schools through property taxes. We also hear about Black writers' and intellectuals' great and often unsung contributions to the struggle, from Phillis Wheatley to W. E. B. DuBois. Simple statistics on the disparity in school expenditures for White and Black students speak volumes about the ongoing inequities in education.

Critical questions include how issues of segregation and funding are being played out in schools today. Students might explore funding in their own districts as compared to a nearby district serving another community. Can a public education system paid for by local property taxes be called "public" when it so plainly discriminates against poor communities? What does integration mean, and what relationship does it bear to social justice and equality? Haskins includes a helpful chronology of events impacting civil rights and education, from the Civil War and Emancipation through a 1995 federal district court judge's ruling that released the Denver, Colorado, public schools from court-ordered busing. Black-and-white photographs give faces to the people who have dreamed of, and struggled for, equal education for African Americans.

20.45 Hoffman, Mary (1997). **An Angel Just Like Me.** Illustrated by Cornelius Van Wright and Ying-Hwa Hu. New York: Dial Books for Young Readers. Unpaged. ISBN: 0-8037-2265-6. Picture Book.

As Tyler's family prepares for Christmas, he discovers that the angel that tops their tree has broken. Wondering why all the representations of angels he has seen are female, pale, and blond, Tyler sets out to find a male Black angel who looks more like him. Through his search, Tyler questions dominant cultural and Christian representations of the angelic and the divine. How can Jesus be blond if he was Jewish and born in the Middle East? Tyler's mother informs him that it is possible to be both Jewish and blond, but Tyler still wonders why Jesus isn't depicted with dark skin and hair and eyes.

The story ends with the appearance of an angel just like Tyler, but his questions remain salient for discussion. Why couldn't Tyler find an image of a male Black angel to identify with in his family's Christian tradition? Why couldn't he find one for sale in any store? With a light touch, this story makes room for us to question how racism and gender stereotypes have shaped not only consumer culture and institutionalized religion, but even individual family traditions and conceptions of spirituality. Tyler challenges the dominant social systems that not only exclude him and deny history, but also stereotype Black males as anything but angelic. Wright and Hu's luminous watercolor illustrations make Tyler and his family come to life.

20.46 Jenkins, A. M. (1997). **Breaking Boxes.** New York: Delacorte. 182 pp. ISBN: 0-385-32513-4. Sophisticated Chapter Book.

Breaking Boxes is a well-crafted tale about sixteen-year-old Charlie, who has lived in a poor neighborhood with his very responsible older brother since their mother died of alcoholism six years ago. Charlie is a loner who is befriended by Brandon, one of the rich kids in town, after an incident in which Brandon ridicules Charlie for not wearing the "in" shoes. We see their friendship grow, and eventually Charlie feels comfortable enough to tell his friend Brandon that Charlie's older brother is gay. Brandon is shocked, feels betrayed, gets incredibly angry, and tells everyone at school about Charlie's brother. The book ends with the story of the eventual reconciliation between Brandon and Charlie.

The issues of homosexuality and homophobia are handled in realistic and appropriate ways for middle-school students. This book invites discussions about friendship, class differences, teenage problems, and homophobia. The publisher suggests that *Breaking Boxes* is written for children fourteen years of age and older. There is a liberal sprinkling of profanity throughout the book, which adds to the believability of dialogue, but which may not be appropriate in certain school settings. There are also scenes that depict teenage drinking and semi-explicit sex. Despite these potential problems, A. M. Jenkins does a masterful job of depicting homophobia in a way that makes the issue accessible for class-room discussions.

20.47 Jiang, Ji-Li (1997). **Red Scarf Girl: A Memoir of the Cultural Revolution.** New York: HarperCollins. 240 pp. ISBN: 0-06-027585-5. Chapter Book.

"Chairman Mao, our beloved leader, smiled down at us from his place above the blackboard." Thus begins the true story of Ji-Li Jiang and her family from 1966 to 1969 during the cultural revolution in China. Twelve-year-old Jiang was an excellent student with the potential to assume an important role in the communist party when Mao Ze-Dong announced the cultural revolution. He commanded everyone to find and destroy "the four olds"—old ideas, old customs, old habits, and old culture. Because of Jiang's family's class status as former landlords, they lived with terror, powerlessness, and confusion as they were publicly humiliated and threatened. Told from Jiang's memories, this compelling story has an honesty, intensity, and integrity that brings to life this frightening period of history.

Critical conversations can begin by examining how the cultural revolution positioned the Jiang family in China. Given some historical background on the McCarthy era, students also could talk about the social, political, and economic forces that positioned American citizens at that time and today. An epilogue and glossary are included.

20.48 Nunez, Sandra, and Trish Marx (1997). **And Justice for All: The Legal Rights of Young People.** Brookfield, CT: Millbrook. 174 pp. ISBN: 0-7613-0068-6. Sophisticated Chapter Book.

Nunez and Marx provide a valuable summary of the legal rights of minors in the United States today, explaining what specific rights children do or do not have. Beginning with a brief sketch of the history of children's rights in the United States, they describe the legal relationships between the state, parents, and children themselves. In recent years, and often for the first time, children's voices are being heard more frequently within the legal system. Each chapter focuses on a different issue, from children's rights and first amendment protections for minors to safety issues and child labor laws. Specific cases are used to illustrate the struggle between minors who demand their own rights, parents who insist on their rights to decide what's best for their kids, and the state which attempts to insure the safety of children.

The strength and spirit of some children, who have challenged not only their families but the entire legal system to provide them with safety and justice, is truly astounding. Issues are presented in a complex, challenging manner, and provide much material for discussion on subjects as diverse as student privacy rights in schools and child protection laws. In the words of Martin Guggenheim, professor of law at New York University, "the book challenges the reader to question the law as it applies to young people, ultimately leaving it to the reader to decide whether the law has gone too far, or not far enough."

20.49 Sapphire (1997). **Push.** New York: Vintage. 192 pp. ISBN: 0-679-76675-8. Sophisticated Chapter Book; adult mediation required.

The adults in Precious Jones' life either brutalize or ignore her. Her mother beats her, her father rapes her, healthcare workers blame her for two resulting pregnancies, and teachers pass her through school even though she can't read. But after she seeks help at the alternative school where Ms. Rain is her teacher, Precious struggles to rewrite the devastating story of her life in her own words.

This is partly a story of what happens when the adults responsible for nurturing and supporting a child act in brutalizing and neglectful ways. Larger questions are raised concerning the systems of meaning in society that neglect or do violence to Precious because she is young, Black, and female. This novel shouldn't be left on shelves for students to read on their own; it raises too many issues that would be overwhelming for kids to deal with alone. Rather this novel pushes us, along with Precious, to ask each other questions about racism, sex, abuse, poverty, and inequities in education. These are important questions that impact kids' lives and often aren't addressed in school settings. One of the most crucial questions raised is where kids can turn, and what social and personal resources they can call upon, when adults hurt them. Precious Jones' story, told partly in the language of a sixteen-year-old just learning to read and write, is also a moving testament to the power of literacy and of courageous teachers. This book passionately reminds us that a prerequisite for learning—for entering into multivalent, literate conversation—is for children to believe that their voices will be heard.

Examining Distance, Difference, and "Otherness"

Primary Reviews

20.50 Abelove, Joan (1998). **Go and Come Back.** New York: Dorling Kindersley. 177 pp. ISBN: 0-7894-2476-2. Sophisticated Chapter Book.

When two female anthropologists arrive at a village in the Peruvian jungle to study agriculture and infant care, the local residents see their actions as both bewildering and foolish to the point of being entertaining. Although some are suspicious at first, most of the villagers end up agreeing that "They ask many stupid questions. But they are not mean. . . . just incredibly ignorant." Told from the point of view of Alicia, an adolescent villager, this is a story of stark contrasts and vast cultural differences. In a society where it is beautiful to be fat and women are encouraged to have relations with several men in order to be assured of giving birth to a healthy baby, there are myriad communication problems that arise between the visitors and their hosts.

Although they never come to understand each other completely, the anthropologists and the villagers are able to connect on some deep issues that touch them all: life, death, and survival in the jungle. Critical conversations could explore how being smart or stupid, "with it" or clueless, is always contextual, and how our perceptions of success or failure depend on the context in which we find ourselves. The story raises questions about how different cultural groups are positioned and how judgments made about people we don't really understand can be seriously flawed.

20.51 Ancona, George (1997). **Mayeros: A Yucatec Maya Family.** New York: Lothrop, Lee & Shepard. Unpaged. ISBN: 0-688-13465-3. Picture Book.

That Ancona chose the title *Mayeros*—the name by which Yucatec Maya call themselves—sets the tone for his respectful and lively photodocumentary of the daily life of a Yucatec Maya family. We meet two young brothers, Armando and Gaspar, as well as their parents, sisters, grandparents, and extended family as they prepare and eat meals, build a ring for a bullfight, and dance to celebrate the feast of saints. Ancona, himself a descendent of the Yucatec Maya, masterfully juxtaposes ancient Mayan carvings and paintings with his photos. We see a carving of a stone house from the ruins at Uxmal that mirrors the family's house, and a painting of a woman grinding corn just as Dona Satulina does today.

Throughout the book, Ancona explores the ways in which the mix of Mayan and Spanish life has come to shape how the family lives today. Although there is room to ask questions about history and economic disparity—how Spanish colonization affected the Yucatec Maya or how the grandmother might benefit from modern medical care after she hurts her wrist—this is not primarily a story of poverty or oppression. Rather, Ancona's lens portrays the life of the family as rich with tradition, laughter, connectedness to people and land, and resilient adaptability to change. (See also **3.56**)

20.52 Browne, Anthony (1998). **Voices in the Park.** New York: Dorling Kindersley. 30 pp. ISBN: 0-7894-2522-X. Picture Book.

An overprotective wealthy mother, her lonely son, an unemployed father, his outgoing daughter—these are the four character voices in Anthony Browne's extraordinary picture book *Voices in the Park*. When these four gorilla characters go to the park, we see their experiences from four very diverse perspectives. Browne uses a different font for each character to tell his or her story—a font that visually represents the personality of the voice. He does a masterful job of letting us see how the same incident is lived and understood in four completely different ways. For example, we see Albert the dog portrayed as an unruly, scruffy mongrel who is bothering a pedigreed Labrador; as the energetic pet of a dejected man who wishes he had half his dog's energy; as a friendly dog who is having a great time (the kind of experience the boy wishes he were having at the park); and as a loving pet who is always in a hurry to be let off of his leash and to have fun.

On the surface this is the story of a simple trip to the park, but readers are soon confronted with issues of class, gender, unemployment, first impressions, prejudice, and cultural stereotypes. One of the ways that Browne is able to accomplish so much in such a short book is through his stunning illustrations, which help to convey the four perspectives. On one page we hear the rich mother describing how she sees her child Charles talking to "a very rough looking" girl. From the illustration, however, we see that there is no way the mother can actually see how the girl looks because the girl and Charles are standing too far away to be seen in detail. This type of interplay between text and illustrations adds wonderful layers of meaning to the story. This unique picture book is appropriate for all age groups.

20.53 Dines, Carol (1997). **Talk to Me: Stories and a Novella.** New York: Delacorte. 223 pp. ISBN: 0-385-32271-2. Sophisticated Chapter Book; adult mediation required.

Truth is I came here with an agenda . . .
Lose my virginity
Become an intellectual
Define my future.

So begins Lez Boy's trip to Paris. Wes—known as "Lez Boy" because he lives with his mother and her partner—needs to find himself psychologically as well as sexually. Like his mother and her partner, Wes has to escape from Woodberry County and the Puritanical attitudes that prevail. In Paris he falls in love, learns to talk openly about his home situation, and begins to take an active role in defining what kind of life he wants to live and what kind of person he wants to be. This is just one of several powerful short stories in *Talk to Me.* In "Pillow Talk," Lise finds herself in love with Mathias, a boy just coming to grips with his own homosexuality. In "Listening to My Father's Silence," a teenage boy has to come to grips with his mother's cancer and his desire not to face the new realities of his family life. In "Boy Crazy," a teenage girl is just that. "You have the face of an angel, the hair of Bonnie Raitt, the body of Madonna, but you are the daughter from hell," her mother tells her, and their relationship goes downhill from there. In "At the Edge of the Pool," Leah finally gets a summer job teaching water aerobics at a senior center. When Dorey, one of the senior citizens, befriends her, everyone gets concerned about this "unnatural" relationship. In "Payback Time," Jess has to decide who will be his permanent guardian. He loves his mother, his stepfather, and his biological father, and has a difficult time deciding between them. In "Locker-Room Talk" (the novella), Pete, Naylor, and other members of the football team start a campaign to get Mary Fortunato—the frequent subject of locker-room jokes—elected homecoming queen. When Principal Rickover charges the boys with having violated the school's sexual harassment policy and consequently rules them ineligible to play in the homecoming game, Pete is led to rethink the effects of his behavior on Mary, her family, and himself.

This volume is extremely well written, and each story pushes us to confront our own beliefs, values, relationships, and stereotypes. The worlds in Carol Dines' short stories are socially constructed, and readers are invited to think beyond themselves to consider how what they do, say, and believe affects others. Although a coming-of-age theme runs through the volume, these stories are meant to start among teenagers much-needed conversations about many issues, and at the exact age when they should be taking place. Lest teachers reading this review conclude these issues are too sentitive for students and therefore become skittish about using this book, the question remains: If these issues can't be discussed in the safety of the classroom, where can they be discussed?

20.54 Fleischman, Paul (1997). **Seedfolks.** Illustrated by Judy Pedersen. New York: HarperCollins. 69 pp. ISBN: 0-06-027471-9. Chapter Book.

This amazingly complex but short novel is told from the perspectives of thirteen different residents of an ethnically polarized inner-city neighborhood in Cleveland. Fleischman does a masterful job of intertwining the narratives and lives of each of the characters. Kim, a nine-year-old Vietnamese girl, plants dried lima beans in a trash-filled vacant lot in an attempt to spiritually connect with her father, a farmer who died soon after her birth. While Kim plants the seeds, she is watched by Ana, an elderly neighbor who lives across the street from the lot. Ana's suspicion that Kim is hiding drugs leads to a series of human interactions that transform an ugly trash heap into a community garden, a place where people who had previously been distrustful of each other come together with a common purpose. In the course of this book, we hear the believable voices of residents who are ethnically, linguistically, and culturally diverse. We hear the pain of their lives, and we hear their triumph as they slowly and tentatively make connections and become part of a community. Each chapter is titled with the name of the character who tells his or her story, and is accompanied by a simple but effective black-line portrait by illustrator Judy Pedersen.

Many important social issues arise from the individual and collective stories of the thirteen characters. Stimulating and provocative classroom discussions can center around the topics of ageism, the social toll of economically depressed inner cities, the immigrant experience, the difficulties with and ways of getting action from city hall, victims of violence, pregnant teenagers, racial prejudice, vandalism, and how to get beyond cultural stereotypes. This inspirational book can serve as a compelling demonstration of what a community action project might look like in students' own communities. (See also **7.66**)

20.55 Walter, Virginia (1998). **Making Up Megaboy.** Illustrated by Katrina Roeckelein. New York: Dorling Kindersley. 64 pp. ISBN: 0-7894-2488-6. Sophisticated Chapter Book.

In this remarkable book, Virginia Walter weaves together popular culture, ethnic tensions, youth violence, and strained interpersonal relationships to create an extremely disturbing, realistic, and well-crafted tale. On his thirteenth birthday, Robbie Jones walks into Mr. Koh's convenience store, pulls out his father's gun, then shoots and kills the elderly Korean proprietor. The story is presented through the voices of community members as they try to figure out why this horrible killing happened. We hear from Robbie's disbelieving mother, a glib television news reporter, Robbie's disapproving father, a Vietnam veteran, the local barber, Robbie's classmates, the girl Robbie had a crush on, Robbie's teacher, Robbie's best friend, a correctional officer, and many others. This book reads like a television drama, and because of the disturbing content and treatment, it is probably best used as a read-aloud text followed by a class discussion.

Walter brings us face-to-face with real-world issues that we read about regularly in newspaper headlines, but that have no easy answers, including teenage violence, the proliferation of guns, the plight of victims of violence, adult responsibilities, callous classmates, small-town prejudice, and lonely children. We also are confronted head-on with how the perceptions of others position us, and how powerful this positioning can be. Some would say that it is a weakness of this novel that Robbie's character is not well developed and we don't learn about the motivation that led to the killing, but by presenting Robbie as a construction of others, Walter places readers in the realistic situation of community members who have been confronted with a "senseless" act of teenage violence, are struggling to understand its source, and don't have a lot of information. Although not a traditional novel, this book is a very convincing postmodern tale. Katrina Roeckelein's striking graphics are powerful, aptly reflect popular media images, and add to the cultural impact and tone of the book.

20.56 Wilson, Nancy Hope (1997). **Old People, Frogs, and Albert.** Illustrated by Marcy D. Ramsey. New York: Farrar, Straus and Giroux. 58 pp. ISBN: 0-374-35625-4. Chapter Book.

Albert is a fourth grader with more than just a reading problem—he's also very uncomfortable about walking by Pine Manor, a nursing home that he passes on his way to and from school each day. The people who sit on the porch and call out to him are not only old and wrinkled, but not in the best of health either. When his reading tutor and friend Mr. Spear has a stroke and ends up at Pine Manor, it's almost too much for Albert to bear. But when he surprises himself by reading a whole book without help and without focusing on the terrifying fact that he is reading, Albert gets the courage to overcome his fear and share his success with the residents of Pine Manor. He learns that the people he has been avoiding are different, yet have much to offer as friends.

This book makes the point very poignantly that being old or sick has nothing to do with being interesting and fun, and that negative feelings about others often disappear when we get to know them. Many children and adolescents share Albert's initial distaste for dealing with incapacitated or elderly people; this book encourages them to rethink their beliefs.

Secondary Reviews

20.57 Birdseye, Debbie, and Tom Birdseye (1997). **Under Our Skin: Kids Talk about Race.** Photographs by Robert Crum. New York: Holiday House. 30 pp. ISBN: 0-8234-1325-X. Picture Book.

In this book, six twelve- and thirteen-year-olds speak in their own words about their perceptions and experiences of race in the United States. They describe their own ethnic traditions, their experiences of racism and prejudice, and their ideas and hopes for race relations in America. One of the kids we meet is Janell, a Native American dancer from Oregon, who tells us that her school friends are curious about life on the reservation. Another is Jason, an African American who offers incisive perspectives on continuing social and economic inequities. The title of the book comes from Jason's observation that "It's not what color the skin is, but what's under our skin that counts." Crum's photographs of each kid in different settings—with friends, with family, at church, cooking traditional foods, at a school dance—complement the multifaceted individual portraits that emerge in the text. This focus on kids' individual voices provides a great starting point for discussion of how students experience the impact of race and ethnicity in their own lives, including the differences that make each of us distinct, the problems of racism and prejudice, and possibilities for social change.

20.58 Lears, Laurie (1998). **Ian's Walk: A Story about Autism.** Illustrated by Karen Ritz. Morton Grove, IL: Whitman. Unpaged. ISBN: 0-8075-3480-3. Picture Book.

Julie and her big sister Tara are on their way to the park to feed the ducks, but now their brother Ian wants to come. Through simple language and Ritz' luminous watercolor illustrations, this book explores not only the range of emotions Julie feels being the sibling of an autistic child, but also the ways in which Ian himself experiences and senses the world differently. On the journey to the park, Ian wants to smell bricks, not flowers, and once there, he lies with his cheek on the concrete instead of feeding the ducks. The illustrations capture the immense range of Julie's feelings: understanding, annoyance, anger, embarrassment, protectiveness, guilt, love, and affection. After Ian becomes lost in the park, Julie tries hard to enter his world and figure out where Ian would go. In so doing, she not only finds her brother, but also finds a way to connect with him and share experiences together.

Lears manages to validate all of Julie's feelings and to convey both the responsibility and opportunity Julie has to reach outside of herself and into her brother's world. This book could spark great discussions with kids about the way we feel toward people we perceive as somehow different, and what changes when we open ourselves up to trying to understand our differences and connect with each other.

20.59 Senisi, Ellen (1998). **Just Kids: Visiting a Class for Children with Special Needs.** New York: Dutton. 40 pp. ISBN: 0-525-45646-5. Picture Book.

This documentary-like book offers a look at "special kids" and "special classes" through the eyes of Cindy, who is a regular education student. Because she really does not know any special needs kids, Cindy makes a hurtful comment to a child in the special needs class. To help her better understand the special needs of some learners, Cindy is asked to join their class for one-half hour each day over the course of two weeks. Every day, the teacher describes the needs of one of the special kids to Cindy. The teacher offers readily understandable information on learning disabilities ranging from autism and dyslexia to epilepsy. She explains the difference between physical therapy, occupational therapy, and speech therapy. The teacher answers all of Cindy's questions about this class, and encourages her to interact with the students.

Through Cindy, the reader comes to know and appreciate the nine learners in this special needs classroom. Each page of this book is highlighted with photographs taken in an actual special needs classroom, which the author acknowledges in her preface. These photographs give faces to the children as they are described by the teacher. The pictures enhance the text, and allow the reader to see the individuals behind the special needs labels. This book offers both clear and concise information regarding the special needs of some learners, as well as a sensitive account of the feelings of the children who carry the labels of special education. It offers an entry point into discussions surrounding these sensitive issues.

20.60 Van Camp, Richard (1998). **What's the Most Beautiful Thing You Know about Horses?** Illustrated by George Littlechild. San Francisco: Children's Book. 30 pp. ISBN: 0-89239-154-5. Picture Book.

The most beautiful thing about this book is that it provides space for us to see the world and ourselves in entirely new ways. Richard Van Camp, the author, is the main character. In his hometown of Fort Smith in the Northwest Territories of Canada, on a day so cold that he says the ravens refuse to fly, he cannot go outside. He decides to ask his friends and family a question he has been thinking about: "What's the most beautiful thing you know about horses?" On the surface, the book appears to be a clear demonstration of what it truly means to be an inquirer. However the perspectives offered to Van Camp in response to his question set up the possibility for a number of conversations to take place regarding stereotypes, ethnic differences, biracial issues, language and power, animal rights, and cultural perspectives. His search for responses to his questions appears to be a playful and gentle reminder that critical issues can arise or be teased out of conversations that are not primarily centered on such issues. George Littlechild offers bold and bright illustrations that encourage curiosity, and therefore invite other inquiries.

Other Ideas for Text-Sets

Full bibliographic information and reviews for the titles in the following groups are included elsewhere in this chapter; see the cross-reference in boldface type at the end of each entry.

Child Labor and Children's Rights

Dash, Joan. **We Shall Not Be Moved: The Women's Factory Strike of 1909.** (See **20.23**)

Jiménez, Francisco. **The Circuit: Stories from the Life of a Migrant Child.** (See **20.36**)

Martinez, Victor. **Parrot in the Oven: Mi Vida.** (See **20.4**)

McCully, Emily Arnold. **The Bobbin Girl.** (See **20.30**)

Parker, David L. **Stolen Dreams: Portraits of Working Children.** (See **20.15**)

Springer, Jane. **Listen to Us: The World's Working Children.** (See **20.17**)

Literacy as Power

Hesse, Karen. **Just Juice.** (See **20.35**)

Mora, Pat. **Tomás and the Library Lady.** (See **20.39**)

Rodriguez, Luis. **América is Her Name.** (See **20.7**)

Sapphire. **Push.** (See **20.49**)

Thomas, Rob. **Slave Day.** (See **20.42**)

Multiple Perspectives

Birdseye, Debbie, and Tom Birdseye. **Under Our Skin: Kids Talk about Race.** (See **20.57**)

Browne, Anthony. **Voices in the Park.** (See **20.52**)

Fleischman, Paul. **Seedfolks.** (See **20.54**)

Fletcher, Ralph. **Flying Solo.** (See **20.34**)

Thomas, Rob. **Slave Day.** (See **20.42**)

Walter, Virginia. **Making Up Megaboy.** (See **20.55**)

Wolff, Virginia E. **Bat 6.** (See **20.43**)

Author Index

Illustrator Index

Subject Index

Title Index

Contributors

Dale Allender, associate executive director, NCTE, Urbana, Illinois

Cheryl Alley, parent and former elementary teacher, Champaign, Illinois

Janet Alsup, doctoral student in English education, University of Missouri, Columbia

Marilyn Andre, first-grade teacher, Lee Elementary School of Expressive Arts, Columbia, Missouri

Linda Aulgur, elementary methods instructor, Westminster College, Fulton, Missouri

Susie Bargiel, multiage intermediate teacher, Captain Elementary School, Clayton, Missouri

Cathy Beck, eighth-grade English teacher, Wydown Middle School, Clayton, Missouri

Sandra Beecher, graduate student in comparative cultural and literary studies, University of Arizona, Tucson

Kathleen Bennett, librarian, Lincoln Trail Elementary School, Mahomet, Illinois

Beth Berghoff, assistant professor of language education, Indiana University–Purdue University, Indianapolis

Joan Bownas, third-grade teacher, Emerson Magnet School, Westerville, Ohio

Amy Breau, graduate assistant in language education, School of Education, Indiana University, Bloomington

Laura Burch, graduate student in French literature and women's studies, University of Minnesota, Minneapolis–St. Paul

Jenay Burck, media and research skills teacher, Indian Creek Elementary School, Indianapolis, Indiana

Sally Burgett, kindergarten teacher, South Side Elementary School, Champaign, Illinois

Caroline Carlson, early childhood resource teacher, Native American Studies Department, Tucson (Arizona) Unified School District

Julie Carlton, director, First Presbyterian Preschool, Las Vegas, Nevada

Ruby Clayton, kindergarten teacher, Cold Spring Elementary School, Indianapolis (Indiana) Public Schools

Kathleen Marie Crawford, assistant professor in curriculum and instruction, Illinois State University, Bloomington

Trina Crawford, elementary media specialist, Hawthorne Elementary School, Lincoln, Nebraska

Sandra Montiel Costell, bilingual teacher, Carrillo Intermediate Magnet School, Tucson (Arizona) Unified School District

Patricia Tefft Cousin, formerly associate professor of education, Indiana University–Purdue University, Indianapolis

Carol Cribett-Bell, librarian, Carrillo Intermediate Magnet School, Tucson (Arizona) Unified School District

Caryl Gottlieb Crowell, bilingual/multiage primary classroom teacher, Borton Primary Magnet School, Tucson (Arizona) Unified School District

Lisa Dapoz, first-grade teacher, Emerson Magnet School, Westerville, Ohio

M. Ruth Davenport, assistant professor of education, Eastern Oregon University, La Grande

Mary Diener, third-grade teacher, Lincoln Elementary School, Clinton, Illinois

Maureen Dietzel, Title I teacher, LeClaire Elementary School, Edwardsville, Illinois

Carolyn Dye, first-grade teacher, Lee Elementary School of Expressive Arts, Columbia, Missouri

Pennie Dye, second-grade teacher, Edwards Elementary School, Las Vegas, Nevada

Diane Elliott, fifth-grade teacher, South Side Elementary School, Champaign, Illinois

Stacie Cook Emert, curriculum specialist, Maxwell Middle School, Tucson (Arizona) Unified School District

Susan Flynn, recent graduate, Southern Illinois University–Edwardsville

Lauren Freedman, assistant professor of education, Western Michigan University, Kalamazoo

Carol Gilles, assistant professor in literacy and language education, University of Missouri–Columbia

Cyndi Giorgis, assistant professor in literature education, University of Nevada–Las Vegas

Barbara Greenberg, teacher librarian, Tucson (Arizona) Unified School District

Denice Haines, sixth-grade teacher, Cold Spring Elementary School, Indianapolis (Indiana) Public Schools

Jerome C. Harste, distinguished professor of language education, Indiana University, Bloomington, Indiana

Jill M. Hartke, sixth-grade teacher, Hopedale (Illinois) Elementary School

Katherine Hawker, pastor, Evangelical United Church of Christ, St. Louis, Missouri

David Heine, assistant professor of education, St. Cloud State University, Minnesota

Patricia Heine, assistant professor of education, St. Cloud State University, Minnesota

Janice Henson, special education teacher, Columbia Catholic School, Columbia, Missouri

Karen Hildebrand, library media director, Willis Middle School, Delaware, Ohio

Lynda S. Hootman, classroom teacher, Tremont (Illinois) Elementary School

Angela Humphrey, fourth-grade teacher, Sheridan Grade School, Bloomington, Illinois

Sang Huang, doctoral student, English as a second language, University of Missouri–Columbia

Christine Inkster, reference librarian, St. Cloud State University, Minnesota

Carol M. Jones, elementary schools librarian, Champaign (Illinois) School District

Frank Kazemak, associate professor, Department of Teacher Development, St. Cloud State University, Minnesota

Jan Keenoy, fifth-grade teacher, Glenridge Elementary School, Clayton, Missouri

Alice Kiruma, first-grade teacher, Panahou Elementary School, Hawaii

Dick Koblitz, multiage intermediate teacher, Captain Elementary School, Clayton, Missouri

Dottie Kulesza, reading specialist, Paradise Professional Development School, Las Vegas, Nevada

Patty Leahey, secondary language arts teacher, James Campbell High School, Ewa Beach, Hawaii

Veronica Lee, multicategorical classes teacher, Fairview Elementary School, Columbia, Missouri

Christine Leland, associate professor of education, Indiana University–Purdue University, Indianapolis

Mitzi Lewison, assistant professor of language education, Indiana University, Bloomington

Jenine Loesing, first-grade teacher, Fairview Elementary School, Columbia, Missouri

MariBeth Loesing, sixth-grade student, Lange Elementary School, Columbia, Missouri

Kathy Lohse, bilingual kindergarten teacher, Borton Primary Magnet School, Tucson (Arizona) Unified School District

Miki Maeshiro, sixth-grade teacher, Kamehameha Elementary School, Honolulu, Hawaii

Carmen M. Martínez-Roldán, graduate student in language, reading, and culture, University of Arizona, Tucson

Janelle B. Mathis, assistant professor of education, University of North Texas, Denton

Beth Mayberry, parent and graphic artist, St. Louis, Missouri

Joyce Madsen, second-grade teacher, Tremont (Illinois) Elementary School

Amy McClure, professor of reading and children's literature, Ohio Wesleyan University, Delaware, Ohio

Elizabeth Mena, third-grade teacher, Four Seasons A+ (Fine Arts) Elementary School, St. Paul, Minnesota

Claudette Mitchell, kindergarten teacher, Inglewood Elementary School, Nashville, Tennessee

Jocelyn Mokulehua, first-grade teacher, Waiau Elementary School, Pearl City, Hawaii

Norma Nelson, sixth-grade teacher, DuBray Middle School, Ft. Zumwalt, Missouri

Shari Nelson-Faulkner, parent, The Family Center, School District of Clayton, Missouri

Beatrice "Bea" Nez, fourth-grade teacher, Tucson (Arizona) Unified School District

Sheilah Nicholas, graduate student, American Indian Studies Department, University of Arizona, Tucson

Anne Ociepka, graduate student in language education, Indiana University, Bloomington

Anne O'Connor, multiage primary teacher, Glenridge Elementary School, Clayton, Missouri

Sally Omalza, sixth-grade teacher, Mililani (Hawaii) Middle School

Marcia Omura, graduate student in education, University of Hawaii–Manoa

Penny O'Shaunessey, sixth-grade teacher, Lincoln Environmental Elementary School, Grand Rapids, Michigan

Peggy Oxley, second-grade teacher, St. Paul's School, Westerville, Ohio

Jann Pataray-Ching, assistant professor of language and literacy studies, University of Nebraska–Lincoln

Pat Pearman, fifth-grade teacher, Four Seasons A+ (Fine Arts) Elementary School, St. Paul, Minnesota

Virginia Pfannenstiel, elementary methods instructor, Central Methodist College, Fayette, Missouri

Kathy Phillips, assistant professor of language and literacy studies, University of Nebraska–Lincoln

Gracie Porter, principal, John Early Middle School, Nashville, Tennessee

Sylvia Raschke, third-grade teacher, Oak Hill Elementary School, St. Cloud, Minnesota

Laurie Reddy, first-grade teacher, Iroquois West Elementary School, Gilman, Illinois

Elizabeth M. Redondo, interactive literacy teacher, Safford Engineering/Technology Magnet Middle School, Tucson (Arizona) Unified School District

Pam Riggs, seventh-grade communication arts teacher, Buehler Middle School, Marshall, Missouri

Charles Robb, parent and former teacher, Moberly, Missouri

Sandra Schmidt, high-school global studies teacher, Comstock Park (Michigan) High School

Sharon Schneegerger, project construct leader, Columbia, Missouri

Stephanie Shafer, early childhood education student, Central Methodist College, Fayette, Missouri

Betsy Shepar, librarian, Wakefield Middle School, Tucson (Arizona) Unified School District

Kathy G. Short, professor of language, reading and culture, University of Arizona, Tucson

Karen Smith, associate professor of curriculum and instruction, Arizona State University, Tempe

Katrina Smits, third-grade bilingual teacher, Carrillo Intermediate Magnet School, Tucson (Arizona) Unified School District

Jane Soelhke, intermediate teacher, Illini School, Fairview Heights, Illinois

Marilyn Soucie, teacher mentor, Teaching Fellowship Program, Fairview Elementary School, Columbia, Missouri

Sharon Stemmons, fourth-grade teacher, Mill Creek Elementary School, Columbia, Missouri

Della Stevens, elementary media specialist, Rice Lake Elementary School, Lino Lakes, Minnesota

Anna Sumida, second-grade teacher, Kamehameha Elementary School, Honolulu, Hawaii

Pamela Swinford, remedial reading teacher, New Palestine (Indiana) School Corporation,

Shelli Thelen, kindergarten teacher, Pilot Grove (Missouri) Elementary School

Nancy Tolson, assistant professor in English, Illinois State University, Bloomington

Beverly Johns Vick, third-grade teacher, Patrick Henry Elementary School, Fairfax, Virginia

Vivian Vasquez, assistant professor of reading and language arts, American University, Washington, D.C.

Joan Von Dras, fifth-grade teacher, Glenridge Elementary School, Clayton, Missouri

Lillian Webb, elementary schools gifted education teacher, Worthington, Ohio

Karla Hawkins Wendelin, elementary library media specialist, Norris School, Firth, Nebraska

David Whitin, professor of elementary and early childhood education, Queens College, Flushing, New York

Phyllis Whitin, assistant professor of elementary and early childhood education, Queens College, Flushing, New York

Jean Williams, acquisitions and collection development librarian, Kalamazoo (Michigan) Public Schools

Sandra Williams, associate professor, Center for Information Media, St. Cloud State University, Minnesota

Jennifer L. Wilson, seventh-grade teacher, Reed-Custer Middle School, Braidwood, Illinois

Susan Wolf, fifth-grade teacher, Glenridge Elementary School, Clayton, Missouri

Allison Young, assistant professor of education, Western Michigan University, Kalamazoo

Editor

Kathryn Mitchell Pierce is a multiage primary classroom teacher in the School District of Clayton, Missouri. She has served on the Children's Literature Assembly of the National Council of Teachers of English, and as a member of the committees to select the NCTE Notable Children's Books in the Language Arts and the Lee Bennett Hopkins Poetry Award. Pierce has served as co-editor (with Carol Gilles) of the "Talking about Books" department in *Language Arts*, and (with Kathy Short) of the "Children's Books" department in *The Reading Teacher*. Her publications include *Talking about Books: Literature Discussion Groups K–8* (with Kathy Short), *Cycles of Meaning: Exploring the Potential of Talk in Learning Communities* (with Carol Gilles), and a chapter in *Teaching Language Arts: Learning through Dialogue* (Judith Wells Lindfors and Jane S. Townsend, editors).

This book was typeset in Palatino and Helvetica by Precision Graphics.
Typefaces used on the cover were University Roman and Palatino.
The book was printed on 50 lb. White Lynx Opaque by Versa Press.